The life of

Evelyn Beatrice Hall

Alpha Editions

This edition published in 2022

ISBN : 9789356898851

Design and Setting By
Alpha Editions
www.alphaedis.com
Email - info@alphaedis.com

Contents

CHAPTER I

THE BOYHOOD

IN 1694, when Louis XIV. was at the height of that military glory which at once dazzled and ruined France, there was born in Paris on November 21st a little, puny, weak, sickly son.

The house into which the infant was born was the ordinary house of a thoroughly comfortable well-to-do *bourgeois* of the time and place. A notary was M. Arouet *père*. *His* father had been a prosperous linen-draper; and Arouet the son, shrewd and thrifty in affairs, had bought, after the custom of his time and his profession, first one post and then another, until he was a man of some wealth and, for his class, of some position. Among his clients he could number the Dukes of Sully and of Richelieu, memoir-writing Saint-Simon, the poet Boileau, and the immortal Ninon de l'Enclos. He had a country house at Châtenay, five miles from Paris. Plenty of sound common-sense, liberal, practical, hospitable; just enough taste for literature to enjoy a doze over a book in the evening when his day's labour was done; eminently respected and respectable; decently acquiescing in the national religion as such, and with no particular faith in anything but hard work and monetary prudence; not a little hasty in temper and deadly obstinate—such was Maître Arouet.

At thirty-four years old he had been prosperous enough to marry one Mademoiselle d'Aumard, of Poitou, whose gentle birth and a certain refinement of type, not at all shared by her husband, formed the chief part of her dowry. The biographers of her younger son have done their best to prove the d'Aumard family something more noble, and the Arouet family something less *bourgeois*, than they were. They need not have troubled. The man who afterwards called himself Voltaire valued his ancestry not at all, and owed it nothing. The most painstaking research has been unable to prove that there was a single one of his forbears who had the smallest taste for literature, or mental endowments above the common. Some have pretended that he owed to his mother the delicacy of his wit, as he certainly owed to her the delicacy of his body. Beyond the fact that she was the friend of her husband's brilliant and too famous client Ninon, and of three abbés—clever, musical, and profligate—who were the *amis de la maison* Arouet and always about it, the theory is without the smallest foundation. Her great son does not mention her half a dozen times in that vast bulk of writings he left the world. To him she was but a shadow; to the world she must needs be but a shadow too.

She had two living children when this last frail baby was born on that November Sunday—Armand of ten and Catherine of nine. She had lost two infants, and she never really recovered this last one's birth.

He himself had at the first but a poor chance of life. He was hurriedly baptised on Monday, November 22, 1694, by the names of François Marie. Every morning the *nourrice* came down from the attic where she tended him to say he could not live an hour. And every day one of those abbés, who had taken on himself the office of godfather and was called Châteauneuf, ran up to the attic to see the baby and suggest remedies to the nurse.

Perhaps the nurse did not try the remedies. At any rate, the puny infant disappointed the expectations of his relatives, and lived. Zozo they called him, or, from the wilfulness of his baby temper, "le petit volontaire." Châteauneuf's interest in him increased daily. He must have detected an extraordinarily precocious intelligence in the small creature, since, when he was but three years old, the abbé had begun to perform his godfatherly duties as he understood them, and to teach the child a certain ribald deistical poem by J. B. Rousseau called "Le Moïsade."

It is not too much to say that at this period, and for about a hundred years afterwards, the name of abbé was synonymous with that of scoundrel. Free liver and free thinker, gay, base, and witty—"qui n'était d'église que pour les bénéfices," as that little godson said of him hereafter— Châteauneuf was not worse than most of his kind, and perhaps, if anything, was rather better. He accepted, indeed, the emoluments of a religion in which he did not only not believe but at which he openly scoffed, in order to live at his ease a life quite profligate and disreputable. It is said, or he said, that he had the honour of being Ninon de l'Enclos' last lover. But he was both goodnatured and kindhearted, and after his fashion was really fond of the little godson and doing his best to lead his baby mind away from a superstition which he himself had found, to be sure, tolerably profitable.

What a strange picture it is! This child lisped scoffings as other children lisp prayers. He had very big brown eyes, bright with intelligence, in his little, wizened, old man's face. The precocity greatly entertained Châteauneuf. Père Arouet may have been amused too, in private, at this infant unbeliever—the state of the Church making it hard then for any man, at once honest and reasonable, to put faith in her teachings. The society of her three abbés and her Ninon must have made delicate Madame pretty used to free thought.

So the little boy learnt his "Moïsade" by heart and was taught to read out of the "Fables" of La Fontaine.

He was but seven when his mother died. Sister Catherine of sixteen was already thinking of a *dot* and a husband, as a prudent French girl should. Brother Armand of seventeen—"my Jansenist of a brother"—had imbibed extreme religious opinions at the seminary of Saint Magloire and was an austere youthful bigot.

So Zozo scrambled up as best he might among mortgages, bonds, and shares; designed from the first by his father to be *avocat* (wherein the family influence would be powerful to help him), a lonely and precocious little creature, and still the infant *protégé* of Châteauneuf.

In the December of 1704, when he was ten years old, he first affixed his name—his baby name of Zozo—to a letter which Brother Armand dutifully wrote at his father's request to wish an aunt in Poitou the compliments of the New Year 1705. That letter may be taken as the small beginning of one of the most enormous correspondences in the world, which new discoveries are still increasing in bulk, and which, as has been said, seems likely to go on increasing until the Day of Judgment.

In that very same year 1704, Zozo was sent to the Jesuit College of St. Louis-le-Grand as a parlour boarder. The school was only a few minutes' walk from his own home. But in that home there was no one to look after him save the busy middle-aged notary fully occupied in affairs. Catherine was married. Armand had already succeeded in repelling a volatile child's spirit with his narrow harshness. So Zozo went to school, and took up his place in the very lowest class.

St. Louis-le-Grand—"the Eton of France"—had two thousand pupils, mostly belonging to the French aristocracy. Louis XIV. had visited it, and left it his name. It was entirely under Jesuit influence, and taught, or omitted to teach, exactly according to the royal pleasure and the fashion of the day.

A very thin-faced, keen-witted little youth was its new ten-year-old scholar. It did not take him long to conceive a passion for Cicero, for Horace, and for Virgil. He soon discovered that he was learning "neither the constitution nor interests of my country: not a word of mathematics or of sound philosophy. I learnt Latin and nonsense." But he applied himself to that "Latin and nonsense" with that passionate voracity for information, useful or useless, good, bad, or indifferent, which he retained till his death. He must have been one of the quickest boys that ever Jesuit master taught. He had an intelligence like an arrow—and an arrow which always went straight to the mark. Before he was eleven he was writing bad verses with a facility and enthusiasm alike extraordinary. The masters were, with one exception, his friends and admirers. While the other boys were at their games this one would walk and talk with the Fathers; and when they told him that he should play like the others, he looked up with those brilliant eyes that lighted the little, lean, sallow face like leaping flames—"Everybody must jump after his own fashion," said he.

His especial tutor was a certain Abbé d'Olivet, then a young man, for whom the promising little scholar conceived a lifelong friendship. Another tutor, called Tournemine, was also first the boy's teacher and then his pupil. Yet another Father, called Porée, would listen long and late to the child's sharp questions on history and politics. "That boy," said he, "wants to weigh the great questions of Europe in his little scales."

He had friends among the boys too, as well as the masters. It was at school he met the d'Argensons—afterwards powers to help him in the French Government—Cideville and d'Argental, his lifelong friend, whom he called his guardian angel.

In 1705, those fluent verses he had written came to the notice of Godpapa Châteauneuf. As a reward the abbé took him to see Ninon de l'Enclos, that marvellous woman who was as charming at eighty as at eighteen, who "looked on love as a pleasure which bound her to no duties and on friendship as something sacred," and was in some sort an answer to her own prayer, "God make me an honest man but never an honest woman!" She received the child in the midst of her brilliant circle with that infinite tact and kindness which have made her as immortal as her frailties. His bright, quick answers, his self-confidence, his childish store of information delighted her. Châteauneuf said that she saw in him "the germ of a great man." Perhaps she did. When she died a few months later, she left him two thousand francs in her will, with which to buy books. And the "great man," many years after, wrote an account of the interview as if it had happened yesterday.

He went back to school after that episode and learnt, and knew he was learning, though he was only twelve years old, "a prodigious number of things" for which he had no talent.

Porée taught him a good deal of Latin, and the primers a very little Greek. He learnt no history, no science, and no modern languages. That he acquired a knowledge of the history and government of France is as undoubted as that he was never formally taught it.

Young Abbé d'Olivet inspired him with his own love of Cicero. Châteauneuf had taught his godson to worship Corneille; and young Arouet championed him valiantly against Father Tournemine's dear hero, Racine.

Other seeds which Châteauneuf had sown in a childish heart were growing and ripening fast. His one enemy among the masters, Father Lejay, answered a too brilliant and too daring retort with the words, "Wretch! you will one day be the standard-bearer of Deism in France!"

The enterprising Deist was still only twelve when, encouraged by Ninon's pension perhaps and the success of some impromptu verses made in class, he attempted a tragedy called "Amulius and Numitor." He burnt it thereafter—very wisely no doubt. But verse-making was in his blood, though his blood was Maître Arouet's and the noble, dull Aumards' of Poitou. Play-acting at the school prize-givings encouraged a love of the drama, also inborn. François Marie Arouet was not yet thirteen when he wrote a versified petition to Louis XIV. to grant an old soldier a pension, wherein the compliments were so delicately turned as to attract the momentary attention of the best flattered monarch who ever sat upon a throne. The old soldier obtained his pension, and François Marie enough fame and flattery to turn a youthful head.

When he was fifteen, in 1709, Châteauneuf died, Malplaquet was lost, and France starving to pay for her defeats. In the midst of that bitter winter of famine, when young Arouet's high place in class always kept him away from the comforting stove, he called out to the lucky dullard who was always near it, "Get out, or I'll send you to warm with Pluto!" "Why don't you say hell?" asked the other. "Bah!" replied Arouet; "the one is no more a certainty than the other."

Here spoke the religious influence of the priestly godfather,

NINON DE L'ENCLOS

who, before he died, had tried to form the godson's mind by recounting to him some of Ninon de l'Enclos' most marvellous adventures.

In 1710, at the midsummer prize-giving, Arouet, runs the story, took so many prizes as to attract the notice of the famous J. B. Rousseau, the author of the "Moïsade," the first poet in France, and once shoemaker to the Arouet family. The great man congratulated and encouraged the boy who was to be so much greater. To be sure he was an ugly boy for all that keen look of his! Ugly boy and mediocre poet were to fight each other tooth and nail hereafter, with the ugly boy the winner for ever.

If young Arouet was anything like an older Voltaire, he knew how to play as well as how to work, and how to work gaily with a jest always ready to relieve the tedium.

The defeat of Blenheim had shadowed the year 1704 when he went to school. In 1711, when he left it, three heirs to the throne died one after the other as if the judgment of God had already fallen upon their wicked house. Abroad, were Marlborough and defeat; at home, death, hunger, and religious persecution. Arouet had a heart always sensitive to misfortune, but he was gay, seventeen, and fresh from drudgery.

When he came home from St. Louis-le-Grand in that August of 1711 it was with every intention on his father's part, and no kind of intention on his own, that he should become *avocat*.

Was it the passing success of that poetical petition to the king which had put the idea of literature as a profession into his head? Was it Ninon's pension? or the approval of poet Rousseau? The love of letters had been in this boy always, a dominant taste, a ruling passion, which he could no more help than he could help the feebleness of his body or the astounding vigour of his mind.

He took the earliest opportunity of announcing to his father that he intended to devote himself to writing.

M. Arouet received the announcement exactly as it might have been expected he would. Literature! Better be a lackey or a play-actor at once. Literature! What did that mean? The Bastille for a couplet, ruin, poverty, disgrace. Rousseau himself had just been degraded from the highest place to the lowest for verses he was only supposed to have written. "Literature," said Maître Arouet with the irate dogmatism which takes no denial, "is the profession of the man who wishes to be useless to society, a burden to his relatives, and to die of hunger." The relatives, fearing the burden, vociferously agreed with him.

Arouet *père* had most unluckily once taken wine with the great Corneille and found that genius the most insufferable old bore, of the very lowest conversation. The indignant parent made the house of Arouet exceedingly unquiet with his fumings and growlings. Pressure was very strong and François Marie was eighteen. The youth who said that his motto was "To the point" was soon engaged in the matchless intricacies of French law, as yet unsimplified by a master mind into the Code Napoleon.

What would be the natural result of a distasteful occupation, youth, wit, and gaiety in eighteenth-century Paris? Such a result supervened with young Arouet almost at once. Boy though he was, Châteauneuf had already introduced him into a brilliant, libertine society called "The Epicureans of the Temple." At its head was the usual abbé—one Chaulieu—"the dissolute Anacreon" who drew a revenue of thirty thousand francs from his benefices to pay for his excesses. Vile, witty, and blasphemous, he was not more so than the noble and titled company over which he presided. It had every vice but one—that of dulness. Most of its members were old men, and as literary critics of the evanescent literature of the hour, unrivalled. To them, it is said, virtue and faith were alike the prejudices of fools. The notary's son, who was nobody and had done nothing, had but two claims for admission to such a society: one was the mental emancipation he had received from his godfather, and the other the daring brilliancy all his own. The Temple suppers were soon incomplete without him. Young Arouet was already showing himself a versifier of astounding audacity. The company of dukes and nobles, of men vastly his superior in age and acquirements, did not daunt him in the least. A penniless boy, he had that careless ease with great people—a certain charming air of familiarity—which never offended if it made old men smile at a boyish vanity, and which he never afterwards lost. Some of his *mots* at those suppers have come down to posterity, and were not less acceptable to the Temple because they are no longer transcribable. At an epicurean supper at the Prince of Conti's, young Arouet could turn to the company and exclaim, "Here we are all princes or poets!"

One poet received very short shrift from respectable, sensible old M. Arouet *père*, when he came home in the small hours of the morning from these orgies. The determined old man locked the house and went to bed, and behold! François Marie must pay for his amusements by walking the streets till morning. That did not daunt him. Nothing daunted him. He was young and enjoying himself, with the keenest sense of the ludicrous, and perfectly willing to take his pleasures—at a cost. One day, finding himself shut out as usual, he went to sleep in the porter's chair in the Palais de Justice, and was carried, still asleep, the next morning, into a café hard by, by two legal wags, his friends. The recollection of Brother Armand's long, disapproving face at home only lent additional piquancy to Arouet's revels abroad. Another day, a noble lady with literary aspirations gives him a hundred louis for tactfully correcting her bad rhymes. Young Arouet, idly watching an auction, bids for a carriage and pair and has them knocked down to him. He drives about Paris all day with his friends, and at three o'clock in the morning takes the carriage home and tries to get the horses into his father's stables. The noise wakes up Maître Arouet, who turns his scapegrace out of doors there and then, and sells the horses and carriage the very next day. One likes the peppery old father with his dogged determination. He would have won the battle over any other son but this one, and deserved to win. He sent the prodigal to Caen in disgrace, and Caen fell in love at once with a youth so clever and amusing, and turned the exile to a delight. There was a charming literary lady here also, who abandoned her *protégé*, however, when she found he could write indecorous verses too, and there was a Jesuit Father who prophesied a great future for this brilliant madcap. Then the old notary at home sent a message to his François Marie—if he would come back and settle to work he would buy him a good post; in time, get him made Counsel to the Parliament of Paris. "Tell my father," was the answer, "I do not want any place that can be bought. I will make one for myself that will cost nothing."

Twenty-six years after, one Voltaire, in his "Life of Molière," wrote that all who had made a name in the *beaux-arts* had done so in spite of their relations. "Nature has always been much stronger with them than education;" and again, "I saw early that one can neither resist one's ruling taste, nor fight one's destiny." It was so in this boy's case at any rate. Some of the monetary prudence inherited from the old notary, and which was so greatly to distinguish a later Voltaire from most of his brothers of the pen, was in embryo within him now. Yet when he got back to Paris after those few months at Caen he was as gay, wild, and determined as ever, and M. Arouet, in despair, procured for him the post of page or *attaché* to the Marquis de Châteauneuf (brother of the abbé) and shipped him off with that ambassador to the Netherlands in the September of 1713.

The Marquis de Châteauneuf and suite reached The Hague on September 28, 1713, but did not formally enter the town until later. "It is amusing," one of the suite wrote, "to make an entry into a city where you have already been living several weeks."

Page, *attaché*, or diplomat, whichever people called him, *this* page, *attaché*, or diplomat was going to enjoy himself. Before they were well established at The Hague he must needs fall head over ears in love with a certain Olympe Dunoyer, the daughter of an adventurous mother who lived by her wits and an audacious society periodical called *The Quintessence*. Olympe, or, more endearingly, Pimpette, was one-and-twenty. She knew something of the world already. With such a mother and the impecunious roving life they had led, that was inevitable. She was not pretty, her lover said long after. She was what is a great deal more dangerous—fascinating and impulsive. He gave her from the first a boy's honest ardent affection. He wrote her immensely long, vigorous, passionate epistles. He originated the most beautiful youthful scheme by which Protestant Pimpette (Madame Dunoyer and her daughter were Protestant) was to be brought back to the true Church, and to Paris, where her Catholic father and sister were living. For a couple of months, the worldly mother not suspecting its existence, the course of true love ran smoothly. But one fatal night Arouet coming home late after a blissful interview, encountered his chief. Madame Dunoyer will certainly disapprove of the addresses of a penniless boy of nineteen! Having a wholesome fear of that libellous "Quintessence," the ambassador felt bound to disapprove too. The *attaché* must go back to France to-morrow. The *attaché*, with his irresistible energy and daring, got forty-eight hours' grace. His valet, Lefèvre, was his accomplice; a certain shoemaker was Pimpette's. A further unavoidable delay in the time of Arouet's departure came to the lovers' assistance. One moonlit night Arouet disguised himself, signalled beneath his mistress's window, and drove her away to Scheveningen, five miles off, where he made her write three letters which were designed to help his scheme of getting her to Paris. Sometimes they met at the obliging shoemaker's, daring, frightened, and happy, with the shoemaker's wife for a sentinel outside.

Of course the ambassador got wind of the interviews and forbade his *attaché* to leave the embassy. But the irrepressible lover *would* see his mistress—"though it bring my head to the block." He let himself down from a window by night, and met a trembling Pimpette who had escaped, heaven knows how! from the Argus-eyed mother—outside her home.

Then the ambassador offered this impossible *attaché* his choice—to leave Holland immediately—or in a week's time with a solemn vow not to leave his quarters meanwhile. Arouet chose the week and the vow. He sent Lefèvre with a letter to Pimpette. "If I cannot come to you, you must come to me! Send Lisbette at three o'clock and I will give her a parcel for you containing a boy's dress." The mad night came, and Pimpette, the most endearing boy in the world, with it. The whole escapade was wild enough. It says something for this impassioned Arouet of nineteen that at its worst it was nothing but an escapade. "My love is founded on a perfect esteem," he had written, and "I love your honour as I love you." He rallied her, not a little gaily, in prose and verse, after that dear meeting. She was such a pretty boy! "I fear you did not take out your sword in the street, which was all that was needed to make a perfect young man!" "But while I am teasing you I learn that Lefèvre suspected you yesterday." Of course he did. But Lefèvre would not betray his master to the ambassador, who had more than a suspicion of the interview. And the next night Arouet broke his parole, got out of the window, and met Pimpette outside her house once more. The ambassador heard of this too, wrote a furious letter to Maître Arouet describing the whole affair, and on December 18, 1713, the lover was despatched home.

He went on writing to Pimpette, of course. It was *her* fate that agitated him—not his. She must be sure to burn his letters—she must not expose herself to the fury of that termagant of a mother. She must take heart; she must be true to him! The letter from the boat which was carrying him to France was full of that capital, clever plan for bringing her over to the Jesuits—to be converted, as near to Arouet as possible, in Paris. All these love letters to Pimpette are much more loving than witty. They are so enthusiastic and earnest and young, so energetic and devoted, so unselfish and hopeful! They make one feel young to read them. It has been said that they are not the letters of Mirabeau. They are those of an honester man.

The very first thing Arouet did when he reached Paris on this Christmas Eve of 1713 was exactly what he had told Pimpette he would do. He went straight to his old master, Father Tournemine, at St. Louis-le-Grand, to whom he had already written some of the circumstances, to arrange with the Jesuits for bringing back the lost Protestant sheep to the Roman fold. Arouet did not think it necessary to mention that the lost sheep was, in point of fact, a lamb—charming, and one-and-twenty—or that he had ever seen her. Good Tournemine promised to do his very best to get Pimpette's father to take her in. In fact the whole scheme was working beautifully when that irascible and dogged old Maître Arouet, who had received not only the ambassador's version of the affair but the furious Madame Dunoyer's, positively obtained a *lettre de cachet* for his scapegrace son, with which to get him arrested and imprisoned.

Young Arouet had not been home, which was very prudent of him. His presence would only have further exasperated his father. The *lettre de cachet* was not put into effect. The lover went on loving, adoring, and writing to his mistress. What was an angry father after all? A necessary rôle in the comedy. What was distance or opposition, what was anything or anybody to Arouet if Pimpette only loved him? Of the two, she was far the more cool and reasonable. She urged him to study law as his father bade him. And for her sake he did even that. A year or two later she became Countess of Winterfeld. Some years later still, he had the pleasure of seeing some of his own love letters to her figuring in a scandalous work of her mother's called "Lettres Historiques et Galantes." Even these events did not disturb a certain tender respect for her memory which he bore to the end of his life. When he was imprisoned in the Bastille four years later, he still carried about with him a little, undated, misspelt letter about one of those dear, stolen interviews—half maternal, half tender in tone—the only letter of Pimpette's which has come down to posterity.

January, 1714, then, beheld Arouet at the bidding of Pimpette, and having made the most abject apologies to his father (François Marie was nothing if not thorough), installed as clerk to a Maître Alain, and living with that dull and worthy solicitor and his wife. He learnt something of law here, no doubt. Nay, he must have learnt a great deal to be hereafter that shrewd and capable man of affairs he proved himself. But it was a dull time and an unfortunate. Maître Arouet kept his prodigal very close in the matter of money; and his prodigal affixed his name to certain bills which gave him trouble hereafter. Pimpette's letters were getting fewer and fewer. Pimpette was false. Then, in the August of this 1714, young Arouet tried for a prize offered by the French Academy for a poem celebrating the King's generosity in giving a new choir to Notre Dame; and failed. The failure attacked La Motte, the judge—the unjust judge, Arouet thought him—with epigrams, and then wrote a satire, called "Mud," on La Motte's "Fables." Old Arouet was furious again, and young Arouet's only consolation in life was the friendship of one Theriot, also clerk to the Alains, an idle, goodnatured, amusing scapegrace, nobody's enemy but his own, and to be Arouet's friend, though not always a faithful friend, for sixty years.

Caumartin, an old Temple acquaintance, reappeared on young Arouet's horizon again presently. Caumartin had an uncle, a famous old magistrate, the Marquis de Saint-Ange, living at Saint-Ange, nine miles from Fontainebleau. When young Caumartin conveyed an invitation to old Arouet that his prodigal should go and stay with Saint-Ange and resume his studies there, the notary naturally supposed an acceptance would be the best thing for Arouet's legal prospects.

And not for his legal prospects only. The boy had that satire, couplets, and epigrams running through Paris. He did not yet know what message he had to deliver to the world; did not know perhaps that he had any message. But he was fast learning the language in which it was to be spoken, and speak in that language he must, were the whole earth peopled by angry fathers and conscientious Alains.

So it was as well that the autumn of 1714 saw him away from Paris and established in the fine old château of the Saint-Anges.

The old magistrate, however, was not magistrate only, or chiefly; he was also a man of the world, and courtier. So it soon came about that, instead of learning maxims of the law, the keen-witted visitor sat and listened, a most eager and intelligent audience, to gossip, scandal, *bons-mots* of the Court of a bygone day—anecdotes of Henry of Navarre and personal recollections of Louis XIV. The château had a splendid library. But it was hardly needed—"Caumartin carries the living history of his age in his head," said his courtly young guest in a quatrain.

It was while he was at Saint-Ange he dashed on to paper the beginning of what was afterwards the "Henriade"; and started that vast collection of anecdotes which formed the material for the "Century of Louis XIV."

Arouet stayed several months in the château, occasionally paying a flying visit to the capital. The end of the Sun King's reign was fast approaching. The famous Bull Unigenitus was the one great topic of all men's conversation; and no doubt was freely discussed at Saint-Ange. If the young visitor had come there meaning to be author, he left a hundred times more fixed in that idea. In August, 1715, Louis XIV. was dying. Arouet hastened to Paris to see the strange things that death would bring about.

In his pocket he had a play, "Œdipe," on which he had now been working for two years.

In his soul were the courage, the conscious power, the clear outlook to a future all unwarranted by the present, which are the consolations of genius.

Arouet was beginning the world.

CHAPTER II

EPIGRAMS AND THE BASTILLE

AT the death of Louis XIV. Paris was still the typical Paris of the old *régime*. Magnificence and squalor, dirt and splendour, a few men living like gods and most men living like beasts; narrow and filthy streets, and the sumptuous glory of the Court of the Sun King; a hungry *canaille*, and a *noblesse* whose exquisite finish of manner concealed the most profound corruption of morals the world has seen. Such was the Paris of 1715.

For the last few years of his life a woman and a priest had absolutely ruled the absolute King. "France forgave Louis his mistresses," said Arouet, "but not his confessor." The great Bull Unigenitus, that thunderbolt hurled at once against Jansenism and liberty, was the first rock on which the French monarchy struck. Everybody was to think as the King did! And France, who had starved patiently to pay for his conquests and his pleasures, received with open joy the news of the death of the man who had tried to strangle her soul with Unigenitus. Paris was flooded with satires as it had never been flooded even with panegyrics. The Court shook off the mantle of austerity which it had of late been wearing over its depravity. The flagrant vice of the Regency flaunted boldly in daylight, and men laughed openly at a religion in which for years they had concurred devoutly—with the tongue in the cheek.

The world wagged thus when Arouet came up from Fontainebleau. The great majority of men go through life accepting what they find in it without question—supposing that because things are, they will be and ought to be. But this boy had the order of mind which takes nothing for granted. A state religion? Well, what had it done for that state and for the souls of men? A paternal government that left its children to starve? Arouet had from the first "lisped in numbers, for the numbers came;" but when he saw on the one hand the crowded prisons and brutalised peasantry, and on the other the luxurious debauchery of the Regent's Court, the numbers began for the first time to have a careless little note in them of a most piquant satire.

Louis died on September 1, 1715. Arouet was at his funeral—that funeral which was gayer than a *fête*. When a burlesque invitation to the obsequies of the Bull Unigenitus appeared, there were not wanting fingers to point at the notary's son of one-and-twenty, who had come back to Paris more audacious than ever, and had immediately resumed his connection with his wild friends of the Temple.

He read aloud his "Œdipe" to them presently. That, and his epigrams, quickly opened to him half the salons in Paris. Then Chaulieu—President of the Temple—introduced him to the magnificent Duchesse du Maine, "that living fragment of the Grand Epoch," and mistress of the famous "galères du bel esprit" at Sceaux. Madame must have him, and at once, in her salon. To be sure the boy has nothing but his play in his pocket and is of no birth at all! But what a wit and daring in his spirit! What a matchless sarcasm in those piercing eyes! The Duchess and her set worshipped cleverness and hated the Regent. It was the only religion they had. What could they do but fall in love with this "little Arouet" who could hardly have been dull if he had tried; and was much more than suspected of the authorship of a too-telling epigram on Philip of Orleans and his infamous daughter, du Berri?

"Little Arouet" read aloud "Œdipe" to the Duchess's court. He was at ease in this society as he was at ease in all societies. "Men are born equal, and die equal." "It is only externals which distinguish them." Those were the sentiments of one Arouet de Voltaire. He must have known, not the less, that here, there was no one who was *his* equal. But he sentimentalised gaily in the moonlit gardens of Sceaux—her "white nights" the Duchess called them—and watched senile old Chaulieu making love to the Duchess's companion, Mademoiselle de Launay; wrote wicked satirical poems to please his hostess; and was so clever and daring that at last all the bold brilliant things that were whispered in Paris were fathered on the presumptuous youth, the son of Saint-Simon's notary.

In the spring of 1716 he stayed with Saint-Ange again. In May he was back in the capital. He did say, no doubt, when the Regent put down half the horses in the royal stables, that he would have done better to have dismissed half the asses who had surrounded the late King. Then a shameful epigram on the shameful du Berri came to the ears of the persons chiefly concerned. Young Arouet was exiled to Tulle—Tulle being changed pretty easily, at his father's request, to Sully. No reason was assigned by the Government for this order of exile.

The Duke of Sully readily became a most hospitable host. The Duchess had a most charming poor companion, Mademoiselle de Livri. It was but an exile *pour rire*, after all—a warning fatherly rap from that paternal Government on the knuckles of an impertinent child.

It is strange to see how the boy chafed under that agreeable courtly life of hunting and conversation. "It would be delightful to stay at Sully," he wrote, "If I were only allowed to go away from it." The Duke was the most delightful of hosts, and his estate most charmingly situated. The young people of the château, in pairs, sonneted the midsummer moon in the gardens; and wrote each other dainty little quatrains and flatteries. Arouet loved verses and the society of charming and vivacious young women in general, and, here, of one charming and vivacious young woman in particular; and he was two-and-twenty. But he wrote himself back to Paris by poetic compliments to the Regent so finely turned that the author must have had some unusual spur on his imagination. He was, in fact, beginning to wonder if there was not a work waiting for him in the world.

If it was not his fault, it was the fault of the reputation he had made, that when there appeared in Paris, immediately he returned to it in the spring of 1717, two stinging satires on the state of France and the Regent's manner of life called respectively "J'ai Vu" and "Puero Regnante," they should at once be assigned to him.

"Puero Regnante" is a dog-Latin inscription.

A boy reigning;
A poisoner
Administering;
Councils ignorant and unstable;
Religion more unstable;
An exhausted treasury;
Public faith violated;
Injustice triumphant;
Sedition imminent;
The country sacrificed
To the hope of a Crown;
The inheritance anticipated;
France perishing.

The "J'ai Vu" is a short poem.

I have seen ... the prisons full;
I have seen ... the people groaning;
I have seen ... Port Royal demolished—

"I have seen," in short, everything to which a prudent person with a proper regard to his safety would have been conveniently blind.

Arouet had not written them. But that did not matter. He might have written them. They were after his manner. Besides, had he not been in exile and disgrace, and was he not still so wicked that his good old father would not have him in the house, and he was living an outcast in furnished lodgings? These reasonings would have been conclusive alone. Then he was known to be the moving spirit at Sceaux, and Sceaux was but another name for disaffection.

A spy, Beauregard, swore to a conversation he had had with Arouet, in which Arouet, with a most unnatural imprudence, avowed himself the author of both satires with much circumstantial detail; and added "things not mentionable" about the Duchesse du Berri.

He went his way quite gaily for a while, however. His "Œdipe" had been accepted, and was actually in rehearsal at the theatre. Here was a triumph indeed. He was still beloved of all the salons and the women— dear, delightful, dangerous. He had the keenest sense of humour to help him through these little *contretemps* of existence. He would, now at least, hardly have missed his *mot* to save his skin—and he held that dear, as the physically weak are apt to do. He was sauntering one day, on May 15, 1717, through the Palais Royal Gardens, runs the story, when he was called into the presence of the Regent, also sauntering there.

"I bet you, M. Arouet," says Philip, "I will show you something you have never seen before."

"What is that, Monseigneur?"

"The inside of the Bastille."

"I take it as seen," replies Arouet airily.

He could, all things considered, have been very little surprised when on May 16th, Whitsunday, while he was still sleeping calmly in bed, he was served with a *lettre de cachet*, his room and person ignominiously searched, and himself removed the next day to that historic prison. Perhaps he smiled a little, but not bitterly, when they discovered on him Pimpette's poor little note. "I am not made for the passions," he said a year or two later. He was not. A great work and a great passion seldom run together. The work must be the only passion one has.

The prison was not very painful, it appears. Arouet was allowed an excellent room, books, a fire, good wine, first-rate coffee, the use of the bowling-green and the billiard-room, visitors, to a reasonable extent, and often a seat at the governor's dinner-table. Some of the King's guests might be rotting forgotten for unknown crimes in the dungeons beneath; but, although almost all the literary men of the period were bastilled some time or other in their lives, they unite in praising the prison as very reasonably comfortable.

The present prisoner was nothing if not a philosopher. Since I am here, I may as well be as easy as I can! The captives were allowed to make purchases. Arouet entered the Bastille, Monday, May 17, 1717. On the following Thursday he signed a receipt for a couple of volumes of Homer, two Indian handkerchiefs, a little cap, two cravats, a nightcap, and a bottle of essence of cloves. He had everything he wanted, in fact, save two things. For the first few weeks of his imprisonment it seems almost certain that he was not allowed pen and ink.

But if he could not write, he could and did compose. There was that poem. Should it be called the "League," the "Henriade," or "Henry of Navarre," or what? What's in a name after all? He had a memory so marvellous and so exact that he could not only invent, without committing to paper, whole cantos of that infant epic, but remember them. The subject possessed him. He said he dreamt in his sleep, in the Bastille, the second canto on the Massacre of Saint Bartholomew exactly as it stands to-day. It is not unlikely. Now and ever when he was writing, *what* he was writing was to him food, air, warmth, light, life. "His prison became his Parnassus," said Frederick the Great in his funeral oration on Voltaire. Hundreds of projects besides that epic, to be called the "Henriade" finally, coursed through that brain, which was surely the most active ever given to man. From his captivity he could look out on his world. What was there not to do there? He must have asked himself a thousand times what part his was to be on the great stage of human existence.

"I knew how to reap benefit from my misfortune," he wrote afterwards. "I learnt how to harden myself against sorrow, and found within me a strength not to be expected from the lightness and follies of my youth."

And at Court, honest memoir-writing Saint-Simon was apologising for mentioning to his readers so insignificant a fact as that one Arouet, "the son of my father's notary," was imprisoned for some audacious verses; while at home that good old notary announced vindictively: "I told you so! I knew his idleness would lead to disgrace. Why did he not go into a profession?"

Something else Arouet did in the Bastille besides dreaming epics. He changed his name. It is now generally thought that he called himself by that one with which he has gone among the gods, after a family who were his mother's ancestors. Before the existence of this family was discovered some supposed that Voltaire was an anagram on the paternal Arouet—Arouet, L. J. (*le jeune*). Others believed that, remembering not untenderly from a prison those who had called him "le petit volontaire" in his childhood's home, he corrupted and abbreviated it into the Voltaire he was to make immortal. As to the reason for the change—"I was very unlucky under my first name," he wrote; "I want to see if this one will succeed any better." Beyond the wildest dream that ever Hope dreamt, "this one" was to succeed indeed.

The real author, a certain Le Brun, confessed to that terrible "J'ai Vu" presently, and the irrepressible supposed author, who was imprisoned for it, sat down in his prison and wrote a burlesque and very profane poem on his arrest, which had taken place, it will be remembered, on Whitsunday.

As he now had only that dog-Latin epigram, the "Puero Regnante" hanging over him, Voltaire was released from the Bastille on April 11, 1718, and exiled merely to his father's house at Châtenay. The authorities do not seem to have thought it necessary to apologise for their little mistake—a mistake which kept a brilliant boy of three-and-twenty shut up in a prison for eleven months for somebody else's rhymes. The little justice there was in France in those days miscarried so frequently that miscarriage was more the rule than the exception. The ex-prisoner wrote from Châtenay letters to the authorities begging to be allowed to return to Paris, and denying that "abominable inscription, the 'Puero,'" pretty vigorously. Only allow me to return to Paris, if but for a couple of hours, and throw myself at the feet of the Regent and explain all! I have proof now of the double-dealings of the spies who betrayed me! "A little journey, situated as I am, would be like the drop of water to the wicked rich man in the parable!" He was permitted to make that little journey, and to see Regent Philip.

"Be prudent," said Orleans, "and I will provide for you."

"I shall be delighted if your Highness will give me my board," replied the audacious young wit, "but beg that you will take no further trouble about my lodging."

Some authorities place this story at a later date and under different circumstances. If the present be its true place and time, the *mot* did not greatly help Arouet to regain his freedom, though a *mot* had done something to lose it. He was allowed to pay flying visits to the capital, but it was not until October 12, 1718, that he was given official permission to return to Paris and to stay there as long as he liked.

Either now, or before the Bastille adventure, he must needs fall in love with that pretty Mademoiselle de Livri, the Duchess of Sully's companion and relative, who would fain be an actress, with a Voltaire to teach her elocution and tenderness. The pair rode about Paris together in a bad hackney coach, and had bad suppers together—in Elysium. A friend of Voltaire's, de Génonville, fell in love with Mademoiselle presently, and she with him—to Voltaire's passing displeasure. He vented his feeling in a few graceful verses—and it vanished into air. The whole thing was but an episode after all, a *penchant* more than a passion, the light fancy of the senses that touched the deeper soul not at all. But posterity should be grateful to Mademoiselle. Voltaire had his portrait painted for her by Largillière, and may be seen to-day as he looked then—flowing wig, wide mouth, the ruffled hand thrust lightly in the waistcoat; a lover, young, satisfied with his mistress, himself, and all the world; and in the eyes and forehead, latent but present, power and will extraordinary. The mockery, the humour, and the cynicism which make later portraits of Voltaire like no other man's, are not in this one. His relations with women—niece or mistress—always show him in some respects in his best light; patient, forbearing, and faithful; generous to the memory of a false woman, giving honour where honour was due, respecting intelligence, and never weary of trying to turn a fool into a sensible companion.

But he had now other things to think of besides the sentiments. He had made his *début*, as has been well said, in epigrams. If he had not written "J'ai Vu," he *could* have written it a thousand times more damning and deadly. The most beautiful sting that ever wasp concealed beneath a gay coat, he was keeping for his enemies yet. He was still the despair of M. Arouet and the spoilt child of salons. He had a reputation but the more widespread for being evil. He was rather vain and inimitably amusing. He was so clever—he might surely do anything! He was, in fact, that most unsatisfactory creature in the world—a youth of promise.

The performance was to come.

CHAPTER III

"ŒDIPE," AND THE JOURNEY TO HOLLAND

ON November 18, 1718, there was produced in Paris the tragedy of "Œdipe," by M. Arouet de Voltaire.

The subject of the play is classical and the plot entirely impossible. Love interest there is none. The style is not a little bombastical and long-winded. The characters are always talking about what they are going to do, instead of doing it. The good people are very, very good, and the bad ones very, very bad. At the best they are brilliant automatons—masks, not faces.

The play has indeed the perfect smoothness and elegance dear to the French soul. All the unities are nicely observed, and there is never an anachronism. But to make it the astounding success it was, it must have had in it something better even than the brilliant ingenuity of a Voltaire—something better even than a Voltaire's perfect knowledge of the human nature for which he was writing. It contained the first trumpet call of the Voltairian message.

The house was crowded. It was the custom of the day for the playwright to beat up his friends and engage them to applaud the first steps of the child of his brain. But here also were enemies and neutrals—all Paris agog to see the next move in the game of a daring player. Among the audience, half grumbling, half delighted, was old Maître Arouet. "The rascal! the rascal!" he muttered, as some bold touch brought down the house. Brother Armand should have been there too, to have heard the strangely passionate enthusiasm with which was received the couplet which, after all, merely referred to the pagan priesthood of a long dead age:

Our priests are not what a foolish people think them!
Our credulity makes all their knowledge.

But "when fanaticism has once gangrened a brain, the malady is incurable," said Voltaire; and neither he nor any other could alter an Armand. A certain Maréchale de Villars—*galante*, coquette, with all the easy *ton* learnt in Courts, and all the French woman's *aplomb* and grace to make five-and-thirty more dangerous than five-and-twenty—leant curiously out of her box presently to watch a young buffoon of an actor who was doing his best to ruin M. de Voltaire's play. The high priest, in a scene essentially grave and tragic, has as train-bearer a lean-faced, narrow-shouldered, boyish-looking youth who must needs take *his* part as comic, and make a fool not of himself only but of his high priest also. Who is the ridiculous boy? M. de Voltaire. It appears deliciously piquant to the Maréchale that an author should run the risk of damning his own work for a jest. What a refreshing person to have to stay when one is a little bored! Madame receives him in her box—he knows quite well how to behave and how to be as affable, daring, and amusing as could be wished—and they begin a friendship, not without result.

There were some allusions to the Regent and Madame du Berri in "Œdipe," very vociferously applauded, which must have made Maître Arouet groan in spirit and think that after all his Armand, his rigid "fool in prose" at home, was safer to deal with than this "fool in verse" on the boards, who would *not* be warned and *must* come to the gallows. But the Regent, like a wise man, hearing of that astounding first night and the allusions, presented the author with a gold medal and a thousand crowns; talked with him publicly at the next Opera ball, and made a point of coming to the performance to show that the arrows could not have been really intended for him after all.

As for the Duchesse du Berri, *she* came five nights in succession to the piece. And of course all the little, witty, disaffected Court of Maine were there too, enjoying those allusions and looking hard at their enemies, the Regent and his daughter.

The curtain went down on perhaps the most successful *début* that ever playwright had made. "Œdipe" ran for forty-five nights. Clever Philip commanded it to Court to be performed before the little Louis XV. The enterprising and energetic young author asked, and obtained, permission to dedicate it, in book form, to downright old Charlotte Elizabeth, the Regent's mother. He sent a copy, with a flaming sonnet, to George I. of England; and yet another copy to the Regent's sister, the Duchess of Lorraine, with a letter wherein is to be found his first signature of his new name, Arouet de Voltaire. When the Prince de Conti, his old Temple companion, complimented "Œdipe" and its author in a poem of his own, "Sir," said Voltaire airily, "you will be a great poet; I must get the King to give you a pension."

The young playwright gained from "Œdipe"—not including the Regent's present—about four thousand francs, besides a fine capital of fame. He was the old notary's son to some purpose after all, and began to invest money. As to the fame, he took *that* very modestly. When the women declared his "Œdipe" to be a thousand times better than his old hero Corneille's play on the same subject, the young man made the happiest quotation from Corneille himself, disclaiming superiority.

He attended every one of the forty-five performances—a learner of his own art and of the actors'.

He must have gone back gay and well pleased enough on those evenings to his furnished room in the Rue de Calandre.

In the spring of 1719 the faithless and charming Mademoiselle de Livri insisted on his using his influence to get her a good part in his play. Perhaps she, Voltaire, and "little de Génonville" enjoyed themselves about Paris together as before. "Que nous nous aimions tous trois!... que nous étions heureux!" the forsaken lover wrote ten years later in his graceful poem to the memory of de Génonville.

Mademoiselle was no actress, though she wished to be one. Her very accent was provincial. She was laughed off the stage when "Œdipe" was revived after Lent, and Voltaire very nearly came to blows with one of the laughers, Poisson, who was one of the actors too. He had Poisson thrown into prison, and then himself obtained his release. Poisson and the public were right after all, and Voltaire soon knew it.

Mademoiselle retired from the boards, and married.

When a few years later, Voltaire went to call on her in her fine house when she was the Marquise de Gouvernet, and her huge Swiss porter, not knowing him, refused him admission, he sent her "Les Vous et Les Tu," one of the most charmingly graceful and bantering of all his poems. In his old age at Ferney, when the first rose of the year appeared he would pluck it and kiss it to the memory of Mademoiselle de Livri. Perhaps it was of her he thought when he wrote one of the few tender lines to be found in his works, and one of the tenderest in any poetry:

C'est moi qui te dois tout, puisque c'est moi qui t'aime.

On his last great visit to Paris, when he was nearly eighty-four and she not much younger, the two met for the last time—ghosts out of shadowland—in a strange new world.

In this same spring of 1719 there appeared in Paris another satire on the Regent, called the "Philippics." M. de Voltaire had not written it, to be sure. But it was clever, and sounded as if he had. Besides, he was known to be the friend of the Duchesse du Maine, at the present moment shut up, with her Court, in the Bastille; of the gorgeous Duke of Richelieu and of the Spanish ambassador who were accomplices in a conspiracy against Orleans. So in May the authorities requested M. de Voltaire to spend the summer in the country; and he spent it at Villars.

If the Maréchale had been charming in Paris, she was a thousand times more so here. If she had flattered a brilliant young author in her box at the theatre, she flattered and petted him a thousand times better now she had him to herself, an interesting young exile. Such a clever boy! so witty! so cynical! so amusing! He certainly ought to have been clever enough to guess that this woman of the world was only playing with him. But he was vain too—and did not guess it. "Friendship is a thousand times better worth having than love," he wrote disconsolately in a letter after a while. "There is something in me which makes it ridiculous for me to love.... It is all over. I renounce it for life." The renunciation was not so easy as he expected. He was, at least for a time, out of gear, restless, discontented. The husband, Louis XIV.'s famous marshal, had a thousand anecdotes of the Sun King to relate. And the future author of the "Century of Louis XIV." was almost too *distrait* to listen to them. He forgot Paris and his career. He forgot the dazzling success of "Œdipe." He would not indeed have been Voltaire, but some lesser man, if he had let this or any other passion ride over him rough-shod. He had the "Henriade" and a new play with him. He turned to his work—worked like a fury—until he had worked the folly out of him. But, not the less, "he never spoke of it afterwards but with a feeling of regret, almost of remorse."

By June 25, 1719, he was at Sully, where he wrote most of his new play, "Artémire," and spent the autumn and part of the winter. Paris had gone mad over the financial schemes of John Law, and it was well that a young man of five-and-twenty, with a taste for speculation and money in his pocket for the first time, should be out of the way of temptation. From Sully he went back to Villars, and from Villars to the Duke of Richelieu's. "I go from château to château," he wrote. He liked the life well, no doubt. It was gay, easy, witty. For anyone else it would have been idle too; but not for a Voltaire.

He had already complained that his passion for his Maréchale de Villars had lost him a good deal of his time. But, all the same, by February, 1720, "Artémire" was finished, and its author was back in Paris superintending its rehearsals.

Its first appearance took place on February 13, 1720. It is not too much to say that it was a most dismal failure.

Adrienne Lecouvreur, the great tragic actress, had hoped everything from it. At a private reading a certain Abbé de Bussi had shed so many tears at its pathos that he had caught cold from them. The public was not so soft-hearted. It was in no mood for plays. Law had just ruined half Paris. When the crash came—"Paper," said Voltaire, with his usual neat incisiveness, "is now reduced to its intrinsic value." Someone says that this mot was the funeral oration of Law's system. Law's system was the funeral oration of "Artémire." It was a dull, feeble play. Not all its author's rewritings and correctings and embellishments—and it was his custom to rewrite, correct, and embellish all his works until labour and genius could do no more for them—could ever make it good enough for him to publish as a whole. But when the public took it exactly at his own valuation, he was not a little hurt. It was a later Voltaire who said that he envied the beasts because of their ignorance of evil to come and *of what people said of them*. He was not less sensitive now than then. The last performance of the rewritten "Artémire" took place on March 8, 1720. When, soon after, the "Henriade" was criticised at a private reading, he threw it disgustedly into the fire; and President Hénault saved it at the price of a pair of lace ruffles. Perhaps the fire was not very bright, or the author had a very shrewd idea that one of his friends would not let a masterpiece be lost to posterity.

He went to stay again with Richelieu after his "Artémire" disappointment; and from there wrote to Theriot telling him to copy out, in his very best handwriting, cantos of the "Henriade" which were to be propitiatingly presented to the Regent. From Richelieu Voltaire went to Sully, and from Sully to La Source, the home of the great St. John, Lord Bolingbroke, and his French wife.

In the June of 1721, he went back to Villars again. He could trust himself to see his Maréchale now. They had "white nights" here as at Sceaux and at Sully. They gaily astronomised through opera glasses in the long, warm, starlit summer nights in the garden—with the assistance of that fashionable "Plurality of Worlds" by M. de Fontenelle. "We mistake Venus for Mercury," Voltaire wrote to him gaily in verse, "And break up the order of the Heavens."

From that modish courtly life the man who had been François Marie Arouet was summoned home in the December of 1721 to the death-bed of his old father. A strange group gathered round it—Catherine, Madame Mignot, a middle-aged married woman; Armand, the austere and surly Jansenist of eight-and-thirty; and the most brilliant man in France. Good old Maître Arouet went the way of all flesh, trusting greatly neither in his "fool in prose" nor his "fool in verse," but leaving Prose a post in the Chamber of Accounts which brought in thirteen thousand francs yearly, and Verse a sum which afforded him four thousand odd francs per annum. He had appointed a trustee and guardian, with whom Verse, who was always what his valets thereafter charitably called *vif*, immediately quarrelled.

The guardian was indeed such a dilatory old person that it took him four years to divide the estate among Maître Arouet's children; and two years after his father's death Voltaire was writing lugubriously to Theriot, "I shall be obliged to work to live, after having lived to work."

Things were not quite so bad as that, however. When he left the Bastille the Regent had given him a pension of twelve hundred francs. And now, a few days after his father's death, in January, 1722, the boy King, Louis XV., made him a further pension of two thousand francs. From this moment Voltaire never spent his whole income.

In no other concern of his life has he been so much misrepresented as in his dealings with money matters.

It is hard to see why for all other men independence should be considered honourable and a freedom of the spirit, and grinding poverty an inspiration and liberty only to the man of letters. But the peculiarly foolish idea that genius cannot be genius if it understands its bank-book, and that great truths can only come from a garret and an ill-fed brain, is not yet extinct. Many of Voltaire's biographers feel that they have to apologise for him paying his bills regularly, hunting out his creditors, and investing his money with shrewdness and caution. It would have been so much more romantic to have flung it about royally—and then borrowed someone else's!

But Voltaire knew that "poverty enervates the courage." He never uttered a truer word. If it was his mission to whip the world's apathy into action with unpalatable truths, he could not depend on that world for the bread he put into his mouth and the coat he put on his back. "Ask nothing of anyone; need no one." "My vocation is to say what I think *fari quæ sentiam*." If Voltaire had been insolvent the Voltairian message could never have been uttered.

In this May of 1722, he further sought to improve his monetary position by running to earth, for Cardinal Dubois—the first, greatest, and vilest of the Regent's Prime Ministers—a spy, one Salamon Levi. Voltaire does not appear to have thought the occupation a derogatory one. Nor did it hurt his cynic and elastic conscience to flatter "Iscariot" Dubois to the top of his bent both in verse and prose, and declare that he (Voltaire) would be eternally grateful if Dubois would employ him somehow, in something.

The pension from the King—very irregularly paid at first, and soon not paid at all—was not taken by him as the authorities must have hoped it would be, and neither shut his mouth nor quenched his spirit. It was nominally a tribute to a talented young playwriter. He took it virtually as such. His old talent for getting into mischief was as lively as ever; and spies at this period seem to have had an unlucky fascination for him. One night in July, 1722, at the house of the Minister of War he met Beauregard, the spy who had been the instrument of putting him into the Bastille. "I knew spies were paid," he said, "but I did not know that it was by eating at the minister's table." Beauregard bided his time, and fell on the poet one night on the Bridge of Sèvres as he was crossing it in his sedan chair, beating him severely. To give blows with a cane was thereafter translated "*Voltairiser*" in the mouth of Voltaire's enemies. He had many of them. He had made so many *mots*! They denied him his proper share of physical courage. D'Argenson, his friend, though he said he had in his soul a strength worthy of Turenne, of Moses, and of Gustavus Adolphus, yet added that he feared the least dangers for his body and was "a proven coward." He was certainly, now and ever, a most nervously organised creature. When he was at fever heat he could be plucky

J. B. ROUSSEAU

From an Engraving after a Picture by J. Aved

enough. But there is as little doubt that he dearly loved his safety as that he spent his whole life in endangering it.

He pursued Beauregard with a most nimble, passionate, vivid intensity. He must have had an extraordinary persistence to get that unwieldy mass of muddle and jobbery which called itself French law to administer any kind of justice; but he did it. It took him more than fifteen months to compass his revenge, and cost him immense sums of money as well as immense labour. The game was not worth the candle. But Voltaire was never the person to think of that. To him the game was everything while he pursued it. It was to this characteristic he owed some of his success in life.

The affair of the Bridge of Sèvres was, not the less, one of the most unfortunate incidents of his experience. To the day of his death it was a whip in the hands of his enemies which they used without mercy and without ceasing.

He must have been tired of fighting and failure, and in need of quiet and change when one of his philosophic marquises—a certain Madame de Rupelmonde—"young, rich, agreeable," took him with her in July, 1722, as her guest, on a trip to Holland. Her witty companion of eight-and-twenty was in no sense her lover. The few *convenances* there were left in those days quite permitted such an association. The two had for each other merely a gallant friendship. Madame was a widow, of easy virtue, and fashionable enough to have religious doubts—to wish to be taught to think. As they jolted leisurely in her post-chaise over the rough roads of old France they had plenty of time to discuss fate, free will, life, death, and the theologies. Voltaire found time, too, during the trip, to answer Madame's questions by an "Epistle to Uranie"—in which he gave, in a few graceful pages, and with the admirable terseness and lucidity which were to be the hall-mark of all his writings, the most powerful objections to Christianity. It was his first open avowal of Deism. How long he had cherished that belief and outgrown all others, cannot be told. The whole temper of his mind was rationalistic. Christianity had come to him through the muddy channel of French Roman Catholicism in the eighteenth century. He began by disbelieving the shameless superstitions with which the Churchmen darkened and debased the understanding of the people. He ended by disbelieving everything which his reason could not follow. The process is easy and not uncommon.

The philosophic pair were much fêted *en route*. "Œdipe" was performed when they were at Cambrai, as a delicate compliment. There was a Congress going on there too; and Voltaire wrote gaily therefrom to Cardinal Dubois (who was archbishop of the place but had never even seen it) one of those audacious, easy letters which were his *forte*, and which Dubois and Theriot between them passed round the salons of Paris. Voltaire and Madame were at Cambrai for some five or six weeks, and then went on to Brussels. Here lived now J. B. Rousseau, fifty-two years old, who from wit and licence had passed to dulness and orthodoxy. Of course the poets met. Voltaire had not seen Rousseau since he was a schoolboy, and Rousseau had been shown him as a prodigy for imitation. To the gay, unsparing logic of the younger poet the old one did not appear at all in the light of a prodigy now. "He despises me because I neglect rhyme, and I despise him because he can do nothing but rhyme," said Voltaire carelessly.

At first, however, all went well. Voltaire read his "master" as he called him, a part of the "Henriade." Rousseau praised it, only criticising such passages as would be likely to give offence to the Church. Then came a meeting, when the poets read to each other some of their minor poems; and Madame de Rupelmonde was a gracious and sympathetic listener. Rousseau read his satire, the "Judgment of Pluto"; which was nothing but an account of the wrongs which had exiled him. And Voltaire said the "Judgment" was unworthy of the Great and Good Rousseau. Then Rousseau must needs read out his "Ode to Posterity," on the same subject. "That is a letter, master," says Voltaire, "which will never reach its address." Then Voltaire takes his "Epistle to Uranie" and reads *that*. "Stop, stop!" cries old Rousseau, still smarting under the audacious boy's criticisms. "What horrible profanity!" And Voltaire asks since when the author of the "Moïsade" has become devout.

There was the making of a very pretty quarrel here. The one sun was rising, the other setting. Both men were not a little vain, sensitive, and jealous. Henceforth, it was war to the knife. They parted; and if Voltaire forgave at the last, Rousseau never did.

Rousseau recorded afterwards how Voltaire attended Mass on the first day of his arrival at Brussels and shocked the congregation by his profanity. The story was true, though it was written by an enemy. Voltaire was born irreverent. When he left Brussels he did not even revere that hero of his youth, Rousseau.

By October, 1722, he and Madame had gone on to The Hague and Amsterdam.

The young man was always out dining and playing tennis there, reading aloud his works, keen, active, enjoying himself. His health, of which he was exceedingly fond of talking and complaining was better than it had ever been; but that did not prevent him from drinking up one day as a kind of medical experiment—"from greediness," said Madame de Rupelmonde—a bottle of medicine from her bedside which she was going to have taken, from necessity.

Perhaps in the midst of gaiety and enjoyment Voltaire recalled the last time he was here, Pimpette, and that wild episode of his youth. But this was the man who was always agog for the future; never a dreamer of the past—a doer, an actor, the most energetic spirit in history.

When he was at The Hague he was busy arranging for the publication of his "Henriade" there, in that freer country, and continually reading and reciting extracts from it to his friends. After a few weeks' visit he started on his journey home. Madame de Rupelmonde had a house at The Hague, and as there was no other agreeable marquise with a travelling carriage returning to France just then, M. de Voltaire did the journey on horseback alone, and as economically as he could.

He was at Cambrai again on October 31, 1722, announcing the forthcoming publication of his epic. At the beginning of the new year, 1723, he was once more staying at La Source, near Orleans, with that exiled Lord Bolingbroke who had, said his guest, "all the learning of his own country and all the politeness of ours." The guest read aloud that dear epic. He called it "The League or Henry IV." now, or "The League," or "Henry IV." only. He advertised it industriously at every château he stayed at. In Paris Theriot was trying to get subscriptions for it, and to propitiate the censor. From La Source Voltaire went to stay with other friends at Ussé, who were also friends of a charming early friend of his own, Madame de Mimeure.

By February 23, 1723, he was back again in Paris seeing a new play by Alexis Piron, called "Harlequin Deucalion," wherein the failure of "Artémire" was piquantly satirised. "Deucalion" is remarkable as having obeyed a prohibition of the censor, designed to stop comic opera in Paris, that not more than one person should appear on the stage at a time, and as having succeeded in spite of that obedience.

Then the active Voltaire was off to Rouen, where lived his old friend Cideville. Then he went on to Rivière Bourdet, near Rouen, the country home of the Bernières, a married couple, also very much his friends. All the time he was planning, scheming, working, for the production of his "Henriade." Almost all his letters of the year 1723 are to Theriot or Madame de Bernières, and almost all on this topic. In May he was staying at the Bernières town house, on what is now the Quai Voltaire and was then the Quai des Théatins, opposite the gardens of the Tuileries. The "Henriade" was finished at last. The subscription lists had not gone well; their ill-success had been burlesqued in the play which succeeded "Deucalion." That was mortifying. Still, it was but the chagrin of a moment. The "Henriade" was about to appear. It must and should succeed! Had not its wary author read parts to the Regent, and changed phrases which might have offended Dubois? The only thing he would not do was to alter its principles to suit the blindest and most autocratic powers that ever brought a country to ruin.

It must take its chance! It took it, and was prohibited by the censor immediately.

CHAPTER IV

THE "HENRIADE," AND A VISIT TO COURT

CONSIDERED as a poem, the "Henriade" is the kind of fighting epic which is the delight of schoolboys and a little apt to bore their elders.

The subject is the life of Henry of Navarre; the chief event, the Massacre of St. Bartholomew. Truth, Discord, and other abstract virtues are embodied, and talk at some length. The poem is modelled on, if not imitated from, Horace and Virgil. Regarded on the surface it is nothing but a dramatic story, easy, swinging, smooth, and with the lilt and rhythm such a story requires.

But beneath that surface, not seen but felt, beneath the easy couplets and running rhymes, there beats a spirit alert for liberty—the wings of the wild bird against the cage which keeps it from life, sunshine, and freedom. The pivot on which the poem turns is that supreme intolerance, the Massacre of St. Bartholomew. Its atmosphere throughout is that of hatred of priestly power, fanaticism, superstition; the love of peace, justice, enlightenment. Its religion is Deism. And its dedication to Louis XV. contains these astounding words: "You are king only because Henry IV. was a great man; and France, while wishing you as much virtue, and more happiness than he had, flatters herself that the life and the throne you owe to him will bind you to follow his example;" and "The astonishment we feel when kings sincerely love the happiness of their people is a thing very shameful to them." Voltaire himself said afterwards that he had advocated in it peace and tolerance in religion and told Rome many home truths. No wonder the censor damned it.

If anything had been needed—but nothing was needed—to make Voltaire more alert, eager, and determined to give his epic to the world, it would have been that ministerial prohibition. Its publication in Holland was conditional on its publication in Paris. Voltaire, as has been well said, had not written an epic to keep it in a portfolio. He lost no time. With the help of the Bernières and ever ready and good-natured Theriot, he surreptitiously printed two thousand copies at Rouen. That occupation took at least five months—from the June of 1723 until the October. He was himself mostly in Paris, staying with the Bernières on the Quai des Théatins, where the noise nearly drove him distracted; or in a very poor lodging of his own. Garret or château, what did it matter? The "Henriade" was everything—his world.

In September he was back at Rivière Bourdet. Everyone concerned in the scheme was infinitely active and secret. "Little de Génonville" died in this September of a very bad kind of smallpox then epidemic in Paris. Voltaire mourned him much and long. He had a new tragedy in hand to keep his mind from the tragedies and trials of life, and turned to "Mariamne" for the comfort and change of thought he needed. It was finished early in November, and the author put it in his pocket and went to stay with his friend M. de Maisons, at the Château of Maisons, in the forest of St. Germains, nine miles from Paris, where were fêtes, parties, gaieties, and where Adrienne Lecouvreur was coming to read "Mariamne" to the guests.

Maisons was but four-and-twenty, delicate, noble, accomplished; destined, it seemed, for all great things, but to die too soon. Madame, his wife, was the friend of that old love of Voltaire's, Madame de Villars.

By November 4th, at least two of the guests, Voltaire and Adrienne Lecouvreur, had arrived. Two days later Voltaire developed smallpox.

No one can gain an adequate idea of his character without realising in what "a thin and wretched case" Nature had enveloped "what is called my soul." No other great man, perhaps, ever fought such a plucky fight against physical weakness, weariness, and infirmities. Voltaire was not always ill, but he was never well. One of his valets said that his state of indisposition was natural and permanent and accompanied him from the cradle to the grave. He himself said he had never passed a single day without suffering, and could not even imagine what it must be like to be in robust health. But he had what he called his "infallible secret"—work. Others have used physical weakness as an excuse for mental idleness, and indisposition as a natural holiday from labour. But not Voltaire. He dictated when he was too ill to write and when he was too ill to think, he read dull books for information which he might find useful and make amusing; and when he was yet worse, and could do nothing else, he read and wrote that gay mockery of his leisure, his "Pucelle." The body was but the ragged covering of the soul at its best; at its worst, it was a subtle and seducing enemy, and one must be ever up and at it, with a thrust here and a lunge there, lest by any means it get the mastery. Voltaire fought it his whole life long—and always won. "Toujours allant et souffrant" was his definition of himself. He hardly ever made a happier.

In the present case, his disease was of that confluent type which a couple of months earlier had killed de Génonville. Voltaire was very ill. He went so far, he said, as to call the *curé*, make his confession, and his will, "which, you will well believe, was very short."

But he was placed under the enlightened care of a Doctor Gervasi, physician to the Chevalier de Rohan, who saved his life with much lemonade and more common-sense.

Voltaire had always that interest in medicine which by no means implies faith in doctors. With two famous exceptions—Gervasi was one—he mistrusted that eighteenth-century faculty as it deserved to be mistrusted. He wrote afterwards a very minute description of his symptoms and treatment for the benefit of an old Baron de Breteuil, the father of Madame du Châtelet.

Adrienne Lecouvreur, it is said, who once had been something more than Voltaire's friend, never left his bedside until Theriot, whom she had summoned, came to be with him.

The Maisons were prodigal of kindnesses. The day after he was out of absolute danger, the patient was writing verses. On the twenty-sixth day from his seizure, that is December 1, 1723, he left for Paris. He was not more than two hundred feet away from the château when the wing he had been occupying caught fire and was burnt to the ground.

As such accidental disinfectants were the only ones known to that age, the conflagration was a blessing in disguise. But Voltaire naturally felt overwhelmed with compunction, as if he had burnt the château himself. As for the Maisons, the letters they wrote him are examples of that exquisite grace and tact known to complete perfection only to France, and to the France before the Revolution.

In the very early days of 1724 certain innocent-looking, plodding agricultural vans arrived in Paris from Rouen. By the exertions of Madame de Bernières the great packages they contained got through the *douane*—somehow. Theriot was ready in the capital with his two thousand bindings. Voltaire's injunctions that his child should be properly clad had not been in vain.

The August of 1723 had seen the death of Cardinal Dubois; the December the death of the Regent. Surely the time was favourable! The censor had condemned the book—what advertisement could be better?

And lo! on a sudden the "League" was all over the city—on the toilet tables of the women, in the salons, in the coffee-houses; aye, and in the King's palace itself. It was of course a thousand times more tempting and delicious for being forbidden fruit.

Was it absurdly imitated from the "Æneid?" Did Henry of Navarre and Elizabeth of England, who never met in real life, meet in the poem for an immense interview? Well, what of that? It was daring, impetuous, and prohibited. That was enough. It was soon all over Europe translated into many languages, fulsomely admired, parodied, burlesqued, abused, pirated, copied. It had all the successes. A year

LOUIS XV.

From the Picture by Carle Van Loo in the Museum at Versailles

later Voltaire could say truthfully in his airy manner that he had made poetry the fashion.

The production of his tragedy "Mariamne" at the Comédie Française in this March of 1724 came like a dash of cold water on his rising spirits. It was a failure. A wag in the pit spoilt the critical moment of the heroine's death with a foolish *mot*.

The author withdrew "Mariamne" to rewrite it, as was his indefatigable fashion, and went to recover his disappointment and his always ailing health at the waters of Forges, near Rouen, whither he was accompanied by the young Duke of Richelieu.

At Forges the invalid drank the waters, lost his money at faro, wrote a gay little comedy called "L'Indiscret," and made the acquaintance of the French Court, then at Chantilly, near Forges.

The French Court then consisted of a King of fourteen; the Duke of Bourbon, who had obtained the post of Prime Minister simply by asking for it; and the Duke's mistress, Madame de Prie. The mistress may be said to have ruled the kingdom, since she ruled the Duke, and the Duke ruled the King.

This wary Voltaire propitiated her, dedicated to her "L'Indiscret," and made her his very useful friend. Drinking the waters ("There is more vitriol in a bottle of Forges water than in a bottle of ink," he wrote; "and I do not believe ink is so very good for the health") was brought to a tragic conclusion by the Duc de Melun, who was out hunting with Richelieu, being gored to death by a stag. The hunt was at Chantilly, and the unhappy Melun died in the arms of the Duke of Bourbon and in the presence of the Court. Voltaire, who never abandoned a friend, stayed another fortnight to console Richelieu, and then went back to Paris, which he had reached by August 15th.

He had a lodging in the Rue de Beaune now, but the unbearable noise of the street drove him into an *hôtel garni*, and the discomforts of the *hôtel garni* back again to the Rue de Beaune. Finally, he completed an arrangement begun the year before, and rented a room from the Bernières in their noisy house.

Wherever he was, he was working as usual. He rewrote "Mariamne." He obtained for Theriot the offer of the secretaryship to Richelieu— Richelieu having been appointed ambassador to Vienna. And M. Theriot is too idle to be bothered with regular work, and twice declines the offer. Voltaire was not a little mortified, and found forgiveness difficult; but he forgave. His letters on the subject are an admirable lesson in the arts of friendship and of forbearance.

In April of the next year, 1725, the rewritten "Mariamne" was produced, with that gay little *bagatelle*, "L'Indiscret," after it. "L'Indiscret" was said to justify its name in that it took too much liberty with the upper classes. "Mariamne" was very fairly successful now. But, after all, the author had had it and "L'Indiscret," as well as the "Henriade," all printed at his own expense, and at a very great expense. Fame, he observed, was agreeable but not nourishing. His thrifty soul began to look out for the nourishment.

In this summer of 1825, Louis XV., aged fifteen, was to be married to Marie Leczinska, aged twenty-one, daughter of Stanislas, ex-King of

Poland. Madame de Prie gave Voltaire the refusal of rooms in her house at Fontainebleau, where the royal honeymoon was to be spent. Here was an opportunity! He had said not a year ago that he had renounced Courts for ever through the weakness of his stomach and the strength of his reason.

But in many respects, and in this respect above all, he was nothing if not inconsistent. He cried for royal favour as a spoilt child cries for the moon; and when he had it, it bored, wearied, and irritated him. But in his day, if the King, and the person who ruled the King, did not smile on talent, talent had small chance of success. "To make one's fortune," Voltaire wrote bitterly hereafter, "it is better to speak four words to the King's mistress than to write a hundred volumes."

So on August 27, 1725, he came up to Madame de Prie's house at Fontainebleau. The festivities were in full swing, though the marriage was yet to come. Voltaire was one-and-thirty. He was there by his own choice. He knew himself to be for the first time in his life well placed. Yet his visit had not lasted three days when he wished himself away again. There was a dreadful rumour, too, that all the pensions were to be discontinued, and a new tax imposed instead to pay for the bride's chiffons! Then Voltaire wrote a little *divertissement* to amuse the royalties, and the master of the ceremonies preferred "Le Médecin Malgré Lui." On Wednesday, September 5th, the wedding took place. Then the bride accorded her gracious permission to M. de Voltaire to dedicate to her "Œdipe" and "Mariamne." Things were a little better! Her father, with whom Voltaire was to have much to do hereafter, begged for a copy of the "Henriade" on his daughter's recommendation. Voltaire was presented to her Majesty. Things were better still. "She has wept at 'Mariamne,' she has laughed at 'L'Indiscret,' she talks to me often, she calls me her 'poor Voltaire.'" Charming! charming! but just a little bit—well, unsubstantial. And then she allowed her poet a pension of fifteen hundred livres.

Voltaire's state of mind at Court was the state of mind of many— perhaps of most—courtiers. It is a dreadful bore to be here—but it is very advantageous! The cage is really so exquisitely gilded that one must try not to see the bars through the gilt! I want to get out, and I could get out—but I am so very lucky to be here, and so many people envy me, that I certainly will *not*. What an inexplicable and yet what a very common state of mind it is!

Voltaire could now count on the friendship, not only of the Queen, but of Madame de Prie, and of the minister Duverney. He was a pensioner of both their Majesties. The Court acknowledged him the first poet in France. Epigrams and the Bastille were in the background. He had hopes of being useful to his friends.

All this was not ungenerous payment for three months' ennui at the finest Court in the world. But was it sufficient? Voltaire had indeed his gift of satiric observation to make the dullest entertainment amusing. "The Queen is every day assassinated with Pindaric odes, sonnets, epistles, and epithalamiums," he wrote; "I should think she takes the poets for the Court fools; and if she does she is right, for it is a great folly for a man of letters to be here." The boredom was stronger than the satisfaction after all. To hang about in the antechamber, tickling the jaded fancy of the Court gentlemen with one's *mots*—to try and rouse the sleepy selfishness of a callow king with one's finest wit—to flatter and cajole a duke's mistress and a poor, honest, simple little foreigner because she happened to be a king's wife—to play for apples of Sodom that turned to dust and ashes at one's touch—was it worth while? "It is better to be a lackey of wits than a wit of lackeys"— better to do any work than none—better any life than this narcotic sleep of easy idleness. In Voltaire's ear that siren, Verse, was always whispering and calling him away. In his heart were passionate convictions throbbing to be spoken. He had been glad to go to Court. He was more than glad to get away.

His zeal for a fight must have been more to the fore than ever after those three months of amiable apathy. He had it soon enough.

It was in the December of 1725 that the great Chevalier de Rohan, meeting this lean, brilliant, impertinent upstart of an author at the opera, said to him scornfully, "M. de Voltaire—Arouet—whatever your name is— —?"

The Chevalier de Rohan was himself the representative of the haughtiest and most illustrious family in France, and of the same house as that Rohan who was to drag its pride through the mud of the episode of the Diamond Necklace.

A middle-aged debauchee; "a degenerate plant, a coward and a usurer"—in the vigorous words of a contemporary—was this great Chevalier whom Voltaire met that night.

He made no answer at the moment. Two days after, at the Comédie Française—most likely in Adrienne Lecouvreur's box there—Rohan repeated the question.

"I do not drag about a great name, but I know how to honour the name I bear," was the answer. There is another version of it: "I begin my name; the Chevalier de Rohan finishes his." Or, as Voltaire himself wrote after in "Rome Sauvée":

My name begins with me: your honour fend
Lest yours with you shall have an end.

The answer was at least one which made the Chevalier raise his cane; and Voltaire clapped his hand on his sword. Adrienne, of course, fainted, and the incident closed.

A few days later Voltaire was dining with the Duke of Sully. He was called from the table to speak to someone in a carriage outside. He went unsuspiciously enough. A couple of Rohan's lackeys fell on him and beat him over the shoulders. Rohan, it is said, looked out of the window of his coach and called out: "Don't hit his head! something good may come out of that!" And the bystanders, cringing to rank and success as they needs must, observed admiringly, "The noble lord!" Voltaire, beside himself with fury, flung off his assailants at last, rushed back to Sully, begged him to redress the wrong, to go to the police, to speak to the minister. Voltaire had been as "a son of the house" for ten years, and had immortalised Sully's ancestors in the "Henriade." But Sully was not going to brave the wrath of such a great man as his cousin Rohan for a *bourgeois* author with a talent for getting into disgrace. Voltaire left the house—never to enter it again. He went straight to the opera, where he knew he would find Madame de Prie, told her his story, and enlisted her sympathy. For a few days it seemed as if she would succeed in getting her lover, the Duke of Bourbon's, influence for Voltaire. But the friends of Rohan showed the Duke an epigram on his one eye, which sounded clever enough to be Voltaire's, and ruined his credit at once. He was baffled on every side. Marais, that keen old legal writer of memoirs, declares that, though he showed himself as much as he could in town and Court, no one pitied him, and his so-called friends turned their backs. He had been publicly caned! He was ridiculous! And the fear of being absurd was a thousand times stronger than the fear of hell in eighteenth-century Paris. Any other but Voltaire would have hidden his head in obscurity and have been thankful to be forgotten.

But with this man an insult raised all the vivid intensity of his nature. "God take care of my friends," said he; "I can look after my enemies myself." For more than three months he led a life of feverish indignation and was every moment busy with revenge. He learnt fencing. He had no aptitude for any bodily exercise. But he perfected himself in this one with all the persistency and thoroughness of his nature. If he was not normally courageous, he had plenty of daring now. The Rohans, anyhow, feared him so much that they kept him under police supervision. On April 16, 1726, the lieutenant of police recorded that Voltaire intended to insult Rohan with *éclat* and at once; that he was living at his fencing master's, but continually changing his residence. On April 17th Voltaire went to Adrienne Lecouvreur's box at the Comédie, where he knew he would find Rohan. Theriot accompanied him and stood without the box, but where he could hear everything. "Sir," said Voltaire, "if you have not forgotten the outrage of which I complain, I hope you will give me satisfaction." The great man agreed. The hour fixed was nine o'clock the next morning; the place, St. Martin's Gate. But before that, Voltaire found himself for the second time in the Bastille. One can hardly fancy a meaner revenge. By March 28, 1726, the influence, cunning, and poltroonery of Rohan had succeeded in getting signed the warrant for his enemy's arrest and detention. Rohan, in fact, was a great noble; and Voltaire, as his rival playwright Piron said to himself, was "nothing, not even an Academician." Armand and his faction were only too glad to be rid of such a stormy petrel.

It is not hard to understand what a passion against the bitter injustice of his gorgeous day must have surged in Voltaire's heart. "You do not hear in England," he wrote but a very short time after, "of *haute*, *moyenne*, and *basse* justice." It was in fact literally true that in France at that period there was not only really, but avowedly, one "justice" for the noble, another for the *bourgeois*, and a third for the *canaille*. Voltaire was in the Bastille only a fortnight. He was very well treated. "Everyone he knew," wrote Delaunay the governor, came to see him; so his visitors had to be limited to six a day. Theriot brought him English books. He dined at Delaunay's table. Also imprisoned in the Bastille was the famous Madame de Tencin—young, clever, and corrupt. "We were like Pyramus and Thisbe," Voltaire wrote, "only we did not kiss each other through the chink in the wall." He could still write gaily. As some people never speak without a stammer, Voltaire never spoke without a jest. But what food in his heart for new strange thought! Under what crushing laws was this great French people bound in darkness, wretchedness, ignorance! "We are born in slavery and die in it." It has been said that Voltaire left France a poet and returned from England a philosopher. But that fortnight in the Bastille must have made him realise, if he had not known already, that he was born for a destiny far weightier and greater than that of a Corneille or a Racine.

"What is done with people who forge *lettres de cachet*?" he asked the lieutenant of police one day, when he was in prison. "They are hanged." "Good!" was the answer, "in anticipation of the time when those who sign genuine ones shall be hanged too."

A few days after his imprisonment he wrote to the Minister of the Department of Paris:

"Sieur de Voltaire humbly represents that he has been assaulted by the brave Chevalier de Rohan, assisted by six cut-throats, behind whom the chevalier was courageously posted; and that ever since Sieur de Voltaire has tried to repair, not his own honour, but that of the chevalier, which has proved too difficult."

He went on to beg permission to go to England. His order of liberty was signed on April 29, 1726. But there were many formalities to be observed before it could be put into execution. On May 2d, Delaunay received it with its accompanying conditions. Voltaire was free—to go to England, accompanied as far as Calais by Condé, one of the turnkeys of the Bastille, to see that he really *did* go there.

The businesslike prisoner asked Madame de Bernières to lend him her travelling carriage to take him to Calais. She, Madame du Deffand, and Theriot came to say good-bye to him. He left the Bastille on May 3d. On May 5th he was writing to Theriot from Calais. He stayed there three or four days, and about the end of the first week, in May, 1726, landed at Greenwich.

CHAPTER V

ENGLAND, AND THE "ENGLISH LETTERS"

IT was the last year of the reign of George I. Swift was Dean of St. Patrick's. Pope was writing that masterpiece of brilliant malice, the "Dunciad," at Twickenham. Gay, Young, and Thomson were in the plenitude of their poetic powers. Sarah, Duchess of Marlborough, was compiling her memoirs at Blenheim. Bolingbroke, Hervey, and the Walpoles shed their lustre on politics. Even at the boorish Court there was one brilliant woman—Caroline, Princess of Wales. Newton was near his dying. And Locke being dead yet spoke.

It was one of those rare spring days, with a cloudless sky and a soft west wind, when Voltaire first set foot in England. Greenwich was *en fête*, with its Fair in full progress—Olympian games and the pretty daughters of the people, whom, in their gala dress, the traveller mistook for fine ladies. When he met the fine ladies that very evening in London, most likely at the house of his old friend Lord Bolingbroke, their hauteur and malice disgusted him, and he said very frankly that he preferred the maidens of Greenwich.

He tells how the very next morning he went to a coffee-house in the City, and gives a gay description of the phlegmatic apathy of the company. If they were laughing in their sleeves at the foreigner, the foreigner's description of them remains to-day a notable example of that keen, clear-cut, airy, bantering humour of which he was so perfect a master.

But if he wrote lightly hereafter, his mood when he landed in England was no laughing one.

This *vif* and sensitive child of fortune could not forget that he was an exile—and exiled unjustly. His pensions both from King and Queen had been stopped. He had an exchange letter on a Jew in London, but before he presented it the Jew was bankrupt and could not pay him, and he was forced to accept a few guineas King George I. "had the generosity to give me." His health was as indifferent as usual. He was in a country of which he knew little or nothing of the language or the customs. He had begun the world brilliantly perhaps, but he had greatly fallen. Those first few weeks in England are likely to have been among the unhappiest in his life.

He had been on English shores but a very short time when he slipped back *incognito* to Paris (he had promised the paternal government to *go* to

England, not to *stay* there), and, with his life in his hands, waited about in the capital for two months for the man Rohan, "whom the instinct of his cowardice hid from me." Theriot knew of the escapade, but no one else. Voltaire wrote him an account of it on August 12, 1726.

He was hardly back in England again when, in September and in the first budget of letters he had had in his exile, he received the news of the death of his sister Catherine. She was nine years older than himself. She had long been married to M. Mignot, and had children and cares of her own to engross her affections and her thoughts. It does not seem that Voltaire had of late seen very much of her. But all the mothering he had had since he was seven years old she had given him. Her death filled his soul with a gloomy despair. "I should have died and she have lived," he wrote to Madame de Bernières. "It was a mistake of destiny." To the end of his days he benefited her children with a large generosity. Bearing evident reference to her death is that letter, called the Letter of Consolation, written from England in 1728 to a friend in sorrow. No reader of it who has himself suffered will doubt that its writer knew how to suffer too, and will find in that wise and patient philosophy a soothing of the troubles common to a Voltaire and to all men.

He had plenty of introductions in England. His acquaintance with the Count de Morville, the intimate of the Walpoles, gave him the *entrée* of the great Whig houses. Bolingbroke, who had returned from France in 1723, would present him to the Tories. He further knew, it is said, Lord Stair and Bishop Atterbury. He had a talent—that delightful French talent—for making new friends. And he was soon engrossed in an astounding application to the English language, and a study of its government, laws, literature, and progress which remains the best ever made by a Frenchman.

It is doubtful if, when he landed here in May, 1726, he knew a single syllable of English except what he had gathered from the English books Theriot had procured for him when he was in the Bastille. There is a letter to a wine merchant, in very bad English certainly, but still in English, which he is supposed to have written when he had been at the most a few months in England.

The year 1726 was not out when he was writing to other friends in that intricate tongue and attacking its idioms with a splendid dash and audacity.

In 1727, he composed some melodious English verses to Lady Harley; and in his English letters of this and the next year to Theriot and others it will be seen that the language was sufficiently his own for him to stamp it with his inimitable style. Authorities differ as to how good or how bad was the accent with which he spoke.

He is said, when he discovered that the word "plague" was pronounced as one syllable, to have wished that plague would take one half of the language and ague the other; and to have complained a good deal of a tongue in which a word spelt *handkerchief* was pronounced *'ankicher*. That he was fluent in it there is no doubt. An uncharitable person declared that he had soon mastered the language, even to the oaths and curses. Why not? Oaths and curses adorned the polite conversation of the day, and why should a Voltaire omit them? But besides that dinner-table English he could soon speak easily the very different English required for discussing science, philosophy, religion—the speciality of an English expert, in that expert's mother tongue.

Soon after he returned to France he declared, in the dedication of his play "Brutus" to Lord Bolingbroke, that, having "passed two years in a constant study of the English language," he found it awkward to write in French. "I was almost accustomed to think in English."

Thirty years after he had left England behind him forever, he wrote English letters to English friends. He quarrelled in that tongue with his mistress in middle life, wrote a couplet in it when he was eighty, and talked in it with his friends in his extreme old age.

He made his headquarters at Wandsworth, already a colony of French refugees, with one Everard Falkener, whom he had met in Paris, the best type of an English merchant, cultivated, hospitable, enlightened. The two bore each other a lifelong friendship. The visitor was never of the idle kind, waiting about to be amused. He was always, on the other hand, indefatigably busy. He was supremely interested in everything, greedy of information, matchlessly quick to observe. Besides, he could never have been very long together at Falkener's Wandsworth villa.

Three months out of the thirty-four he spent in England he stayed at Lord Peterborough's. He was constantly at Lord Bolingbroke's, either at his town house in Pall Mall or in the country. He speaks himself of having known Bishop Berkeley, and Gay of the "Beggar's Opera." Before he left England he had visited almost every celebrated person in it.

It is easy to understand Voltaire's passionate admiration for a country in which genius was everywhere the best passport to glory, riches, and honour. He had lived under a system so different! Here his own talent immediately procured him an entrance into that noblest aristocracy, the aristocracy of intellect. When was it that he went to stay at Bubb Dodington's at Eastbury in Dorsetshire, and at that Liberty Hall of the Muses met Young of the "Night Thoughts" and Thomson of the "Seasons"? The man who was to be English parson and author of those solemn religious periods of the "Thoughts" was now writing his "Satires" and had not a little in common with the sceptical, cynic Frenchman of the "Epistle to Uranie." The one was as brilliant a conversationalist as the other. As for the "Seasons," though Voltaire politely praised them, he considered Nature an ill-chosen subject for a Scotchman who knew nothing of the warmth and glow of the South.

At Lord Peterborough's Voltaire met Swift—"Rabelais in his Senses," that greater than any Rabelais—"one of the most extraordinary men that England has produced." That was Voltaire's judgment of him. He did not like him the less because he was "a priest and mocked at everything." At bottom, the dark and awful genius of Swift and the vivid and passionate inspiration of Voltaire had something in common. At Peterborough's table there sat then the two finest masters of invective who ever lived.

Voltaire was still quite new to the country when he made the acquaintance of little, crooked, papist Mr. Pope of Twit'nam. It has been maliciously said that on the occasion the visitor talked so blasphemously and indecently that he sent Pope's poor old mother shuddering from the room. But as at the time Voltaire did not know English and Pope and his mother did not know French, the story may be taken for what it is worth. A great and very natural admiration had the French author, to whom precision, the unities, and poetical neatness were so dear, for the polished easy rhythm of Mr. Pope; but that did not prevent him, long after, when he was talking to James Boswell of Auchinleck at Ferney, from diagnosing the respective merits of Pope and Dryden in a truly Voltairian criticism. "Pope drives a handsome chariot with a couple of neat nags, and Dryden a coach and six stately horses." Nor did his love of Mr. Pope's style prevent him loathing Mr. Pope's philosophy.

One day he went to see old Sarah Marlborough at Blenheim, and audaciously asked her to let him see the memoirs she was writing. "You must wait," answered Sarah; "I am just altering my account of Queen Anne's character. I have begun to love her again since the present lot have become our rulers." Is it hard to fancy the delighted cynic humour on her guest's shrewd face at that naïve reply?

Goldsmith says that she *did* show him the memoirs, and when he remonstrated with her for abusing her friends therein, seized them out of his hands in a rage. "I thought the man had sense, but I find him at bottom either a fool or a philosopher."

Presently Gay was reading aloud to him that "Beggar's Opera" before its publication; and he went to see old Congreve, who spoke of his plays as trifles beneath notice, "and told me to look upon him merely as a private gentleman." That literary snobbishness was very little to the taste of a Voltaire. "If you had the misfortune to be only a gentleman like any other," he answered, "I should never have come to see you." It is to be hoped the foolish old playwright felt duly snubbed.

The great Lord Chesterfield—"the only Englishman who ever recommended the art of pleasing as the first duty of life"—invited Voltaire to dinner. When he was asked a second time, he had to decline, as the gratuities expected by the servants were too much for his slenderly equipped pockets.

He visited Newton's niece, Mrs. Conduit, who told him the famous story of Newton and the apple. Voltaire twice repeated it in his works, and thus preserved it for posterity. He frequently met and talked with Newton's friend and disciple, Clarke.

In 1727, he was introduced at the English Court. Had he not dedicated "Œdipe" to its King? Just as in 1728 he was to dedicate his English edition of the "Henriade" to "that amiable philosopher on the throne," Caroline, the wife of George II. At Court, doubtless, he met that lean malice, my Lord Hervey, and Lady Hervey, "beautiful Molly Lepell." He met everybody, in fact, and saw everything. He went to Newmarket races and to a Quakers' meeting. He was continually at the play. He mixed with bishops and boatmen, lords, play-actors, merchants and politicians. When on one of his rambles round London he was insulted by a mob, he mounted on a few handy steps: "Brave Englishmen!" said he, "am I not already unfortunate enough in not having been born among you?" And they were with him at once.

Perhaps he was not sorry to get away from the wits and the parties, to the quiet of Falkener's villa. He had always something better to do than to be a social light for his own or other men's entertainment.

When he was at Wandsworth he wrote, in English prose, the first act of "Brutus." In these thirty-four months he composed nearly the whole of his "History of Charles XII." of Sweden. In 1727, he took up his abode for a time at the Sign of the White Peruke, Maiden Lane, Covent Garden, that he might the more conveniently arrange for the publication by subscription of the new edition of his "Henriade." "The English generally make good their words and promises," he said long after. They did in 1728. The book went into three editions. From them Voltaire had omitted the tale of the noble exploits of Rosny, the ancestor of his false friend Sully.

Swift pushed the "Henriade" in Ireland. The English were inclined to think it too Catholic, as the Catholics had thought it too Protestant. But, in their character of a free and generous people, they bought and read it not the less.

After a few months' residence in the country this amazing Frenchman was turning "Hudibras" into French verse.

After eighteen months, he wrote, in English, a little volume containing two essays: "An Essay upon the Civil Wars of France," and upon "The Epick Poetry of the European Nations." A presentation copy of the first edition of this daring little work, published in 1727, may still be seen in the British Museum with a few words in Voltaire's handwriting in the corner—"to Sr. hanslone from his most humble servant voltaire." Sir Hans Sloane was the President of the Royal Society. This book is now so rare as to be practically unobtainable. It went into a second edition in 1728, and into a fourth in 1731.

By it, by "Brutus," and the "Henriade" Voltaire gained a sum of about two thousand pounds.

The chronology of the events of his English visit remains, and must remain, very imperfect. He wrote very few letters during that period and dates are not the *forte* of his English hosts. So much, however, is certain. He arrived in England about the end of the first week in May, 1726. By September, he had paid his stolen visit to France and returned to these shores. In January, 1727, he was presented at Court. On March 28th, he was at Newton's lying-in-state in Westminster Abbey. In July the French authorities gave him permission to return to France for a while to see to some business, but he did not go. He spent the greater part of the year preparing his English edition of the "Henriade" and writing "Charles XII." In December, 1727, appeared the two English essays. The year 1728 saw the publication of the English edition of his "Henriade."

Archibald Ballantyne's "Voltaire's Visit to England" gives the best and most exhaustive account of that visit yet published.

By far the most momentous and the most influential, both on Voltaire's own fortunes and on the public intellect, of any of his works written for the most part in England, were his "English Letters" or the "Philosophical Letters."

They were originally written to Theriot; but they must always have been meant for publication. They are not the best example, but they are no bad example, of the Voltairian manner—polished, easy, witty, sarcastic, not so much daring in word as daring in meaning, more remarkable for what they imply than for what they say—yet of all letters in the world, perhaps, those which have had the most far-reaching as well as the profoundest effect on the human mind.

Read casually, they are chiefly remarkable for their luminous and amusing criticisms on the genius of England, and on the men and events of that day.

Voltaire found Shakespeare exactly, after all, what a Voltaire *would* have found him—"nature and sublimity," "force and fecundity," "an amazing genius"—he was too great a genius himself not to recognise in a Shakespeare such matchless traits as these. But Voltaire was also an eighteenth-century Frenchman, with his dramatic gift pinioned by the unities, by a hundred prim, foolish, and artificial rules, and he was the writer who above all other writers valued style, polish, finish, and culture. How should he have forgiven Shakespeare what he called his "heavy grossness," his "barbarisms," his "monstrosities"? Voltaire did not know, with the moderns, that many of the clowns and the clownish jokes to which he took a just objection were interpolations, not Shakespeare himself. And what wonder that this most impressionable child of a country and an age where an abstraction called Taste was as a god, should have missed its polite influence in a Shakespeare, and have found the rugged grandeur of that vast intelligence imperfect without it? Not the less, it was Voltaire who first revealed this man, who had been "the ruin of the English stage," to the French; who copied and translated him; and then abused him so fiercely in the famous preface to "Semiramis" and the quarrel with Letourneur, as to make him of as supreme an interest on the Continent as in his own country.

Voltaire wrote one admirable letter "On Mr. Pope and other famous Poets," another "On Comedy," a third "On Tragedy," and a fourth "On Nobles who cultivate Literature." He praised Swift; adored "the judicious Mr. Addison"; and did due homage to Wycherley and Congreve. But if the "English Letters" had been nothing but a series of literary criticisms, however brilliant, they would not have been the Letters which made Lafayette a republican at nine, and which Heine spoke of as a stepping-stone to the Revolution.

In the "Henriade" the bird's heart had throbbed against the bars of the cage; in the "English Letters" it had found the gate of liberty and taken its first sweeping flight through free air.

Voltaire came straight from the Bastille to the most liberal and enlightened country in the world. What wonder that he conceived that hero-worship for England and the English which no time could change, and which in his old age at Ferney was still a burning and a shining light?

He was from the first an impassioned admirer of almost every Anglican institution. "The English, as a free people, chose their own road to heaven." "You do not see any imbeciles here who put their souls into the keeping of others."

"You have no priests then?" said I. "No, friend," answered the Quaker; "and we get on very well without them." "When the English clergy know that in France young men famous for their excesses and raised to the prelature by the intrigues of women, make love publicly, amuse themselves by composing love songs, give every day elaborate and elegant suppers and go straight from them to ask the illumination of the Holy Spirit and boldly call themselves successors of the Apostles, they thank God that they are Protestants. But they are vile heretics, fit for burning with all devils, as Master François Rabelais said; that is why I do not mix myself up with their affairs."

The last touches are admirably Voltairian.

The live-and-let-live policy of a country where thirty religions dwelt together quite amicably and comfortably could not but appeal to the man who was Armand's brother and who remembered Unigenitus.

As for the government—what a contrast he saw there too! In this country the sovereign was only powerful to do good "with his hands tied from doing evil"; the great were "great without insolence and without vassals"; and "the people share in the government without disorder." What a contrast indeed! what a glaring contrast! The pen trembled in the man's nervous hand as he wrote; and his soul was on fire. "It has taken seas of blood to drown the idol of despotism; but the English do not think they have bought their laws too dearly." How much more dearly France was to buy hers, this man, who himself expended the work and genius of his life to gain Frenchmen a little liberty, had no idea. He had seen Newton buried at Westminster with the honours due to so great a genius. When Voltaire was very old it is said "his eye would grow bright and his cheek flush" when he said that he had once lived in a land where "a professor of mathematics, only because he was great in his vocation," had been buried "like a king who had done good to his subjects."

What a country to live in! to be proud of! where there were better ways to glory than the favour of a royal mistress or the unearned virtue of an ancestral name!

He saw Mrs. Oldfield, the actress, buried with the honours due to her far different and very inferior talent. Perhaps the honours were greater than her desert. But Voltaire, with his passion for the stage, was not the man to think of that.

Thirty-five years later he recalled how he had heard when in England that the daughter of the poet Milton was in London—old, ill, and poor. "In a quarter of an hour she was rich."

"What would you have done if you had been born in Spain?" said his secretary to Voltaire long after. "I would have gone to mass every day: kissed the monks' robes: and set fire to their convents. I was not made to live in Spain, nor in France." "Where then?" "In England."

But if Voltaire loved the tolerant English religion and the liberal English government and the generous English people, he loved far more "the noble liberty of thinking." His Letters on Bacon and on Locke, on Descartes and Newton, on the History of Attraction and on Newton's Optics, are a worship of that free thought that dared to doubt, that searched and tried the old truths which men believed because they *were* old and for no better reason, and which found them too often to be no truths, but a prejudice, a delusion, and a lie. Voltaire passionately declared that it was the theologians, and not the Lockes, the Bayles, the Hobbes, the Spinozas, who sowed "discord in a state." He spoke of Locke as "the wisest of human beings"; of Bacon as "the father of experimental philosophy." "A catechism reveals God to children," he said; "but Newton has revealed Him to sages." "Before Locke, the great philosophers had positively decided what the soul of man is, but as they did not know in the least, it is only natural they should all have been of different opinions.... Locke dares sometimes to speak positively but he also dares to doubt." "How I love English daring!" he cried *à propos* of Swift's "Tale of a Tub." "How I love people who say what they think! We only half live if we dare only half think."

Voltaire was fully alive at all events. However widely one may differ from his opinions they are at least entitled to respect. They were passionately genuine, the vivid convictions of his soul. He was no *dilettante*, fine-gentleman unbeliever—too bored and idle to find in the world "the footmarks of a God." He was from this time henceforth and always one of the most zealous seekers after truth who ever lived. It was to be no more "a fountain sealed"; no more a luxury for a few, but the common property of all. To free Frenchmen by bringing to them the light and knowledge of England—to destroy, so far as in him lay, everywhere and for all men, darkness, ignorance and superstition—that was the Voltairian mission. "He swore to devote his life to that end, and kept his word."

CHAPTER VI

PLAYS, A BURLESQUE, AND THE APPEARANCE OF THE "LETTERS"

IN the middle of March, 1729, there was a man calling himself M. Sansons, living over a wigmaker's at St. Germain-en-Laye. At the end of the month M. Sansons came to Paris, and lived for a while at the house of one of his father's old clerks. Being so advised by his friends he applied for a warrant, annulling his order of exile. He obtained it; and lo! M. de Voltaire, after an absence of nearly three years, is returned from his English travels, and once more at work on his profession in the capital.

He had no thought at present of bringing out those "English Letters." The time was not yet ripe; and discretion here, certainly, was the better part of valour. He applied himself instead to his "Charles XII." He spoke of it himself as his favourite work, and "the one for which I have the bowels of a father." Its breathless race of incident swept him along, and he had hardly time even to be sociable. Refusing one of Theriot's invitations to dinner on May 15th, he said that he would drop in at the end of the entertainment "along with that fool of a Charles XII." The subject engrossed him, as the subject he had in hand always engrossed him. Then, since he was no more an exile, he set to work with Theriot to get his pensions restored—and, succeeded.

One night when he was out at supper he heard talk of a lottery formed by Desforts, the controller-general. One of the guests observed that anyone who took all the tickets in the lottery would be greatly the gainer. Voltaire was as swift to act as swift to see. He formed a company who bought up all the tickets: and found himself the winner of a large sum. To be sure he had offended Desforts, who was thus written down an ass. So off went the poet to Plombières with Richelieu in August for a visit. When he returned to Paris the squall had blown over, and M. de Voltaire had made an uncommonly successful speculation.

He made others, too, about this period, and never again was in need of money.

In this December of 1729 Voltaire invited the actors of the Comédie Française to dinner and read them his new play, "Brutus." It was accepted, rehearsed, and then suddenly and mysteriously withdrawn. Voltaire said there was a plot against it—a cabal of Rohan and his kind, and of Crébillon—famous rival playwright and gloomy tragic poet. But worse than any plot was the feebleness of the play itself and its fatal absence of love interest. The actors themselves thought it unworthy of a Voltaire and his public. Voltaire knew it to be so himself, and at once set about revising and rewriting it.

On March 20, 1730, there died after four days' acute anguish, aged only thirty-eight, the great actress, Adrienne Lecouvreur. Her death was the supreme event of this period of Voltaire's life. Perhaps it was one of the supreme events of his whole life. He had been, he said, "her admirer, her friend, her lover." If the last word is to be taken literally, that relationship had long ceased. But he had for ever a passionate admiration for her talents. The last piece she played in was "Œdipe," and she was taken ill upon the stage. Voltaire with his quick instinct of a passionate pity, hastened to her bedside, and she died in his arms in agonies for which there could be found no remedy. She was an actress, so she could have neither priest nor absolution, and dying thus, was refused Christian burial, and taken without the city at night and "thrown in the kennel," like a dead dog.

What wonder if Paris was stirred to its soul? And if Paris was stirred, what must a Voltaire have been? Adrienne, it has been well said, had "all the virtues but virtue." She was generous and disinterested to a high degree. She was a woman of supreme talent and achievements. She was at least morally no worse, as she was intellectually far greater, than those kings' mistresses over whose graves prelates had thought it no shame to lift their voices in eulogies and orations, and who had been buried with royal honours and splendour.

In Voltaire's mind England and Mrs. Oldfield's burial were still fresh impressions. Injustice had begun to play the part with him that the lighted torch plays to the fagot. His soul was ablaze at once.

It is not fashionable to look upon him as a man of feeling. In the popular idea he is the scoffer who jeered at everything. Read the "Poem on the Death of Adrienne Lecouvreur" written, not on the passionate impulse of the moment, but many months later, and see in it a soul stirred to its profoundest depths—the ebullition of a feeling as deep as it is rare.

"Shall I for ever see ... the light-minded French sleeping under the rule of superstition? What! is it only in England that mortals dare to think?"

"Men deprive of burial her to whom Greece would have raised altars." "The Lecouvreur in London would have had a tomb among genius, kings, and heroes." "Ye gods! Why is my country no longer the fatherland of glory and talent?"

Such words were enough to endanger its author's safety.

It was well that when Theriot was showing them about the salons of Paris in June, 1731, Voltaire was living *incognito* in Rouen, and was supposed to be in England.

Paris forgot; but not Voltaire. For sixty years he never ceased to try and improve the condition of actors. Thirty years after Adrienne's death he wrote as if it had happened yesterday: "Actors are paid by the King and excommunicated by the Church; they are commanded by the King to play every evening, and by the Church forbidden to do so at all. If they do not play, they are put into prison; if they do, they are spurned into the kennel. We delight to live with them, and object to be buried with them; we admit them to our tables and exclude them from our cemeteries. It must be allowed we are a very reasonable and consistent nation." In his old age, his one dread was not the mysterious Hereafter, but that he too, dying unabsolved, might be "thrown into the gutter like poor Lecouvreur."

By the spring of 1730, "Charles XII." was almost ready for the press. The censor—its satire of current superstition was so very delicate the good man had not noticed it—passed the book.

The author was delighted, and was more than busy in preparing a large edition of the first volume for the press.

By the autumn of 1730, when he had two thousand six hundred copies on the eve of publication, the whole edition was suddenly seized by the paternal government. The censor had passed it? True. But a change in the political outlook made France uncommonly nervous of displeasing Augustus, the usurping King of Poland, of whom Voltaire, forsooth, had spoken disrespectfully. "It seems to me," he wrote very reasonably, "that in *this* country Stanislas [the Queen's father and ex-King] ought to be considered rather than Augustus."

It is easy to fancy what a maddening irritation such a prohibition, and the delays, worries, and waste of time it caused, must have had on such an impatient and energetic temperament as Voltaire's.

But he never gave up hope, as he never gave up work.

On December 11th of this year 1730 the rewritten "Brutus" was performed: very favourably received on the first night—by an audience composed entirely of the author's friends—and damned with faint praise on the second. The author had quite enough vanity to be bitterly mortified. But, not the less, he wrote the kindest and most considerate of letters to the terrified *ingénue* of fifteen who had played one of the chief parts hopelessly badly. "Ce coquin-là," one of his bitterest enemies said of him, "has one vice worse than all the rest; he has sometimes virtues."

The last performance of "Brutus" took place on January 17, 1731. There had been but fifteen in all. In the Revolution it was revived, and received with tumultuous applause. Its *motif*, that of a father sacrificing his sons for the common good, appealed to those stirring times of reckless deeds, but not to the cultivated and sentimental *dolce far niente* of 1731.

By February, Voltaire was writing to Cideville at Rouen that the new edition of the "Henriade" was tacitly permitted in Paris by the authorities. While they had been busy suppressing it, those authorities had also been busy reading and admiring it themselves. Henceforth, it was allowed in France.

In March, M. de Voltaire announced his intention of returning to his dear England, and insinuated that he was going to print "Charles XII." at "Cantorbéry." In truth, Cideville had found his friend "a little hole" in Rouen—a very dirty and uncomfortable little hole as it turned out—where he could live *incognito* and superintend the secret printing and publishing there. He removed from the first little hole to the house of Jore, his printer and publisher, with whom he was to have only too many dealings in the future. He passed as an English gentleman. He had the society of Cideville to console him. He was five months in Rouen altogether, from March of 1731 until August. One of these months he spent in bed. Part of his time he was in the country. The whole time he was correcting the proof-sheets of the first part of "Charles XII." and writing the latter, and composing two tragedies—"The Death of Cæsar" and "Ériphyle."

He returned to Paris in August, 1731. On September 13th died the noble young Maisons, aged only thirty-one, of the smallpox which had spared him before. "He died in my arms," said Voltaire, "not through the ignorance but through the neglect of the doctors."

In October the secretly printed "Charles XII." was introduced surreptitiously into Paris, as the "Henriade" had been. Like the "Henriade," it became the mode and was read by all the educated classes; and soon, in translations, by the educated of other countries as well.

It is indeed a bold and vigorous story. Plenty of anecdote and action—a vivid drama wherein the characters play their parts with extraordinary spirit and energy. In the heat of so many battles the author has no time for reflections. But throughout, not the less, he shows very plainly his contempt for his hero, and his love for all those strange things— peace, liberty, enlightenment—which that hero had done so much to crush.

Many of his facts he had obtained first-hand from the Duchess of Marlborough, who remembered her husband's dealings with Charles; and from Baron Goertz, who had been Charles's favourite minister and then Voltaire's personal friend.

Voltaire, as has been seen, loved his "Charles XII." himself; and as usual had spared nothing to make it as good as he could.

"My great difficulty," he wrote, "has not been to find memoirs, but to sift out the good ones. There is another inconvenience inseparable from writing contemporary history. Every captain of infantry who has served in the armies of Charles XII. and lost his knapsack on a march, thinks I ought to mention it. If the subalterns complain of my silence, the generals and ministers complain of my outspokenness. Whoso writes the history of his own time must expect to be blamed for everything he has said and everything he has not said; but these little drawbacks should not discourage a man who loves truth and liberty, expects nothing, fears nothing, asks nothing, and who limits his ambition to the cultivation of letters."

By December of this year 1731 Voltaire was staying with a certain gay old Comtesse de Fontaine Martel who had a house in the Palais Royal, to which she made her visitor free, as to her carriage, her opera-box, and her fine company.

His friendship with the Bernières had cooled by this time. To be sure, he was no small acquisition to this corrupt old Countess, whose one aim in existence was to be amused if she could. "To be bored near Voltaire! Ah, Dieu! that is not possible!" said an enthusiastic lady admirer thereafter. He sonneted his hostess now, as only he knew how—delicate, graceful, French, delightful. "Ériphyle" was performed at her house very early in 1732. The guests were much too polite not to sob at its pathos and applaud it to the echo.

On March 7, 1732, it was played to a public who received it with a very tepid warmth; until the fifth act, of which they unmistakably disapproved. "One forgives the dessert when the other courses have been passable," Voltaire wrote cheerily to Cideville. But one of his critics was not far from the truth when he said that if it had not been for its hits at the great, at princes, and at superstition, it would have had nothing of Voltaire in it at all.

It was dull; and Voltaire knew it. He employed the Easter holidays in writing a very good prologue to it. But if a bad dessert cannot spoil a good dinner, a good *hors d'œuvre* will not save a bad one. On May 13th Voltaire wrote to Theriot that he was resolved not even to print it, and it was withdrawn from Jore's hands at the last moment. Some of its material was used in "Semiramis."

The author of "Œdipe," of the "Henriade," and of "Charles XII." had already not unnaturally turned his thoughts to that mistress who was the object of all literary men's hopes, vows, and adorations—the French Academy. By December, 1731, there was a vacant chair there. Who had a right to it if not he? He was almost forty years old. He had already done great things; he was ripe to do greater. Even the authorities could not be blind to his deserts and to his powers. Richelieu was his friend, and used all his influence to help him. The thing was as good as done, when by secret malice, or very ill fortune, there appeared in print in the spring of 1732 that luckless "Epistle to Uranie," written ten years earlier to that fair travelling companion, Madame de Rupelmonde.

There is nothing in that poem but its grace, cleverness, and sincerity which would excite comment if it appeared in a magazine to-day. Voltaire had called it "Le Pour et le Contre," but it was certainly much more *against* revealed religion than *for* it. Yet it is in no sense offensively anti-Christian. It is not the poem of a scoffer, but of one who seeks truth diligently and "gropes through darkness up to God."

The fact did not soften the authorities in the least.

"What do you think of it?" said the Chancellor of France to his secretary.

"Voltaire ought to be deprived of pen, ink, and paper," was the answer. "That man has a mind which could destroy a state."

"Uncertain Uranie" had before this solved *her* doubts by going into a convent. Her mentor saw but one course open to him. It was a very characteristic course—and used by him afterwards very freely. He denied the authorship of the ill-omened little work *in toto*; and, true to his principles of doing everything thoroughly, declared that the Abbé Chaulieu was the writer thereof, and that he (Voltaire) had heard him recite it at the Temple.

Nobody believed the story, it appears. At any rate, the Academy doors remained closed to him.

Many worldly-wise old friends of Voltaire's—Fontenelle and Madame de Tencin among others—took the opportunity of the failure of "Ériphyle" to beg him about this time to give up that dramatic career for which he was evidently unsuited.

"What answer did you make?" someone said to him.

"None; I brought out 'Zaire.'"

"Zaire" was written in twenty-two days.

"The subject carried me away with it; the piece wrote itself." It is a tragedy full of love and pathos, which still in some degree keeps its popularity. It has been ably criticised as being not the best of Voltaire's tragedies, but the most inspired. It reads as if its author were a lover of five-and-twenty—quick with the emotions he describes. "Whoso paints the passions has felt them," he said himself. What an unknown Voltaire "the tender Zaire" must have revealed to his friends! It was his first real dramatic success since "Œdipe." It was a greater success than "Œdipe" had been. At the first performance, indeed, on August 6, 1732, the pit was somewhat noisy, and vociferously called attention to defects arising from hasty writing. But, after all, the play moved the heart. At the fourth performance the author was called from his box to receive the unanimous plaudits of the house. He himself wrote a notice of the play in the "Mercure"—the first time such a thing had ever been done. On October 14th it was played before the King and Queen at Fontainebleau. It brought its author much of what he called "that smoke of vainglory" for which he had written 'Ériphyle' and 'Brutus' all over again, and in vain. He himself superintended the performance. He was at Court six weeks. "Mariamne" was also performed; and the "Gustave" of that rival playwright, Alexis Piron, was *not*. Voltaire met Piron at Court one day. "Ah! my dear Piron, what are *you* doing here? I have been here three weeks. The other night they played my 'Mariamne'; they are going to play 'Zaire.' How about 'Gustave'?" Bitter Piron himself tells the story. It does not sound like truth. An enemy's ill-luck nearly always killed the Voltairian spite at a blow. But if it be true, it is easy to understand that this cool, witty Arouet, the son of the notary, was not precisely popular. While at Court he rewrote his "English Letters" on "Newton" and "Gravitation"; read aloud to Cardinal Fleury, with a few judicious omissions, that one on the Quakers, and corresponded with a man who was now his scientific teacher and, to be, his admired friend and his bitter enemy. His name was Maupertuis.

When Voltaire had returned to his comfortable quarters at the Palais Royal, "Zaire" was acted there by amateurs in January, 1733. Voltaire himself took the part of Lusignan, the heroine's father, in spite of his health, which was so bad that "I dread being reduced to idleness, which to me would be a terrible disgrace."

In that very same month of January the Comtesse de Fontaine Martel died very suddenly. She had her card parties and her salon to the last. She was quite old, wicked, godless, charming and generous, a perfect type of her class and her age. Voltaire was at her bedside when she died. "What time is it?" she asked with her last breath. Before she could be answered—"Thank God!" said she, "whatever time it is, there is somewhere a *rendezvous*."

Voltaire said that he lost, by her death, a good house of which he was the master, and an income of forty thousand francs which was spent in amusing him.

He stayed on in her house for some time. He was there when there swept over him one of the noisiest hurricanes of all his stormy existence.

In 1731, that envious old exiled J. B. Rousseau had circulated in Paris a very venomous letter on the subject of Voltaire. The brilliant success of 'Zaire' was the signal for him to attack it with fury. The criticism was so manifestly unjust and so manifestly dictated by jealousy, that Voltaire might have been well content to leave it alone. But almost the only thing he could not do was to do nothing. So he wrote "The Temple of Taste."

"The Temple of Taste" is a brilliant burlesque, half prose, half verse. Pope's "Dunciad" is the only English poem with which it can be compared. Its story is that Cardinal Fleury and the poet go together to the "Temple of Taste" criticising every foible of the age on their way there. Near the entrance they meet the candidates for admission to the "Temple," great among whom is J. B. Rousseau.

The "Temple" is one of the most graceful and easy of the works of an author who always possessed those two qualities in an extraordinary degree. It shows, as no other writing of Voltaire's had yet shown, his delicate and perfect critical judgment. He expresses his damning opinion—so gaily, so charmingly, so innocently—on many other over-rated celebrities besides Rousseau. The piquancy of the thing lies in the fact that three fourths of those celebrities were then living. It hits off every passing craze. Every line contains a deadly allusion. Every other word is a *mot* almost. No translation can give any idea of the full and deadly effect of that easy, trifling, bantering style. "The Temple of Taste" is a flame which still leaps and shines, though it burns no more.

By February "the Temple," wrote its builder, "had become a Cathedral." In April it was in the hands of the censor. Voltaire quite expected to be given a privilege for it. The censor did not seem to see anything objectionable in it.

It is easy to fancy what a success a work so gay, witty, and daring would meet with, when it dropped red-hot from the press, while it was still in the hands of the authorities awaiting the coveted yellow seal. If it *was* a cathedral, it was one which afforded the author no sanctuary. The old dangers and the old outcries, to which he should have been getting wearily used by now, met him as usual. There was a threatened *lettre de cachet*. "Here is little villain of a writer who ought to be sent over the sea again," said Marais.

All Paris was up in arms in fact. "This 'Temple of Taste' has roused those whom I have not praised enough for their liking," Voltaire wrote to Theriot on May 1st, "and still more those whom I have not praised at all ... add to that the crime of having printed this *bagatelle* without a permission, and the anger of the minister against such an outrage; add to that the howlings of the Court and the menace of a *lettre de cachet*, and, with all, you will have but a feeble idea of the pleasantness of my position and of the protection afforded to literature."

"I must then rebuild a second Temple," he added cheerfully; and he positively set to work to do it, missing out some of the stones of offence in the first.

On May 15th he left the late Comtesse de Martel's comfortable house and went to live at the mean lodging of his man of business—"in the worst quarter of Paris in the worst house"—opposite the Church of St. Gervais. "The place is more deafened with the sound of bells than a sacristan," said he, "but I shall make so much noise with my lyre the bells will be nothing to me."

One hardly knows whether to admire more the man's admirable indifference to things material, or that genius for hard work which stood him in as good stead in a garret as in a palace.

He was not long alone in these rooms. He soon had with him two literary *protégés* whom he fed, lodged, and entertained "like my own children." One of them, Lefèvre, died young. For the other, Linant, Voltaire had done his very best to get the good offices of Madame de Fontaine Martel. But that worldly-wise old person, who had already been much tried by friend Theriot, declined to accommodate Linant in her house. Then Voltaire besought Madame du Deffand for him.

The *protégés* were always going to do great things and never did them. Voltaire believed in them exactly as devout and simple persons will long believe in the reclamation of the irreclaimable. "I am persuaded," he had said in that "Temple of Taste," "that if a man does not cultivate a talent it is because he does not possess it; there is no one who does not write poetry if he is a poet; or music, if he is a musician."

MADAME DU CHÂTELET

From an Engraving after Marianne Loir

But his heart was softer than his judgment. Now, as later, he believed in the capacity as in the generosity of his fellows, with an enthusiasm which outlasted experience, and wholly contradicts the gay cynicism of his utterances.

On July 3, 1733, there is a little innocent, ominous sentence in a letter of Voltaire's to Cideville. "Yesterday I began an epistle in verse on Calumny, dedicated to a very amiable and much calumniated woman." That nameless lady, who had Voltaire's Richelieu for a lover, had already written to Richelieu highly praising Voltaire's new play, "Adélaïde du Guesclin." In this July she, a certain Comte de Forcalquier and a gay young duchess, paid a surprise visit to Voltaire in his dingy lodging, which occasioned the poet to break into charming verse and to compare his guests to the three angels who visited Abraham. The summer also saw him busy buying pictures, writing an opera, "Samson," to music by Rameau, and rewriting his

"Adélaïde." It was to have been performed in the April of this 1733, but the illness of the chief actress delayed its appearance, and gave the author more time to correct and improve it.

But paramount in his mind to any opera and tragedy, aye, to any amiable and calumniated woman of fashion too, was his haunting fear, which never left him all through this year, that the "English Letters," which were being printed at Rouen privately and under his own supervision, should slip out and become public property before he gave the signal at what he took to be the psychological moment. By July they were already published in England—free England who received them with delight. "The Letters philosophical, political, critical, poetical, heretical, and diabolical are selling in English in London with great success." But here?

The outcries against "The Temple of Taste" were still loud and vehement. Voltaire's terror lest "our incorrect Jore" should play him false with regard to this far more dangerous work, vibrates passionately in every letter of the period he wrote. "These cursed Letters," he called them. They were damned on their reputation alone in Paris, before anyone had seen them. It is almost impossible now to believe that any government should have thought it dangerous to the state and its citizens to understand the theory of gravitation or the principles of light. But, after all, those authorities were not such fools as they looked. Once allow the people to reason, and the Bourbon dynasty would fall like a pack of cards.

The author had already toned down some of his freer utterances. But he could never tone the free soul which breathed in them.

He had "a mortal aversion to prison," he wrote. He had a reason, a stronger reason than he had ever had in his life, for wishing to remain quietly in France. But speak his message to the world he must. "The more liberty one has, the more one wants." He had tasted of that deep nectar of the gods, and his countrymen must drink of it with him. He feared his gay manner of conveying grave truth would offend. "If I had not lightened matter, nobody would have been scandalised; but then nobody would have read me."

The *vif* and anxious author paid Jore and worried him freely enough. And then he tried to propitiate the fickle French public, as he had propitiated it before, by a play. On January 18, 1734, was performed the long-delayed "Adélaïde du Guesclin." The first act was received with hisses, which redoubled in the second. In the fifth, the ruin was completed by one of those *mots* at which a Parisian *parterre* is only too apt. On the second evening Voltaire spoke of himself as attending Adélaïde's funeral. One critic, indeed, and no mean critic, had found the play "tender, noble, and touching." But then that critic already looked on Voltaire with eyes more than friendly. "Adélaïde," far from smoothing the way for the "Letters," was but another stumbling stone in it.

Then the versatile Voltaire, at once a friend and a notary's son, must needs arrange personally for the marriage of his friend Richelieu to Mademoiselle de Guise.

To be sure, Richelieu was *amant volage* if ever man was; but he took Mademoiselle without a *dot*, and the manners of the time were such that neither husband nor wife would in any case have expected fidelity of the other. Voltaire left for Montjeu, near Autun, the residence of the bride's parents, on April 7th. "I have drawn up the contract, so I shall not write any verses," said he. But he did his duty all the same a few days after, and composed an "Epithalamium." The bridegroom left shortly to join his regiment. Among the wedding guests was that old love of Richelieu's, the tender critic of "Adélaïde," "the most amiable and calumniated of women," Émilie de Breteuil, Marquise du Châtelet. Between composing love verses for the newly married pair, and perhaps some on his own account, Voltaire enjoyed a brief holiday, idle and content. Then the storm burst in such a clap of thunder as had never shaken even his world before.

By April 24, 1734, the "English Letters" had appeared without the slightest warning to the author and with his name on the title-page, and were running through Paris like a firebrand. Appended was his Letter on the "Thoughts of Pascal," in which he had dared to doubt the omniscience and infallibility of that thinker, and which he had done his best to suppress altogether. Jore was thrown into the Bastille. The book was denounced. On June 10th it was publicly burnt in Paris by the hangman as "scandalous, contrary to religion, to morals, and respect for authority." Voltaire's lodging in the capital was searched. When the officer arrived to arrest him at Montjeu on May 11th he was told that he had gone five days earlier, that is, on May 6, 1734, to drink the waters of Lorraine, not yet a French possession.

But in reality Voltaire was making his way quietly to the Château of Cirey-sur-Blaise, in Champagne, a country home of the Marquis and the Marquise du Châtelet.

CHAPTER VII

MADAME DU CHÂTELET

IN 1706, there was born one Émilie, the daughter of the Baron de Breteuil. Émilie grew up into a tall slip of a girl with very long legs, very bright eyes, very little grace, and a great deal of intelligence. She was about eight years old, and presumably living in Paris with her parents, when she saw one day, possibly at the house of Caumartin, that lean-faced scapegrace, François Marie Arouet, of twenty. Arouet was not yet out of love with Pimpette Dunoyer. Émilie was a child who ought to have been thinking about games and dolls and was thinking, with a quite undesirable precocity, of lessons and learning. The meeting made not the slightest impression on either of them. Arouet went on climbing the steep and rugged way that leads to glory. Émilie learnt Latin and Italian, devoted herself to the Muses, and at fifteen began to write a versified translation of the "Æneid."

In the eighteenth century learning was a mode among women which they put on exactly as they put powder on their hair and patches on their cheeks. They talked philosophy as charmingly as they had once talked chiffons. They sentimentalised over the Rights of Men, neglected their children, and treated their servants like dogs. Culture was hardly a pose with them, as it has been with less clever women since, but it was a garment which they wore when and as they chose. There have been few women in any age "devoted from all eternity to the exact sciences," impassioned for learning for learning's sake, capable of that keen delight in the discovery of a new truth which is like the delight of the sportsman when he has run his quarry to earth. There were few such women even in the eighteenth century. But there were some: and Émilie de Breteuil was one of them.

She was married at nineteen to the Marquis du Châtelet. It was hardly even an episode in her career. This *bonhomme* was so stupid and so earthy! Madame always appears to have agreed with him well enough. But there were so many other things to think about! First of all, there was a Marquis de Guébriant. When he was false, his vehement young mistress took so much opium that she would have died, but for his timely assistance. The brilliant Duke of Richelieu became her lover presently: and she wore his portrait in a ring and loved him, temporarily, but sincerely enough, and exacted from him, if this girlish Marquise was anything at all like a later Madame du Châtelet, a quite extraordinary amount of attention and devotion. Pretty early in her career she became addicted to that modish pastime, gaming. She played on the spinet and sang to it. She loved dress and had a very bad taste in it. She loved society and talked in it much and brilliantly. She was an amateur actress of no mean ability. She had three children who interfered with her scheme of life not at all and on whom she seems to have wasted none of that effervescent emotion she felt for her lovers. There are many strange portraits in the great gallery of eighteenth-century France before the Revolution, but no one stranger than that of this bony, long-limbed woman, whose flashing intelligence made her harsh-featured face almost beautiful, who was familiar with Horace and Virgil, with Cicero, Tasso and Ariosto, with Locke, with Newton and with Euclid—a philosopher with a passion for metaphysics—a being at once excitable and sensual, who united to an entire lack of the moral sense, intellectual passions the most pure and sincere that ever raised a woman above the pettiness, the backbitings, and the meannesses common to her sex.

In 1731, before Voltaire knew her personally, her learned reputation had reached him and he had written her some lines on the Epic Poets. To 1732 belongs an "Ode on Fanaticism," also addressed to the "charming and sublime Émilie."

Early in 1733, when Madame was seven-and-twenty years old, studying mathematics under Maupertuis, one of the courtiers of the Duchesse du Maine at Sceaux reintroduced her to Voltaire, famous and forty. Then, with her modish Duchess and Marquis as chaperons, she visited him in his rooms. It took the man but a very little while to recognise in her a kindred passion for that noblest liberty, enlightenment; to see reflected in her his own genius for hard work; to find out that she too was tired of this Paris "at once idle and stormy" and would fain find a life where there should be more of the gods' best gift—time—to think, to write, to speak one's message for the benefit of that world which *must* listen at last.

He had soon written her an Epistle on her scientific connection with Maupertuis, as well as that one dated 1733, to the "respectable Émilie," on Calumny.

By August 14, 1733, he was writing to his dear Cideville "You are Émilie in a man and she is Cideville in a woman": and a few days later to the Abbé de Sade giving his brilliant first impressions of his Marquise. In November he was writing to Sade again, proudly telling him how Émilie had learnt English in a fortnight.

Then she was with him at Richelieu's wedding. Far from finding the situation embarrassing, she was in heaven, she said—until the fear of Voltaire's arrest, and the news that it would not be safe for him to remain in France made her discover that men were insupportable. "I shall retire at once to my château," she added. For her Château of Cirey was on the extreme edge of France; on the borders of Lorraine, and but a stone's throw from safety.

Its position thus decided two destinies.

Of what did Voltaire think as he fled from Montjeu through the pleasant, budding country on those spring days, towards that desolate spot he was to make famous? The Marquise was not with him. She was going to Paris to use her noble name and influence at Versailles to obtain the revocation of that horrible *lettre de cachet*. Voltaire was already her lover; though he was not now, any more than he was hereafter, in love with her. He had a boundless and most generous admiration for her talents—the warmest enthusiasm for her whom he called "a great man whose only fault was being a woman." He was indeed as faithful to her person as he was faithful to his belief in her great intellectual gifts. She was for ever his ideal of feminine erudition—"who listens to Virgil, and Tasso, and does not disdain a game of picquet," "who understands Newton and loves verses and the wine of Champagne as you do"—the sorceress whose charms worked all their magic on his mind, but never touched his heart. To be at once a great creative genius and capable of an all-absorbing love passion is given to few men. It was not given to Voltaire. No doubt, as his carriage jolted along the roads under the May sunshine towards quiet, peace, and safety, he honestly supposed himself to be devotedly in love with his "divine Émilie." He had chosen her to be the companion of life. Those eight volumes of his letters to her, which were destroyed at her death, were very likely in some sort the letters of a lover; but, arguing from the known to the unknown, they must have been the letters of the lover who worshipped his mistress's scientific acquirements, her passion for knowledge, and her matchless intellectual industry, a thousand times more than any qualities of her heart and soul.

By May 23, 1734, Voltaire was at Bâle and writing from there to Madame du Deffand. She, as well as Madame du Châtelet, was doing her best to get him back into ministerial favour. They were of the opinion that the usual disavowal would be the best thing. Very well! "I will declare that Pascal was always right ... that all priests are disinterested: that the Jesuits are honest ... that the Inquisition is the triumph of humanity and tolerance: in fact I will say anything they like, if they will but leave me in peace." Of course, no one could believe the disavowal. But they could pretend they believed it. Madame du Châtelet worked harder than ever among her influential friends and, when her mind grew easier respecting her lover, continued her lessons from Maupertuis. She spent the summer at Versailles. The government no doubt had never been very anxious to bring back such a troublesome fugitive as Voltaire. The matter dropped.

In June, 1734, Voltaire first saw the Château of Cirey. No one was there when he arrived. The obliging Marquis was with his regiment. He was generally with his regiment when he was not wanted at home. And he was very seldom wanted at home. It was the custom of the day for a fine lady to have a lover. The husband was the last person in the world to object to an arrangement so ordinary. Provided everything was done with a decent respect for the *convenances*—why, then, one might do anything. "Modesty has fled from our hearts and taken refuge on our lips" said Voltaire. The words may stand as the motto of French eighteenth-century morality. It shuddered horror-struck at the ill-bred word and connived gaily at the coarse thing. No one thought the worse of Émilie for her lovers; and rather thought the better of her for keeping them so long. One of Voltaire's biographers has adduced as an excuse for that "Pucelle" of his that chastity was the peculiar boast of the Church, so that Voltaire, hating the Church, despised chastity too. Perhaps that excuse might serve for his attachment to Madame du Châtelet. But he himself considered that no excuse was needed at all. He was following the usual custom of his age. If the Church objected to immorality it was in theory only. In practice, the abbés who had influenced his boyhood and been the companions of his youth were a thousand times more vicious than he had ever been. That he never showed himself to better advantage than in that position, does not make his long connection with the Marquise less reprehensible. But it remains a fact, that he was loyal and patient when she was shrewish and unreasonable: that he was true to what he knew was no bond, and had long become a bondage: faithful when she was faithless: abundantly generous in appreciation of her mental gifts: and staunch to her false memory to the end.

Cirey-sur-Blaise is situated in Champagne, to the south of the wine country. It is surrounded by almost impenetrable forests. It lies one hundred and forty bad miles from Paris, four from Vassy, the nearest village, eight from St. Dizier, a little town. It is near Domrémy, the birthplace of Joan of Arc. In 1734, a coach came two or three times a week from Paris, bringing news of the world, some of the necessaries and a few of the luxuries of life. The château itself was utterly tumbledown, old, huge, bare, and desolate. A chapel adjoined it, and the gardens had long fallen into overgrown neglect. A lady visitor, who came there in 1738, spoke of the place in words which were at least admirably descriptive of her own character, and said it was "of a desolation shocking to humanity, four miles from any other house, in a country where you can see nothing but mountains and uncultivated land and where you are abandoned by all your friends and hardly ever see anyone from Paris." The last words denoted the climax of horror in the vulgar little mind of roundabout Madame Denis, Voltaire's niece. *She* had not "the insurance of a just employment" against ennui and melancholy.

The first sight of its solitary beauty may have been delighting her uncle's soul when in Paris his "English Letters" were being burnt by the hangman and himself denounced by every opprobrious term in the vocabulary of the government. He had been there but a very short time when he heard news of a duel in which the Duke of Richelieu was engaged; and hastened to the camp of Philippsburg near Baden, where he arrived on July 1, 1734. The duel had arisen out of Richelieu's marriage: so Voltaire, having made that, felt responsible for the duel too. Richelieu was at Philippsburg with his regiment. His injuries were not serious. The camp received Voltaire with so much *éclat* and delight that Madame du Châtelet warned him the French authorities were offended and he returned to Cirey. He had scarcely set foot in its tangled garden before he became a gardener, busily setting it to rights: or looked at the tumbledown château, before he was, in his own words, "mason and carpenter." He had never had a home before. What matter if the place were desolate, ruined, and forlorn? It was on the borders of safety; it could be repaired, improved, beautified. He fell in love with it, with that impulsive idealism which was always a part of his nature and always at variance with the gay, deadly, careful cynicism of nearly all his writings. He had "a passion for retirement," he said. He lent the absent Marquis forty thousand francs (at five per cent. interest, "never paid") that the repairs might be set on foot. By August they were well in train and the house becoming habitable.

Voltaire hunted boar in the forest and exchanged country produce with an amiable neighbour, Madame de la Neuville. He wrote gallant letters to another, the fat and good-natured Madame de Champbonin, who was to be hereafter, a constant visitor at Cirey. He was working of course—at his "Century of Louis XIV."—at new plays—at a certain "Treatise on Metaphysics" and some "Discourses on Man," at once light and wise. The glory of summer was on the land. Voltaire was now a man of substance through his shrewdness and economy rather than through his writings. To the money he derived from them he was always strangely indifferent. For them he was to be paid, not by gold, but by their gigantic influence on the human mind.

On the whole, those first few solitary months at Cirey must have been some of the happiest he knew. The future shone rosy like dawn. Peace, love, and work—there is no better life. That was the life to which Voltaire looked forward now.

In October he spent, for some reason not certain, a few weeks at Brussels: and then returned to Cirey.

In November, there arrived from Paris, laughing and vigorous, not having slept a single wink on the journey, and preceded by mountains of chiffons and books, boxes, pictures, necessities, luxuries, and superfluities—Madame du Châtelet.

The extraordinary pair wasted no time at all in sentiment. They turned their energetic attention to the dilapidated house and grounds at once. Madame became "architect and gardener." She found the secret, with plenty of old china and tapestry to help her, "of furnishing Cirey out of nothing." Voltaire had valuable pictures to contribute to the general effect. Both workers were so thoroughly practical, so indefatigable, so clever! It was in these early days of happiness that Voltaire wrote a blissful quatrain which was placed over one of the summer-houses in the garden and which may be broadly translated by the quatrain of another poet:—

A Book of Verses underneath the Bough,
A Jug of Wine, a Loaf of Bread—and Thou
Beside me singing in the Wilderness—
Oh, Wilderness were Paradise enow!

The du Châtelet children, little Pauline of eight and Louis of six (the third had died a baby in the January of this year, 1734), kept much in the background, were, if anything, an additional charm to the illustrious visitor. He found Louis a *doux* and sensible little boy: discovered him a tutor on one occasion: gave him a silver watch on another: and saved his life, for the guillotine, by dosing him with lemonade when he had smallpox. Pauline, early sent to Joinville, sixteen miles away, to be educated, was frequently recalled therefrom when, a little later, she was wanted to act in the Cirey theatricals, for which, like her mother, she had a pretty talent.

Madame la Marquise did not herself pretend at any time to a great interest in her offspring. When her husband foolishly returned presently from his regiment she wrote to her old lover, Richelieu, that her situation was very embarrassing, "but love changes all thorns into flowers." She and Voltaire both spoke of the Marquis as *le bonhomme*. Beyond being a sad bore in conversation, and as incapable of appreciating wit in others as he was of originating any himself, he seems to have given no trouble provided he had his meals regularly: and remains for posterity what he was for his contemporaries—a stupid, good-natured, complacent, slip-slop person whom one could neither much dislike nor at all respect.

When he was at home, his wife and her famous guest left him to his sport, his dinner, and his nap, and themselves plunged into work of every kind, but particularly into that intellectual work which was the passion of their lives. It was a strange household in that tumbledown château in the depths of primæval forests—a strange mixture of the laxity and wickedness of the evil Paris of the day and of the highest mental effort and enjoyment—of the meanest sensual indulgence and the noblest aspirations towards light and liberty—the clear voices of children and the biting and dazzling sarcasms of a Voltaire against those who would keep men in bondage and ignorance, children for ever.

In the December of 1734, Madame du Châtelet went to Paris, taking with her to d'Argental a new tragedy Voltaire had written, called "Alzire."

At the end of 1734, Voltaire first makes allusion in his letters, to one of the most famous—and certainly the most infamous—of his works, the "Pucelle." The idea of it had been suggested at a supper at Richelieu's— Richelieu, equally celebrated for both kinds of gallantry—in 1730. The "Pucelle" is Joan of Arc, the Maid of Orleans. Dull Chapelain had spoilt the subject already. It did not occur as a promising one to poet Voltaire. Richelieu and his guests over-persuaded him to try his hand upon it. In a very short time, he was reading aloud to them the first four cantos of that gay masterpiece of indecent satire. How very little he could have guessed then what a plague, danger, torment, solace and delight "my Jeanne," as he called her, was to be to him for the rest of his days! He had indeed many other things to think of. "Jeanne" could only be an interlude to weightier occupations. He turned to her as one man turns to gaming and another to dissipation. She was the self-indulgence of his life, and it must be owned a very pernicious one.

He must have found Cirey's neighbourhood to Domrémy inspiring. By January, 1735, eight cantos were complete.

Voltaire received in March the revocation of his *lettre de cachet*—the end for which his friends had used all their influence. He was told almost in so many words that he might go back to Paris if he would be a good boy. On March 30, 1735, he *did* go back. The capital was always to him the gorgeous siren who fascinated him from far and disillusioned him near. Cantos of that dangerous "Pucelle" were already flying about the salons. Voltaire busied himself in finding a tutor for little Louis du Châtelet and characteristically engaged that Linant, his unsatisfactory *protégé*—ignorant and indolent—"for fear he should starve"—and trusting to the Marquise's Latin to improve the master's. The Marquis had desired that the tutor should be an abbé. It looked more respectable! But when Voltaire said decisively "No priests chez les Émilies!" the *bonhomme* contented himself with the stipulation that the youth should have a *penchant* for religion.

One night when in Paris, Voltaire supped with the famous Mademoiselle Quinault, actress of the Théâtre Français. She told him how she had seen at a fair a dramatic sketch with a good idea in it—and of which she was going to tell Destouches, the comic playwright. The other playwright listened in silence: but the next morning he brought her the plan of a comedy on the subject and vowed her to secrecy. Not only was the idea not to be divulged, but the very name of the author of the play, which was called "The Prodigal Son," was to be a mystery. Theriot knew of course, and one Berger. "It is necessary to lie like the devil," Voltaire wrote to them, "not timidly or for a time but boldly and always. Lie, my friends, lie. I will repay you when I can."

He thought, not wrongly, that if its authorship were known, the play, good, bad, or indifferent, would be hissed from the stage. "I made enough enemies by 'Œdipe' and the 'Henriade,'" he said.

He was weary, as he might well be, of quarrels, of dangers, and of jealousies. The visit to Paris was a very flying one. He left there on May 6th or 7th. On May 15th he was writing to Theriot from Lunéville, soon to be the Court of Stanislas, ex-King of Poland, and where Voltaire now found a few philosopher friends and the charming and accomplished bride, Madame de Richelieu. He was there but a very short time.

How good it was to see the Cirey forest again—the garden growing daily into order and beauty—balconies and terraces being built here—an avenue planted there—and within, everywhere delightful evidence of Madame's clever touch! He rode about the country on her mare, Hirondelle. He urged on the workmen—and enjoyed doing it. He flung himself with ardour and enthusiasm into small things as into great. He had so many interests and was so much interested in them, no wonder he was happy. There was that idle Linant to spur to industry, and Mesdames de la Neuville and de Champbonin to vary the home party. Cirey was *Cirey-en-félicité*—Cireyshire, in memory of that dear England. Émilie was still "the divine Émilie," "the goddess," the cleverest, the only woman in the world.

In August, 1735, Voltaire's play "The Death of Cæsar," imitated from (Voltaire thought it an improvement on) the "Julius Cæsar" of Shakespeare, was played by the pupils of the Harcourt College on the day of their prize-giving. "I have abandoned two theatres as too full of cabals" wrote the author gaily, "that of the Comédie Française and that of the world." The truth was "The Death of Cæsar" was unsuited to the stage, and of what its author called "a Roman ferocity." It had no love interest and no female characters.

Voltaire was not a little indignant when the piece appeared in print in Paris—totally unauthorised and shamefully incorrect. "The editor has massacred Cæsar worse than Brutus and Cassius ever did," said he. Its appearance was the chief trouble of this autumn of 1735. In its November, Algarotti, the Italian *savant*, and the friend of Prince Frederick of Prussia, came to stay at Cirey. He read aloud his "Dialogues on Philosophy": and Voltaire read aloud a canto of the "Pucelle," or "Louis XIV.," or a tragedy.

The rest of the time they laughed over their champagne and studied Newton and Locke. What extraordinary people! The *bonhomme*, if he was there at all, did not count. The Marquise, who, as has been seen, had learnt English in a fortnight, already translated at sight and had her inborn genius for philosophy and science.

The year waned in such studies. Algarotti left. In eighteen months, besides the seventy-five pages of the "Treatise on Metaphysics" which he had written in answer to Émilie's question as to what she was to think on life, death, God, man, and immortality, Voltaire had also written a comedy—"my American Alzire," "my savages"—the three-act tragedy "The Death of Cæsar," cantos of the "Pucelle," chapters of "Louis XIV.," some part of "The Prodigal Son" and at least four of the rhymed "Discourses on Man." His letters of the period which survive, and which only include a single fragment out of the number he must have written to Madame du Châtelet, fill a fourth of a large volume. Add to this that he was personally supervising the building and decorating, that he was the lover of the Marquise—a position that always occupied a good deal of time with that *exigeante* lady—correcting the incorrigible Linant, busy making all kinds of chemical experiments and collecting old pictures by proxy in Paris, and it will be seen that he was the living proof of his own saying, "One has time for everything if one chooses to use it."

CHAPTER VIII

A YEAR OF STORMS

AFTER the death of Madame du Châtelet, Longchamp, Voltaire's secretary, rescued from the flames in which many of her papers were burning, a number of letters in a very small handwriting. They were the "Treatise on Metaphysics." Voltaire dedicated them to her in a quatrain which is as graceful in the original as it is clumsy in the translation.

He, who wrote these metaphysics
Which he gives you as your own,
Should die for them, as a traitor,
But he dies for you alone.

They were intended only for her eye. They contain the whole Voltairian creed in brief, but in every essential. They were indeed, in the opinion of that day, fit matter for the hangman, and to bring their author to the Bastille.

The title is not alluring, it must be confessed. But the matter has that witchery of style which Voltaire's writings never missed. There is no thinking man but must some time or other have asked himself such questions on God and the soul, free-will, liberty, vice, and virtue, as Voltaire here proposes and answers. Like his hero Newton, he knows how to doubt. He passionately seeks truth and pursues that quest even when he has found the truth is not what he wishes it to be. No man ever made a more clear, logical, and honest statement of his religion, as far as it had then progressed, than Voltaire in the "Treatise on Metaphysics": and no student of his works or character can afford to pass it by.

The "Discourses on Man" form seven epistles in easy verse: and may be said to be founded on Pope's "Essay on Man" in much the same way as the ribald "Pucelle" was founded on the "Maid of Orleans" of the dull and respectable Chapelain. Their sentiments certainly differ widely from the comfortable optimism and orthodox theology of Mr. Pope. In this work, as in all his others, Voltaire was not so much the enemy of religion, as of *a* religion: and less the foe of Christianity than of that form of it called Roman Catholicism. The Epistles are upon the Nature of Pleasure, the Nature of Man, True Virtue, Liberty, the writer's favourite subjects. They are easy reading—light, graceful, delicate, witty. In brief, they are Voltaire.

On January 27, 1736, was produced in Paris Voltaire's Peruvian comedy "Alzire." "My Americans" he called it usually. It was a brilliant success, and ran for twenty consecutive nights. Voltaire gave all the proceeds to the actors. He had no great opinion of it. "As for comedy, I will have nothing to do with it: I am only a tragic animal," said he: and again, "You must be a good poet to write a good tragedy, a good comedy only requires a certain talent for versemaking." He was right—with regard to himself at least. His comedies are all sprightly and vivacious, but not much else. Between the lines, indeed, even of "Alzire"—which the author, with a twinkle in his eye, called "a very Christian piece ... which should reconcile me with some of the devout"—may be read the most characteristic of the Voltairian opinions. But he was too true an artist to allow those opinions to override his play, and never forgot to disguise the powder in a great deal of jam. It was twice performed at Court.

He was living quietly at Cirey when it was pleasing the popular taste of Paris. One is not surprised that overtaxed Nature had her revenge at last. By February, he was thoroughly ill. Madame du Châtelet sat on the end of his bed and read aloud Cicero in Latin and Pope in English. They were not wasting their time anyhow! One of them, at least, considered it nothing short of "a degradation" to allow bodily ill-health to stop mental industry.

In March, he wrote that he was "overwhelmed by maladies and occupations." By April, he was well enough to be plunged into a quarrel with the faithless Jore, bookseller of Rouen.

If Voltaire was a very good friend, he was also a very good enemy. A more hot-headed, energetic, pugnacious foe certainly never existed. While he hated, he hated well. He lashed his enemy with such brilliant invective, such delicate gibes, such rollicking sarcasms, that one must needs pity the poor wretch if he deserved his fate ever so fully. Did he get up and retaliate, Voltaire was at him again in a moment, dancing round him, goading him to madness with the daintiest whip flicked with *mots* and jests and little cunning allusions, which looked so innocent, and always caught the victim on the raw. Diatribe, gaiety, quip, mockery,—this man had all the weapons. He never used one where another would have done better. He had a dreadful instinct for finding out the weak place in his adversary's armour and logic. "God make my enemies ridiculous!" was one of his few prayers. It was granted in full measure.

But if he was a dangerous and an untiring foe, he was not an ungenerous one. In this case, Jore was certainly the aggressor. He had played Voltaire false in the matter of the "English Letters." He had endangered the author's safety and condemned him to exile. He wrote now from the Bastille saying that if Voltaire would avow himself the author of the book, he, Jore, would be released. Voltaire was as quick to compassion as he was quick to anger. If he had hated a pigmy like Jore with a fierceness he should have kept for a worthier foe, the moment the man was fallen, his enemy became his friend. He wrote the letter asked of him, declaring himself to be the writer of the abominable thing. Then Jore demanded fourteen hundred francs, the cost of the confiscated edition. On April 15th Voltaire hurried up to Paris. There he saw Jore, and, though denying that he had any claim upon him, offered him half the sum he had demanded. Jore refused it: brought a lawsuit against Voltaire, and published a defamatory account of him. Voltaire's quick passions were up in arms in a moment. He was as much agog to get at his enemy as a terrier is agog for a rat. He would have shaken the wretched little bookseller in just such a terrier fashion, if he could have got hold of him. But all Voltaire's friends advised compromise with such insistence that he at last yielded. He spent twelve breathless indignant weeks in the capital. He had to pay Jore five hundred francs, in lieu of the fourteen hundred he had demanded. "I sign my shame," he wrote. But he signed and paid all the same. He returned to Cirey in July sick in mind and body, baffled, bitter, and sore. In a year or two Jore professed penitence, and lived for the rest of his life on a small pension allowed him—by Voltaire.

While he was in Paris, two seats had fallen vacant in the Academy. But what chance could there be of one for the hero of a public scandal, a notorious firebrand, like Voltaire? Villars and Richelieu did their best for him—in vain.

He professed himself gaily indifferent, and *was* bitterly disappointed. He had to further postpone too the production of his "Prodigal Son." He could not give that son, he said, so unpopular a father.

The man needed rest after his battles. He had soon what was far better than rest to one of his vivid temperament—a victory. In August began his correspondence with Prince Frederick of Prussia, afterwards Frederick the Great. It comprises many letters remarkable on both sides, extraordinary on Voltaire's. It lasted for many years—before they met, in the early golden days of an almost lover-like infatuation—and long after they had quarrelled and parted. Voltaire was not the man at any time to be insensible to the honour of being the correspondent of one who was "almost a king." He was a great deal too impressionable not to be in some sort the child of his age. In all his glowing dreams of liberty, he never wished royalty abolished—only restrained, enlightened, ennobled. And behold! the means were given him now, himself to show a king the way in which kings should walk—to influence a man who would influence a great people—to teach Europe, by a master to whom it *must* listen, those emancipating truths which were the passion of Voltaire's own soul. What an opportunity! It was characteristic of the man that he realised and seized it at once.

"Believe that there have never been any good kings save those who, like you, have begun by teaching themselves, by knowing men, by loving the truth, by hating persecution and superstition. There is no prince who, thus thinking, cannot bring back the golden age to his country. Why do so few sovereigns seek this great good? You know why it is, monseigneur; it is because they all think more of royalty than of humanity."

These words occur in Voltaire's very first letter, written August 26, 1736. They are the text of all the others. If there were compliments and flatteries, French grace and *politesse*, and the adulation of the "Solomon of the North" somewhat overdone, those were the inevitable courtly trappings which adorned all letters of the time. The monitor of Solomon, as shown in that very first letter, knew himself to be the monitor; and, for all that exquisite turn of phrase and those pretty eulogies, was going to remain the monitor to the end. The flattery was by no means all humbug either. This royal pupil was the aptest that ever man had. He answered his Voltaire, not unworthily. At five-and-twenty he was himself philosopher and thinker: as great a natural genius as he was a natural barbarian. All learning and cultivation left him as much the one as the other.

The correspondence, once started, went on its way with a will. On Voltaire's side it was from the first profoundly philosophic. His style was as clear, easy, and lucid when he wrote on the deepest and subtlest problems of free-will and personal identity as when he wrote scandal to Theriot or *bagatelles* to Mademoiselle Quinault. He wrote on the most abstruse subjects with a limpid simplicity of language, unachieved by any other writer before or since. It is the greatest glory of Voltaire as an author in general, as well as the author of the letters to Frederick the Great, that he made profound truths, common truths, and the knowledge that had been the heritage of a few, the heritage of all.

Madame du Châtelet read the letters, of course, before they were despatched from Cirey. One fills eleven large pages of print and is practically an Essay on Personal Liberty—reasonable enough, said Madame, to bring its author to the stake. Theriot showed Frederick's letters about the salons of Paris: the prudent Voltaire thinking that the correspondence with a king might just as well do him all the good it could, and proclaim to his enemies that *all* temporal powers did not hate and fear him. At Cirey, the royal association certainly gave pleasure at first. Madame was singularly superior to kingly attractions: but Frederick was a thinker as well as a prince and loved philosophy as she did. She had not begun to look upon him as a rival in her lover's affections. In his very first letter Voltaire had declined an invitation to be his visitor on the score that friends should always be preferred before kings.

The bloom of that summer of 1736 came and went on Cirey. Jore was hardly silenced and by no means forgotten when Voltaire flung aside his princely philosopher, as it were, to reply to a long, scandalous, and very personal attack which bitter old J. B. Rousseau, infuriated by the "Temple of Taste," had made upon his rival, in a publication called the "Bibliothèque Française." That attack dated from the May of this year. It was not until September 20th Voltaire decided to answer it. He had been very patient, or had crouched awhile for a surer spring. His answer is a masterpiece of gay and biting satire. "Rousseau has printed in your journal a long letter on me in which, happily for me, there are only calumnies, and, unfortunately for him, there is no wit. What makes the thing so bad, gentlemen, is that it is entirely his own ... it is the second time in his life he has had any imagination. He has no success when he is original.... As for his verses, I can only wish for the sake of all the honest people he attacks, that he should go on writing in the same style."

And in answer to Rousseau's insinuations on Voltaire's origin, "I have a valet who is his near relative and a very honest man. The poor youth begs me every day to pardon his relation's bad verses."

And in reply to that little story Rousseau had once circulated about Voltaire's profane behaviour at a mass, "Do you think ... it sits well on the author of the 'Moïsade' to accuse me of having talked in church sixteen years ago?... Thank God, that Rousseau is as clumsy as he is hypocritical. Without this counterpoise he would be too dangerous." The letter finishes by recalling all the humiliating episodes in Rousseau's life he would have most wished forgotten.

From which it will be seen that Voltaire did not scruple to employ his adversaries' weapons—and to use them with a most deadly skill and finish.

On October 10, 1736, a play called "Britannicus" could not be played at the Théâtre Français in Paris on account of the illness of the principal actress. A new comedy called "The Prodigal Son" by an anonymous author was therefore produced in its stead, and performed to a crowded house with enormous success.

It had been acted already by a company beaten up in that desolate neighbourhood of Cirey. Voltaire had written reams of letters about it to Mademoiselle Quinault, filled with rather doubtful jokes—which were apparently, however, to the taste of Mademoiselle and of the period. The "Prodigal" is in verse and five acts, and perhaps reaches a higher level than most of Voltaire's easy comedies. There were many surmises as to its authorship. Voltaire himself suggested that it was by one Gresset. Before he withdrew the veil of anonymity, "The Prodigal Son" had been lavishly praised by most of its father's enemies.

He had other pleasures just now, too, besides that success, to distract him from the thoughts of his health which, as usual, "went to the devil." "Émilie, reading Newton, ... terraces fifty feet wide, balconies, porcelain baths, yellow and silver rooms, niches for Chinese trifles, all that takes a long time," he wrote to Theriot. Passing travellers too came to Cirey, and told travellers' tales about it when they returned to Paris. In this year, 1736, Voltaire began an immense correspondence with a Parisian agent of his, an Abbé Moussinot, to whom he wrote about investments and speculations, and whom he commissioned to buy tapestries, diamond shoe-buckles, and scrubbing brushes; reflecting telescopes and hair powder; thermometers, barometers, scent, sponges, dusters—everything in the world. "If you do not want to commit suicide, always have something to do" was one of his own axioms.

Even now, unfortunately for him, all these varied occupations did not give him so much to do that he could not read, re-read, delight in, and talk about until it became public property, a certain little *bizarrerie* of his versatile mind called "Le Mondain." A gay little piece is the "Mondain," three or four pages long, in very flowing verse, a little impertinent, perhaps, and quite volatile and careless. It was written about the same time as "Alzire." It contains a flippant allusion to Adam and Eve, and the famous expression "le superflu, chose très nécessaire." Those are the most memorable things in it. The most memorable thing about it is the fury of persecution it brought down on the author and the storm of hatred it excited. The offence was supposed to lie in the allusion to our first parents. The real offence was the name and reputation of Voltaire.

On December 21, 1736, he received a warning letter from his friend d'Argental in Paris, telling him that the "Mondain" rendered its author's position once more unsafe. It is said that the authorities thought of warning the Marquis that he must no longer give refuge to such a firebrand. Voltaire and Madame had a hurried consultation. Madame wept not a little: for though she was a philosopher she was also a woman, and as a woman, and after her capacity, she loved Voltaire. She strongly opposed the idea of his taking refuge with Prince Frederick: but agreed that he must fly across the frontier. She went with him as far as four-mile distant Vassy, and they parted there, with many tears. The man's heart was hot with anger and bitterness. The old serpent of injustice and oppression entered into every Eden he found. Madame only remembered that she loved him and that he must leave her. The strange *convenances* of the day, which permitted so many things, had a few rules, and those few had to be observed rigidly to make up for many laxities. If the Marquise could have gone with Voltaire to England or Prussia, all would have been well. But that was not permitted. Neither she could go with him nor he stay with her. They said good-bye in a bitter cold. It was winter—the winter had come so soon! A few days later there arrived in Brussels, in deep snow, one M. Renol, merchant.

No personal injustice which he ever suffered so deeply affected Voltaire as this one. In some cases if he did not deserve, he at least tempted, the anger of the authorities. But here! "Is it possible that anyone can have taken the thing seriously?" he wrote. "It needs the absurdity and denseness of the golden age to find it dangerous, and the cruelty of the age of iron to persecute the author of a *badinage* so innocent." He went to Antwerp, to Amsterdam, and to Leyden. At Brussels "Alzire" was performed in his honour—for all that he was travelling *incognito*, and M. Renol, merchant, had no reason to be more interested in "Alzire" than anybody else. At Leyden crowds flocked to see him, and he was introduced to Boerhaave, the great doctor. He was at Amsterdam in January, 1737, received with all honour, "living as a philosopher," studying much, working at Newton—as Voltaire alone knew how to work—at any hour of the night and day, passionately, thoroughly, devotedly. He superintended the printing of his "Elements of Newton's Philosophy" then in the Dutch press. He tried to forget. But he could not. The offence was rank and smelt to heaven. He was abroad until March. Then in answer to the tears and prayers of his Marquise, he gave out he was going to England—and went to Cirey. But for those tears, but for that faith unfaithful which kept him falsely true, he *would* have gone to England as he said. "If friendship stronger than all other feelings had not recalled me, I would willingly have spent the rest of my days in a country where at least my enemies could not hurt me: and where caprice, superstition, and the power of a minister need not be feared.... I have always told you that if my father, brother, or son were Prime Minister in a despotic state I would leave it to-morrow. But Madame du Châtelet is more to me than father, brother, or son." She was. She had been not a little sore and wretched while he was away. Prudence had made his letters perforce so cold! "He calls me 'Madame'!" The overwhelming vigour of her affection brought him back to her. But even *her* entreaties for prudence could not keep him from writing a "Defence of Le Mondain," and an answer to the criticisms thereon, called the "Use of Life." His heart was hot within him. Fifteen years later the fever burnt still.

"You will say fifteen years have passed since it all happened" he wrote to d'Argental. "No! only one day. For great wrongs are always recent wounds."

CHAPTER IX

WORK AT CIREY

THE spring of 1737 passed quietly enough. Voltaire and Madame du Châtelet were occupied in scientific experiments, and as delighted as two children with wonderful discoveries and a dark room. They paid very little heed to the summer which was coming, tender and fragrant, to crown desolate Cirey with loveliness. Nothing was so unfashionable as Nature in the eighteenth century. Even the poets neglected her—save one ploughman in his barren North. To painters she served only as the unheeded background to a trim Watteau shepherdess courting a bashful shepherd on a fan. To Voltaire and his Marquise she hardly formed even a background. In all his writings there is not the slightest evidence that he had so much as a perception of natural beauty. He was fond of pointing out how much better off was a modern, cultivated, luxurious Frenchman, than a happy Adam in some wild Eden, and hereafter was quickly irate, after his fashion, with that absurd theory of Jean Jacques Rousseau's that the "state of Nature is the reign of God."

About midsummer there arrived at Cirey on a visit, one Kaiserling, a Prussian, young, gay, delightful, with a pretty talent for making French verses—*tant bien que mal*—and the social ambassador of Prince Frederick. Kaiserling brought his master's portrait as a present to his master's guide, philosopher, and friend, and the warmest of greetings and messages, besides the second part of somebody's Metaphysics and the whole of somebody else's Dissertations. He was received, he said, as Adam and Eve received the angel in Milton's garden of Eden, only the hospitality was better and the *fêtes* more gallant. There were plays and conversations. Eve, as Madame du Châtelet, was the easiest and most delightful hostess in the world, who sang to the celestial organ, played the spinet, spoke all languages, and no doubt amused the visitor, if he were not of nervous habit, by driving him about the country in her "phaeton for fairies drawn by horses as big as elephants."

In the evenings, if one did not read aloud a canto of that wicked "Pucelle" or a chapter of "Louis XIV.," there were fireworks, the most beautiful fireworks with letters of flame spelling Frederick's name and surrounded by the motto "To the Hope of the human race." It is not a little curious to note the naïve delight Voltaire took to the very end of his days in these, and such, amusements. He had always something of the child in him—the child's love of laughter, the child's love of the gaudy, as well as the child's hot temper, generous impulse, and quickness to forgive. Nothing was so small that he was too great to be amused by it. "Rire et fais rire" was one of his mottoes. He threw himself into those firework preparations as thoroughly as a very few months later, and after days passed in the most abstruse studies, he devoted himself body and soul to marionnettes, charades, and a magic-lantern. To say that he was a versatile Frenchman is some explanation: but it is not a sufficient one. He worked and thought so hard that the more frivolous the recreation, the more it recreated. "The divinity of gaiety," Catherine the Great called him. "If Nature had not made us a little frivolous we should be most wretched," he said himself. "It is because one can be frivolous that the majority of people do not hang themselves." It was because Voltaire could always laugh and work that it could be truly said of one of the most impressionable and sensitive of human creatures that "sixty years of persecution never gave him a single headache."

After three weeks' stay, Kaiserling left, taking with him to his Prince a part of "Louis XIV." and some short poems. They both wanted—and begged—just a few cantos of the "Pucelle." But on this point the goddess of Cirey was perfectly firm. "The friendship with which she honours me does not permit me to risk a thing which might separate me from her for ever," Voltaire wrote. Entrust King and Kaiserling with a bomb which might explode at any moment and scatter love, liberty, peace, to atoms! Madame was too clever a woman for that. The guest left without his "Pucelle," and Émilie and Voltaire plunged deeply again into the scientific studies and experiments which were the particular madness of the hour.

At the end of the year 1737, the lazy Linant, the tutor, was very rightly discharged by Madame du Châtelet. She had extended her kindness to both his mother and sister. But the sister was as unpromising as the brother. They left Cirey. Voltaire said he had given his word of honour not even to write to his former *protégé*; "but I have not promised not to help him." Through a mutual friend he was weak and generous enough to send this "enfant terrible," as Diderot called him, fifty livres: and thereafter took no little pride and interest in Linant's third-rate writings.

There are some very characteristic letters of Voltaire's written at this period in which he economically tries to arrange, through Moussinot, for the engagement of a young priest, who is also to be something of a chemist, so that he can say mass in the Cirey chapel on Sundays and Saints' days and devote himself to the laboratory all the others. This *factotum* did not turn out a success, and a separate young man had to be engaged for each occupation.

In the November of 1737 died M. Mignot, the husband of Voltaire's dead sister Catherine. M. Mignot left behind two slenderly portioned and unmarried daughters—and behold! the versatile Voltaire in the part of the paternal uncle, seeking them husbands and furnishing them with *dots*. He wanted Louise, the elder, to marry the son of his Cirey neighbour, the stout, good-natured Madame de Champbonin. But Louise, who was a bouncing young woman of four-and-twenty, with a pronounced love of pleasure and the sound of her own voice, entirely declined to be buried alive for the rest of her life in an impossible country neighbourhood: and expressed these sentiments quite distinctly to Uncle Voltaire. In practice, as well as principle, he was for freedom of action. In his day, the father, or the person who stood in place of the father to a marriageable girl, disposed of her literally without consulting her, and exactly as it seemed best to himself.

"They are the only family I have," Voltaire wrote of his nieces rather sadly. "I should like to become fond of them.... If they marry *bourgeois* of Paris I am their very humble servant, but they are lost to me." But he had said too that to restrict the liberty of a fellow creature was a sin against Nature. So on February 25, 1738, Louise Mignot married a M. Denis, who was in the Commissariat Department in Paris, and received from Uncle Voltaire a wedding present of thirty thousand francs.

In March, the young couple came to spend part of their honeymoon at Cirey. It has already been said that Madame Denis found the country horribly, abominably, and dismally dull. There was a theatre, to be sure! But where was one to find actors in this desert? The bride had to put up with a puppet show, which, indeed, was very good, she added grudgingly. They were received in "perfect style" too. That must have been comforting to the soul of a Madame Denis. Uncle Voltaire was building "a handsome addition to the château"—also comforting perhaps to the Denisian temperament. The bride added naively that her uncle was very fond indeed of M. Denis, "which does not astonish me, for he is very amiable."

But what an eerie enchanted castle it was amid these tangled forests of Champagne! Its sorceress—pretty and charming as well as clever, niece Denis found her—brewed every potion that could keep a lover, humoured his whims, dressed for him, sang to him, decorated the house to his fancy and—strange love-philtre!—quoted him "whole passages of the best philosophers." The captive was an unconscious captive, but a captive still. The chains were gold, but there were chains. And even gold chains chafe and bruise and eat into the flesh at last. The commonplace niece saw much to which the brilliant Madame and her Voltaire were both as yet blind. She loudly regretted that her uncle should be lost to his friends and bound hand and foot by such an attachment. Voltaire and Émilie parted from the bride and bridegroom, it may be assumed, pretty cheerfully. They were not only still happy in each other, they had a prodigious amount of work to get through. And your idle people, not content with doing nothing themselves, are the surest prevention of work in others and grudge the industry they will by no means imitate.

In the June of 1738, the second Mademoiselle Mignot was married to a M. de Fontaine. Voltaire did his duty and gave the bride twenty-five thousand francs: but he hated weddings and was not to be persuaded to go to this one, any more than to Madame Denis's.

Lazy, good-natured Theriot came to stay at Cirey in October, and no doubt did *his* idle best to wean his indefatigable host from the scientific labours to which he was devoted, soul and body. The Cirey goddess did not care about M. Theriot. If she was not married to Voltaire she was at least wifely in her failings, and not at all too disposed to like her lover's old friends. Voltaire went into the parting guest's bedchamber, and under pretence of helping him to pack, slipped into his box fifty louis. He was a man of substance by now. It is estimated that at this period his income must have been about three thousand pounds per annum (English money). Few men who have made wealth as hardly and thriftily as he did, and are of temperament naturally shrewd and prudent, have been as generous with it when made. Voltaire was not only fully alive to the claims of his relatives and to the needs of his friends, but had a strangely soft spot in his cynic heart for anyone who was forlorn and poor. It was in 1737 he had written to Moussinot to go, from him, to a certain Demoiselle d'Amfreville and, for no better reason than that she was needy and had once had "a sort of estate" near Cirey, "beg her to accept the loan of ten pistoles, and when she wants more, I have the honour to be at her service."

Ever since Voltaire returned from England he had been the most enthusiastic hero-worshipper of the great Newton and the great Newtonian system. In England, he had talked with Clarke, the dead Newton's successor and friend. The year following his arrival at Cirey he had devoted himself to science as only a Voltaire understood devotion. At his side was the woman who was the aptest pupil of Maupertuis and almost the only other person in France who understood Newtonianism, save Maupertuis himself, Voltaire, and one Clairaut. The rest of the world was Cartesian. The philosophy of Descartes was *de rigueur*. Fontenelle's "Plurality of Worlds," which clothed that philosophy with all the grace and charms of a perfect style, was on the toilet table of every woman of fashion. The government said Descartes was infallible, so he *must* be infallible. With what a passion of zeal those two people set themselves to seek truth for truth's sake—to seek truth whether it agreed with the fashionable belief and the text-books or whether it did not—to find it, and to give it to the world! To make Newton intelligible to the French people—to present his theories so that they would read as delightfully as a romance—to teach his countrymen to think boldly as Newton had thought—to weigh, to ponder, and consider whether the popular faiths were the true faiths—to believe intelligently or to deny, not afraid—that was Voltaire's aim. "Nothing enfranchises like education." "When once a nation begins to think, it is impossible to stop it." The French were to be taught to think by the "Elements of Newton's Philosophy." The censor prohibited the work with its dangerous and terrible anti-Cartesian theories when it appeared. But in ten years' time, the Cartesian theories were proscribed in the schools of Paris and the Newtonian taught everywhere in their stead. Voltaire hardly ever won a finer victory.

In 1735, there had begun, then, to arrive by that bi-weekly coach from Paris air-pumps, crucibles, prisms, compasses, almost every kind of scientific appliance then known. One day the coach brought a practical young chemist (not a priest)—also purchased by the useful Mouissinot. Voltaire and Madame were by no means going to be content with reading of Newton's experiments. They must try them themselves! One day, with a good deal of outside help, it may be presumed, they weighed a ton of red-hot iron. The dark room gave an almost childish pleasure to them both. Voltaire tried experiments of his own. He was so absorbed in them that he neglected his correspondence even. For the time being he was the most scientific scientist who ever breathed—in a fever of interest in his work, agog to know more, for more time, more power to labour, longing for a body that never wanted sleep or rest, change or refreshment. "How will you be the better," a friend inquired of him, "for knowing the pathway of light and the gravitation of Saturn?" It was a stupid question, to be sure, to ask a Voltaire. All knowledge was a priceless gain, he thought. We must open our souls to all the arts, all the sciences, all the feelings! Poetry, physics, history, geometry, the drama—everything. What! to miss knowing what one might have known! to have a mind only ready for one kind of learning, when it had room in it, if properly arranged, for every kind! Friend Cideville had mistaken his man.

The Marquise was no whit less enthusiastic. Voltaire's own mathematical education had been neglected. But not hers. The pupil of Maupertuis could help out her lover's defects. Metaphysics was her passion. She had the accuracy of Euclid, Voltaire said, and algebra was her amusement. In his dedicatory Epistle to the "Elements," which was the fruit of their joint labour, he spoke of her in terms which were, at once, high-flown compliment and hard fact. She *had* penetrated "the depths of transcendent geometry" and "alone among us has read and commented on the great Newton." She *had* "made her own by indefatigable labour, truths which would intimidate most men," and had "sounded the depths in her hours of leisure of what the profoundest philosophers study unremittingly." She had corrected many faults in the Italian "Newtonianism for Ladies" written by their visitor Algarotti, and knew a great deal more about the subject than he did himself. It is not hard to understand how Voltaire came by what he called his "little system"—that women are as clever as men, only more amiable. He had Madame du Châtelet always with him— Madame whose whole aim in life then was to work, and to please him. Her industry was as great as his own. The word "trouble" was never in her vocabulary. He loved her intellect if he did not love her. They should have been happy. If they ever were, it was over the "Elements of Newton's Philosophy."

The book was ready at last. To make the theory of gravitation clear— and entertaining—had been Voltaire's chief difficulty. If any man was adapted to enlighten obscurity, he was that man. His own mind was not only extraordinarily brilliant, but it was extraordinarily neat. In the "Elements" sequence follows sequence, and effect, cause, as incisively as in a proposition of Euclid.

It has been seen that while Voltaire was in Holland in the spring of 1737 he was superintending the printing of these "Elements." Before forwarding the last chapters to the printers he sent the whole book for the inspection of the Chancellor of France, full of hope. "The most imbecile fanatic, the most envenomed hypocrite can find nothing in it to object to," he wrote in his vigorous fashion. Six months passed, and no answer. And then the French authorities sent a refusal. "It is dangerous to be right in things in which those in power are wrong," wrote Voltaire. Very dangerous. And how unmannerly of this presumptuous Voltaire to dare to treat the beloved Descartes with cool logic and relentless scrutiny just as if he were not sealed, signed, and stamped by the infallible decree of fashion!

But, though it was not permitted, as Voltaire said, to a poor Frenchman to say that attraction is possible and proved, and vacuum demonstrated, yet, as usual, the pirate publishers would by no means miss their chance.

The printers of Amsterdam produced an edition of the work which they called the "Elements of Newton's Philosophy Adapted to Every Capacity" (*Mis à la Portée de Tout le Monde*). Of course there was not wanting to Voltaire an enemy to say the title should have been written *Mis à la Porte de Tout le Monde*—shown the door by everybody. The author raged and fumed not a little over the printers' blunders and incorrectness.

The usual host of calumnies attacked him again. Society and the gutter press united in feeling that a person who dared to doubt their darling Cartesian system *must* be of shameful birth and the most abandoned morals.

They insulted him with all "the intrepidity of ignorance." He was accused of intrigues with persons he had never seen or who had never existed. The vile licence of that strictly licensed press is the finest argument for a free press to be found: the freest is less scurrilous than those much watched and prohibited journals of old France.

Not the less, the storm which heralded its birth thundered the "Elements of Newton's Philosophy" into fame. It is forbidden: so we *must* read it! If Fontenelle had made the system of Descartes intelligible, Voltaire made the system of Newton amusing. In 1741, he brought out an authorised edition. In ten years, as has been said, there were hardly so many Cartesians in France.

To this same year 1738 belongs a Prize Essay which Voltaire wrote for the Academy of Sciences on the "Nature and Propagation of Fire." There were plenty of foundries near Cirey, where he could make practical observations on the subject. So he went and observed. Time? The man had on his hands, to be sure, a lawsuit, a tragedy, a history, an enormous correspondence, a "Pucelle," a love affair, an estate, and a couple of chattering lady visitors who had to be amused in the evenings with music, with readings, and charades. He had nearly finished writing the essay when Madame du Châtelet, whose opinions differed from his and who always had the courage of them, must needs write, in secret, a rival essay on the same subject.

She began to work on it but a month before it had to be sent in. She could only write at night, since Voltaire did not know she was doing it. Her husband—strange confidant!—was the only person in the secret. For eight nights, she only slept one hour in each. Every now and then she thrust her hands into iced water to refresh herself, and paced her room rapidly. The idea possessed her. "I combated almost all Voltaire's ideas," she said herself.

He once very happily defined their connection as "an unalterable friendship and a taste for study." It *was* friendship and would have been happier for both if no softer feeling had entered it. They were friends who could intellectually differ and be friends still: who never sacrificed truth to sentiment, and whose bond of union was not a passion for each other, but for knowledge.

Both of them sent in their efforts. Madame's was chiefly remarkable for the statement that different-coloured rays do not give an equal degree of heat: since proved indisputably correct by repeated experiments. Voltaire's paper, as well as Émilie's, contained many new ideas. That of itself was sufficient to disqualify their efforts for the prize. It did do so. It was divided between three other competitors, who were correctly orthodox and anti-Newtonian.

Then Madame told her secret, and Voltaire wrote a favourable anonymous review of that essay which contradicted his own, and should have made Madame du Châtelet famous in a better way than as his mistress.

Both of them were as disappointed as two children might have been at their failure. "Our Essays really *were* the best!" they wrote and told Maupertuis, almost in so many words. They were, although neither of them is now worth much as science. Some of their theories have been superseded; or proved absolutely wrong. But they were wise for their age, and brilliantly expressed. That may be said, but not much more than that, for all Voltaire's scientific works. They were the alphabet of the language—to teach a scientific childhood to think for itself. It is because they accomplished that aim to the full that they are forgotten to-day.

CHAPTER X

PLEASURE AT CIREY

ON December 4, 1738, there arrived at Cirey, having been almost upset out of her post-chaise, and actually compelled to wade through the midwinter mud of the worst roads in France, a visitor, Madame de Graffigny.

Fat and forty was Madame: a vulgar, cheerful, gossiping old nurse, already an ardent hero-worshipper of Voltaire, whom she had met at Lunéville, and with something of literary taste on her own account. The Graffigny had, in fact, caught that eighteenth-century epidemic which showed itself in easy wit, easy writing, and easy morals. She had a brute of a husband from whom she had just obtained a divorce. She had no money. She had any number of friends. Voltaire seems to have liked her because she was poor, good-natured, and adored him. He came to meet his guest in her room when she arrived at two o'clock on that December morning, with a flat candlestick in his hand, and looking for all the world, said the effusive lady, like a monk. Émilie was there, too. Her greetings were only a shade less warm than her lover's. Madame de Graffigny was left alone: so that she could then and there sit down to her writing-table and for the benefit of a dear confidant, called Panpan, ring up the curtain on one of the most intimate and minute of domestic comedies ever given to the public.

Some years later Madame de Graffigny obtained some contemporary celebrity by her "Letters of a Peruvian." They are altogether forgotten. But her "Vie Privée de Voltaire et de Madame du Châtelet" will live as long as the fame of that strange pair and the popularity of gossiping memoirs.

Since their arrival there in 1734, both Voltaire and Émilie had been busy in improving, not only the outside, but the inside of their thirteenth-century château. Voltaire had a little wing to himself which, by the irony of fate or choice, adjoined the chapel. He could open his bedroom door and sacrifice to the *convenances* by seeing mass performed, while he went on with his own occupations. Sometimes the visitors fulfilled their religious duties in this way too. They were all very particular not to miss the attendance on Sundays and *fête* days. Their religion was a concession to social laws, like powdering the hair. When Voltaire was ill in bed, which was pretty often, he had his door opened so that he could hear the penitential litanies being recited, and had a screen drawn round him to exclude draughts. His rooms were very simply furnished, for use not show, spotlessly clean, so that you could kiss the floor, said Madame de Graffigny, in the enthusiastic hyperbole of her early letters. There was very little tapestry and a good deal of panelling which formed an admirable background to a few good pictures. There was a small hall, where their guests took their morning coffee sometimes, where a stove made the air like spring, and where there were books and scientific apparatus, a single sofa, and no luxurious armchairs at all. The dark room—still unfinished—led out of the hall, and there was a door into the garden.

The Goddess's apartments were far more gorgeous. The lady visitor went into ecstasies over that bedroom and boudoir upholstered in pale blue and yellow—even to the basket for the dog—the pictures by Watteau and the fireplace by Martin, the window looking on the terrace, and the amber writing-case, a present from the politic Prince Frederick.

The rest of the castle was ill-cared for enough, she said. The thirty-six fires which blazed in it daily could not keep it warm. In her own room, in spite of a fire "like the fire of Troy," she sat and shivered. On Christmas Eve the draught from the windows blew out the candles—although the visitor had solemnly vowed those draughts should be stopped with canvas bags, "if God gives me life." It may not unfairly be surmised that most of the guests suffered as she did. Voltaire was a very good host—hospitable, kind, warm-hearted, very anxious they should not be bored, and indefatigable in amusing them with entertainments in the evenings and talking to them at meals. But their comfort in their rooms was naturally not his province. He did not think of it, and Émilie did not care. She did not object to visitors so long as they left her plenty of time and solitude to work: and then was ready enough to be charming in the evenings. Experimental science and good housekeeping are not necessarily incompatible: but each must have its own hours. Science had all Madame du Châtelet's. She seems to have been the sort of mistress who provided a liberal table for her friends because it is much less trouble to be liberal than economical, and had occasional fits of frugality which took the form of feeding her servants very meanly. She was sublimely inconsiderate towards them, as she was, in a lesser degree, inconsiderate towards her own friends. She was of her age! The *noblesse* of that time treated their dependents exactly as if they were animals, and animals who were at once dumb, deaf, blind, and stupid. Behind their masters' chairs, the valets listened to theories on which the masters talked and the servants acted. Longchamp, who was later half secretary, half valet to Voltaire, and before that in Madame du Châtelet's service, has left on record how he assisted at her toilet as if he had been her maid. For her, he was not a human creature but a thing—not a man, but a machine.

When Madame de Graffigny arrived she found two fellow-visitors also at Cirey—Madame de Champbonin, Voltaire's near neighbour and distant relative, and her son. Madame de Champbonin was variously and elegantly known as the "fat lady" or the "great tomcat." Voltaire made her in some sort a confidante. Perhaps the stout placidity of her disposition was restful after the tumultuous emotions of the "effervescent Émilie." The son was employed as Émilie's amanuensis, and copied for hours and hours manuscripts of which he did not understand a single word. The two lady visitors seem to have walked about the castle a good deal and admired its beauties, sympathised with each other concerning the draughts and the hostess's sublime indifference to such trifles, and hugged themselves with delight at the thought that half France was dying to be in their position as guests at Cirey. To be sure, there were drawbacks even in this earthly Paradise: but half France did not know that, and the daily journal addressed to Panpan was still rapturous.

Presently the Abbé de Breteuil, Madame du Châtelet's brother, also came to stay. He was *grand vicaire* at Sens. He was in every sense a typical abbé of the period—not much pretending to believe in the religion he professed—with a pronounced taste for broad stories—and "assez bon conteur" himself. The connection between his sister and Voltaire seemed to him only a thing to be proud of. He had countenanced it by his presence here before. The Marquis countenanced it too. Why should anyone else be particular? The abbé had come to enjoy himself, and he did.

While he was there the day began with coffee in Voltaire's hall between 10.30 and 11.30. Even Madame du Châtelet seems to have roused herself dimly to the sense that she had visitors and that something might be expected of her in the way of entertaining them. Both she and Voltaire tore themselves away a little oftener and for a little longer time from their beloved Newton, during Breteuil's visit. Everybody stayed with them in the hall till noon, when the Marquis and the two Champbonins went off to their *déjeuner*. The Marquis was always threatening to go to Brussels to see about an endless lawsuit he was concerned in there, and putting off his departure; which was a pity, as no one wanted him. After coffee, Voltaire, the abbé, Émilie, and Madame de Graffigny talked on all things in heaven and on earth for a while, and then separated.

The Marquise drove her great horses in her *calèche* sometimes in the morning. Once she would have insisted on nervous Madame de Graffigny going with her, but Voltaire interfered and said people must be happy in their own way. So Émilie, who had herself no time for nerves, went out alone.

Sometimes the party met again for *goûter* at four—sometimes not till the nine o'clock supper. That was the appointed hour for relaxation. Who would not have been of those evenings? Voltaire was inimitably gay, brilliant, and amusing. Madame de Graffigny had him on one side of her, and that pitiless bore, the unfortunate Marquis, on the other. *He* said nothing, fell asleep, and "went out with the tray."

The supper was elegant and sufficient, without being profuse. Voltaire had his valet always behind his chair to look after him, besides two other lackeys also in attendance. Émilie was geometrical no more. She was a woman of the world, trained in the first Court in Europe, witty, easy, charming, delightful. The stories had been broad at previous suppers; but they were broader than ever now, for the especial benefit of Breteuil. He told some of the same kind himself which entertained everybody immensely and which Madame de Graffigny, who had laughed at them fit "to split her spleen," retailed for Panpan's benefit the next day. The company drank Rhine wine or champagne which loosened their tongues and brightened their wits, though they were a temperate little gathering, by nature as well as from prudence. Voltaire improvised verses over the dessert, or read something aloud, or quoted from memory. The bare mention of J. B. Rousseau or Jore or any other enemy drew from him a quick torrent of vivacious indignation. One night, after dessert and the perfume handed after the dessert, there was a magic-lantern. Voltaire showed it with "*propos* to make you die of laughing," said Madame de Graffigny. Another night there were charades. A third, there was a reading of the "Mondain." A fourth, the entire party migrated to the bathroom—an exquisite room with porcelain tiles, marble pavement, pictures, engravings, and *bric-à-brac*—where Voltaire read aloud a canto of the "Pucelle." Panpan's correspondent avowedly enjoyed *that* immensely. So did everyone else. To hear something really shocking and dangerous read aloud in a bathroom with closed doors—how *piquant*! Madame de Graffigny gave Panpan epitomes of the cantos she heard, and lived to wish she had not. After the cantos they amused themselves by making punch.

Another evening they rehearsed "The Prodigal Son" and a farce Voltaire had written, "Boursouffle." Private theatricals were one of the Cirey manias. The little theatre was reopened for Breteuil's benefit. Pauline du Châtelet of twelve was interrupted in her education at Joinville to play the part of "Marthe," which she learnt in the post-chaise coming home. One night they danced in the theatre. Another, Voltaire read one of the "Discourses on Man." Yet another they discussed Newtonianism. Once, Voltaire showed them the scientific apparatus—which still stood in the hall awaiting the completion of the dark room—and they looked at globes and through telescopes. Twice he read his new play "Mérope" to them, and on the second occasion the effusive Graffigny "wept to sobs." She had also told them her own melancholy family history, when it had been Voltaire's turn to weep, and Madame du Châtelet was unable to pursue her geometrical studies for the evening.

Breteuil did not stay more than a week or so in all. The fun had been fast and furious while it lasted. It may be surmised that Voltaire and Émilie were not sorry to relax their efforts to keep the social ball rolling. They plunged deeper than ever into hard work. Madame worked all day as well as all night—and never left her room except for the morning coffee and the evening supper. Voltaire often could not tear himself from his desk until that supper was half over, and directly it was finished could hardly be prevented from returning to his writing. He did his best—he had the true French *politesse* all his life long—to talk and tell stories and amuse his guests; but his thoughts were far away. He was shut up in his own room the whole day too, now, except for a few minutes when he called on his two lady guests. He would not even sit down. "The time people waste in talking is frightful," he said on one of these brief visits. "One should not lose a minute. The greatest waste possible is waste of time." Madame de Graffigny was thrown on the stout lady for all companionship, and was in the melancholy position of the person who has to pretend she likes quiet, solitude, and reflection, and does not. After a very little while her graphic and garrulous pen goes much less easily and gaily over the paper.

Voltaire and Madame du Châtelet had troubles of which their guest did not know the cause, but of which she felt the effect. The Christmas Day of 1738 was one of the darkest of both their lives. To be unhappy is seldom to be very amiable. This Graffigny too was, on her own showing, something of a fool. Voltaire and Madame lived in a Paradise about which a serpent, called the French authorities, was for ever lurking, ready to spoil. Voltaire was always writing something he should not have written. And Madame de Graffigny was always writing those voluminous, gushing, confidential, imprudent epistles to Panpan. What *did* she say in them? On December 29, 1738, a tempest which had long been gathering in petty mistrusts, small jealousies, opened or kept back letters, suspicions, fears, hatreds—burst in a clap of thunder. There was a constrained and silent supper. Then Voltaire came to Madame de Graffigny's rooms and accused her of having betrayed his trust and endangered his safety by having copied cantos of the "Pucelle" and sent them to Panpan. She denied the accusation *in toto*. Voltaire, beside himself with fury, made her sit down and write and ask Panpan and Desmarets, her lover, both for the original canto she had sent and the copies which had been made of it. The unfortunate lady entirely lost her head. Then enter Madame du Châtelet in a rage royal, besides which Voltaire's was calmness, temperance, and reason. She produced a certain letter from her pocket as a proof of infamy and flung it, very nearly literally, in her guest's face. She accused her of having stolen a canto of the "Pucelle" from her desk. She reminded her that she had never liked her, and had only invited her to Cirey because she had nowhere else to go. The Graffigny was a monster, the most *indigne* of creatures—all the opprobrious things in the du Châtelet dictionary, which was a very full one. Voltaire put his arm round his furious mistress and dragged her away at last. The quarrel was so loud that the Graffigny's maid, two rooms off, heard every word of it. Madame de Champbonin came in, in the middle, but very prudently retired at once. When Madame de Graffigny was calm enough to read the letter which Emilie had flung at her, she discovered it was one of Panpan's which Emilie had intercepted and read and wherein was the remark "The canto of 'Jeanne' is charming." Madame de Graffigny was able to explain to Voltaire in a very few words that this sentence referred to her description of the pleasure one of those readings of the "Pucelle" had given to herself, and that there had been no question of stealing, copying, and sending a canto to anybody in the world.

Cannot one fancy how that little, sensitive, *vif*, angry Voltaire was on his knees to his offended guest at once, begging her a thousand pardons, kissing her hands, apologising, furious with Émilie and ashamed of himself? It was already five o'clock in the morning. But Émilie was recalled not the less (Megæra, poor Graffigny named her now). Voltaire argued long with her, in English, to bring her to reason, and was so far successful that the next day she coldly apologised to her guest. She was too much in the wrong to forgive easily or thoroughly. As for Voltaire, *he* asked pardon again and again with tears in his eyes. He could not do too much to make up for his suspicions and mistake. Émilie was diabolically cold and haughty. The unfortunate visitor was "in hell," she said. But she had no money and nowhere to go to. There were silent uncomfortable suppers. Voltaire's "pathetic" excuses and nervous anxiety for her comfort and well-being, when he came to see her in her rooms, did not make her position much easier.

After waiting three weeks Madame de Graffigny obtained confirmation of her story from Desmarets and Panpan.

Émilie at last relented so far as to give her guest the very doubtful pleasure of driving her out in that *calèche* of hers, and talking to her more freely and amicably. But though such wounds as Madame de Graffigny had received may heal, the scars remain for ever.

On January 12, 1739, the mathematical Maupertuis, Madame du Châtelet's tutor, came to stay a few days. The unlucky Graffigny suffered a good deal from her eyes about this time, and stayed much in her room. Voltaire himself was in wretched health; so there was no play-acting. Madame de Champbonin left for Paris on a mission of whose nature the

Graffigny was ignorant. On January 18th the Marquis du Châtelet went to Seineville bearing with him many letters and messages for dear Panpan. Early in the next month, Desmarets, the lover of Madame de Graffigny, came to stay and Cirey roused itself to another burst of gaiety. It acted "Zaire" and "The Prodigal Son" and a play called "The Spirit of Contradiction." One rehearsal lasted till three o'clock in the morning. Once the party spent the whole day in Émilie's room where she was "in bed without being ill." The next, she was singing to the clavecin, accompanying herself. Another, she sang through a whole opera after supper. She and Desmarets went out riding. In one twenty-four hours the company had rehearsed and played thirty-three acts of tragedies, operas, and comedies. Desmarets read Panpan's letters to the Graffigny while she was at her toilette, as she had no time herself. Desmarets was "transported, intoxicated"—enjoying himself immensely.

His mistress may be presumed to have been more unhappy than ever, since the first thing he had done on his arrival at Cirey was to tell her he no longer felt for her the feelings of a lover. He went away.

About the middle of February, 1739, Madame de Graffigny herself left Cirey, having been there less than three months—not six, as the title-page of her book declares. For the rest of her life Voltaire was one of the most staunch and generous friends she had in the world.

Nothing in Madame de Graffigny's "Vie Privée de Voltaire et de Madame du Châtelet" is so interesting as the light she throws on their relationship to each other. The golden chains had begun to eat into the flesh. Voltaire and Madame du Châtelet, like lesser persons, had to pay the inexorable penalty of a breach of moral law. "Wrong committed—suffering insured." Their punishment was the severest of all—it came, not from outward circumstances, but from themselves. The very relationship which had been a sin and a delight, was now at once sin and torment. The gods are just.

The visitor was not long in discovering clouds in the blue heavens of Voltaire's "Cirey-en-félicité." There was the "eternal cackle" of Émilie's tongue, and her sublime indifference to trifles like the hours of meals. Did not she love power too? Not only to have power but, womanlike, to show she had it. One day her lover's coat does not please her. He shall change it! He agrees—for peace, one may suppose, since the coat is good enough and he does not wish to catch cold by putting on another—and his valet is sent for; but cannot be found. Let the matter rest! Not Madame. She persists. They quarrel with a great deal of vivacity, in English. They always quarrel in English. Voltaire goes out of the room in a rage, and sends word to say he has the colic. They are very like two children. Presently they are reconciled—also in English and tenderly. "Mais elle lui rend la vie un peu dure."

Another time the quarrel is about a glass of Rhine wine. Rhine wine disagrees with this imprudent Voltaire! The imprudent Voltaire, is, not to put too fine a point upon it, very much out of temper with Émilie's interference in the matter. And it takes the united and warmest persuasions of Breteuil and Graffigny to make him read "Jeanne" after supper as he has promised.

At one of the readings of "Mérope," Madame du Châtelet, with her abominably clever tongue, turns it into ridicule and laughs at it. She knows her vain and sensitive Voltaire's tender places, it seems, and for the life of her cannot help putting her finger on them just to see if he will wince. He always winces. He will not speak all supper time. After supper it is the nymph's turn to be cross, and Voltaire shows the visitors his globes while she sits sulking in a chair, pretending to be asleep.

What an old, old story it is! What a weary, dull, aggravating old story! and what a happy world it might be still if all the miseries men carefully manufacture for themselves were taken out of it!

Yet another day, and there is a very bitter quarrel about some verses. Émilie says she has written them. Voltaire does not believe it. They both lose their tempers, and it is even said Voltaire takes a knife from the table and threatens her with it, crying, "Do not look at me with your squinting, haggard eyes!" Perhaps the story is exaggerated. It is to be hoped so. Madame de Graffigny speaks too of Voltaire's wretched health; of his system of doctoring and starving himself; of his disposition at once kind, nervous, and petulant. He told her one day, she says, that Émilie was a terrible woman who had no "flexibilité dans le cœur" although that heart was good. The Graffigny adds on her own account that it was not possible to be more "spied" than Voltaire was, or to have less liberty. It must indeed be remembered that the Graffigny was speaking of a woman of whose superior powers she was always jealous, and whom she had learnt to hate. Émilie had at least one great good quality: she never abused other women behind their backs.

It has been said that lovers' quarrels are but the renewal of love. There was never a falser word. Every quarrel is a blot on a fair page; forgiveness may erase it, but, at the best, the mark of the erasure is there for ever and the page wears thin. Perhaps Voltaire and Madame du Châtelet acted on the dangerous assumption that, since they could be reconciled to-morrow, it was no matter if they quarrelled to-day. Their attachment had now lasted not quite five years. It lingered nearly another ten. Every day Émilie drew the cords by which her lover was bound to her tighter—and a little tighter still; until that dramatic moment when she cut them for ever. As for Voltaire, he still warmly admired her genius; wrote her verses; forgave her temper, and held himself unalterably hers.

The life at Cirey—already the subject of a burlesque in Paris—was not what he had dreamed it might be. He was himself hasty, capricious, not easy to live with. But he was also most generous, most affectionate, and most forgiving. And faithful to the end.

CHAPTER XI

THE AFFAIR DESFONTAINES

IN 1724, when Voltaire was thirty years old and in Paris, Theriot had introduced to him Desfontaines, then a journalist, and an ex-abbé. Their acquaintance was of the slightest. It had lasted only a few weeks when Desfontaines was accused of an abominable crime (then punished by burning), arrested, and cast into the Bicêtre. The impulsive Voltaire must needs get up off a sick bed, travel to Fontainebleau, and throw himself at the feet of the influential Madame de Prie and obtain Desfontaines's discharge—on the sole condition that he should not live in Paris. Not content with this good office, he obtained from his friend Madame de Bernières the permission for Desfontaines to reside on her estates. Finally, he procured the revocation of the edict of banishment. Desfontaines could live in Paris and pursue his calling as before. All this for a man he hardly knew, who was an ex-priest, and a very bad writer, if not a very bad man. It was generous, unnecessary and imprudent. In brief, it was Voltaire.

He might have expected gratitude. He did expect it. Desfontaines wrote him a letter of warm thanks. Eleven years later he was scoffing in a weekly Parisian paper at Newtonianism, as revealed to the French in Voltaire's "English Letters." Then he must translate the "Essay on Epic Poetry," which Voltaire had written in English, into French, very badly, so that the tireless author felt the necessity of re-translating it himself. Then, forsooth, M. l'Abbé must damn with faint praise "Charles XII." and the "Henriade." Even a sensitive Voltaire could only laugh at bites from such a miserable gnat. "I am sorry I saved him," he wrote lightly in 1735. "It is better to burn a priest than to bore the public. If I had left him to roast I should have spared the world many imbecilities." But even a gnat may hurt if it sting often and long enough. The early bliss of Cirey was disturbed by that petty malice. Now in one way, now in another, Desfontaines showed the truth of the shrewd saying that the offender never pardons. The gnat bites grew feverish and swollen. Voltaire had reason to believe, though he still found it hard to believe, that Desfontaines was in league with those other enemies of his, Jore and J. B. Rousseau. Was it possible? Could there be such ingratitude in the vilest thing that lived? It is to the credit of Voltaire's character, that he gave his abbé the benefit of the doubt till there was doubt no longer. It was in 1736 he wrote that memorable "I hear that Desfontaines is unhappy, and from that moment I forgive him." And the Thing stung again in a criticism on Voltaire's "Elements of Newton"—

meant to be offensive. He was again forgiven. Then he stung once more, and turned his benefactor into the liveliest, keenest, deadliest foe that ever man had.

When Algarotti was at Cirey in the November of 1735, Voltaire had addressed to him a few gay and graceful lines, meant only for his own eye, and in which the real nature of the relationship between the poet and Madame du Châtelet was plainly acknowledged. The verses fell into the hands of Desfontaines. He wrote to ask permission to publish them in his journal. Publish them! If all the world knew that Voltaire was Émilie's lover, all the world had at least the decency of feeling to pretend that it knew nothing of the kind. Publish them! Voltaire, Émilie—nay, the dull *bonhomme* himself—protested passionately. Publish them! Not for a kingdom! But they were published. And Voltaire woke to revenge.

He would have been a worse man than he was if every bitter feeling in his soul had not been stirred now. He was always acutely sensitive to any slight put on his mistress's name, honour, intellect—on anything that belonged to her. If he was a good fighter when he was roused on his own account, he was a ten times better fighter when he was roused on hers. He was roused now. And he wrote the "Préservatif."

It begins by a collection of all the slips, mistakes, misstatements, printers' errors and illiteracies which he was able to find in two hundred numbers of Desfontaines's weekly paper which was called "Observations on New Books." They were grouped together with all a Voltaire's ability—never a point missed, and so arranged as to make M. l'Abbé supremely ridiculous. The "Préservatif" purported to be by a Chevalier de Mouhy, a real person. At the end, the Chevalier presents to the public a letter he has received from M. de Voltaire giving the whole history of the Desfontaines affair in 1724—only not mentioning the nature of the crime of which the abbé had been accused.

The "Préservatif" ran through Paris at the end of 1738 as such a pamphlet would. With it, there ran a deadly epigram, and then a caricature, with another epigram beneath. Neither epigrams nor caricature would be tolerated by a decent age. They were all from the pen of M. de Voltaire. They told the nature of the abbe's crime. They were a shameful weapon, shamefully used: and most deadly. Voltaire gave Madame de Graffigny the "Préservatif" to read. To mention the name of Desfontaines to him had soon the same effect as a red flag on a bull. He was beside himself when he thought of the man's base treachery and ingratitude. He was beside himself when he wrote the epigrams and drew the caricature. It is their only excuse. They need one.

He also wrote against Desfontaines, anonymously, a little comedy called "L'Envieux": but it was never played.

On that Christmas Day of 1738, Madame du Châtelet received a document by the post. She read it alone and said nothing about it to Voltaire. Whatever else she was, she was a woman of very strong sense and very just judgment. The document she had received was the "Voltairomanie" by Desfontaines—the retort to the "Préservatif"—the blasphemous shriek of a lunatic—"the howl of a mad dog." She herself wrote a reply to it—still preserved. Voltaire must not see it! His health was wretched as ever. He had just had an access of fever. He was acutely sensitive. She did right to hide it from him. He was not less considerate. He had also received a copy of that "gross libel" and was hiding it from *her*. There must have been something good in the feeling these two people had for each other—in spite of quarrels and bickerings and the testimony of all the old women visitors in the world—they were so anxious to save each other pain. They discovered their mutual deception on New Year's Day, 1739, and were the easier for being able to talk over the affair together.

The "Voltairomanie" is too savage to be sane. It brought that old accusation against Voltaire—a lack of personal courage. It recalled the affair of the Bridge of Sèvres and the affair of Rohan in terms which practice had made perfect in falsehood and offensiveness. It declared Voltaire liar as well as coward. In the "Préservatif" he had said that Theriot had shown him a libel Desfontaines had written against his benefactor, while Desfontaines was staying with the Bernières at Rivière Bourdet and only just released, by that benefactor's efforts, from Bicêtre. "And behold!" says Desfontaines in the "Voltairomanie," "M. Theriot has been obliged to deny all knowledge of the affair."

Cirey at first was pretty calm, even under the matchless audacity of this last statement. Theriot had been staying at Cirey last October and had told with his own lips that very story just as Voltaire had told it in the "Préservatif." Voltaire did not take the matter so much to heart as Madame du Châtelet had feared. He decided at once to treat Desfontaines's attack as a criminal libel, and to take legal proceedings against him. He had witnesses as to the truth of *his* story. Madame de Bernières herself was one of them and prepared to write the most violent letters on behalf of a friend. And Theriot—Theriot whom Voltaire had made, loved, and trusted—why, Theriot had nothing to do but tell his tale as he had told it in letters to Voltaire and over the Cirey supper-table last autumn.

And Theriot never uttered a word. How hardly and slowly the conviction of his treachery took possession of Voltaire's mind, there is evidence in his letters to show. Theriot false! Theriot time-server, coward, frightened of the sting of a Desfontaines—impossible! The softest spot in Voltaire's heart was for this easy-going ne'er-do-weel who had been the friend of his youth—confidant and intimate for five-and-twenty years. Another man convinced of such a baseness as that, would have shaken the creature off—flung himself free of the traitor who had eaten his bread, accepted his money, lived on his fame, fattened on his benefits—and denied him.

And Voltaire wrote pleading, persuading, imploring: counselling repentance, eager to forgive: as a woman might have written to a scapegrace son whose sin she knows, whose reformation she hopes, and whom she must needs love for ever.

"Will you not have the courage to avow publicly what you have written to me so many times?... My honour, your honour, the public interest demand ... that you should own that this miserable Desfontaines *did* write an abominable libel called the "Apology of Sieur Voltaire" and had it printed at Rouen, and that you showed it me at Rivière Bourdet."

"I am your friend of twenty years.... Will it be to your honour to have renounced me and the truth for a Desfontaines?"

"Once again, do not listen to anyone who will counsel you to drink your champagne gaily and forget all else. Drink, but fulfil the sacred duties of friendship."

"Make reparation, there is still time."

"Everybody helps me but you. Everyone has done his duty, save you only." And at last, "All is forgotten, if you know how to love."

There are many such letters of the early days of this year 1739—generous and pathetic enough. It was certainly Voltaire's interest to make Theriot speak the truth. But it may be believed that it was Voltaire's heart that was hurt by his silence. Émilie wrote to the false friend, imploring: so did the easy-going Marquis, and the fat lady watered *her* letter with her tears. The affair would not have been Voltaire's if he had left a single stone unturned. Madame du Châtelet wrote for him to obtain the influence of his prince—Frederick of Prussia. And all the wretched Theriot would say was, that if the episode had occurred, he had forgotten all about it. Madame de Graffigny recorded how, when she was at Cirey in that February of 1739, Voltaire received letters which threw him into a sort of convulsions, and Émilie came into her guest's room ("with tears in her eyes as big as her fist") to say the comedy they were to have played must be put off. The Graffigny was too graphic a writer to be literally accurate. But there is no wonder if Voltaire and Madame were greatly agitated and harassed as to what course to pursue next. The mission which took Madame de

Champbonin, who must certainly have been one of the most good-natured women who ever breathed, to Paris in January, 1739, was to try the weight of *her* moral influence on Theriot. And at last the wretched creature, buffeted on all sides by letters at once heart-breaking, entreating, and indignant, *did* so far repent of his treachery as to eat his words and consent to appear in some sort as the accuser of Desfontaines.

And now Voltaire, having won his Theriot, must move heaven and earth that in all points his libel suit may be carried to a successful issue. It was the custom of that day for as many of the complainant's friends as possible to appear before the magistrate when the suit was brought—just to see how they could influence impartial justice. "Nothing produces so great an effect on a judge's mind," the plaintiff in the present case wrote off plainly to Moussinot, "as the attendance of a large number of relatives.... Justice is like the kingdom of Heaven. The violent take it by force." Voltaire had, then, not a friendly acquaintance in Paris who was not to be roused to help him. It was judged best that he himself should remain at Cirey. So Moussinot became his agent, and a very active agent he had to be. He was to hire carriages for the friends. He was to pay their expenses. All other business was to go to the winds. He was to search out nephew Mignot— Madame Denis's brother—so that he might be useful in stirring up *his* relatives. He was conjured to pursue the affair "avec la dernière vivacité." "No *ifs*, no *buts*: nothing is difficult to friendship," the energetic Voltaire wrote cheerfully. The Marquis du Châtelet was sent up to Paris to see what *he* could do. Voltaire's old school friends, the d'Argensons and d'Argental, were not a little active. Prince Frederick wrote influential letters to his Court at home. Paris was in a ferment. Europe itself was interested. It was a *cause célèbre* of quite extraordinary vivacity. Through January, February, and March of 1739, Voltaire himself was working feverishly at Cirey. He rained letters on his friends. He wrote anonymous ones on Desfontaines to be circulated in Paris, not at all decent and very much to the taste of the age. He was certainly a matchless foe. He thought of everything. The resources of his mind were as wonderful as its energy. He had the gift of making other people very nearly as enthusiastic as he was himself. To read his letters of this time, in cold blood one hundred and sixty years after, stirs the pulses still. The most apathetic reader himself feels for the moment Voltaire's dancing impatience for revenge, his hot anxiety for fear miserable Theriot should be false at the last after all, his throbbing, vivid determination that he *shall* be true.

The vigour of the man seems to have worn out at last even the malice of his enemies. Desfontaines was told that he must disavow his "Voltairomanie"—or go to prison. So the honourable magistrate drew out a formula in which the honourable Desfontaines repudiated with horror, and in sufficiently servile terms, all idea of his being the author of that blasphemy and expressed "sentiments of esteem" for M. de Voltaire! The whole case may be said to have rained lies. Everybody lied. Desfontaines's final lie was "done in Paris, this 4th of April, 1739." Moussinot was commissioned to give Madame de Champbonin two hundred francs— which, to be sure, she deserved—and one hundred to the needy and complaisant Mouhy, who had been dubbed the author of the "Préservatif," "telling him you have no more."

The buffeting of that storm left Voltaire panting, feeble, and exhausted. "There are some men by whom it is glorious to be hated," was an axiom of his own. Desfontaines was certainly one of them. But Desfontaines's hatred had power to the end of his life to rouse him to a frenzy of indignation. "Take honour from me and my life is done," had not, alas! been the spirit of either defendant or plaintiff in this case. But it had one good thing about it, though only one,—Voltaire's dealing with Theriot. Theriot was forgiven as if Voltaire had been the Christian he was not.

On May 8, 1739, the two du Châtelets, Koenig (Madame's mathematical professor—a very good mathematician and a very dull man), M. de Voltaire and suite left Cirey for Brussels. Voltaire had been at Cirey nearly five years. He had learnt to love its solitude, its calm, its facilities for hard work. He had learnt to dread towns if he had not learnt to love Nature. But Émilie wanted a change, so was quite sure that a journey and a different air were the very things for her lover's deplorable health. The process of reasoning is not unusual. Was there not too a certain du Châtelet lawsuit, of which they were always talking, which was already eighty years old and could only be settled in Brussels? So to Brussels they went.

Voltaire had to be dragged away from a tragedy, from "Louis XIV.," from elaborate corrections which he was making to the "Henriade," and from the study of Demosthenes and Euclid. Madame had an iron constitution herself, and could be at a dance all night and up at six the next morning studying mathematics—for fear Koenig should find her a dunce. *En route* for Brussels, they stopped at Valenciennes, where they were entertained with a ball, a ballet, and a comedy. They had no sooner reached their quiet house in the Rue de la Grosse Tour, Brussels, than they left it to visit some du Châtelet relations, at Beringen, ten miles distant, and at Hain. They were back in Brussels by June 17th. The city put herself *en fête* for them. J. B. Rousseau, who lived there, was "no more spoken of than if he were dead." Anyone with a human nature must have been pleased at *that*. Voltaire exerted himself and had a beautiful garden-party with fireworks one of those fine days to the Duc d'Aremberg and all the other polite society in Brussels. Of course he must needs superintend the firework preparations himself. Two of his unfortunate workmen fell from the scaffolding on to him, killing themselves, and nearly killing him. The event affected him not a little.

Then the Duc d'Aremberg invited his entertainers to stay with him at Enghien. The gardens were so exquisite that they almost reconciled even a Voltaire and a Marquise du Châtelet to a house where there was not a single book except those they had brought themselves. They played *brelan*: they played comedy: and the author of the "Century of Louis XIV." listened to the Duke's anecdotes of the days when he had served under Prince Eugene. They were back in Brussels by July 18th. Useful Moussinot was there too. On September 4, 1739, and after an absence from it of more than three years, Voltaire found himself again in Paris.

If he had not wished to move to Brussels, he had much less wished to move to Paris. But "the divine Émilie found it necessary for her to start for Paris, *et me voilà*." That was the situation. They were both immediately engulfed in a social whirlpool—suppers, operas and theatres, endless visitors and calls—"not an instant to oneself, neither time to write, to think, or to sleep." Voltaire wrote rather sorrowfully of the dreadful ennui of these perpetual amusements to placid old Champbonin, at Cirey. As for Madame du Châtelet—

Son esprit est très philosophe,
Mais son cœur aime les pompons

her lover had written of her to Sade in 1733, in perhaps the most apt and descriptive couplet ever made. She was enjoying the *pompons* now. Paris was *en fête* for the marriage of Louis XV.'s eldest daughter to a prince of Spain. Madame was as energetic in her amusements as she was energetic in acquiring knowledge. She gratified her tastes for dress, talk, and gaiety and her taste for mathematics all together. Koenig had come to Paris with them. Poor Voltaire wrote of her, not a little dolorously and enviously, "Madame du Châtelet is quite different; *she* can always think—has always power over her mind." But to compose plays in this tumult!—it was impossible to the man at this time at any rate. His health was really as wretched as Madame said. It is not a little characteristic of him to find him ill in bed being copiously bled and doctored on Sunday, and gaily arranging a supper party on Thursday. But even his versatility and courage, even the good-humoured patience with which he watched Émilie enjoying herself, were not inexhaustible. He had two plays to be produced in Paris. He did not wait to see either of them even rehearsed. Early in November, 1739, he and Madame du Châtelet were spending a week or two at Cirey on their way back to Brussels.

CHAPTER XII

FLYING VISITS TO FREDERICK

SINCE that first letter of the August of 1736 the correspondence and friendship between Voltaire and Prince Frederick of Prussia had grown more and more enthusiastic. The devoted pair had from the first interspersed abstract considerations on the soul and "the right divine of kings to govern wrong" with the most flattering personalities and hero-worship. Each letter grew more fervent and more adoring than the last. By 1740 Voltaire was Frederick's "dearest friend," "charming divine Voltaire," "sublime spirit, first of thinking beings." In Voltaire's vocabulary Frederick was Marcus Aurelius, the Star of the North, not a king among kings but a king among men. Voltaire dreamt of his prince "as one dreams of a mistress," and found his hero's Prussian-French so beautiful "that you must surely have been born in the Versailles of Louis XIV., had Bossuet and Fénelon for schoolmasters, and Madame de Sévigné for nurse."

Not to be outdone, Frederick announced that his whole creed was one God and one Voltaire.

There was indeed no extravagance of language which this Teutonic heir-apparent of six or seven and twenty and the brilliant withered Frenchman of six-and-forty did not commit. They *did* adore each other. For Voltaire, Frederick was Concordia, the goddess of Peace—the lightbringer—the hope of the world—veiled in the golden mist of imagination, unseen, unknown, and so of infinite possibility and capable of all things. While heir-apparent Frederick was quite shrewd enough to know that a Voltaire might add lustre even to a king's glory, and be as valuable a friend as he was a dangerous foe.

By 1740 and the return of Voltaire and the Marquise from Paris to Brussels, Frederick had begun compiling the most sumptuous and beautiful *édition de luxe* of the "Henriade" ever seen. He counselled his author friend to omit a too daring couplet here and there, and his author would have none of such prudence. Then Frederick must turn writer himself, and sent his Voltaire a prose work called "Anti-Machiavelli" and an "Ode on Flattery."

"A prince who writes against flattery is as singular as a pope who writes against infallibility," said Voltaire. The "Anti-Machiavelli" is a refutation in twenty-six prosy chapters of the entire Machiavellian system. Voltaire called it "the only book worthy of a king for fifteen hundred years," and declared it should be "the catechism of kings and their ministers." He wept tears of admiration over it. He had it bound and printed. He wrote a preface for it. His transports of delight were sincere enough, no doubt. He was also sincere enough to criticise it to Frederick pretty freely, and to recommend "almost a king" to be a little less verbose, and to cut out unnecessary explanations. It must be confessed that the "Anti-Machiavelli" appears a very dull and trite composition to-day, and that the beautiful moral sentiments on the iniquities of war and the kingly duty of keeping peace lose a good deal of their weight when one knows that a very few months after they were written their author invaded Silesia and plunged Europe into one of the most bloody wars in history.

But when Voltaire waxed enthusiastic over the princely periods at Brussels in the January of 1740 he had no premonition of that future. Compared with other royal compositions "Anti-Machiavelli" *is* a masterpiece. Even to one of the shrewdest men who ever breathed it might well have given hopes that its author would be a king not as other kings, a benefactor and not an oppressor of humanity, a defender of all liberal arts, a safeguard of justice, freedom, and civilisation. Old Frederick William was dying. The time was at hand when his son might make promise, practice. On June 6, 1740, he wrote to Voltaire: "My dear friend, my fate is changed, and I have been present at the last moments of a king, at his agony and at his death"; and prayed friend Voltaire to regard him not as king but as man. And Voltaire replied to him as "Your Humanity" instead of "Your Majesty," and saw in the heavens the dawn of a golden day, and on earth all things made new.

On July 19th, Voltaire arrived at The Hague to see about recasting and correcting a new edition of the "Anti-Machiavelli," now being printed there. There were certain things in it safe enough for a crown prince to have written anonymously, but hardly prudent to appear as the utterances of a king.

Voltaire was quite as active and thorough on that King's behalf as on his own. He wasted a whole fortnight of his precious time on Frederick's business in Holland. He had infinite trouble with the printer, Van Duren, and stooped to trickery (to be sure, Voltaire thought it no abasement) to get the necessary alterations made in the royal manuscript. At length this most indefatigable of beings himself brought out an authorised version of the "Anti-Machiavelli." Voltaire's corrected edition and Frederick's original version both appear in a Berlin issue of the Works of King Frederick the Great. A comparison of the two shows the versatile Voltaire to be the most slashing and daring of editors. He cut out, as imprudent, as much as thirty-two printed pages of the royal composition. The time had not yet come when Frederick was grateful for such a hewing and a hacking as that. But the time was very soon to come when he would have been but too glad if Voltaire had flung into the fire the whole of "Anti-Machiavelli," and the memory thereof.

The friendship between editor and author grew apace, meanwhile, daily. They sent each other presents of wine and infallible medicines. Voltaire had an escritoire, designed by Martin, specially made in Paris for Frederick's acceptance. But they had long discovered that the handsomest of presents and the most adoring of letters were but a feeble bridge to span the space that separated them, and the question of a meeting, long and repeatedly urged by Frederick, became imminent.

Since Frederick's first letter it had been the *rôle* of Madame du Châtelet to stand by and watch a comedy in which she was not offered a part. To be a passive spectator was little to the taste of her supremely energetic temperament. It was not long before she learnt to be jealous. She was a great deal too clever not to know from very early times that, but for her, Voltaire would have been a satellite to the Star of the North, instead of to any woman in the world. When his friendship with Frederick began he was no doubt true to her because he wished to be true. But how short a time was it before he was true only from a sense of duty! Madame du Châtelet, with her vigorous passions, was not the woman to be satisfied with a cold, conscientious affection like that. She must be first—everything! Her woman's instinct told her to mistrust Frederick, and she did mistrust him. Then the mistrust grew to dislike; dislike to hate; and hate, war to the knife.

Oh what beautiful compliments that pair exchanged through Voltaire, or directly in the most flattering letters to each other—in those four years between 1736 and 1740! Frederick said the most charming things about Émilie. She was always the goddess, the sublime, the divine. Flattery costs so little and may buy so much.

When he read her "Essay on the Propagation of Fire," he wrote to Voltaire that it had given him "an idea of her vast genius, her learning—and of your happiness."

Did Madame look over her lover's shoulder and smile not a little grimly with compressed lips at those last words? "Of your happiness"! Very well. Leave him to it then. What can your court or kingship give him better than happiness, after all? It is to be feared that if Émilie had rendered Voltaire's life "un peu dure" in the time of Madame de Graffigny she rendered it much harder now, and that there was not much question of real happiness between them. To be fought over was a much more trying position for a nature like Voltaire's than to be one of the fighters. And there is no hell on earth like that made by a jealous woman.

Within easy reach too, in tempting sight, were the pleasures of a king's congenial society, honours to which a worldly-wise Voltaire could be by no means insensible. Yet in almost all his letters to Frederick he reiterates his decision that he will not leave his mistress; that he is bound to her in honour and gratitude; that he has chosen his fate and must abide by it.

In the spring of 1740 she had published her "Institutions Physiques," in which she now championed Leibnitz against Newton, as Voltaire had championed Newton against Leibnitz. Frederick went into ecstasies over it—to its authoress; and damned it with very faint praise indeed to his confidant, Jordan. Madame may have suspected that perfidy. King Frederick, when he became king in that May of 1740, guessed he had met his match in that resolute woman whom he addressed variously as "Venus Newton" and the "Queen of Sheba." If Frederick wanted to see Voltaire—well, then, he must have Venus too. Of that, Venus was determined. Voltaire returned to Brussels from The Hague in the early days of August, 1740. It was not the slightest use Frederick's writing to him on the 5th of that month from Berlin: "To be frank ... it is Voltaire, it is you, it is my friend whom I desire to see, and the divine Émilie with all her divinity is only an accessory to the Newtonian Apollo"; and more plainly still the next day, "If Émilie *must* come with Apollo, I agree; although I would much rather see you alone." Madame du Châtelet was for Voltaire a sovereign far more absolute than any on earth. He pulled a very wry face, shrugged his shoulders, and resigned himself to her determination with as much good-humour and nonchalance as he could compass. It was arranged that Frederick should meet Voltaire and Venus at Antwerp on September 14th, and should return with them for a brief visit, *incognito*, to the du Châtelet's hired house in Brussels.

One can fancy the baffled rage of the Marquise when at the very last moment the news arrived that that subtle Frederick had artfully developed an attack of ague which would quite prevent him meeting Émilie at Antwerp and Brussels, but need be no obstacle in the way of Voltaire, alone, coming to see his sick friend for two or three days at the Château of Moyland, near Cleves. Even Madame du Châtelet's jealousy and resource could find no excuse to keep her lover now. He went—feeling no doubt rather guilty and very glad to get away—the precise sensations of a schoolboy who has escaped for a day's holiday from a very exacting master. He was not going to play truant for long! After all, Madame *had* been dreadfully *exigeante*! One thinks of her with pity somehow—Voltaire thought of her with something very like pity too—left alone in Brussels, beaten, angry, and restless, and adding daily to an already magnificent capital of hatred for Frederick.

That meeting at Moyland is one of the great *tableaux* of history. Voltaire himself painted it in letters to his friends when its memory was green and delightful; and twenty years after, with his brush dipped in darker colours. The ague, though convenient, was not a sham. Voltaire found Solomon, Marcus Aurelius, the Star of the North, huddled up in a blue dressing-gown in a wretched little bed in an unfurnished room, shivering and shaking and most profoundly miserable. "The sublime spirit and the first of thinking beings" sat down at once on the edge of the royal pallet, felt the King's pulse and suggested remedies. The day was Sunday, September 11, 1740: very cold and gloomy, as was the disused château itself. It is said Voltaire recommended quinine. Any how, the fit passed, and by the evening Frederick was well enough to join a supper of the gods.

Three men, who had been visitors at Cirey and were all renowned for learning or brilliancy, were of it—Maupertuis, Algarotti, and Kaiserling. Frederick forgot his ague, and Voltaire his Marquise. They discussed the Immortality of the Soul, Liberty, Fate, Platonics. On the two following nights the suppers were repeated. At one of them Voltaire declaimed his new tragedy "Mahomet." Frederick wrote of him just after as having the eloquence of Cicero, the smoothness of Pliny, the wisdom of Agrippa, and spoke, with a more literal truth, of the astounding brilliancy of his conversation. As for Voltaire, he found for a brief space the realisation of his dream—the incarnation of his ideal. Here was the philosopher without austerity and with every charm of manner, forgetting he was a king to be more perfectly a friend. Writing after twenty years—after strife and bitterness—Voltaire still spoke of Frederick as being at that day witty, delightful, flattering—aye, still felt in some measure what he felt in fullest measure at the Château of Moyland in 1740, the siren seduction of the King's "blue eyes, sweet voice, charming smile, love of retirement and occupation, of prose and of verse." With a mind keenly acute and searching, Voltaire was youthfully susceptible to fascination. He had to the end a sort of boyish vanity, and Frederick greatly admired him. But that alone would not account for the fond pride and affection with which he regarded this young King—and which might have been almost the partial and sanguine love of a father for a promising son. No man ever wore better than Frederick the Great that fine coat called Culture. He fitted it so well that even a shrewd Voltaire thought it his skin, not his covering; and when he flung it on the ground and trampled on it, still regretfully loved him—not for what he had been, but for what he had seemed.

The three days came to an end. On September 14th, Frederick took Maupertuis to Paradise, or Potsdam, with him, and condemned Voltaire to Hell, or Holland (this is how Voltaire put it), where he was to stay at The Hague in an old palace belonging to the King of Prussia and complete his arrangements for the publication of his edition of the "Anti-Machiavelli." The Marquise was at Fontainebleau paving the way for Voltaire's return to Paris, and writing to Frederick to ask him to use his influence to win Cardinal Fleury, the Prime Minister's, favour, for "our friend." Fleury had formerly met Voltaire at the Villars', "where he liked me very much"; but that liking had since turned to dislike. Madame worked at once with enthusiasm and with wisdom—that rare combination of qualities which can accomplish everything. She said herself, not a little bitterly, that she gave her lover back in three weeks all he had laboriously lost in six years: opened to him the doors of the Academy; restored to him ministerial favour. He sent a presentation copy of the "Anti-Machiavelli" to Cardinal Fleury presently, and the powerful Cardinal, now that Voltaire was a great King's friend and the active Marquise was at Court, suddenly discovered that he never had had any fault but youth. "You have been young; perhaps you were young a little too long"—but nothing worse than that; really nothing. The two exchanged flattering letters. Then came events which changed the face of Europe. On October 20, 1740, died the Emperor Charles VI. He was succeeded by Maria Theresa of three-and-twenty. The Powers were looking hard into each other's faces to see if peace or war were written there. "The slightest twinkle of Fleury's eyelashes" was hint sufficient for this daring and versatile Voltaire to try a new *rôle*. When he started off to Remusberg on November 4 or 5, 1740, to pay another little visit, already arranged, to friend Frederick, he went not only as a visitor, but to discover the pacific or bellicose disposition of Anti-Machiavelli who had already written, a little oddly, that the Emperor's death upset all his peaceful ideas.

The journey from The Hague to Remusberg took a fortnight. Voltaire had as companion a man called Dumolard, whom Theriot had recommended for the post of Frederick's librarian. Their travelling carriage broke down outside Herford, and Voltaire entered that town in the highly picturesque and unpractical costume of his day on one of the carriage horses. "Who goes there?" cried the sentinel. "Don Quixote," answered Voltaire.

Remusberg was *en fête* when they reached it. There were suppers, dances, and conversation, a little gambling, delightful concerts—the gayest Court in the world. Frederick played on the flute and was infinitely agreeable. The Margravine of Bayreuth, his sister, was of the party. Voltaire showed Frederick Cardinal Fleury's complimentary letter on the "Anti-Machiavelli." There was no change on the King's face as he read it; or if there was a change, it escaped even a Voltaire. If Voltaire had been brilliant at Moyland he was twice as brilliant here—in spite of the fact that he could only describe himself to Theriot as "ill, active, poet, philosopher, and always your very sincere friend." He busied himself in procuring for that faithless person a pension from Frederick, for having been the King's agent in Paris. All the time, through the suppers and the talk and the parties, he was watching, watching, watching. The visit lasted six days. Voltaire had never in his life tried to find out anything for so long without finding it. But when he parted from Frederick at Potsdam he had not the faintest suspicion that that invasion of Silesia upon which the King was to start in twelve days' time was even a possibility.

Frederick pressed his guest to prolong his stay. He went to Berlin for a brief visit to pay his respects to the King's mother, brother, and sisters; but left there on December 2 or 3, 1740, and then returned to Potsdam to say good-bye to his royal host—and to look into the royal heart, if that might be. But it was not to be.

Voltaire was anxious to be back in Brussels in time to receive Madame du Châtelet on her return from Paris, where her husband had just bought a fine new house. He wrote a little epigram to his host before he left, in which he gaily reproached the King as a coquette who conquers hearts but never gives her own. He had been at least astute enough to divine that there was Something his master hid from him. And his master responded with a little *badinage* on that other coquette who was drawing Voltaire to Brussels.

They parted friends—and warm friends. But there was a highly practical side to both their characters which came to the fore when Frederick bade Voltaire send him the bill of his expenses at The Hague, and Voltaire added to that bill the expenses of the journey to Remusberg, taken at Frederick's request. It was a large total—thirteen hundred écus—but it was not an unjust one. It has been happily suggested that it at least contained no charge for Man's Time, and this man's time was of quite exceptional value. "Five hundred and fifty crowns a day" grumbled Frederick to Jordan; "that is good pay for the King's jester, with a vengeance." But when the King's jester is a Voltaire, the King must expect to pay for him. That was Voltaire's view of the question, no doubt.

A series of accidents befell him on his journey home. He was a whole month getting from Berlin to Brussels, and twelve days of the time ice-bound in a miserable little boat after leaving The Hague. In a wretched ship's cabin he worked hard on "Mahomet" and wrote voluminous letters.

One of them, dated "this last of December," 1740, was to Frederick—cordial, flattering, and expansive. Having been dutiful enough to tear himself away from "a monarch who cultivates and honours an art which I idolise" for a woman "who reads nothing but Christianus Wolffius," Voltaire was a little disposed to grudge that act of virtue, and to make the most of it. He was anxious, too, to prove to Frederick that he had left him chiefly to finish the du Châtelet lawsuit—not merely "to sigh like an idiot at a woman's knees." "But, Sire ... there is no obligation I do not owe her. The head-dresses and the petticoats she wears do not make the duty of gratitude less sacred." The last cloud of illusion must have been dispelled long before the Marquise du Châtelet's ex-lover could have written those words.

He saw her now not only as she was, but at her worst. "Men serve women kneeling: when they get on their feet they go away." Shall it not be accounted for righteousness to a Voltaire that he got on his feet and went back to her?

CHAPTER XIII

TWO PLAYS AND A FAILURE

BEFORE Voltaire reached Brussels—nay, before he had written to Frederick that letter from the ice-bound boat off the coasts of Zealand—he had received one of the greatest mental shocks of his life. The news of the invasion of Silesia came upon him like a thunderclap. This—after the "Anti-Machiavelli"! This—after all they had hoped, planned, dreamed! Where was that smiling kingdom, Arcadia, wherein all liberal arts were to flourish, where were to be for ever peace, tolerance, plenty? Where indeed? But Voltaire was nothing if not recuperative. There is not a single instance in his life when he sat down and cried over spilt milk. He was disillusioned now—and bitterly disillusioned. "After all, he is only a King," he wrote; and again, "He is a King, that makes one tremble. Time will show"; and to English Falkener, in English, "My good friend the King of Prussia, who wrote so well against Machiavelli and acted immediately like the heroes of Machiavelli ... fiddles and fights as well as any man in Christendom." Fiddles and fights! Well, since it was impossible to adore Frederick as Concordia, one might as well admire him as Mars. Making the best of it was part of Voltaire's creed. He did what he could to live up to it now. He congratulated Frederick on his victories. The pair continued to write each other long letters, much interspersed with facile rhymes. They were still friends. But it was no longer the boy-hero, the Messiah of the North, the youthful benefactor of human kind whom Voltaire adored: it was a far cleverer and a far less lovable person—the real Frederick the Great.

Voltaire's interminable journey did near its end at last. By January 3, 1741, he was in Brussels. Did he feel a little bit like the truant schoolboy returning in the evening expecting a whipping, and all his excuses for so long an absence disbelieved? Of course Madame du Châtelet disbelieved them! A month getting back from Berlin to Brussels! That was a very likely story indeed, and quite on a par with friend Frederick's artful ague at Moyland! Had quite planned to be back in Brussels before I arrived from Paris! Had you indeed? And you expect me to believe that too?

The unhappy Marquise had been eating her heart out in suspicion and impatience, waiting for him. "I have been cruelly repaid for all I have done for him," she wrote to d'Argental out of this angry solitude; and again, "I know the King of Prussia hates me, but I defy him to hate me as much as I have hated him these two months." She overwhelmed Voltaire with reproaches directly she saw him. Her tongue was dreadfully voluble and clever. The Marquis was away, as usual. There was nothing to distract her attention, and Voltaire's excuses *did* sound very lame indeed. He had a very bad quarter of an hour; but, after all, it was only a quarter of an hour. They were reconciled—and tenderly. If Madame was scolding and exacting, devoted to the metaphysics of Christianus Wolffius, extraordinarily clad and with a painful taste in headgear, she loved her lover and had done much for him. And Frederick the Great had invaded Silesia. If that invasion was a triumph for him, it was also a triumph for one of the bitterest foes he had, Madame du Châtelet.

At Brussels, in that January of the year 1741, there was then, for a time, some sort of renewal of the brief honeymoon days of Cirey, before the Prussian heir-apparent's earliest letter, when the chains that bound the first man in Europe to his Marquise were forged of warm admiration and not barren duty.

Voltaire was soon writing that it was not Frederick's perfidy that had hastened his return—that if he had been offered Silesia itself he would have come back to his mistress just the same. She had never seemed so far above kings as she did now. Her unjust reproaches even were sweeter than the flatteries of all courts. He had left her once for a monarch, but he would not leave her again for a prophet. And she—a true woman after all—wrote that Frederick could take as many provinces as he pleased, provided he did not rob her of the happiness of her life.

Voltaire was busy in these early months of 1741 with his play "Mahomet," for which he had a quite fatherly love and admiration. The English Lord Chesterfield, with whom he had dined in London, was a visitor at Madame du Châtelet's Brussels establishment, and to him Voltaire read selections from the new drama. It would have been immediately produced in Paris; but the best actors were unable to take part in it, and it was judged better to postpone its appearance there.

In this April Voltaire and Madame du Châtelet went to Lille, to stay with Madame Denis and her husband. At Lille, "Mahomet" was performed by a company of French players, who had been half engaged by Voltaire to go to Prussia in the employ of Frederick, and then thrown over by that busy monarch. The audience, each of the three nights the play was performed, was numerous and passionately enthusiastic. The clergy of Lille were powerfully represented and entirely approving. M. Denis and his plump three years' bride of course came to clap the latest effort of Uncle Voltaire. Uncle Voltaire had a keen eye on the face, and a lean forefinger on the pulse of that audience to see how certain daring passages affected it.

What Lille applauded, Paris might pass. On the first night, at the end of the second act, a despatch from the King of Prussia was handed to M. de Voltaire in his box. He read it aloud. "It is said the Austrians are retreating, and I believe it." It was the declaration of the victory of Mollwitz. Lille had its own reasons for being passionately Prussian, and received the news with shouts of delight. If anything had been needed to complete the success of "Mahomet," that despatch would have done it. The bearer of good news is always a popular person. But nothing was needed. The clergy of Lille begged, and were granted, an extra performance of the play for their especial benefit at the house of one of the chief magistrates. Orthodoxy seemed to be taking this Voltaire under her strong wing at last, and Voltaire accepted the situation with a very cynic grimace and a great deal of satisfaction. He and Madame du Châtelet left Lille with the most sanguine hopes of seeing "Mahomet" shortly and successfully produced in Paris. Until November, 1741, they were mostly in Brussels, watching the progress of the du Châtelet lawsuit. Madame had a little quarrel on hand with her tutor Koenig, in which Maupertuis joined.

In November they went to Paris and stayed, not in that splendid Palais Lambert which the Marquis du Châtelet had bought, but which was not yet completely furnished, but in Voltaire's old quarters—the house which had belonged to Madame de Fontaine Martel. In December they returned to Cirey for a month; and in the January of the new year 1742 were again in Brussels. The lawsuit was positively progressing, and so favourably that they felt justified in spending the rest of the winter in Paris. Immediately on their arrival in the capital they were plunged into that "disordered life" which the Marquise loved and Voltaire loathed. "Supping when I ought to be in bed, going to bed and not sleeping, getting up to race about, not doing any work, deprived of real pleasures and surrounded by imaginary ones"—as a description of fashionable life the words hold good to this day. "Farewell the court," he wrote again; "I have not a courtier's health." He spoke of himself as being always at the tail of that lawsuit— which the indefatigable and persistent Marquise *must* pursue to the bitter end.

They lingered in Paris through May, June, July—in their fine Palais Lambert now—and all the time no "Mahomet." Voltaire should have been used to disappointments and delays, if any man should. He brought out everything he ever wrote at the point of the sword. There were always anxiously waiting to take offence the acutely susceptible feelings of a Church, a king, a court, a nobility, and a press censor. This time, first of all, it was the Turkish envoy who was being *fêted* in Paris, "and it would not be proper to defame the Prophet while entertaining his ambassador," said the polite Voltaire. The second cause of delay was much more serious. Exactly at a moment when the policy of Frederick the Great appeared peculiarly anti-French and that monarch was enjoying the brief but vivid hatred of Paris, there crept out one of Voltaire's rhyming letters to the Prussian King, in which the courtly writer lavishly praised and flattered his correspondent. M. de Voltaire had to be alert and active in a moment. He pursued his old line of policy. First of all, I did not write the letter. Secondly, if I did, it has been miscopied. Thirdly, if I did write it and it has not been miscopied, the reigning favourite of Louis XV., Madame de Mailly, must help me out of my dilemma. Voltaire wrote and asked her assistance. She could not do much. But Cardinal Fleury still looked upon Voltaire as a person to be conciliated as an influence on Prussia. He read the play, and approved. The censor did likewise. The murmur of the streets and the *cafés* was still against the too Prussian Voltaire. But for once the authorities actually seemed to be with him.

On August 19, 1742, "Fanaticism, or Mahomet the Prophet" was performed to a house crammed with the rank, wit, and fashion of Paris, who applauded it to the echo. D'Alembert appeared for literature. The Bar and the Church were generously represented. The author himself was in the pit. This might be another "Zaire," only a "Zaire" written in the plenitude of a man's mental powers—stern, not tender—grand, not pathetic—the expression of matured and passionate convictions, instead of vivid, impulsive feelings. Voltaire was eight-and-thirty when he produced "Zaire," and eight-and-forty when he produced "Mahomet." How fully he had lived in those ten years! Then he felt: now he knew. He had often dared greatly in his plays: in "Mahomet" he dared all.

Lord Chesterfield had regarded the tragedy as a covert attack on Christianity. It must have been the sceptical reputation of M. de Voltaire which made Lord Chesterfield so think. No impartial person reading it now could find an anti-Christian word in it. It is a covert attack on nothing. It is an open attack on the fanaticism, bigotry, intolerance, which degrade any religion. It is a battle against the "shameful superstition which debases humanity." Worth, not birth, is its motto. "All men are equal: worth, not birth, makes the difference between them," says Omar, one of the characters. In this play is found that famous and scornful line, "Impostor at Mecca and prophet at Medina." There is scarcely a sentence in it which is not a quivering and passionate protest against the crafty rule of any priesthood which would keep from the laity light, knowledge, and progress. "I wished to show in it," said Voltaire to M. César de Missy, "to what horrible excess fanaticism can bring feeble souls, led by a knave."

If there were dissentient voices—and there were—the applause of that brilliant first night drowned them. The play was repeated a second time and a third. Voltaire may have begun to feel safe: to congratulate himself that at last free thought uttered freely was permissible even in France. He was always hopeful. But his enemies were too mighty for him. Working against him always, untiring, subtle, malicious, was the whole envious Grub Street of Paris led by beaten Desfontaines and jealous Piron. The man in the street was now bitterly against him too. The Solicitor-General, who, on his own confession, had not read a word of the play, much less seen it acted, was soon writing to the Lieutenant of Police that he "believed it necessary to forbid its performances." On the valuable evidence of hearsay, he found "Mahomet" "infamous, wicked, irreligious, blasphemous," and "*everybody says* that to have written it the author must be a scoundrel only fit for burning." It was still in the power of this remarkable officer of most remarkable justice to prosecute Voltaire for the "Philosophic Letters," which he threatened to do, if "Mahomet" were not removed. Feeling ran so high that friend Fleury himself was compelled to advise the withdrawal of the play. It was performed once more—that is, in all four times—and then withdrawn.

A man of much more placid disposition might have been roused now. But this time Voltaire was too disgusted, too sick at heart with men and life, to have even the strength to be angry. He and Madame du Châtelet left for Brussels on August 22d. He was ill in bed by August 29th—ten days after that first brilliant performance—trying to sit up and make a fair copy of the real "Mahomet" to send to Frederick the Great.

The spurious editions, shamefully incorrect, which were appearing all over Paris, must have been the overflow of the invalid's cup of bitterness.

"It is only what happened to 'Tartuffe,'" he wrote from that sick bed to Frederick. "The hypocrites persecuted Molière, and the fanatics are risen up against me. I have yielded to the torrent without uttering a word.... If I had but the King of Prussia for a master and the English for fellow-citizens! The French are nothing but great children; only the few thinkers we have among us are so splendid as to make up for all the rest." And a day or two later to another friend: "This tragedy is suitable rather for English heads than French hearts. It was found too daring in Paris because it was powerful, and dangerous because it was truthful.... It is only in London that poets are allowed to be philosophers."

The words sound as if the writer were weary, *las*, at the end of his tether. On September 2, 1742, he went for a very few days' rest and refreshment to Aix-la-Chapelle to see Frederick the Great, who had just signed a treaty of peace. Madame du Châtelet did not object to that brief holiday, and entertained no idea of making a third person thereat herself. She was more confident of her Voltaire now—hopeful that he was hers, body and soul, for ever. When he was at Aix, Frederick offered him a house in Berlin and a charming estate—peace, freedom, and honour for the rest of his life. And Voltaire said he preferred a second storey in the house of his Marquise—slavery and persecution in Paris, to liberty and a king's friendship in Berlin. "I courageously resisted all his propositions," was his own phrase. For this man when he was virtuous always knew it, and keenly felt how much pleasanter it would have been to be wicked instead. Fleury approved of the little visit, and though it *was* a holiday and Frederick *was* his friend, Voltaire did still his best to subtly find out the royal disposition towards France.

On September 7th he returned to Brussels, not having been absent a week. Madame du Châtelet longed to get back to the gaieties of Paris, though Voltaire, who was ill enough to be able to write nothing but verses, said Madame, was well content in Brussels.

He went back to the capital, however, in this November of 1742, and was not a little *vif* and active in getting imprisoned certain publishers who had produced "the most infamous satire" on himself and Madame du Châtelet.

He was soon also busy on a scheme which he had tried successfully ten years before. When "Êriphyle" failed he brought out "Zaire." When the authorities damned "Mahomet" he produced "Mérope. " Ten years—ten years of battles and disappointments, of wretched health and domestic vicissitudes—had not robbed him of one iota of his pluck, energy, and enterprise. He flung off that lassitude and despair of life which came upon him in those few dismal days in Brussels: searched among his manuscripts: discovered "Mérope," and went out to meet the enemy with that weapon in his hand. It had been written in the early days at Cirey, between 1736 and 1738. It was the play over which Madame de Graffigny had "wept to sobs." Voltaire had wept over it himself. He felt what he wrote when he wrote it, so acutely that there was no wonder his readers were moved too. His own wit and pathos always retained their power to touch him to tears or laughter whenever he read them, which is more unusual.

"Mérope" is a classic tragedy—"a tragedy without love in it and only the more tender for that," wrote Voltaire to Cideville. It turns on maternal affection. The idea is uncommon and daring enough. Would the venture be successful? Madame de Graffigny had wept indeed; but then Graffignys weep and laugh easily, especially when the author is also the host. Mademoiselle Quinault and d'Argental had told him that "Mérope" was unactable to a French *parterre*.

The Marquise had mocked at it; but then the Marquise had happened to be in a very bad temper with the playwright. Who could tell? If taking pains could make it succeed, a success it would be. The author, himself no mean actor, attended the rehearsal and coached the players. When Mademoiselle Dumesnil, who was cast for "Mérope," failed to rise to the height of tragedy demanded in the fourth act where she has to throw herself between her son and the guards leading him to execution, crying "Barbare! il est mon fils!"—she complained she would have to have the devil in her to simulate such a passion as Voltaire required. "That is just it, Mademoiselle," cried he. "You *must* have the devil in you to succeed in any of the arts!" There was never a truer word. He did manage to put a good deal of the devil into Mademoiselle. She became a famous actress. His own fervour was infectious. The players, who had disliked the play at first, caught his own enthusiasm for it at last. On February 20, 1743, it was first represented to a house crowded with persons who had admired "Mahomet" and sympathised with the treatment of "Mahomet's" author. It was the best first night on record. Mademoiselle Dumesnil kept the house in tears throughout three acts, it is said. For the first time in any theatre the enthusiastic audience demanded the appearance of the author. He was in a box with the Duchesse de Boufflers and the Duchesse de Luxembourg and entirely declined to present himself on the stage. His Duchesses tried to persuade him, with no better success than the audience. He kissed the Duchesse de Luxembourg's hand and left the box, "with a resigned air," and tried to hide himself in another part of the house. But he was discovered, and drawn into the box of the Maréchale de Villars for whom he had once felt something more than the feelings of a friend. How long ago that was—Villars and its white nights—a young man of five-and-twenty, and Madame, gracious, *svelte*, and woman of the world to the tips of her fingers! She had become *dévote* since. "She was made to lead us all to Heaven or Hell, whichever she chooses," wrote Voltaire airily. As for himself, *he* had his Marquise du Châtelet. The moment was not one for reminiscences in any case. The *parterre* was not to be silenced. The story runs that it vociferously insisted that Madame de Villars, the young daughter-in-law of his old love, should kiss M. de Voltaire. The Maréchale ordered her to do so, and Voltaire wrote after that he was like Alain Chartier and the Princess Margaret of Scotland—"only he was asleep and I was awake."

He enjoyed that evening as only a Frenchman can enjoy. He was all his life intensely susceptible to the emotions of the moment; vain with the light-hearted vanity of a very young man; loving show and glitter, applause and flattery—a true child of France, though one of the greatest of her great family. Was it not a triumph over his enemies too? What might not follow from it? Voltaire said thereafter that the distinction between himself and Jean Jacques Rousseau was that Jean Jacques wrote in order to write, and he wrote in order to act. Of what use was the dazzling success of "Mérope" if it could not buy him a place he had long coveted and gratify one of the darling desires of his soul?

On January 29th of this same year 1743 had died Voltaire's friend, Cardinal Fleury. He left vacant one of the forty coveted chairs in the French Academy. Who should aspire to it if not the man who had written the "Henriade" and the "English Letters," "Zaire," "Alzire," "Mahomet," and "Mérope"? It would be no empty honour, but a safeguard against his enemies: the hall-mark of the King's favour.

The King was for his election; so was the King's mistress, Madame de Châteauroux; but against it, and bitterly against it, were Maurepas, Secretary of State, and Boyer, Bishop of Mirepoix, and tutor of the Dauphin. Voltaire always called Boyer the "âne de Mirepoix" from the fact that he signed himself "anc: de Mirepoix," meaning that he was formerly bishop of that place—and it must be conceded that, if conscientious, he was one of the most narrow-minded old prelates who ever fattened at a court. He has been well summed up as a man who "reaped all the honours and sowed none." *His* argument was that it would offend Heaven for a profane person like M. de Voltaire to succeed a cardinal in any office. To be sure, the chairs in the Academy were designed to reward literary, not ecclesiastical, merit. But what was that to a Boyer?

Voltaire wrote long letters which are masterpieces of subtlety and special pleading to prove what a good Christian and Churchman he was, and how suited in character, as well as ability, to be the successor of a prelate. He did not stop at a lie. In a letter to Boyer written at the end of February he declared himself a sincere Catholic, and added that he had never written a page which did not breathe humanity (which was true enough) and many sanctified by religion (which was very untrue indeed). He conclusively proved (cannot one fancy the twinkle in his eager eyes as he penned the words?) that "the 'Henriade' from one end to the other is nothing but an *éloge* of a virtue which submits to Providence," and that most of the "English Letters," current in Paris, were not written by him at all. The mixture of the false and the true is so clever that it *might* have deceived anybody. Voltaire may have argued with himself that since he knew it *would* deceive nobody, the lying was very venial indeed. What did it matter what he said now? It was the master motives which had ruled his life, the passion for freedom of thought and action, the sceptical temper, the burning longing for light and knowledge which panted in every page of every play, in every line almost of his graver works, which counted against him. He was excluded from the Academy. The Ass of Mirepoix won M. de Voltaire's seat for a bishop—of very slender literary capacity indeed. Voltaire wrote lightly that it was according to the canons of the Church that a prelate should succeed a prelate, and that "a profane person like myself must renounce the Academy for ever."

But he was bitterly disappointed not the less. Frederick the Great, in a kingly pun, said that he believed that France was now the only country in Europe where "âncs" and fools could make their fortunes. In 1743 England elected Voltaire a member of her Royal Society. During the year four other chairs fell vacant at the French Academy. But the greatest literary genius of the age, perhaps of any age, was not even mooted as a candidate. It was Montesquieu, the famous author of "L'Esprit des Lois," who said scornfully of the occasion and of Voltaire:

"Voltaire n'est pas beau, il n'est que joli. It would be shameful for the Academy to admit him, and it will one day be shameful for it not to have admitted him."

In what a far different and far larger spirit it was that Voltaire criticised his critic—"Humanity had lost its title-deeds. Montesquieu found them and gave them back."

CHAPTER XIV

VOLTAIRE AS DIPLOMATIST AND COURTIER

VOLTAIRE had a little distraction from his disappointment about the Academy in the April of this 1743 in the marriage of Pauline du Châtelet, the vivacious little amateur actress of Cirey. Pauline was fresh from a convent and aged exactly sixteen. The Italian Duc de Montenero-Caraff, the bridegroom, was distinctly elderly, and, as sketched in a few lively touches by Voltaire, very unprepossessing. The Marquise maintained *she* had not arranged the alliance. But *mariages de convenance* were the established custom of the day. Who knows? Voltaire had been for freedom of choice in the case of niece Denis, it is certain. Pauline was not his to dispose of. He would appear to have shrugged his shoulders and given her his blessing. With it, she disappears out of the history of his life.

In June he had another chagrin. The performance of his play, "The Death of Cæsar," already acted in August, 1735, by the pupils of the Harcourt College, was stopped on the very evening before it was to have been produced in public. Not many days after, M. de Voltaire left Paris on his fourth visit to Frederick the Great. Frederick wanted him socially as the wittiest man in the world, the most daring genius of the age. If the French Academy would have none of him, the Prussian Court knew better. Besides—besides—could not this subtle Solomon of the North rely on himself to find out from his guest something of the temper and the disposition of France toward Prussia? The guest was not less astute. The *rôle* of amateur diplomatist pleased his fancy and his vanity. What if he had not been successful in it before? A Voltaire could always try again. He left Paris then in June pretending that his journey was the outcome of his quarrel with Boyer, but really as the emissary of Richelieu on a secret mission to Frederick to warn him of the danger of allowing King George of Hanover and England to help Maria Theresa to her rights, and meaning to win over the cleverest monarch in Europe to an alliance with France. It was a beautiful scheme. It had first "come into the heads" of friend Richelieu and Madame de Châteauroux; then the King had adopted it, and Amelot, the Minister for Foreign Affairs. It was ambitious enough to particularly appeal to Voltaire's audacity. The King of France was to pay all expenses: which was not unjust. The Bourbons seldom spent their money so wisely. Madame du Châtelet was the only person intrusted with the secret of the journey's real object. She felt that it was due to herself to have a fit of hysterics since her Voltaire was leaving her for this Frederick, and she had it. But she kept the secret. If she was a little proud in her heart of the honour such a mission implied, yet her grief at the departure of her "ami" was so unrestrained as to make her and it the laughing-stocks of Paris. Frederick "is a very dangerous rival for me," she wrote on June 28, 1743. "If I had been in Voltaire's place I should not have gone!" "I am staying here in the hopes of getting 'Cæsar' played and so hastening his return."

Voltaire set off in very excellent spirits. It would so annoy Boyer to see his enemy protected by the most powerful monarch in Europe—and by a monarch who was not at all above making *mots* on an "anc: de Mirepoix"! "I had at once the pleasure of revenging myself on the Bishop ... of taking a very pleasant little trip, and being in the way of rendering services to the King and the state." In July he was writing to his friends, and to Amelot, from "a palace of the King of Prussia at The Hague"—a little humanly proud of being able to date his letters from such a place, keen for the fray, sick in body as usual, and vividly alert in mind.

On August 31st he arrived at Berlin. The first news he had to communicate to Amelot was the victory of George II. of England at Dettingen. What honours could be too great for a man who, at such a juncture, made Prussia the friend of France? Madame du Châtelet, keeping her counsel at home, must have had high hopes for her Voltaire. And her Voltaire, at Berlin, cherished them for himself.

To all appearances indeed the visit was but a *fête*, and a gorgeous *fête*. Berlin was gay with balls, operas, and parties. Sometimes there were ballets, and nightly almost those royal suppers where, said the guest, "God was respected, but those who had deceived men in His name were not spared." Voltaire had a room adjoining Frederick's, and the King came in and out of the visitor's apartment familiarly. The old potent charm which these two men had for each other was at work again. But not the less, through the glamour, the wit, the wine, and the laughter, each pursued his secret object, adroit, thorough, and unsleeping.

Voltaire played the *rôle* of diplomatist as he played all *rôles*—brilliantly. He was delightfully gay and easy. He seemed so volatile and so gullible. He threw himself into the pleasures of the hour with all his French soul. An ulterior motive? The man was *bon enfant, bon conteur, bon* everything. He had come to enjoy himself and was doing it to the full.

"Through all," he wrote, "my secret mission went forward." He despatched immense diplomatic documents to his country *via* Madame du Châtelet. He drew up a famous series of questions, to which friend Frederick was to append such answers as would bare the secrets of his Prussian soul to France. The diplomatist had immense conversations with the monarch, which he reported. Frederick wrote Voltaire a most beautiful open letter to show in Paris, wherein he complimented France on her Louis XV., and Louis XV. on his Voltaire. He renewed his pressing invitations to Voltaire to come and live at Berlin—nay, did more. He worked behind his back so as to further embroil him with Boyer, and make France too hot to hold him. "That would be the way to have him in Berlin."

Frederick was his guest's friend, and his devoted friend. But he thought it no breach of friendship to trick him where he could, and kept closed the book of his intentions and his soul.

The fact was that where Voltaire was but a brilliant amateur, Frederick was the sound professional; that what this daring Arouet took upon himself for the nonce, was the business of the King's life. Voltaire was not above trickery: but Frederick tricked better. His answers to that famous series of questions are evasive, or buffoonery. Voltaire counted that he had not done badly in his mission. But Frederick had done better.

The visit finished with a fortnight at Bayreuth in September, 1743, where Voltaire and the King were the guests of the King's sisters, where were gaiety, laughter, and wit—"all the pleasures of a court without its formality." Voltaire distinguished himself by writing three charming madrigals to the three royal ladies. They do not admit of translation. It is only in their original tongue that their grace, ease, and delicacy can be appreciated. But for that kind of versifying they are the model for all time. If Voltaire had not far more splendid titles to fame, he would have gone down the ages as the daintiest and wittiest writer who ever made sonnets on his mistress's eyebrow, trifled with graceful jests, and flattered with daintiest comparisons.

In the early days of October he was back in Berlin for a few days *en passant*. On October 12th he and his King parted there, not without much show of sorrow, and some of the reality of it.

Voltaire had found out "that little treason" whose aim was to keep him in Prussia; but at these parting moments "the King excused himself and told me he would do what I liked to make reparation." As for Frederick, he, in Voltaire's own words, had "scented the spy." They could no longer trust each other. To the misfortune of both, they loved each other still.

On October 12th, then, Voltaire left for Brussels. On the 14th his travelling carriage was upset and he was robbed by the people who came to his assistance. The wretched village in which he hoped for shelter that evening, he found in the process

MADAME DE POMPADOUR

From the Painting by François Boucher in the Possession of Baron Nathaniel de Rothschild

of a conflagration. At last he reached Brunswick, where for a few days he was royally entertained by the Duke. Finally, he returned to Brussels.

It is not to be supposed that the divine Émilie had been sitting contented and smiling in Paris while her lover was addressing tender rhymes to princesses in Bayreuth. Voltaire had been away four months—four heart-burning, chafing, angry months. What unsatisfying food for the heart were diplomatic despatches after all! Voltaire was one whole fortnight without writing a single letter to his mistress. She had to learn his movements "from ambassadors and gazettes." "Such conduct would alienate anyone but me," she wrote to d'Argental, always her confidant. Then, to add insult to injury, was that delay at the court of the Duke of

Brunswick. Courts and kings! Madame du Châtelet was weary of them. She started up in a passion and left Paris: was ill with a nervous fever at Lille, and feverishly reproachful still when she met her Voltaire at last. That inevitable storm blew over as it had blown over before. The sun came out again, though it was a sun in a clouded sky. The pair went to Paris together about the middle of November, 1743: Voltaire to report on his mission and to be, he hoped, substantially rewarded.

But the ill-fortune which always dogged him beset him now. Amelot, the Foreign Minister, fell out of favour, and with him his *protégé*, Voltaire.

No two people in the world were so used to chagrins and disappointments as the two who returned to Brussels in February, 1744, and in the spring to Cirey, and applied their old panacea for every evil in life—work. It succeeded. It was generally successful. Very few letters belong to the early months of this year. There was not time even for letter-writing. Monsieur Denis died in April, leaving behind him a bouncing widow of seven-and-thirty.

It was in April too that Voltaire received a very satisfactory little courtly consolation, to compensate him for many rebuffs. Richelieu engaged him to write a play for the wedding festivities of the Dauphin and the Infanta of Spain, which were to take place in the autumn, and which would presently demand the presence of M. de Voltaire at Versailles.

It is not necessary to say that Voltaire took immense trouble over this *bagatelle*, because he always took immense trouble over everything. All his works are as good as he could make them. He called his play "The Princess of Navarre." He laid the scene there in delicate compliment to the Infanta—and for the practical reason that he could introduce into it both French and Spaniards, with their gorgeous medley of costume. Rameau was to write the music. There were to be the loveliest ballets, processions, and songs. The scenery was to be unique in splendour. "The Princess of Navarre" is what would now be called a comic opera, and as such was certainly unworthy of the genius of Voltaire. But it was not unworthy of his shrewdness. If it would but gain him some trifling post at Court, the favour instead of the fear of the King, why, then it would give him, too, the right to live where he liked in peace, would cripple the power of Boyer, of censors, of Desfontaines, might open to him the doors of the Academy and gain him liberty to think—aloud. It *was* worth while after all. He worked at it night and day. He wrote immense letters about it to Richelieu and to d'Argenson. Cirey was delightful, priceless—"Cirey-en-félicité" once more. "To be free and loved ... is what the kings of the earth are not." Nevertheless, to be free and loved in Cirey alone was not enough. "I am engaged in writing a *divertissement* for a Dauphin and Dauphiness whom I shall not divert," said he, and again to Cideville: "Me! writing for the Court! I am afraid I shall only write foolery. One only writes well what one writes from choice."

But he wrote, rewrote, altered, improved, not the less. On July 7th, President Hénault, the friend of Voltaire's friend Madame du Deffand, came to spend the day at Cirey. He found it "a delightful retreat, a refuge of peace, harmony, calm, and of mutual esteem, philosophy, and poetry." Voltaire was in bed when the guest arrived: working hard there, as usual. Summer was on the land. The house was a marvel. Madame, recalled from her exact sciences, was a charming hostess. If Voltaire was fifty years old and ailing, if he had to look back on many honours missed and favours given to meaner men, his "Princess of Navarre" was but the more delightful a compliment for being paid so late and so unexpectedly. He read it to the President, who wept (though the "Princess" is not at all pathetic), and was very nearly as interested in it, and as pleased with it, as the eager author himself.

In September, Voltaire and Madame came up from Cirey to Champs-sur-Marne, a village only five leagues from Paris, to take part in the rejoicings which celebrated Louis XV.'s recovery from an illness and return from a campaign, and to arrange about the production of the "Princess."

One night Madame insists on her Voltaire driving up with her those five leagues to Paris, to witness the fireworks and festivities. Madame has her own carriage and her country coachman, unused to the city. She is in *grande tenue* and diamonds. The carriage gets into a crowd—that light-hearted, light-headed mob of Paris—and cannot move an inch until three o'clock in the morning. Out gets Madame followed by her lean Voltaire (not a little disgusted and amused and having the very greatest admiration for this extraordinary woman's pluck and spirit), pushes her way through the crowd, marches straight into President Renault's house in the Rue Saint-Honoré and takes possession of it. The President is away from home. Madame sends for a chicken from the restaurant, and she and her Voltaire sit down to supper with perfect philosophy and enjoyment, and drink to the President's very good health.

Voltaire recounted the story to Hénault a few days afterwards. The man who had undertaken to write a court *divertissement* had laid himself open to all kinds of social adventures, amusements, boredoms. In the beginning of the January of 1745 he took up his abode at Versailles to superintend rehearsals, arrange scenery, and accommodate his verses to Rameau's music.

It was twenty years since Voltaire had stayed at the French Court. Did he remember how it had wearied and sickened him? He forgot nothing.

The Court was but a means to an end then, and was but a means to an end now. He wrote to Theriot that he felt there like an atheist in a church. "Don't you pity a poor devil who is a king's fool at fifty?" he asked Cideville; "...worried to death with musicians and scene-painters, actors and actresses, singers and dancers." He complained how he had to rush from Paris to Versailles, and write verses in the post-chaise; how he must take care to praise the King loudly, the Dauphine delicately, the royal family softly, and to conciliate the Court without displeasing the town. Since it must be done, Voltaire was the man to do it as it had never been done before.

On February 18, 1745, died Armand Arouet, aged nearly sixty. Voltaire received the news only seven days before the *fête* was to take place, and hastened from the Court to the funeral of his "Jansenist of a brother." The two had met little of late. But they had always been separated by a gulf wider than that of any physical distance—a diversity of character and ideas. Voltaire could no more understand an Armand than an Armand a Voltaire. Long after, at Ferney, Voltaire told Madame Suard how his brother had had so great a zeal for martyrdom that he had once said to a friend, who did not seem to care about it, "Well, if *you* do not want to be hanged, at least do not put off other people!"

The fanatic left the sceptic as little of his fortune as he dared, having due regard to public opinion. Voltaire was enriched by his brother's death only by six thousand francs per annum. He feigned no overwhelming sorrow at his loss. He was back at Versailles before the contents of the will were known to him, putting the last touches to his "Princess."

The *fêtes* began on February 23d. They were as gorgeous as that old *régime* knew how to make them—with a prodigal gorgeousness which perished with that *régime* itself and will be no more for ever.

A special theatre had been built in the horse-training ground near the palace. Time, labour, money—the lavish expenditure of each was incalculable. At six o'clock on the evening of February 25th there assembled one of the most brilliant and splendid audiences that ever gratified the heart of a playwright. The King, who was certainly nothing in the world if he was not an imposingly decked figurehead, was there with his royal family. The great ladies glittered in diamonds. The nobles were in the splendid robes of their order. It was a night to remember.

"The Princess of Navarre" was acted to an audience who talked gaily all through it and went into raptures of delight and applause when it was finished. M. de Voltaire compared the chatter to the hum of bees round their queen. But the King—that dullest of all gross mortals—condescended to express himself amused. He commanded a second performance. If that fashionable audience *did* make more noise than the *parterre* of the Comédie, Voltaire could afford to shrug his shoulders. "The King is grateful. The Mirepoix cannot harm me. What more do I want?" he wrote to d'Argental. His Majesty told Marshal Saxe that that "Princess" was above criticism, and Voltaire thereupon told Madame du Châtelet that he looked on Louis XV. as the very best critic in the kingdom. The moment was one of laughter and triumph. To be sure, it had not been gained without hard work. In addition to the "Princess," Voltaire had written a poem on the "Events of the Year" (1744) in which he may be said to have fooled Louis to the top of his bent, and paid that monarch the most outrageous compliments upon his personal courage and his popularity.

But it was the means to an end—an end which, to Voltaire, justified any means. This brilliant M. de Voltaire was so very entertaining and fair-spoken that he must on the spot be made Historiographer of France at an annual income of two thousand francs, and on the very next vacancy Gentleman-in-Ordinary to Ourself! What nobler reward could wit and merit hope for? On April 1, 1745, the brevet of Historiographer was signed by Louis XV. On April 16th Voltaire and Madame du Châtelet hastened to the bedside of her son, sick of the smallpox at Châlons, to save him, if that might be, from the "ignorant tyranny of the physicians." Voltaire, as has been said, did so save him, with much lemonade and a little common-sense. He became ambassador in England under the Ministry of Choiseul; and, at last, victim of the Revolution.

After forty days of quarantine the Historiographer of France rejoined the Court.

CHAPTER XV

THE POPE, THE POMPADOUR, AND "THE TEMPLE OF GLORY"

THE new favour Voltaire had obtained had to be paid for like any other advantage of fortune. Then, as now, the finer the post, the more ennui and exaction in filling it. The nearer he climbs to the sun, the more scorched and weary the climber. Voltaire found out that simple fact of nature very soon.

The truth is he was a great deal too clever to be wasted. Was it a diplomatic letter that was required? The Historiographer had had practice in such things, and would naturally do them better than anyone else. A poem? He was a poet. An epigram? Once upon a time his epigrams had been so dangerously clever that he had positively been bastilled for them. Four days after the *fête* the newly made courtier had written to Theriot that he was so utterly weary he had neither hands, feet, nor head. He spent the whole day hunting up anecdotes and the whole night making rhymes. He had the reputation of a wit, and the Court felt defrauded if he did not make a *bon mot* every time he opened his lips. Then came the French victory of Fontenoy over the English—and of course the Historiographer must celebrate that historical event in an ode. It is but just to Voltaire to say that if he was in some sort belying his principles by being at Court at all, when there, he did, in so far as might be, live up to them. He had pleaded for peace pretty openly in those official documents, and pointed out better ways to glory than the way of battle.

But, after all, though war is deplorable, if war there must be, let *Us* win by all means if we can. Even a peace advocate might feel some such sentiment. One peace advocate, with his facts drawn direct from a letter of d'Argenson's, written from the scene of action itself about May 16, 1745, sat down in a fine glow of enthusiasm and produced his heroic poem, of three hundred lines and entitled "Fontenoy," on the spot. Paris was delighted. The King was content. Five editions were sold in ten days. The Historiographer, of course, corrected, embellished, altered, indefatigably. "This battle has given me a great deal more trouble to celebrate than it gave the King to win it," he observed, very truly. He was plagued out of his life by the Court ladies who really *must* insist on the poet flattering in his poem all their cousins and lovers who had taken even the smallest part in the fight. "My head swims," he wrote. He grumbled. But he was not ill content. Presently, "Fontenoy" received the compliment of being clumsily burlesqued, and a gay Voltaire answered the burlesques in a "Critical Letter from a Fine Lady to a Fine Gentleman of Paris"—dainty, light, rallying, graceful—and as good-humoured as witty. If his "Princess" had won him favour, "Fontenoy" had sealed it. He had gained the King. To keep him there remained but to gain also the woman and the priest who ruled him.

Looking back long after on this period of his life—"It was not the time of my glory if I ever had any," said Voltaire. It was not. To fawn on that sensual stupidity the King, to cajole the Pope, to flatter the mistress—they were not occupations that commended themselves to a man with such a passion for work and such a supreme consciousness of a mission in life crying aloud to be fulfilled, as Voltaire. But the end—the end was everything. How should he speak truth if he were gagged? What hope of freedom to speak in these times without the royal indulgence? The means were contemptible enough, be it granted. But they were the only means. What matter how dirty the road if it led to the goal? That was Voltaire's idea—not high-minded, nor quite without excuse, and perfectly characteristic. He plunged through that Court mire alert, gay, and vigorous; flattered the women; amused the courtiers; was eternally witty and gallant; and just sarcastic enough in his wit to make himself respected.

And then he set to work to gain the Pope. Hardly any other transaction of his life shows him as matchlessly clever and ingenious as this one. He *was* a sceptic—that is, if a sceptic be one who believes in a creed of his own rather than the creed of other persons. He had the reputation of an atheist. The Church had banned his books, and discovered some subtle innuendo against herself in every line he wrote. Worse than all, the man was a satirist, a jester, a mocker, who viewed the huge pretensions and the gigantic claims of Rome with a cynic gleam in his eyes and a laugh on his lips.

He started his bold campaign by reading the whole of the Pope's works and complimenting that very good-natured representative of St. Peter, Benedict XIV., on their ability. Benedict thereupon sent his "dear son" a couple of beautiful medals with his own portrait engraven thereon as a return civility. "He looks like a *bon diable*," wrote the graceless Voltaire to d'Argenson, "who knows pretty well how much *all that* is worth."

And then on August 17th Voltaire wrote to beg permission to dedicate that "Mahomet," which Lord Chesterfield had considered a covert attack on Christianity, to his Holiness himself. The letter with which he sent the play is a masterpiece of subtlety. The Voltairian daring and adroitness, which are without their counterpart in history, succeeded of course. If one can be at once supremely bold and supremely clever, success is a foregone conclusion. Voltaire was lucky in his man—and knew his man to perfection. Benedict XIV. was *bonhomme* rather than an ideal pope, and *did* accept his own infallibility and the astounding assumptions of his Church, with a great many comprehensive qualifications.

He was quite wise enough in his generation to perceive that it was better to have a subtle Voltaire for a friend than an enemy. He therefore sent him his Apostolic Benediction: and accepted the dedication of "your admirable tragedy" in a charming letter dated September 19th. Voltaire, on his part, said he laid a work against the founder of a false religion at the feet of the chief of the true religion: "kissed the Pope's holy feet" and "sacred purple" indefatigably in every letter he wrote; flattered the cardinals and went into ecstasies over Benedict's virtues. The correspondence between the two was printed as a preface to a new edition of "Mahomet" in French and Italian; and M. de Voltaire, with his tongue in his cheek and not a little satisfaction in his soul, is proclaimed before all men the *protégé* of Rome!

Long before this desirable consummation, as far back as May 3d of this 1745, he had written with a gay confidence that the devout might now ask *his* protection for this world and the next. The subject never ceased to afford his sense of irony the most delicious amusement. But better than being amused he was henceforth "covered from his enemies by the stole of Heaven's vicegerent." The Pope, it has been seen, did not accept the dedication of "Mahomet" until September. Before that Voltaire was hard at work to win another influence—the influence of Madame d'Étioles, afterwards the Marquise de Pompadour.

The summer of 1745 was but a dull summer at Court. In May the King joined his army. What were the courtiers and flatterers to do with no one to flatter and toady? The firmament was dark without its Sun: and would have been darker yet but for the steady rising of one brilliant star. Clever head and cold heart, a cool and persistent ambition, a most subtle intellect, and a morality which never interfered with an early and plainly avowed intention to become the King's mistress—such was the woman who "with her harlot's foot on its neck" ruled France for nineteen years, lost it India and Canada, and spurred it, galloping, to the Revolution. With every charm, every grace, every accomplishment that can make a woman irresistible—all carefully learnt for that one noble end, the King's subjugation—five-and-twenty years old, the wife of a wealthy *bourgeois*, M. d'Étioles, living in the country, and having already begun, and coolly waiting to finish, her conquest of the royal heart—such was the Pompadour when Voltaire first knew her. In May he was her correspondent. In June he was her visitor—drinking her tokay, and paying her the loveliest compliments, and discussing with her gravely all subjects in heaven and earth, for she had not only natural cleverness, but a fine cultivation, and, in her heart, said Voltaire, was always "one of us." She confided in him her design on—she called it her passion for—the King.

In July Voltaire was addressing verses to his "dear and true Pompadour" and saying he might well call her in advance by a name which rhymed with "amour" and would soon be the loveliest name in France. She was formally created Marquise and came up to Court. She was the mistress of Louis. She was the mistress of France. And—she was the friend of Voltaire.

If he had thought it necessary to justify himself for that friendship, only he did not think it necessary at all, he might have argued, as he might have argued as to his alliance with the Pope, that it was a pity kings should be governed by priests and women; but that since they were, the best and wisest thing to do was to get the influence of the priests and women on the right side. What might a Pompadour not do? "One of us"—that meant a philosopher, mentally capable of seeing new points of view, acquiring new truths, breaking from old superstitions. In the hollow of her hand she held the happiness or the misery of thousands. Not only the welfare of a proud kingdom but the well-being of those silent suffering units who peopled the kingdom, hung, as too often before, on a shameless woman's smile or frown. And if she could make or mar a country and a nation, how much more a Court poet?

Voltaire had begun writing to Rameau's music an opera called "The Temple of Glory," to celebrate Louis XV.'s victories in his campaign. It was just as well from Madame de Pompadour's point of view to be on the right side of such a very poignant wit as M. de Voltaire's. She *was* on the right side of it. With all his usual audacity the poet inserted in his opera the most unmistakable and complimentary allusions to her and her King and to the relations between them. He was busy with other work too. Only one disease—it was an internal complaint this time—and an opera on hand at once would have been idleness indeed. All through the autumn of this 1745 he was writing the authorised historical account of the King's campaigns, an honour which d'Argenson had procured for him, and which afterwards swelled into his "History of Louis XV." Now, it was known as the "Campaigns of the King." With a very rare love of justice, at a time when national feeling ran high, he wrote to Sir Everard Falkener, now secretary to the Duke of Cumberland, to ask him for first-hand facts regarding the war so that the historian might do justice to the "many great actions done by your nation"—our enemies, the English. He had time to read the back numbers of three past years of the "London Magazine" in English. Madame du Châtelet was always with him. In June they had been at Châlons for a fortnight with Madame du Deffand. In October they went to Fontainebleau—Madame creating not a little talk and scandal by insisting, on the way there, on a right, or a supposed right, of her family to ride in the best place in the first coach after the Queen's—to the exclusion of other noble and indignant ladies, who had, or thought they had, similar rights.

In the comparative quiet of Fontainebleau Voltaire worked at his "Campaigns"—"as I always work—with passion."

He and Madame returned to Versailles in November in time to welcome the King. On the 26th of that month the Sun was beaming graciously in his firmament again—after a campaign in which he had done nothing but look on from a very cautious distance. And on November 27, 1745, appeared "The Temple of Glory."

The two principal characters in it are Trajan, great in war but the friend of peace, emperor, Roman—and lover; and Plotine, the beloved. The dullest among the audience must have seen whom these characters represented.

Ta plus belle gloire
Vient du tendre amour,

sang the chorus to Trajan. And did not *amour* rhyme with Pompadour for ever and ever? Among the spectators were the injured Queen, who had no reason now to love this M. de Voltaire; and Madame du Châtelet, taking advantage of another hereditary right and sitting in her royal mistress's presence. Rameau's music was delightful and the dancing perfection. Richelieu had superintended the *mise-en-scène*. The curtain went down on a tumult of applause. And Voltaire, with that boyish French capacity of his for being intoxicated by the very thin wine of a social success, strolled up to the royal box and said to Richelieu, to be overheard of the King, "Trajan est-il content?"

There are a dozen versions of the story. There are several vehement denials that any such incident took place. But there is no smoke without fire, and the episode is characteristic enough of a pleased and audacious Voltaire. He does not ever allude to it himself: but that may be accounted for by the fact that Trajan was *not* very content with the too daring question. He had reason to be a little sulky at his royal name being so openly coupled—with Plotine's. One authority has it that he turned his back on Voltaire and addressed compliments to Rameau.

But "The Temple of Glory" was repeated; and the Sun came out from behind the little cloud as bright as ever.

The next court *divertissement*, performed on December 22d, was not indeed written by Voltaire, but by Jean Jacques Rousseau, citizen of

Geneva, with whom Voltaire was now brought into a polite correspondence, and with whom he was hereafter to fight as he had never fought even with Rousseau's old exiled namesake at The Hague.

On January 16th of the new year, 1746, Longchamp entered as a kind of confidential valet into the service of Madame du Châtelet, and from her service was shortly drafted into that of M. de Voltaire. Half secretary, half servant, and all observer, Longchamp lived to write memoirs of unusual interest and fidelity, and to make Voltaire a proof of the fallacy of the saying that no man is a hero to his valet. Longchamp, Collini, Wagnière, who were in turns the servant-secretaries of Voltaire, have all painted his picture as most generous, hasty, and kind, with the sensitive temper of genius and the forethought and consideration for others, even for dependents, which genius too often lacks. To Voltaire's generation the *canaille* were as dirt beneath the feet; but not to Voltaire. Irritable and impulsive in speech, he had at times to his servants the manners of the old *régime*; but he had ever the heart of a better age.

Abundantly generous—"a miser of nothing, but his time"—one servant speaks in warm terms of his "solid and durable indulgence and goodness," and another of his kindness, sympathy, and forgiveness. The character that masters give their servants is often unreliable through ignorance or weak indulgence; but the character that servants give their masters rarely falls into either of these errors.

From that fiery inquisition, the inquisition of the domestic eye, Voltaire is one of the few great men in history whose character comes out better than it went in.

All the early months of 1746 were taken up in keeping the vantage ground he had gained and in gaining more. He wrote letters to Italian cardinals in Italian. He reminded the Pope of the dutiful existence of his dutiful son. He pleased Madame de Pompadour. He amused sulky Trajan. He began a regular Voltairian battle against Charles Roy, an old scurrilous minor poet, who stood not ill at Court, himself hoped for a chair in the Academy, and had written an unsuccessful rival piece to Voltaire's "Princess." These occupations were very fatiguing. But they were essential. On March 17th a fresh vacancy fell in at the French Academy, and who should have it if not Voltaire? The gods were more favourable now. The candidate canvassed for himself feverishly. He wrote an artful letter to the Lieutenant of Police and a beautiful one to Father La Tour, one of his old schoolmasters, expressing a warm affection for religion and the Jesuits. If the thing was to be done at all it must be done thoroughly.

On April 25, 1746, the greatest literary man of the age, who was fifty-two years old and a member of almost every other Academy in Europe, was at last formally elected to the Literary Society of his own country. On May 9th he read before it his preliminary discourse, Voltairian in every line.

CHAPTER XVI

THE ACADEMY, AND A VISIT

WHO is it that having climbed to a height does not look on the prospect that it affords him, and wonder if that prospect be worth the bogs and the mire, the stones and the boulders, the steep places and the thorns that lay on the way to it? Voltaire was not given to useless reflections. Yet it could but occur to his cynic soul that his friendship with a king's mistress had gained him a reward that all his writings and genius could not; just as he had declared in a verse, whose gay bitterness is Voltaire's only, that his "Henriade," his "Zaire," and his "Alzire" had not won him a single glance of kingly favour, while for a "farce of the fair," "The Princess of Navarre," honours and fortune had rained on him. He might well be a cynic.

What use would that coveted chair among the Forty be to him now he had it? Was it the hall-mark, the sign and seal of talent? That sign and seal were on every line the man had written. He, who had made by his works so startling an impression on the human mind that, though he had a host of enemies, adorers, fearers, none could be indifferent with regard to him, had surely no need of the cold distinction of an academical honour. But he thought that it would be valuable as a refuge from *lettres de cachet* and official interference. It conferred various legal privileges. It would be his passport, obtained from red-tapeism, to be flaunted in the face of it, to show the Voltairian right to say what a Voltaire pleased. The position further gratified a naïve and very human vanity. And now I *am* here I will be so uncommonly active, lively, and reforming as to drive my thirty-nine solemn, pompous, formal, conservative, elderly brethren pretty well distracted!

It was *de rigueur* in the inaugural address to do nothing but praise Cardinal Richelieu and flatter one's predecessor in the chair. And up gets M. de Voltaire and delivers a brilliant discourse on the French language and French taste—smooth, polished, graceful, and with the grip of the iron hand felt always through the velvet glove.

"Gentlemen, your founder put into your society all the nobility and grandeur of his soul: he wished you to be always free and equal."

"No great things without great trouble."

"It is precisely, gentlemen, because there is so much wit in France that there is so little real genius."

No doubt those thirty-nine literary fogies had some sort of notion what a daring spirit they had admitted into their prosy body before that discourse was ended. The artful Voltaire did not forget to introduce into it dainty compliments to such varied persons as the King of France, the Empress of Russia, and the Pope; Frederick the Great and Maupertuis (who spoke and wrote the great French language as if it were their own); Montesquieu, Fontenelle, and Hénault, who adorned it; and my old schoolmaster, d'Olivet.

Sympathising and delighting in his genius and success was a certain new obscure young friend of Voltaire's, who had just come up to Paris to seek his fortune, and who was named Marmontel.

"Sine virtute amicitia existere non potest," says Cicero. If a man may be judged by the company he keeps, Voltaire's character should not be meted a wholly unmerciful sentence. He had too in himself, in an extraordinary degree, the noble talent of friendship.

Fifty years after his school days he was still writing to Abbé d'Olivet, in terms of tenderest respect and affection. He began, as has been seen, his lifelong attachment to his "guardian angel," d'Argental, at the same date and place. "I am not like most of our Parisians," he wrote to Cideville, "I love my friends better than superfluities; and I prefer a man of letters to a good cook and two carriage-horses. One always has enough for others when one knows how to restrict oneself." He acted on that principle through life. There must surely have been something more than commonly lovable in a character which three years earlier than this, in 1742, had commanded the love and admiration of Vauvenargues, the young soldier, the splendid thinker—daring spirit and noble mind. That friendship appealed not in vain to Voltaire on the finest side of his character, at the very moment when a Court, a king, a Pompadour, worldly gain, and the bauble of official favour tempted him on his worst. The pair wrote each other long letters, philosophic, thoughtful, enlightened. Vauvenargues loved to call Voltaire his "dear master." And the master had for the pupil the tender respect, the generous admiration which a great father might feel for the possibilities of a son whom his fond hopes love to fancy greater still. The son went the way of all flesh in 1747, aged thirty-two. He left the world only one work; but those "Maxims" have been justly said to give the soul of man an impetus towards truth. They are too little known.

Marmontel was of a different *calibre*. A young, struggling, literary man in the provinces, he wrote to the chief of his profession, now sunning in court favour, for his advice. "Come up to Paris," wrote the impulsive Voltaire at the end of 1745. He thought letters the noblest of all professions. To be sure, it was one not merely precarious, but generally

ruinous. But then, to deliver one's message—to help truth by speaking it—
a Voltaire, if he could, would have encouraged the merest stutterer to do it,
such as Marmontel was not. In the midst of the preparations for "The
Temple of Glory" he had time to obtain the promise of a post for his *protégé*
from the Comptroller-General of Finance. Up comes Marmontel to Paris,
six louis in his pockets, and a translation. And the Comptroller-General has
fallen out of favour and has no place to give away! Voltaire broke the news
as gently as he could. Perhaps he looked the while out of his brilliant eyes
to see how this new metal stood the furnace. Marmontel said that Adversity
was his oldest acquaintance and that he was not afraid of her. And M. de
Voltaire took upon himself to provide for him until his talents should make
him independent. A hundred and fifty years ago and in Paris such conduct
does not strike the reader as nearly so generous and Quixotic as if the same
event had occurred in London and to-day. Yet the profession of letters was
very much worse then than it is now. Voltaire had had unsuccessful literary
protégés dependent on him for an unpleasantly long time before this, it will
be remembered. *He* remembered it, no doubt. He was more fortunate in
the present instance. Taught, advised, encouraged by Voltaire, Marmontel
became the Marmontel of successful tragedies, of the "Contes Moraux," of
"Bélisaire," and of the "Memoirs."

In his hope that his chair at the Academy would afford him a little
peace and rest, Voltaire was at first very much mistaken. His new honour
was a signal for every enemy he had in the world—and he had a great
many—to set upon him. Every envious, snarling cur of the scurrilous Grub
Street of Paris came yelping at the mastiff's heels. Old Roy burlesqued and
lampooned him; and the thin-skinned poet, who should have been true
enough to his own philosophy to have laughed at such a poor, miserable,
effete old foe, was up and at him in a trice, whipping and stinging him with
verses and epigrams whose rancour still glows and burns.

Other skits and satires followed. And Voltaire, with authority on his
side for once—to say nothing of Madame de Pompadour—hunted out,
accused, prosecuted the authors in a vehement activity and enthusiasm. To
be sure, on one occasion, in his zeal he had the wrong person arrested, and
had to pay damages in a law court for false imprisonment; besides
promising after the fashion of the time, never to do anything so naughty
again.

These skirmishes lasted for many months; nay, the Travenol case, for
wrongful imprisonment, went on for two or three years. Voltaire came out
of such affairs with neither success nor glory. He was always both too quick
to anger, and too quick to forgive. The latter quality was as much a snare to
him as the former.

By the August of 1746 this energetic courtier had reached the fourth act of a play written to order for the Dauphine, and entitled "Semiramis." The Dauphine died at that juncture; but its author continued "Semiramis" all the same. He paid a flying visit in September to a very old friend, the Duchesse du Maine. In October he and Madame du Châtelet came up to Fontainebleau with the Court, and stayed at Richelieu's house there, which he had lent them. Just as she was about to leave Versailles, the whole of Madame's servants, except Longchamp, had left her in a body. Now, as at Cirey, she was a mistress not a little expectant and inconsiderate, and by fits and starts, if not habitually, mean. The invaluable Longchamp saved the present situation. He was not sorry when, at Fontainebleau, he was allowed to renounce a post in which he sometimes appears to have acted, literally, as the Marquise's lady's maid, for that of secretary to the quick-tempered and kind-hearted M. de Voltaire.

A new weapon was put into Voltaire's hands in December wherewith to defend himself from his enemies, and, having been promised the post for two years, he was made Gentleman of the Chamber to Louis XV. What an honour, what a splendid honour, for the author of the "Henriade" and the "English Letters"—for the man who had already begun to inaugurate a new era of thought in Europe, and who was to make Voltairism such a power in the world that it would one day shake Catholicism on her immemorial foundations! What an honour—what a noble honour! M. de Voltaire did not meet with at all a warm reception from his brother Gentlemen. Bah! the creature was but a *bourgeois*. Where were his pedigree and his letters-patent of nobility? In his books? We do not want any literary hacks among Us! One youthful Gentleman of the Chamber, noble, but very uncertain as to his spelling, wrote to his uncle that the appointment of "ce Voltere" was a "dezoneur" to gentlemen of name and arms, and the King really should have known better. The naïve youth consulted his "respequetable oncle" as to whether it would not be best for the Chamber to refuse to receive "this Person named Arouet." But at a very early date this Person named Arouet showed himself more than a match for the noble young gentleman and all his brethren at once.

Talking of the coming marriage of a lord's daughter with a Farmer-General—that synonym for dishonesty and extortion—one of the Gentlemen inquired where the pair would be married. "At the tax-office," suggested someone. "There is no chapel there," said another. "Pardon me, gentlemen," said Voltaire, who hitherto had not spoken a word, "there is the Chapel of the Impenitent Thief."

It may be guessed that the Gentlemen of the Chamber at least learnt to respect a brother with such a killing tongue.

He passed the early months of 1747 busy with his Travenol lawsuit, taking patent pills which he was always warmly recommending to Frederick, and "making his court" to Madame de Pompadour. On July 2d he was congratulating the Minister of War on the French victory of Lawfeld; which he afterwards celebrated in an epistle, not at all equal to his "Fontenoy."

He had now reached the climax of his favour. The Historiographer of France, the Gentleman of the Chamber, and the favourite of the mistress, may well have seemed a fixture at Court.

He was not sorry to escape from it on August 14th for a few days' visit to the Duchesse du Maine, now at Anet. Voltaire must have altered greatly since he was first her guest as a promising boy of twenty-one, two-and-thirty years ago. The promise had become fulfilment. Once, he had been honoured in being the Duchess's visitor; now, she was honoured in being his hostess. She allowed him to bring Madame du Châtelet with him, because he would by no means have been allowed to come without her. The Duchess was still the "sublime personage" Voltaire remembered. With her haughty and imperious temper, her brilliant grace and wit, her stately courtesy, and her magnificent condescension, she was the living type of those women who went later to the guillotine, scornful to the last of the *canaille* that brought them there—the women who lived so ill, and died so well. A little deformed was the great Duchess: very small; fair-haired; loving amusement and hating boredom above everything in this world and

MARIE LECZINSKA

From the Picture by Carle Van Loo in the Louvre

the world to come; seventy years old, but as appreciative of a Voltaire as she had been at forty.

With her was Madame de Staal, formerly Mademoiselle de Launay, whom Voltaire already knew; half maid, half companion, very observant and with a brilliant, satirical pen, much in use for writing famous Memoirs and recounting the gossip of the Maine court to Madame du Deffand in Paris.

There were various other visitors. The Duchess liked society, she said, because everybody had to listen to her and she had to listen to nobody.

Play-acting was much in vogue. Cleverness was *de rigueur.* To be moral was unnecessary—but to be a bore, that was not to be dreamt of. It was upon this court that the erratic Émilie, with her lover and a great quantity of luggage in her train, descended very late on the evening of the day before she was expected.

There was a fine fuss, according to the acid, elderly de Staal. The pair wanted supper. One of the visitors had to give up his bed to Madame du Châtelet, who complained of it the next morning. She tried two other rooms, and grumbled at *them.* She was determined, as usual, to carry on her studies, and required a bedroom where she could have silence, not so much by night, as by day. She shut herself up there and worked hard at Newton, joining the other visitors only in the evenings. Sublimely indifferent to social obligations was the Marquise. The stupid rules which govern guests in most polite societies she ignored entirely. She preferred work to tittle-tattling with the other women; so she worked. There were not enough tables in her room for her papers, her jewels, and her *pompons;* so she made a foraging expedition round the house and appropriated six or seven for her use. Anyone with a taste for occupation, and condemned to polite idleness, will understand and sympathise with Madame du Châtelet. It is also easy to understand that the old Duchess, who invited her guests solely to amuse herself, was offended. And that Voltaire, whose own passion for work kept him shut up alone almost as much as Émilie, felt it necessary to atone for their conduct by writing the Duchess lovely, gallant verses, and when he *did* appear, by being delightfully amusing and agreeable.

In a few days the company began to rehearse Voltaire's farce "Boursouffle," which had formed the amusement of a Cirey evening nine years before. Madame du Châtelet took a part and would not submit, wrote the acrimonious de Staal, to the simplicity of costume it demanded, but persisted in dressing it like a Court lady.

She and Voltaire had a passage of arms on the point, de Staal added. "But she is the sovereign, and he the slave"; and of course the slave had to submit. It is noticeable here, again, that it was the other women who abused Émilie, and not Émilie the other women. Perhaps her eternal Newton, at which they sneered, kept her from the meanness and the backbiting which disfigured their own conduct. Let her sublime inconsideration for other people's feelings and her childish fondness for fine clothes be granted. Those failings were common to most of the great ladies of the eighteenth century, and, no doubt, to Émilie's detractors among them. Her passion for work and her noble intellectual endowments were her own alone.

"Boursouffle" was an immense success. Voltaire and Madame took leave of the Duchess on August 25, 1747, the morning after its performance, and in their usual confusion of bandboxes, chiffons, and papers, left "Boursouffle" behind them. Madame de Staal, whose temper was perhaps rendered uncertain by her post of polite maid-of-all-work to all the Duchess's guests, received agonised letters from Voltaire imploring her to send the farce by a safer means than the post, for fear it should be copied, and to keep the list of characters "under a hundred keys." He and Madame were back at Court again—with the sun of kingly favour shining on them, it seemed, as brightly as ever. Six weeks passed without any distinguishing events. On October 14, 1747, the Court was at Fontainebleau, and Voltaire and Madame du Châtelet, its constant attendants, still staying at the house of the Duke of Richelieu in the same place.

CHAPTER XVII

COURT DISFAVOUR, AND HIDING AT SCEAUX

IT was one of the very doubtful privileges of Madame du Châtelet's rank that she was permitted to play cards at the Queen's table. Émilie had never done anything in moderation in her life. She not only loved, worked, and dressed to excess, but she gambled to excess also. High play was in the air of that eighteenth century. In England, as well as in France, men lost an estate or a fortune in an evening, and women staked the diamonds on their breast and the doweries of their children.

The thrifty Voltaire regarded the dangerous craze in Madame du Châtelet with not a little apprehension. He had known poverty not by name, but in person; and had no desire to renew the acquaintance.

One night at Fontainebleau, probably at the end of October, 1747, but the actual date is not quite clear, Émilie lost four hundred louis. She must have exerted all her power over the man who had ceased to love her, but not to fear her or to be faithful to her, to make him lend her two hundred more. She played again the next evening, and lost those. One can fancy the scene—the crowded ante-chamber of royalty; the flushed and excited players; lights, laughter, and talk; Émilie, desperate and breathless, forgetting alike her fine clothes which were the sign she was but as other women, and her cool reason which set her far above them—and at her side, Voltaire, urging her in fervent English whispers to come away, that the game was played, and the loss must be accepted with a shrug of the shoulders and as good a grace and philosophy as one could muster.

A fly buzzing at her ear could not have moved her less. The intoxication of play was upon her. She sent out and raised from her man of business and a friend, Mademoiselle du Thil, three hundred and eighty louis more. She lost them. Luck had been against her. It *must* turn now! She played on and on. At last she owed eighty-four thousand francs. The quick Voltaire at her elbow, robbed of all prudence and discretion (to be sure, he never had much of either), bent over her desperately at last and said in an agitated whisper in English: "Don't you see you are playing with cheats?" The words were hardly out of his mouth before he realised that they had been overheard and understood, or before one of the quickest intelligences that ever man had, had decided on action. Madame du Châtelet, sobered suddenly, was herself far too clever not to see the danger of the situation. The pair rose at once and left the palace. The room was full of their enemies; noble Gentlemen-in-Ordinary jealous of a brother whose pedigree was his brain and who had no birthright but genius; and women angry with Émilie for her absurd airs of youth, and her passion for learning which must be affected in *her*, because it certainly would be affected in *us*!

Would Madame de Pompadour's patronage save her brilliant *protégé*? By no means. The play was at the Queen's table; and the silent Queen had no reason to love the Pompadour's friends. Historiographer of France and Member of the French Academy—even that would not save a Voltaire, with a Voltaire's record behind him, from the consequences of such an utterance as this.

The two returned post-haste to Richelieu's house where they had their quarters. It was half-past one in the morning. They waited for nothing. The horses were put to at once. Longchamp was sent in search of their servants who were lodging at different houses in the place. Émilie's *femme de chambre* had only time to throw together a few packages of chiffons. She, Voltaire, and Émilie got into the carriage just as the October day was breaking. Longchamp was left behind to pack. The carriage was driven towards Paris, and the desperate pair within hastily sketched in the details of their scheme of action. A wheel of the carriage broke when they were near Essore, and the wheelwright, who had no mind to be cheated of his dues even by fine folk in gala attire, declined to let the carriage proceed till his bill was paid. Neither Voltaire nor Émilie had a single sou. A *lettre de cachet* and the Bastille loomed much too close for delays to be endurable. Luckily, an old acquaintance of the du Châtelets, coming by post-chaise from Paris, recognised Madame and paid the wheelwright. They drove on. At a little village near Paris, Voltaire alighted. Madame proceeded to the capital. It had been arranged that there she should make arrangement for the payment of her gambling debts, and if possible smooth the way for Voltaire's return. She was used to that office.

From a wayside inn Voltaire wrote to the Duchesse du Maine, now hard by at Sceaux; and sent the letter by messenger. He had asked his old friend for hiding, shelter, refuge, till the storm blew over. She responded, telling him to come that night to the château, where one Duplessis, known to Voltaire, would meet him and conduct him to the rooms she was keeping for him. He did as she said. He entered the house unknown to any save Duplessis and the Duchess.

For not less than a month he lived in those rooms on the second floor, with the shutters barred night and day. Longchamp joined him there, bringing luggage, books, and papers. All day long the master wrote and the valet copied. Voltaire never slept more than five or six hours; but wrote, wrote, wrote by that eternal candle-light. At two o'clock every night, when the rest of the house was asleep, he came softly downstairs into the Duchess's bedroom, where the little, great lady was already in bed and where, propped on pillows, she royally waited to be amused by her guest. She was never disappointed. A servant, the only one in her confidence, brought M. de Voltaire a little supper which he ate on a little table between his hostess's bed and the wall. The valet left the room. During the meal the old Duchess told her visitor the most delightful, wicked stories of the Court of Louis XIV.—from her own experience. And then, M. de Voltaire produced a manuscript and read to the Duchess the charming result of his imprisonment—those miniature masterpieces of romance, "Zadig," "Scarmentado," "Micromégas," and "Babouc."

Only children of that astonishing eighteenth century could have enacted such a scene entirely without awkwardness, self-consciousness, or exaggeration. It was worth days of labour and darkness to find a listener as acute, as sympathetic and intelligent as this little old woman who had lived so fully and knew human nature to the core.

While this lean M. de Voltaire with his startlingly brilliant eyes, and the sardonic mouth and drooping hook-nose more nearly meeting year by year—his conversation alone could turn night into day, and make one forget that such things as fatigue, ennui, sleep, are part of man's portion. Out of gratitude for her goodness—gratitude was never a virtue he lacked—he was wittier now than ever. Gratitude guided his pen as well as his speech, and made his stories the most easy, graceful, and delightful in the world.

Voltaire had not been a romancer hitherto. He did not find it in him to invent plots now. "Zadig" is founded on a story by English Thomas Parnell; and "Micromégas" pretty openly taken from Cyrano de Bergerac's "Journey to the Moon." But as the "amazing genius" of Shakespeare took the stillborn children of lesser men's brains and breathed on them the breath of life, so did Voltaire. Everything that makes a story immortal is his own in those matchless *contes*. Charm, wit, delicacy, an exquisite lightness of touch, the finest taste in satire, humour, variety, epigram, gaiety—with that ever-present undercurrent of biting meaning—almost all the Voltairian gifts are here. Every story is a pungent satire on the King, Court, *régime*, or religion of that evil day. The characters are very palpably drawn from life. In "Zadig" there is a certain Yebor who could by no possibility be anyone else than Boyer, the Âne of Mirepoix.

The graceless old Duchess, sitting up in bed, thoroughly enjoyed hearing her order castigated. She laughed loud and long to see how this Voltaire always had his whip on the raw.

No wonder she was eager for the tales to be given to the larger public of her court. The imprisonment was becoming wearisome. The unlucky Longchamp was ennuied to death. Voltaire's health began to suffer for want of light and fresh air. The secret of his whereabouts had been kept so well, that his enemies at Court supposed him to be on the road to Frederick and Berlin.

Everybody was glad when one fine day, probably about the end of November, Madame du Châtelet appeared with the news that the storm had blown over, that the unlucky utterance was more or less forgotten, and the gambling debts settled—somehow. The autocratic little Duchess was not going to part with her Voltaire now she might enjoy him openly. He and Madame du Châtelet joined her throng of gay satellites. There were comedies, operas, and balls. Voltaire, Émilie, and Madame de Staal all took parts in his play of "The Prude," imitated from Wycherley's "Plain Dealer," and now played for the first time—December 15, 1747. They acted "Issé" by La Motte, "Zélindor" by Moncrif, and "Les Originaux," a comedy by Voltaire, first performed at Cirey. Émilie took the part of *Issé*; was *Fanchon* in the "Originaux," and *Zirphé* in the opera of "Zélindor." If she *was* one-and-forty years old and *would* dress her parts, not to suit them, but her own love of finery, it must be confessed that she was matchlessly accomplished and versatile.

Voltaire, after the manner of the days when he was lover indeed, improvised gay verses of compliment to her. "Madame du Châtelet," he wrote to a friend, "sang *Zirphé* correctly and acted with nobility and grace: a thousand diamonds were her least ornament."

Besides play-acting there was an orchestra of marquises and viscounts. Dancers from the Opera amused the pleasure-loving little court. A delightful girl of thirteen carried that art to its highest perfection and charmed everyone with her grace and talent. And, in the bad quarter of an hour before dinner, Voltaire read the *contes* composed for the Duchess, to the Duchess's guests gathered together in the great salon.

The visit came to an end about the middle of December, when Voltaire had been at Sceaux about two months. Once more in Paris, he busied himself with a very pretty little *ruse*, by which he evaded the piracy of publishers and had two hundred private copies of "Zadig" printed to give to the Duchess and her friends, before the rest of the world had read it.

Then came the pleasing news that on December 30th "The Prodigal Son" had been played in the private apartments before the King by a distinguished company of amateurs: and that his Majesty had deigned to be amused. Amateur theatricals had a vogue only second to gaming in eighteenth-century France. To play the smallest parts in the feeblest piece in the King's presence, men and women made incredible sacrifices of fortune, of honour, and of truth. Madame de Pompadour's *femme de chambre* obtained a commission in the army for one of her friends by procuring, for a duke, the very minor *rôle* of a policeman, who had only two lines in his part, in "Tartuffe." The clever Pompadour herself was an actress of no mean ability. She took a part in the "Prodigal." Voltaire had not been behindhand in encouraging her histrionic tastes. He does not appear to have been present at this performance of his comedy. When a play had already been performed in public (and "The Prodigal Son," it will be remembered, was played, anonymously, in October, 1736), it was not etiquette to invite its author to witness its *début* before royalty. But it pleased his bored Majesty so much that, on the strength of it, Madame de Pompadour obtained for her brilliant Voltaire the delightful right and privilege of being henceforth always a spectator at the plays acted in the private apartments. And this unlucky Voltaire, in his enthusiasm and gratitude, must needs look among his papers and discover a poem, which, with a little artful alteration, will express his thanks to the mistress.

Nothing would ever have made Voltaire cautious. Audacity was in his nature, and there was no preventing it oozing out, like Bob Acres's courage, at the tips of his fingers whenever he got a pen in his hand. To be sure, if he had been circumspect he could not have been half so witty. If wit is not spontaneous, it is rarely wit at all. And this verse really would not have done him the slightest harm, if the favourite had but kept it to herself.

Every grace and charm and art,
Pompadour, in you is found.
And it is alike your part
To be the treasure of one heart
And a Court's delight.

So much blest, then, live for aye
Lovely years with pleasure crown'd.
The King brings peace with him. Oh may
Your foes be nothing: and alway
You both your conquests keep!

But, after all, though she was an astute, cool-blooded Pompadour, she was a woman too and loved a compliment; and that her *entourage* should be aware she received such beautiful ones as that.

It soon reached the ears of poor Marie Leczinska, patient and dignified in the dreary and respectable seclusion of her apartments. The days were long gone when, a bride of one-and-twenty, she had called

Voltaire "my poor Voltaire" and pensioned him from her own purse. The ugly daughters, Mesdames, too, had still some influence over their royal father, the King, and were not slow to use it.

Old Roy took occasion to sententiously point out in a dreary poem how abominable it was to allude to royal—mistakes: and how the loves of gods and kings were never meant for the comment of the vulgar. The unlucky Voltaire was further suspected at the moment of having been the author of some lines to the Dauphine, whose gay philosophy offended the King. He denied the authorship, of course, *in toto*. But that was very little use. It was whispered that Mesdames, the daughters, so worked upon Louis that he signed a decree of banishment for Voltaire, without even consulting Madame de Pompadour. That would seem to have been an addition to make a good story better. There was most likely no edict of banishment on paper. Voltaire himself denied that there was ever any idea of such a thing. But on January 13, 1748, coming gaily to Versailles and not in the least anticipating any evil effect from the charming audacity of his verses, he found the Court too hot to hold him. He dined in Paris that night at a coffee-house, with a few other literary men. He arrived rather late. He had come straight from Versailles, and alone of the company knew what had occurred there. He made his dinner, after his frugal fashion, off seven or eight cups of black coffee and a couple of rolls, and was very talkative and amusing. The conversation turned on the newly imposed tax on playing-cards, and on luxury. When the dinner was over other visitors at the coffee-house gathered round him and "plied him with questions."

He was not exiled. But he had committed an offence which made it expedient to Go. He knew the Pompadour much too well to suppose she would put her position in jeopardy by trying to save a friend, even if he were a Voltaire. "Circumspection is all very well," he had once written to d'Argenson, "but it is a melancholy thing in poetry: to be reasonable and cold is almost the same thing." For his part, he would rather write even compliments and madrigals as he chose, and be banished for them, than remain at Court, tongue-tied and careful. If the Historiographership and the Academy and the solemn joy of signing oneself Gentleman-in-Ordinary to the King did not give one freedom, they were useless. Neither Voltaire nor Émilie had seen Cirey for many months. On the whole, it was best to go. They left Paris in the deep midwinter at nine o'clock on a January evening, 1748, with the snow thick on the ground and a temperature many degrees below freezing-point.

CHAPTER XVIII

THE MARQUIS DE SAINT-LAMBERT

ONE of Madame du Châtelet's idiosyncrasies was to travel only by night; and another, to overload the travelling carriage with luggage. She insisted on having her way in both particulars this time. It has been aptly said of Voltaire that he was at once patient and hasty. He certainly must have been patient to take the road with a woman whose packages frequently numbered a hundred and who could never travel without her lady's maid. That he usually lost his temper on such journeys, is simply to say that he was human.

On the present occasion, as they were nearing Nangis, the hind spring of the carriage broke, and the overladen vehicle fell over on the side of Voltaire. Madame du Châtelet, large and bony, the *femme de chambre* (whose weight and figure history does not record), and a vast quantity of bandboxes and parcels, came tumbling on the top of him. He relieved his feelings by uttering "piercing shrieks." Two footmen, by getting on the roof of the overturned carriage and dragging their mistress, the lady's maid, and the bandboxes up through the doors "as from a well," at last released M. de Voltaire in the same manner. It was bitterly cold and a brilliant starlight night. The two footmen, aided by the postillions, tried to set the carriage straight again, and failed. One of the postillions rode on into the next village for further assistance. And Voltaire and Émilie sat by the roadside on the carriage cushions, and would have been "perfectly happy" shiveringly studying astronomy, if they had only had a telescope. They *were* philosophers, after all.

The carriage was mended at last. But it had not gone fifty paces before it broke down again. The workmen, who considered Madame had underpaid them, had to be brought back by force—and promises. At last the carriage was able to proceed at a walking pace the nine miles to the Château of Chapelle, where the travellers halted. They reached Cirey about the middle of January, 1748, without further adventure.

The month they spent there was a gay one. Neither was anxious for too many *tête-à-têtes*. The honeymoon had set for ever. When they were alone, each wrote all day; in the evenings they read aloud together or played trictrac. Émilie had an aggravating habit of keeping her Voltaire waiting till supper was cold while she finished "a little calculation." That her Voltaire, himself orderly and punctual, was extremely *vif* at the delay need not be doubted. Madame du Deffand had once said that he followed Émilie like a faithful dog with the collar round his neck. Well, the dog was faithful still. But the collar irked and worried him; and there were times when he snapped at the hand that had put it there.

Madame de Champbonin reappeared on the scene very soon, with a hoydenish twelve-year-old niece in her train. She had been very warmly invited—if only to finish that solitude *à deux*. The whole neighbourhood received invitations presently to act in, or to witness, theatricals. Émilie wrote charades for the occasion. She played comic parts as well as any other. Sometimes the servants were pressed into the cast and acted too. The *bonhomme* would seem to have been conveniently absent, as usual. Voltaire doubtless enjoyed the freedom of private life after the slavish etiquette of the Court. He was certainly able to enjoy theatricals to his last breath.

About the middle of February he and Madame went to visit another Court, at Lunéville, where the etiquette was not slavish at all, and where a king was a great deal more anxious to have them than ever dull Louis had been.

Stanislas, once King of Poland, had been not a little thankful to exchange that quarrelsome and much quarrelled over kingdom for the peaceful little duchy of Lorraine, the tranquil enjoyment of a pipe six feet long and the *dolce far niente* of his lazy and easy-going mistress, Madame de Boufflers. He still had the title of King. He still had a position—he was the father of Marie Leczinska. His miniature Court had all the pleasures and intrigues of a greater, with no weary formalism. Stanislas had his Jesuit, Menou, to rule him just as other kings had their priests to rule them. The priest fought the mistress for the command of the royal puppet, in the approved, courtly fashion; and the mistress fought the priest, when she was not too lazy.

The little Court was further ornamented by a child dwarf, who could sleep in a *sabot*, and a most beautiful young guardsman, six feet high.

Following the example of Frederick, Stanislas was a feeble author himself and a very enthusiastic admirer of the literary Voltaire. The literary Voltaire was not sorry to show the offended Court of France that he stood well with its offended Queen's royal father. So the visitors and the visited were gratified alike.

The visit was a gay one. "Issé" was played; and "Mérope," when everyone sobbed just as they had done in Paris. In the evenings they played lansquenet or talked. It was an agreeable, idle life. Voltaire, ailing as usual, was humoured and made much of by the King. Émilie overwhelmed the inert and voluptuous Madame de Boufflers with her energetic friendship. And then—

The Marquis de Saint-Lambert is one of the most picturesque figures of his century. Poet and soldier, handsome, haughty and cold, with just enough disdain in his perfect manner to make every woman adore him and long to thaw that flawless ice—he had almost every quality which makes riches superfluous. He was, in fact, nothing but the officer of a company of Lorraine guards. He was much in Lunéville because he had, said the world, a fancy for his King's mistress, Madame de Boufflers. His own age accounted him celebrated because he wrote the loveliest drawing-room verses and was the author of a poem called "The Seasons"—much duller than Thomson's. The present age only knows him as the man who robbed Rousseau of Madame d'Houdetot and Voltaire of Madame du Châtelet.

In 1738, when Madame de Graffigny, who was a friend of his, was at Cirey, she had corresponded with him. He had much wished to be asked to stay there. Since he knew how "to read and rest in his own room during the day" and would only expect to be amused in the evenings, Madame du Châtelet desired to have him for a visitor. But the plan, probably owing to the rupture with Madame de Graffigny, had never been carried out.

Madame du Châtelet was now two-and-forty years old, and, on the unanimous testimony of all her female friends, not at all beautiful. But that inflammable temperament, which years before had made her fling honour and prudence to the winds and give her heart and life to Voltaire, was hers still. Age had not quenched the fire. Abstruse thought and long devotion to the exact sciences had still left her, on one side of her nature, passionately a woman. Voltaire had passed quickly and easily from love to friendship— but not Émilie. Her jealousy of Frederick the Great was a proof that she loved her lover as he had long ceased to love her. As early as 1741, in Brussels, after his return from his second Prussian visit, she had bitterly reproached him with no longer caring for her. He had replied to her in verses of which the following give the keynote.

If you want me still to love
Give me back love's golden morn;
To the twilight of my days
Join, forsooth, love's happy dawn.

Even the sunrise touches night.
One hour is mine: and is no more.
We pass: the race which follows us,
Another follows: all is o'er.

In the year after he first met her, on the occasion of Richelieu's marriage to Mademoiselle de Guise, in April, 1734, he had written:

Love not too much: and so you may
Love alway.
For were it not the better far to be
Friends for eternity
Than lovers for a day?

He had always been honest at least. If he had been still lover indeed, it might yet never have occurred to him that there could be cause for jealousy of Émilie of two-and-forty and a young guardsman of one-and-thirty.

When did that wild passion begin? Did it begin in those idle, early days of the Lunéville visit, gradually nourished by propinquity, that gay, easy life, those lovely society verses, and the tantalising fact that Saint-Lambert was a little bit in love with that stupid, lazy, self-indulgent de Boufflers? It would have been an irresistible temptation to Émilie's cleverness and energy to win away such a man from such a woman.

But it seems more likely that she had no time for designs, that she fell head over ears in love madly, recklessly, and at once—with that utter *abandon*, all foolish and half pathetic, with which an old woman too often loves a young man. Was it the handsome face and cold manner and heart that attracted her? The whole eighteenth century found them attractive. Saint-Lambert had so much, too, of that particularly vague quality called taste! He liked being amused, though he found it too much trouble to be amusing himself. And here was one of the cleverest women of her day, or of any day, who could not be dull if she tried and wanted nothing better than to entertain him. She was an invigorating change from the sleepy de Boufflers, at any rate. He was not sorry, too, to obtain the *cachet* which would accrue to him for having robbed a Voltaire.

But whether the passion on both sides was born full-grown, dominant, and irresistible, or had slower roots in vanity and idleness, matters not. It was soon an accomplished fact. Madame du Châtelet wrote her Saint-Lambert the most mad, adoring letters on rose-coloured or sky-blue notepaper with an edge of lace. She put the letters in Madame de Boufflers's harp in the salon. And when everyone had gone to bed, the young guardsman came and found them there. He replied of course. If he did not adore, he graciously submitted to be adored. "Come to me as soon as you are up," wrote the deluded woman. And sometimes, secretly creeping round by the thickets of the garden, *she* would visit *him*. She hardly thought her conduct required apology. She loved him. That was enough. Or if it did, well then, for years Voltaire had been but her friend when he should have been her lover. "I loved for both." "I had reason to complain and I forgave all." She had tried to be satisfied with friendship: but she could not. She wrote thus to d'Argental in a letter not devoid of genuine feeling and even of pathos. She *had* some excuse. But she made the common mistake of thinking that an excuse and a justification are the same thing.

The Abbé Voisenon has recorded how once Madame du Châtelet, after, it may be guessed, a quarrel with Voltaire, spoke of herself as entirely alienated from him. The Abbé took down one of the eight volumes of Voltaire's manuscript letters to her and read some aloud. All his love letters contained, says the Abbé, more epigrams against religion than madrigals for his mistress. But when the reader stopped, Émilie's eyes were wet. She was not cured yet. A few years later, in 1749, her priestly friend tried the same experiment. She listened unmoved. She was cured indeed: and the doctor had been Saint-Lambert.

The Lunéville visit lasted from about February, 1748, until the end of April. Then Madame du Châtelet left the Court, and returned to Cirey, where she and Saint-Lambert may have spent a few blissful, uninterrupted days together. Voltaire prolonged his visit to Stanislas a short time. By May 15th he and Madame du Châtelet were both once more at Cirey *en route* for Paris.

During her stay at Lunéville the energetic Marquise had not only found a lover, but obtained for her *bonhomme* the lucrative post of the Grand Marshal of the Household to Stanislas, and a commission in the army for her son.

But her thoughts were not with husband, son, or friend (as, she still called her Voltaire), but with M. de Saint-Lambert. Wherever she was she wrote to him continually—letters filled with passion, *abandon*, tenderness, bitterness, doubt. He had purposed taking a journey in Italy, but renounced it at her pleading. She thanked him with the melancholy effusion and the humiliating gratitude of the woman who has obtained from her master a sacrifice she knows to be unwilling. She and her unsuspecting Voltaire came up to Paris. If she spent her time writing to her lover, Voltaire spent his in superintending the rehearsals of his new tragedy "Semiramis." One day his versatility appeared in a new character, and he wrote a prologue for his "Death of Cæsar" for a girls' school that proposed to act it. It is characteristic of the man that he adapted himself to this entirely new *rôle* with the most perfect flexibility and thoroughness. The prologue's chief characteristics are its "ease and orthodoxy." He wrote it leaning on a mantelpiece, on the spur of the moment. He included a charming little letter to the Sister Superior and even begged the prayers of that good lady on his behalf!

On June 28th he and Madame du Châtelet left Paris for Commercy, another seat of Stanislas, where that King then was.

Voltaire was ill and miserable and Madame a more impossible travelling companion than ever. On their route, at Châlons-sur-Marne, she must needs engage in the most vociferous, fatiguing dispute with the landlady of an inn over a basin of soup.

Commercy was as gay as Lunéville. There were the inevitable operas and comedies, and on July 14th Providence kindly arranged a total eclipse of the sun to further amuse the little Court. One of its number had astronomised ever so many years ago at Sceaux and at Villars: and had not forgotten those times.

On August 26th he returned to Paris, leaving Madame du Châtelet behind him. She did not complain of his neglect this time. King Stanislas also came up to Paris to stay for a few days with his daughter, the Queen. Voltaire arrived in the capital on the very day of the production of "Semiramis"—probably August 29, 1748.

There had long been forming a cabal against the piece, headed by enemy Piron and joined by most of the adherents of that dismal old playwright Crébillon, who had himself written a clumsy "Semiramis" in 1717. Well, conspiracy for conspiracy. What weapons you use against me, I have the right to use against you. That was Voltaire's theory now as ever. He met cunning with cunning. He bought up half the seats in the house. He gave them to persons who could be absolutely relied upon to clap and cry at the right moments, and to drown all hisses with applause. Theriot helped him. The d'Argental husband and wife had been already active on his behalf. Voltaire too had boldly asked the patronage of King Louis and Madame de Pompadour, and the King, in consideration of the piece having been originally written for the late Dauphine, agreed to pay the expenses of putting it on the stage. If the play but once had a hearing Voltaire believed that no conspiracy could damn it.

The little scheme succeeded fairly well. M. de Voltaire's friends wept and applauded to perfection. But the first three acts were received by the audience as a whole with only a very moderate warmth. And in the fourth, the play was nearly ruined. It was then the custom in France for the spectators to sit and walk about on the stage. During this fourth act, at a scene at the tomb of Ninus, there were so many of them, that the too enthusiastic player who took the part of the sentinel and was guarding the tomb, called out: "Make way for the ghost, if you please, gentlemen. Make way for the ghost!" which set the house in a roar. The playwright, to be sure, had no reason to find the incident amusing. He complained to the Lieutenant of Police, and in future performances of "Semiramis" the abuse was corrected.

That first night, then, was by no means so decidedly successful as its author had hoped.

On the second night, August 30th, M. de Voltaire, wanting to hear what his friends as well as his enemies said of the piece behind his back, disguised himself and went to the famous Café Procope, opposite the Comédie Française, and largely frequented by literary and theatrical people. He had been an amateur actor to some purpose, and understood the art of make-up as well as any professional on the boards. With cassock and bands, an old three-cornered hat, and an immense full-bottom unpowdered wig that showed hardly anything of his face except the sharp end of his long, pointed nose, he looked the part of an abbé to perfection. He put a breviary under his arm; arrived at the *café*; possessed himself of a newspaper; chose a dark corner; put on his spectacles, and read the paper over a modest repast of a cup of tea and a roll. The *café* filled presently—journalists, actors, some of the partisans of Crébillon and some of Voltaire—all fresh from the play and all anxious to air their views thereon. That sensitive, thin-skinned, long-nosed abbé in the corner had to exercise all his self-control to keep himself from contradicting an enemy who criticised unjustly, or a friend who praised foolishly. But he did it. The *rôle* pleased his sense of humour. And one or two of his critics quoted some of his fine passages not amiss. He sat there for an hour and a half, keenly attentive to the conversation. The result as a whole was not unsatisfactory. The play would do.

It ran for fifteen nights in succession. When a month or so later a vile parody appeared on it, Voltaire, supported by her father's friendship, begged Marie Leczinska to suppress that parody. But the Queen, remembering Voltaire not as the man whose "Indiscret" and "Mariamne" had charmed her youth, but as the imprudent friend of Madame de Pompadour, coldly declined to interfere. The Pompadour herself could do little. But the parody did not much harm the original after all. On October 24, 1784, "Semiramis" was performed at Fontainebleau and well received. The play is still of interest to English people—not for itself, but for the "Advertisement" which precedes it: and which contains the most famous and the most adverse criticism upon Shakespeare in the world. He was "a drunken savage"; and "Hamlet" "a coarse and barbarous piece which would not be endured by the dregs of the people in France or Italy." In his head "Nature delighted to bring together the noblest imagination with the heaviest grossness." This was Voltaire's most remarkable word on the great Englishman. But it was not his last.

Before "Semiramis" was performed at Court Voltaire had returned to Lunéville. The excitements of Paris had been too much for him. From being always ailing, he was now really ill. Longchamp was his travelling companion. By the time they reached that unlucky Châlons, on September 12th, Voltaire was in a high fever and compelled to take to his bed in a wretched post-house. Longchamp, seeing that his condition was critical (Voltaire never gave in to illness until he could neither stand nor speak), told the bishop and intendant of the place. They hastened to the patient and offered him hospitality, which he declined; and then they sent him a doctor. He listened to the professional advice very patiently. Long ago, at Cirey, Madame de Graffigny had noted his good humour and politeness in sickness: and recorded how he was grateful even for advice and prayers! His gratitude for advice fortunately did not extend to following it. On the present occasion he heard meekly and replied laconically when he was told he must be bled and swallow various violent and nauseous mixtures. But he was not bled and he did not take the medicines. Temperance and exercise in health, and abstinence and rest in illness, were the main principles of the system which he followed all his life. That with a wretched constitution and a fatal habit of taking too little sleep and doing far too much brain-work, he lived to be eighty-four at a period when the threescore years and ten of the Psalmist were accounted very old age, is a proof that his *régime* was not wholly a mistaken one.

On the present occasion he was so ill that he thought himself dying. But he still read and still dictated letters to Longchamp; though he was so weak he could only sign himself "V." After a few days on a self-imposed diet of tea, toast, and barleywater, the fever left him. He was far too feeble to stand. But he made Longchamp wrap him up in his dressing-gown and carry him into the post-chaise, in which they proceeded towards Lunéville. He was still so ill that he travelled thirty miles without uttering a single word. Before this, unknown to him, Longchamp, who was very sincerely attached to him, had written to tell Madame du Châtelet and Madame Denis of his condition. Once, Émilie would have hastened to him, and half killed him with her vigorous, overwhelming affection and attentions. It was as well for his health that she was quite engrossed with her lover at Lunéville and simply sent a courier with a message.

That message cheered the sick man a little. If he was but her friend, he was her very faithful friend. And friendship meant much more to Voltaire than to most people.

He was better by the time he reached Lunéville. The urgent desire to get well as soon as possible, on that old principle that illness was a kind of degradation, may have helped his recovery.

Madame du Châtelet insisted upon his being cheerful because she felt so herself. He was soon fairly well again, and that miserable journey faded into a bad dream.

In the early part of the October of 1748, Stanislas, and his little Court with him, moved again to Commercy. The guilty loves of Madame du Châtelet and Saint-Lambert were still not even suspected by Voltaire. The guardsman, who soon resigned his commission to become Grand Master of Stanislas's Royal Wardrobe, seems to have been not a little embarrassed by the vehemence of Émilie's passion. But in exact proportion as he was cold, she was ardent. His letters to her have not survived; but from hers to him it is evident that while she was imprudent, headlong, and reckless, he was at least cool enough to see danger and discourage the maddest of her schemes.

The discovery of their secret was of course only a matter of time. One night early in that October of 1748 at Commercy, Voltaire walked into Madame du Châtelet's apartments, unannounced as his habit was, and there in a little room at the end of the suite, lighted by only one candle, he found the handsome young soldier and his clever, foolish, elderly mistress "talking upon something besides poetry and philosophy."

CHAPTER XIX

THE DEATH OF MADAME DU CHÂTELET

IF the invasion of Silesia by King Anti-Machiavelli-Frederick-the-Great had given Voltaire a moral shock difficult to recover from, he experienced a shock far greater in degree and kind now.

He had been slow to see anything. But when he did see, he saw all. He broke into the most passionate and violent reproaches. The lofty Saint-Lambert responded that no one had the right to criticise *his* conduct, and that if M. de Voltaire did not like it, he had better leave the château. The remark irritated Voltaire to a frenzy. Émilie stood by, nonplussed for once in her life, not at all ashamed, but in very considerable difficulty. One can fancy the half dark study, the abominably aggravating coolness of Saint-Lambert, and the inarticulate fury of Voltaire. He flung himself out of the room in one of the greatest passions of his life. He called Longchamp, said that he must beg, borrow, or steal a post-chaise, and make ready to start for Paris that very night. The artful valet went straight to Madame du Châtelet for an explanation. "No post-chaise is to be found on any consideration," said Émilie. An outcry would ruin her reputation. (It is inconceivable, but true, that Madame du Châtelet considered her reputation as yet immaculate.) At two o'clock in the morning Longchamp came to his master's rooms and announced that a post-chaise was an impossibility. Then ride to Nancy at daybreak and get one! M. de Voltaire's passion had not yet spent its force. He went to bed. And Longchamp crept down again to Madame du Châtelet. That marvellous woman was writing at her desk, and announced the extraordinary intention of going to see M. de Voltaire herself, then and there, and bring him to reason.

She did it. She took a seat on the end of his bed. She spoke to him in English, that old language of their quarrels and love, and by a tender name, long disused. Longchamp lit a couple of candles and retired—to listen to the conversation through the wall. It was the most marvellous conversation in the world. They spoke in French now. Émilie tried to excuse herself—somehow. The lean, furious, exhausted, unhappy man in bed started up.

"Believe you!" he cried. "Now! I have sacrificed health and fortune for you, and you have deceived me."

And Émilie proceeded to explain with a perfect plainness of speech that Voltaire had long ceased to love her as a lover, and that since she *must* love someone, he should be pleased that her choice had fallen on a mutual friend, like M. de Saint-Lambert.

How the piercing eyes in the thin face on the pillow must have looked her through and through! Voltaire answered with a very fine irony: "Madame, you are always right; but if things must be so, do not let me see them."

Before she left him, she embraced him. She had succeeded in her aim so far that he was calmer.

The rest of the night the energetic woman spent in appeasing Saint-Lambert, who considered Voltaire had insulted him.

Voltaire was ill in bed the next day. It must be allowed he had an excuse for illness this time. And behold, as the evening drew in, the young Marquis comes in person to make inquiries after the invalid's health, and the invalid admits him. Saint-Lambert makes very handsome apologies for the hasty words which had escaped him in a moment of agitation. Voltaire takes him by both hands and embraces him. "*Mon enfant*, I have forgotten all. It was I who was wrong. You are at the happy age of love and pleasure. Make the most of both."

The very next day the three met at supper at Madame de Boufflers's, and all enjoyed themselves immensely. All idea of the post-chaise and Paris was dismissed. Did Voltaire recall that gay episode of his youth when he and de Génonville had shared the smiles of Mademoiselle de Livri?

In 1749, he actually wrote Saint-Lambert a beautiful gallant poem on the event which had for the time being so much disturbed his peace:

Saint-Lambert, it is all for thee
The flower grows:
The rose's thorns are but for me:
For thee, the rose—

and went on to say in flowing couplets how the "astronomic, Émilie" had renounced mathematics and inky fingers for those "beautiful airs which Love repeats and Newton never knew."

By October 17th, the ex-lover, the lover, and the mistress had returned to Lunéville with Stanislas's Court (of which Voltaire justly complained as being "a little ambulant") on terms of perfect amity. The whole episode had occupied only a few days. And presently Voltaire was once more engrossed heart and soul in his "History of Louis XV."

The explanation of his conduct lies, as ever, in character.

He was angry at first because he had an uncommonly quick temper and a great provocation. But he was always a philosopher as he grew calmer. It was a very bad world. That was his lifelong conviction. So much the more reason to make the best of it! He had lost a selfish, irritating, and exigeante mistress. But there was no reason why he should not keep a clever woman for a friend. Émilie had, after all, but acted on a principle which was his as well as hers; that, in the relation of the sexes, when duty ceases to be a pleasure, it ceases to be a duty also. (It is but just to Voltaire and to Madame du Châtelet to say that they did not carry this remarkable theory, not yet out of vogue, into any other department of morals.)

The age looked upon such irregularities simply as subjects for a jest or an epigram. And every man sees in some degree with the eyes of the time in which he lives.

So Voltaire wrote "Louis XV." The pain passed, as sharp pains are apt to do, quickly. He and Madame du Châtelet, unaccompanied by Saint-Lambert, left Lunéville for Cirey about December 20, 1748. The journey was very like a hundred they had made in old times. At that fatal Châlons, Émilie *would* call on the bishop and keep the post-horses waiting the whole day while she played cards, and Voltaire lost his temper with her just as if he had been her lover still. Once at Cirey, he was engrossed in hard work, and she wrote a preface to her Newton when she was not writing love letters to Saint-Lambert. Her infidelity would hardly have altered the course of her life were it not for that rigorous law that "every sin creates its own punishment."

The events that followed are such as are best passed over in the fewest words possible. In this December of 1748 at Cirey, Madame du Châtelet found that she was again to be a mother. Saint-Lambert was summoned. He, Voltaire, and the unhappy woman consulted together on what course they would take. Émilie was in tears at first; and they all ended in laughter. They decided on a daring comedy. The Marquis—that simple *bonhomme*—was summoned home, fêted, caressed—and deceived. It is sufficient to say that he was delighted with his wife's prospects, and thought he had reason to be so delighted. He left Cirey, spreading the good news abroad. And Madame du Châtelet complacently considered that her reputation was saved.

Nothing damns the eighteenth century deeper than the fact that this loathsome story was its darling anecdote; and that his criminal connection with Madame du Châtelet, and the sinister events which were its consequence, made Saint-Lambert the very height of fashion. Every memoir of the period has the tale in detail. Longchamp gloats over it. The fine ladies of Paris made *mots* upon it, of which in our day a decent bargee would be ashamed. If the French Revolution immolated some of the very persons who brought it about, was the injustice so gross? A Voltaire shared the vices of the social conditions he condemned, and was himself in some sort a part of that system which set itself above decency and duty and which he knew to be fatal to the good of mankind.

He came out of this unclean comedy less smirched than the other actors therein. But that is to say very little. To be a part of it at all was defilement enough.

By February 17th of the new year 1749 Voltaire and Émilie were installed in the Rue Traversière-Saint-Honoré in Paris.

The *bonhomme* had rejoined his regiment. Saint-Lambert was in attendance at Lunéville.

Voltaire had written a "Panegyric of Louis XV." which was to be recited to his Majesty by Richelieu when the Academy went in a body on February 21st to offer their congratulations to the King upon the establishment of peace. But, as so often happened with Voltaire's writings, the thing had become public too soon. Friend Richelieu, enraged at hearing his recitation being murmured and quoted by the courtiers about him, would not recite it at all. Voltaire was not present on the occasion. When he heard what Richelieu had done, he flung his old friend's portrait into the fire in a rage.

March 10th saw a brief revival of "Semiramis": but all the same it was the fashion just now to prefer Crébillon and his "Catilina."

On May 27th, Voltaire obtained the privilege of selling his useless post of Gentleman-in-Ordinary, while he was allowed to retain its title. But privilege or no privilege, he did not stand well at Court. King Stanislas had written a work called the "Christian Philosopher": in which his good daughter, Queen Marie Leczinska, saw, disapprovingly, the freethinking influence of Voltaire. He still courted Madame de Pompadour; but no Pompadour ever yet imperilled her own position for any friend in the world.

Another king and court were, indeed, particularly anxious that Voltaire should return to them, but Voltaire refused Frederick's invitation firmly. He *was* really ill, as he said. But there was another reason. He had resolved not to leave Madame du Châtelet until the dark hour that was coming upon her had passed.

They fell, even in Paris, into their old habit of hard work. Émilie worked to kill thought, to stifle a dreadful foreboding which was with her always. She studied mathematics with Clairaut, who had once visited Cirey and was "one of the best geometricians in the universe." She shut herself up with him for hours and hours, resolving problems. She plunged into all kinds of gaiety. Her letters to Saint-Lambert are the letters of a very unhappy woman—tortured with jealousy and doubts, *exigeante*, fearful, unquiet. He was true to her—and cold. She tried to thaw his ice at the fire of her own passion. "I do not even love Newton," she wrote; "only you. But it is a point of honour with me to finish my work."

One day, she and Clairaut were so engrossed in their labours, that Voltaire, whose philosophy never could endure being kept waiting for meals, bounded up from the supper-table, ran upstairs "four steps at a time," found the door locked, and smashed it in with his foot in a rage. "Are you in league to kill me?" he cried as he went down again, followed by the too-zealous mathematicians, who had the grace to be ashamed of themselves. There was a very cross, silent supper *à trois*. The next morning Madame du Châtelet, feeling she owed her friend a reparation, suggested that she should take her morning coffee in his rooms. She did so, out of a priceless porcelain cup and saucer, which Voltaire, whose temper was still rather irritable, broke by a clumsy movement. Madame reproached him sharply. He retaliated. He grumbled a good deal at the exorbitant sum he had to pay to replace the *bric-à-brac*. Both he and Émilie were at the end of their tether. Yet they were good to each other. Émilie felt she owed Voltaire much for his pardon, and his reasonableness. And Voltaire never appears even to have thought that her faithlessness as his mistress could exonerate him from fidelity to her as his friend. He knew that she was unhappy. Compassion was in his nature. It is that quality which made him to the last hour of his life, in spite of his gibes and cynicisms, something more than commonly lovable.

In April, Stanislas had come up for a fortnight to the French Court. The unhappy Marquise had then been able to make arrangements for a future sojourn at Lunéville, of great importance to her: and of which she wrote, eagerly and feverishly, to Saint-Lambert.

Voltaire was now writing a play, "Nanine"—founded on Richardson's "Pamela." When it was produced on June 16, 1749, he had followed his old plan of filling the house as much as possible with his friends. There were a few spectators in the gallery, however, who would talk aloud. The nervous and sensitive author could by no means endure *that*. Up he got on to his feet. "Silence, you boors, silence!" he cried; and silent they were. Whenever he saw his own plays he found it impossible to contain himself. He not only trained the actors beforehand; but he must lead the laughter and the tears of the *parterre* at the performance. And, to be sure, if there is anyone who should know where a play is pathetic and where it is comic, it is the man who wrote it.

He and Émilie were in Paris from February until the end of June. Frederick repeated his invitation warmly. "You are not a *sage-femme* after all," he wrote to Voltaire scornfully, "and Madame will get on very well without you." Any sarcasm penetrated Voltaire's thin skin. But he replied gravely, "Not even Frederick the Great can now prevent me fulfilling a duty I believe to be indispensable. I am neither doctor nor nurse, but I am a friend and will not leave, even for your Majesty, a woman who may die in September."

He was true to his word. Late in June, while "Nanine" was still running, he and Madame du Châtelet went to Cirey at her urgent desire. When they were there, the most versatile of human creatures, the author of the "Pucelle" and the prim prologue for a girls' school, wrote at her request a eulogy of Saint-Louis, and a very good eulogy too, for an abbé who had to deliver one before the Academy and could by no means compose it himself.

It was at Émilie's desire, too, that they left Cirey, after only a fortnight's stay there—"these delightful rooms, books and liberty, to go and play at comets" at Lunéville. A few days at Commercy had preceded their stay at Lunéville, which they reached on July 21, 1749. It was there that Madame would find Saint-Lambert. It was there that the event which she dreaded more every day was to take place. Voltaire was not only sick to death of that wearisome mockery of astronomy with which Stanislas's little Court was still amusing itself, but was further annoyed by being very uncomfortable and ill-attended to in his rooms, in which he shut himself up as much as he could. He bore the discomfort—not at all in silence indeed—but he bore it.

A quarrel on the subject with Alliot, who was commissioner-general of the household of Stanislas, and a very economical commissioner too, burst out on August 29th, and Voltaire relieved his feelings in some *vif* little notes: one of which he addressed to the King himself, and besought his Majesty to remedy the defects in the meals, lighting, and firing supplied to his guest. Émilie, who had so urgent a reason for remaining at Lunéville, did her clever best to soothe her *ami*. He was soothed apparently.

Meanwhile the little Court went its usual way. Madame de Boufflers was her smiling, easy self—that *dame de volupté* "who," as she said in her epitaph, "for greater security, made her Paradise in this world." There were also the austerer, priestly influences trying to gain Stanislas. Poetry was a fashion among the guests and the courtiers, as also the inevitable play-acting. Saint-Lambert was still at work on that lengthy poem, "The Seasons." The summer was waning. Émilie plunged into every excess of gaiety, and every excess of work. She forgot that she was three-and-forty, not three-and-twenty. To forget everything—that was her aim—to have no time to think of past or future. His duties often called Saint-Lambert away to Nancy, and when he was absent the wretched woman endured torments of loneliness, helplessness, and foreboding. He reassured her when he was there. He was always so calm! As September drew near she sent for Mademoiselle du Thil from Paris, that ill-advised friend of hers, once her lady-companion, who on one memorable occasion had lent her money—to lose at the Queen's table. The *bonhomme* appeared on the scene. Voltaire was writing constant letters to his friends, anticipating the coming event gaily. Madame had a herculean constitution. All would be well! She was still constantly at her desk. She employed many hours in doing up her manuscripts and letters in parcels, and giving Longchamp directions as to the persons who were to receive them—if—if——. It was a point of honour with her, as she had said, to finish Newton. On August 30, 1749, she wrote her last letter to Saint-Lambert. "I am wretched to a degree which would frighten me if I believed in presentiments," she said.

On September 4th, Voltaire was writing delightedly to announce the birth of a little girl and the well-being of the mother. The infant was sent straight into the village to be nursed, and in the stress of the painful events which followed, died almost unnoticed. Madame du Châtelet progressed favourably. The little Court was in the highest spirits and spent most of its time in her room. On September 9th, the weather being exceedingly hot, the patient asked for an iced drink. It was given her and she was seized with convulsions.

Stanislas's physician hastened to her and for the moment she seemed better. The next day, September 10th, the convulsions returned: and two doctors from Nancy were called in. The Marquise again appeared better. In the evening Voltaire and the Marquis du Châtelet went down to supper with Madame de Boufflers—still not the least anticipating any danger. Longchamp, Saint-Lambert, and Mademoiselle du Thil were left in the room with the sick woman. Eight or ten minutes later, they heard a rattle in her throat. They did what they could. Mademoiselle hastened downstairs to tell Voltaire and the Marquis. The horrified supper-party hurried to the bedroom and a scene of dreadful confusion ensued. Madame du Châtelet was already quite unconscious. No one had time to think "of priest, of Jesuit, or of Sacrament." But the Marquise was past their help. "She knew none of the horrors of death," wrote Voltaire. "It was her friends who felt those."

His own anguish of spirit, when the dreadful truth was borne in upon him, rendered him beside himself. He and Saint-Lambert remained by the bed awhile. And then Voltaire, who had loved his mistress longer and better than his supplanter, dragged himself away, blind and dull with misery. He stumbled at the foot of the staircase without, and when Saint-Lambert, who had followed, would have helped him, Voltaire turned upon him with a bitter reproach. Its terms are so unrepeatable that the eighteenth century repeated them *ad nauseam*: and the twentieth may as well forget them if it can.

The brief remainder of that fatal day Voltaire spent in writing the bitter news to his friends.

If any proof be needed of the vehemence and sincerity of his feeling for the dead woman, those letters give it.

The next day Madame de Boufflers took from the Marquise's ring a portrait of Saint-Lambert and bade Longchamp give the ring to the Marquis du Châtelet. A little later Voltaire asked Longchamp for the ring in question. Thirteen years before, he had given Émilie his own portrait for it, with these lines,

Bavier 'graved this likeness for you.
Recognise it, and his art.
As for me, a greater Master
Has engraved you—on my heart.

His portrait had displaced one of the Duke of Richelieu's—and now his, in its turn, had made way for Saint-Lambert's.

Voltaire might well turn away saying that all women are alike; and trying to comfort himself with the antique and barren reflection that, after all, it was the way of the world.

Among Madame du Châtelet's effects was a large parcel of letters. She left a memorandum to beg her complaisant husband to burn them unread. "They can be of no use to him and have nothing to do with his affairs." He did so, on his brother's prudent advice. But Longchamp observed him make a very wry face at certain ones of which, being uppermost, he caught sight. The cautious valet rescued from the flames the whole of Voltaire's "Treatise on Metaphysics" and some letters, afterwards also burnt. Among the destroyed manuscripts were historical notes of Voltaire's, of which he deplores the loss in his preface to his "Essay on the Manners and Mind of Nations." It has been thought, but it is not certain, that the whole of his eight volumes of letters to Madame du Châtelet also perished in this conflagration. If they did not, a new Voltaire, a new world, rich in human interest, as no doubt in wit and philosophy, still remains to be discovered by some literary Columbus. At present, of all the letters he wrote to her, the human being with whom he was most intimate and who shared the deepest secrets of his soul and the highest aspirations of his genius, there can be found but one gay little note.

Madame du Châtelet was buried with all honour at Lunéville. Paris had already flayed her dead body with epigrams. She had not been too immoral for its taste. That was impossible. But she had been far too clever. One indignant person said that it was to be hoped the cause of her death would be the last of her airs. "To die in childbed at her age is to wish to make oneself peculiar: it is to pretend to do nothing like other people." Frederick the Great wrote her epitaph. "Here lies she who lost her life in giving birth to an unfortunate infant and a treatise on philosophy." Maupertuis and Marmontel spoke of her in terms of warm admiration. And Voltaire prefixed to her translation of Newton, published in 1754, at once the kindest and the truest estimate of her character yet made.

Madame du Châtelet was intellectually a very great woman. She had a mind essentially clear and logical—the mind of a clever man. She had not only a passion for learning rare in her sex, but for exactly the kind of learning in which her sex generally fails. She had, too, an intellectual fairness strangely unfeminine. She was long the champion of Leibnitz against Newton; and then, convinced of her mistake, acknowledged it, and made it the business of her life to prove it and to translate and explain Newton for the benefit of the French people. In an age busily idle, she was distinguished by a noble and untiring industry. In an age of scandal, she was charitable. For all those terrible fine clothes and that passion for high play and taking youthful parts in amateur theatricals, the laugh of the de Staals and the du Deffands at her expense turns against them now.

Still preserved among her letters are her "Reflections on Happiness." She plainly avows there that "rational self-indulgence" was her idea of it. Upon that rock her barque split. She chose pleasure before duty and gained a faithless Richelieu, fifteen jealous, feverish years with Voltaire, and a wretchedness from the cool love of the lofty Saint-Lambert, of which every letter she wrote him is proof.

Out of the picture painted by Loir there still looks down the shrewd, smiling face—reflective eyes, clever forehead, mobile lips, drooping nose—of the woman who was at once Voltaire's curse and blessing—who, if she had been all good might have been his blessing only, and if she had been all bad would have been curse alone. At the Revolution, some wretches broke open her coffin to steal the lead.

There had been gold in her heart once, but the world and the flesh had overlaid it in dross.

CHAPTER XX

PARIS, "ORESTE" AND "ROME SAUVÉE"

THE death of Madame du Châtelet marks one of the great epochs of Voltaire's life.

For a while he was utterly crushed and broken. He wrote of himself to his friends as the most wretched of men. He was alone, abandoned, dying. Everything that made life worth having had been taken from him— and he would live no longer.

There is not the slightest doubt that he felt passionately every word he wrote, and that he suffered wretchedly. It was characteristic of his nation and himself to give grief words. It was characteristic of himself to remember nothing but good of that "friend of twenty years" who had been taken from him. He recalled Cirey and the springtime of their passion, and forgot Lunéville and Saint-Lambert. He remembered the woman of a splendid intellect and a most just judgment: who was learned without affectation of learnedness; who had "the genius of Leibnitz, with feeling"; and the literary style of a Pascal or a Nicole. He remembered "her imperial sympathy" and not her "shrewish temper." "The *pompons* and the world are of her age, and her merit is above her age, her sex, and ours," he had written to the Abbé de Sade in 1733. He thought that now. Her brilliant and ready understanding of his philosophies, thoughts, aims, came back to him overwhelmingly. She had sinned against him in the flesh. Her mind had been his for ever.

It would indeed have been impossible but that a fifteen years' connection with such a woman as Madame du Châtelet should have had lifelong effects upon a character so impressionable as Voltaire's. Her relentless logic and her passion for hard facts did a work, and a good work, upon his vivid, sensitive, bantering, and versatile intelligence. She added correctness to a style which has no equal in the world for interest, gaiety, and satire. She forced him to sound the depths his matchless sparkle hid, to examine first principles, to advance step by step in argument with the stern accuracy of a Euclid.

From his acquaintance with her he formed his conviction of the mental equality of women with men. In his first grief at her loss, says Longchamp, he wrote of her:

The world has lost her! She, sublime, who, living
Loved pleasures, arts, the truth. The gods in giving
Her their soul and genius, kept but for their own
That immortality which is for gods alone.

Voltaire denied the verses. He was in no mood for making mediocre rhymes, he said. But in 1754 he certainly *did* write that noble eulogy of her which forms the preface to her translation and commentary of Newton, and never afterwards spoke of her—and he spoke of her often—but in terms of a reverent and a passionate admiration.

For the first few days his grief was overwhelming. King Stanislas was full of compassion, and three times a day mingled his tears with the mourner's.

Lunéville was now naturally horrible to Voltaire. He thought of going to stay with a certain priestly friend at the Abbey of Senones. Perhaps he would go back to England! He would have preferred the grave—or thought he would have preferred it—to either of these alternatives. About September 14, 1749, he ended by accompanying the Marquis du Châtelet to Cirey.

It is not difficult to realise that such a temperament as Voltaire's might derive a melancholy consolation from revisiting the scene "de ces heureux jours quand nous étions si malheureux!" It was for the last time. Every room in the house must have recalled her. Every corner in the garden had its own memory. There was that inscription over the summer-house—

A Book of Verses underneath the Bough ...
A Jug of Wine ... and Thou....

Here, they had been tender. There, they had quarrelled. It is not always the most perfectly loved who are the most bitterly mourned. The keenest grief is called remorse.

That good-natured old lady—Madame de Champbonin—came to Cirey to mingle her tears with Voltaire's.

Longchamp was kept busy packing books, furniture, *vertu*, to be transmitted to Paris. Voltaire and the Marquis settled their money affairs—much to the advantage and the satisfaction of that remarkable *bonhomme*. It was arranged that Voltaire should take the whole of the house in the Rue Traversière-Saint-Honoré in Paris—of which hitherto he had only rented a part from the Marquis. They parted at the end of a fortnight: "on the best of terms," though they never saw each other again. Voltaire also retained a friendship—for Saint-Lambert.

He left Cirey about September 25th, and proceeded by melancholy, slow stages to Paris. He stopped for a day or two at kindly Madame de Champbonin's; at Châlons, and at Rheims, and finally reached the capital.

If the unhappy man had been miserable at Cirey he was a thousand times more so in Paris. He was alone. The house was in a dreadful confusion with the du Châtelet furniture being moved out and the Voltaire furniture being moved in. Voltaire was as sick in body as in mind. He tried to work. He did work—with his loss and his wretchedness thrusting themselves on his consciousness all the time. Sometimes in the dead of night, half dreaming, he would get up and wander about the disordered rooms, and fancying he saw Madame du Châtelet, call to her. Once, in the dark and cold, he got up and walking a few steps was too weak to go farther and leant shivering, supported against a table—"yet reluctant to wake me," says Longchamp. The unhappy man stumbled into the next room presently, and against a great pile of books lying on the floor. Longchamp found him there at last, speechless and half frozen, in the chilly dawn of the October morning. All his letters of the month are miserable enough. A few chosen friends were admitted to see him after a while—Richelieu, the d'Argentals, nephew Mignot, and Marmontel. They would come and sit by his fire in the evenings and try to distract his thoughts with talk of the drama, which he had loved. They did their best to rouse him. He had certainly never needed rousing before. Frederick the Great wrote brusquely to Algarotti that this Voltaire talked about his grief so much he was sure to get over it quickly. Marmontel speaks of him as one moment weeping and the next laughing. Tears and laughter were both genuine enough, and to such a temperament, quite natural. There was something of the child in this Voltaire to the very last—the warm, quick emotions, so keenly felt, and so keenly felt to be eternal. That they were not eternal does not impair their sincerity in the least.

He was so lonely and miserable during that dismal autumn in Paris that one day, exactly upon the same principle as a sorrowing widower marries his cook and with much the same disastrous results, he asked his niece, Madame Denis, to come and live with him. She could not do so till Christmas. Before then, Longchamp declares he had helped his master's cure by showing him some letters in which Madame du Châtelet had spoken slightingly of him. There was certainly bark in that tonic if it was administered, which seems a little doubtful. How did Longchamp come by such letters?

There was a sharper bark in the fact that while Voltaire was weeping for a woman who had been false to him, that dreary old Crébillon was making fine headway at Court, had a pension from the false Pompadour, and all Paris applauding his bad verses.

It was his enemy, not his friends, who roused Voltaire at last. He woke as after a disturbed dream—at first dazed; shook himself; looked round; and began life afresh.

He was, to be sure, fifty-five years old. But fifty-five in a Voltaire, though it meant an old and decrepit body, meant a vigorous and eager mind, thirsting for life and action. He was a man of substance, and a man whose time was his own. He had no ties. He had a reputation not a little feared. He had the world before him yet, and a world only he could save. The fighting zest to turn "dead Catilina of Crébillon into 'Rome Sauvée' of Voltaire" was the spur that urged him back to "life and use and name and fame."

"Rome Sauvée" had been written in a fortnight in this August of 1749, at Lunéville. "The devil took possession of me, and said 'Avenge Cicero and France: wash out the shame of your country.'" Crébillon had made the subject a weariness and a foolishness in "Catilina." How could a Voltaire better avenge France and himself—particularly himself—than by turning the same subject into a masterpiece and a *furore*?

The pages of "Rome Sauvée" were still wet, when he took another dull play of Crébillon's—"Électre"—and turned it into "Oreste."

He called together a few friends at the house of his "angels," the d'Argentals, and a few of the chief actors and actresses, for a reading of "Rome Sauvée"; and read them "Oreste" instead. The truth was the actors were in want of a play to act immediately, at the end of a week. If M. de Voltaire could not give them one—well, there were other playwrights who could! M. de Voltaire considered that his "Rome Sauvée" would require at least six weeks' rehearsal; so he read "Oreste." He went in person to obtain the censor's permission for it, and did obtain it. "Oreste" appeared in public on January 12, 1750, to a house equally crowded with the author's friends and with the faction of Crébillon, headed by Piron as usual. Voltaire had written an opening speech in which, with a touching innocence, he disclaimed all idea of being the rival of Crébillon and "Électre." Half the house received the play with applause which had nothing to do with its merits, and the other half with hisses which had nothing to do with its defects. The impulsive author, who was in the d'Argentals' box and supposed to be *incognito*, forgot all about *that*, and leant over the side, crying, to encourage a burst of applause, "Courage, brave Athenians! This is pure Sophocles." For a few nights the vivid energy of Voltaire

FREDERICK THE GREAT

From an Engraving by Cunejo, after the Painting by Cunningham

kept the piece going. He was improving and correcting it the whole time. "Voltaire is a strange man," said Fontenelle. "He composes his pieces during their representation." He kept the actors and actresses to their work with a dreadful determination. He was always altering and adding to their parts. Mademoiselle Clairon received at least four notes from him, full of the handsomest compliments and of apologies for making so many changes; but making them all the same. Mademoiselle Desmares at last totally declined to have her lines changed any more, or even to receive Voltaire. So, never baffled, on a day when she was giving a dinner-party he sent her a *pâté* of partridges—and behold! each partridge had a little note in its beak containing emendations to her *rôle*.

If the story be true or not, the fact remains that Voltaire was a very *exigeant* manager. He had dedicated "Oreste" to the Duchesse du Maine; and took the pains to write her a very long letter to reproach her for not having attended the first performance. But in spite of all pains "Oreste" was hardly a success. It was exceedingly tragic and had no love interest. It was revived, after being withdrawn for a time, which the author spent in rewriting it, and on its revival it was acted nine times. Its last performance took place on February 7, 1750.

Voltaire's grief was certainly by this time on the high road to a cure. He had to fight so hard there was no time to sit at home, dull and wretched. He did not realise at first the strength of his enemy, Crébillon. The truth is, the Court was afraid of the Voltairian pen, and meant to stand by Crébillon and applaud his dulness to the echo, only because he was Voltaire's rival. The Comédie Française—good, loyal toady—must needs think like the King. When Voltaire realised the nature of the conflict, he resolved to fight the enemy by a new method of warfare.

At Christmas, 1749, Madame Denis had come to live with him. A plump widow of forty, not at all disinclined to try matrimony again, was Madame Denis by this time. She had attempted to be a playwright when Voltaire was at Lunéville; and her dear uncle had written with dreadful plainness of language to d'Argental that to write mediocre plays was the worst of careers for a man and "the height of degradation for a woman."

Not the less, he saw his niece as a rule through very kindly spectacles, and let his good nature so far warp his judgment as to make him think, or at any rate say, that if she was no playwright she was an actress of the highest ability. It is true that she was very fond of that amusement, having a vast appetite for pleasure of any kind. At the beginning of the year 1750 both she and her sister, Madame de Fontaine, were in the Rue Traversière; and Madame Denis was making a very goodnatured, easy-going hostess for her uncle's guests.

Voltaire had begun to go out and about again, too. It was at some very inferior amateur theatricals one night that he discovered an uncommonly good amateur actor: sent for him, and received the trembling and delighted youth the next morning. He embraced him, and thanked God for having created a person who could be moved, and moving, even in speaking such uncommonly bad verses. The pair drank chocolate together, mixed with coffee. Lekain—that was the youth's obscure name— announced his intention of joining the King's troupe. Voltaire offered to lend him ten thousand francs to start on his own account. Eventually, he received the young actor and his company into his house, and paid all his expenses for six months—"and since I have belonged to the stage I can prove that he has given me more than two thousand crowns," says the famous Lekain in his "Memoirs."

There was plenty of space in the house in the Rue Traversière now the Marquis du Châtelet no longer shared it. Voltaire turned the second floor into a theatre capable of holding a hundred and twenty persons, and in a very short time had there a playhouse, players, and plays which were the height of the mode and made Court and Comédie, with all their hopes pinned on poor old Crébillon of seventy-six, green with jealousy.

The Voltairian amateurs began with "Mahomet." There were only half a-dozen intimates, and a few of the servants, as spectators. Lekain was in the title *rôle*, and the heroine was played by a shy little girl of fifteen, who—thanks, partly at least, to the energetic coaching of M. de Voltaire—became a pleasing actress. Actors and audience all stayed to supper; and, after it, M. de Voltaire produced the parts of "Rome Sauvée," distributed them, and begged the actors to learn them as soon as they could. He coached and rehearsed his company himself. He superintended the scenery. He saw personally to the smallest details. Nothing was too much trouble if Voltaire could but outvie Crébillon, and "Rome Sauvée" "Catilina." The audacious playwright actually had the coolness to make Richelieu get him the loan of the gorgeous costumes in which "Catilina" had been played at the Comédie.

"Rome Sauvée" appeared on the boards of the theatre of the Rue Traversière before an audience composed almost exclusively of the greatest literary men of the age and country. Here were d'Alembert, the prince of mathematicians, and, to be, perpetual secretary of the Academy; Hénault, President of the Chambre des Enquêtes, and of at least two of the most famous salons in Paris; young Marmontel, rising in the world; Diderot, the encyclopædist of unclean lips; gallant and accommodating friend Richelieu; and schoolmaster d'Olivet. The performance was a brilliant success. "Rome Sauvée" was worthy of its author.

At a second representation that untiring person himself played the part of Cicero, and excited the enthusiasm of the audience.

The fame and ability of the troupe of the Rue Traversière reached the ears of Court and Comédie of course. They had players as good; but where were they to find such plays?

One of the aims of the performance of "Rome Sauvée" in the Rue Traversière was attained when on February 28th, "after long hesitations," that shifty Pompadour—a little bit to oblige Voltaire and chiefly because no other play so suitable could be found—had "Alzire" acted by a distinguished company of amateurs in the royal apartments.

Madame de Pompadour herself played "Alzire." The Queen was not present; nor her daughters; nor the Dauphin; nor the playwright himself.

But on March 6th "Alzire" was repeated: with Voltaire in the audience. The King was well pleased with "Alzire," but not with its author.

When the play was over he said loudly that he was astonished that the author of so good a play as "Alzire" could also have written "Oreste"; and the writer of "Oreste" had to swallow that royal rebuff in silence.

It was in this same March of the year 1750 that Voltaire was stung to fresh action by the attacks of Fréron, enemy and journalist, the tool of Boyer, and the acknowledged foe of all the light and knowledge in France. Fréron had written an unsuccessful poem on the victory of Fontenoy, and had never forgiven Voltaire for winning where he had failed. All the aggressions seem to have been on the part of Fréron. Voltaire was only aggravatingly successful and good-humoured. Fréron had not found it an easy task to goad him to anger. But he had done it at last. "That worm from the carcase of Desfontaines" was Voltaire's vigorous epithet for him now. And when in this March there was question of this "worm" being made Parisian correspondent to Frederick the Great—"to send him the new books and new follies of our country"—Voltaire flung on to paper a warm remonstrance to his King against any such appointment; and then recommended in writing to Darget, Frederick's friend, the Abbé Raynal for the post instead. Raynal was not appointed; but then neither was Fréron. For many years, Fréron was to Voltaire the wasp who stung, and stung, and stung again—with a sting not deadly indeed, but infinitely annoying and malicious.

The death of Madame du Châtelet had, not unnaturally, been the signal for King Frederick to renew his pressing invitations to Voltaire to visit him. In the November of 1749 this most persistent of monarchs and of men had written to reproach his friend for making excuses for not coming. They must be excuses now! And Voltaire was so apt in them! In December the King wrote again. In the January of 1750, more persistently still. In February—"well, I will not press an immediate visit: but I will hold you bound to come when the weather is better and Flora has beautified this climate of mine."

It was all very flattering. Voltaire felt it to be so. He was in the not uncommon position of the man who likes to be asked but does not want to go. There were many reasons against his going. He had just settled into his house in Paris. Niece Denis had come to look after it for him. All his friends lived hard by. The feverish events of the past year had made rest and quiet peculiarly desirable. His health made them almost necessary. Travelling was exceedingly expensive. But if these were all good reasons for remaining in the Rue Traversière-Saint-Honoré, there were better ones for leaving it.

Running now through Paris were those gay satirical *contes* of his which ridiculed every vice of the old *régime* and made King, Court, and confessor supremely ridiculous. The graceless old Duchesse du Maine, sitting up in bed at three o'clock in the morning, had laughed to hear her order burlesqued in "Zadig." But all her class had not her saving sense of humour. The satire was too keen not to cut—the portraits too lifelike to be unrecognised.

If he had stopped at "Zadig," at "Barbouc," at "Scarmentado," there was no reason in the world why Voltaire should be a popular member of the society he had chastised with such whips. And when he chastised it with the scorpions of that deadly pamphlet of brief paragraphs called the "Voice of the Sage and the People," there was very small wonder that he should once more find Paris getting too hot to hold him.

The "Voice of the Sage and the People" is the voice of the man who could sting with bald truths as well as lively satires. It hacked at superstition and the Mirepoix with a hatchet that always went to the root of the tree. "A government in which it is permitted a certain class of men to say, 'Let those pay taxes who work: we should not pay because we are idle'—is no better than a government of Hottentots." "A woman who nurses a couple of children and spins does more for the State than all convents have ever done." "The Church ought to contribute to the expenses of the nation in proportion to its revenues.... The body set apart to teach justice should begin by giving an example of it." Forty years later these truths were enforced by the blood of the Revolution.

Could Voltaire have thought even in 1750 that they were politic truths to utter in a city where he had just bought a house and was much minded to settle down and be at peace? It is to his infinite and lifelong credit that he seldom cared whether a truth were politic or not. The moment he saw it to be truth he must utter it in scorn of consequence.

Even "Rome Sauvée" and "Oreste" could not shield a man responsible for the paternity of such writing as this, nor the uncertain smile of a Pompadour save him from its consequences. Well, he had better go! He had always wished to travel in Italy. He would take Potsdam and Berlin *en route*. His visit there could be brief. On May 8, 1750, he wrote to Frederick saying that, though he was rich, "even very rich for a man of letters," his house in Paris and the du Châtelet affairs had made him so short of money that he must beg the royal permission for Mettra, an exchange dealer of Berlin, to advance him four thousand crowns for the expenses of his proposed journey. The delighted King wrote back on May 24th enclosing a letter of exchange for sixteen thousand francs. He was willing to pay, and to pay highly, for a man who was "a whole Academy of *belles-lettres* in himself." Voltaire was gratified of course. But he wrote dismally that he was more in need of a doctor than a king, and on June 9th spoke of himself to that King, in verse which was meant to be gay and sounds a little dreary, as "your very aged Danaë, who leaves his little home for your star-spangled dwelling-place, of which his years make him unworthy." A little home is so much more comfortable than a star-spangled dwelling-place, after all! Voltaire in fact needed a spur to make him undertake that long-talked-of visit with alacrity. And he had it.

Among the many other poor and generally worthless literary hangers-on, whom the most generous literary genius of any age had commissioned his agent Moussinot to assist with gifts of money, was one Baculard d'Arnaud. A conceited young writer of very fluent rhymes and three, dull, unacted tragedies, was d'Arnaud.

But he was needy and a man of letters. That was enough for Voltaire. He procured him the post of Paris correspondent to King Frederick for which Raynal and Fréron had competed unsuccessfully, and on April 25, 1750, young d'Arnaud arrived in Berlin, with letters and verses from Voltaire to the King. A personable young man was Baculard. A gay head, very easily turned. Was it to pique Voltaire that Frederick gave Voltaire's *protégé* a pension of five thousand francs yearly, and compliments much above his merits? If so, that aim failed at first. On May 19th, Voltaire wrote to young d'Arnaud the kindest of friendly letters. On May 31st, d'Arnaud wrote to Voltaire saying that he was waiting for him "as a child awaits his father." The father was not hurrying himself, it appears.

On June 22d, Voltaire and his company of clever amateurs were at Sceaux, and played "Rome Sauvée" to the Duchesse du Maine and her court, Voltaire taking Cicero, and Lekain, Lentulus Sura.

On June 23d, Collé, writer of memoirs, meets Theriot, that idle gossip of a Theriot, who tells Collé a most *piquant*, incredible story about the great Frederick and little Baculard d'Arnaud. Then friend Marmontel, also writer of memoirs (and of memoirs written, it must be remembered, many years after the events they chronicle), tells how he and Theriot went together to see Voltaire one morning and found him writing in bed as usual. Theriot played the part of candid friend. "I have news to tell you," says he. "Well, what is it?" asks the writer in bed. "D'Arnaud has arrived at Potsdam and the King has received him with open arms." "With open arms?" says Voltaire. "And that d'Arnaud has written him an Epistle." "Dull and bombastic, I suppose?" "On the contrary, very good, and so good the King has replied by another Epistle!" "What! the King of Prussia an Epistle to d'Arnaud?" says the person in bed, roused a little. "Someone has been gaming you, Theriot." But Theriot produces copies of the two Epistles from his pockets. Voltaire stretches out a lean hand, seizes and reads them. "What rubbish! What platitudes!" says he, reading d'Arnaud's verses to Frederick. But Frederick had not thought so. Then he comes to Frederick's verses to d'Arnaud, and reads "for a moment in silence and with an air of pity."

D'Arnaud, by your genius fair
You will warm our bleak North air;
And the music of your lyre
Kindle quick my muse's fire—

and so on; and so on. Not much in *that*, to be sure. But when he came to the last verse—

The French Apollo 'gins to die
And his term of fame is nigh.
Come then, you, and take his place,
Rise and shine: outgrace his grace.
The sunset of a gorgeous day
A finer sunrise brings alway—

he sprang out of bed as if he had been stung and danced about the room in a fury. "I will go! I will go!" he cried, "if only to teach him to know mankind!"

That "sunset" had accomplished Frederick's purpose. Perhaps he had guessed it would. He was certainly too astute to really think that a d'Arnaud's twinkle would show at all in a sky where the sun of a Voltaire's genius beamed and burnt.

"To sit high is to be lied about." Many of Marmontel's "facts" are conspicuously inaccurate. But if this story be true—and having regard to Voltaire's character it sounds at least as if it had truth in it—no doubt remains that he was quite clever enough to disguise his anger. A gay little versified reproach to Frederick dated June 26, 1750—that was all. The very reproach was written from Compiègne, whither the Gentleman-in-Ordinary had gone to beg the permission of Louis XV. to visit Frederick II. Frederick was to pay all expenses of the journey. Voltaire would put the *cachet* of genius on the King's prose and verse which just missing that, just missed everything. He left his house in the Rue Saint-Honoré in the joint care of Longchamp and Madame Denis, giving the latter a handsome income for its maintenance. He apologised to his friends for leaving them.

And on June 26th the "domestique" of the King, as he called himself, was at Compiègne, as has been seen, taking leave of his master. The farewell was hardly a success. Louis wanted the dangerous Voltaire gone, and was offended at his going. What room was there in France for the author of those shameless *contes* and that loud passionate "Voice of the Sage and the People"? None. That "Voice" had been the sensation of the year among the orthodox. A hundred "Voices" had been raised to answer it—in parody, in refutation, in agreement. Even Madame de Pompadour was offended—this clever Voltaire had whispered in her ear too apt and impudent a couplet. True, when he took farewell of her, she smiled on him a little and sent her kind regards to King Frederick. When Voltaire gave the message, that astute boor of a monarch curtly observed, "I do not know her"—and the artful Voltaire wrote the Pompadour some very pretty verses to tell her that he had the honour to give Venus the thanks of Achilles!

As for his French Majesty, when Voltaire begged permission to visit the Prussian, *he* turned his back on the greatest man in his kingdom and said indifferently, "You can go when you like."

Even now, a word would have detained Voltaire. But that word was far from being spoken. After he was gone, there arose at Court one day some question of the royal treatment of this child of genius. "After all," said Louis, "I have treated him as well as Louis XIV. treated Racine and Boileau.... It is not my fault if he aspires to sup with a king;" and proceeded to add that if he had been too good-natured to talent "*all that*"—which included d'Alembert, Fontenelle, Maupertuis, Montesquieu, Prévost—"would have dined or supped with me." Comment is needless.

Voltaire left France with Boyer keeping the conscience of King and Dauphin; and keeping from the people light, knowledge, and advancement. The *ânes* of Mirepoix were the sworn enemies, not of Voltaire alone, but of all his friends, of all the intellect of France. Fréron, that "worm from the carcase of Desfontaines," was their tongue and pen. They were busy now refusing the Sacrament to dying Jansenists who could not produce a certificate to show they had accepted the Bull Unigenitus. Voltaire could not resist a parting shaft at them. Two little pamphlets, gently satirical and both directed against the clergy, were the final bolts which shut the gates of Paris upon him for eight-and-twenty years. In the belief that he was leaving it for a very few months at the most, he set out from Compiègne on a day towards the end of June; but precisely what day is not certain. On July 2d he was at Cleves. On July 10, 1750, he arrived at the palace of King Frederick the Great, at Potsdam.

CHAPTER XXI

GLAMOUR

CLEAN, quiet Potsdam stands on the river Havel and is sixteen miles from Berlin. In 1745, the great Frederick had begun to build there the little, white, one-storied palace called Sans-Souci. He desired to be buried at the foot of a statue of Flora on one of its terraces—"when I am there I shall be *sans souci.*"

The French tastes of the royal architect are everywhere evident. Sans-Souci is a kind of miniature Versailles. It stands on a hill. Formal terraces slope to a formal park. Here are statues, and a fountain—all the artificial and no natural beauties. Within the palace may still be seen, almost unaltered, the rooms where the great King lived and died—his chair, his clock, his portrait. In the picture gallery he walked and talked with Voltaire. And in the west wing is the room occupied by that favoured guest, and before him by the Maréchal de Saxe.

Voltaire arrived then at Sans-Souci on July 10th, after a journey which cost thrifty Frederick 600*l*., and during which the traveller had visited the famous battlefields of Fontenoy, Raucoux, and Lawfeld.

It was ten years since Voltaire had escaped from his Madame du Châtelet to first see in the flesh the hero of his dreams. It was fourteen years since the pair had first exchanged adoring letters. Their friendship was of European fame. They were the two greatest men of their age. Half the world watched their meeting—and awaited results.

The pair fell metaphorically, and perhaps literally too, into each other's arms. This day had been so long delayed. The host had worked for it so persistently, doggedly, and consistently! The visitor had so warmly wanted it when it had been wholly impossible—and when it was inevitable had done his best to recall that early enthusiasm.

The enthusiasm may well have come back to him now. It did come back. Instead of sulky Louis's cold shoulder, was *"my* Frederick the Great," flattery, honour, and consideration. Potsdam was gay and busy with preparations for a splendid *fête* to be held in Berlin in August. But it forgot gaiety and business alike to do honour to Voltaire.

Saxe's apartments left nothing to be desired. The royal stables were at the guest's disposal. There were music and conversation. On July 24th, the guest sketched Potsdam for d'Argental—"one hundred and fifty thousand soldiers ... opera, comedy, philosophy, poetry, grandeur and graces, grenadiers and muses, trumpets and violins, the suppers of Plato, society and liberty—who would believe it? Yet it is very true."

And on August 1st to Thibouville, "To find all the charms of society in a king who has won five battles; to be in the midst of drums and to hear the lyre of Apollo; ... to pass one's days half in *fêtes*, half in the delights of a quiet and occupied life"—here was glamour indeed.

And then on a day before August 14th, and before Voltaire had been five weeks at Potsdam, Frederick, who perfectly understood the policy of striking while the iron is hot, offered his dearest friend, if he would but stay with him for ever, the post of Chamberlain, a Royal Order, twenty thousand francs per annum, and niece Denis a yearly pension of four thousand francs if she would come and keep her uncle's house in Berlin.

The offer was so sudden and so brilliant! That impetuosity which had made all his shrewdness of no avail a hundred times before, was still at once Voltaire's charm and stumbling-block. He forgot "Anti-Machiavelli" and d'Arnaud. Everything that makes life delightful surrounded him at the moment. Behind him lay the Bastille of his youth, flight to Holland, hiding at Cirey, the "English Letters" burnt by the hangman, the fierce persecution for that babbling trifle the "Mondain," the Pompadour's false smile, the kingly scowl, Crébillon, Desfontaines, Boyer. At its best his country had given him grudging and empty honours. If he had won fame and fortune, it had been in spite of Courtly malice and for ever at the point of the sword. He was sick to the soul of gagging and injustice. It was not the least part of his bitterness against his Louis, that he had cringed to and flattered such a creature—in vain. He was fifty-six years old. The fifty-six years had been one long persecution. He had still the daring spirit of a boy. He had still such deeds to do that the gods would make him immortal, if need be, to do them. A new heaven and a new earth lay before him. He accepted the offer—and began the world again.

There is still preserved his letter to Madame Denis, dated August 14, 1750, wherein he tells her of Frederick's bounty. It has the spontaneous enthusiasm of youth. "You *must* come, niece Louise," it says in effect. "Think of the magnificence of the offer! And then—Berlin has such operas!" (shrewd Uncle Voltaire!) He had hardly been given time to breathe, much less to think, since he arrived at Potsdam. Pleasure had succeeded to pleasure and flattery to flattery. For three hours at a time he would criticise his royal host's writings. Crafty Frederick gave up whole days to *belles-lettres*. There was everything to intoxicate the excitable brain of this French child of genius. The great Frederick was cool enough. *He* had no glamour. Does it make the great Voltaire less lovable that he saw things all *en rose or en noir*, was led dangerous lengths by his emotions, and for all that rasping cynicism could be a dreamer of dreams, a visionary, and a sentimentalist?

Practical niece Denis, with her vulgar, shrewd instincts, wrote back and said that no man could be the friend of a king. Toady or slave—but friend, never. And Voltaire, carried to Berlin in the whirl of the Court for the Carrousel, wrote to d'Argental begging him to persuade her, and asking d'Argental's forgiveness for the course upon which he was resolved.

On August 23d, Frederick, having read Madame Denis's letter, condescended to write with his own royal hand from his private apartment to beg Voltaire to stay with him. What more flattering? Yet even now Voltaire was not quite sure he was wise. He took such immense pains to prove himself so. But he had decided irrevocably—and flung the responsibility of that choice on destiny at last. "I abandon myself to my fate," he wrote on August 28th, "and throw myself head foremost into that abyss."

The fall was soft enough at first.

The Carrousel had begun about August 8th.

Berlin was crowded with noble and distinguished guests from all lands. Frederick rode about the city on horseback, personally supervising the preparations for the *fête*. Red of face, portly of figure, eight-and-thirty years old, and much addicted to snuff—one of his English guests thus described him, not ungraphically. With his five great battles behind him and such a future before him as might well surpass the wildest flights of fancy, he was a great man to call "friend."

And in Berlin, among the notables of all Europe convened to celebrate a Carrousel which should make Louis XIV.'s famous *fête* of the Tuileries dull and obscure, the great Voltaire was only less honoured than the great Frederick himself. He may be forgiven for thinking he had chosen well.

Among the guests was the Margravine of Bayreuth, Frederick's sister, and very much Voltaire's friend. In 1743, he had spent ten days with her at Bayreuth. French plays were acted—but, strangely enough, no plays by M. Arouet de Voltaire. He was a spectator on the occasion. He had said truly of himself that he loved good verses so much that he loved other people's—"which is a great deal for a poet." On August 17th the French players acted the "Mauvais Riche" of his vain little rival, Baculard d'Arnaud. But Voltaire was in the mood when he was ready to be pleased with anything. On August 26th was played the "Iphigénie" of Racine, and on the 27th the "Médecin Malgré Lui."

"The language least talked at Court was German," said Voltaire. "Our tongue and literature have made more conquests than Charlemagne." He wrote delightedly of the King's brother and sister, Henry and Amelia, as the most charming reciters of French verse. His spectacles were rose-coloured indeed.

August 25th was the crowning point of the *fête*, one of those splendid revelries which were the boast of the old *régime*—and died with it. The Carrousel of the Sun King had been glorious. The Berlin Carrousel far outvied it. It was, too, one of the golden nights of Voltaire's life, and lives in history for that reason.

The courtyard of the great palace in Berlin had been turned into an amphitheatre. Three thousand soldiers under arms lined the approaches to the place. Forty-six thousand lights illuminated it. Tier above tier, brilliantly apparelled, blazing with jewels, the nobility of all lands, sat the spectators. Among them were Lord Melton and Jonas Hanway—"a chiel amang ye, takin' notes"—and Collini, a young Florentine. Save only the royal box, every seat was occupied. The hush of expectation was on the audience. And then, on a sudden, gorgeous in dress, as that period alone knew how to be gorgeous, "among a group of great lords," a lean figure moved towards the King's enclosure. For an instant the house was silent. And then there swept through it a murmur like the wind among the trees—"Voltaire!" "Voltaire!"

It was a moment worth life and worth death. A stranger and foreigner raised by genius alone to that mighty eminence of fame to which genius, a proud line of royal ancestors, and five great battles had raised Frederick the King! Every eye was upon this son of a notary, this Paris *bourgeois*, Voltaire. Collini noticed the delight in the piercing eyes, and a certain modesty of demeanour very pleasing. Voltaire *had* chosen rightly after all! There could have been no doubt in his impressionable mind at that magnificent minute.

Then in the arena the tournament began. Voltaire described it as fairyland, the *fête* of Chinese lanterns, and the Carrousel of Louis the Magnificent, all in one. The competitors in the fray were royal, and a princess—Venus and the apple—gave away the prizes. After the tournament was a supper, and after the supper a ball. Voltaire did not go to that. He was surfeited with delight—*las* with adulation. He had already written of his great host that he scratched with one hand and caressed, with the other. To-night it had been all caresses. And would surely be caresses for ever! "When a clever man commits a folly, it is not a small one."

The plan as now formed was that Voltaire, with Prussia as home, should travel in Italy in this autumn of 1750 and so gratify a desire of years, and that in the spring of 1751 Madame Denis should join him in Berlin. In the meantime, Prussia was heaven.

On September 12th, he wrote again to his niece earnestly trying to persuade her of its charms. And would have succeeded very likely if she had not had particular reasons of her own at the time for preferring Paris.

Even at Berlin and during a Carrousel Voltaire had entire liberty. Or at least as much liberty as fame and distinctions allow any man. His days were his own. In the morning he studied "to the sound of the drum." In the evening queens asked him to supper, he said, and were not offended when he denied them. He spent hours correcting Frederick's works, and observed gallantly "Cæsar supra grammaticam" to excuse the noble pupil's defects in that department. He gave up the kingly dinners presently—there were too many generals and princes, forsooth, for this M. de Voltaire.

On September 14th, "Rome Sauvée" was played in the rooms of the Princess Amelia at Berlin and on a stage especially erected by its author, who took the part of Cicero as he had done at Sceaux and in the Rue Traversière. He also trained the company and lost his temper with them, exactly as he had lost it with his troupe in Paris. When the tumult of *fêtes* was past the Court went back to Potsdam. Life was a thousand times more delightful than ever. "I have my whole time to myself, I am crossed in nothing." "I find a port after thirty years of storm. I find the protection of a king, the conversation of a philosopher, the charms of an agreeable man united in one who for sixteen years consoled me in misfortune and sheltered me from my enemies.... If one can be certain of anything it is of the character of the King of Prussia." "I have the audacity to think that nature has made me for him. I have found so singular a likeness between his tastes and mine that I have forgotten he is the ruler of half Germany and the other half trembles at his name...." "The conqueror of Austria loves *belles-lettres*, which I love with all my heart." "My marriage is accomplished then. Will it be happy? I do not know. I cannot help myself saying 'Yes.' One had to finish by marriage after coquetting for so many years."

Even the d'Arnaud affair "does not prevent the King of Prussia from being the most amiable and remarkable of men." Nay, d'Arnaud himself was "bon diable" after all. And the Prussian climate so rigorous? Not a bit of it. What are a few rays of sunshine more or less to make us give ourselves such airs? The glamour was complete.

All the letters from which these extracts are taken were written less than four months after Voltaire's arrival in Prussia, and when the contrast between his treatment there and the treatment meted to him in France, was fresh and glaring. All the letters were written to persons who only half approved or wholly disapproved, of what Lord Chesterfield called Voltaire's "emigration."

His friends, enemies, and niece were all united in fearing and disliking it. In Paris a caricature was being sold in the street: "Voltaire the famous Prussian! Look at him with his great bear skin bonnet to keep out the cold! Six sous for Voltaire the famous Prussian!"

At the French Court the offended attitude of King Louis had not changed. King Frederick wrote very civilly to borrow the great Voltaire from his brother of France. And his brother of France, says d'Argenson, replied he should be very glad to make the loan, and turning to his courtiers, added that there would be one fool more at the Court of the King of Prussia "and one fool less at mine."

On October 27th, Voltaire wrote to tell the d'Argentals that his post of Historiographer had been taken away from him; though Madame de Pompadour had told him, in a little note, that King Louis had had the goodness to allow him to keep an old pension of two thousand livres.

"I do not know why the King should deprive me of the Historiographership and let me retain the title of his Gentleman-in-Ordinary," Voltaire wrote rather disgustedly to Madame Denis on October 28th. But after all, what did it matter? In return for the Historiographership he had the post of Chamberlain to the King of Prussia, that Royal Prussian Order, and that yearly Prussian pension.

He had exchanged strife for peace; slights for honour; and Louis XV. for Frederick the Great. How *could* he be wrong?

It is always far harder to guess the mind of Frederick on any given occasion than the mind of Voltaire. Frederick at least was sure that Voltaire was worth keeping even at a heavy price to be "the glory of one's own Court and the envy of the world." Gay, witty, and easy—a past master of the art of conversation—and with an impulsive susceptibility to the impressions of the moment wholly fascinating—the King was not wrong in placing a high estimate on the companionship of Voltaire. The King knew genius when he saw it. He meant to keep it now he had it. So, after a day spent in the ardours of government and military duty, at five he became the verse-maker, the man of ease and letters, the polished Frenchman instead of the great German soldier.

At seven, he had his evening concert, small, select, delightful. "If you think the King loves music," said someone, "you are wrong. He loves only the flute and only his own flute." (To be sure, such an egoism has been known as a love of music both before and since.) No women were admitted. Frederick the Great's dislike of that sex is historical, and was always consistent and unmoved. And then, at nine o'clock began those immortal suppers of the gods. Voltaire was of course of them from the earliest days of his stay in Prussia.

Half Europe watched them from afar. Much more than half the genius of Europe would have paid a high price to have been of them. They generally consisted of about ten persons. The only language spoken was French, and more than half the *habitués* were of that favoured nation. The other half included two Scotchmen, one Prussian, and that great Prussian-Frenchman, Frederick himself. Baculard d'Arnaud, though living at Potsdam and under the immediate eye and favour of the King, was not invited. The meal was severely sober and frugal. The King rose at twelve, as clear-headed as he had sat down. Sometimes his guests prolonged that feast of reason far into the morning. The servants who waited on them contracted, it is said, swellings in the legs from too much standing. Occasionally, Frederick was not of the party at all. He supped with Colonel Balby instead. "What is the King doing this evening?" it was asked of Voltaire. "Il balbutie" was the ready answer.

Great among the *convives* of the supper was Maupertuis, the pompous and touchy geometrician, the President of the Berlin Academy, and once the friend and the tutor of Madame du Châtelet. He had stayed at Cirey in 1739. Voltaire had never liked anything about him but his talents. Surly, solemn, and unsociable, he was already antipathetic in every attribute of his character to the brilliant Frenchman.

Another visitor of Cirey, was also of the suppers—Algarotti, the amiable Italian, the agreeable man of the world, the "Swan of Padua," whose "Newtonianism for Ladies" Émilie's Newton had so completely eclipsed.

Here too was La Mettrie, a freethinking French doctor of medicine, with his ribald rollicking stories and his bold atheism, "the most frank and the most foolish of men." He had become notorious as the author of a book called "The Man Machine" in which he had gaily proved, to his own satisfaction, the material nature of the soul.

Then there was "the brave Major Chasot," an excellent type of a gallant eighteenth-century French gentleman. He had saved the King's life at the battle of Mollwitz, but owed the coveted *entrée* to the suppers less to that heroism than to the facts that he was French and flute-player.

Here too was d'Argens, a profligate French marquis, whom Frederick loved for "his wit, his learning, and his person"; and who was at once credulous and sceptical, freethinking and superstitious.

The other Frenchman was Darget, reader, confidant, and secretary to the royal host, very discreet, reserved, and judicious, a man to be trusted. It did not take a subtle Voltaire long to recognise the value of the friendship of this friend of the King. Frederick often wrote to Voltaire through Darget, and Voltaire replied to Darget in terms of tenderness and admiration.

Then there was the French ambassador of Irish birth—Lord Tyrconnel—famous for giving heavy dinners, whose *rôle* "was to be always at table," and who had the brusque honest speech of British forbears. Lady Tyrconnel had receptions in Berlin and presently acted in Voltaire's company of noble amateurs.

The Scotchmen were the two brothers George and James Keith, Jacobites and gentlemen, "not only accomplished men, but nobles and warriors," the only friends of the King whom his bitter tongue spared. Nay more, George Keith was, says Macaulay, "the only human being whom Frederick ever really loved." Earl Marischal of Scotland, he had fought with his brave young brother for that forlorn hope, the cause of the Stuarts, in 1715. They had long wandered on the Continent, and at last found a home in Potsdam with Frederick.

The only Prussian of the suppers was Baron Pollnitz, and he was cosmopolitan, had many times visited Paris, and had a rich store of travellers' tales. Clever and well born, he was extravagant and miserably poor; and since he could not afford to lose Frederick's favour, was the butt of his royal master's cruellest jokes—the wretched scapegoat who could not escape and whose very helplessness goaded Frederick's bitter wit to new effort.

Of such an assembly as this, versatile and brilliant though it was, Voltaire and the King were the natural leaders.

Sulzer, who had listened to it, declared that it was better to hear the conversation of Voltaire, Algarotti, and d'Argens than to read the most interesting and best written book in the world. The talk was on "morals, history, philosophy." It was the boast of the talkers that they had no prejudices. They explored all subjects as one explores a newly discovered country, knowing neither whether it be sterile or fertile, rich or poor—eager to learn, sharp-set to see—and without fear of consequence. No topic was debarred them. The only intoxication was of ideas. "One thinks boldly, one is free," said Voltaire. "Wit, reason, and science" abounded. Frederick stimulated the conversation by always taking one side of a question when his guests took the other. His own tongue was so caustic that it has been said that it is difficult to conceive how "anything short of hunger should have induced men to bear the misery of being the associates of the great King." But that is to take a very one-sided view of his character. If one hand could scratch, the other could caress. If on one side of his nature he was a brutal jester, an untamed barbarian, on the other he was a thinker and a philosopher with all the light, the ease, the charm, and the cultivation of France.

Besides, there was one man at the suppers whom the King feared. Frederick's satire was a saw; but Voltaire's was a knife: and the clumsier instrument dreaded the finer. A needy Pollnitz or a patient Darget might bear the royal insolence in silence. But it did not yet dare to encounter that "most terrible of all the intellectual weapons ever wielded by man, the mockery of Voltaire." Saw and knife seem both, for the while, to have been quietly put away.

A Voltaire with his splendid capacity for living in the present moment may sometimes have forgotten the very existence of the King's weapon. "No cloud," "far less a storm," marred the harmony of those suppers.

Between them, operas, receptions, correcting the royal compositions, and spending long days with his own, the September and October of this autumn of 1750 passed away. Now and again a courtly Voltaire went to pay his devoirs at the Court of the Queen Mother and read her cantos of the "Pucelle," which he assured the good Protestant lady was nothing in the world but a satire on the Church of Rome. Nor did he neglect to attend the dull and frugal receptions of Frederick's unhappy wife, the pretty and accomplished Elizabeth Christina. Hanbury Williams was in Berlin in September as English envoy, and made Voltaire complimentary verses on "Rome Sauvée." The exile continued to write long letters to his friends, speaking of his speedy return to France and of the thousand delights of life in his present "paradise of philosophers."

He *had* chosen rightly after all! All would be well. All *was* well. But—

—

CHAPTER XXII

THE RIFT WITHIN THE LUTE

ON November 6, 1750, at Potsdam, and after he had been in Prussia rather less than three months, Uncle Voltaire took his versatile pen in hand and wrote to Louise Denis a famous letter—the letter of Buts. Prussia had fulfilled all his hopes, nay, had exceeded them, but—. "The King's suppers are delightful, but—." "My life is at once free and occupied, but—." "Operas, comedies, carousals, suppers at Sans-Souci, military manœuvres, concerts, study, readings, but—." "Berlin splendid with its gracious queens and charming princesses, but—." "But, my dear, a very fine frost has set in."

That letter might serve not only as a description of life at Potsdam, but of all human life. A most delightful world, but—. The truth was that Voltaire had begun to feel the grip of Frederick's iron hand. On November 17th he wrote again to his niece and told her a little, ugly story. Secretary Darget had lost his wife. And the great Frederick wrote to him a letter of sympathy, "very touching, pathetic, and even Christian"; and the same day made a shameful epigram upon the dead woman. "It does not bear thinking about," wrote Voltaire. Whose turn might it not be next? "We are here ... like monks in an abbey," he added. "God grant the abbot stops at making game of us!"

There was another source of trouble going on at the same time. Who could have expected that a Voltaire and a d'Arnaud could share a kingdom in peace? "Do you not know," Voltaire said once, "that when there are two Frenchmen in a foreign court or country one of them must die?" He had forgiven that "rising sun" affair; but he had not forgotten it. This d'Arnaud, too, was the most absurd, conceited, ungrateful simpleton imaginable.

Voltaire had not only lent him money. He had done much more than that. He had tried to make his *protégé* fit for some good post—to make him improve, for instance, a shameful handwriting. He had introduced him to Helvétius. He is "as my son," "he has merit," "he is poor and virtuous." In return Baculard had paid his master some fine compliments; and in 1739 had written a preface for a new edition of M. de Voltaire's works, in which the flattery was so fulsome that M. de Voltaire himself cut out, or toned down, some of the most eulogistic passages.

Then came Baculard's invitation to Prussia. He gave himself the finest insolent airs. He pretended to be surprised at the smallness of the handsome pension Frederick had given him. If he was not of the suppers, he had every other honour. He was received by the princes, and play-acted with them. The story goes that being given a part in "Mariamne" too small for his conceit, he did it as badly as he could; and Voltaire lost his temper with him and cried out "You are not clever enough for the *rôle*; you do not even know how to speak the words!" But Baculard's hot head was turned. The princes, and that negligible quantity, Frederick's wife, had taken him up and were playing him off against Frederick's Voltaire. Then the misguided young man was positively foolish enough to ally himself with Voltaire's enemy, Fréron, and to attack the wickedest, cleverest foe that ever man had. Baculard wrote Fréron a letter to be shown about Paris, in which he not only denied the authorship of that flattering preface written in 1739, but added that Voltaire himself had inserted therein "horrible things" against France.

And of a sudden, Voltaire flung off the encumbering mantle of comfortable prosperity he had worn for so short a time and was at his foolish bombastical minor poet, tooth and nail.

On November 14, 1750, he wrote to tell his Angel of the affair. Then he wrote to King Frederick and insisted on Frederick taking his part—cool Frederick who would fain have conciliated both parties. "I cannot meet the man, Sire! He is going to-day to Berlin in Prince Henry's carriage, why should he not stop there to study, to attend the Academy—whatever you like! I do not mention the word *renvoi*, but that is what I mean. And I leave all to the goodness and prudence of your Majesty."

On November 24th a very triumphant uncle wrote to his niece that "the rising sun has gone to bed." D'Arnaud in fact had been ordered to leave Berlin in twenty-four hours and—the King had forgotten to pay the expenses of his journey. Voltaire was victorious. Most of his friends and all his enemies both in Paris and Berlin had been watching that quarrel with a scrutiny seemingly out of all proportion to its importance. D'Arnaud had gone into obscurity for ever. But the easily elated Voltaire was not long elated this time somehow. Here again was food for thought. If one favourite was lost as suddenly as a bright exhalation in the evening and no man saw him more, why not another? "And when he falls, he falls like Lucifer, never to hope again."

The victory left Arouet strangely pensive.

D'Arnaud had not only wrought mischief, it appears, but left a train of it behind him. His patron, Prince Henry, had long desired a copy of that firebrand, that stormy petrel, the "Pucelle." Just before his dismissal, the obliging d'Arnaud had helped the Prince to corrupt Voltaire's secretary, Tinois; and paid him to copy some cantos of the poem for the Prince, by night. Tinois was a young man whom Voltaire had taken into his service when he was at Rheims in October, 1749, for no better reason than that he had written rather a pretty verse after reading "Rome Sauvée." On January 3, 1751, Voltaire wrote to Madame Denis that he had dismissed Tinois, and that Prince Henry had sworn to keep the "Pucelle" secret and safe. But if "put not your trust in princes" had long been the burden of Madame du Châtelet's and of his niece's warnings, it had sunk into Voltaire's soul now. He was not at ease.

The successor of the faithless Tinois gave him further trouble.

The new secretary's name was Richier. He had a friend called Lessing who was to be the great German writer, but who was now obscure, poor, and unknown, two-and-twenty years of age, and trying to make a livelihood in Berlin by copying and translating. Richier introduced him to the great Voltaire; and the good-natured Voltaire gave Lessing work and became very much his friend. Then the foolish Richier lends Lessing a volume of Voltaire's "Century of Louis XIV."—the work and pride of so many years—and now almost ready for the press. Lessing leaves Berlin—with the volume. Considering the fact that the upright character of Lessing was not then a notorious thing, it is not wonderful that Voltaire was alarmed. Suppose Lessing should publish the volume on his own account, and in its imperfect state! Voltaire wrote Lessing a very courteous letter asking for its return. And Lessing sent back the manuscript with some very ill-timed jokes. Lessing, it must be remembered, was nobody, and young; and Voltaire was past middle life and the most famous literary man of his period. The offender never forgave Voltaire for having suspected that he would make dishonourable use of his manuscript. But, after all, Voltaire seems to have been more sinned against than sinning.

There were, too, going on at the same time various mean domestic disagreeables—literally storms in teacups. Formey, writer of memoirs, but not always of reliable memoirs, records how Voltaire complained to the King of the bad sugar, coffee, tea, and chocolate served to him; how the King apologised, and altered nothing; and how angry the great Voltaire demeaned himself to be over these trifles. Did he remember that he had written hotly to Alliot, King Stanislas's chamberlain at Lunéville, in 1749, just before the death of Madame du Châtelet, on a like subject? "I can assure you at Berlin I am not obliged to beg for bread, wine, and candles." And now! The truth is best summed up by the most thorough and minute of all Voltaire's biographers, Desnoiresterres. "He used, and thought he was entitled to use largely, a hospitality which he had only accepted after many invitations and prayers." He asked his friends to dine with him on "the King's roast" without any fear of exceeding his rights as a guest. Formey adds that he appropriated the candle-ends which were the servants' perquisites; and records that, through meanness, when the Court was in mourning he appeared in a borrowed black suit and returned it to its portly owner, cut to the dimensions of the lean Voltairian figure. The story seems to be that lie which is part of the truth. True or false, it is not worth examination. No doubtful anecdotes are needed to prove that Voltaire was the sensitive philosopher whose delicate body made him singularly unphilosophic in trifles; or that in money affairs he was at once exceedingly generous and prudently thrifty.

But he had to do now with a money affair in which his prudence, alas! was only conspicuous by its absence.

In November of 1750 had begun his too-famous affair with Hirsch, Jew usurer of Berlin.

He had been first brought into relations with the shifty Israelite on November 9th. On the day following he played "Cicero" in his "Rome Sauvée"—a blaze of jewels, borrowed from the Hirsch father and son. On November 23d he received Hirsch *fils* (Hirsch *fils* transacted all the business, Hirsch *père* being well stricken in years) in his room at Potsdam quite close to the unconscious Frederick; and there, forsooth, M. de Voltaire, with the aid of M. Hirsch, plans to do on the quiet a little illegal stock-jobbing. Several years before, the Elector of Saxony had established a bank in Dresden. It issued such an immense number of notes that "the currency of Saxony was inflated: for a time a note of one hundred thalers was worth but fifty." Frederick, when the Silesian war made him master of Dresden, stipulated that *Prussian* subjects holding these notes should be paid in full. This went on for three years; but in 1748, Frederick, yielding to the remonstrances of the Elector, forbade his subjects to purchase these notes or to bring them into the Prussian kingdom at all. Such notes it was, which on this fatal November 23, 1750, a cunning M. de Voltaire commissioned Hirsch to purchase, and then to sell again in Saxony, receiving of course their full nominal value. To effect this purchase, Voltaire gave Hirsch negotiable bills worth 2,500*l.*

One of these bills was a draft on Voltaire's Paris banker for 1,600*l.*, "not payable for some weeks." Bill two was a draft for 650*l.* by old father Hirsch—or Hirschell, as Voltaire called him—on Voltaire himself. In exchange for these two bills, Voltaire held the borrowed jewels.

There is nothing more remarkable about Voltaire, considered in his character of a literary man, than the fact that he was always speculating, and except on this occasion, hardly ever unsuccessfully. But a Court is no place for a secret. By November 29th some rumour of his guest's little affair had reached Frederick. On December 1st that procrastinating Hirsch had not even started on his journey to Dresden. Hirsch is pretty cool about the whole business, it appears, and not inclined to hurry himself. Voltaire's dancing, agitated impatience spurs him off at last. From December 1st to 12th he is in Dresden—delaying, making excuses and cashing never a Saxon note. (All he *did* do was to raise money on the Paris draft for 1,600*l.* Voltaire had given him, and trade on his own account.) Voltaire entirely loses his temper, stops the payment of that draft on his Paris banker, and summons Hirsch home at once. He comes. Still pretty cool is M. Hirsch. Rather injured, if anything, in fact. It is not pleasant, M. de Voltaire, "to have sold a bill of exchange which the drawer protested;" and that is what happened to me about that Paris draft of yours! I have the paper now—entirely worthless of course. But M. Hirsch takes care to keep it very securely all the same. For a Hirsch to have such a document signed Arouet de Voltaire may be rather an awkward thing for the King's visitor; and so, a profitable one for a Hirsch, as giving him a hold over his client. He has, or fancies he has, the whip hand of M. de Voltaire, who cannot make himself very disagreeable, thinks Hirsch, since the whole affair is illegal and under the rose.

On December 16th, Voltaire, come to Berlin with King and Court for the Christmas carnival, receives Hirsch. The two draw up a document, "a complete settlement." Hirsch gives back Voltaire his unused drafts "and expressly engages to return the bill upon Paris." Voltaire, in exchange, is to buy

MOREAU DE MAUPERTUIS

From an Engraving after a Painting by Tourmere

some of the Hirsch jewels he holds, and to give Hirsch the expenses of his journey and "compensation" for his time and trouble. The dangerous affair is at an end. M. de Voltaire supposes he has done with it for ever. He and Hirsch part satisfied. Then Hirsch discovers that Voltaire considers 9*l.* compensation sufficient. The Jew does not. Voltaire consults another money-lender, Ephraim, the enemy of the house of Hirsch, who tells him the jewels he holds are not worth what Hirsch said they were. "Then you must have changed them," says Hirsch. That is the declaration of war.

Until the Christmas Day of that 1750, daily stormy meetings between Hirsch and Voltaire took place in Voltaire's room in the palace. Voltaire was convinced the Jew meant to extract money from him by means of the Paris bill: and return that bill Hirsch would not. No one who remembers the character of a youthful and middle-aged Arouet will be in the least surprised to hear that an Arouet of fifty-six chased the Jew round the room at last, shook his fist in his face, pushed him out of the door in a rage, and banged it after him like a passionate child.

The "final total explosion" took place at a meeting at "brave Major Chasot's" lodging when the *vif* infuriated Voltaire sprang at Hirsch's throat and sent him sprawling.

The affair had been noised abroad. If Hirsch still thought—and he did still think—that it would be so singularly unpleasant and impolitic for Voltaire to have the transaction made public and that he would submit to any indignity rather than to that catastrophe, he had mistaken his man. He had reckoned without the marvellous imprudence, mettle, and vivacity of the enemy of Rohan and Desfontaines and Boyer. Here was he who never made a compromise, and in his whole life never once bought peace by submitting to be cheated.

The fuse had been put to the gunpowder: and on December 30th came a shock which startled Europe.

The great Voltaire, the guest of the King of Prussia, *versus* Messrs. Hirsch & Son, Jew money-lenders of Berlin! Here was a *cause célèbre* with a vengeance!

Voltaire was quite as active and excited as he had been in the affair Desfontaines. He engaged the best counsel he could get. On January 1, 1751, he obtained a warrant to throw old Hirsch into prison for wrongly detaining papers belonging to M. de Voltaire. Hirsch was released therefrom in a few days on bail—and the lawsuit began.

To unravel the truth from that complex tissue of lies has been the effort of all Frederick's and of all Voltaire's biographers. None have wholly succeeded. The case is infinitely intricate. The Hirsches lied very freely, and were inartistic enough not always to adhere to the same lie. It has been seen that though Voltaire preferred truth and honesty (which is already something) *he* was not above lying—when there was necessity. *His* case, in brief, was, "I *lent* Hirsch money to help his business at Dresden in fur and jewels." (This was the pretext on which the Jew had undertaken the journey.) "Some diamonds I took from him in part payment are not worth what he said they were; and he illegally retains my draft on my Paris banker, and has not kept to the agreement he signed."

Hirsch's case was, "M. de Voltaire *sent* me to Dresden to deal in Saxon notes for him. The diamonds I gave him *were* worth what I said. He has changed them for diamonds of less value. The agreement he produces, signed by me, was altered by him, to his advantage, after I had signed it."

Documents were produced on both sides. That famous paper of agreement which Hirsch had signed and of which he now accused Voltaire of altering the wording, after he, Hirsch, had signed it, has been reproduced in facsimile.

It proves nothing. The document *has* been palpably altered. But who is to say if those illiterate and careless alterations were made before, or after, Hirsch had signed it? If after, then Voltaire was the most blundering and ignorant of forgers. But those early chafing months in a notary's office must have given a shrewd head such as his a knowledge of law and legal documents which would have made him a better swindler than this forgery proves him. Voltaire's cleverness, not his virtue, exonerates him from that crime.

The man's mind was on the rack while the case lasted. His fury against the Hirsches blinded him to the folly and indignity of having been drawn into such a suit at all. "I was piqued. I was mad to prove I had been cheated," he wrote penitently afterwards. Wretched old Hirsch died during the progress of the trial—of a broken heart, said his son pathetically. King Frederick preserved a very ominous silence indeed. His guest's health was miserable. He had a fever—of the soul—and Berlin and Paris were watching, as at a play.

On February 18, 1751, the case was decided in favour of Voltaire. Hirsch was condemned on every count with which Voltaire had charged him. The purpose for which Voltaire had advanced the money was not, said the court shrewdly, the court's business. But all the waiting and watching world knew what that purpose had been, and so did the waiting and watching Frederick. Hirsch was to restore the Paris exchange bill. The diamonds were to be valued "by experienced jewellers on their oaths." Voltaire's seizure of the person of Hirsch was declared just and right. As to the famous agreement, Hirsch was fined ten thalers for denying he had signed it; and Voltaire was to make an affidavit that he had not changed its wording.

It is said that he asked upon what book he was to take his oath, and when he was answered, "The Bible," cried, "What, on that book written in such bad Latin! Now if it were only Homer or Virgil!" If the story is true, it was but a flash of the old mocking spirit. Voltaire was in no mood for jesting. He had won, it is true. But his victory was a sorry one.

It was such a sorry one that the unlucky victor had perforce to go about congratulating himself loudly thereon, if only to make other people congratulate him too. Even now, the settlement was not complete.

The jewels had to be valued. That would take time. Voltaire was worn body and soul by a case which had kept him at a fever heat of passion from December 1, 1750, until this February 18, 1751. And in a deadly silence the King sat aloof in a rage. Voltaire's friends implored him to end an affair which had been degrading to everyone concerned in it. And at last he did come to some sort of compromise with the determined Hirsch. A few minor points appear to have been still undecided as late as the December of 1751.

Throughout a whole three months Frederick had uttered never a word.

His attitude towards this case was at once natural and justifiable. It was a poor, mean, despicable business at the best. Kingly hands, of all hands in the world, if they touch pitch are defiled therewith. Frederick shut ears and eyes to the shriekings and the cheatings of this pair of low money-lenders—and his guest. At first, indeed, his fury with that guest had got the better of him. On January 12, 1751, the King of France announced at his *levée* that the King of Prussia had dismissed Voltaire. Angry Frederick *had* turned to Darget, saying, "Write and tell him that he is to be out of my dominions in four-and-twenty hours." Well for Voltaire that he had cultivated the friendship of the discreet secretary! Darget pleaded for him. "Wait till the case is tried, Sire! If he is guilty, then will be time enough to send him away." Frederick agreed; but during January and February they never met. Voltaire was for the most part in Berlin, and the King at Potsdam, but sometimes they were in the same palace divided by a few planks of wood—and the Jew lawsuit.

The versatility of Voltaire had hardly ever been better exemplified than by the fact that during this very December and January when rage and anxiety were tearing him to pieces, and he was breathlessly waiting the judgment of his case, he was play-acting with the princesses in Berlin exactly as if nothing were happening, and as if he were in full favour with the King. On January 5th, "Zaire" was acted and Voltaire played Lusignan as he had done in happier days at Madame de Fontaine Martel's: the Princess Amelia was Zaire; the Princes Henry and Frederick also took parts; and the Queen was enchanted. "The Death of Cæsar" was also acted, and other plays. Throughout the winter too Voltaire gave audiences to great persons; and received marshals, princes, statesmen, and nobles.

Yet, through it all, the man was appealing passionately to the King by Darget. "Throw yourself at the King's feet and obtain for me that I may retire to the Marquisat" (a country house near Potsdam). "My soul is dead and my body dying."

When he was not drawing tears from the spectators in that moving part of the old father, tears of rage and bitterness were very near his own eyes. "It is not sufficient to be courageous," he said himself; "one must have distractions." He had need of them if any man had.

On January 22d, the King summed up the case to the Margravine of Bayreuth as "the affair of a rascal who is trying to cheat a sharper.... The suit is in the hands of justice, and in a few days we shall know who is the greater scoundrel of the two." On January 30th, Voltaire himself wrote to the Margravine with a very wry face: "Brother Voltaire is here in disgrace. He has had a dog of lawsuit with a Jew, and, according to the law of the Old Testament, he will have to pay dearly for having been robbed."

Then Voltaire wrote direct to the King and pleaded and argued with him personally. Only receive me into favour and I will anger you no more! And on February 2d Frederick wrote again to the Margravine, softened not at all; and *she* wrote on February 18th to her friend Voltaire: "Apollo at law with a Jew! Fie then! that's abominable." Then Voltaire appealed again to Frederick. "All the genius of our modern Solomon could not make me feel my fault more than my heart feels it."

Finally Solomon *did* give Apollo that Marquisat he had asked for; and Voltaire's "quarrel with the Old Testament," as he called it, being settled, the King wrote to him icily on February 24th from Potsdam: "D'Arnaud had done nothing. It was because of you he had to go.... You have had the most detestable affair in the world with a Jew. It has made a frightful scandal.... If you can make up your mind to live like a philosopher I shall be glad to see you." If not ... "you may as well stay in Berlin."

On February 27th, Voltaire replied, volubly explaining, regretting, apologising. He owned himself in the wrong with a candour and humility rather engaging.

"I have committed a great fault. I ask pardon of your Majesty's philosophy and goodness.... Do with me what you will." His health was suffering dreadfully at the time. "The winter kills me"—especially the winter of our discontent. Even hard work at "Louis XIV." could not make him forget that. He pleaded very hard indeed.

On February 28th, Frederick accorded a cold permission to him to come to Potsdam if he would.

By March 11th he was established at the Marquisat with, as he said, "pills and pill-boxes" and the fifth canto of a poem by King Frederick entitled "The Art of War."

The King no doubt had missed Voltaire's conversation. He had missed too his brilliant, delightful, inconsequent, unreliable personality. The old subtle charm drew the two men together—in spite of themselves, and the imprudence of their connection. They were sure to quarrel! But, like many a lover and his mistress, they were dying to see each other, if it were only to discover fresh reasons for disagreement. "I have committed a folly," wrote Voltaire to Madame Denis, "but I am not a fool." He was something so infinitely removed from a fool that his living touch of genius alone could raise, if anything could raise, Frederick's poems from a dead mediocrity and the dreadful limbo of dulness. "To the Prussians" and "The Art of War" were very important factors in the Treaty of Peace.

Very early in his stay in Prussia the indefatigable Voltaire had begun learning a little of the despised German language—of which, says Morley, he never knew more "than was needed to curse a postilion." To correct the King's works, he needed none. By October 28, 1750, he was busy overseeing the second edition of Frederick's history of his country, written in French and entitled "Memoirs of the House of Brandenburg," and trying to modify the royal author's round abuse of his own grandfather. But Frederick only loved truth the better if it burnt. "After all," said Voltaire with a shrug of his lean shoulders, "he is your grandfather, not mine; do as you like with him."

The critic was not generally so accommodating, however. He was not a critic *pour rire*. He gave himself an enormous amount of work. He ran a thousand risks of offending his royal pupil. He cavilled at this, queried that, suggested endlessly. The manuscript of "Aux Prussiens" is still extant, with remarks in Voltaire's little handwriting all over it. His minuteness and care were extraordinary. It would have been at least a hundred times easier for him to have praised lavishly and indifferently. Any author will accept flattery—on trust. It is only for blame and disagreement that the critic must give clear reason and proof; and chapter and verse for his alterations and amendments. If Voltaire had been a toady and had not loved his art better than all monarchs, he would have wasted much less of his dearly prized time in "rounding off a little the works of the King of Prussia." His "official fidelity, frankness, and rigorous strictness" are a high testimony to his character. "The Art of War" is a much more ambitious work than "To the Prussians" and was subjected to the same relentless criticism. The eager critic wanted, he said, to enable his royal master to do without his help. Sometimes Frederick would leave a wrong word purposely. "We must give him the pleasure of finding some fault," he wrote to Darget. But on the whole he accepted not only verbal emendations, but alterations of his very opinions with a generosity and fairness which prove the true royalty of the royal soul. This quick, thorough, breathless, aggravating schoolmaster would be satisfied with nothing less than his pupil's best. If a man could be made a great writer without being born one, Frederick the Great's literary efforts would not be mouldering in the libraries to-day.

The reconciliation between the teacher and the taught seems for a while to have been complete. The worry of the Hirsch affair had made Voltaire really ill. But Frederick was all goodness to the sufferer. He had a room kept for his use at Sans-Souci. Formey records how one day he went to the Marquisat to call upon Voltaire and found him in bed. "What is the matter with you?" "Four mortal diseases," answers the invalid. "Your eyes look nice and bright though," says the ill-advised Formey, meaning consolation. "And don't you know," shouts the sick man with all his strength, "that in scurvy people *die* with their eyes inflamed?" It must be conceded that though Voltaire never allowed his ailments to stop his work, he liked to have full credit for them, and took care never to be ill without impressing upon his friends that he was dying. All the same, he began to attend those gay, frugal, philosophical little suppers once more—and was once more permitted to dispense with the ponderous dinners. Yet once more too, except for that ill-health, the life here was all he dreamed it. Frederick wrote him little friendly notes—"I have just given birth to six twins.... The 'Henriade' is engaged to be their godmother. Come to the father's room at six o'clock this evening"—the six twins being six cantos of "The Art of War." And Voltaire would answer, "Sire, you have the cramp, and so have I; you love solitude, and so do I." The pair were again as lovers, in fact; writing nothings, only for the sake of writing something. The winter was past, and the summer blossoming again.

The trip to Italy, postponed from the autumn of 1750, had been arranged to take place in this May of 1751, but was finally abandoned altogether; partly on account of the Inquisition, but partly also, it may be surmised, because Frederick having found Voltaire again, was in no mind to lose him.

Through the summer host and guest were hard at work with their respective secretaries. Both knew at least one of the receipts for happiness. Prussia *was* heaven. Only—only—there was a delightful earth called Paris where d'Argental was doing his vigorous best to get the authorities to permit the performance of "Mahomet"—an earth from which he wrote on August 6th of this 1751, one last, long, pleading appeal to Voltaire to return, while he could yet return, with honour. Madame Denis, resolved not to join her uncle in Prussia, added her entreaties. The foolish woman, who had a *tendresse* for handsome young Baculard d'Arnaud in the days when he was her uncle's *protégé* in Paris, was now coquetting with a certain Marquis de Ximenès, or Chimenès, as Voltaire called him, and less minded than ever to leave the capital.

The wild La Mettrie, too, was for ever calling on Voltaire—volubly homesick for Paris himself. Voltaire would have gone, perhaps; but in August his "Louis XIV." was actually in the press of Berlin, he had a hundred prospective engagements, and—he thought Frederick was his friend.

It was at the end of this same month of August that La Mettrie, calling on Voltaire, swore to him that he had heard Frederick say of him: "I shall want him at the most another year: one squeezes the orange and throws away the rind." Voltaire would not believe the story. La Mettrie redoubled his oaths. Voltaire wrote the scene to Madame Denis on September 2d in his quick, vivid fashion. "Do you believe it? Ought I to believe it ... after sixteen years of goodness ... when I am sacrificing all for him?... I shall be justly condemned for having yielded to so many caresses.... What shall I do? Ignore what La Mettrie has told me, tell nobody but you, forget it, wait?" If Voltaire thought he really could do these things, he could have known little of his own character. He did try to forget. But that rind of an orange! It rankled, it rankled. *Could* Frederick have said it? Impossible! But he had written the "Anti-Machiavelli" and spilled blood in war like water; condoled piously with Darget and made an epigram on his wife; caressed d'Arnaud and ruined him. It made one thoughtful.

On September 30th "Mahomet" was successfully performed in Paris. That was another voice urging Voltaire to return.

"The orange rind haunts my dreams," he wrote to Madame Denis again, on October 29th. "I try not to believe it.... We go to sup with the King and are gay enough sometimes. The man who fell from the top of a steeple and finding the falling through the air soft, said, 'Good, provided it lasts,' is not a little as I am."

On November 11th, the tale-bearer, La Mettrie, died from having consumed a whole *pâté* (composed of eagle and pheasant, lard, pork and ginger!) at Lord Tyrconnel's house. He would make mischief no more. But, then, he could not undo the mischief he had made. "I should like to have asked La Mettrie when he was dying," Voltaire wrote sombrely to Madame

Denis on Christmas Eve, "about that rind of an orange. That good soul, about to appear before God, would not have dared to lie. There is a great appearance that he spoke the truth.... The King told me yesterday ... that he would give me a province to have me near him. *That* does not look like the rind of an orange."

Between doubting and hoping, mistrusting, fearing he knew not what, in health always wretched ("my distempers ... make me utterly unfit for kings"), homesick, uneasy, longing at once to go away and to be persuaded to stay, Voltaire spent his second winter—in heaven. Hirsch had made the first something very like pandemonium. But there was life, interest, excitement in a fight. The dull anxiety, the ugly care to wake up to in the dead nights and the dark mornings—these were worse a thousand times. Well for Voltaire that now, even more than ever, he had to comfort him that best relief from all the fears, doubts, problems, and presentiments of life—hard work.

CHAPTER XXIII

THE QUARREL WITH MAUPERTUIS

IN December, 1751, there appeared in Berlin, in two volumes octavo and anonymously, "The Century of Louis XIV." by Voltaire.

The earliest idea of it was conceived by a wild Arouet of twenty listening to personal recollections of the Sun King from the old Marquis de Saint-Ange at Fontainebleau.

Arouet had heard with his own ears the strange tales told in Paris at that monarch's death. In 1719, when he was five-and-twenty and falling in brief love with the exquisite Maréchale de Villars, her husband recounted him more anecdotes of that magnificent and miserable age. To write it had been a relief from Émilie's shrewish tongue and inconvenient emotions, at Cirey. It was Voltaire's "chief employment" in that first lonely summer there, before she joined him. He worked hard at it in Brussels. He found in it consolation for his mistress's infidelity: and for her death. It involved him in an enormous amount of reading, and unparalleled labours in research. Since he came to Prussia, he hardly wrote a letter without alluding to it. He found in it balm for the wounds inflicted by a d'Arnaud, a Hirsch, and a king. As it drew nearer completion, his interest and excitement in it deepened daily. "I am absorbed in Louis XIV." "I shall be the Historiographer of France in spite of envy." Before the author had finished reading the proofs, a pirated edition of his work appeared in Holland and elsewhere. There was the usual scramble among the publishers for the profits. Voltaire appealed to Frederick; and wrote to Falkener, in English, trying, through him, to get a correct edition circulated in England. His efforts were astonishingly fruitless. An author had then not only no right to the moneys his brain had earned, but was not even allowed the privilege of correcting the work of that brain: and the more famous the author the worse his chances in both respects. No anonymity could conceal a Voltaire.

Boyer prohibited "The Century of Louis XIV." in France, and its circulation in that country was enormous. The first authorised edition printed in Berlin was sold out in a few days. Eight new editions appeared in eight months. In those times, when to be educated was a rich man's privilege and not a pauper's right, such a success was unique. That it was deserved is proved by the fact that this is still the most famous history of that reign.

Voltaire had written it, as he always wrote, as a free man. But this time he had written, as he did not always write, as a free man who has no desire to offend the prejudices of the slave-dealers. He himself loved the glitter of that Golden Age: its burning and shining lights of literary genius, and the glory it gave to France. So far as he could be true and tactful, he was tactful. He did not run amok at abuses with that "strident laugh" which has been said to fill the eighteenth century, as he had run amok at them in that "Voice of the Sage and the People"—and in a hundred of his writings a thousand times before. When he wrote the latter part of the book in Prussia, it was in his mind always that he might some day—one day—soon—who could tell?—be not sorry to come back to France. If he could still tell the truth and not offend the authorities! If any man could have done it, that man was Voltaire. There is no writer in the world who so well knows, if he chooses, how to put blame as if it were praise, to turn censure into a dainty compliment, and to trick out harsh realities in a charming dress.

But now, as too often before, his reputation damned him in advance. Besides, did he not give the place of, and the witnesses to, that secret marriage of Louis XIV. and Madame de Maintenon? How imprudent! Some patriots "raised a noble clamour" against him for having praised Marlborough and Eugene, and a great party of churchmen condemned him for having gently laughed at Jansenism and Molinism.

The book was full of reason; that in itself was enough. "My book is prohibited among my dear countrymen," wrote Voltaire to Falkener on January 27, 1752, "because I have spoken the truth." And again, to President Hénault, "I have tried to raise a monument to truth and my country, and I hope they will not take the stones of the edifice to stone me." The style, too, of the book, that style which has kept it alive, fresh, and vigorous for a hundred and fifty years, made it offensive in the nostrils of the solemn and approved historians of the period who held that an author cannot be learned without being dull, and if he is readable can be by no means worth reading. "Louis XIV." is a bright example of Voltaire's own aphorism, "A serious book should not be too seriously written." Though he had spent years of his life, and endless trouble and activity in gathering his information, he wrote with the same spontaneous life and vigour as he wrote the *contes* he read to the Duchesse du Maine and her gay court; with not less inspiration than he flung on to paper in the morning the "Henriade" he had dreamt at night on his prison bed in the Bastille. In a word, "I tried to move my readers, even in history." His own countrymen now understand him better; but it is to be feared many of his foreign students still suspect the fidelity of his facts because he puts them so gracefully, and fear that a sense of humour and a sparkling style are incompatible with sound judgment and deep learning, and that if an historian is really clever he must prove it by being excessively dull.

The success of the book must have exceeded its author's eager hopes. It delighted England. D'Alembert, in his lodging over the glazier's shop, and all the nobility of intellect in Paris, rejoiced in it. What matter if the Court frowned? Pirated editions appeared in Edinburgh, as well as London, Prussia, and Holland. The publishers were scrambling wildly for the proceeds. The author did at last get something—and shrugged his shoulders and was not ill-satisfied. After all, he had a better success than a monetary one. Lord Chesterfield called the book "the history of the human mind written by a man of genius." Condorcet spoke of it as "the only readable history of the age." Renault declared its author "le plus bel esprit" of the century. "Louis XIV." excites men's curiosity at every page. If the author had been deprived of the Historiographership of France, he *was* the Historiographer not the less.

"Louis XIV.," and correcting Frederick's works, were not all of Voltaire's literary work in Prussia. He was always composing *bagatelles* and compliments for the two Queens and the Princesses. He wrote Frederick— in the room next to him—gay verses as well as many letters: and was also busy with his famous philosophical poem called "Natural Law," not published till 1756. He began here his great "Philosophical Dictionary"; and was further fanning the flame, by innumerable suggestions, of that light- bringer of the eighteenth century, that torch in a darkness which could be felt, the "Encyclopædia" of Diderot and d'Alembert. Its preface appeared in 1750 and its first volume in 1751. Voltaire called it "the dictionary of the universe"—"the bureau of human learning," and should have found in its splendid audacity—a quality so dear to his soul—an antidote for many afflictions. Perhaps he did. It was never because he had idle hands that Satan found them mischief still to do. But he was homesick. He was in that pitiable state of body which makes the mind irritable and despondent. Paris had been stormy enough. But here one lived always over a volcano. That orange rind rankled still. If one royal hand caressed, there was the other that might scratch at any moment. The never-sleeping anxiety affected Voltaire's *vif* temper, just as anxiety affects the temper of lesser persons. He was in a mood when he was sure to be offended by someone. This time the person was Maupertuis.

Born in 1698, in Saint-Malo, Maupertuis was four years younger than Voltaire, and in his precocious intelligence, ardent imagination, and unquenchable thirst for knowledge, not unlike him. But there the likeness stopped. Maupertuis studied in Paris, and then became that rare anomaly, a *savant*-soldier. He was also elected a member of the Academy of Sciences; and in 1728 spent six months in England, where he was made a member of the Royal Society and imbibed Newtonian opinions. In 1740, after an Arctic expedition which roused much public interest, he was made by Frederick President of the Berlin Academy, that he might form it "as you alone can form it." Maupertuis married one of the Queen-Mother's maids of honour, and lived in a fine house in Berlin close to the Royal Park, which his zoological tastes led him to turn into a kind of menagerie. Precise, pompous, and positive; boring society with his worrying exactness upon trifles even more than society bored him; inordinately vain, and with a sensitive temper made yet more inflammable by brandy and self-love; acutely conscious of his dignity, and without any sense of humour, the ex-tutor of Madame du Châtelet was the sort of person with whom, sooner or later, her lover was sure to disagree. Added to these facts, Voltaire's pension from King Frederick exceeded that of Maupertuis by two thousand crowns; and while Maupertuis was socially dull, at the King's suppers Voltaire's conversation was even more brilliant than his writings.

On October 28, 1750, the naturalist Buffon had written to a friend, "Between ourselves, Voltaire and Maupertuis are not made to live in the same room."

The first tiff between the uncongenial pair took place, in point of fact, in that very October of 1750, the autumn after Voltaire's arrival in Prussia. There was a vacant chair in the Berlin Academy. Maupertuis wished it given to d'Argens—Voltaire, further seeing, to that Raynal, already his friend, afterwards the famous philosopher and historian. Voltaire won, with the help of Frederick; and Maupertuis was left surly and jealous. In the Hirsch affair Voltaire asked his help, and Maupertuis refused it. Maupertuis read "Louis XIV." and compared it to "the gambols of a child"—heavy Maupertuis who could not have gambolled to save his soul.

Then, at the end of the year 1751, a certain book entitled "Mes Pensées," by a young French adventurer called La Beaumelle, made some little stir in Berlin. The "Thoughts" were desultory, unequal, and very ill put together. D'Argenson wrote of the book that half of it was excellent, a quarter mediocre, and the other quarter bad. From the excellent part he quoted a shrewd axiom—"Happy the State where the king has no mistress, provided that he also has no confessor!" Two Berlin readers, at the least, included in the bad quarter this extraordinary sentence: "There have been greater poets than Voltaire, but never one so well paid.... The King of Prussia overwhelms men of letters with kindness for precisely the same reasons that a little German prince overwhelms with kindness a jester or a buffoon." The passage was the joke of one of the royal suppers. But if Frederick and Voltaire laughed at it, it was not the less a joke that left a taste in the mouth. Then up comes La Beaumelle to Berlin. On November 1, 1751, he calls on the great Voltaire; and Voltaire, though he asks him to dinner and wastes on him four hours of his time, treats him with a civil chilliness which surprises La Beaumelle, who appears to have no idea that Voltaire has seen those "Pensées"; and attributes his cold manner to an indigestion.

La Beaumelle is much with Lord Tyrconnel, seeks to gain the good graces of Darget, perhaps even to sup with the King. He has owned to an admiration for Maupertuis. Voltaire bethinks himself presently of a little ruse to rid his path of this bramble. "Will you lend me your 'Thoughts,' M. Beaumelle?" Beaumelle lends the book; and after three days Voltaire returns it with the page containing the offensive remark upon himself and the King turned down.

But La Beaumelle did not take the hint.

On December 7, 1751, the King and Voltaire arrived in Berlin from Potsdam, and foolish La Beaumelle went again to see Voltaire. He attempted to explain away that remarkable sentence. But it was hardly capable of a favourable interpretation. Voltaire, on La Beaumelle's own showing, behaved with self-control and dignity.

"Who showed the passage to the King?" says La Beaumelle.

"Darget," answers Voltaire.

So La Beaumelle goes to Darget. "You had better leave Berlin," the prudent secretary advises. Then La Beaumelle seeks, and finds, better consolation in Maupertuis. "Voltaire gave the passage an offensive interpretation," says the President. "Send the King a copy of your book." But though La Beaumelle not only did this but addressed petitions to the King, he received no answer and was not invited to the suppers.

In a sentimental affair of La Beaumelle's, which was the next scene in his adventures, Voltaire took his enemy's part good-naturedly enough, and did his best to get Beaumelle out of the prison into which an injured husband had thrown him. He had some reason for wishing to conciliate the foolish young man. La Beaumelle had in his possession autograph letters of Madame de Maintenon which would have been of infinite value to the author of "The Century of Louis XIV." At their first interview Voltaire had asked to look at them; and La Beaumelle had made excuses. The persevering Voltaire tried again and again to attain his aim; and at last after a furious interview, the two parted for ever, La Beaumelle crying bitterly that his hatred would long outlive Voltaire's verses. Voltaire had not obtained the de Maintenon letters; and La Beaumelle, after leaving Berlin in May, 1752, revenged himself on his enemy by bringing out a pirated edition of "Louis XIV." which positively ran parallel to Voltaire's own, and to which La Beaumelle added "Remarks" offensive to the author and dealing also, with a dangerous freedom, with the Royal Family of France.

To be sure, Voltaire was fair game; but the House of Bourbon!

In a very little while M. La Beaumelle was expiating his imprudence in prison.

Throughout the affair Voltaire seems only to have taken offence, and the audacious Beaumelle to have given it. He was nothing after all. He might rot in the Bastille and be forgotten. He had no significance, except that Maupertuis defended him.

In the spring of 1752, while the affair of the "Pensées" was amusing Berlin, events of importance to Voltaire had occurred both in Paris and in the King's *entourage* in Berlin.

On February 24th, "Rome Sauvée," much altered and improved by its author, was successfully performed in Paris through the exertions of d'Argental and Madame Denis. The niece, not content with superintending Uncle Voltaire's plays, had written one herself called "The Punished Coquette." Voltaire was in agonies for fear the thing should be a failure; but his feelings were spared and it was not performed.

On March 2d, Lord Tyrconnel died in Berlin, and on March 4th Darget left the King's service; nominally, and perhaps in part really, for his health's sake. But he was glad to go, and he came back no more. Voltaire lost in him a very faithful friend. "I ought to go too," he wrote thoughtfully.

Then Longchamp had been triumphantly discovered by Madame Denis committing the unpardonable sin of copying his master's manuscripts with two accomplices who had been servants in the employ of Madame du Châtelet. Madame Denis abused him for her own satisfaction, and exposed him for his master's.

Was it only because Longchamp knew too much and had in his possession dangerous writings which were more likely to be coaxed than to be scolded out of him, that his master wrote to him very gently and offered pardon in return for the truth? The goodness and generosity which made all his servants love him must have had some foundation in fact. On March 30th of this 1752, Longchamp replied penitently and burnt the copies he had made. Voltaire gave him a handsome sum of money over and above the wages due to him, and Longchamp became a map and chart dealer. Twenty-six years later he came to see his old master, when he was on his last visit to Paris.

But the danger that Longchamp's perfidy had threatened had been no light one to the man who had already begun to look on that very sensitive and touchy French capital as a possible refuge, and was soon to find Prussia too hot to hold him.

Before the end of the year 1751 Frederick had begun to intercept and keep copies of Voltaire's and Madame Denis's letters. Voltaire wrote bitterly that the Golden Key tore his pocket, that the ribbon of the Order was a halter round his neck, that nothing in Prussia gave him a grain of happiness. "I have lost my teeth and my five senses," he wrote on February 6, 1752, "and the sixth is leaving me at a gallop. I doubt if even 'Rome Sauvée' will save *me*." He was sick now with such a homesickness as only a Frenchman knows. All these things, taken together, doubled his natural imprudence.

Before La Beaumelle left Berlin in May had begun a quarrel, into which Voltaire was to plunge headlong, between Maupertuis and the mathematician Koenig, who had stayed and worked for two years with Madame du Châtelet at Cirey.

Koenig was a member of the Berlin Academy and a strong partisan of Leibnitz, as Voltaire and Maupertuis were of Newton; but was all the same a warm friend and admirer of Maupertuis, whom in September, 1750, he had visited in Berlin. It was not unnatural that when these two partisans came to discuss Leibnitz and Newton they should quarrel. They did quarrel. Koenig, however, apologised handsomely to the touchy President, and returned to Holland where he lived. There he wrote an essay on the subject of their dispute—the principle of the least action—or the theory, which Maupertuis claimed to have discovered, that Nature is a great economist and works with the fewest materials with which she can possibly attain her purpose. Koenig disproved this theory, and quoted in his support a letter written by his dear Leibnitz. He submitted the essay to Maupertuis, who apparently did not read it, for he sanctioned its publication, and it appeared in March, 1751, in Latin. Then Maupertuis did read it, and was deeply offended. Produce these letters of Leibnitz from which you quote, M. Koenig! I am certain Leibnitz is of *my* opinion in the matter! Produce the originals! But only copies and not the original letters were forthcoming. They were undoubtedly genuine. Every page bore the unmistakable stamp of the Leibnitzian style. But there are none so blind as those who won't see.

On April 13, 1752, Maupertuis, as President, called together a meeting of the Academy, and caused Koenig to be expelled therefrom as a forger.

Then Voltaire, hard at work at Potsdam, looked up from his books, thrust aside La Beaumelle, Darget, and those home worries of Madame Denis and Longchamp, and must needs go down to the shore just to see the storm coming up and wet his imprudent feet a little in the surf. "I am not yet well informed," he wrote to Madame Denis on May 22d, "as to the details of the beginning of this quarrel. Maupertuis is at Berlin, ill from having drunk a little too much brandy." Soon after June 8th the Berlin Academy, to which Koenig had appealed, ratified its shameful sentence. By now Voltaire at Potsdam was chafing and snorting to get into the battle. There were so many spurs to urge him there! One day he had been giving a dinner-party at which Maupertuis was a guest. Voltaire airily complimented the President on a pamphlet he had written on Happiness—Voltaire having really found "Happiness" very dry and depressing. "It has given me great pleasure—a few obscurities excepted—which we will discuss later." "Obscurities!" cries the touchy President. "Only for you, Sir!" And Voltaire, with his lean hand on the presidential shoulder and his eyes uncommonly bright and malicious, answers, "Je vous estime, mon Président; you want to fight—you shall. In the meantime, let us go to dinner."

On July 24th, he wrote Madame Denis another little story. Maupertuis had said that the King having sent Voltaire his verses to correct, Voltaire had cried "Will he never leave off giving me his dirty linen to wash?" And Maupertuis had told the anecdote, "in the strictest confidence," to ten or twelve people. The King had heard of it, of course. Then, after the death of La Mettrie, had not Maupertuis declared that Voltaire had said that the post of the King's Atheist was vacant? True, *that* story did not reach the King. But every story was a whip to goad Voltaire into the forefront of the fray. He hated tyranny and wrong wherever he found them. But being human, and chafing and longing to fight with him, he hated Maupertuis' tyranny above other persons'. On September 18th, there appeared an anonymous pamphlet defending Koenig and entitled "A Reply from an Academician of Berlin to an Academician of Paris." It was supposed to be from the pen of Voltaire—the first arrow from his quiver. A few days later Koenig produced his own "Appeal to the Public," which easily proves his case to any fair-minded person. There was one man, however, who meant to stand by his President, as his President, and to defend him right or wrong. King Frederick would not even read Koenig's "Appeal." By October 15th he had himself produced a "Letter to the Public," which was nothing, said Voltaire, but an attack on Koenig and all his friends. "He calls those friends fools, jealous, and dishonest." Voltaire wrote an account of the thing to his niece, in which he spoke out as only a Voltaire could speak. In the letter are these ominous words: "Unluckily for me, I also am an author, and in the opposite camp to the King. *I have no sceptre, but I have a pen.*"

Then Maupertuis produced an extraordinary series of letters which certainly do not read like the composition of a sane person. He advocated in them the maddest scientific schemes, such as blowing up one of the

Pyramids with gunpowder to see why they were built; and making an immense hole in the earth to find out what it contains.

In a preface he had very unpromisingly stated that he should follow no sequence or order, but write on the impulse of the moment, and no doubt contradict himself! Voltaire wrote that Maupertuis had previously been in a lunatic asylum and was now mad. It did seem as if drink and vanity had turned the poor wretch's brain. But Frederick stood by his President; and on November 5th, while recommending him rest and repose, gravely congratulated him on his book.

On November 17th, from that room looking on to the terrace at Sans-Souci, Voltaire wrote a letter to Koenig, easy, graceful, and not exactly impolite to Maupertuis, but explaining that that solemn Infallibility had been in the wrong. As for those twenty-three scientific letters, why one must pity, not blame, him for them. And no doubt, M. Koenig, the same mental misfortune which made him write them, inspired his conduct to you!

It was a dainty glove thrown down; but it was a declaration of war not the less.

Frederick was far too shrewd and sane a person not to know very well who had right and reason on his side in such a dispute. He and Voltaire continued to meet as friends, and supped together as of old. Now Tyrconnel and La Mettrie were dead, Darget gone away, and Maupertuis too sick and sore to attend them, the suppers would have been small and dull indeed without Voltaire. He had been always the real soul of them. At one, only this last September, the daring idea of "The Philosophical Dictionary" had been started; and in a day or two he had sent the King that matchlessly audacious first article, "Abraham," which would have made the Pope laugh and might have made a Frederick forget that "Reply from an Academician of Berlin" which Voltaire had written, under a thinly veiled anonymity, but a few days earlier. But though the chain which bound the royal Damon to his Pythias still held, it was weak in every link. Voltaire declared of himself that he was a hundred years old—that the suppers were suppers of Damocles—the world a shipwreck—"sauve qui peut!" He was, in fact, too wretched to fear anything, and so ready to dare all. There was a pause. The tiger crouched a moment before it sprang, and then leapt on Maupertuis in the "Diatribe of Doctor Akakia."

There is no more scathing and burning satire in literature. The deadly minuteness of Swift's malign and awful irony is not so terrible as the pungent mockery of this jester who laughed, and laughed; looked up and saw his victim writhing and mad with impotent rage, and held his sides and laughed the more. The great English-Irishman at least paid his victims the compliment of taking them in some sort seriously; of bringing great and terrible weapons to slay them; and gave them the poor satisfaction of feeling like martyrs if they wished. But Voltaire made Maupertuis a byword and a derision; the sport of fools, the laughing-stock of Europe: a buffoon, a jest, a caricature: such that men seeing, stopped, beheld open-mouthed, and then laughed to convulsions. Akakia means guilelessness; and Akakia is a physician who takes the remarkable effusions of Maupertuis with a serious innocence, very deadly; who asks the most simple questions in the world; and turns upon the President's theories the remorseless logic of the gayest and easiest commonsense. Read a hundred and fifty years after, when of necessity many allusions must be missed and the point of many a jest be lost, "Akakia" is still one of the wittiest productions in the French language.

There could have been no style better than Voltaire's for making Pomposity mad. One can still see the "sublime Perpetual President" writhing under that pitiless mockery and that infectious laugh of malicious delight. The wickedest, cleverest little picador in all the world goaded this great, lumbering, heavy-footed old bull to impotent frenzy. The lithe tiger, agile as a cat, sprang on his foe, showing all his teeth in his grin, and, grinning still, tore him limb from limb.

"I have no sceptre," Voltaire had said, "but I have a pen." He had indeed.

Before that mild letter to Koenig was written from Sans-Souci on November 17th, the first part of "Akakia" had been finished. But if nothing could stop a man writing imprudence, under the absolute monarchy of Prussia there was everything to stop him printing it. Trickery was in Voltaire's blood; and practice had made him perfect in the art. Frederick had dealt treacherously with him; so why not he with Frederick? He went to the King, and read aloud a pamphlet he had written on Lord Bolingbroke. Will his Majesty sign the royal permission for that pamphlet to be printed? By all means. Frederick signs the last page of the manuscript. Voltaire sends it to the printers; asks for it back, to make some trifling alterations, and puts "Akakia" in front of Bolingbroke. What more simple?

It only remained to get a few printed copies sent out of Prussia, and then one could face destiny bravely. One story runs that Frederick, who heard everything, got wind of this "Akakia," and that Voltaire, armed with the manuscript, brought it to the King; and the King, who loved wit very nearly but not quite so much as he loved his own greatness, laughed till he cried. How should a Frederick the Great, with his bitter humour, not laugh at a Maupertuis thus ridiculed by a Voltaire? Under the rose, one could laugh at anything—God, man, or devil—even one's own Perpetual

President. If those "Matinées du Roi de Prusse, écrites par lui-même" are genuine, Frederick stands proven as one of the most accomplished actors on the world's stage. "One must think according to the rank he occupies," says he. So he laughed "to dislocation" and added that there must be no publishing of such a wicked, delightful, malignant document—and then laughed afresh. Voltaire flung the manuscript on the fire, as a proof of good faith. He could afford to be thus generous. Frederick rescued the papers, says the story, and burnt his sleeve. And the friends parted, still vastly entertained—and each pair of clever eyes looking into the other pair—wondering—wondering——.

The anecdote, though it is recorded by two different persons and is picturesque, is, however, of doubtful veracity. The more probable truth is that Frederick, first discovering on November 20th that "Akakia" had been printed at Potsdam by his own printers and in his own printing-office, and on the strength of the permit signed by himself, was furiously enraged. He sent off Fredersdorff—his servant, valet, friend—post-haste both to the printer, who confessed all, and to the author; and warned the author, who simply denied everything as usual, of awful consequences to follow.

Then Frederick wrote Voltaire that famous letter, very badly spelt, which under the circumstances was not immoderate. "Your effrontery astonishes me.... Do not imagine that you will make me believe that black is white.... If you persist in going on with the business I will print everything, and the world will see that if your works merit statues, your conduct deserves chains."

And the irate host put, it is said, a sentinel outside the guest's door.

Voltaire wrote his answer on the foot of Frederick's letter and continued to deny everything. The whole thing is a hideous calumny, and I am very ill! But Frederick was not moved; and the sentinel was not moved either. Fredersdorff was sent to Voltaire again—this time bearing with him the signed confession of the printer. Then the crafty Voltaire thought he had better turn the matter into a joke. A joke! On November 27th, Frederick wrote out for him a very elaborate promise to be a good boy. Voltaire did not sign it. He wrote beneath it, calling attention to its weak points instead. But, not the less, Frederick, on November 29th, was able to console Maupertuis with the news that Voltaire had been forced to give up the whole edition of the "Diatribe," which had been solemnly burnt in the royal presence. He had also been forbidden to print the thing elsewhere. So, poor, mad, beaten Perpetual President, you can be at peace!

After an "arrest" of eight days the sentinel was removed from Voltaire's door. He had behaved abominably. But he was very amusing—and so still infinitely worth having.

On December 10th the King announced comfortably to Maupertuis, "The affair of the libels is over.... I have frightened Voltaire on the side of his purse (by the threat of a fine), and the result is as I expected." Before December 16th the Court came up to Berlin for Christmas. Voltaire lodged at a friend's house, the house of M. de Francheville, whose son he employed as a temporary secretary. There seems no doubt he would have been again of that *société intime*, the suppers—but for one little event.

One edition of "Akakia" had been burnt; but M. de Voltaire had known very well it was not the only one. King and Court had hardly arrived at Berlin, when lo and behold! "Akakias" sprang up all over it as quickly and plentifully as mushrooms and to be far longer lived.

Berlin hated Maupertuis and enjoyed "Akakia" as it had never enjoyed anything before. The neat, staid town went mad with laughter and delight. And in his lodgings the father of "Akakia" looked thoughtfully to the future. "The orange has been squeezed—one must think now how to save the rind." The words were written to Madame Denis on December 18th, and Voltaire, with the scales fallen at last from the sharpest eyes that ever man had, added his "little dictionary as used by kings."

"*My friend* means my *slave*.

"*My dear friend* means *I am more than indifferent to you.*

"*For I will make you happy* read *I will endure you as long as I have use for you.*

"*Sup with me to-night* means *I shall mock at you this evening.*"

Voltaire might well feel that that three years' dream was over, and that it remained only "to desert honestly."

On the afternoon of the Christmas Eve of 1752, Collini, that intelligent young Italian who had seen Voltaire at the Carrousel at the giddy height of glory and had now become his secretary, was standing at the window of his master's lodgings. There was a great crowd in the street, watching a fine bonfire. Italian Collini did not understand the meaning of the scene. But Voltaire, with his rich experience, knew in a flash. "I'll bet it's my Doctor!" said he.

It was.

CHAPTER XXIV

THE FLIGHT FROM PRUSSIA

WITH the exception of the Hirsch affair there is no episode in Voltaire's life about which so many statements (usually conflicting) have been made as about the quarrel with Maupertuis and Voltaire's flight from Prussia. Collini wrote *his* version of the story. Prussia naturally has its own. Voltaire has *his* own. All the Lives of Voltaire and of Frederick—French, English, and German—have their versions. To quote authorities for every statement is the general custom of the biographer. But the sifting for truth is surely a process which may be well carried on behind the scenes; and then the result of that sifting given clear and clean to the public. If the public cannot trust the ability or the honesty of the biographer, the sources of his information are not inaccessible, and the public with a little extra trouble can verify his facts, even though he does not assist it by cumbering his text with that annihilation of all interest, the perpetual footnote. If the subject is not considered worth the extra trouble, the reader may well take the biographer—on faith. It may be added that the custom of learning a man's life and character from other people and not from himself, is far too closely followed. After all, the great do not tell so many lies about themselves as their too partial friends, their malicious enemies, and their interested, gossiping servants tell about them. The best biographer of Voltaire is Voltaire himself. If any writer can lead his reader to throw away the biographies, even his own, and study Voltaire at first-hand—his letters, the wittiest in the world, and his works, which in matchless adroitness can be compared to no other production of the human mind—he will have done much and should be well satisfied.

The light of that Christmas bonfire made "Akakia," as it might have been expected to make it, more conspicuous than ever. Thirty thousand copies were sold in Paris in a few weeks. By January, 1753, in Prussia, twelve presses were kept busy printing it night and day. The Prussian newspapers held up their hands at it in holy horror, and did their best for it by their abuse. For a week Voltaire lay *perdu*. He had thoughts of escaping to Plombières on the very good excuse of his health. A flight to England was often in his mind.

On New Year's Day, at half-past three in the afternoon, he sent back to Frederick "the bells and the baubles he has given me," which comprised the Cross and Ribbon of the Order of Merit and the Chamberlain's Key.

On the outside of the packet he wrote the well-known quatrain:

Oh! tenderly I took your tender gifts
And sadly render them to you again,
As bitter lover to lost love gives back
Her pictured image, in his hot heart's pain.

He accompanied the parcel with a letter—a melancholy reflection on the Vanity of Human Wishes. "My resignation is equal to my sorrow. I shall remember nothing but your goodness. I have lost everything; there only remains to me a memory of having once been happy in your retreat at Potsdam.... I made you my idol: an honest man does not change his religion, and sixteen years of a measureless devotion are not to be destroyed by a single unlucky moment."

His sorrow was genuine; but so was his determination to go.

At four o'clock on this afternoon a *fiacre* drew up at the door of his rooms. Fredersdorff had come from the King, bringing back the Order and Key. There was a long consultation. Collini, who was apparently eavesdropping in the next room, said his master only consented to receive them again after a very lively argument. The King's Chamberlain, in fact, made a very wry face at finding himself his Chamberlain still. Go he would; but go with peace and honour he certainly would if he could. On January 2d, he wrote his King a conciliatory letter. "Do with me what you will," it said. "But what in the world *will* you do with me?" it *meant*. As for the suppers—I will be of them no more.

On January 18th, Voltaire published a declaration denying the authorship of "Akakia." It was a form—hardly a deceit, in that it deceived nobody. It was to oblige the King—the King who still hungered and thirsted for his Voltaire and could not let him go. True, it was a humble, obedient, penitent, reformed Voltaire he wanted—in short, an impossibility.

Frederick went back to Potsdam on January 30th, and begged his Chamberlain to come back there too, to his old quarters.

"I am too ill," says the Chamberlain, but inconsistently pleased with the friendly offer and taking care to have it recorded in the newspapers, and to tell it to all his correspondents in Paris. Still, in the very letters in which he announced the King's favour like a pleased child, the shrewd man was arranging to leave. On February 16th, he was still at Berlin with dysentery. His royal host sent him quinine. But that did not cure him. Nothing would cure him but some air which was not Prussian air—some diet which the kingly table could not produce—some company which was not Prussian company.

He could not go to Potsdam; but about March 1st he wrote to beg formal permission for leave of absence, to journey to French Plombières and take there the waters which were much recommended for his complaints. He awaited the answer with a feverish impatience. He made Collini arrange his papers and pack his things. Here was a book to be returned to the royal library; then, there were the coming expenses to be considered. But no answer came from Frederick. Voltaire, restless and irritable, must needs, on March 5th, move from the rooms he occupied in a house in central Berlin to another in the Stralau quarter—almost in the country. Here he lived at his own expense with Collini, a manservant, and a cook. His doctor, Coste, came to see him—Coste, who was not afraid to say Plombières was the only cure for his patient's health, though he knew the recommendation would be displeasing to the King.

What if the King refused permission? Such things had been done by men of his temperament, and might be done again.

Voltaire would walk in the garden of that Stralau house with young Collini. "Now leave me to dream a little," he would say. And he paced up and down alone—conjecturing, fearing, scheming. He *must* go somehow. He invented the wildest, absurdest plans of escape; and laughed at them gaily enough with that capacity for seeing the humorous side of the worst troubles, which was the best gift the gods had given him.

At last Frederick broke his silence; and Voltaire wrote to his niece on March 15th that the King had said there were excellent waters in Moravia! "He might as well tell me to go and take waters in Siberia."

Not the least curious of the many human documents preserved in the archives of Berlin is that famous dismissal which at last, on March 16, 1753, Frederick the Great flung upon paper in a rage.

"He can quit my service when he pleases: he need not invent the excuse of the waters of Plombières; but he will have the goodness, before he goes, to return to me the contract of his engagement, the Key, the Cross, and the volume of poetry I have confided to him. I would rather he and Koenig had only attacked my works; I sacrifice *them* willingly to people who want to blacken the reputation of others; I have none of the folly and vanity of authors, and the cabals of men of letters appear to me the depth of baseness."

The Abbé de Prades put that dismissal in a politer official form, and thus sent it to Voltaire. But this keen-sighted Arouet was not minded to be expelled like a schoolboy by an angry master. Wherever he might go, that master's iron arm could reach him. He wrote, therefore, a gay letter of entreaty to Prades, asking for a parting interview with the King. Permission was granted him. On March 18th, after a stay of thirteen days at Stralau, Voltaire went to Potsdam. That evening he was once more installed in his old rooms at Sans-Souci.

The next day, after dinner, he and the King met in private, and once again met as more than friends. It has been said before that there was between these two men something of the glamour and the fitfulness of passion. "I could live neither with you nor without you," wrote Voltaire after they had long parted for ever. "You who bewitched me, whom I loved, and with whom I am always angry." That was the summing up of their whole relationship. The enchantment was at work again to-night. It is said that they talked over the Maupertuis affair. Collini affirms that they laughed at the President together. The harsh dismissal was altered into a gracious royal permit for a necessary change and holiday. Voltaire was to drink the waters, recover his health, and return. He was still the King's Chamberlain. He was to retain his Cross, his Key, and alas! alas!—the royal volume of poems. The interview lasted two hours. Voltaire came from it radiant and satisfied. For a week Potsdam laid herself out to delight him. Perhaps she and the King would be so charming, Voltaire would not want to leave them even for a time! Frederick may have hoped so. Voltaire submitted to the blandishments; nay, enjoyed them. But behind the bright eyes and the gay, vain, susceptible, pleasure-loving French heart lay the purpose and iron resolution which make greatness. Voltaire was going. On March 26, 1753, about eight o'clock in the morning he went on to the parade ground where Frederick was holding the last review of his regiment before he started for Silesia.

"Sire, here is M. de Voltaire, who comes to take his orders."

"Eh bien! M. de Voltaire, you are resolved then to set out?"

"Sire, urgent business and my health make it necessary for me to do so."

"Monsieur, I wish you a pleasant journey."

They never met again.

Voltaire hurried back to his rooms. Everything was ready for flight. Collini had arranged all money matters. The travelling carriage was at the door. Voltaire hastily wrote a brief farewell to d'Argens. By nine the travellers were *en route*. They never paused or looked back. By six o'clock in the evening of March 27th they had covered ninety-two miles of road, and were in the rooms prudent Voltaire had engaged in advance at Leipsic. Did he then recall and wonder at that strange tragi-comedy of the last three years? Whatever his lips uttered, his heart knew he had left Frederick for ever. The time had not yet come, though it did come, for regret, remorse, and affection.

Voltaire had brought with him in that travelling carriage two supplements to his "Doctor Akakia." Almost his last words from Potsdam, in a letter to Formey, were, "When I am attacked I defend myself like a devil; but I am a good devil and end by laughing." But it was better to be attacked by a Voltaire than to be mocked by him—which Maupertuis, when he read those supplements, once more knew to his cost.

On April 3d, that very ill-advised person saw fit to write a threatening letter to Voltaire at Leipsic, in which he said, almost in so many words, If you attack me again, nothing shall spare you. "Be grateful to the respect and obedience which have hitherto withheld my arm and saved you from the worst affair you ever had."

Voltaire's answer was a new edition of "Akakia" with the two supplements added, a travesty of the letter he had just received from Maupertuis, and a burlesque epistle to Formey in his official character of Secretary of the Berlin Academy. If the first part of "Akakia" had been laughable, the second was exquisitely ludicrous. It reached Frederick soon enough, as everything reached him.

On April 11th, he wrote a very memorable and famous order to his Resident at Frankfort—one Freytag. The King commanded Freytag to demand of Voltaire, when he passed through Frankfort, the Chamberlain's Key, the Cross and Ribbon of the Order of Merit, every paper in his Majesty's handwriting, and a book "specified in the note enclosed." If Voltaire declined to do as he was told, he was to be arrested. On April 12th, Frederick wrote to his sister of Bayreuth a letter wherein he spoke of his "charming, divine Voltaire," that "sublime spirit, first of thinking beings," as the greatest scoundrel and the most treacherous rascal in the universe; and said that men were broken on the wheel who deserved it less than he.

The Margravine confessed that, for the life of her, she had not been able to keep her countenance while reading that second part of "Akakia"; but her brother was in no laughing mood. To soothe Maupertuis he had caused his curt dismissal to Voltaire of March 16th to appear in the newspapers. "Akakia" may be fairly said to have been one of the most famous jokes of the eighteenth century, and to have been the delight of every person who read it, save only Maupertuis and Frederick the Great.

For two-and-twenty days Voltaire passed his time not unhappily at Leipsic. He visited the University there. He arranged his books and papers. He had with him, besides Collini, a copyist and a manservant, both of whom he employed in literary work. He now was busy defending "Louis

XIV." against La Beaumelle's criticisms. To be sure "Louis XIV." was its own defence; but it was never in Voltaire's irritable and pugnacious nature to let the curs bark at his heels unheeded. He must be for ever kicking them or stinging them with his whip and so goading them to fresh fury. To sit serene above the thunder was quite impossible to this god: he was always coming down from his Olympus to answer the blasphemies of the mortals and to fight the meanest of them.

On April 18th, after he had been in Leipsic rather less than a month, the travelling carriage stood once more at his door. The luggage which was heaped into it did not contain the book to which Frederick had alluded in his letter to Freytag. That luckless volume, in which were compiled the poetic effusions of Frederick the Great, freethinking, imprudent, and not a little indecent, had been given in charge of a merchant of Leipsic, who was to forward it, with many other of Voltaire's books, to Strasburg.

Chief among the royal poems was a certain "Palladium," imitated from the "Pucelle," but very much more ribald and insulting to the Christian religion; and, in that it abused other kings who might be dangerous foes, certainly not a work of which King Frederick would care to own himself the author. It had been secretly printed in the palace at Potsdam in 1751.

Voltaire hoped to meet at Strasburg, not only his books, but the person whom Frederick spoke of as "that wearisome niece." The criminal's next stopping-place after Leipsic was Gotha. M. de Voltaire and suite intended to put up at the inn there, but were not installed in it when the delightful Duchess of Saxe-Gotha, not the least charming of Voltaire's philosophic duchesses and with whom he had corresponded when he was at Cirey, begged him to be her guest, in her château. Forty years old, gentle, graceful, accomplished, with that love of learning without learnedness which was the peculiar charm of the women of the eighteenth century, Voltaire may well have found her, as he did find her, "the best princess in the world." "And who—God be thanked," he added piously, "wrote no verses." She received him and his attendants with a delighted hospitality. She had a husband, who was not of much account on the present occasion. And there was a Madame de Buchwald, who also had all that fascination which seems to have been the birthright of the women of that time.

In all lives there are certain brief halcyon periods when one forgets alike the troubles that are past and the cares that are to come and enjoys oneself in the moment, defiant of fate, and with something of the *abandon* of a child. This month was such a period for Voltaire. After the fights and the worries of the past three years, he was peculiarly susceptible to the soothing flattery and the caressing admiration of this couple of gracious women.

He read them his "Natural Law." He read them new cantos of the "Pucelle." (Modesty was the lost piece of silver for which the woman of this period never even searched.) Nothing was bad about Gotha save its climate, said he. To please his dear Duchess and to instruct her son, the obliging Voltaire embarked here on a popular history of the German Empire from the time of Charlemagne.

"Annals of the Empire" is one of the least successful of Voltaire's works. Truth compels the critic indeed to say that it comes very near to being hideously, preposterously, and unmitigatedly dull. It was written to order and without inspiration. It is laborious, monotonous, and long. That its conscientious list of Kings, Emperors, and Electors, and its neat little rhyming summary of each century, may have proved useful to the young gentleman they were designed to instruct, is very likely. But Voltaire did not put his soul in it. In the mechanical effort it required of his brain he was soon indeed to find great, and greatly needed, soothing. The month passed on winged feet. But Voltaire had to proceed, leisurely it might be, but still to proceed to Strasburg to embrace his niece.

He had had an idea of visiting the clever and delightful Margravine of Bayreuth with whom he so often corresponded; but all the circumstances considered, he thought she was too nearly related to Frederick, and that a visit to her might endanger the little liberty he had obtained.

No doubt, as he lumbered along in the great travelling carriage, he congratulated himself on at last getting out of Prussia, at once easily and gracefully.

He left Gotha on May 25, 1753.

He rested a night or two with the Landgrave of Hesse at Wabern, near Cassel. At Cassel, Baron Pollnitz of the suppers was staying; as Frederick's spy, Voltaire seems to have suspected. By May 30th the travelling party were at Marburg. After leaving there they passed through Fredeburg, where they visited the Salt Springs. And on May 31, 1753, Voltaire reached the "Golden Lion" at Frankfort-on-Main, meaning to proceed on his journey the next day.

CHAPTER XXV

THE COMEDY OF FRANKFORT

FREDERICK THE GREAT had the misfortune to suffer now from subordinates so loyal that they went beyond their master's commands, and officials with a blundering zeal not according to knowledge.

The second part of "Akakia" had flung him into one of the greatest furies of his life. The unmeasured terms in which he wrote of Voltaire to his sister have been recorded. Wilhelmina's propitiating answer did not propitiate him. Voltaire was maddeningly and devilishly clever. The sting of the "Akakia" supplements lay in part for Frederick the Great in the fact that he could hardly prevent himself from laughing at such an exquisite humour, nor withhold his admiration of such a dazzling and daring genius. But add to this, that in making a fool of his President, Voltaire had also made a fool of the President's friend and King; that that King had cringed to win Voltaire to Prussia, and cringed to keep him. Still extant were the royal letters filled with the wildest hyperbole of devotion and of admiration. He had stooped to entreat. He had licked dust to keep the Frenchman his property; and he had done it in vain. It may be forgiven him that, like Naaman the Syrian, he went away in a rage.

Before he went to Silesia he had caused to be written on April 11th that memorable order to Freytag, before alluded to, wherein he commanded Freytag to deprive Voltaire on his arrival at Frankfort of that Key, Cross and Order, all papers in the King's handwriting, and—"the book specified in the note enclosed." Only—there was no note enclosed, and no book specified at all.

A conscientious and fussy old busybody was Freytag; worryingly anxious to do right, and fretfully and rightly suspecting himself to be no match for Voltaire. Back he writes to Potsdam on April 21st, asking further instructions about that unspecified book; and "If Voltaire says he has sent on his luggage ahead, are we to keep him a prisoner at Frankfort till he has brought it back?"

"Yes," comes back the answer on April 29th. "Keep him in sight till the luggage is brought back and he has given to you the royal manuscripts, especially the book called 'Œuvre de Poésie.'"

For six weeks, while Voltaire was amusing himself with his Duchess and his "Annals," fussy Freytag awaited him. Voltaire spent the night of

May 31st in perfect tranquillity at the inn of the "Golden Lion." On June 1st, Freytag, Councillor Rucker, who represented a Councillor Schmidt who was ill, and Lieutenant Brettwitz called upon Voltaire at eight o'clock in the morning at the "Golden Lion," and in the name of his Prussian Majesty requested his Prussian Majesty's ex-guest to deliver up immediately all the royal manuscripts, the Key, the Cross and the Order.

It was not wonderful, perhaps, that at this request Voltaire flung himself back in his chair and closed his eyes, overcome. Even to Freytag's unemotional vision the Frenchman appeared ill, and was nothing better than a skeleton. Collini ransacked Voltaire's trunks at his order. He delivered up all the royal manuscripts—save one which he sent to Freytag the next morning, saying he had found it later under a table. The Key and the Ribbon—that Key which had long torn his pocket, and that Ribbon which had been a halter round his neck—he also gave to Freytag. He sent on to him in the evening his commission as King's Chamberlain. As for the "Œuvre de Poésie"—why, *that*, says Voltaire, I packed up with other books in a box, and, for the life of me, cannot tell you whether the box is at Leipsic or at Hamburg.

Considering the passionate nature of his desire to be out of this Prussia; considering his wretched health, which really did need Plombières waters, or some waters or some great change of scene and of air; considering the affront that was being put upon him; considering the fact that that "Œuvre de Poésie" was his own, a present from the King, corrected and embellished by M. de Voltaire himself, it must be conceded that he took the news that he was to be a prisoner at the Frankfort inn until that unlucky book was forthcoming, pretty philosophically. He did indeed beg vainly to be allowed to pursue his journey. It was not pleasant to have to sign a parole not to go beyond the garden of one's hotel; to have for host a man under oath not to let his guest depart. It was not pleasant to have three blundering German officials turning over one's effects for eight consecutive hours, from nine in the morning till five o'clock in the afternoon. The facts that Freytag—who certainly meant very well—confided Voltaire's health to the best doctor in the place, and offered the captive the pleasure of a drive with himself, the great Freytag, the Resident, in the public gardens, were insufficient consolations for delay and indignity. Freytag signed a couple of agreements wherein he declared that as soon as the book arrived, Voltaire could go where he liked. One copy of the agreement Voltaire kept. He and Collini declared that Freytag spelled Poésie, *Poëshie*; and on the second copy which Voltaire sent to Madame Denis, to reassure her, her uncle wrote "Good for the Œuvre de *Poëshie* of the King your master!" Voltaire could still joke; and still work. He was not all unhappy.

He went on with his "Annals." He received visitors—as a famous person whose extraordinary detention had already got wind in the town. He walked in the garden with Collini. He wrote several letters, without even alluding to his present circumstances. He was still a laughing philosopher. He enjoyed that *Poëshie* joke immensely. He also enjoyed boxing the ears of Van Duren, once printer at The Hague and now retired to Frankfort, who waited on him with a bill thirteen years old. Collini found his master, as ever, good and benevolent.

Five days later he had begun to grow a little impatient. Worthy Freytag was shocked when he visited his captive on that fifth day of his detention, June 5th, to hear him ask if he could not change his residence, and go and call on the Duke of Meiningen; and, worst of all, break out into invectives against that solemn old conscientious stupidity, the Resident himself. Freytag, not a little flurried, went home and wrote for more explicit commands from Potsdam. Since that first order, dated April 11th, none had proceeded directly from Frederick. He was still away on his tour: and to Fredersdorff in Potsdam and Freytag in Frankfort, his too zealous servants, belongs most of the dishonour and ridicule the affair heaped on the name of Frederick.

Freytag was no sooner out of the house than Voltaire, who still pursued his old, old policy of leaving no stone unturned, sat down and wrote a very cunning letter to the Emperor of Austria beseeching his interference in his, Voltaire's, behalf. The day before, on June 4th, he had written a similar one to d'Argenson, showing how it would really be to the best interest of the French Ministry to come to his rescue. On June 7th, he wrote to d'Argental of his detention with a calm and philosophy which, as has been well said, people keep as a rule for the misfortunes of others.

On the ninth day of his captivity, that is to say, June 9, 1753, there drew up at the door of the "Golden Lion" a post-chaise containing a very fat, hot, breathless, and excited lady of uncertain years, who fell upon the captive's neck and fervently embraced him, crying out "Uncle! I always said that man would be the death of you."

Marie Louise Denis was at this time about three-and-forty years old. Idle, self-indulgent, and extravagant, she was a good-humoured person enough if a vast appetite for pleasure were gratified to the full. Voluble, bustling, and impetuous; foolish, but not without a certain vulgar shrewdness; affectionate, until the objects of her affections were out of sight, when she entirely forgot all about them; vain, greedy, and good-natured; much too lazy to be long offended with anyone, and quite incapable of speaking the truth—Madame Denis was a type of woman which has never been uncommon in any age. So long as she was happy and comfortable herself, she was quite ready to allow her neighbours to be so too. She was a cordial hostess; and talked a great deal and at the very top of her voice. With a mind as wholly incapable of real cultivation as was her heart of any great or sustained feeling, from long association with Voltaire she caught the accent of cleverness, as after living in a foreign country one catches the accent of a language though one may know nothing of its construction, its grammar, or its literature.

If Voltaire had been in many respects unfortunate in the first woman who influenced his life, he was a thousand times more so in the second. If Madame du Châtelet had had a shrewish temper, she had had transcendent mental gifts; Madame Denis had the shrew's temper with a mind essentially limited and commonplace. Madame du Châtelet had once loved Voltaire; Madame Denis never loved anything but her pleasures. From the first moment of her connection with him, his niece was a worry and a care to him—making him, as well as herself, ludicrous with her *penchant* for bad playwriting and her elderly coquetries. It is not insignificant that Longchamp, Collini, and Wagnière hated her from their souls. (Collini, indeed, politely praised her in his memoirs, written long after the events they chronicled, and roundly abused her in his letters written at the time.) Voltaire kept her with him, partly no doubt because the tie of relationship bound them. But his enemies may concede that if he had not been in domestic life one of the most generous, patient, good-humoured, forbearing, and philosophic of men, he would have snapped that tie in the case of Louise Denis without compunction.

It must be briefly noted here that those enemies declare that there was another tie between Voltaire and Madame Denis than that of uncle and niece. But if there had been why should it not have been legalised by marriage? An appeal to the Pope and the payment of a certain sum alone were necessary. Voltaire was not too moral, but he was too shrewd, and had had far too much experience of the painful consequences of acting illegally, to do so when it was totally unnecessary. He had been, too, but a cold lover to Madame du Châtelet with her *éblouissante* personality. What in the world was there to make a decrepit uncle of nine-and-fifty fall in love with a lazy, ugly niece of forty-three, who bored him? The thing is against nature. The tone in which he speaks of Madame Denis in his letters—good-humoured and patronising—is certainly not the tone of a lover. Add to this, that the foolish relict of M. Denis was always the victim of gallant *penchants* for quite other persons than Voltaire, now for d'Arnaud, now for Ximenès, presently for young secretary Collini, and a handsome major of twenty-seven.

The age was a vile one; and Voltaire was in it and of it. No woman, were she ever so old and ugly, could have been at the head of his house and escaped calumny. But he may be exonerated from being his niece's lover. It was a sin he had no mind to.

He was undoubtedly very sincerely glad to see her at the present moment. And if she was not quite heroic enough to keep herself from saying, "I told you so!" she was quite good-natured enough to sympathise with her uncle, even if he had brought his misfortunes at least in part upon himself. This meeting, too, had been so long planned, written of, and delayed. Both uncle and niece—not yet knowing each other as fatally well as they were soon to do—had heartily desired it. One of the very first things practical Madame Denis did was to sit down and write on June 11th a very sensible and moving letter to Frederick the Great, which, if her uncle did not help in its composition, is an example of the truth of the axiom that one intuition of a woman is worth all the reasoning of a man. It was not Madame Denis's fault that that appeal to Frederick to let Voltaire go free did not reach Frederick until it was too late to be of use. She had already implored the good offices of Lord Keith, who had been of Frederick's suppers, and was now in France as Prussian envoy; and the prudent Scotchman had replied advising her to recommend Uncle Voltaire to keep quiet, and to remember that "Kings have long arms." Nothing daunted, Madame Denis wrote to Keith again. This letter, too, though in the niece's hand, bears evidence of the uncle's brain. The energetic pair (Madame Denis declared in every letter that they were both very ill) further wrote to d'Argenson and Madame de Pompadour to lay before France the astonishing facts of their case.

It only remained for Madame Denis after this to try and cheer the captivity of the prisoner of the "Golden Lion," and to help him entertain the illustrious local notables who came to call upon him.

Early on the morning of Monday, June 18th, the chest containing that famous "Œuvre de *Poëshie*" was delivered at Freytag's house. "Now we can go!" thinks Voltaire. He completed his preparations. He sent Collini to Freytag's house to be present at the opening of the parcel. But cautious Freytag was awaiting clearer orders from Potsdam: and would not open the case. Voltaire sent Collini many times during that morning; nay, many times in a single hour: and Freytag sent him away again. At noon comes a despatch to Freytag from Fredersdorff. "Do nothing," says that official, "until the King returns here next Thursday, when you shall have further orders." And Freytag, in a note of the most excessive politeness, conveys this message to Voltaire.

Voltaire's patience had had eighteen days to run out: and the supply was pretty well exhausted. At his side was his niece dying to go, and anticipating, not unnaturally, that Frederick intended something very sinister indeed by these delays. Voltaire went to Freytag and asked to see Fredersdorff's despatch. And Freytag refused, in a rage. That night Madame Denis wrote to the Abbé de Prades—as the intimate of Frederick—telling him of this new insult and delay. And Voltaire resolved upon action.

Leaving Madame Denis to look after the luggage and await events at the "Golden Lion," on Wednesday, June 20th, about three o'clock in the afternoon, Voltaire and Collini slipped out of the inn and went to another hostelry, called the "Crown of the Empire," where they got into a post-chaise which was returning to Mayence. A servant followed them as far as the "Crown of the Empire" and put into the post-chaise a cash-box and two portfolios. But for the fact that one of the escaping criminals, sombrely dressed in black velvet for the occasion, dropped a notebook in the city and spent four minutes of priceless time looking for it, they would have been out of Frankfort and the jurisdiction of Freytag before that breathless and flurried official caught them up and arrested them, with the assistance of the officer at the Mayence gate, which they had actually reached.

It is not necessary to say that Voltaire did not submit to this arrest tamely. He argued with no little passion and adroitness. Collini supported all his statements impartially. "The worst bandits could not have struggled more to get away," said unfortunate Freytag. But the Resident had might on his side, if not right. He left Voltaire and Collini under a guard of six soldiers and "flew" back to the Burgomaster of Frankfort, who confirmed the arrest. When the unhappy official got back to the city gate, he found Voltaire had spent his time burning papers. What he did not know, was that Voltaire had further taken advantage of his absence to abstract a sheaf of manuscript from one of the portfolios and to give it to Collini, saying, "Hide that somewhere about you."

Freytag brought his prisoners back to the city in his carriage, which was surrounded by a guard of soldiers, and very soon by a crowd. He took them to the house of that Councillor Schmidt (whose office had been temporarily filled on June 1st by Councillor Rucker) because, said Freytag, the landlord of the "Golden Lion" would not have Voltaire in his house any longer "on account of his incredible meanness." Freytag then made the prisoners give up the cash-box and their money. "Count the money," said Schmidt; "they are quite capable of pretending they had more than they really had." From Voltaire were also taken "his watch, his snuff-box, and some jewels that he wears." Collini recounts that Voltaire feigned illness to soften the hearts of his captors. But this very transparent ruse failed entirely; as might have been expected. After two hours' waiting, Dorn, Freytag's clerk, a disgraced solicitor of Frankfort, took the pair to a low tavern called the "Goat," where Voltaire was shut up in one room guarded by three soldiers with bayonets; and Collini in another. Voltaire's cash-box and portfolios had been left in a trunk at Schmidt's, and the trunk padlocked.

Madame Denis, hearing of Voltaire's arrest, had flown to try the effect of feminine eloquence upon the Burgomaster.

He replied by putting her under arrest at the "Golden Lion"; and presently sent her, under guard of Dorn and three soldiers, to the "Goat" tavern, where she was placed in a garret with no furniture in it but a bed; "soldiers for *femmes de chambre*, and bayonets for curtains." Madame Denis appears to have spent the night in hysterics. The miscreant Dorn actually persisted in taking his supper in her room and emptying bottle after bottle in her presence and treating her with insult. The truth was, Freytag and Dorn did not believe in her nieceship to Voltaire and mistook the poor lady for a wholly disreputable character.

Collini spent *his* night, dressed, on his bed. Beneath the shelter of its curtains he drew forth from his breeches that sheaf of manuscript Voltaire had given him at the Mayence gate. It was the manuscript of the "Pucelle," so far as it was then written.

If Voltaire spent *his* night in a rage, he had every excuse for it. At ten o'clock in the evening he wrote to that good friend of his, the Margravine, laying his desperate case before her and begging her to send his letter on to her brother. He had broken his parole—true; but not until Freytag had broken his written agreement that when that "Œuvre de Poëshie" arrived he should go where he listed. He had borne a most galling delay not impatiently. For being in possession of a book which had been given to him, he, his niece, and his servant had been hustled, jostled, and insulted. If the book was blasphemous, indecent, and a dangerous work for a king to have written, was that Voltaire's fault? He had but corrected its blunders and its grammar. If its model was the "Pucelle"—the royal author had chosen that model himself. Voltaire suffered for the King's imprudence and for the King's official's folly. He was in a situation not too common to him—he really was not the aggressor.

The following day, Thursday, June 21st, the Potsdam mail arrived bringing orders dated June 16th from Frederick—just returned from his tour—that Voltaire, on giving his promise and a written agreement that he would send back the "Poëshie" to Freytag within a given time, and without making any copies of it, was to be allowed to go "in peace and with civility."

That is all very well, thinks fussy Freytag. But when the King wrote that, he did not know this Voltaire had set at naught his Resident's solemn authority and had had the audacity to try and escape. He must wait to go until we hear what the King's commands are when he knows of this abominable breach of discipline.

Voltaire, goaded to desperation, wrote again to the Margravine of Bayreuth, begging her to send to his Majesty a most indignant statement of the wrongs done to Madame Denis—the statement having been drawn up by that outraged lady herself. As a good niece, she also wrote again passionately, direct to the King, on behalf of her uncle. He himself implored Freytag in quite humble terms to at least let them go back to the "Golden Lion," which was a more decent habitation than the "Goat"; and, besides, would save the prisoners from paying for two prisons.

A few hours after, he appealed again to the mercy of that harassed and unfortunate jailer. All these letters are of June 21st. It must have been a busy day. It is strange that at such a juncture Voltaire himself did not write direct to the King. It could not have been his pride that prevented him. If pride was an obstacle in the way of attaining his end, an impulsive Voltaire could always kick it aside. Besides, he stooped to entreat a Dorn and a Freytag. In answer to his requests Madame Denis and Collini were allowed to go out of doors. But Voltaire was kept to his room in that wretched "Goat" and guarded by two sentinels as if he had been a dangerous criminal awaiting hanging. Four days went by. Then, on June 25th, came clearer and more positive orders from Frederick to let the prisoners go. Frederick was sick of the business and ashamed of it. But still, argues Freytag, when he sent those orders, he did not know of the attempt to escape. So the only effect of them was that the guards were removed from the door, and Voltaire was put on his honour not to leave the room.

The chest of books from Strasburg had meanwhile been opened; and the *"Poèshie"* extracted therefrom. But for the punctilious idiocy of one dull official, Voltaire might long ago have been at his Plombières and have done with Prussia for ever. The very burgomaster began to pity him. Frankfort was near regarding him as a martyr. Freytag, a little nervous, splendidly allowed the captive the freedom of the whole inn; and then he and that captive fought tooth and nail over money matters. For Voltaire had not only endured the miseries of arrest and detention, but had had to pay their whole expenses. He and Collini swore they had been robbed of jewels, money, and papers, and of various trifles as well.

On July 5th—after they had been detained thirty-five days—came sharp orders from Potsdam that Voltaire was to be released at once. Even a Freytag could doubt and delay no more. On July 6th the party returned to the "Golden Lion": where Voltaire called in a lawyer and laid before him a succinct account of the events of those five-and-thirty days. Collini completed their preparations for departure. On the very morning when they were going, the impetuous Voltaire caught sight of Dorn passing his door and rushed out at him with a loaded pistol. Collini intervened. They had been in scrapes enough already.

On July 7, 1753, Voltaire and Collini left Frankfort. That fighting, scrambling, wearying month of folly and indignity was over. The same night they reached Mayence-on-the-Rhine—a city which knew not Frederick. The day following, Madame Denis left Frankfort for Paris.

Nothing is more remarkable about the Frankfort affair than the moderation Voltaire, considering he was Voltaire, displayed in it. When the Margravine wrote on the subject to her brother and described Voltaire as "intense and bilious" and "capable of every imprudence," the description was not unfair. When Frederick wrote to his sister and said plainly that Voltaire and Madame Denis lied in their descriptions of the event and coloured it and embroidered on it to suit their own ends, he was not precisely lying, though he was not precisely truthful, himself. But leaving the account of Voltaire, Madame Denis, and Collini altogether alone, from the account of Freytag the prejudiced, it is proved that Voltaire behaved, all things considered, with a great deal of philosophy and an unusual amount of patience.

Why?

He was leaving Prussia—with enormous difficulty to be sure—but he *was* leaving it at last. He was returning, as he hoped, to France. He had made a final trial of courts and kings—and found them wanting. Liberty was whispering and wooing him again—the siren he had loved and deserted, and whom he was to love again and desert no more. His blessed monotonous work at his "Annals" made him "forget all the Freytags." For five hours a day, whether he was living in palaces or in prison, with princes or with jailers, he "laboured tranquilly" at that book. The comic side of the situation appealed to him. He knew, or said he knew, that he deserved some of his misfortunes. And above all—far above all—the dream and the night were ending, and with the dawn of a new day came the courage, the fight, and the energy to win it.

CHAPTER XXVI

THE "ESSAY ON THE MANNERS AND MIND OF NATIONS"

THE arrival of Voltaire at Mayence rang down the curtain upon the greatest act of one of the most famous dramas of friendship in the world. It left Frederick enraged: first of all with himself; secondly, with blundering Freytag, whose blunders the King ostensibly approved, according to his principle, in a formal document written for that purpose; and only thirdly with Voltaire. With his muse taught by that Voltaire, Frederick abused the teacher in spiteful epigrams, and then dealt him a blow which shook Voltaire's whole life, as a lover will kill the mistress who has been false to him not because he has loved her too little, but too much.

As for Voltaire, he was both angry and sorry. In that mean, world-famous story of their quarrel he must have known well enough that he had been too often most aggravating, *méchant*, and irrepressible. Yet that letter he wrote on July 9th from Mayence to Madame Denis, seen and meant to be seen by Frederick, gave a view of the situation not wholly false. The King "might have remembered that for fifteen years he wooed me with tender favours; that in my old age he drew me from my country; that for two years I worked with him to perfect his talents; that I have served him well and failed him in nothing; that it is infinitely below his rank and glory to take part in an academical quarrel and to end as my reward by demanding his poems from me at the hands of his soldiers."

Adoring and quarrelling, passionately admiring and yearning for each other when they were apart, admiring and fighting each other when they were together—that is the history of the friendship of Frederick and Voltaire. If it be true that the great are no mates for common people, still less are they mates for each other. Even in fabled Olympus, gods could not live in peace with gods.

It is not unworthy of remark that their connection conferred far greater benefits on the King than on the commoner. Voltaire *had* consistently trained and taught the royal intellect from that first letter written in August, 1736, to the Prussian heir-apparent. He had been such a master as kings do not often find—and his royal pupil had gained from him such advantages as kings are seldom wise enough to use.

But for Voltaire himself—for the most fruitful literary producer of any age—those three years in Prussia were comparatively barren and unprofitable. True, in 1751, "The Century of Louis XIV." had appeared; but all the materials for it had been collected, and by far the greater part of the book written, before Voltaire came to Prussia at all. The "Poem on Natural Law" (not published till 1756), a few improvements to "Rome Sauvée," the beginnings of that "magnificent dream," "The Philosophical Dictionary," were, as has been seen (except "Akakia"), his only other works written in Prussia. For a while the author of the "Henriade" and the "English Letters" was chiefly famous as the enemy of d'Arnaud, Hirsch, and Maupertuis; as the hero of the low comedy of Frankfort; and as the guest "who put his host's candle-ends into his pockets."

If without Voltaire the glory of Frederick would have been something less glorious, without Frederick the great Voltaire would have been greater still.

Flourishing Mayence, with its Rhine river flowing through it, its fine castles, its fine company, its indifference to the opinion of Frederick, and its warm enthusiasm for Frederick's guest, friend, enemy, might well have seemed Paradise to Voltaire. He was free. His social French soul was delighted with many visitors. He worked hard too. He spent three weeks in "drying his clothes after the shipwreck," as he phrased it himself. But for one fear, he would have been happy. It was not only in Prussia that Frederick was Frederick the Great. His name was everywhere a power and terror. Why should prudent France embroil herself with the greatest of European sovereigns for the sake of clasping to her breast an upstart genius who was always making mischief whether he was at home or abroad, and who had been punished for his abominable, free, daring, unpalatable opinions a hundred times without changing them?

Voltaire had arrived in Mayence on July 7, 1753. On July 9th he was writing to Madame Denis that letter for the public eye in which he gave *his* account of the affair with Frederick; and went on to prove that he had never been a Prussian subject, or anything but a Frenchman to the bottom of his soul, which was true enough; and to assert, the truth of which he felt to be very doubtful, that Frederick would be the first to ask of the King my master (I am still Gentleman-in-Ordinary, you will be pleased to remember) that I may be allowed to end my days in my native land. Madame Denis was working hard to attain that same end in Paris: and thought herself likely to succeed. Her sufferings in Frankfort had been such that the emotional lady had to be bled four times in a week, she said. She still hoped, in italics, that her old prophecy that the King of Prussia would be the death of Uncle Voltaire would not be fulfilled after all; and recalled Frankfort in terms so agitating that there was no wonder her uncle—who greatly overestimated his niece's goodness in coming to him there—harped on the treatment she had received, on Freytag, Fredersdorff, and the "Goat," in every letter he wrote. In one at least, written at this period, he ominously signed himself Gentleman of the Chamber of the King of France. Voltaire was coming home.

He and Collini left Mayence on July 28th for Mannheim, where Charles Theodore, the Elector Palatine, had invited Voltaire to stay with him. They passed a night at Worms *en route*. Voltaire's spirits were light enough for him to pretend to be an Italian for the benefit of the Worms innkeeper, and make the supper what his secretary called "very diverting." At Mannheim, the Elector Palatine's Court being in the country, Voltaire spent a short time putting money matters in order, and changing his German money into French. He was nearly in his "patrie"; no wonder he was lighthearted. In a few days the Elector fetched him to Schwetzingen, his country house, where was held the gayest and most charming of little Courts. Voltaire always dined with the Elector, and after dinner read aloud to him one of his works. There were *fêtes* and concerts. The court theatrical company came to visit the author of "Zaire" and "Alzire," of "Mahomet" and "Mérope." Four of his own plays were acted. He was only too delighted to show the actors how to render this passage, and give to that character its true weight and significance. He began here ("like an old fool," he said) a new love drama called "The Orphan of China." If liberty was the passion of his life, the drama was the pet child of his leisure. An agreeable fortnight passed away. The distinguished guest was taken to see the Elector's library at Mannheim and presented to it the companion volume to that ill-omened "Poëshie" of the King my master—Frederick's "Memoirs of the House of Brandenburg."

While unconscious Voltaire was still at Schwetzingen, training actors, or reading the "Annals" to the Elector, d'Argenson, Voltaire's old school friend and member of the French Cabinet, recorded in his diary "Permission to re-enter France is refused to M. de Voltaire ... to please the King of Prussia."

On August 16th, Voltaire and Collini reached Strasburg and put up there at a poor little inn called the "White Bear," because it was kept by the father of a waiter at the inn at Mayence; and good-natured Voltaire had promised to patronise it to oblige him. He moved shortly to a little house outside the city gate, and received there everyone of note in Strasburg.

He was still hard at work on the "Annals." He spent the evening sometimes with the agreeable Countess de Lutzelburg, who lived near. He took counsel about his "Annals" with Schoepflin, the German historian. Altogether he would have passed a couple of months quite after his heart— if—if—Madame Denis had been able to tell him that it was safe for him to proceed further into France. Alsace was the borderline. On it was written, it seemed, "Thus far shalt thou come, but no further." But still—patience, patience! Voltaire did not yet despair. He knew nothing of that entry in d'Argenson's diary. But much bitter experience had taught him that discretion is the better part of valour. On October 2d he left Strasburg, and arrived the same evening at Colmar.

Colmar was a well-chosen spot for several reasons. One was that Schoepflin's brother, who was a printer, was going to print Voltaire's "Annals" for him there. Another was that Colmar had plenty of agreeable literary society. And a third—and most important—it was very conveniently situated for the receipt of Madame Denis's communications. Within a drive of it was Lunéville. Two days' journey from it was Cirey. Its upper classes all spoke French. And though the Jesuits were no small power in it, Voltaire seems to have forgotten that unpleasant little fact, when he came. He went into modest rooms; and was his own housekeeper, with a young peasant girl called Babet, whose gaiety, simplicity, and volubility much entertained him, as cook. He played chess after dinner with Collini. His way of life delighted tastes always modest; and his health improved rapidly. He drew plans for his "Orphan." With a brilliant play he had successfully defied his enemies before. Why not again? But the dramatic muse required much wooing this time; and the most versatile writer in the world began compiling articles for the "Encyclopædia" instead.

In this October Voltaire buried himself in the village of Luttenbach, near Colmar, for a fortnight, where he was happy enough proof-correcting his "Annals" and still hoping for good news from France. On October 28th, he came back to Colmar, had a fit of the gout, and, as usual, gaily bemoaned his ill-health in all his letters.

He still liked Colmar. He still thought he was creeping home. Prussia was behind him; and, though he was nearly sixty years old and always talked of himself as dying, he knew there was still a world before.

And then, in this December of 1753, Fate struck him one of those stunning blows she had too often dealt him.

Just as he was hoping for the best, as his friends in Paris were straining every nerve to smooth the way for his return, as he was laboriously wooing the histrionic muse that he might captivate the capital with a comedy; just as he had renounced Frederick and Prussia and remembered that he was Gentleman-in-Ordinary to his French Majesty and a Frenchman body and soul, and no Prussian after all, there appeared at The Hague, in a shamefully incorrect pirated edition, the most ambitious, the most voluminous, the most characteristic, and the most daring of all Voltaire's works, the "Essay on the Manners and Mind of Nations."

If Madame du Châtelet "despised history a little," it had not the less been her and her lover's chief employment at Cirey. "The Century of Louis XIV." was not enough to occupy such an energy as Voltaire's. That cramped him to one time and to one country. And behold! there was the world to look back upon; the history of all nations to study—the progress of mankind to regard as a whole.

The "Essay on the Manners and Mind of Nations" is of all Voltaire's works the one which has exerted the most powerful influence on the mind of men. On July 10, 1791, when his body was taken to Paris and placed on the ruins of the Bastille on the very spot where he himself had been a prisoner, on the funeral car were written the memorable words, "He gave the human mind a great impetus: he prepared us for freedom." That line might have served as the motto of his great essay. It prepared men for freedom. It records the history of human progress from Charlemagne to Louis XIII. It was the first history which dealt not with kings, the units, but with the great, panting, seething masses they ruled; which took history to mean the advance of the whole human race—a general view of the great march of all nations towards light and liberty. It was the first history which struck out boldly, and hit prejudice and oppression a staggering blow from which they have not yet recovered. Yet its style is infinitely frank, gay, and daring. It is such easy reading, so light, clear, and sarcastic. It is the one book of its kind the frivolous will finish for pleasure. It has such a jesting manner to hide its weighty matter. It is infinitely significant; and yet sounds as if it were simply meant to be amusing. It is said that Voltaire put it into such a form to overcome Madame du Châtelet's dislike of history. But it was his lifelong principle as a writer that to be dull is the greatest of all errors. He was always wishing that Newton had written vaudevilles; and praying that his own taste might never be "stifled with study." What Frederick the Great called the "effervescence of his genius" bubbles over in the "Essay on the Manners and Mind of Nations," as in all his works. But it must be remembered that easy reading means hard writing; and that this "picture of the centuries," this "history of the human mind," needed, as its author declared, "the patience of a Benedictine and the pen of a Bossuet." When he wrote "Finis" on the last page of the last edition in 1775, the book numbered six volumes, and was in every sense the greatest of its author's works. Parton has justly said that to it "Grote, Niebuhr, Gibbon, Colenso, and especially Buckle, are all indebted." That it is full of mistakes which any fairly well-educated person of to-day could easily correct does not make it a less extraordinary production for the age in which it was produced. That it is now obsolete, only proves how thoroughly it accomplished its aim. The great new truths for which Voltaire fought with his life in his hand are the commonplaces and the truisms of to-day.

But then he made them so.

Jean Néaulme, the pirate publisher at The Hague, said he had bought the manuscript from a servant of Prince Charles of Lorraine—Charles having obtained it either by persuasion or treachery from Frederick the Great. Voltaire had given a manuscript copy of the book to his royal friend. In his present state of mind, it was only natural he should suspect Frederick of foul play.

However this might be, the thing was printed. It was called, and miscalled, "An Abridgment of Universal History." It was filled from end to end with astounding, and, very often, wilful blunders. It confused the eighth century with the fourth, and the twelfth with the thirteenth, and Boniface VIII. with Boniface VII. The unhappy author, with tears in his eyes, called it "the disgrace of literature." He had, of course, never corrected the proofs. Since writing that first

LEKAIN

From an Engraving after a Painting by S. B. Le Noir

manuscript, intrusted to Frederick, he had written other manuscripts wherein he had not only modified but actually changed his first ideas. This time at least, when he followed his old plan of loudly disavowing the work, he had much justification. The "pretended Universal History," as he called it, *was* his "Essay," but so mauled and disfigured he may be forgiven for refusing to acknowledge it.

But far stronger than any merely literary reasons for denying such a paternity was the bold, free-spoken character of this son of his genius. Voltaire knew that no work he had ever written would so bar his way back to his country as this one. Every line glowed with some truth hateful to Boyers and to tyranny. There was never any mistaking a Voltaire's meaning. Now, more than ever, he had written in luminous words which, like sunbeams, being much condensed, greatly burnt. His principles were as lucid as daylight. There was hardly a phrase which would not draw upon him "the implacable wrath of the clergy." How could he forget in it such remarks as the following—"Rome has always decided for the opinion which most degraded the human mind and most completely annihilated human reason"?

"Whoso thinks makes others think."

How could he help remembering that he had taken the Protestant Reformation as a new tyranny—not an emancipation; that he had degraded war "from the highest to the lowest place in the historian's regard"; and had declared that "Tyrants sacrifice the human race to an individual"—a dangerous sentence in itself, and which that abominable pirate publisher had rendered a thousand times more dangerous by misquoting as "Kings sacrifice the human race to a caprice"? He had offended every powerful class, and every cherished prejudice. But action was now, not less than ever, his *forte*. If it could not save him from his enemies, it could save him from himself—from that worst combination, idleness with misery.

On December 28, 1753, he wrote to Néaulme, and told M. Jean his candid opinion about that edition. He also wrote not a little piteously, a very few days after, to his old friend Madame de Pompadour—the publication of that "Essay" forcing him to prove, he said, his innocence to his master the King—of France.

But it was in vain he reminded Louis XV., through her, that he had spent years of his life in writing the history of Louis's predecessor; "and alone of the Academicians had had his panegyric translated into five languages." That surly Bourbon, with that intuition which saved his degraded race a hundred times from earlier and completer ruin, saw in the genius of Voltaire the fuse which was to set ablaze the gunpowder of sedition and misery with which his France was undermined. He turned to Madame de Pompadour and said that he "did not wish" Voltaire to return to Paris. It is not difficult to imagine the exile's state of mind. "I have no comfort but in work and solitude," he wrote; and to Cideville, on January

28th of this new year 1754: "My dear Cideville, at our age one must mock at everything and live for self. This world is a great shipwreck. *Sauve qui peut!* but I am far from the shore."

On what shore would he be allowed to land if he could gain one?

Colmar, he soon discovered, was "a town of Hottentots governed by German Jesuits." On February 17th, he wrote a very meek, artful letter to one of those Jesuits, Father Menou (whom he had known at the Court of Stanislas and of whom he speaks in his "Memoirs" as "the boldest and most intriguing priest I ever knew"), pleading his cause with him. He pleaded it, too, with the Archbishop of Paris through M. de Malesherbes. But it was all in vain. The Church was as offended as the King.

On February 20th, pushed to extremity, and neither able to leave nor to stay in this wretched Colmar without the sanction of his French Majesty, the unhappy man asked d'Argenson to "sound the King's indulgence"—to know if he might travel.

On February 22d, he called in two notaries, who compared the correct manuscript of his "Essay" with the two incorrect volumes published at The Hague; and drew up a formal declaration in which they affirmed that the Dutch edition was "surreptitious, full of errors, and worthy of all contempt," and that the real "Essay" was at least eight times longer than the false one. But that also was useless. Neither Court nor Catholic meant to be convinced.

Then, as if her uncle's cup of misfortune were not brimming over already, niece Denis's bad management and extravagance with his money in Paris forced him to appoint an agent to look after her affairs; and she, living on his bounty, turned and accused him of avarice. No public wrongs are so cruel as private ones. Beside Madame Denis's ingratitude, excommunication, said Voltaire, would have been a light penalty. He had given her an ample fortune—a larger one than old Maître Arouet had left his Voltaire. Her reproaches were the unkindest cut of all.

That they were singularly ill-timed may be gathered from the fact that sixty thousand francs of Voltaire's income were derived from annuities or bonds of the City of Paris, of which at any moment angry Louis might deprive him, by a line of writing and the royal signature, for ever. Two kings were now his enemies. Jesuitical Colmar hated him. Prussia and France were barred to him. Denis had turned upon him. The Pompadour was helpless. The "Essay," filled with blunders and pregnant with daring and danger, was all over Europe. Such was Voltaire's position in the month of March, 1754.

CHAPTER XXVII

THE ARRIVAL IN SWITZERLAND

RECEIVING no answer to his request to be allowed to travel, Voltaire prudently resolved to consider that silence gave consent. But he was still not a little nervous that if he took refuge in a foreign country Louis XV. might consider himself justified in seizing the pensions of his truant subject.

And then, where was he to go? It seems most likely that if it had not been for that unromantic disorder called *mal de mer* he would have ended his days in Pennsylvania. He had still his *bizarre* liking for the Quakers; and America was the country of the free. To be sure *mal du pays* was a worse and a longer lived disorder with him than the other: and if he had tried Pennsylvania on one impulse, he would quickly have left it on another.

He looked back lovingly, too, on bold little England, "where one thinks as a free man." And on March 19, 1754, he asked M. Polier de Bottens, who had been a Calvinist minister at Lausanne, if he could assure him of as much freedom in Lausanne as in Britain. Meanwhile, there was no reason why, in the near future, that long-deferred and greatly discussed Plombières visit should not take place.

And, for the time, he was in Colmar. On January 12th of this year he had sent his Duchess of Saxe-Gotha twelve advance copies of those "Annals of the Empire" written at her request, and just printed under Voltaire's own eye at Colmar by Schoepflin. In return, Madame had done her gracious best to reconcile him with Frederick. He was anxious to be reconciled. Frederick could influence France to receive back her prodigal, as could no one else. "Brother Voltaire," as he signed himself in his letters to her, also pleaded his cause once more with the Margravine of Bayreuth; and then sent Frederick himself a copy of those "Annals" as a tentative olive branch. Frederick accepted the book, and declined the peace overtures in a letter, dated March 16, 1754, which contained bitter allusion to the Maupertuis affair and showed that the kingly heart was still sore and that the kingly soul still angrily admired the great gifts of his Voltaire.

The famous suppers "went to the devil" without him. But if the King missed his wit much, he dreaded it more; and if Voltaire wanted the King's powerful friendship—he did not want the King's society. They were better apart. And, for the first time, both were wise enough to know it.

To this spring belongs a very active correspondence between Voltaire, the most voluble correspondent who ever put pen to paper, and Madame du Deffand. Blind, bored, and brilliant, the friend of Horace Walpole, a courtier at Sceaux, and the head of one of the most famous salons in Paris, Madame du Deffand had long been a friend of Voltaire's, and had visited him in the Bastille in 1726, just before his exile in England.

If she thought, as Frederick the Great wrote to Darget on April 1st of this same year 1754, that Voltaire was "good to read and bad to know," her cynic old soul loved his wit if she feared it. Perhaps she even loved him—though mistrustingly. Blindness had just fallen upon her. And "the hermit of Colmar"—neither now nor ever only *méchant*—wrote to her with the finest sympathy and tact, cheering, amusing, rallying her. "My eyes were a little wet when I read what had happened to yours.... If you are an annuitant, Madame, take care of yourself, eat little, go to bed early, and live to be a hundred, if only to enrage those who pay your annuities. For my part, it is the only pleasure I have left. I reflect, when I feel an indigestion coming on, that two or three princes will gain by my death: and I take courage out of pure malice and conspire against them with rhubarb and sobriety."

As Voltaire could have had nothing to gain by continually writing to amuse this blind old *mondaine*, it may be conceded that he did it out of kindness; and that if he loved her cleverness, he also pitied her misfortune. The eighteenth century, which failed so dismally in all other domestic relationships, perfectly understood the art of friendship.

On the Easter Day of this 1754, Voltaire, having first confessed to a Capuchin monk, received the Sacrament. *Faire ses Pâques* declares the laxest Catholic to be still a son of the Church. What Voltaire's motives were in this action, it is not easy to see. It is said that his anxious friends in Paris recommended the action as an answer to the charges of unbelief brought against him. But a Voltaire must have known well enough that such an answer as that would impose on no one. Besides, it was not like him to be governed by the advice of fools—even if they happened to be his friends. The reasons he himself gave for the action were that at Rome one must do as Rome does. "When men are surrounded by barbarians ... one must imitate their contortions.... Some people are afraid to touch spiders, others swallow them." "If I had a hundred thousand men, I know exactly what I should do: but I have not, so I shall communicate at Easter, and you can call me a hypocrite as much as you like."

The hypocrisy was but ill acted. Voltaire received the Sacrament with an irreverence painful to believers and harmful to his own reputation. To him the thing was a jest—"the contortions of barbarians." He was quite mocking and gay. When he got home, he sent to the Capuchin convent a dozen of good wine and a loin of veal. I despise you too much to be ill-natured to you! If you believe in this mummery, you are fools! If you connive at it, unbelieving, you are knaves! Knaves or fools, I can laugh at you quite good-humouredly. If ever present conveyed a message, this was the message conveyed by the dozen of wine and the loin of veal.

To justify Voltaire for this act is not possible. It was at best a *méchanceté*. It was the mocking, jesting nature of the man getting the upper hand alike of his prudence and of his consideration for others. He was himself a Deist, and a firmly convinced Deist. To him the religion of Rome was not merely a folly but the stronghold of tyranny and of darkness. The fact that millions of faithful souls had found in her bosom consolation for the sorrows, and a key to the mysteries of life and of death, did not soften him.

In Voltaire was lacking now and ever that "crown of man's moral manhood," reverence. To find in "the last restraint of the powerful and the last hope of the wretched" only subject for a laugh was the greatest of his faults. If he had been a nobler nature, he would have seen the beauty and the virtue which lie even in the most degrading theologies: and respecting them, would have stayed his hand from the smashing blow, and for the sake of the virtue which sweetens corruption, have let corruption alone.

It has been done many times. "No man can achieve great things for his country without some loss of the private virtues." A reverent Voltaire— what a contradiction in terms!—to spare some goodness, must have spared much vice. To arouse eighteenth-century France, steeped to her painted lips in superstition, and the slavery which had debased her till she came to love it, the shrieks and the blasphemies of a Voltaire and a Rousseau were necessary. No calmer voice would have waked her from her narcotic sleep. "Without Voltaire and Rousseau there would have been no Revolution." No honest student of eighteenth-century France can doubt that that Revolution, though it crushed the innocent with the guilty and left behind it some of the worst fruits of anarchy, left behind it too a France which, with all its faults, is a thousand times better than the France it found.

By the middle of April the Plombières arrangements were well advanced. The d'Argental household was to be there; and Madame Denis, more or less penitent and more or less forgiven, had asked to join the party. The waters would be good for a health—ruined, said her temperate uncle, by "remedies and gourmandising." Voltaire would come, with a couple of servants at the most. He was anticipating the change with pleasure when at the very last minute Madame Denis wrote to tell him that Maupertuis was at Plombières too. It was certainly not big enough to hold both him and his enemy. The events of the last months had taught even Voltaire some kind of caution. He was absolutely *en partant* when Madame Denis's letter came; but on June 8th, though he left Colmar, it was to stop halfway between it and Plombières, at the Abbey of Senones, as the guest of Dom Calmet, who had himself been a visitor at Cirey. Calmet had a splendid library. His visitor, who was condemned, as he said, to work at a correct edition of that "General History, printed for my misfortune," made good use of it, during his three weeks' visit. Absurd reports were noised abroad—which the Dom did not contradict—that he had converted "the most pronounced Deist in Europe." But, as the Deist himself said, his business was with the library—not with matins and vespers. Directly Maupertuis left Plombières, Voltaire took leave of Calmet and his monks, and on some day not earlier than July 2d left for Plombières, where he found not only his dear d'Argentals and Madame Denis, but her sister, Madame de Fontaine, as well.

The little party passed here an agreeable fortnight or so. About July 22d, Voltaire returned to Colmar with Madame Denis, who from this time forth managed, or mismanaged, his house for him till his death. The "Universal History" greatly occupied him after his holiday. But there was another subject which was even more engrossing.

It was the idea of living in Switzerland. Since March the plan of seeking "an agreeable tomb in the neighbourhood of Geneva," or possibly near Lausanne, had been growing—growing. There were many reasons why the little republic was a suitable home for Voltaire. In the first place, it *was* a republic. It was quite close to France, though not in it; and though France might not like to have such a firebrand as Voltaire burning in her midst, she would not object to be lit by his light if it were burning near.

Then Switzerland was Protestant—and in Voltaire's English experience of Protestantism he had found that faith singularly tolerant and easy-going—in practice, that is, not in principle. By August he was negotiating actively with M. de Brenles, a lawyer of Lausanne, about "a rather pretty property" on the lake of Geneva. It was called Allamans; and Voltaire was not a little disappointed when his negotiations for buying it fell through. In October he was inquiring if a Papist could not possess and bequeath land in the territory of Lausanne. He urged secrecy on de Brenles; and entered fully into money matters. If he bought land, it was to be in the name of his niece, Madame Denis. There was a danger throughout these months of that bomb the "Pucelle" bursting—into print—"and killing me." That fear made the Swiss arrangements go forward with a will.

On October 23d, Voltaire went to supper at a poor tavern of Colmar, called the "Black Mountain," with no less a personage than his friend Wilhelmina of Bayreuth. She overwhelmed him with kindness and attention; asked him to stay with her; begged she might see Madame Denis, and made a thousand excuses for the bad behaviour of brother Frederick; so that impulsive Voltaire jumped once more to that favourite conclusion of his that "women are worth more than men." To be sure, if he had seen an account of the interview his clever Princess wrote to her brother, he might have thought something less highly of her and her sex. But he did not see it; nor Frederick's bitter reply. If he had, neither flattery nor opprobrium would have moved him now from one fixed resolve—to shelter in Switzerland.

On November 11th, Voltaire, Collini, Madame Denis, a lady's maid, and a servant left Colmar to visit the Duke of Richelieu at Lyons. Voltaire had lived at Colmar on and off for thirteen months—among Jesuits who five years earlier had publicly burnt the works of Bayle, the prophet of tolerance. He could not have left with regret. Just as they were starting off, Collini declares that his master, finding the travelling carriage overladen with luggage, gave orders that everything should be taken out except his own trunk and Madame Denis's; and that he told Collini to sell *his* portmanteau and its contents. The hot-tempered young Italian refused to do so, and gave notice on the spot. On his own showing, his impetuous master made at once the handsomest apologies for his little burst of temper; gave the secretary generous presents of money as a peace-offering; and made him re-pack his portmanteau and put it back in the carriage. The storm blew over; but Collini, like almost all Voltaire's servants, was beginning to take advantage of his master's indulgence, and to trespass on a kindness which Voltaire made doubly kind to compensate for his irritability.

By November 15th, the party were installed in a very bad inn, called the "Palais Royal," at Lyons. Voltaire complained that it was "a little too much of a joke for a sick man to come a hundred *lieues* to talk to the Maréchal de Richelieu." But he and Richelieu were not only very old friends but, in spite of little disagreements such as that affair of the "Panegyric of Louis XV." at Court in 1749, very faithful friends. The brilliant author and the brilliant soldier had still for each other the attraction which had been potent twenty years earlier in those June days at Montjeu, when Voltaire had negotiated the marriage between Mademoiselle de Guise and the gallant Duke. The charming wife had died young; and her husband and Voltaire had met little of late. But Voltaire received Richelieu in the bad inn, and clever Richelieu made the five days he stayed at Lyons so infinitely soothing and agreeable for his much tried and harassed friend, that when Richelieu left, Voltaire said he felt like Ariadne in Naxos after the desertion of Theseus.

While he was at Lyons the enterprising traveller also went to call on Cardinal de Tencin, head of the Church there, uncle of d'Argental, and brother of that famous Madame de Tencin who had played Thisbe to Voltaire's Pyramus when Voltaire was in the Bastille in 1726. The wary Lord Cardinal stated to M. de Voltaire that he could not ask a person in such ill-favour with his Majesty of France to dine with him. Voltaire replied that he never dined out, and knew how to take his own part against kings and cardinals; and, so saying, turned his back on his Eminence and went out of the room. As he and Collini were returning from that brief visit, the visitor observed absently that this country was not made for him. The officer in command of the troops in Lyons received him in much the same way. All the authorities were cold, in fact, to propitiate that Highest Authority at the Court of France, who was colder still. However, their disapproval was not very afflicting. The town of Lyons saw Voltaire with bolder eyes. It acted his plays at the theatre; and when he appeared in his box there, loudly applauded him. On November 26th, he formally took his seat in the Lyons Academy, of which he had long been an honorary member. Then, too, Wilhelmina was in Lyons; and Wilhelmina used her shrewd influence with de Tencin, and at a second interview, behold! the Church and Deism on quite friendly terms.

As a whole, the Lyons visit was a success; or would have been but for Voltaire's ill-health and "mortal anxieties" about "that cursed 'Pucelle.'" He was afraid that it was in the possession of Mademoiselle du Thil, once companion to Madame du Châtelet, who had found it among Émilie's effects. The ill-health, too, which took the form of gouty rheumatism this time, was so painful and annoying that many of his friends had strongly recommended him to try for it the waters of Aix-in-Savoy. In the meantime he had been lent "a charming house halfway." On December 10, 1754, he, Madame Denis, and Collini left Lyons for ninety-three miles distant Geneva, which they reached on December 13th and found gaily celebrating a victory gained in 1602 over the Duke of Savoy. The gates of the city were shut for the night when they arrived. But the great M. de Voltaire was expected: and they were flung open for him. He supped that night in Geneva with a man who was to be till his death one of the best and wisest friends he ever had, the famous Dr. Tronchin.

No account of Voltaire's life in Switzerland could be complete without mention of that honourable and celebrated family, who in the eighteenth century nobly filled many important posts in the Swiss republic and whose descendants are well known in it to the present day. One Tronchin, the Swiss jurisconsult, is celebrated as having provoked, by certain "Letters from the Country," the famous "Letters from the Mountain" of Jean Jacques Rousseau. Another, the Councillor François Tronchin, the most delightful and hospitable of men, was at once the constant correspondent, the legal adviser—in brief, the factotum of Voltaire.

But the most famous of the family, as well as the one most intimately associated with Voltaire, was Theodore Tronchin, the doctor. Handsome face, noble mind, fearless spirit, with the stern uprightness of the Puritan, and an infinite benevolence and compassion all his own—if greatness meant only goodness, friend Theodore was a greater man than his great patient, Voltaire.

Yet, though no spark of the Voltairian genius was in him, he was the most enlightened doctor of his age. It is not only as the intimate of that "old baby" as he called him, the Patriarch of Ferney, that Tronchin may well interest the present day: but as the earliest discoverer—after eighteen centuries of stuffiness—of the value of fresh air; as the first of his class who preached the Gospel of Nature; recommended temperance, exercise, cleanliness in lieu of the drugs of the Pharmacopœia; and, after years of labour, taught the woman of his age to be very nearly as good a mother to her children as is the lioness to her cubs. Tronchin deserves to be famous.

It was he who discountenanced the idea of Voltaire trying the waters of Aix. Tronchin's diagnosis always went through the body to the soul. No doubt he saw that this *vif*, irritable, nervous patient—torn to pieces with the quarrels and the excitement of the last five years—wanted, not the waters of Aix, but of Lethe: peace, quiet, monotony, and a home.

After four days' stay in Geneva, Voltaire and suite reached the "charming house" which had been lent him, and which was ten miles from Geneva and called the Château of Prangins. It stood on very high ground, overlooking the lake from thirteen immense windows. There was too much house and too little garden. The house was only half furnished, and beaten by every wind that blew. And it was mid-winter in Switzerland. Was it really so charming? Madame Denis was volubly discontented. Italian Collini, who felt he had been cheated out of going to Paris, was extremely cross and cold. His master and mistress were always calling him to make up the fires, shut the windows, and bring them their furs. The draughts were really abominable. And what was one to do here? "Be bored; in a worse temper than usual; and write a great deal of history; be as bad a philosopher as in the town; and have not the slightest idea what is to become of us." This was discontented Collini's account of Prangins. He was pluming his wings for flight, and not at all in the mood to make the best of things.

It was Voltaire who did that. Between the grumbling niece and secretary, acutely sensitive himself to physical discomfort, not a little worried by the memory of that "abortion of a Universal History," compelled to wait for a package of absolutely necessary books that ought to have come from Paris and had not, so ill that by January 3, 1755, he could not even hold a pen, he was still, in spite of angry Collini's insinuations, the same true philosopher who had astronomised with Madame du Châtelet sitting by the roadside on a January evening on the cushions of their broken-down carriage. He was still busy and cheerful. "*They* have need of courage," he wrote of his companions, very justly. As for himself, he worked and forgot the cold. It was in these early days of his life in Switzerland that he arranged with the Brothers Cramer, the famous publishers of Geneva, to bring out the first complete edition of his writings. Then he heard from d'Argental that the public of Paris resented his exile. What warmth and comfort in that! "Nanine" was played there with success; and a play of Crébillon's was a failure. That would have made one glow with satisfaction in any climate. And if Prangins was cold, two at least of the influential persons in the neighbourhood had written warmly to assure the famous newcomer of their good offices.

And better than all, better a thousand times, through this chill, discontented January, Voltaire was eagerly looking for a house and property of his own, in this free little Switzerland, where he might settle down at last and be in peace. On January 31, 1755, he was in active negotiation about two houses. On February 1st there appeared in the Registers of the Council of State of Geneva a special permission to M. de Voltaire—who alleged the state of his health and the necessity for living near his doctor, Tronchin, as a reason for wishing to settle in Switzerland—to inhabit the territory of the republic under the good pleasure of the Seigneury.

On February 8th or 9th the Councillor Tronchin bought a property quite close to Geneva, called Saint-Jean, which he let on a life lease to Voltaire, and which, in a characteristic enthusiasm and before he had had any practical experience of it, Voltaire rechristened "Les Délices." Thus he was enabled to evade the law of the republic, and, Papist though he nominally was, to live and hold property under the Genevan republic.

A few days later he acquired a second house, called Monrion, on the way from Lausanne to Ouchy.

He was now sixty-one years old. Strong in his heart all his life had been his love of a home. For a while Cirey had seemed like one. But it had never belonged to him. It was, too, in France; and there had been often the painful necessity of leaving it as quickly as possible, and without any surety of being allowed to come back again. The man's whole life had been a buffeting from pillar to post.

But the fretted youth in Paris, the restless middle age at Lunéville, Brussels, Cirey, and the angry hurry of Prussia were over for ever.

When he settled in Switzerland Voltaire took a new lease of his life. He entered upon its last, greatest, noblest, and calmest epoch.

CHAPTER XXVIII

THE DÉLICES, AND THE "POEM ON THE DISASTER OF LISBON"

IN 1755, the little republic of Geneva contained twenty thousand of some of the most simple, honest, frugal, and industrious persons in the world. Calvin had been dead two centuries. But his influence yet lived in laws which regulated not only the worship but the food and the drink of his followers; which bade them rise at five in summer and at six in winter, under penalty of a fine; allowed but two dishes at their tables; and made more than one fire in a house appear unjustifiable extravagance. In many respects the Genevan Calvinists of the time of Voltaire were not unlike a certain section of Scottish society. Austere in morals, and shrewd in mind, narrow, laborious, economical, equally exempt from degrading poverty and degrading luxury, content with stern pleasures, and a brief and rigid creed—the Calvinist was but a severer Presbyterian after all. By the middle of the eighteenth century, indeed, one party of the Genevans had been influenced not a little, on the side of their intellect, by the new science, the new literature, the new philosophy, which were remoulding Europe; and beneath the Calvinistic gloom still felt the gay heart-beats of the Frenchman. But the other and larger party were Puritan to the marrow—who believed, with all the morbid intensity of their founder, that enjoyment was sinful, musical instruments had been invented by the devil, and play-acting was the abomination of desolation.

It was among such a people that this cynic Voltaire, whose motto was "Rire et fais rire," whose darling amusement was the drama, and whose incorrigible indulgence was the "Pucelle," had elected to live.

On the very day, February 9, 1755, when he completed his negotiations for buying the lease of Délices, a certain Pastor Vernet wrote to him, begging him to respect religion, and saying that the serious persons of the neighbourhood were not without their apprehensions on that count. But when it came to writing, Voltaire was more than a match for any pastor who ever lived. He responded by a letter brilliantly ambiguous; to which Vernet could take no exception, but in which he must have found much food for thought.

Les Délices stood on the top of a hill on the Lyons road and quite near to the town of Geneva. It was therefore in that republic, while it was ten minutes' walk from the Sardinian province of Savoy, half an hour's ride into France, and an hour's ride into Vaud. Altogether, a most prudent situation for a Voltaire. Lake Leman lapped the foot of its terraces. It was surrounded by gardens, whose beauty was only marred by high walls which shut out the lovely surrounding country. His signature on the lease was still wet when this enthusiastic Voltaire began pulling down those walls that he might look uninterruptedly upon one of the most beautiful views in Switzerland—across the city of Geneva, the junction of the rivers Arne and Rhone, to the Jura and the Alps. He called the place the Délices, he said, because "there is nothing more delightful than to be free and independent." Certainly, the Delights were his torments in some respects. He complained that the architect of Prangins had forgotten to make a garden, and the architect of Délices had forgotten to make a house. Its builder had built for himself; and the guest-rooms were inadequate and uncomfortable. But such defects could be remedied. The last occupant of Délices was the son of that Duchess of Saxe-Gotha who had inspired the "Annals." *That* seemed like a good omen.

Monrion, the second purchase, was on the way from Lausanne to Ouchy—at the other end of the lake from Délices. "Les Délices will be for the summer, Monrion for the winter, and you for all seasons," Voltaire wrote to Lawyer de Brenles, the very day he acquired Délices. "I wanted only one tomb. I shall have two." Monrion was comfortable and "sheltered from the cruel north wind"—"my little cabin," "my winter palace"—a "clean, simple house" such as its master loved. After his time it was inhabited by Tissot—a celebrated doctor, only second in reputation to Tronchin.

It is pleasant to see the keen youthful enjoyment and ardour with which Voltaire turned to the improvement of his new homes. The first letter he wrote from Délices is dated March 5, 1755, but, as has been noted, even before that date he was enthusiastically pulling down walls in the garden and planning new rooms for the house. By March 24th, he and Madame Denis were actually in the midst of building the "accommodation for our friends and our chickens—planting oranges and onions, tulips and carrots. One must found Carthage." The new fascination—the safest and best he had ever known—the fascination of home and garden, of country life, of pride in simple things—took possession of the most susceptible of men. He said with his cynic smile that he "was born faun and sylvan." He was at least strangely free from love of the pavement for a man who had spent on it all the most pliable years of his life. He wrote in this March that his whole conversation was of "masons, carpenters, and gardeners." Even Madame Denis, whose "natural aversion to a country life" her poor uncle was to have bitter cause to lament, liked the hurry and bustle of moving, and was for a while content.

There was much to be done, too, within doors. For himself, Voltaire's own tastes were always quite frugal and simple. He wanted neither fine furniture nor many servants. And as for rich eating and drink, from those, if he had ever desired them—which he had not—his health would have precluded him. His sternly frugal fare and love of simplicity about him should have pleased his Calvinistic neighbours. But he was a friend before all things. And Délices and Monrion were to be open to all his friends— who must be received with every hospitality and with every generous comfort of which their host could think. For them he would live like a rich man. For them he began spending that comfortable fortune he had acquired with so much sagacity, and very often with so much self-denial. He bought half a dozen horses and four carriages. He kept a couple of lackeys, a valet called Boisse, a French cook, and a cook's boy; maidservants, coachmen, a postilion, and gardeners; beside Collini, whose duties were only less universal than Longchamp's had been. That French cook soon had to provide a great many dinners for a great many diners; and generous suppers after evening theatricals. The carriages had to be sent to bring the economical, quiet-going neighbours to and from the dinner parties. The carriage Voltaire kept for his own use was of antique build, with a blue ground speckled with gold stars; but it was his fancy always to drive this remarkable equipage into Geneva with four horses to it—to the great excitement and astonishment of the grave little republic. On one occasion the people so crowded round him to see him alight from this extraordinary conveyance, that he called out, "What do you want to see, boobies? A skeleton? Well, here is one," and he threw off his cloak. The establishment of Délices was further completed by a tame bear and a monkey. The monkey, who bit the hand that caressed him, was called Luc. So in his letters of the time Voltaire soon began to allude to a certain royal friend as Luc too.

Voltaire had been established at Délices about a month, when in April his first visitor, Lekain the actor, came to stay with him. Lekain, who in 1750 had been nobody at all but a clever young dependent on the bounty of the famous M. de Voltaire, was himself famous now, as one of the best tragedians in Paris. Of course the amateur dramatic talents of Délices took advantage of the professional genius of Lekain. "Zaire" was rehearsed; and then read aloud in one of the large rooms of the house. Denis and Lekain were in the principal parts. Voltaire took his favourite *rôle* of Lusignan, and declared gaily that no company in Europe had a better old fool in it than himself. The frigid Calvinists and the Tronchins, who formed the audience, were in tears. Lekain had more sentiment than voice, said Voltaire; and was so moved sometimes as to be inaudible. But then he moved his audience too. That was the great thing. He and his amateurs also read some part of the new play, "The Orphan of China"; and when Lekain left he carried away most of it in his box with the view of producing it in Paris.

But even at Délices the man who had written the "Pucelle" could not long expect to find only the pleasures of play-acting and the agreeable troubles of an estate. Since he began it, in 1730, the thing had been copied, and miscopied, read, re-read, quoted, and travestied a thousand times. It had been imitated by King Frederick in the "Palladium"; and read aloud to the Prussian princesses and the Duchess of Saxe-Gotha. It had been transcribed *for* Prince Henry, and *by* Longchamp. It was everybody's secret; but still it *was* a secret. There was one indecorum it had not yet committed—that of print.

And in this January of 1755 had come that unpleasant news that a manuscript *was* in the possession of Mademoiselle du Thil; and then, like a clap of thunder, the announcement that the thing "was printed and being sold for a louis in Paris."

The publication of such a work would have been disastrous for Voltaire at any moment; but it was doubly disastrous now. Here he was just settling down upon his estate as a sober, respectable country gentleman, very much minded to stand well with his strait-laced neighbours, very fond of his new home, not at all inclined to leave it, and having nowhere to go if he did leave it—yet holding his land and his right to live on it only at the "good pleasure" of a very strict Seigneury. To make matters worse, the printed "Pucelle" was (of course) full of errors; and while it was much less witty than the original, was not at all less indecent. At first there seemed to be nothing to be done but to follow the old, old plan. The thing is not mine at all! Here, for instance, is a passage abusing Richelieu—and Richelieu is my friend! And then, to make assurance doubly sure, Voltaire tried another very artful and most characteristic *ruse*. He employed hundreds of copyists in Paris to copy it as incorrectly as possible. Then all his friends, as well as himself, denied loudly and vehemently that he was the author thereof. A Voltaire write such bad verse—so *fade*, so *plat*, so prosy! Impossible! At the same time, Voltaire sent copies of such a "Pucelle"—or such parts of *the* "Pucelle"—as he wished to avow, to all his acquaintance and all persons in authority. It was a very good idea. It cost a great deal of money, and a great deal of trouble; and might have been of some use if M. de Voltaire's character and writings had not been known and feared these forty years.

On July 26th, Grasset, a publisher of Lausanne, appeared at the Délices and kindly offered to sell M. de Voltaire the incorrect copy of his own "Pucelle" for fifty louis. Voltaire had already written to Grasset to tell him in no mild terms that those "rags of manuscript" were not his "Pucelle" at all, but the work of some person who had neither "poetic art, good sense, nor good morals"; and that of such a thing Grasset would not sell a hundred copies. His rage, therefore, may be imagined. He denounced Grasset to the Genevan authorities; and had the satisfaction of seeing that misguided person made fast in prison—for a time. On July 27th, factotum Collini was sent up to Paris to see if he could not better matters there. But Paris burnt the "Pucelle." The Pope prohibited it; and it sold lustily. It is not a little curious that Voltaire himself never in all his life suffered anything worse from it than frights: though of those he had enough and to spare. In 1757, a Parisian printer was sentenced to nine years at the galleys for printing an edition. Geneva—pretending to believe, and trying to believe, that M. de Voltaire was not its author—burnt the accursed thing as Paris had done; knowing that M. de Voltaire could only be glad to see the destruction of such a wicked travesty of his respectable poem. With what a wry smile he must have watched that bonfire!

The republic, however, for the moment, ostensibly gave him the benefit of the doubt. And then in this very July, just when he ought to have been most cautious and circumspect, if this imprudent, mischievous person does not begin making a stage of inverted wine-barrels, painting scenery, getting together theatrical costumes, flashing sham lightning in a dust-pan, preparing sham thunder by means of the rims of two cartwheels—and, worse than all, a thousand times worse—recruiting a theatrical company from among the young people of Geneva! The young people were only too willing. The Council of State had swallowed—in disapproving silence—that reading of "Zaire" when Lekain had reduced "Tronchins and syndics" to tears. But this was a little too much. So on July 31st the Council met, and, as the result of a solemn confabulation, reminded M. de Voltaire that the drama, played publicly or privately, was contrary to their regulations, and that no Calvinists were allowed to take part in, or to witness, the same. Voltaire replied with a suspicious meekness that his only desire was to obey the "wise laws" of the government. He further wrote to Councillor Tronchin in terms quite abject. "No man who owes to your honourable body the privilege of living in this air ought to displease anyone who breathes it."

In brief, there was a different and quite as good an air in Lausanne, where the "wise laws" of Geneva had no sway. Lausanne loved play-acting; and M. de Voltaire had a house at Monrion.

In Paris, too, on August 20th, "The Orphan of China" was performed with brilliant success. Here was excellent consolation for the solemn resolutions of Genevan Councils. They might take offence at "Zaire," but Paris applauded "my Chinese baboons" to the echo. Poor Marie Leczinska, indeed, who not unnaturally saw evil in everything this sceptic, this Pompadour's favourite, did, saw it here too. But even her objections, that the piece contained lines hostile to religion and to the King, were too obviously unjust to harm it. The censor had passed it. Its first performance declared it Voltaire's greatest success since "Mérope." If Lekain *did* fall into his old fault and speak dreadfully indistinctly, Mademoiselle Clarion made the most charming of heroines, and the play was "all full of love"—tender, graceful, picturesque. It was played twelve or thirteen times in Paris; and when it was moved to Fontainebleau the Court delighted in it as much as the capital had done. In the annals of the French stage it is still remembered as the first play in which the actresses consented to forego their *paniers*.

Collini was present on the opening night. Even his grumbling pen allows that his master had made a very palpable hit. The pleasure-loving secretary had spent six weeks in Paris, almost entirely engaged in enjoying himself, before Voltaire recalled him in the friendliest of terms.

On August 30, 1755, Voltaire wrote from Délices one of his most famous letters; perhaps one of the most famous letters in the world. It was to Jean Jacques Rousseau, and thanked him for the "Discourse on the Origin of Inequality among Men," which Rousseau had written as a prize essay at the Academy of Dijon, and now sent for the approval of the great master. The "Discourse" was nothing but an elaboration of Rousseau's famous theory—the advantage of savage over civilised life. Years before, at the French Court in 1745, Voltaire and Rousseau had had dealings with each other. They now renewed that acquaintance. Voltaire's letter began, "I have received, Sir, your new book against the human race.... No one has ever employed so much wit in trying to make us beasts: one longs to go on four paws when one reads your book, but, personally, it is sixty years since I lost the habit, and I feel it is impossible for me to resume it." He went on to agree with Jean Jacques that literature and science brought many troubles to their votaries; and instanced his own case with as quick a feeling as if all his wrongs were of yesterday. But, "literature nourishes, rectifies, and consoles the soul ... one must love it, in spite of the way it is abused, as one must love society, though the wicked corrupt its sweetness: as one must love one's country, though one suffers injustice from it; and one's God, though superstition and fanaticism degrade His service."

On September 10th, Rousseau replied from Paris in warm terms of friendship, and agreeing with the superior wisdom of his master's argument. As yet, each could see the other's genius—and reverence it. They could disagree and be friends.

The autumn at Délices was further marked by the visit of Patu, a poet, who was a friend of David Garrick's and wrote him an ecstatic account of his boyishly energetic host; and by a *fracas* with Madame Denis.

The facts that that foolish person was fat, short, forty-five years old, and squinted, did not, it has been said, make her less fond of admiration from the opposite sex, or less prone to make a fool of herself in a flirtation when opportunity offered.

In the present case Uncle Voltaire suspected her of being a party to a theft her old admirer, the Marquis de Ximenès, had made of some manuscript notes for Voltaire's "Campaigns of the King." Ximenès had sold the notes to a publisher. Madame Denis's voluble denials would certainly prove nothing. Voltaire was already quite aware of what Madame d'Épinay discovered after a very short acquaintance with her, that his niece was constitutionally a liar.

And then, on November 24th, came news which staggered Voltaire's soul; and beside which all petty trouble seemed shameful. On November 1, 1755, Lisbon was destroyed by an earthquake. It was All Saints' Day, and the churches were full. In six minutes, fifteen thousand persons were dead; and fifteen thousand more were dying.

In these days, when every morning has its "crisis" and every evening its "appalling disaster," it is difficult to realise the effect of the earthquake at Lisbon upon the eighteenth century. The less news there is, the more is that news felt. In the eighteenth century, too, all thoughtful persons saw signs in the heavens and the earth of some great change; and felt in the social order throes, which might be the death pangs of the old world, or the birth pains of a new. Further, men had begun to think and to reason for themselves: to ask why? from whence? to what end? and to brush aside the answers of the old theologies to those ancient questions as trite, unproven, and inadequate.

And if this was the temper of mind of most thoughtful persons, how much more of a Voltaire!

The news took nearly a month to reach him. For many months after he received it, there is hardly one of his letters which does not allude to it in terms of a passionate horror or a passionate inquiry. "The best of all possible worlds!" "If Pope had been there would he have said 'Whatever is, is right'?" "All is well seems to me absurd, when evil is on land and sea." "I no longer dare to complain of my ailments: none must dare to think of himself in a disaster so general." "Beaumont, who has escaped, says there is not a house left in Lisbon—this is *optimism*." Over and over again he reverts to the comfortable dogmas of Mr. Pope's "Essay on Man"—conceived sitting safe and easy in a Twickenham villa. The stories of the earthquake reached Voltaire exaggerated. But the bald truth was enough. "Voltaire," said Joubert, "is sometimes sad; he is moved; but he is never serious." He was serious once—over the Earthquake of Lisbon.

When the horrors were still fresh in his mind, when the burning questions to which they gave rise were still loudly demanding an answer, he wrote the most passionate and touching of all his compositions; one of the most vigorous and inspired works of any author of the age.

The "Poem on the Disaster of Lisbon" is only two hundred and fifty lines long; but it contains a statement of almost all those searching problems which every thinking man, of whatever belief or unbelief he be, has to face at last.

What am I? Whence am I? Whither go I? What is the origin of evil? What end is accomplished by the suffering and sorrow I see around me? "Why is Lisbon engulfed while Paris, no less wicked, dances?" Your "whatever is, is right" may be an easy doctrine for the happy, the rich, the healthy; but a hard saying for the poor, the sick, and the wretched. I will none of it! All Nature gives it the lie. The lips that utter it in prosperity to-day will deny it in misery to-morrow. At the end, the note of consolation is struck in the story of the caliph who, dying, worshipped God in the prayer "'I bring to Thee all that which Thou hast not in Thy immensity—faults, regrets, evils, ignorance.' He might have added also Hope."

The philosophy of "The Disaster of Lisbon" is the philosophy of "In Memoriam."

Behold, we know not anything;
I can but trust that good shall fall
At last—far off—at last, to all,
And every winter change to Spring.

Voltaire's poem has not the tender beauty of the other: but it is not less reverent, and not less religious.

One line of it, at least, has found a place in the immortalities of poetry:

Que suis-je, où suis-je, où vais-je, et d'où suis-je tiré?

and one phrase, "Autres temps, autres mœurs," has become part not only of the French language, but of our own.

On January 1st of the new year 1756, Voltaire sent an incomplete copy of the poem to the Duchess of Saxe-Gotha. On the margin he wrote the word "Secret." But on January 8th he was telling d'Argental, "My sermon on Lisbon was only for the edification of your flock. I do not throw the bread of life to dogs." So many confidences and so many confidential friends had their usual result. "The Disaster of Lisbon" appeared in Paris. With it was also published the "Poem on Natural Law," begun in Prussia in 1752.

CHAPTER XXIX

"NATURAL LAW," THE VISIT OF D'ALEMBERT, AND THE AFFAIR OF BYNG

THE "Poem on Natural Law" was an answer to Frederick the Great's version of the stupendous question of Pilate—"What is truth?" The poem is in four short parts and an "easy and limpid versification." In it, Voltaire calls it a "seeking for the law of God." Condorcet says it is "the most splendid homage man ever paid to Divinity." Desnoiresterres speaks of its "incontestable orthodoxy." At once profound and simple—the simple expression of profound problems—"Natural Law" and "The Disaster of Lisbon" are almost the only works of the man who has been called the Prince of Scoffers which are completely reverent. They are pre-eminently *not* the writings of an atheist, but of one who gropes for a God he knows to exist, though he knows neither how nor where.

But, not the less, the whole world, and all the Churches fell upon them both, tooth and nail. In 1759, "Natural Law" was publicly burnt by the hangman in Paris; and immediately after it appeared, the pious Genevans begged J. J. Rousseau to refute the horrible heterodoxy of "The Disaster of Lisbon." In July, 1757, Marie Leczinska, going to mass, saw a copy of "Natural Law"—which was then commonly entitled "Natural Religion"—on a bookstall. On her return from church she took the pamphlet and tore it across, and told the astonished shop woman ("who had supposed, from its title, the work to be one of edification") that if she sold such things her licence should be taken from her. It is true, there was a smile for Voltaire and all the world in such stories. There is a smile still in the fact that works far more freethinking than "Natural Law" and "Lisbon" are avowed now by persons who continue to call themselves not only Christians, but orthodox Catholic churchmen.

The January of 1756 passed quietly at Monrion, where Voltaire had arrived for the winter at the end of December. In spite of his opinions, Lausanne ministers, always more liberal-minded than the Genevans, came much to see him. He liked them not a little. "They are very amiable and well read," he wrote. "It must be granted there is more wit and knowledge in that profession than in any other. It is true I do not listen to their sermons." Other visitors were Lawyer de Brenles and his charming young wife. Voltaire, disappointed of his play-acting in Geneva, had greatly encouraged a scheme for building a theatre here in Lausanne. But the earthquake had made all men thoughtful. They mistrusted their love of the drama, and filled the churches instead.

That wave of austerity swept also over Paris and the Court. They were in the vanguard of this new mode of seriousness, as of every other. To quite propitiate an angry heaven Madame de Pompadour renounced her connection with the King. His private entrance to her apartments was closed; and in February Madame was created Maid of Honour (of honour!) to the Queen.

Voltaire had dedicated "Lisbon" to a certain courtier friend—the Duc de la Vallière—grandson of the hapless Louise de la Vallière, the mistress of Louis XIV. In return, possibly, for the compliment of that dedication the good-natured Duke consented to be the emissary of Madame de Pompadour, and to write from Court on March 1st to make a really most advantageous proposal to M. de Voltaire. We are all serious here now, you know! Can you not take advantage of our seriousness and versify some of the Psalms which I, the Duke, will at once have printed at the Louvre? The typical wit of the eighteenth century has no doubt lost something by the fact that Voltaire's two letters in reply to this proposal are missing. He did not versify the Psalms. Condorcet says that he could not be a hypocrite even to be a cardinal. It seems, if not certainly, at least very likely, to be true that a red hat *was* held out to him—in those fairest of white hands—as an inducement to fall in with the grave vogue of the Court and employ that matchless irony and that scathing wit for, instead of against, the established religion.

It was the chief duty of the mistresses of Louis XV. to keep him from being bored; and the Pompadour knew her business to perfection. What reason was there why Voltaire, who could do it so well, should not help her to "*égayer* the King's religion"—for a reward? That age had had worse cardinals than he would have been. It still remembered Iscariot Dubois, traitor, usurer, debauchee; and Mazarin, that synonym for lies.

Carlyle, who, by every instinct of his character and every racial trait, was necessarily out of sympathy with such a man as Voltaire, said of him, "that he has never yet in a single instance been convicted of wilfully perverting his belief; of uttering in all his controversies one deliberate falsehood."

He was at least too honest a man to be a cardinal. A little later he did write "a free, too free imitation" of Ecclesiastes and the Song of Solomon. But he cannot be charged with pandering in these works to the popular creed. His Notes on his paraphrases are profane and coarse; and the paraphrases themselves miss all the dignity and beauty of the original. The only merit they have is that they truthfully express the unpalatable opinions their writer held—to his loss.

In May, Voltaire paid a brief visit to Berne. On June 12th, Collini left his service. He had been with him four years. Bright-witted, quick-tempered, too fond of pleasure, and "loving women," said Madame Denis, "like a fool," Collini had never been a satisfactory servant. It is only a very noble character which can remain unspoilt by spoiling. Voltaire certainly did not understand the Napoleonic principle of government—to be feared before you are loved. He had apologised to Collini. He had forgiven him a hundred times; nay more, when it was the servant who was in the wrong it was the master who had won him back to good temper by a thousand injudicious indulgences. Voltaire was lax enough on the subject himself, heaven knows; but now his foolish secretary must needs conduct himself in a love affair in a manner which offended even this easy-going master. Then, Collini speaks ill of us behind our backs! That seemed one of the worst failings in the world to a man who understood the art of friendship so completely as Voltaire. And then—then—the foolish secretary—called away suddenly to get a carriage for Madame de Fontaine, who was just going to arrive at Délices from Paris—leaves open on his desk a letter in which he had laughed at Madame Denis; and Madame Denis's maid, coming in, reads the letter and carries it to her mistress. Voltaire had been infinitely loyal to Madame du Châtelet. He was not less so to this chattering *bourgeoise* of a niece. He gave the secretary his *congé* the next day—sadly, but firmly at last—as a decision that admitted of no appeal. Collini must go! Collini implies in his Memoirs that a kind of flirtation between himself and Madame Denis was one of the causes of his dismissal. Madame Denis was certainly foolish enough. It is also on his testimony that when his master said good-bye to him, he talked with him for more than an hour and asked if he had enough money for his journey to Paris—"and to last some time." As he spoke Voltaire went to his desk and took from it a *rouleau* of louis, saying "Take that: one never knows what may happen." And Collini adds, "with tears in my eyes I left the Délices." Three years later, Voltaire procured a post for him at the Court of the Elector Palatine, which Collini is believed to have kept till his death. Written long after their parting are many friendly letters from the master to the servant.

Collini had his significance and his uses. From his "Séjour auprès de Voltaire," wherein he tries to make Voltaire appear as faulty and himself as faultless as he can, the master still comes out better than the servant. There is no more reliable testimony to character than that wrung out of an unfriendly witness. On one point at least the ill-tempered young Italian has cleared his master's reputation for ever. "Stinginess never had a place in his house I have never known a man whose servants could rob him with greater ease. I repeat it, he was miser of nothing but his time."

Collini's place was at once filled by Wagnière, a Genevan boy, now sixteen years old, who had been in Voltaire's service since 1754. As if he had nothing else to do in the world Voltaire taught him Latin and trained him in his duties himself.

Collini's departure for Paris seems to have suggested to his master that he too would like to pay a visit to the capital—just a very flying visit to see about some business. So he wrote off to one d'Argenson, to ask him to get the requisite permission from the other d'Argenson, the Secretary of State. But in spite of that old school friendship, the minister was not at all too friendly just now to this presumptuous exile. The permission was refused: and Voltaire revenged himself by an epigram. He had a richer revenge, if he had wanted it in the January of the next year, 1757, when the Secretary was banished to please her Mightiness the Pompadour. But he did not want it. The spiteful epigram relieved his feelings and his temper. And it will be remembered of an earlier Voltaire, that from the moment an enemy became unfortunate, this inconsistent person could not help regarding him as a friend.

In August, J. J. Rousseau wrote, as the Genevan ministers had asked him, to remonstrate with Voltaire on that unorthodox "Disaster of Lisbon." Jean Jacques permitted himself to admire the grace and beauty of M. de Voltaire's poem, while continuing to find the optimism of Mr. Pope much more consolatory, and deducing from the earthquake a splendid argument for his darling theory of the advantages of savage over civilised life. Do you not see, my dear M. de Voltaire, that if people did not build themselves houses seven stories high and huddle together in great towns, earthquakes really would not be nearly so disastrous?

The letter was scarcely one which called for a serious reply. But it was instinct with all the glow and passion of that matchless style which made men forget to examine the common-sense of the ideas it clothed; and it fitted in admirably with the fashionable optimism which was naturally popular with the well-to-do and the powerful. The world *did* take it gravely. And in September M. de Voltaire sent a reply of airy badinage.

"Madame de Fontaine has been in danger of her life, and I have been ill too; so I am waiting till I am better and my niece cured, to dare to think as you do."

The note was a little trifling, certainly; but Rousseau wrote to Tronchin that he was charmed with it. As for Voltaire, the very idea of that further scathing rollicking answer that was to come had not yet even occurred to him. He had as little time as desire to quarrel with anybody at the present moment. Besides all his new duties as a landed proprietor, a tragedy, history, verses, correspondence, he was engrossed with d'Alembert as a visitor and the "Encyclopædia" as a hobby.

The story of the foundling who, thirty-nine years earlier, had been discovered on the steps of a Parisian church, is hardly less familiar to our own century than it was to the eighteenth. Brought up by a compassionate poor woman, a glazier's wife, it was not until he had become the great d'Alembert, the first geometrician and philosopher of the day, that the false mother who had borne and abandoned him—Madame de Tencin, the old acquaintance of Voltaire—would fain have avowed a child so creditable. But that child had not a characteristic in common with her. He denied her. He had no mother but the glazier's wife. In her home he grew up to be one of the wisest and gentlest of great men. In her home he learnt the blessings of peace and privacy, of work and obscurity. "Simple, sober, and proud," too well acquainted with Poverty to be afraid of her, he always shunned a society which could give him nothing and might rob him of the time to work out the work of his life. Above that glazier's shop, after long throes and travail of delightful pain, he brought forth in 1750 the first-born son of his genius, the Preliminary Discourse of the great "Encyclopædia." In 1756 he became a member of the French Academy. In 1772 he was made its perpetual secretary. His long passion for that most ardent and unhappy woman, Mademoiselle de Lespinasse, was for eleven years of his later life at once its consolation and its despair. As a writer his style has all the clumsiness of the *savant* who has so much to say that he has no time to take care how he says it, and all the coldness of the mathematician. But it was only his writing that was cold.

For all his "stately irony," for all his recluse student ways and frugal life, d'Alembert inspired his century not so much with admiration as with love. Once, when Voltaire was asked to write something in an album, he saw in it the name of d'Alembert. Beneath, he wrote his own—*Hic fuit Dalemberti amicus.*

D'Alembert arrived at Délices some time about August 10, 1756. He stayed five weeks. It must have been a delightful visit. Voltaire had that rare combination of qualities as a host—he knew both how to amuse his guest and how to leave him to amuse himself. It was during this stay that at a dinner party at Délices, at which Dr. Tronchin and others were present, the company began telling robber stories. Each anecdote was more thrilling than the last. Then Voltaire looked up—"Once, Gentlemen, there was a Farmer-General ..." and he relapsed into silence, with the honours of the evening. That ancient story still has point. How much more it must have had when it was new—in 1756!

The five weeks passed only too quickly. Summer was on that beautiful country. Madame de Fontaine was also staying at Délices. She was now a widow of about forty, rather tall and good-looking, and with a taste for painting—the subjects not too decorous, for choice. Madame was not exactly decorous herself. When she arrived at Délices she had brought with her the Marquis de Florian, her lover. Uncle Voltaire accepted that intimacy with perfect nonchalance and amiability. On the present occasion Madame de Fontaine was useful to keep Madame Denis company, and so leave Voltaire and d'Alembert to themselves.

They had much to do and to say. From 1746 they had been correspondents; but the "Encyclopædia" was a link which had bound them closer far. Founded on the "English Encyclopædia" of Chambers, which had been translated into French about 1743, the "immense and immortal work" of Diderot and d'Alembert wholly eclipsed its prototype. It was, is, and will be, not *an* "Encyclopædia" but *the* "Encyclopædia." It includes, indeed, neither history nor biography: the vast discoveries of modern times make men smile to-day at its science; and its hardy philosophy seems timid to our bolder age.

But it was not the less the Guide to the Revolution, the first great public invitation to all men to drink of that knowledge which enfranchises the soul. To it Grimm, Rousseau, Holbach, Marmontel, and Condorcet were contributors. There was not an enlightened man in France who did not recognise it as the primer of a new language—the handbook to a better country. The authorities burnt it. Voltaire loved it. It suggested to him his own Philosophical or, as he called it, "pocket Dictionary." To the "pocket Dictionary" could be relegated what was too bold even for the Encyclopædia. It has been seen that in Prussia he wrote articles for it, and reams of letters about it. It was not his own. He called himself "the boy in your great shop"; and his contributions to it "pebbles to stick into the corners of the immortal edifice you are raising." But he loved it as if it had been his own, and as he loved the d'Alembert who had created it.

That summer visit at Délices was the cause of the most famous and fought-over article the "Encyclopædia" contains. Geneva delighted in d'Alembert. Besides being gentle, modest, and accomplished, it also knew him to be hostile to the Church of Rome; and naturally concluded that hostility to Rome meant friendliness to Calvin. The ministers flocked to Délices, and gave parties themselves for their host and his guest. The guest was quite as charmed with them as they were with him. They were so free from superstition, so learned, tolerant, and open to reason! It was equally pleasant and surprising to find a religion—and the ministers of a religion— nearly as agnostic as the philosophers themselves.

The next thing to do when I get back to Paris is to write an article on Geneva and compliment the children of Calvin on their freedom of thought! There is no doubt that d'Alembert talked over that proposed article with his host. Nor is there any doubt that Voltaire knew perfectly well that such compliments would set all the Calvinists in Geneva by the ears and create a fracas which would ring through Europe; nor that he anticipated that fight with the richest enjoyment, and secretly and gleefully rubbed his hands together at the prospect of it.

And as you *are* going to write the article, my dear d'Alembert, can you not put in just a few lines to say that the only thing the Genevans really need to make them entirely delightful is to permit theatrical representations among them—not for enjoyment, of course, but just to "improve their taste" and give them "tact and feeling"?

The amiable d'Alembert naturally agreed to oblige his host on so small a matter.

In September he packed up his boxes and went back to Paris with the article on Geneva much in his mind; and those casual observations on play-acting, not to be forgotten.

He was missed at Délices. Madame de Fontaine was ill there in the autumn. Her uncle's cook was too good for both her and her sister, who were always calling in Tronchin to cure them of "a little indigestion." And of course Voltaire (though certainly not from the same cause) was ill himself. "We have been on the point, my dear universal philosopher," he wrote to d'Alembert on October 9th, "of knowing, Madame de Fontaine and I, what becomes of the soul when separated from its partner. We hope to remain in ignorance some time longer."

On December 9th Voltaire received a visit from an old friend, George Keith, Earl Marischal of Scotland.

He did not come as the emissary of Frederick; or to recall, though no doubt he did recall, to Voltaire those early golden days of the Prussian visit when they had sat together at the most famous supper-table in the world. He introduced many of his countrymen to the "old owl of Délices." But that was not the reason either of his visit. He came to plead the cause of Admiral Byng.

Richelieu had just taken Minorca from the English. The fleet sent by England to its relief retired under Byng, before the French. Paris went mad with delight as only Paris can, and sang the exploits of Richelieu in one of those national songs whose glow and vigour keep them fresh for ever:

Plein d'une noble audace
Richelieu presse, attaque la place——

Voltaire was nearly as enthusiastic as Paris. He had prophesied such splendid things of his hero! And it would have been very damping to his ardour to have had his prophecies and hero-worship proved wrong. Then, too, England had been so confident of victory; and so dreadfully rude and aggressive in her confidence. Such pride deserved a fall; and great was the fall of it. To be beaten on the sea by the French seemed to Britain like being struck across the face by the open hand of insult. She forgot that love of fair play which she has some right to call her national instinct. She did what, with all her faults, she very seldom does—she hit a man when he was down, and wreaked upon him, in the bitterness of her disappointment, the anger she should have kept for the blundering ministry who had commanded him impossibilities. Byng was arraigned on a charge of treason and cowardice. But he had a friend—and the friend remembered Voltaire. True, Voltaire was a Frenchman, and the closest intimate of Richelieu. But Keith knew that he was first of all a humanitarian; and that he had a passion for justice and a rage against tyranny which made him love his enemies if they were oppressed, and hate even his friends if they were oppressors. On December 20th, Voltaire wrote to Richelieu telling Byng's story. Richelieu replied in an open letter which generously vindicated the character of his foe. Had Byng continued the fight, the English fleet must have been totally destroyed. A clever sailor and a brave man, his misfortunes were from the Hand of God—and the valour of the French.

Voltaire sent that letter to Byng with a letter of his own. He had known the Admiral as a young man, when he was in England; but he judged it better not now to mention that they were acquainted, lest his interference might be attributed to personal partiality. The sequel is very well known. The miserable ministry wanted a scapegoat. Though Byng was recommended to mercy by the court which tried him, he was shot on March 14, 1757, meeting his death with the courage with which his foes declared he had met them.

He left grateful messages to Richelieu and to Voltaire; and to Voltaire a copy of his defence.

The author of "Candide" added later to that famous satire a few stinging and immortal lines on this *cause célèbre*. "In this country it is good to put an admiral to death now and then, *to encourage the others*."

Voltaire's part in the affair of Byng is not only of importance as being of interest to English people. It began a new era in his life.

The scoffer, the jester, the uprooter had found nobler work for his hands at last. The defender of Byng became the avenger of La Barre, of Sirven, of Montbailli, and of Calas.

CHAPTER XXX

THE INTERFERENCE IN THE SEVEN YEARS' WAR, THE "GENEVA" ARTICLE, AND LIFE AT DÉLICES

ON January 5, 1757, Damiens, an unfortunate lunatic, made a very feeble attempt upon the life of Louis XV. As is usual in such cases, the King was accredited with infinite calm and courage, though his heroism had consisted entirely in being the unwilling victim of a very small wound from a very small penknife. However, he took the penknife to be the chosen instrument of the wrath of heaven; went to bed; sent a contrite message to the Queen; and for ten days declined to have any dealings with the lively Pompadour.

On January 6th, d'Argenson wrote Voltaire a very courtier-like account of the affair. To say that when Voltaire heard that a New Testament had been found in the poor lunatic's pocket he was delighted, is to express his sentiments feebly. A Testament! I told you so! All assassins have "a Bible with their daggers." But have you ever heard of one who had a Cicero, a Plato, or a Virgil?

He turned, twisted, and tossed the subject with all that gibing buffoonery which was his *forte* and other men's fear. Damiens died under tortures which were a disgrace to civilisation. D'Argenson, Secretary of State, and Machault, Keeper of the Seals, who had been bold and foolish enough to suppose that the King would be able to kill time without his Pompadour, united, in her brief disgrace, to crush her. With her return to power, she crushed them. On February 1st they were both exiled. A few days earlier, the other brother d'Argenson (the better friend of the two to Voltaire) had died. Voltaire might well say that his own fate was more worth having than that of a Secretary of State who was banished; and that he would rather scold his gardeners than pay court to kings. In February he received a very flattering invitation from Elizabeth, Empress of Russia, to go to Petersburg to write "The History of Peter the Great," her father. He undertook to write the history. But he declined the invitation. Frederick, too, was trying coquetries on him—such a tender letter, for instance, from Dresden on January 19th! But here again he was firm: "I want neither king nor autocracy. I have tasted them ... that is enough."

The early months of the year 1757 were passing, indeed, not a little pleasantly at Monrion.

The society of Lausanne, living up to its character of being more liberal than that of Geneva, was only too delighted to welcome such an amusing person as Voltaire in its midst. Many Lausannois were French—all French in their social charms and their language—and only Swiss in their sincerity and simplicity. Voltaire said that, as an audience, there were a couple of hundred of them who were worth the whole *parterre* of Paris, and who would have hissed Crébillon's "Catilina" off the stage. What higher praise could he have given to anybody? Lausanne, indeed, would not have been Swiss if there had not been a certain section of its society who held themselves aloof from this volatile Deist and his more volatile entertainments. Nor would it have been a country town if there had not been in it some touchy and discontented persons who were offended with M. de Voltaire because he had not asked them often enough or had asked someone else too often. Voltaire gaily divided the society into two parts: first, the Olympe, which included both the strait-laced and the offended; and, second, the Sensible People. That classification spoke for itself. He was not a little amused one day when, hearing that an Olympe lady had had a parody of "Zaire" acted at her house, he said to a young girl of the same name, "Ah! Mademoiselle, it is you who have been laughing at me!" and the naïve girl replied, "Oh no, Monsieur, it was my aunt!"

But, Olympes notwithstanding, Lausanne as a whole was only too delighted to come to M. de Voltaire's theatricals, and the excellent suppers prepared by his first-rate cook. It did not expect him to pay visits, which he hated. So he and Madame Denis spent all their leisure hours learning parts and coaching their company. Madame Denis lived in a whirl of "tailors, hairdressers, and actors," and being well amused was entirely amiable.

The plays acted were "Zaire," "Alzire," and the "Enfant Prodigue," and a new play of Voltaire's which he now called "Fanine," and which was afterwards called "Zulime."

Voltaire persistently declared that Madame Denis acted "Zaire" infinitely better than Gaussin, "though she has not such fine eyes"; which was a very delicate way of describing her squint.

In March they "preached the 'Enfant Prodigue,' with an opera-bouffe ('Serva Padrona') for dessert." Also in March, they played "Zulime" "better than it will be played in Paris," said its author. He proudly numbered among the audience on its first night twelve Calvinist ministers and their young students, studying for the Church. Here was liberal-mindedness indeed! Besides acting plays, there was the house to improve or to alter. Its master was surrounded with workmen. He had also a parrot and a squirrel. He had turned to play-acting, he said, because though "tranquillity is a beautiful thing—ennui is of its acquaintance and family." But he knew too well, by that old courtly experience, that the worst of all boredoms is perpetual amusement. He was happy at Monrion because there, as everywhere, he knew how to work as well as to play. In articles for the "Encyclopædia," rewriting "Zulime," and beginning "The History of Peter the Great," he justified his existence. He had much to do, so he enjoyed his theatricals and the lovely country in which he found himself, as only the busy can enjoy anything "From my bed I can see the lake, the Rhone, and another river. Have you a better view? Have you tulips in March?... My vines, my orchard, and myself owe no man anything...."

Was it glamour again? If it was, it was a better glamour than had made him dream Prussia heaven, and Frederick the Great a faithful friend.

On June 3th, he went back to Délices for the summer. Madame Denis was still in high good-humour—furnishing the house, entertaining, acting. Voltaire said she was "a niece who made the happiness of his life." Everything was *couleur de rose*. Switzerland had proved a successful venture indeed. By August the man who now signed himself the Swiss Voltaire had acquired yet another house in Lausanne—Chêne, in the Rue de Lausanne, which was the last street in the town on the Geneva side, and from where he had exquisite views of the lake. He rented it for nine years. Quite near it was a house called Mon Repos, which belonged to two of Voltaire's amateur dramatic company, the Marquis and Marquise de Genlis. Very soon these two enthusiasts made, in a barn adjoining their house, a theatre which practically belonged to Voltaire, and where in future nearly all his theatricals were held. His first letter from Chêne is dated August 29, 1757. Here he soon received with great gravity the Lord Bailiffs of Berne: good, sober, pompous people, with a very amusing idea of their own importance, and a strictly limited sense of humour. "What the deuce, M. de Voltaire," said one of them one day, "are you always writing verses for? What is the good of it, I ask you? It leads to nothing. Now *I*, you see, am a Bailiff." And another day, a second observed solemnly, "They say you have written against God. That is bad, but I hope He will pardon you; and against religion, which is worse; and against our Lord, which is worse still: but He will forgive you in His mercy. Only take care, M. de Voltaire, you do not write against their Excellencies the High Bailiffs, for *they* will never pardon you!" It is not difficult to imagine the zest and delight with which Voltaire repeated these stories.

These good Swiss had not only charming scenery, cultivated society, and some kind of freedom, but they were also, without intending it, positively amusing! It would have been well for Voltaire's peace of mind if he could have engrossed himself entirely in their small world, and forgotten wholly that vaster, louder one, which stretched wide beyond Délices, Monrion, and Chêne. But he had ever itching fingers for a fight.

In the August of 1756 had begun the third, longest, and greatest struggle for Silesia, the Seven Years' War. Voltaire did not choose to remember that, though he had tried diplomacy before, he had never tried it successfully. He flung himself, head foremost in every sense, into the contest. He began in the spring of 1757 by inventing a war machine: "an engine of massacre upon the plan of the Assyrian war chariots of old." Certainly, he was a peace advocate. But if men must destroy each other, let them do so by the best and quickest of possible means. He had had, too, a dozen careers already without adding to them that of a scientific inventor. It is marvellous, but true, that this "paper smudger's" idea—the appellation was his own—was really very excellent. The machine was also intended to carry ammunition and forage. The Minister of War thought well of it. The inventor recommended it highly to Richelieu. The Assyrian chariots were not tried until they were used for carrying grape-shot, but they were not the less an uncommonly bright, ingenious, and Voltairian invention.

The inventor relinquished the idea of their immediate use rather sadly. But the war, considered apart from war chariots, was becoming of personal moment to him.

In the spring of 1757, the Petticoats, which were the damnation of France, swept her into it.

In his old Paris days, Voltaire had known, and scornfully liked, a certain rosy-cheeked *bon conteur* of an abbé, called Bernis. Verse-maker and *bon-vivant*—not yet developed into the shrewder and wiser personage his "Memoirs and Letters" reveal him—Voltaire had named the abbé the flower-girl of Parnassus, or Babet, after a famous pretty flower-seller of the day; and loved to tease him on those rosy cheeks and that cheerful air. Babet, who was nothing if not audacious, had asked Boyer (the âne of Mirepoix, who had died in 1755) for a post: and when Boyer told him that as long as he was in power a Babet had nothing to hope for, replied, "Sir, I shall wait." The answer ran through Paris. It was the beginning of success. Madame de Pompadour turned the smile on this round-faced wit; pensioned him; installed him in the Tuileries; and made him ambassador to Vienna, and Secretary for Foreign Affairs. Frederick, who had received the mistress's kind regards, sent through Voltaire, with that curt "I do not know her," had also laughed at Bernis-Babet in the fatal "Œuvre de Poëshie du Roi Mon Maître."

Therefore, on May 1, 1757, "the first minister of the state," Pompadour, made her willing tool, Bernis, sign an offensive and defensive treaty with the ambassador of Austria against Frederick the Great, and plunged France into the blood of the Seven Years' War.

Voltaire's interest in it was varied and conflicting. He was the friend of Richelieu, of Bernis, and the Pompadour: and he was a Frenchman. He had strong sympathy with brave Maria Theresa and with Austria—the allies of his country. Her great enemy, Frederick, was both his friend and his foe: still loved, still admired, and still unforgiven. All through these seven years one sees that fatal affair of Frankfort rankling in Voltaire's heart; struggling with his admiration for Frederick as a king and a soldier: with his pity for him when beaten, with his pride in him when victorious. All through the war Frederick wrote him prose and verse; the deepest sorrows of his soul, reproaches, confidences, yearnings. And Voltaire answered half bitterly and half tenderly, with angry allusions to the past, and brave words to comfort the King's sore heart for the future: never consistent, not seldom spiteful, and yet touched, affectionate, and sympathetic.

Explain the attitude who can.

In July, 1757, Voltaire wrote to Richelieu begging him, if he passed by Frankfort, to send the four ears of those two *coquins*, Freytag and Schmidt.

In August he was busy trying to bring about peace, through the medium of the Margravine of Bayreuth and Richelieu, between Freytag's master and France. This first diplomatic interference of Voltaire's in the war was not badly planned. In his own words, he "wanted Richelieu to add the quality of arbitrator to that of general." The scheme was so far a success

THE CHÂTEAU OF FERNEY

From an Engraving

that, on August 19th, Wilhelmina replied that her brother was as grateful for such a proposal as herself. The moment for it was opportune. Frederick was still bruised and broken by the crushing defeat he had suffered at Kolin on June 18th. He wrote direct to Richelieu on September 6th, asking him to act as an arbitrator; and Richelieu replied that he was very willing. Did the hermit of Délices rub his lean hands and congratulate himself on a good piece of work? Perhaps he knew the temper of an offended woman and a piqued Bernis too well. The blood of her children was as water to these rulers of France. The Court declined arbitration.

The unhappy Margravine wrote to Voltaire on September 12th that Frederick was reduced to frightful extremities. She might well so write. In October Voltaire sent to the King one of the wisest and kindliest letters which he ever penned. He dissuaded Frederick from a contemplation of suicide. He stimulated him by admiration. He deterred him by insisting that such an act would not only sadden his friends, but please his foes. When, in this same month, Voltaire read some dismal verses Frederick had written to d'Argens on the same unhappy topic, he wrote a second letter to the King, diplomatically lauding the verses to the skies, and again passionately dissuading such a poet, and such a man, from the disgrace of suicide.

In those fatal "Memoirs" (meant to be secret) he was now writing at Délices, Voltaire, indeed, avenged himself for Freytag and Frankfort by declaring that much of that Epistle to d'Argens was stolen from Chaulieu and from himself; while that love of justice which was always getting the better of his malice, in spite of himself, made him add that, under the circumstances, it was wonderful for a king to have written two hundred verses at all.

On October 8th, dismal Luc confided to Wilhelmina that he had "laughed" at the exhortations of Patriarch Voltaire; and the very next day wrote to the Patriarch a letter owning that those admonitions had had effect, and ending:

Though the storm beats high
I must fight, not fly,
And a King live and die.

Meanwhile, at Délices, busy Voltaire was trying his hand a second time at peace negotiations. This time his medium was de Tencin—that crafty and haughty Cardinal, who, three years before, at Lyons, had found it impolitic to invite Voltaire to dinner. But the Cardinal loved intrigue, and hated Austria and the Austrian alliance with France, from his soul. When, on November 5, 1757, Frederick beat French and Austrians at Rossbach with "the most unheard-of and the most complete defeat in history" (the vigorous words are Voltaire's), all angry France shared the Cardinal's hatred of the rosy-cheeked Bernis's treaty with the Court of Vienna. De Tencin allied himself with the man he had despised—Voltaire—"to engage the Margravine to confide to him the interests of her brother the King," and so to procure peace between France and Prussia. Prussia was willing enough. Voltaire was the intermediary through whom all the letters passed. He said malignly that he enjoyed the post because he foresaw the disappointment the Cardinal was preparing for himself. In reality, he was something less Machiavellian, and really thought the peace he hoped for might be brought about. De Tencin communicated directly with Louis XV.; and sent him a letter of the Margravine, written to be so sent. But Maria Theresa had bowed her pride to flatter Madame de Pompadour; while Frederick had said "I do not know her." The Pompadour's kingly slave answered de Tencin icily that the Secretary for Foreign Affairs would instruct his Eminence of the royal intentions. So Babet, the "flower-girl," the verse-maker, the *bon-vivant*, dictated to the astute Cardinal the unfavourable reply he was to make to the Margravine. De Tencin had to sign it. He died only a fortnight later—of mortification, said Voltaire.

Thus ended Voltaire's second interference in the Seven Years' War. Both were useless. His interest in the affair was very far from being ended, or even weakened. But in the meantime there were disturbances nearer home.

It was sixteen months since d'Alembert had stayed at Délices, and been charmed by the liberal-mindedness of Calvinism. The result of that visit was, as has been noted, the famous article entitled "Geneva" in the storm-breeding "Encyclopædia." In this December of 1757 the pious pastors of that town heard that they were therein complimented as no longer believing in the divinity of Christ or in hell; as having in many cases no other religion than "a perfect Socinianism," rejecting all mystery; as, among the learned at least, having a faith which had reduced itself to believe in one God, and which was alone distinguished from pure Deism by a cold respect for the Scriptures and for Christ.

It is not difficult to fancy what an effect such statements, uttered by a d'Alembert, and in what was then the most famous book in the world, would have on that strict, simple, pure-living sect. Was it true? Could any of it be true? The dreadful fear that it might be—that that stern, narrow creed, with its brief assertions and its wide negations, might lead, or tend, unknown to its followers, to something very like a barren Deism—appears to have taken possession of their souls.

On December 12th, Voltaire, who had been waiting sixteen months for this *dénouement*, began to enjoy himself. "These droll people," he wrote to d'Alembert "actually dare to complain of the praise you have given them—to believe in a God and to have more reason than faith. Some of them accuse me of having a profane alliance with you. They say they will protest against your article. Let them, and laugh at them."

On December 23d, at a meeting of Calvinistic pastors, they made, with deep heart-searchings, a formal inquiry to assure themselves that none of them had given ground for d'Alembert's—compliments. They then drew up a commission, which appointed Dr. Tronchin, not less a sincere Christian than he was a sincere friend of the Deist Voltaire, to reply to the article in the "Encyclopædia" and "to wipe away the stain" that d'Alembert had affixed to their character. It was Tronchin's charm as a writer that he touched the heart as well as appealed to the head. He refuted the imputations of d'Alembert in terms not a little touching. From Paris, on January 6, 1758, d'Alembert replied, as he could but reply, that he was convinced of the truth of his words: and what he had written, he had written. When Geneva further asked him to name the pastors who had given rise to such opinions, he very honourably declined. On February 8th, the commission produced its Confession of Faith. As it did not insist on the doctrine of Everlasting Punishment, or declare that Christ was equal to His Father, or lay stress on the worship of Him, Voltaire said with some truth, when he wrote to d'Alembert, that they had declared themselves Christian Deists after all, and justified the article in the "Encyclopædia."

"Geneva," in fact, brought home to the thoughtful Calvinist the logical outcome of his religion. The shock was great. To stand face to face with the ultimate consequences of their belief would indeed startle the votaries of many other creeds besides Calvinism.

Their difference on the most vital of all subjects did not affect the friendship of the great Voltaire and the great Tronchin.

During this winter of 1757-58, the Doctor was, for the time being, almost the greater man of the two. He had just returned from Paris, where he had prescribed for all its rank, wit, and fashion; and where he and his inoculation had become a *furore* and the mode. In Geneva he now started a cure, to which flocked all the *mondaines* of Paris to learn the rudiments of hygiene, of temperance, and of common-sense; to be taught for the first time in their lives the value of simple living; and to undergo inoculation.

Voltaire always loved the bold and sensible regimen of this good physician. Like the women, he was also not a little influenced by the great Doctor's charming manner, handsome face, and splendid six feet of height. Then, too, supposing ennui *should* be "of the acquaintance and family" of retirement, this "cure" brought half the wit of the capital to the very doors of the Hermit of Délices. The year 1757 was not over, and their acquaintance was of the briefest, when Voltaire, with his usual impulsiveness, was already in the midst of a delightful intimacy with one of the cleverest and most sympathetic of the Tronchin patients, Madame d'Épinay. Bright, black-eyed, about two-and-thirty years old, the ill-treated wife of a Farmer-General, the head of a salon, and the coquettish friend of Rousseau, Madame d'Épinay reflected in her sparkling little French mind the cleverness of a clever age, and, without ever saying or doing anything which gave substantial evidence of a superior intelligence, had a great deal of that vague quality which is now called culture. Voltaire delighted in her; played with her; laughed with her; talked with her; called her his Beautiful Philosopher; wrote her innumerable little notes about innumerable little nothings; welcomed her constantly at Délices; and in January, 1758, had her to stay there for two or three days with her doctor. Madame's complaint was of the nerves, and the very best cure for that kind of disease is to be amused, as everybody knows. So she was delighted to come to Délices, where Madame Denis was "entirely comic," and "fit to make you die of laughing"; short, fat, ugly; quite good-natured; a liar, simply from habit; clever enough to seem so without being so; always gesticulating, talking, and arguing, especially when that "Geneva" article—just now very much on the *tapis*—was mentioned, when she threw her arms and hands about, abused republics and their laws with a fine generality, and was entirely absurd.

The little, shrewd, shallow visitor was not quite so sure about the great Voltaire. He might have been fifteen, he was so gay, lively, and inconsequent! But then he had a number of quite childish prejudices; and an air of laughing at everybody, even himself. Madame d'Épinay was not at all certain she liked *that*. In Paris she had been taken gravely as a clever woman. The owl of Délices, looking at her through those little, cynic, half-shut and all-seeing eyes of his, regarded her as an ingenious little mechanical toy, whom it amused him to set in motion. That he was very gallant with her was true enough. But gallantry is hardly a compliment to a woman who wants to be looked upon as *savante*.

Madame d'Épinay was not the only one of Tronchin's patients who visited Voltaire. Almost all of them came to peep at him. Here was the Marquise de Muy—"a very little soul in a very little body much debilitated by remedies," said Tronchin—but the *chère amie* of Choiseul the minister, and so to be cultivated by a far-seeing Voltaire.

Here, too, came the nephew and niece of de Tencin, the Montferrats—whom Voltaire received very kindly though he liked neither them nor their uncle.

Among neighbours who were not of Tronchin's "cure," Huber, celebrated as a painter and wit, had been one of the most constant visitors at Délices from the first, and was fast dropping into the position he never afterwards relinquished, of *ami de la maison*. Madam Tronchin—as plain and disagreeable as her husband was handsome and charming—was a guest too. "Et que fait Madame Tronchin?" said someone one day to the sprightly Madame Cramer, herself a visitor. "Elle fait peur," was the answer. Madame Cramer, as the wife of Gabriel Cramer, one of Voltaire's publishers, and as, in her own person, gay, naïve, and witty, was always a *persona grata* at Délices. Her husband and brother-in-law were as successful socially as in their business; acted in their client's theatricals, and were delightfully good-looking and pleasant.

Voltaire's nearest neighbours at Délices, a Professor Pictet and his wife and daughter, were constantly of his parties. The daughter Charlotte was a gay and pretty little person, who had aroused the jealousy of Madame Denis by embroidering Voltaire a cap to wear on the top of the great peruke he always affected. Voltaire repaid the present by trying to find Mademoiselle what he always considered the *summum bonum*, a husband; and Madame Denis was not precisely pleased when Charlotte married a handsome major of eight-and-twenty, for whom the foolish niece herself had had a *tendresse*. In 1757, a Baron Gleichen, who wrote Souvenirs, also visited Délices.

It is no contradiction to say of Voltaire that he was all through his life both the most unsociable and the most sociable of men.

At Délices there were nearly always seven or eight persons to supper. On one occasion at least, the house was so full of guests for theatricals, that Madame Denis, having no bed, sat up all through the night playing cards. When he met his guests no host could have been more agreeable than Voltaire. He had a hundred stories to tell. He made so many *mots* that half the *mots* of the eighteenth century have been fathered upon him by posterity. Sometimes he read aloud, or quoted from memory. He was inimitably gay, good-natured, and courteous. One woman (who did not love him) said that he alone of his age knew how to speak to women as women like to be spoken to. That old quality which had made him revere the intellect of Madame du Châtelet made him respect now whatever was respectable in the intellect of his female companions. That surest sign of inferiority—to be afraid of mental superiority in the weaker sex—was certainly never to be found in Voltaire. If he toyed with a d'Épinay, it was because she was but a toy after all. He searched so diligently for cleverness in his nieces that he actually thought he had found it. Some of the best and most careful letters he ever wrote are those to Madame du Deffand—who was old, poor, blind—but splendidly intelligent.

He certainly took very good care during this social winter of 1757-58—as in all other social winters and summers—not to see too much of his guests, male or female. He worked twelve or fifteen hours a day; and generally kept his secretary writing part of the night as well. He never suffered himself to be interrupted in the mornings; and was fond of saying that he believed less in optimism at that time than at any other.

As in the old days at Cirey, he was often too busy to join his friends at dinner, and ate "no matter what, no matter when," instead.

In January, 1758, he migrated to Chêne, his newly acquired house in Lausanne; and, in the formal phrase of one of his guests there, by "his wit and his philosophy, his table and his theatre, refined in a visible degree the manners" of that town. That guest was an English youth called Gibbon, who, having been led into Roman Catholicism at college, had been sent to a minister at Lausanne to be led out of it again—by Calvinism. In the intervals of falling in love with the *beaux yeux* of Mademoiselle Curchod (afterwards Madame Necker), the self-satisfied young gentleman found time during two winters to pompously approve of M. de Voltaire in various *rôles*—in "Zaire," "Alzire," "Fanine," and the "Enfant Prodigue," played in that theatre in the granary of Mon Repos. Gibbon wrote hereafter, in that solemn, polished, rewritten, immortal Autobiography, that M. de Voltaire's "declamation was fashioned to the pomp and cadence of the old stage, and he expressed the enthusiasm of poetry rather than the feelings of Nature"; while Voltaire, in the gay impromptu of *his* style, declared of himself he was "the best old fool in any troupe. I had rage and tears—attitudes and a cap." He added that Madame Denis was splendid in the *rôle* of mothers; and a little later quite seriously announced that though she had not *all* the talents of Mademoiselle Clairon (!) she was much more pathetic and human! The observing English youth in the audience considered, on the contrary, that the "fat and ugly niece" quite ruined the parts of "the young and fair," and was not nearly clever enough to make the spectators forget the defects of her age and person. When she was playing the heroine in "Zaire" she did herself say, hoping for a compliment, "To take such a part one ought to be young and beautiful!" and a well-meaning *gauche* person replied "Ah! Madame, you are a living proof to the contrary!" Uncle Voltaire would have been very *vif*, no doubt, if he had known of Gibbon's unflattering criticism on his niece. As it was, he was not too pleased on his own account when this heavy young genius must needs, after having heard them only twice, remember and repeat certain lines which Voltaire had written in the first enthusiasm of settling at Délices, and which (of course) contained an allusion which would offend somebody. M. de Voltaire may be forgiven if he wished this blundering Mr. Gibbon and his prodigious memory—in England.

In May, after the *ménage* Voltaire had moved back to Délices, another visitor came to it. She was Madame du Boccage, famous for her learning, as modest as she was accomplished, and a woman quite after her host's heart. He put off a visit to the Elector Palatine to receive her. He gave up his bed to her as being the most comfortable in the house; and got up plays for her benefit. As for Madame, she found him everything that was kind and agreeable, surrounded by the best company—that is, the intellectually best company—and always singing the praises of his rural life. In fact, the only thing she had to complain of was that he was so very hospitable that, like the nieces, she was always having indigestion. She left after a visit of five days, and long corresponded with her host.

Between work and play, the Délices, Monrion, and Chêne, Voltaire had spent more than three years in Switzerland. That they had been happy enough to have made him altogether forget that a Paris, a Louis, and a Pompadour existed—and neglected him—is true enough. But he never forgot. If on one side of his character he was splendidly a philosopher, on the other he was always an "old baby" crying for the moon.

CHAPTER XXXI

"THE LITERARY WAR," AND THE PURCHASE OF FERNEY AND TOURNEY

ON June 21, 1758, Voltaire was writing delightedly to his Angel to tell him that through the offices of the pink-cheeked Bernis, Louis XV. had been good enough to give a formal permit for the greatest Frenchman of the age to retain his title of Gentleman-in-Ordinary.

Frederick said, obviously enough, "*That* will not be the patent that will immortalise you." But the Gentleman himself was quite naïvely delighted. He had always been miserable at Court and in Paris, but he so much wished to feel he could go back there, if he liked! He seems to have regarded this formal permission to keep his title as the thin end of the wedge. But it was not.

"Let him stay where he is," was the Bien-Aimé's sole comment on Voltaire's exile. Marmontel suggested to Madame de Pompadour that it was for *her* to recall him; but Madame could only reply, perhaps not untruthfully, "Ah, no! it does not rest with me."

In July, Voltaire visited another Court, which had never looked askance at him. He spent a fortnight with his old friend the Elector Palatine, at Schwetzingen. The Elector had arranged some money matters for Voltaire greatly to his advantage, so the visit was one of gratitude. It has no importance, except that the story runs that here the guest was so engrossed by a mysterious Something he was writing that he shut himself up in his room for three days, only opening his door to have food and coffee passed in. On the fourth day Madame Denis forced an entry. Voltaire threw a manuscript at her, saying, "There, curious, that is for you." It was the manuscript of "Candide."

The only drawback to the little anecdote is that Madame Denis was not at Schwetzingen at all—having been left behind at home with her sister, learning parts. "Candide" may have been written at the Elector's; but the time for its appearance was not yet ripe.

The summer of 1758 passed without much incident at Délices. Elsewhere, there was only too much. The Seven Years' War—"the most hellish war that ever was fought," said Voltaire—raged with unabated fury. Frederick had recovered Silesia by a great victory at Leuthen on December 5, 1757, when he beat an army of Austrians three times as large as his own.

On August 25th of this 1758 he beat the Russians at Zorndorf. And then his evil star rose again. On October 14th, he was taken by surprise and defeated with great loss at Hochkirch. But he suffered a still greater loss that day in the death of Wilhelmina, Margravine of Bayreuth. Worthy in courage to be the sister of Frederick, and in intelligence to be the friend of Voltaire, both men mourned her as she deserved to be mourned. Frederick wrote that there are some troubles against which all stoicism and all the reasonings of the philosophers are alike useless. He was face to face with such a trouble now. Voltaire, at the King's request, wrote to her memory an ode beginning, "Dear and illustrious shade, soul brave and pure." But it is not always when the writer is himself most moved that his writings are most moving. There are some griefs which paralyse the brain and make every utterance cold. Voltaire was no more satisfied with his poem than was Frederick. He wrote another, which gave the unhappy brother the first moment of comfort he had had, he said, for five months. For a time their mutual loss and grief drew the two friends together as of yore. They put away their grievances. The "old need of communication, of finding each other again, at least in thought," was powerfully present. Over Wilhelmina's grave they forgot for a while Maupertuis and Akakia, Freytag and Frankfort.

Voltaire would have known himself forgotten and obscure if he had ever lived six consecutive months in his life without being plunged in some or other kind of quarrel. That "Geneva" article was still a tree of discord bearing fruit. It will not be forgotten that to oblige the most hospitable host in the world, d'Alembert had introduced into it a few remarks on the beneficial effects of play-acting in general, and the peculiar benefits which would accrue from it to Geneva in particular.

In the October of 1758, from the depths of his forest of Montmorency, Jean Jacques Rousseau—intense, morbid, bitter, with so much amiss in himself that he supposed all other men to be unreasonable and out of gear—wrote to d'Alembert his famous "Letter on Plays."

He had "tried his wings" against d'Alembert's friend, in his reply to the "Poem on the Disaster of Lisbon," and Voltaire had laughed at him gaily and civilly enough. If Jean Jacques's impetuosity had ever waited for reason, there would have seemed none now why he should not enter the lists again, and tilt once more with this active, mocking, sprightly little opponent, whom everybody knew to have inspired d'Alembert's sentiments.

Jean Jacques, it is true, was a strange person to write against plays. He had written them himself. He had a genuine admiration for M. de Voltaire's. If all plays were but like his! But, then, they are not. So he brought to bear against them all the magic and the fervour of his style, and flung on to four hundred pages of paper his astonishing views not only on play-acting, but on women, on love, and on literature.

No one reads "La Lettre sur les Spectacles" now. But everybody read it then, and though the stricter of the educated Calvinists only coldly acknowledged Rousseau as an ally, the common people heard him gladly. The aristocracy of Geneva had enjoyed Voltaire's theatrical evenings too much to bring themselves to disapprove of them.

From Paris the little frail d'Alembert "deigned to overwhelm that fool Jean Jacques with reasons," in a letter full of grave and stately irony. As for Voltaire, he waited, as he could afford to wait. He had taught some at least of the Genevans to be as "mad for theatres" as he was himself; and—he had "Candide" up his sleeve.

Running parallel with that controversy on theatres was another. Of course Voltaire was in it—and the soul of it. That goes without saying. He had been but a short time settled in Lausanne, when one Saurin, a poet-neighbour of his there, begged him to contradict a certain history of Joseph Saurin, his father, as given by Voltaire in a Catalogue of French Writers, added to his "Century of Louis XIV." In that catalogue Voltaire had written of Joseph what not only he, but all the world, believed to be true. Joseph had been a pastor who, hating the life of Switzerland, had allowed himself to be very easily brought back by the preaching of Bossuet to Roman Catholicism and to France. But in France he was poor, and he hated poverty. Presently came rumours of robbery—of robbery he had committed in church. In a letter to a Lausanne pastor, Gonon, Saurin practically confessed to these robberies. This letter was published in the "Swiss Mercury" of April, 1736, and Saurin did not attempt to refute it. He had since died; and now, at his son's suggestion, this energetic Voltaire must needs unearth the whole story, and with a very rash good-nature, set to work to prove that that letter to Gonon was nothing but a forgery after all. He obtained a certificate from three of the Lausanne ministers who had been principally concerned in the affair, declaring that they had never seen the original. This certificate Voltaire put into the second edition of his "Essay on the Manners and Mind of Nations."

But in this October of 1758, some impertinent anonymous person reproduces the whole letter from Saurin to Gonon in another Swiss newspaper, and positively dares to doubt the authenticity of Voltaire's certificate from the three pastors.

On November 15th, M. de Voltaire sits down and writes "A Refutation of an Anonymous Article," wherein he dwells on the useless danger and cruelty to an innocent family of attempting to convict their dead father of heinous crime.

The impertinent unknown (who turns out to be a pastor, Lervèche, who had long objected to Voltaire's theatricals at Mon Repos) writes a "Reply" to the refutation.

Then who should appear on the scene but Grasset, the publisher, and Voltaire's enemy in the latest "Pucelle" fracas. Grasset reprints the whole correspondence, and adds thereto Voltaire's "Defence of Lord Bolingbroke," and other little *brochures* from his pen most likely to give offence. The whole he calls "The Literary War or Selected Pieces of M. de V——."

Literary War indeed! says M. de V——; a literary libel! And do you know who this Grasset is? A scoundrel, a cheat, a common criminal! M. de V——, in short, not only loses his temper, but seems for the moment to lose sight of the Saurin cause, and to devote all his energies to getting Grasset punished. He appeals to all the local authorities. He "knocks at every door," and continues to knock till all are opened. He is once more his own angry, spry, busy little fighting self. Peaceful landowner and householder—all that is forgotten. Behold again the restless and terrible little enemy who fought Desfontaines.

Most people listened to him—and sympathised, if not for his rage with Grasset, at least for his zeal for the Saurins. There was but one man who threw on his enthusiasm the cold water of irony: and that was Haller, the great Swiss genius, *savant*, philosopher, linguist, botanist, poet, philologist. Until Voltaire settled at Délices, Haller had been *the* lion of the neighbourhood. Now he was only *a* lion. The situation hardly needs further explanation. Suffice it to say that Haller was as firm a Christian as Voltaire was a Deist: and that Haller had been a rather sarcastic spectator of M. de Voltaire's theatricals. All generous admiration was on the side of Voltaire, who always had plenty to spare for real talent such as Haller's.

When Haller returned a very cool answer to Voltaire's warm pleadings for the Saurins and suggested that to concern himself in so small a matter was beneath a great man's greatness, Voltaire waited a judicious ten days, and returned a mild and pleading answer.

To be beneath one's greatness to put wrong, right, and to clear a dead man's honour! Haller could have known the Voltaire who was to avenge Calas, very little. The correspondence continued. Haller was not a little stiff-necked and difficult: and Voltaire at once persistent and impulsive. Then Haller published the letters—in which he fancied he himself played a *beau rôle*—and made an enemy, though a very generous enemy, of Voltaire, for ever.

Grimm records how Voltaire one day asked an English visitor at Ferney, from whence he had come.

"From Mr. Haller's."

"He is a great man," cried Voltaire, "a great poet, a great naturalist, a great philosopher—almost a universal genius in fact."

"What you say, Sir, is the more admirable," replied the Englishman, "because Mr. Haller does not do you the same justice."

"Ah!" said Voltaire, "perhaps we are both mistaken."

A like interview is also described as taking place between Voltaire and Casanova in 1760. Casanova stayed with Haller before he went to visit Voltaire; and on leaving his first host observed how much he was looking forward to becoming acquainted with his second.

"Ah!" replied Haller, "many persons, contrary to physical laws, have found M. de Voltaire greater when seen at a distance."

Voltaire had presently the satisfaction of hearing that the sale of "The Literary War" was prohibited, and of seeing Grasset severely censured; though he would have liked better to see him banished.

The Saurin-Grasset-Haller affair had one important influence upon Voltaire. It disgusted him with Lausanne.

In this autumn of 1758 Voltaire wrote to a very old friend, King Stanislas, saying that he had fifty thousand francs which he should like to invest in an estate in Lorraine—that he might not die on the borders of Lake Leman. Cautious Stanislas consulted the French Government. Would this meet its views? Choiseul, representing it, as Bernis's successor, replied, "You know Voltaire well enough to decide for yourself."

So on some date, not before November 20, 1758, Bettinelli—Italian, Jesuit, poet, and literary man—arrived at Délices as the envoy of Stanislas, sent to accept the proposed investment and tell Voltaire how delighted Stanislas would be to have him as a neighbour.

Voltaire was in the garden, gardening, when Bettinelli came, and presented an extraordinary appearance in a long pelisse, a black velvet cap, and a peruke which covered almost all his face except the nose and chin, which by now nearly met. He had a stick in his hand which had a weeding fork at one end and a pruning hook at the other; and observed, when he saw Bettinelli, that his crop from his garden was much more abundant "than from that I sow in my books for the good of mankind."

The pair talked on all kinds of subjects. Bettinelli, who was not a little afraid of Voltaire's cynic wit, nervously remarked the brilliant flash of the eyes and the sarcastic, mobile lips. He thought his host spoke slowly because he was preparing something caustic to say next; but the truth was the host had already lost most of his teeth and spoke slowly in order to be understood. The pair discussed all kinds of subjects—Italy, the Inquisition, slavery, Tasso, Ariosto, Tronchin, Bettinelli's poetry, and the famous book "On the Mind," which Voltaire sharply criticised; and whose author, Helvétius, he summed up "as a fool who wanted to be a philosopher with courtiers and a courtier with philosophers."

They spoke of Madame du Châtelet. In Voltaire's rooms were several pictures of the dead woman. "Here is my immortal Émilie," he said. Bettinelli records that she was the only person of whom he heard Voltaire speak with an unchanging admiration and enthusiasm. Before Bettinelli left he had a little interview with Dr. Tronchin, who congratulated him on having found Voltaire in a mood unusually serene and equable. In fact, the visit had been wholly a success—but for one thing. When Bettinelli handed Voltaire Stanislas's acceptance of his proposal to live in Lorraine, Voltaire took it, saying that he had just bought a little estate near Délices, where he intended to live out the rest of his life. On November 18th, Voltaire had dated his first letter from Ferney. Bettinelli was too late.

Since the middle of this September, 1758, Voltaire had been busy negotiating with a M. de Boisy for the purchase of Ferney—formerly spelt Fernex—and with a Président de Brosses for the life lease of Tourney or Tournay.

There were reasons which made both estates peculiarly suitable to a Voltaire. Ferney was in France, in Burgundy, in the district of Gex; but it was also on the frontier of Switzerland, only three and a half miles from Geneva. Here one could laugh at those strait-laced Genevans as freely as if the three miles were three hundred; and if one offended France, which was only a question of time, what more simple than to drive into Geneva? Then, too, Ferney, lying on the north shore of Lake Leman, almost joined the Délices. Voltaire at first thought it would be a sort of supplement to his first Swiss home. But, as all the world knows, Ferney soon supplanted Délices in its master's affections, and became the literary capital of Europe.

There were equally strong reasons for buying Tourney. It was in France, in Burgundy, as Ferney was; and it was under the direction of a foreign prelate, the Bishop of Annecy. It was on the very frontier of the Swiss canton of Berne; and at the very gates of that rich, powerful, intellectual Geneva, and yet entirely independent of its prim Calvinistic laws. From Tourney one could thus "tease Geneva and caress Paris; brave orders and *lettres de cachet*; have one's works printed without the King's permission, and get away in the twinkling of an eye from all prosecutions." Admirable for a Voltaire, this. Then, too, if Ferney was a supplement to Délices—Tourney was a prolongation of Ferney. Add to this, with the life lease of Tourney went the title of Lord and Count of Tourney. Was not this something to the man who clung so tightly to the empty honour of Gentleman-in-Ordinary? It was very much. Voltaire took an enormous pleasure in calling the attention of his correspondents to his new designation; and presently signed himself, with a solemn pride and joy, "Gentleman-in-Ordinary to the King of France and Count of Tourney." If Tourney was nothing in the world but a tumbledown old country house with a ruined farm attached to it—what difference did that make? What was a Gentleman-in-Ordinary? An exile from France the French King would have none of. The same sort of pleasure which he received from fine clothes was conveyed to Voltaire by fine titles. The characteristic is not a grand or ennobling one; but it is delightfully human.

By September, then, he had these two estates in view—"Tourney for the title, and Ferney for the land: Ferney for a perpetuity, and Tourney only for life." There was not much trouble with M. de Boisy over Ferney. It was bought for 24,000 écus in the name of Madame Denis, who was to inherit it after her uncle's death. The contract for the purchase was not actually signed until February 9, 1759; but in the middle of September, 1758, Voltaire had made a kind of state entrance into the parish, accompanied by Madame Denis. Madame Denis was in her very best clothes, with all the diamonds the *ménage* Voltaire could produce. As for Uncle Voltaire himself, he, in spite of the fact that the weather was still very warm, enjoyed himself vastly in crimson velvet trimmed with ermine. The pair drove in the smartest carriage, and attended High Mass—"droned out—false"—at the parish church, during which the enthusiastic future tenants of the proprietor of Ferney thumped on tin boxes to represent a welcome of cannon! That little, lively, black-eyed French-woman, Madame d'Épinay, has left a vivacious record of the day. If she saw it as comic, Voltaire did not. Once more he justified Tronchin's appellation for him, "an old baby," and enjoyed himself like a schoolboy.

But if the Ferney negotiations had been simple, not so the Tourney.

Président de Brosses and Voltaire were soon engaged in a vast correspondence. A whole book has been written on their relations with each other. There is no doubt that over Tourney Voltaire showed a great deal of that spirit which people call business capacity in themselves and meanness in others.

On September 9th, he made an offer to de Brosses for the life lease of the little estate. De Brosses said the offer was insufficient. After a good deal of trouble and haggling over small items on both sides, Voltaire finally bought the life lease of Tourney (with all seigneurial rights and that delightful title included) for 35,600 livres. He undertook to make certain alterations and repairs. A herd of cattle was included in his purchase. Although he was not to enter into his life tenancy until February 22, 1759, the agreement is dated December 11, 1758; and on December 24th he made his state entrance into Tourney, as three months before he had into Ferney.

The second occasion was much the more magnificent of the two. Madame de Fontaine was with him this time, as well as Madame Denis. Both were in diamonds. Here, too, was their brother Mignot, the abbé; also *tout paré*. The village girls handed the ladies baskets of flowers and oranges. The artillery had come from Geneva, so there was no need to thump upon tin boxes. There were drums, fifes, cannon: all the music of flattery. The spectators were not only peasants, as they had been at Ferney, but all the polite persons of the neighbourhood. There was a splendid banquet, given by the outgoing tenant of Tourney, and served by the innkeeper of a neighbouring village. The curé made M. de Voltaire a beautiful address. M. de Voltaire was wholly delighted—"very gay and content." He answered quite *en grand seigneur*, and as was expected of him, "Ask anything you like for the good of your parish and I will give it you." Lord and Count of Tourney! This most impressionable of men lived up to the part immediately. He wrote an enthusiastic account of the proceedings to de Brosses on the very same day, when he was back again at Délices. "I made my entrance like Sancho Panza into his island. Only his paunch was wanting to me." "My subjects frightened my horses with musketry and torpedoes." The banquet (served by the native innkeeper) "was a magnificent repast in the style of those of Horace and Boileau." In short, the Lord of Tourney saw his new estates all *couleur de rose*, or almost all. It is infinitely characteristic that in this very letter he went on to plead for the restitution of certain tithes to the poor of Ferney, which they had enjoyed for a century, and of which Ancian, the curé of the neighbouring parish of Moens, "the most abominable pettifogger in the district," had deprived them, further "putting them to fifteen hundred francs of law expenses before they knew it." Voltaire had also appealed passionately to the Bishop of Annecy; and did at last obtain his suit, but only after he had paid a very large sum out of his own pocket.

He wrote also to Theriot that evening—tired, no doubt, but too charmed to remember it. "You are mistaken, my old friend; I have four paws instead of two. One paw in Lausanne, in a very pretty house for the winter; one paw at Délices, near Geneva, where good company comes to see me—those are the front paws. The back are at Ferney, and in the county"—a county, if you please, and not merely an estate—"of Tourney."

He went on to point out the advantages of Ferney—how there was plenty of land and wood for the rebuilding operations he already had in hand; how he could get marble by the lake; how the extensive estates would really not be so costly after all. For himself, he would like to live on them quite simply. But my niece, you know—that victim of Frankfort—*she* merits luxury and indulgences. He had already set the peasants to work to mend the neglected roads about Ferney; so that in a month or two he was able to say truthfully that they had earned more in that time than formerly they had been able to do in a year. He had already chartered more than a hundred workmen, that his rebuilding and gardening operations might be put in hand at once.

The year closed full of the happiest expectations. Despite gala entrances to new estates, Madame Denis, indeed, complained that the winter of 1758-59 was dull. It was all spent at Délices: as being more out of the way of the troubling of Grassets and Hallers, than Monrion. True, plenty of visitors came from Lausanne; but there were not many who came to sleep and stay. True, too, the Délices troupe had privately acted ("the only pleasure I have in this country," Madame Denis wrote dismally) "Aménaïde," which was to have its name changed to "Tancred" later; and as "Tancred" become immortal. But Madame Denis apparently was suffering from an indigestion which Tronchin could not cure, for she spoke slightingly of that good physician, and discontentedly of life in general. Uncle Voltaire was so absurdly busy! Trying to do a hundred things at once, and invincibly obstinate. "It is the only sign of old age he has." "If I were not so sensitive I should be very happy." When a lady complains she is sensitive, she always means that she is cross and offended. Uncle Voltaire had shown his invincible obstinacy by persisting in going on with that Saurin controversy when his niece thought he had very much better leave it alone.

Then, too, he was getting more and more engrossed every day with pulling down and putting up, with barns, farms, oxen, sheep, horses; and "adored the country even in winter," while Louise, as he said himself, was "very difficult to reduce to the *rôle* of Ceres, of Pomona, and of Flora, and would much rather have been Thalia in Paris." But when her uncle found Tourney and Ferney, he found a better life than he had ever known; and the dearest and crossest of nieces would not make him relinquish it. The year 1759 was still new-born when he was writing, not once but many times, that he was wonderfully well and happy, stronger and better than he had ever been; that he had only really lived since the day he chose his retreat; that he was so infinitely content "that if I dare I should think myself wise."

"Such is my life, Madame, tranquil and occupied, full and philosophic." "I love to plant, I love to build, and so satisfy the only tastes which gratify old age."

"This kind of life makes one want to live." "Property in paper depends upon fortune; property in land depends only upon God."

"To have found the secret of being independent in France is more than to have written the 'Henriade.'"

CHAPTER XXXII

FERNEY

FERNEY, as has been said, stood on the north shore of Lake Leman, in the district of Gex, three and a half miles from Geneva and almost joining Délices. The village to which it belonged, also called Ferney, was really nothing but a mean hamlet with forty or fifty miserable inhabitants, "devoured by poverty, scurvy, and tax-gatherers." A very ugly little church stood much too near the house.

That house, when Voltaire bought it, was very old, tumbledown, and totally inadequate to his requirements. The entrance was through two towers connected by a drawbridge. If it was picturesque, it was certainly not comfortable. When Voltaire had rebuilt it, it was certainly comfortable, and decidedly unpicturesque.

He had begun that rebuilding three months before the deed of purchase was signed. By December 6, 1758, he had twenty masons at work. By the 24th, what he might well have cynically called his *optimism* led him to think it "a pretty house enough." By June, 1759, it was "a charming château in the Italian style."

By July it was "of the Doric order. It will last a thousand years."

By November it was "a piece of architecture which would have admirers even in Italy." While by the March of 1761 it had grown—at any rate in its master's fancy—into "a superb château."

There have not been wanting to Voltaire enemies to argue persistently and vociferously that Ferney was not at all what he represented it; and that all his geese were swans. They were. Ferney at its best and completest was never anything but a plain, sensible, commodious country house. It had neither wings nor decoration; not any architectural merit, except that its ugliness was simple and not elaborate. Voltaire was his own architect; and owned quite frankly that he knew nothing at all about architecture. The man who had travelled through Holland, Belgium, and Prussia without once stepping out of his post-chaise to look at a famous picture, or an immortal sculpture, or the "frozen music" of a grand cathedral, had as little feeling for art as for Nature.

He thought Ferney a superb château because it was *his* château. Just as he was devoted to flowers and gardens, when they were *his* flowers and *his* gardens.

It is certainly not the best way of loving art or Nature, but it is the only way of many persons besides Voltaire. And, after all, that comfortable feeling of landed proprietorship, that honest pride in his cows and his sheep, his bees and his silkworms, sits pleasantly enough on this withered cynic of sixty-five; and makes him at once more human, more sympathetic—the same flesh and blood as the simple and ordinary.

He had, as he said, plenty of wood and stone for his building operations on the premises—"oak enough to be useful to our navy, if we had one"; and stone, which the architect thought very good, and which turned out to be very bad. He said gaily that when the house was finished he should write on the wall "Voltaire fecit"; and that posterity would take him for a famous architect. As for that marble of which he had talked largely as being brought up by the lake, the man who declared that he preferred a good English book to a hundred thousand pillars of it, did not trouble to obtain much or to make an elaborate use of what he did obtain. He wanted the house "agreeable and useful," and he had it. There was a fine view from it; though not so fine as it might have been, for it faced the high road. Still, as its happy master said, it was situated in the most smiling country in Europe; at its feet the lake gleamed and sparkled; and beyond the warm and gorgeous luxuriance of its perfect gardens could be seen, in dazzling contrast, the eternal snows of Mont Blanc.

When the rebuilding was finished the house was, looked at without prejudice, the well-appointed home of a well-to-do *bourgeois gentilhomme*—with an unusual love for literature. There was an ordinary hall with a stone staircase on the left which led up to the fourteen guest-rooms, all comfortably furnished, said one of those guests, who was an Englishman and had been used to solid English comfort at home. Here and there were some good pictures—or copies of good pictures—copies, most likely, since Voltaire, hardly knowing the difference, would be apt to reflect that a copy would do as well as an original, and be much cheaper. A Venus after Paul Veronese and a Flora after Guido Reni, some of the visitors declared genuine; and some as hotly pronounced spurious. Wagnière, that Genevan boy who lived to write memoirs like the other secretaries, stated that his master had about twenty valuable pictures in all; and some good busts. There were various family portraits about the house: one of Madame Denis; one of Voltaire's young mother; and, soon, a likeness of Madame de Pompadour painted by herself, and by herself given to Voltaire. In Madame Denis's room presently there was a portrait of Catherine, Empress of Russia, embroidered in silk; and a marble statue of Voltaire. There was a copy of this statue, or his bust in plaster, in almost every room in the house.

The library was simple, and, for Voltaire, small. Dr. Burney, the father of Fanny, who saw it in 1770, describes it as "not very large but well filled," and says it contained "a whole-length figure in marble" of its master "recumbent, in one of the windows." At Voltaire's death it contained only 6,210 volumes. But almost every one had on its margin copious notes in that fine, neat little handwriting. Six thousand volumes annotated by a Voltaire! His sarcasm should have made the dullest ones amusing; and his relentless logic the obscurest ones clear. There were a great many volumes of history and theology; dictionaries in every language; all the Italian poets; and all the English philosophers. The Comte de Maistre, who saw this library after Voltaire's death when it had been bought by Catherine the Great, wondered at the "extreme mediocrity" of the books. By this he explained himself to mean that there were no rare old editions and no sumptuous bindings, which the Count took as a sign that Voltaire was "a stranger to all profound literature." It was a sign that Voltaire read to act; that books were his tools, not his ornaments; that he loved literature, not as a sensuous delight, but as the lever that was to turn the world. "A few books, very much marked." That library was infinitely characteristic of the man who was doer, not dreamer; of the mind to which every poet, every philosopher, every scientist acted as a spur to new practical effort; of the man who was to go down the ages not as playwright, or verse-maker, but as he who "conquered the intellect of France, for the Revolution."

The *salle à manger* was distinguished only by a most extraordinary and very bad allegorical picture, called "The Temple of Memory," in which a Glory, with her hair dressed much *à la mode*, was presenting Voltaire (who was surrounded with a halo like a saint) to the God of Poetry who was getting out of his chariot with a crown in his hand. On one side of the picture appeared busts of Euripides, Sophocles, Racine, Corneille, and other great men; on the opposite side were caricatures of Fréron and Desfontaines, who were being most satisfactorily kicked by Furies. Voltaire laughed at, and enjoyed immensely, this part of the picture while he was at meals. The artist was Alix, a native of Ferney, and soon an *habitué* at the château. It was fortunate for him that Voltaire was so much better a friend than he was a judge of art.

His bedroom and salon were both small rooms. The salon, entered by folding doors, contained the master's bust above the stove, six or seven pictures, "more or less good," a portrait of Madame du Châtelet, and casts of Newton and Locke. One of the pictures, after Boucher, represented a hunting scene. There were ten tapestry armchairs, and a table of very common varnished marble. French windows and a glass door led into the garden.

Voltaire's bedroom was principally distinguished by a neatness, cleanness, and simplicity natural to him, but very unusual in his day. The roughly carved deal bedstead one visitor regretfully regarded as "almost mean." It was the fashion then to spend the night in what looked like a large heavily curtained coffin. Voltaire—to the melancholy vexation of the fashionable—seems to have dispensed with most of the curtains, but could not escape a huge baldachino over his head. Inside it, hung a very bad pastel portrait of Lekain; and a candelabra containing three wax candles, so that he could see to read. On either side of the bed hung portraits of Frederick the Great, of Voltaire himself, and of Madame du Châtelet. Placed between the door and the only window were five or six other engraved portraits, all in very simple black frames. The bed hangings and the four armchairs were upholstered alike in pale blue damask.

The room contained five desks. On each were notes for the various subjects on which the author was working: this desk had notes for a play; this, for a treatise on philosophy; a third for a *brochure* on science; and so on. All were exquisitely neat and orderly; every paper in its right place. The writing chair was of cane, with a cover on it to match the bed curtains. Later on, Voltaire had a second writing-chair made, which he used much in the last few years of his life: one of its arms formed a desk, and the other a little table with drawers; and both were revolving.

Just below the master's bedroom was Wagnière's, so that if Voltaire knocked on the floor during the night the servant could hear him. That he did so knock, pretty often, rests on the rueful testimony of Wagnière himself.

Quite close to the house stood a little marble bathroom with hot and cold water laid on. It was a very unusual luxury in those times, and considered a highly unnecessary one. It is pleasant to a century much more particular in such matters than the eighteenth to reflect that Voltaire was always personally cleanly and tidy to an extent which his contemporaries considered ridiculous. That fine and dirty age could hardly forgive his insisting on his ancient perukes and queer old gardening clothes being kept as trim and well brushed as if they were new and grand. His passion for soap and water was one of the complaints his enemies in Prussia had brought against him. Wagnière records that his master was "scrupulously clean" and also his love of washing his eyes in pure cold water. Doubtless the habit preserved them, in spite of the inordinate amount of work they had to do. To the day of his death they never needed spectacles.

Most of the visitors comment on the well-kept appearance of the house; though one, Lady Craven, Margravine of Anspach, said the *salle à manger* was generally dirty and the servants' liveries soiled. It was at Ferney as it had been at Cirey. The master was particular, but the mistress was not. If Madame du Châtelet had been engrossed with science, Madame Denis was engrossed with amusement. Her extravagance and bad household management in that respect were often the cause of disagreements between her uncle and herself. And, that "fat pig, who says it is too hot to write a letter," as Voltaire once described his niece to Madame d'Épinay, was the sort of person who thought no trouble too great for pleasure, but any trouble too great for duty.

It is significant that when she went to Paris in 1768 her uncle seized the opportunity of having Ferney thoroughly cleaned from top to bottom.

It is said that when he caught sight of cobwebs by the pillars and porticoes of the house, which the servants had neglected to remove, he used to vigorously flick a whip, crying out, "À la chasse! à la chasse!" and the whole household, including the guests, had to join in the spider hunt.

He had in his daily employ sixty or seventy persons, and sometimes more. Five servants usually waited at table, of whom three were in livery. Martin Sherlock, the Englishman, says that the dinner consisted of two courses and was eaten off silver plates with the host's coat of arms on them; while at the dessert the spoons, forks, and blades of the knives were of silver-gilt; and adds that no strange servant was ever allowed to officiate at meals. Wagnière records how two of the household having robbed their master, the police got wind of the matter; and Voltaire bade him go and warn the delinquents to fly immediately, "for if they are arrested I shall not be able to save them from hanging." He also sent them some money for the journey. It is pleasant to learn that the hearts of the culprits were touched by this generous kindness, and that, having escaped, they lived honest lives.

It was a rule at Ferney that all peasants who came to the house should have a good dinner and twenty-four sous given them before they pursued their way.

"Good to all about him," was the Prince de Ligne's description of Voltaire. It was not an extravagant one.

If the house at Ferney was simple and comfortable rather than magnificent, the grounds were on a far more elaborate scale. There was enough land to grow wheat, hay, and straw. There were poultry yards and sheepfolds; an orchard watered by a stream; meadows, storehouses, and an immense barn which stabled fifty cows with their calves and served as a granary, and of which its master was intensely proud.

Then, too, there were farms which Voltaire managed himself, and so made lucrative. He was pleased to say, with a twinkle in his eye, that he also did everything in the garden—the gardener was "*si bête*." That he had a field which was always called Voltaire's field, because he cultivated it entirely with his own hands, is certainly true. Before long he had four or five hundred beehives; turkeys and silkworms; and a breeding stable for horses, transferred from the Délices. He was not a little delighted when, in this May of 1759, the Marquis de Voyer, steward of King Louis's stables, made him a present of a fine stallion. As if he had not hobbies enough, he soon became an enthusiastic tree-planter—begging all his friends to follow his example— and sending waggons all the way to Lyons for loads of young trees for his park.

After a while that park stretched in three miles of circuit round the house, and included a splendid avenue of oaks, lindens, and poplars. In the garden were sunny walls for peaches; vines, lawns, and flowers. It was laid out with a charming *imprévu* and irregularity, most unfashionable in that formal day. Voltaire had always a "tender recollection of the banks of the Thames," and made his garden as English as he could. It is indeed melancholy to note that artificial water and prim terraces were soon introduced to spoil—though their master thought they improved—its luxuriant irregularity; and that objects like lightning conductors, and fountains presided over by plaster nymphs, were not considered the least out of keeping with Nature by their lord and master. Near his silkworm house a thick linden-tree with overhanging branches formed what was called Voltaire's study, and there he wrote verses "for recreation." Nature certainly never inspired any of *them*. Now and again there came, it is true, even to this most typical son of the most artificial of all centuries, as he cultivated his field, or pruned and weeded in his garden, such reflections as might have fallen from the lips of his great opposite, Rousseau: "I have only done one sensible thing in my life—to cultivate the ground. He who clears a field renders a better service to humankind than all the scribblers in Europe."

"You have done a great work for posterity" a friend said to him one day.

"Yes, Madame. I have planted four thousand feet of trees in my park."

No more incongruous picture could be painted than that of this "withering cynic," this world-famous hewer, hacker, and uprooter in his old grey shoes and stockings, a long vest to his knees, little black velvet cap and great drooping peruke, tranquilly directing, cultivating, sowing, "planting walnut and chestnut trees upon which I shall never see walnuts or chestnuts," consoling himself for the toads in his garden by the reflection that "they do not prevent the nightingales from singing": and prophesying that his destiny would be "to end between a seedlip, cows, and Genevans."

For the time this country life was his element not the less. He wrote that it was, to Madame du Deffand, a dozen times. True, he had taken to it late. But perhaps always, deep down in him, undeveloped, stifled by Paris and by the burning needs of humanity, had been the peaceful primæval tastes. Cirey had roused them. Délices had nourished them: and Ferney and Tourney confirmed them.

Tourney had given its master a title, but at first it gave him nothing else. It was a county *pour rire*, "the land in a bad state," "a garden where there was nothing but snails and moles, vines without grapes, fields without corn, and sheds without cows," and "a house in ruins." Still, the land could be made fertile; and the house, if it *was* in ruins, boasted an admirable view, and was but "a quarter of a league" from Geneva.

By February, 1759, fifty workmen were putting it to rights; and by November the Count of Tourney could say that he had planted hundreds of trees in the garden, and used more powder (in rock-blasting) than at the siege of a town. Everything needed repairing, he added—fields, roads granaries, wine-presses—and everything was being repaired.

As at Ferney and Délices, the master personally supervised every detail; and so made his farms, his nurseries, his bees, his silkworms, all pay.

In the house at Tourney he quickly made a theatre-room. If some of the guests were disposed to laugh at a stage which held nine persons in a semicircle with difficulty, and to think the green and gold decorations tawdry, Voltaire adored that "theatre of Punchinello" as a child adores a new toy. "A little green and gold theatre," "the prettiest and smallest possible"—he alludes to it in his letters a hundred times. From the September of 1760 he was anxious to transfer it to Ferney. But meanwhile he loved it where and as it was. Tourney also was useful to provide accommodation for the servants of the innumerable guests who came to stay at Ferney.

No idea of Voltaire's life there could be given without mention of that incessant stream of visitors of all nations and languages which flowed through it, almost without pause for twenty years. Half the genius—and but too many of the fools—of Europe came to worship at the shrine of the prophet of this literary Mecca.

As prim Geneva shut its gates at nightfall, every one who came to sup with M. de Voltaire had to stay all night in his house. Ferney had no inn. After fourteen years of his life there, Voltaire might well say that he had been the hotel-keeper of Europe. He told Madame du Deffand, as early as 1763, that he had entertained four hundred English people, of whom not one ever after gave him a thought.

Too many of his guests, indeed, were not merely self-invited: but remained at Ferney with such persistency that their unhappy host would sometimes retire to bed and say he was dying, to get rid of them. One caller, who had received a message to this effect, returned the next day. "Tell him I am dying again. And if he comes any more, say I am dead and buried."

Another visitor, when told Voltaire was ill, shrewdly replied that he was a doctor and should like to feel his pulse. When Voltaire sent down a message to say he was dead, the visitor replied, "Then I will bury him. In my profession I am used to burying people." His humour appealed to Voltaire's. He was admitted. "You seem to take me for some curious animal," said Voltaire.

"Yes, Monsieur, for the Phœnix."

"Very well: the charge to see me is twelve sous."

"Here are twenty-four," said the visitor. "I will come again to-morrow."

He did, and on many to-morrows: and was received as a friend.

But all the importunate were not so clever, and their fulsome flattery was odious to the man who loved it daintily dressed.

"Sir, when I see you, I see the great candle that lights the world."

"Quick, Madame Denis," cried Voltaire. "A pair of snuffers!"

One persistent woman tried to effect an entry by saying that she was the niece of Terrai, the last, and not the least corrupt, of Louis XV.'s finance ministers.

Voltaire sent out a message. "Tell her I have only one tooth left, and I am keeping that for her uncle."

The Abbé Coyer, on his arrival, calmly announced that he was going to stay six weeks.

"In what respect, my dear Abbé, are you unlike 'Don Quixote'? He took the inns for châteaux, and you take the châteaux for inns."

Coyer left early the next day.

Still, in spite of such rebuffs, the visitors were incessant.

One said that he could not recollect there being *more* than sixty to eighty people at supper after theatricals. Voltaire himself said there were constantly fifty to a hundred.

Many visitors stayed for weeks; many for months; some for years.

Madame de Fontaine, with her lover *en train*, could come when she chose—and she often chose. Mignot came when *he* liked. Great-nephew d'Hornoy was a constant visitor.

At different times there were two adopted daughters and two Jesuit priests living in the house. One relative, as will be seen, was at Ferney for a decade—completely paralysed. And hanging about the house were generally a trio or a quartette of gentlemen ne'er-do-weels, who sometimes copied their host's manuscripts, and sometimes stole them.

In the midst of such a household Voltaire pursued his way and his life's work, wonderfully methodically and equably. It was his custom to stay in bed till eleven o'clock, or later. There he read or wrote; or dictated to his secretaries with a distressing rapidity. Sometimes he was reading to himself at the same time. About eleven, a few of his guests would come up and pay him a brief visit.

The rest of the morning he spent in the gardens and farms, superintending and giving orders. In earlier years, he dined with his house party—in an undress, for which he always apologised and which he never changed. Later on, he always dined alone. After dinner he would go into the salon and talk for a little with his guests. The whole of the rest of the afternoon and evening until supper-time he spent in study: in which he never allowed himself to be interrupted. One at least of his guests complained that his only fault was to be *"fort renfermé."*

At supper he appeared in as lively spirits as a schoolboy set free from school. It was the time for recreation: and a well earned recreation too. He led his guests to talk on such subjects as pleased them. When a discussion grew serious, he would listen without saying a word, with his head bent forward. Then, when his friends had adduced their arguments, he advanced his own, in perfect order and clearness, and yet with an extraordinary force and vehemence. He was seldom his best before a large company, especially of the kind that had come, as he said, "to see the rhinoceros." But with a few kindred spirits he was as brilliant as he had been twenty years before over the supper-table at Cirey. At Ferney he must have missed indeed that woman who, having flung off her mantle of science and erudition, became socially what socially all women should be—an inspirer, a sympathiser, a magnet to draw out men's wit—a sorceress who talked so well that she made her companions feel not how clever she was, but how clever they were.

Niece Denis was certainly the most good-natured of hostesses—if she was *gaupe*, as Madame du Deffand said—and was grateful to her uncle's guests for mitigating the ennui of a country life. She was useful too. When Voltaire was tired or bored, he could retire directly after supper to that invariable refuge, bed; and leave his niece to act with his visitors. When he was not bored and there were no theatricals, he sometimes read aloud a canto of the "Pucelle" as in old times; or quoted poetry—any but his own—which he never could recollect; or talked theatres or played chess. It was the only game in which he indulged, and he was a little ashamed of it. Games are so idle!

When he went to bed he started work afresh. It was his only intemperance. If he kept an abundant table for his guests he was still infinitely frugal himself. His *déjeuner* consisted only of coffee, with cream; his supper, of eggs, although there was always a chicken ready for him in case he fancied it. He drank a little burgundy, and owned to a weakness for lentils. Of coffee, in which he had indulged freely in youth, he now took only a few cups a day. He had a habit of ignoring meals altogether when he was busy—a little idiosyncrasy somewhat trying to his secretaries. Wagnière also complained that his master was too sparing in sleep; and called him up from that room below, several times in the night, to assist him in his literary work. When he had a play on hand he was "in a fever."

Many of the visitors who stayed at Ferney have left an account of their life there. Though the accounts always graphically portray the character of the writers, they sketch much less vividly the portrait of Voltaire. But from such accounts—all taken together, and corrected by each other from Voltaire's own descriptions, from Wagnière's and from Madame Denis's—Ferney, and the life there, were as nearly as possible what has been depicted. Changes in habits are inevitable in twenty years. Differing accounts may all be true—at different times. Feverishly busy for Voltaire, idle and sociable for Madame Denis; she carried along by that unceasing stream of guests, and he watching it, half amused and half bored, from his own firm mooring of a great life's work—that was Ferney for its master and mistress from 1758 until 1778. They did not regularly take up their abode there until 1760. They did not give up Délices altogether until 1765. But from the autumn of 1758 Ferney was their real home, the home of Voltaire's heart; inextricably associated with him by his friends and his enemies; the subject of a thousand scandals, and of most beautiful imaginative descriptions. Nearly all great men have had one place dedicated to them—Florence to Dante; Corsica to Napoleon; Stratford to Shakespeare; Weimar to Goethe; and Ferney to Voltaire.

CHAPTER XXXIII

"CANDIDE," AND "ÉCRASEZ L'INFÂME"

ON February 10, 1759, Voltaire's "Natural Law," Helvétius's book "On the Mind," and six others were publicly burnt in Paris by the hangman.

In March the "Encyclopædia" was suspended.

"Natural Law," it will be remembered, was nothing but a seeking for an answer to that everlasting question "What is truth?"

"On the Mind" was the naïve expression of the materialism of the wittiest freethinker in Paris, Helvétius, *maître d'hôtel* to the Queen and Farmer-General. But the Dauphin showed it to his mother, and it received the compliment of burning. "What a fuss about an omelette!" said Voltaire contemptuously. The destruction of his own "Natural Law" disturbed him as little. "Burn a good book, and the cinders will spring up and strike your face" was one of his own axioms. From the flames of its funeral pyre, the thing would rise a phœnix gifted with immortal life and fame.

But the suspension of the "Encyclopædia" hit him hard.

Since the attempted assassination of the King by Damiens the laws against the freedom of the press had been growing daily more severe. True, the poor creature had had a Bible in his pocket, but the churchmen argued somehow that it was the New Learning which had guided the dagger. Then France had had reverses in war. Suppose these misfortunes all came from these cursed philosophers and their "Encyclopædia"! As, later, whole nations attributed the rot in the crops and the ague in the bones of their children to the withering influence of that great little Corporal, hundreds of miles away from them, so in the eighteenth century in France a great party in the State attributed to the extension of learning every disaster which their own folly or foolhardiness brought upon them.

They turned, and brought all their power, influence, and money against the Encyclopædists. D'Alembert was no fighter. Student, recluse, and gentle friend—he was not one of those who could write with a pen in one hand and a sword in the other. "I do not know if the 'Encyclopædia' will be continued," he wrote to Voltaire as early as the January of 1758, "but I am sure it will not be continued by me"; and though the pugnacious little warrior of Délices wrote and passionately urged his peaceful friend not to do what his absurd enemies wished—not to let them enjoy "that insolent victory"—still, d'Alembert withdrew. On February 9, 1759, Voltaire wrote that he seemed to see the Inquisition condemning Galileo.

But it was as he said. The cinders from the burning sprang up and burnt the burners. They could mutilate the "Encyclopædia," but they could not kill it. Its very mutilations attracted interest, and "Natural Law" and "On the Mind" continued to be sold—in open secrecy—a hundred times more than ever.

It will not have been forgotten that with "Natural Law" had originally been published "The Disaster of Lisbon"; and that the doctrines of "Lisbon" had been refuted, by the request of the Genevans, in a long, wild, rambling letter by Jean Jacques Rousseau, wherein that absurd person had pointed out that if we lived in deserts, not towns, the houses would not fall upon us, because there would not be houses to fall.

Answer a fool according to his folly! A few gay bantering lines were all Voltaire's reply at the moment. To strike quickly—or wait long—this man could do both. He loved best to strike at once; but if he could have patience and wait to gather his weapons, to barb his arrows, to poison his darts, why, he was of nature the more deadly. This time he had waited long. The bantering note was but a sop thrown to his impatience. Rousseau's Letter on Optimism bears the date

VOLTAIRE

From the Bust by Houdon

of August, 1756. It was not till the early part of 1759 that there crept out stealthily, secretly, quietly, the gayest little volatile laughing romance called "Candide."

Written in some keen moment of inspiration—perhaps at the Elector Palatine's, perhaps at Délices, where, it matters not—in that brief masterpiece of literature Voltaire brought out all his batteries at once and confronted the foe with that ghoulish mockery, that bantering jest, and that deadly levity which few could face and live.

If the optimists had talked down the passionate reasonings of the "Poem on the Disaster of Lisbon" with that reiterated "All is well," "All chance, direction which thou canst not see—all partial evil, universal good," "Candide's" laugh drowned those affirmations—so loudly and so often affirmed that the affirmers had come to mistake them for argument. In this novel of two hundred pages Voltaire withered by a grin the cheap, current, convenient optimism of the leisured classes of his day, and confounded Pope as well as Rousseau. This time he did not argue with their theories. He only exposed them. In that searching light, in that burning sunshine, the comfortable dogmas of the neat couplets of the "Essay on Man" blackened and died, and Rousseau was shown forth the laughing-stock of the nations.

One of the few literary classics which is not only still talked about but still sometimes read, is "Candide." Nothing grows old-fashioned sooner than humour. The jests which amuse one age bore and depress the next. But it is part of Voltaire's genius in general, and of "Candide" in particular, that its wit is almost as witty to-day as when it was written. It still trips and dances on feet which never age or tire. Nothing is more astounding in it than what one critic has called its "fresh and unflagging spontaneity"—its "surpassing invention." Its vigour is such as no time can touch. It reads like the work of a superabundant youth. Yet Voltaire was actually sixty-four when he wrote it; and if indeed "we live in deeds, not years: in thought, not breaths: in feelings, not in figures on a dial," he was a thousand.

The story is, briefly, that of a young man brought up in implicit belief in the everything-for-the-best doctrine, who goes out into a world where he meets with a hundred adventures which give it the lie. Life is a bad bargain, but one can make the best of it. That is the moral of "Candide." "What I know," says Candide, "is that we must cultivate our garden." "Let us work without reasoning: that is the only way to render life supportable."

As children read the "Gulliver's Travels" of that past master of irony, Jonathan Swift, as the most innocent and amusing of fairy tales, so can "Candide" be read as a rollicking farce and as nothing else in the world.

Who knows, indeed, when he puts down that marvellous novelette, whether to laugh at those inimitable traits of the immortal Dr. Pangloss—"noses have been made to carry spectacles, therefore we have spectacles; legs have been made for stockings, therefore we have stockings; pigs were made to be eaten, and therefore we have pork all the year round"—or to weep over the wretchedness of a humanity which perforce consoles itself with lies, and, too miserable to face its misery, pretends that all is well?

One woman, with her heart wrung by that cruel mockery, speaks of "Candide's" "diabolical gaiety." "It seems to be written by a being of another nature than our own, indifferent to our fate, pleased with our sufferings, and laughing like a demon or a monkey at the miseries of that humankind with which he has nothing in common." Some have found in it the blasphemies of a devil against the tender and ennobling Christianity which has been the faith and the hope of sorrowing millions; and others discover in it only one of the most potent of arguments for embracing that Christianity—the confession that no other system so consolatory can be found. To one reader it is the supreme expression of a genius who, wherever he stands, stands alone—"as high as mere wit can go"; to another, shorn of its indecency, it is, like "Gulliver," but a *bizarre* absurdity for youth; while a third finds it "most useful as a philosophical work, because it is read by people who would never read philosophy."

Perhaps the genius of "Candide" lies partly in the fact that it is both serious and frivolous, ghoulish and gay, tragedy and comedy; and equally perfect as the one or the other.

Voltaire assigned "this little sort of romance" to that convenient person, the Chevalier de Mouhy, on whom, in 1738, had been fathered the "Préservatif." The real author declared that the thing was much too frivolous for him to have written. He had read it, to be sure. "The more it makes me laugh the more sorry I am it is assigned to me." Almost every letter of this spring of 1759 contains a mocking allusion to *optimism*. "Candide" was much to the fore in its writer's mind.

On March 2d, the Council of Geneva condemned the book to be burnt; and once more, as in the case of the "Pucelle," Voltaire watched a bonfire with a very twisted smile. He revenged himself by flooding Geneva with anonymous irreligious pamphlets with such religious names—"Christian Dialogues" and "The Gospel of the Day"—as to deceive the very elect.

But it was not only his suspected paternity in the case of "Candide," but a suspected paternity of an even more dangerous child, that prevented Voltaire in this spring giving up his whole soul peacefully to rebuilding Ferney and laying out gardens. Frederick was in the midst of a disastrous campaign; but, unfortunately, no disaster stopped him writing to Voltaire or composing verses. Wilhelmina's death had only healed the old wounds for a while. They broke out afresh. In March this strange Damon and Pythias were again squabbling over that ancient bone of contention, Maupertuis; and then, as inconsistently as if they had been a couple of schoolgirls, passionately regretting their old amity. "I shall soon die without having seen you," wrote Voltaire on March 25th. "You do not care, and I shall try not to care either.... I can live neither with you nor without you. I do not speak to the King or the hero: that is the affair of sovereigns. I speak to him who has fascinated me, whom I have loved, and with whom I am always angry." Then they remembered Frankfort and Freytag, and began snarling and growling again.

And then—then—a book of Frederick's poems which abused Louis XV. and Madame de Pompadour was opened in the post on its way from Frederick to Voltaire. And in a trice Voltaire is quaking lest he should be thought to have inspired, or positively written, verse so dangerous and disrespectful.

No emergency had ever yet robbed him of his cleverness. He took the packet to the French envoy at Geneva and showed him the broken seal; and then, by the envoy's advice, sent the whole thing to Choiseul, the head of the French Ministry. Choiseul was himself a verse-maker; he wrote a virulent versified satire upon Frederick and sent it to Voltaire. "Tell your King, if he publishes his poems I shall publish mine."

Voltaire says that if he had wished to amuse himself he might have seen the Kings of France and Prussia engaged in a war of verses. But he was the friend of peace as well as the friend of Frederick. He begged Frederick not to shut every door of reconciliation with the King of France by publishing that ode; and added, that in mortal fear of its being attributed to Uncle Voltaire, Niece Denis had burnt it. Frederick would not have been human had he not immediately felt convinced that those ashes contained the finest lines he had ever written. But they *were* ashes. The episode closed.

On July 27, 1759, Maupertuis died at Bâle, "of a repletion of pride," said Voltaire. Akakia, busy with his history of "Peter the Great," and with touching up "Tancred," or his "Chevaliers" as he called it sometimes, must needs push them aside and shoot an arrow or two of his barbed wit at that poor enemy's dead body. "Enjoy your hermitage," Frederick wrote back to him gravely. "Do not trouble the ashes of those who are at peace in the grave.... Sacrifice your vengeance on the shrine of your own reputation ... and let the greatest genius in France be also the most generous of his nation." The counsel was just and noble. Alas! it was even more needed than Frederick guessed. At this very time Voltaire was writing his secret

"Memoirs for the life of M. de Voltaire." They were not published till after his death. They were never meant to be published at all. They contain what Morley has well called "a prose lampoon" on the King's private life, "which is one of the bitterest libels that malice ever prompted."

Its incomprehensible author was still actually compiling it when, for the third time, he took up his *rôle* of peacemaker between France and Frederick.

This time, Tencin and Richelieu having been tried in vain, the medium was to be Choiseul, Choiseul being approached by Voltaire's angel, d'Argental. The moment was favourable. The campaign of 1759 was wholly disastrous to Frederick: and on August 12th he was beaten by the united armies at Kunersdorf. Chased from his States, "surrounded by enemies, beaten by the Russians, unable to replenish an exhausted treasury," "Luc," as Voltaire phrased it, "was still Luc." He still kept his head above the foaming waters that would have engulfed any other swimmer. "Very embarrassed, and not less embarrassing to other people; astonishing and impoverishing Europe, and writing verses," Frederick as if to give himself time—as if, though he never meant to yield to such advances, he yet did not dare to openly refuse them—coquetted with the peace offers of M. de Choiseul, sent through that "Bureau d'adresse," Voltaire. It is not a little wonderful that Voltaire, with his itching fingers for action, could suffer himself to be a "Bureau d'adresse," a passive medium, even for a while. But he did. An immense correspondence passed between himself and Frederick—for the benefit of Choiseul. Frederick was alluded to as Mademoiselle Pestris or Pertris: and very coy was Mademoiselle over the matter. Shall it be peace? shall it not? It was a delicate negotiation, said that "Bureau d'adresse," very truly. It was like the play of two cats—each with velvet paws to hide its claws.

It came to nothing. Though, perhaps, when in December there appeared in Paris a book entitled "The Works of the Philosopher of Sans-Souci," containing those freethinking effusions a Most Christian King had written under the rose, and which he would not at all wish to see daylight, Choiseul's claw had been active in the matter. Fortunately Voltaire could not be suspected. Had not Freytag taken from him at Frankfort that "Œuvre de Poëshie du Roi Mon Maître," which was none other than the "Works of the Philosopher of Sans-Souci" under a different name? Still, the year 1760 opened as 1759 had done, with Damon and Pythias still sparring at each other. "You have embroiled me for ever with the King of France, you have lost me my posts and pensions, you have ill-treated me at Frankfort, me and an innocent woman," writes Voltaire to Frederick from peaceful Tourney in April, 1760.

And in May Frederick wrote back. "If you were not dealing with a fool in love with your genius," what might I not do and say? As it is— "Once for all, let me hear no more of that niece who bores me, and has nothing but her uncle to cover her defects."

The niece who bored Frederick must have been very nearly as bored herself throughout the remainder of this year 1759 as she confessed to have been at the beginning. Uncle Voltaire was always so engrossed with writing, or with those stupid farms and gardens. "The more you work on your land, the more you will love it," he had written to Madame de Fontaine in the summer. "The corn one has sown oneself is worth far more than what one gets from other people's granaries." And then, there were so few visitors.

Valette, a needy, clever, unsatisfactory acquaintance of d'Alembert's, was at Délices in December; and during the year a man named d'Aumard had arrived on a visit. But that was all.

D'Aumard was a young soldier cousin of Voltaire's mother. Of very ordinary abilities, and morals rather below the very low average of his day, that distant cousinship was the only claim he had upon Voltaire's notice. But it was more than sufficient. Voltaire had already sent him presents of money through Madame Denis, and made him a promise of a pension for life. Directly he arrived at Délices he was attacked by what was at first taken to be rheumatism. Tronchin was called in. Voltaire sent d'Aumard to Aix for the waters. But neither the first physician nor the most fashionable cure in Europe was of any avail. D'Aumard became a helpless and hopeless cripple. In 1761, Voltaire said that it required four persons to move him from one bed to another. In this condition he lived in Voltaire's house for at least ten years, and finally died there. His host engaged in a long correspondence about his case with the surgeon of the Royal Footguards, and entered into every detail with infinite pains and minuteness. To a busy and active Voltaire the fate of this young man, shut out of all work and interest—hearing, as he lay on the bed from which he was never to rise, the stir and movement of a life in which he could never join—seemed peculiarly pitiable. He makes a hundred sympathetic allusions to him. That his own conduct was infinitely generous he seems to have wholly lost sight of in the fact that d'Aumard's fate was infinitely sad. Yet Voltaire had a reward if he wanted one. To Madame du Deffand's question if life were worth living he could reply, "Yes. I know a man completely paralysed who loves it, to folly." The man was d'Aumard.

In this year Voltaire obtained, after the exercise of even more than his usual persistence, and after working himself and his friends to death to attain his aim, the grant of two letters-patent for his lands of Tourney and

Ferney. He set great value on these letters as declaring him a French subject.

Also in this year he heard of the loss of that very old English friend of his, Falkener. In 1774, Falkener's two sons came to stay with him at Ferney.

He still kept himself well *au courant* of English affairs and English literature.

It was in 1759 he wrote to Madame du Deffand that there was nothing passable in "Tom Jones" but the character of the barber; and of "A Tale of a Tub" as "a treasure-house of wit." He also read—and yawned over—"Clarissa Harlowe" and "Pamela"; and in 1760 he was criticising "Tristram Shandy." No other great Frenchman of his day got into the heart of English literature and English character as Voltaire did. "An Englishman who knows France well and a Frenchman who knows England well are both the better for it," is one of the shrewdest of his sayings, and he said many shrewd things, on the two races. "The English know how to think; the French know how to please." "We are the whipped cream of Europe. There are not twenty Frenchmen who understand Newton."

But there was another foreign country besides England which was engaging his attention now—Russia.

In this 1759 he produced the first volume of that "History of Peter the Great," which he had undertaken to write two years earlier, in 1757, at the request of Peter's daughter, Elizabeth.

In the spring of 1717, when Arouet was an imprudent young Paris wit of three-and-twenty, awaiting his first introduction to the Bastille, he had seen the great Peter in the flesh, being shown the shops of the capital, the lion of its season—"neither of us thinking then that I should become his historian."

But directly Elizabeth made the suggestion, a Voltaire of sixty-three had embraced it with an enthusiasm which would not have been astonishing in an Arouet of twenty-three, and set to work at once.

The subject bristled with difficulties. First it involved an enormous correspondence with Schouvaloff, the Russian minister. Schouvaloff was ready and eager to shower maps, medals, and documents upon the historian. But the medals, as the historian pointed out, were not of the slightest use; the maps were inadequate; and the documents had too often been tampered with.

Then, too, there was an immeasurable difficulty, for a writer who wanted to tell the truth, in the fact that his hero's own daughter was not only living, but had commissioned him to write the work. When Frederick wanted to know what in the world made Voltaire think of writing the history of the wolves and bears of Siberia, he represented the point of view from which most people then regarded Russia. A cold, ugly, barbarous, uninteresting place—what in the world can you have to say about it? The veil of tragedy and romance which now hangs before that great canvas did not give it the potent charm of mystery in the eighteenth century. Only Voltaire would then have dared to write "Russia under Peter the Great," and only Voltaire could have made it readable.

He took a flying leap into that sea of difficulties, and came up to the top safely as usual. He gave Schouvaloff a plan of the work in advance. First, there are to be no unnecessary details of battles; secondly, the thing will be called not "The History of Peter the Great," but "Russia under Peter I.," as giving me greater liberty, and explaining to my readers in advance the real aim of the book; thirdly, Peter's little weaknesses are not to be concealed when necessary to expose them.

The rough sketch was bold, and so was the finished picture. But to its boldness were united that grace and charm by which Voltaire could make disagreeable truths sound like compliments. If to the world generally Peter was, and should be, but the "wisest and greatest of savages," "only a king," and a badly brought up one at that—to Russia he was, and ought to be, a great man and a hero; and, Peter apart altogether—and there is a good deal of the work from which Peter *is* entirely apart—the book "revealed Russia to Europe and herself," and brought that great country to the knowledge and the interest of other nations.

The style sometimes bears trace of the difficulties its author had to overcome—the fact that the subject was chosen for him, not *by* him. "I doubt," he wrote to Madame du Deffand, "if it will be as amusing as the 'Life of Charles XII.,' for Peter was only extraordinarily wise, while Charles was extraordinarily foolish." All the time he was writing it, "Tancred," Ferney, "Candide," Frederick, were calling his attention away from it.

Not the less, the History was a very successfully executed order, with which the orderer was so pleased that in 1761 she sent the author her portrait set in diamonds.

To the end of 1759 also belongs a very different work of Voltaire's— one of those spontaneous, impulsive, rollicking, daring things which must have been no little relief to his *méchanceté* to turn to from those grave ploddings through Schouvaloff's documents. Encouraged by that burning of "Natural Law" and its companion volumes, and by the suppression of the "Encyclopædia" in the early part of the year, in November a weekly Jesuit organ called the "Journal de Trévoux," edited by one Berthier, furiously assailed not only "Natural Law," which fires could not destroy, but the "Encyclopædia," which prohibitions could not suppress, and all the works of enlightenment in France. Voltaire had always an inconsistent *tendresse* for the Jesuits. They had been good to him in his school days: and among them he still numbered some of his friends. But this thing was too monstrous! Voltaire attacked it with sharpest ridicule, and wrote anonymously that scathing pamphlet called "The Narrative of the Sickness, Confession, Death, and Re-appearance of the Jesuit Berthier." This he followed by another pamphlet, "The Narrative of Brother Grasse." Both were but burlesques. True, there was a hit in every line; and then, if not now, every arrow went home. But the real significance of the pamphlets is in the fact that they were a declaration of war. Gardens and architecture, farms and beehives—in these things is to be found happiness perhaps. But there has been no great man in the world who ever thought happiness enough. That hatred of intolerance, that passion for freedom which had been the motive power of a young and struggling Arouet, was still the motive power of this affluent, comfortable Voltaire of sixty-five. To be sure, it is easier to feel sympathy with the oppressed and the needy when one is oneself downtrodden and poor: and something more difficult when one is oneself prosperous and independent. It must be accounted to Voltaire for righteousness that when he no longer suffered himself, the sufferings of others appealed to him only with a double force. It was in those smiling days of Délices and Ferney that he framed his battle-cry and formulated the creed of all the philosophers, and the aim and the conviction of his own life, into one brief phrase—*Écrasez l'infâme.*

Friend and foe still remember him by that motto. The one has idly forgotten, and the other carefully misunderstands, what it means and meant. To many Christians, *"Écrasez l'infâme"* is but the blasphemous outcry against the dearest and most sacred mysteries of their religion; and *l'infâme* means Christ.

But to Voltaire, if it meant Christianity at all, it meant that which was taught in Rome in the eighteenth century, and not by the Sea of Galilee in the first. If it *was* Christianity at all, it was not the Christianity of Christ. *L'infâme did* mean religion, but it meant the religion which lit the fires of Smithfield and prompted the tortures of the Inquisition; which terrified feeble brains to madness with the burning flames of a material hell, and flung to the barren uselessness of the cloister hundreds of unwilling victims, quick and meet for the life for which they had been created.

L'infâme was the religion which enforced its doctrines by the sword, the fire, and the prison; which massacred on the Night of St. Bartholomew; and, glossing lightly over royal sins, refused its last consolations to dying Jansenists who would not accept the Bull Unigenitus. It was the religion which thrust itself between wife and husband in the person of the confessor—himself condemned to an unnatural life which not one in a thousand can live honestly and aright; it was the religion of Indulgences, and the rich: for those who could pay for the remission of their sins and for large impunity to sin afresh; it was the religion which served as a cloak for tyranny and oppression, ground down the face of the poor, and kept wretchedness wretched for ever.

And above all, *l'infâme* was that spirit which was the natural enemy of all learning and advancement; which loved darkness and hated light because its deeds were evil; which found the better knowledge of His works, treason to God; and an exercise of the reason and the judgment He had given, an insult to the Giver.

If there was ever a chance for the foolish to become learned, *l'infâme* deprived them of it. If the light fought its way through the gross darkness of superstition, *l'infâme* quenched it. It prohibited Newton; burnt Bayle; and cursed the "Encyclopædia." If men were once enlightened, *l'infâme* would be cast down from the high places where it sat—as Pope or as King, as Calvinist or as Cardinal; but always as the enemy of that Justice which drives out oppression, as the sun drives out the night.

L'infâme cannot be translated by any single word. But if it must be, the best rendering of it is Intolerance.

No one can have any knowledge of the career or of the character of Voltaire without seeing that this Thing, to which in the year 1759 was first given the name of *Infâme*, was his one, great, lifelong enemy. Loathing of it coursed in his *bourgeois* blood and was bred in his bones. The boy who had seen France starve to pay for the Sun King's wars, and Paris persecuted to please his mistress and his confessor, had felt surge in him the first waves of that tireless indignation which was to turn a courtier into a reformer, and make a light soul, deep. By the time he himself became the Voice crying in the wilderness of men's sorrows, the utterer of hard truths, *l'infâme* had imprisoned, persecuted, and exiled him. And who is there who does not better hate wrong-doing when he has himself been wronged? He had revealed God to sages through Newton; and the hangman burnt the "English Letters." He had studied history, especially the history of the religious wars, and he knew what *l'infâme* had done in the past as well as in the present. He declared, with that extraordinary mixture of levity and passion which is his alone, that he always had an access of fever on St. Bartholomew's Day. He had seen the works of Boyer—fanatic and tyrant— the product of a shameful system, and not the less harmful in fact because he was honest in intention. He had seen *l'infâme* prompt Damiens's knife; and then, in its besotted inconsequence, avenge the crime of its own scholar by prohibiting all the works of enlightenment in France.

In 1757, in writing to d'Alembert, Voltaire had first given *l'infâme* a name—the Phantom. A few days later he called it the Colossus. Under any name a d'Alembert would recognise it. On May 18, 1759, Frederick the Great spoke of it by that title it was to bear for ever, in one of those bitter yearning letters he wrote to his old friend. "You will still caress *l'infâme* with one hand and scratch it with the other; you will treat it as you have treated me and all the world." And in June Voltaire replied: "Your Majesty reproaches me with sometimes caressing *l'infâme*. My God, no! I only work to extirpate it." And the next year—June 3, 1760—"I want you to crush *l'infâme*; that is the great point. It must be reduced to the same condition as it is in England. You can do it if you will. It is the greatest service one can render to humankind."

Henceforward, his allusions to it in his letters became more and more frequent. Sometimes, he abbreviated it to *Écr. l'Inf.* Sometimes he wrote in one corner "*É. l'I.*" "The first of duties is to annihilate *l'inf.*; confound *l'inf.* as much as you can."

"This Mr. *Écrlinf* does not write badly, said these worthy people." One of his theories was that truths cannot be too often insisted on. "Rub it in! rub it in!" he would cry. He rubbed in his *infâme*. Now in passionate earnest, now in jest, now cynically, now bitterly, he alluded to it at all times and seasons and to all kinds of persons. To Damilaville, who was to take Theriot's place as his correspondent and who himself loathed *l'infâme* with a deadly intensity, Voltaire hardly wrote a letter without that "Crush the monster!" It was a catchword at last. "I end all my letters by saying *Écr. l'inf.*, as Cato always said, That is my opinion and Carthage must be destroyed." By it, he heated the zeal of his fellow-workers in the cause; quickened the "phlegmatic perseverance" of d'Alembert; and rallied to new effort Helvétius, Marmontel, Holbach, and a dozen lesser men.

It has been seen that he had loathed the Thing, a nameless monster, for fifty years. The insults of the "Journal de Trévoux" were the final spur to action. If Berthier had not pushed him to extremities, no doubt some other of "those serpents called Jesuits" would have done it equally effectually. The time was ripe; and Voltaire was ripe for the time. He flung down the glove at last and declared upon *l'infâme* an open war, which was to be war to the knife till he had no longer breath in his body, and the sword—his pen—fell from a dead hand.

CHAPTER XXXIV

THE BATTLE OF PARTICLES, AND THE BATTLE OF COMEDIES

ON March 10, 1760, M. le Franc de Pompignan took the seat in the French Academy left vacant by the death of Maupertuis, and delivered an opening address which was nothing but an attack on the philosophic party.

Marquis and county magnate was Pompignan, rather a good minor poet, a native of Montauban, and, in his own province and his own estimation, a very great man indeed. In 1736, he had written a play with which he had tried, vainly, to supplant Voltaire's "Alzire." He and Voltaire met afterwards, in amicable fashion enough, at the house of a mutual friend. And then Voltaire retired to Cirey and Madame du Châtelet: and Le Franc to his magisterial duties in Montauban.

But by the year 1758 Montauban, and his own vanity, had so impressed the noble Marquis with the idea that his genius was wasted in a province, that he came up to Paris: stood for a vacant chair in the Academy; failed to gain it; stood again for another chair in 1760, and, as has been seen, won it, in succession to Maupertuis. When it is added that Le Franc was also Historiographer of France in place of Voltaire, and that he was practically the only nobleman in the kingdom who was at once clever, educated and orthodox, his design to use that Academical chair as a stepping-stone to the tutorship of the Dauphin's sons—always one of the most influential posts in the kingdom—was not at all a wild ambition. He began his speech by praising his predecessor, Maupertuis, as in duty bound, and also as being sure to raise the ire of that arch-fiend of philosophers, Voltaire; and then abused those philosophers and their works roundly, soundly, and at length.

The chairman of the Academy made reply in a very fulsome speech, in which he compared Le Franc to Moses, and his younger brother, the Bishop of Puy, a not illiberal churchman, to Aaron. "The two brothers are consecrated to work miracles, the one as judge, the other as pontiff, in Israel."

Moses was then granted an interview with the King, in which his Majesty highly praised that Academical discourse as little likely to be applauded by the impious, "or by strong minds"—which he took to be the finest compliment he could pay it.

On March 28th, one of those "esprits forts" was writing comfortably from Délices that he saw all storms, but saw them from the port. The port! Of course someone sent him that Academical discourse. He applied the remarks on the philosophers particularly to himself (to be sure, the cap fitted), and took upon himself to avenge them all.

One fine day there appeared in Paris, without date, without any indication as to the place in which it had been printed, a little *brochure* of seven deadly pages entitled the "Whens: or Useful Notes on a Discourse pronounced before the French Academy on March 10, 1760." They were the little skiff in which Voltaire sailed into the teeth of the storm.

All his works are characteristic in a high degree, but hardly any are so characteristic as those he wielded in this Battle of the Particles.

Exquisitely dainty and gay: as fine and as sharp as needles from my lady's work-basket, and yet as "biting and incisive as a poignard": such are the hall-marks of those little instruments of torture of which the "Whens" was the first.

"*When* one has the honour to be admitted into a respectable company of literary men, one need not make one's opening speech a satire against them."

"*When* one is hardly a man of letters and not at all a philosopher, it is not becoming to say that our nation has only a false literature and a vain philosophy."

"*When* one is admitted into an honourable body, one ought, in one's address, to hide under a veil of modesty that insolent pride which is the prerogative of hot heads and mean talents."

Voltaire would not have been Voltaire, nor of his century, if he had not gone on to remind this highly correct Marquis that in a free youth he had himself coquetted with Deism and translated and circulated "The Universal Prayer"—then commonly called "The Deists' Prayer"—of Mr. Pope. He also added that for his Deistic opinions this proper Le Franc had been deprived of the charge of his province; which was not true, but made the story much better.

It is hardly necessary to say that Voltaire denied the "Whens." "I did not write them," he told Theriot on May 20th, "but I wish I had."

They had roused his party very effectively. If "the shepherd, the labourer, the rat retired from the world in a Swiss cheese," was pushed, as the rat said, into the "deluge of monosyllables," how should the philosophers in Paris escape it? The famous Morellet, abbé, writer, freethinker, one of the "four theologians of the Encyclopædia," whom

Voltaire called *Mords-les* (Bite them) from the caustic nature of his wit, rushed into the fray with the "Ifs" and the "Wherefores"; and a reproduction of the luckless Le Franc's translation of "The Universal Prayer." Délices followed up at once with the "Yeses" and the "Noes," the "Whats," the "Whys," and the "Whos." Délices said that chuckling sustained old age: no wonder *his* old age was so vigorous. There was not a vulnerable inch in the body or soul of that unhappy Marquis which one of those particles did not wound. A riddle ran through Paris, "Why did Jeremiah weep so much during his life?" "Because, as a prophet, he foresaw that after death he would be translated by Le Franc"—Le Franc having compensated for that "Universal Prayer" by writing the most devout works ever since. Later were to come the "Fors" and the "Ahs." Some were by other hands than Voltaire's. But his was the spirit that inspired them all. Some were in verse. All were brief. Then he published extracts from an early tragedy of Le Franc's, making them as absurd as he alone knew how. The affair was the talk of Paris: the most delicious farce in the world. Madame du Deffand spoke of Le Franc as buried under "mountains of ridicule." Wherever he was recognised he excited shouts of laughter. He solemnly and prosily defended his translation of "The Universal Prayer" as a mere exercise in English, which it very likely was. And Paris laughed afresh. Voltaire declared that Tronchin had ordered him to hunt Pompignan for two hours every morning for the good of his health. Poor Pompignan, goaded to madness, presented a petition to the King in which he asked the assistance of their Majesties and recalled to them the splendid welcome they had accorded to himself and his Academical discourse.

But Louis XV. could not prevent Paris laughing nor Voltaire answering by what purported to be an extract from a newspaper of Le Franc's native Montauban, wherein the natives of that place were represented as appointing a committee to go to Paris and inquire into the mental condition of the unfortunate Marquis. But this thing was a *brochure*—a nothing.

Délices had not done with Montauban yet. There was a pause. And then Voltaire produced one of the most scathing and trenchant satires of which even he was capable. It was in verse, and it was called "Vanity." It began:

Well, what's the matter, little bourgeois of a little town?

and contains many lines which still form part of the common talk of France.

Gay, fluent, contemptuous—written scornfully in a colloquialism which, in that day of set and formal phrases, was in itself an insult—

Pompignan, like Maupertuis, was stifled with badinage, and laughed—to death.

Though all the wit of the thing, and more than half its significance, are lost in a translation, even in a translation some idea of the sufferings of that wretched provincial Marquis may be gained still.

The Universe, my friend, thinks of you not at all:
The future less. Look to your house and diet:
Drink: sleep: amuse yourself: be wise: be quiet.
. . . .
Oh, but my beautiful Discourse, they laugh at it!
The malice of their vulgar gibes hurts so,
That, sure of justice, to the King I'll go.
. . . .
He'll make it law to find my writing good
I'll tell him of it all without delay
And get the laugher's licence ta'en away.

The poem ends with lines which, as Voltaire wrote them, stabbed straight to the enemy's heart:

Ruined great Alexander's tomb and town:
And for great Cæsar's shade no home there be,
Yet Pompignan thinks a great man is he.

He thought so no longer. "Vanity" was his deathblow. The very Dauphin laughed at it. The Marquis went home to his province, and never again dared to appear at the Academy.

In 1769, when his play, "Dido," was acted in Paris, the Comédie Française announced quite innocently that it would be followed by "The Coxcomb Punished" of Pont-de-Veyle. Everything was against poor Pompignan. He died in 1784. The turn of his priestly brother, Aaron, was yet to come.

If Pompignan had been nothing but a self-satisfied nobleman who over-estimated his own talents and under-estimated those of the philosophers and the Academicians, he would certainly not have deserved the fury of ridicule with which he was assailed, and the laugh would have turned against the laughers.

But this was no harmless fool. It may have been a small thing that, as Voltaire wrote, "if Le Franc had not been covered with ridicule, the custom of declaiming against the philosophers in the opening discourse of the

Academy would have become a rule." But it would have been no small thing that a Pompignan should be tutor to the Dauphin's sons; should teach the boy who was to rule France a narrow hatred for the light and learning which alone could save it; and preach the principles of *l'infâme* to the susceptible youth who would one day practise them to the ruin of a great kingdom.

Écrasez l'infâme! Pompignan was but a victim to that purpose. Voltaire kicked him aside with his foot, and looked out for other foes to vanquish.

There were always plenty of them. He had on hand at the moment a satire called "The Poor Devil," which set out to be an account of the adventures of that Valette, the friend of d'Alembert and the guest of Délices, but which ended as a fiercer "Dunciad," "more than a satire, more than a *chef d'œuvre* of incomparable verve and malignity," and which reveals to our own day many an ugly secret of the literary life and men of that strange epoch.

But the general satisfaction of whipping a multitude is nothing to the personal satisfaction of whipping a unit.

While the Pompignan affair was still running high, news came one morning—on April 25, 1760—that a comedy by a certain Charles Palissot, entitled "The Philosophers" and bitterly ridiculing that party, was about to be played in Paris. "Very well," says Délices; "I cannot prevent that. But what I can and will do is to withdraw "Tancred," already in rehearsal." So "Tancred" is withdrawn.

On May 2d, Palissot's "Philosophers" was performed for the first time.

A clever journalist was Charles Palissot, who, in 1755, had been Voltaire's guest at Délices with Patu the poet. His play was clever too, a rollicking comedy in three acts, which not only laughed at the philosophic party but represented them as dangerous to society and the State. Helvétius, Diderot, Duclos, Madame Geoffrin, and Mademoiselle Clairon were openly satirised. J. J. Rousseau, declared Voltaire, was represented on all fours, with a lettuce in his pocket for provender.

The "Encyclopædia" was mentioned by name. Two noble ladies openly gave the play their patronage. One was the Princess de Robecq, the mistress of Choiseul the minister, and so a force to be reckoned with.

"The Philosophers" had carefully omitted to attack the two greatest of the philosophers, d'Alembert and Voltaire. But the one wrote an account of the thing to the other, and that Other began to inspect his weapons.

True, he tried mild measures at first. Palissot sent him a copy of the play. And Voltaire wrote back trying to win its author over to the right side, or at least to an impartial attitude of mind. But Palissot did not mean to be convinced. Then Abbé Morellet-Mords-Les-Bite-Them was flung into the Bastille, at the instigation of the Princess de Robecq and the command of Choiseul, for having sneered at the Princess in his comic answer to Palissot's comedy, called "The Preface to The Philosophers." These things were not precisely soothing. To meet ridicule with reason had failed. Gibe for gibe, then; foolery for foolery! If Voltaire was one of the two who could play at that game, he was always the winner when he played.

He had another, older, deadlier foe than Palissot, who would also be the better for a beating. The older foe was Fréron. And the beating he received with Palissot was called "The Scotch Girl."

Fréron was still a very cool, clever, opulent, successful Parisian journalist: still the bitterest and shrewdest foe of the philosophers, and the sharpest tool of the Court. Voltaire, it will be remembered, had no reason to love this "worm from the carcase of Desfontaines," the defender of Crébillon, the supporter of d'Arnaud, the founder of "The Literary Year," that review which, appearing every ten days, had been for twenty-three years "a long polemic against the Encyclopædia in general and Voltaire in particular." But Voltaire seldom made the mistake of underrating his enemy's powers. He spoke of Fréron as the only man of his party who had literary taste. He acknowledged him to be of an amazing energy and courage, of great self-command, and an excellent critic.

But when it came to sharply criticising "Candide" in that "Literary Year" and scornfully twitting "Candide's" author with his dear title of Count of Tourney, the Count was foolish enough not only to lose his temper but to enumerate his grievances against Fréron in a letter to "The Encyclopædic Journal," the rival organ of "The Literary Year."

There was certainly a fine air of coolness and indifference in the letter. But the *vif*, warm genius of a Voltaire only assumed these qualities. Fréron really had them. Hence, Fréron was a powerful foe.

Athirst for revenge, then, alike on Palissot and on Fréron, Voltaire wrote "The Scotch Girl" in eight days. An English play, if you please, by Mr. Hume, brother of the historian; translated into French by Jérôme Carré; and before it appears, to be read, discussed, laughed over, and recognised in every boudoir in Paris as a satire on Fréron and on Palissot's "Philosophers." Everything fell out as the author had desired, and laboured that it should. If he *was* buried at Délices and hundreds of miles of vile roads from Paris, he had friends there only something less active and angry than himself. He had in himself the vigour and genius which can span space and move mountains.

On July 25th, the day before the play was to appear, he caused to be circulated in Paris a letter in which Carré, the translator, complained of the immense efforts Fréron had made to damn "The Scotch Girl" in advance. These advertisements were perfectly successful. On the first night— Saturday, July 26th—crowds besieged the door of the theatre before it opened; some, the friends of Fréron, some of Palissot, some of Voltaire; and all knowing enough of the piece to be quite sure they should be amused. In a prominent place in the auditorium shrewd Fréron had placed his pretty wife, to excite compassion for himself, and anger against his foes. He himself sat among the orchestra. Malesherbes, the minister, had a place hard by him. Palissot was in a box. Many neutral persons, piqued only by curiosity, found seats in the house. It was upon their pulse Fréron kept his finger. It was their displeasure or approval which would give the real verdict of the piece.

"The Scotch Girl" is not at all a good play. But it is witty, topical, and infinitely audacious. "It is not sufficient to write well: one must write to the taste of the public," said Voltaire. He had not written well: but he had written for the psychological moment. His audience had expected him to take a bold spring from the footboard: and he jumped from the roof. His old experience of England enabled him to give one of the first sketches of a comic Englishman ever seen on the French stage. The character of Freeport is the best in the piece: and the saving of it. The scene is laid in a London coffee-house—the sub-title of the play being "Le Café." Fréron appeared as Frelon: which, being translated, is wasp or hornet. Wasp is a Grub Street hack "always ready to manufacture infamy at a pistole the paragraph." "When I discover a trifle, I add something to it: and something added to something makes much." The tactics of scandalous journalism are unaltered to this day. "The Philosophers" was broadly burlesqued: and to philosophy were gravely ascribed all the evils under the sun.

The play was received with delight. Foe as well as friend laughed aloud. Pretty Madame Fréron nearly fainted when she saw her husband thus travestied; and did not make matters better by naïvely replying to a friend, who assured her that Wasp did not in the least resemble her husband who was neither slanderer nor informer, "Oh! Monsieur, it is too well done! He will always be recognised."

The performance took place at five o'clock in the afternoon. The next day, July 27th, was a Sunday, and the day for the appearance of a number of "The Literary Year." It contained an account of that first night under the title of "The Account of a Great Battle," written in that cool and easy style, principally remarkable for its moderation and self-restraint, which was the finest weapon in Fréron's armoury. It ended with a "Te Voltairium," a sort of parody of the Te Deum, which was licensed by the censor, to the great indignation of the philosophers who had so often been profane—and unlicensed.

Meanwhile, at his Délices, Voltaire wrote *his* account of that first night—"An Advertisement to the Scotch Girl." The little, pricking, red-hot needles of his style were much less effective for his purpose now than the judicial calm of M. Fréron. But, after all, Voltaire was the winner. "The Scotch Girl" had what d'Alembert called "a prodigious success." The provinces received it with rapture. It was played three times a week in Paris. Its last performance there took place on September 2d.

And on September 3d it was replaced by "Tancred."

No man in the world better understood the force of contrast, and the infinite value of the striking and the *bizarre* upon the minds of his countrymen, than Voltaire. In France, if anywhere, he who strikes must strike at once; must appeal immediately to emotions which are sooner at boiling point and sooner cooled than the emotions of any other nation in Europe. "The Scotch Girl" had made Paris laugh: and Paris loved laughter. It had quite forgotten for the moment that it had also loved Fréron, its dear, clever, sociable, amusing journalist, who was pleasantly renowned for giving charming little suppers, and as the favourite of the great. Here, then, was the moment for this Swiss exile, who belonged to the wrong party, who persistently thought—and said—the wrong things, and was infinitely able and dangerous, to strike in with his "Tancred." To ensure its success a hearing was all that it wanted. Its genius could be trusted to do the rest. Voltaire took at the tide that flood which leads on to fortune, and sailed straight into harbour.

He began "Tancred," it is said, in his joy on learning of that decree which, in April, 1759, forbade spectators henceforth to sit on the stage. On the 19th of the next month, May, he wrote that this day an old fool finished a tragedy begun on April 22d. At first he called it "Aménaïde," or "My Knights," or "The Knighthood," and designed to have it played by Lekain or Lauraguais as the work of "a young unknown." "I have changed the metre," he wrote on May 29, 1759, "so that that cursed public shall not recognise me by my style."

In the October of 1759 he and his amateur company had acted it at Tourney. It moved the author and Madame Denis to tears; but as he very justly observed, they were too near relations to the piece for their emotion to count for much. When Marmontel had stayed at Délices in the summer of 1760 he, too had wept over it—had returned the manuscript with his face bathed in tears, which told the author, he said, all he wanted to know.

Every omen was good. For several weeks during the summer of 1760 the d'Argentals had the manuscript in their charge in Paris. They had seen it put into rehearsal. Then Voltaire had withdrawn it to punish a company which dared to produce "The Philosophers." But that brave "Scotch Girl" had effectually killed "The Philosophers." The time was ripe indeed.

The theatre was crowded to the full. No more piquant contrast could be imagined than between the rough English burlesque of last night and the polished, romantic Sicilian tragedy of this. Yesterday there had not been a grave face in the house, and to-day every eye was wet. Madame d'Épinay was there, in the most fascinating grief. "Satan, in the guise of Fréron," who was in the amphitheatre, spoke of the thing as having "the simplicity and natural beauty of the classic, above all of the Odyssey." When d'Alembert saw it for the third time the whole audience was in tears. Mademoiselle Clairon surpassed herself as the heroine: so that the author, always largely generous in such appreciations, said that the piece owed to her all its success; and d'Olivet, Voltaire's old schoolmaster, declared there had been no such acting since the days of Roscius. As for Lekain—"nothing is comparable to Lekain, not even himself." The truth was, luckily for Voltaire, that the play was so moving that few were sufficiently masters of themselves to criticise coolly, and did not even carp at the author for writing in a metre with which they were wholly unfamiliar. Marmontel, who wept over it, had declared very justly not the less, that the style was not equal to that of Voltaire's earlier tragedies; that it was sometimes tedious, and a little wanting in vigour. But, after all, he had wept. Marmontel's attitude describes "Tancred" exhaustively.

Satan in the amphitheatre criticised the piece with the only criticism that need ever really hurt—a just one. He had mingled praise with his blame. Voltaire was sensible enough to recognise the weight of censure so tempered.

Fréron continued to conduct his "Literary Year" until his death in 1776. When he gave any of the actors—such as Lekain or Clairon—a bad notice, they simply revived "The Scotch Girl." And M. Wasp mended his manners at once.

In September Voltaire dedicated his "Tancred" to Madame de Pompadour. But that "chicken-hearted fellow" as he called her, made, at the time, no acknowledgment of the compliment. The truth was, as twice before in their history, some jealous scandal-monger about the Court had read an evil meaning into his flatteries.

Meanwhile the hermit of Délices, if ever in his life, was independent of her favours. Délices was charming: Ferney nearly finished: and Tourney the most histrionic place in Europe.

In the June of 1760 Marmontel had come to stay at Délices. Marmontel was a great man now: a successful playwright; and the author of that once much read and now wholly forgotten novel, "Bélisaire." He was not ungrateful to the benefactor who fourteen years earlier had launched him on the literary sea of Paris; while Voltaire on his side had always a fellow-feeling for that brave heart which at eighteen had begun the world on a capital of six louis, hope, cleverness, and a translation. Marmontel brought with him one Gaulard; and found at Délices a M. Lécluse, the King of Poland's dentist, who, when he was not mending Madame Denis's teeth acted and sang most agreeably.

Of course, Marmontel found Voltaire in bed, dying. And of course the moribund read aloud the "Pucelle" in the most lively and delightful manner in the world; took the visitors to see the view from Tourney, and discussed with them theatres, Frederick the Great, J. J. Rousseau—everything under heaven. He also played chess with Gaulard, and listened to Marmontel's poetry. And after a three days' visit, thereafter recorded in minutest detail by Marmontel, the visitors left.

Another burst of gaiety marked the autumn. "To get rid of public misfortunes and my own," the arch-foe of Fréron conducted another theatrical season, and asked so many people as actors or audience that, one night at least, Délices, Tourney, and Ferney all together would not hold them, and they had to be drafted into neighbouring houses. Ferney was neither finished nor furnished, but there were attics ready which accommodated a few guests and their servants. Sometimes the plan was to dine at Délices, see a play at Tourney, and sleep at Ferney—"on the top of each other," as the host said. The theatrical troupe would stroll about the gardens of Tourney in the moonlight in the intervals of their labours; and as they were young, and of both sexes, they no doubt took advantage of so excellent an opportunity for a little love-making. Corrupter of youth! cried Geneva, who was by no means best pleased just now with a Voltaire who a little earlier had fought Dr. Tronchin tooth and nail to establish a troupe of comedians of doubtful morals, only a quarter of a league from Geneva, though on French soil. Dr. Tronchin won—for the time; the comedians were ordered away, and Voltaire and his good doctor were excellent friends again; but it is not in the Calvinistic temperament in general to forget or to forgive easily.

And then this autumn season was marked by the presence of a most dissipated *roué* of a duke, the Duke of Villars, who was a patient of

Tronchin's, and considerably madder upon theatricals than his host himself. He had acted from his earliest youth at Vaux Villars, where a Voltaire of five-and-twenty had fallen in love with that gracious Maréchale, Villars's mother. But her son, though he thought great things of himself and *would* coach the company in general, was a poor performer. He casually asked Voltaire one day how he thought he acted. "Why, Sir, like a duke and a peer," answers Voltaire. Poor Cramer, the actor-publisher, was so misinstructed by his noble friend, that it took him a fortnight to unlearn the lesson of this bad master. When he had done so, Voltaire cried out to Madame Denis, "Niece, thank God! Cramer has disgorged his Duke!"

Also of the company was Mademoiselle de Bazincourt, Madame Denis's pretty, poor companion, who was destined to a convent from which Voltaire could not save her, and who meantime played the parts of "Julia, her friend," to perfection.

On September 29th, a house-warming took place at Ferney, in the shape of the marriage there of M. de Montpéroux, the envoy of France. Voltaire gave a great dinner in his new house to celebrate the event, and from henceforth lived there—at first generally, and at last entirely.

On October 20th, he and his theatrical company were sharply reminded by the Council of Geneva that "Sieur de Voltaire had yesterday a piece played at Saint Jean, the territory of the republic, in distinct violation of a promise he had made in August, 1755." They went on acting as gaily and continuously as ever. It is to be feared that to this wicked Voltaire prohibitions were only sauce to the *plat*, and made it a hundred times the more irresistible.

In the December of this 1760, which was one of the most full, varied, and active years of one of the most energetic lives ever lived by man, Voltaire appeared in a new *rôle*. He adopted a daughter.

In estimating his character no trait in it has been more lost sight of than that which, for want of a better word, may be called his affectionateness. Yet the man who was the lifelong friend of false Theriot, as well as of faithful d'Argental, who kept a warm corner in his heart for ungrateful servants and ne'er-do-weel relatives, who supported tiresome nephews and at least one trying niece, to say nothing of that crippled profligate d'Aumard, had that quality in a very high degree. Satire and cynicism were in his every lively utterance. But in his acts were a tenderness, a generosity, and a charity, to which better men than he have not attained.

Mademoiselle Marie Corneille was the great-niece of the great Corneille. Poor and provincial, her father came up one fine day to Paris and claimed his cousinship with the great Fontenelle. But Fontenelle had so long lost sight of this branch of the Corneille family that he thought the man an impostor, and left his money elsewhere. Then who but Fréron must needs take compassion on this hapless little family of three persons—father, mother, and daughter—and have a play of their uncle's performed for their benefit? But even five thousand five hundred francs do not go far, when out of the sum debts have to be paid, three persons to live, and one to be educated. Marie, of nearly eighteen, had to be removed from her convent. A friend took charge of her for a while. And then Le Brun, secretary to the Prince of Conti and a second-rate poet, conceived the happy idea of enlisting Voltaire's sympathy for her in an ode.

It is not an exaggeration to say that Voltaire adopted her on the spot. His only feeling seems to have been one of complete delight at having the opportunity of doing good in such a charming way; and he considered it, he said, an honour for an old soldier to serve the granddaughter of his general.

On November 5th, he was arranging details for her journey and her education with Le Brun.

He wrote to her direct to assure her she should have every facility for the practice of her religion, for reading, and for music; that Madame Denis would supply her with a wardrobe; that she should have masters for accomplishment; and learn to act so that in six months she would be playing *Chimène*.

In the second week in December Mademoiselle arrived. Quiet, gentle, and good, as naïvely ignorant as she was ingenuously ready to learn, tenderly and faithfully attached to the father she had left as she was to grow girlishly fond of the father she had found, Marie Corneille comes like a fresh and virgin air across the tainted and heated atmosphere of that eighteenth century, like some human angel to the Voltaire who hardly ever, perhaps never before, had intimately known a good woman.

He began at once to give her lessons in reading and writing, and in grammar. Mademoiselle had not much aptitude for that "sublime science," or for any science. She had come out of her convent as widely and profoundly ignorant as even those good nuns could leave a girl. And the cleverest man of his age taught her to write, and made her send him little notes, which he returned to her with her very doubtful orthography corrected; made history as amusing as a novel, and all the teaching go gaily "without the least appearance of a lesson." She was to have a tutor presently, when one good enough could be found. Meanwhile Voltaire taught her by word of mouth, while she looked up into his lean face with her clear candid eyes, and he looked back and delighted in her round girlish prettiness—"a plump face like a puppy's"—and her adorable *naïveté*.

Madame Denis forgot her comforts and her flirtations to nurse her when she was "a little ill," and to teach her needlework when she was well. All the servants adored her, and vied with each other to serve her. Presently she had her own *femme de chambre*. Every Sunday Voltaire and his niece took her to mass. Voltaire did not only preach tolerance. He did more even than leave her, when she prayed, "her early Heaven, her happy views." He made every careful provision, as he had said he would, for her to follow the faith of her fathers. The sneer on his lips and the scorn in his soul died as he looked at Marie Corneille. Trust, simplicity, innocence, appealed not in vain to Voltaire, as they have appealed not in vain to far worse men. There is a noble touch in that confession of his that, though he loved her well enough to set a very high value on her love for him, he liked nothing more in her than her unforgetting attachment to her father. To that father (who was, it may be added, a very cavilling and trying person) he wrote himself, thanking him with the finest tact and delicacy for a loan so delightful, and repeatedly congratulating himself on being the host of so charming a visitor. Voltaire certainly knew how to confer a favour.

It was not unnatural that, when the news of this adoption reached them, the devout should call out loudly at a lamb being entrusted to such a wolf. But it is noticeable that none of the devout offered to support the lamb in their own sheepfold. They only demanded a *lettre de cachet* to get her away from Voltaire.

There was another trouble too. Fréron, though he had helped her himself, was bitterly angry and jealous at Voltaire's adoption. In his "Literary Year" he inserted, with a very venomous pen, calumnies on her father, and on the mode of education Voltaire was providing for her. Without the smallest ground for such a charge he declared that her tutor was to be Lécluse, the dentist and amateur actor, whom Fréron represented as a kind of disreputable mountebank.

Voltaire instantly rose to the provocation. He always rose. But when its subject was an innocent girl, he may be forgiven that he was more furious than wise. He demanded justice from the minister Malesherbes, and a formal apology from Fréron: and failed to get either. So there appeared first a cutting epigram, and then an exceedingly scurrilous publication called "Anecdotes of Fréron," which Voltaire vehemently denied, but which that very best and most trustworthy of all possible editors, Beuchot, has included, not the less, in his Works.

Fréron's calumnies were not without effect. They lost Marie Corneille a husband: who must have been well lost, since the sting of a wasp frightened him away.

Meanwhile the life at Ferney and Délices went a busy and tranquil way; and Papa Voltaire began to cast about in his mind the means for providing a *dot* for his daughter.

CHAPTER XXXV

BUILDING A CHURCH, AND ENDOWING A DAUGHTER

The novel of the winter season of 1760-61, was "The New Eloïsa," by Jean Jacques Rousseau.

It is hardly possible to write a life of Rousseau or of Voltaire without comparing them. Voltaire, all sharp sense: and Rousseau all hot sensibility; Rousseau, visionary, dreamer, sensualist, sentimentalist, madman: and Voltaire, the sanest genius who ever lived, practical, businesslike, brilliant, easy, sardonic. The one's name stands as a synonym for a biting wit, the other's for a wild passion.

Yet they had much in common. Both belonged to the great philosophic party. In the burning zeal of their mutual hatred of *l'infâme* Voltaire sometimes lost his head; and Rousseau lost his heart. Both fought tooth and nail all their lives for Tolerance and for Liberty. Both foresaw that stupendous change called the French Revolution, and both foresaw it bloodless, serene, and glorious.

By January 21, 1761, "Eloïsa", which had been written in the little cottage Madame d'Épinay had lent Rousseau in the Montmorency forest, had been read at Ferney.

Rousseau had already been in opposition to Voltaire both on the subject of a theatre in Geneva, and on optimism.

But still, though they had greatly disagreed, they had not been ("Candide" notwithstanding) exactly enemies.

And then, in the October of 1760, Voltaire had written gaily on the theatre subject—"Jean Jacques showed that a theatre was unsuitable to Geneva: and I, I built one." Jean Jacques was at once too womanish, too impulsive, and too vain to keep long on good terms with a cynical person who could airily agree to differ in that way. He admired his rival's "*beaux talents*," but he was jealous of them. He was jealous, too, of his power and influence in Geneva. By the June of 1760 he had worked himself into something like hating this Voltaire; and, Rousseau-like, he sat down and wrote a letter to tell him so. Voltaire, still perfectly cool, observed to Theriot on June 26th that Jean Jacques had become quite mad. "It is a great pity."

And then came "The New Eloïsa."

That tissue of absurdities and genius, of fine, false sentiments and highly ridiculous social views—set forth with the warmth, the energy, and the passion which are Rousseau's alone—would in any case have aroused Voltaire's contempt.

But when he added to it their present differences on the theatre topic, and their past differences on optimism, and the childish rancour of Rousseau's last letter—above all, when he saw that those owls, the public, opened their stupid eyes and were quite dazzled and delighted with the sham glitter of this false romance about the highly improper Julie and her no more respectable tutor—his ire was roused.

He dubbed "Eloïsa" "foolish, *bourgeois*, impudent, and wearisome." It was "one of the infamies of the century" to have admired it. And he wrote to Theriot: "No novel of Jean Jacques, if you please. I have read him for my misfortune; and it would have been for his if I had the time to say what I thought of it."

The last words were only the blind which hoodwinked nobody. "There is time for everything if one likes to use it." Staying at Ferney at the moment was the Marquis de Ximenès, ex-admirer of Madame Denis and now forgiven that unpleasant little business of the stolen manuscript of a few years back.

There quickly appeared four letters on (or rather against) "The New Eloïsa," the first of which bore the signature of the Marquis, and all of which bore unmistakable traits of a famous style.

Voltaire denied them, according to custom.

But it was the denial *pour rire.*

The wise d'Alembert wrote and remonstrated with his friend for "declaiming openly" against Jean Jacques, who, after all, was of their party and with a warmth and ardour which might serve it well.

But Rousseau had begun to sting and irritate the sensitive skin of his great rival, and would by no means be shaken off. In the October of 1761 Voltaire said that Jean Jacques wrote about once a fortnight to incite the Genevan ministers against theatres.

In the meantime, fortunately for them both, Voltaire had interests which eclipsed even that excited by a sentimental rival's annoying Puritanism or long-winded romance.

He was fighting the Jesuits and building a church.

On January 1, 1761, he wrote to tell Helvétius that he had reclaimed from the Jesuits of Ornex, his neighbours, with whom he had hitherto been on good terms, the estate belonging to six poor brothers, of which the Jesuits had robbed them during their minority.

To compass this act the Jesuits had allied themselves with a Calvinistic Councillor of State of Geneva. There is no doubt at all that Voltaire delighted, as he said, in thus triumphing over both Ignatius and Calvin; or that the defeat of the Jesuits gave him as much pleasure as the victory of the brothers. But when it is added that he had lent those brothers, without interest, all the money necessary to reclaim their heritage: that he spent on them an incalculable amount of that time which was more valuable to him than any money, it must be allowed that if his motives were mixed, good preponderated in the mixture.

And then he turned his extraordinary mind towards building a church.

The church scheme had been on the *tapis* as far back as the August of 1760. The truth was that the old church at Ferney was not only very hideous and tumbledown, but spoilt a very good view from the château. If churches there must be to enslave men's souls, thinks Voltaire, why, they need not offend their eyes as well. I will build a new one!

Every Sunday it was now his habit not only to attend mass with Marie Corneille and Madame Denis, but to be duly incensed thereat as lord of the manor. He also looked after his poor, and behaved very much as a conscientious country landowner ought to behave, but as, in the eighteenth century, he very seldom did.

But still this sceptic, this freethinker, this wicked person who had just successfully brought home to the good Jesuits an accusation of robbery, was certainly a character whose every act the devout might well eye suspiciously.

Voltaire cautiously obtained the permission of the Bishop of Annecy to change the site of the church, and then began pulling down with a will. He was to bear all the expenses himself. If the deed was not strictly right in law, it was so excellent in morals that it had been done with impunity hundreds of times before.

In the rasing operations, part of the churchyard wall had to be taken down, and a large cross, which dominated the churchyard, removed.

All would have been well, however, if this unlucky Voltaire had not had, as usual, an enemy on the spot. When he first came to Ferney, it will be remembered that he had successfully fought Ancian, the curé of the neighbouring parish of Moens, for a tithe of which Ancian had long deprived the poor of the neighbourhood. Ancian, whom Voltaire vigorously described as "brutal as a horse, cross-grained as a mule, and cunning as a fox," had not forgiven that affront easily. But worse was to come.

On December 28, 1760, a young man, wounded and nearly bleeding to death, had been brought to the doors of Ferney. Voltaire did not only take him in and care for his body. With that passionate love of fair-play which was so fatal to the ease and comfort of his life, he determined to ferret out the rights of the case and get justice done.

It appeared that three young men had been supping, after a day's hunting, at the house of a woman of whom Ancian was commonly reported the lover. Ancian, and "some peasants his accomplices," rushed in and violently attacked the three men, nearly killing Decroze, the one who had been brought to Ferney.

Here is a pretty state of things! says Voltaire. A priest who is not only thief but murderer as well! He set to work at once. He moved heaven, earth, and the authorities to get M. Ancian "employment in the galleys." He found out Decroze's father and sister. He tried to rouse the father's timidity and apathy to action. The sister told him, on her oath, that her confessor had refused her absolution if she did not force that father to renounce his son's cause.

By January 3, 1761, Voltaire was passionately complaining that a "feeble procedure" against the criminal had hardly been begun. The province was divided on the subject. All Voltaire's letters of the time are full of it. But Ancian was protected by his order. It was thought, as it has been often thought before and since, that the scandal of punishing the crime would be greater than the scandal of leaving it unpunished.

Ancian had to pay Decroze a sum down; but he kept his living, and nursed his revenge.

When he saw M. de Voltaire pulling down the churchyard wall and removing the cross, he knew that the time had come. He assured his brother curé of Ferney and the simple people of the place that this atheist of a Voltaire had profaned their church; that he had not only moved the cross without first fulfilling the usual formalities, but had cried out, "Take away that gibbet!" Ancian, therefore, on the biblical principle of an eye for an eye and a tooth for a tooth, denounced Voltaire to the ecclesiastical judge of Gex as guilty of sacrilege and impiety, and involved him in a "criminal suit of a most violent character."

But Ancian did not know, though he ought to have known, the sort of man with whom he had to deal. Voltaire's blood was up. A criminal lawsuit, forsooth, for "a foot and a half of churchyard and two mutton cutlets which had been mistaken for disinterred bones"! There was an angry note in that laugh which meant fight. Further, his enemies were saying publicly that they hoped to see him burned, or at least hanged, for the glory of God and the edification of the faithful; and meanwhile his church-building operations were stopped.

It was an old principle of his always to turn their own weapons against his foes. He had not forgotten it. He put himself into correspondence with an able ecclesiastical lawyer of Lyons. He read up ecclesiastical histories, and ancient volumes of Church law; and then suddenly flung at the head of the enemy such a mass of rules and precedents, of dreary old parallel cases of mouldering decrees which councils had forgotten to revoke, of long-winded formulas and by-laws whose existence and orthodoxy were as indisputable as they had been unheeded, and of authorities who were infinitely sound, obscure, and confusing—that the priestly party put its hands to its ears, cried "Peccavi!" and confessed itself beaten on its own ground.

In the meanwhile its surprising little foe, who "passionately loved to be master," had rased the whole church at Ferney to the ground, "in reply to the complaints of having taken down half of it," had removed the altars, the confessional boxes, and the fonts, and sent his parishioners to attend mass elsewhere.

To crown all, and to leave nothing undone that could be done, by June 21st he had forwarded the plan of his church to the Pope and applied to his Holiness for a bull granting him absolute power over his churchyard, permission for his labourers to work on *fête* days, instead "of getting drunk in honour of the Saints" according to custom, and for sacred relics to place in the church.

The letters to Rome are, very unfortunately, lost. But, through Choiseul, they reached there; and the requests were granted in part. On October 26, 1761, the Holy Father sent a piece of the hair shirt of St. Francis of Assisi—the patron saint of François Marie Arouet. On the same day, in tardy recognition for the dedication of "Tancred," came a present of the portrait of Madame de Pompadour. "So you see," wrote Voltaire, "I am all right both for this world and the next."

When his church was finished he inscribed on it *Deo Solo* (sic), which by September 14, 1761, he had altered to *Deo erexit Voltaire*. He was fond of saying that it was the only church in the universe which was dedicated to God alone, and not to a saint. "For my part I had rather build for the Master than for the servants."

He had designed his own tomb jutting out from the wall of the church. "The wicked will say that I am neither inside nor out."

In March a public event distracted his thoughts for a moment from "Eloïsa," Ancian, and the church building. The Dauphin's eldest son died; and Pompignan, as Historiographer of France, lifted his diminished head from Montauban and from those "mountains of ridicule" which covered him, and wrote a eulogium of the little boy, which alas! for foolish Pompignan, was also another attack on the philosophers. Voltaire waited a little. Then he wrote two pieces of "murderous brevity"—the "Ah! Ahs!" and the "Fors."

Down went the head of Pompignan again. If it even peeped up for a moment, which it still did now and then, Ferney shot an arrow at it from the richest quiver and with the deadliest aim in the world.

But he had better things to do now than hitting an enemy who was down.

That dear spoilt daughter of the house, who might interrupt even the chess or the verse reading of *vif* Papa Voltaire with impunity—who was pretty and naïve enough to do anything in the world she liked with him—still had no *dot*.

On April 10, 1761, Voltaire wrote to Duclos, secretary of the Academy, and proposed that he (Voltaire) should edit and annotate Corneille's works, in an edition of the classics then appearing under the patronage of the Academy, for the benefit of the great Peter's great-niece.

To say that Voltaire put his whole heart, soul, and body into the thing and worked at it like a galley slave, and worked till he made all Europe work too, is no exaggeration. He began by getting up a subscription, which remains one of the best managed, if not *the* best managed, and certainly the most successful thing of its kind ever undertaken. He advanced all money for preliminary expenses himself. The King of France, the Empress of Russia, the Emperor and Empress of Austria, Choiseul, and Madame de Pompadour figured imposingly and attractively on his list. The nobles and notables of France, courtiers, farmers-general, and literary men quickly followed suit. In England the givers included good Queen Charlotte, Lords Chesterfield, Lyttelton, Palmer, Spencer, and the great Mr. Pitt. To Pitt, Voltaire wrote, in the English he was always clever enough to remember, when expedient; and Pitt replied favourably.

By May, only a month after the subscription was started, and before a single copy of the work was ready, enough money had come in to afford Marie Corneille a yearly income of fifteen hundred francs.

Voltaire was far from finding the labour congenial. To the vigour of his creative genius work that was so largely mechanical soon became irritating and tiresome. Still, it consoled him, as he said, for those public disasters in the Seven Years' War which were fast making France the fable of the nations and the laughing stock of Europe; and presently for that crushing defeat of the French by Frederick the Great at Villinghausen on July 15th.

That he was an excellent commentator is proved by the fact that his Commentary remains unrivalled, and is still *the* text-book on Corneille. With an ear as exquisitely delicate for a harmony as a discord, with that single-minded love of good literature which equally prevented him being flatterer or caviller, Voltaire was the critic who, like the poet, is born, not made. He admired warmly; but he blamed candidly. "It is true that Corneille is a sacred authority; but I am like Father Simon, who, when the Archbishop of Paris asked him what he was doing to prepare himself for the priesthood, replied, 'Monseigneur, I am criticising the Bible.'"

When Martin Sherlock was at Ferney in 1776 he observed that the English preferred Corneille to Racine. "That," said Voltaire, "is because the English do not know enough of the French language to feel the beauties of Racine's style or the harmony of his versification. Corneille pleases them better because he is more striking; but Racine for the French because he has more delicacy and tenderness."

When the Commentary was finished it numbered many volumes, and "served to marry two girls, which never before happened to a Commentary," said the Commentator, "and never will again."

By a peculiarly delicate thought, *poor* literary men received copies as gifts.

The autumn of 1761 was not dull at Ferney. Among the visitors were Abbé Coyer and Lauraguais, wit and playwright, and one of those highly unsatisfactory clever people who *can* do everything, and do nothing.

Besides the visitors, the autumn was marked by the progress of the quarrel with de Brosses, from whom Voltaire had bought Tourney, and with whom he was still deeply engaged in a lawsuit for "fourteen cords of firewood."

The man who gave a home to d'Aumard, to Marie Corneille, and to Father Adam, and who pensioned his poor relations without in the least accounting it to himself for righteousness, was incredibly sharp and mean over this firewood with de Brosses, and wasted his time and his talents in the fight. The details of the quarrel are long, uninteresting, and profitless. But it must in justice be said that it shows Voltaire "at his very worst:

insolent, undignified, low-minded, and untruthful." Besides quarrelling with de Brosses, with Ancian, and Rousseau, editing Corneille, writing "Peter the Great," revising the "Essay on the Manners and Mind of Nations," and looking after three estates, this wonderful man also found time in 1761 for his usual gigantic correspondence, and to write two plays. The correspondence alone comprises letters to a king and cardinals, prime ministers, and actresses, *savants* and *salonières*, besides letters to old friends like Panpan and Madame de Champbonin; letters in English and Italian, and in rhyme; and letters *from* people he had never seen. In this July a burgomaster of Middleton had written to inquire of him if there is a God; if, supposing there be one, He troubles about man; if Matter is eternal; if it can think; and if the soul is immortal. The burgomaster added that he would like an answer by return of post. "I receive such letters every week," Voltaire wrote to Madame du Deffand. "I have a pleasant life."

From 1760 until 1768 he was also writing constantly to that Damilaville who was so steady a foe of *l'infâme*, and who took Theriot's place as Voltaire's Parisian correspondent. Theriot had long sunk into a good-natured parasite of any rich man who would give him a good dinner and an idle life; while Damilaville, if he *was* heavy and mannerless, as Grimm said, was a patient and tireless disciple; who ran all Voltaire's errands in Paris for him; despatched to Ferney constant packets of books, manuscripts, and news; and, in brief, loved and worked for Voltaire as sincerely as he loathed, and worked against, *l'infâme*.

On October 20, 1761, Voltaire wrote to tell his Angels that the fever took him on Sunday and did not leave him till Saturday—which, being interpreted, meant that at sixty-seven years old he had composed in six days the tragedy of "Olympie."

But even in a Voltaire—a Voltaire of whom Joubert justly said that "his mind was ripe twenty years sooner than other men's and that he kept it, in all its powers, thirty years later"—such quick work could not mean his best work.

The Angels recommended revision.

"It was written in six days," wrote Voltaire to a friend whose opinion he desired. "Then the author should not have rested on the seventh," was the answer. "He did, and repented of his work," replied Voltaire. The play written in six days took six months to correct.

In the meantime, and for fear one should get idle and the brain rust, he flung on to paper a versified comedy called "Seigneurial Rights" ("Le Droit du Seigneur"). It had been rehearsed at home by December 17th. It was to pose as the work of one Picardet, an Academician of Dijon, until its success was established.

But once again Voltaire had to reckon with an old enemy. Crébillon of eighty-eight was still envious, and now censor of plays. He recognised the style of Picardet, Academician of Dijon, and refused to license his play unless a scene from his (Crébillon's) hand was added. Chafing Voltaire called this scene a carnage of all his best points.

Early in the new year 1762, Crébillon died, at peace with all the world, it was said, even his profligate of a son—and M. de Voltaire. But Voltaire had too much to forgive in return. He wrote the "Éloge de Crébillon," and once more peaceful d'Alembert had to complain of his *vif* friend's losing his temper—"a satire under the name of a eulogy." "I am sorry you chose the moment of his death to throw stones on his corpse." "He had better have been left to rot of himself: it would not have taken long."

D'Alembert was right, as he had been before.

Meanwhile "Seigneurial Rights" had been produced on January 18, 1762, and had met with a success far above its slender merits.

January also saw another temporary resurrection of poor Pompignan. It was Voltaire himself who had provoked the poor man to turn in his grave this time, by writing to a popular tune and in a catching metre "A Hymn Sung at the Village of Pompignan."

This he sent round to his friends with a guitar accompaniment. It became *the* air of Paris; and the street boys, it is said, sang it *at* the Pompignans as they passed. A little later Voltaire wrote a burlesque "Journey of M. le Franc de Pompignan from Pompignan to Fontainebleau," and replied to an attack Brother Aaron de Pompignan, Bishop of Puy, had been foolhardy enough to make upon the philosophers, with such a running fire of pamphlets, epigrams, and irony as might have slain a far abler foe.

And so *exeunt* the Pompignans for ever.

In January, too, Voltaire published a pamphlet called "The Extract of the Opinions of Jean Meslier," Meslier having been a curé who left at his death papers seeking to prove the falsehood of the religion which he had professed. Voltaire put it into shape. It was a curious and a very human document. He was not a little disgusted that "tepid" Paris did not receive it with more enthusiasm.

But if Paris was tepid, that cold King seemed to be getting a little warmer. Voltaire wrote to tell Duclos on January 20th that his Majesty had restored to him an old pension.

"What will Fréron say to *that*? What will Pompignan?" wrote the delighted pensioner naïvely. There was also a rumour that his Majesty has been pleased to recall M. de Voltaire. That was false. And Voltaire, since he could not reach the grapes, took the very sensible *rôle* of declaring that they were sour. No doubt they really were. The fruit of his own labours was at least far sweeter. To work in the Ferney garden with Lambert, his stupid gardener—"my privateer"—was safer too. "Love like a fool when you are young—work like a devil when you are old," was one of Voltaire's rules of life. He had to his hand new work, beside which even gardening at Ferney was dull and useless, and waiting in a king's antechamber a shame and a contempt.

On March 10, 1762, Jean Calas was broken on the wheel.

CHAPTER XXXVI

THE AFFAIR OF CALAS

IN 1761 and 1762, Toulouse, the capital of Languedoc and the seventh city of France, was one of the most priest-ridden in the kingdom. The anniversary of that supreme crime of history, the Massacre of St. Bartholomew, was always legally celebrated as a two days' festival. The Revocation of the Edict of Nantes had been commemorated by two frescoes erected at the public expense. In Toulouse no Protestant could be a lawyer, a physician, a surgeon, an apothecary, a bookseller, a grocer, or a printer; he could not keep either a Protestant clerk or a Protestant servant; and in 1748, an unhappy woman had been fined three thousand francs for acting as a midwife without having first become a Roman Catholic.

The city was further celebrated for its monastic orders, the White, the Black, and the Grey Penitents; and for a collection of relics which included bones of the children massacred by Herod and a piece of the robe of the Virgin.

In such a place, not the less, Jean Calas, a Protestant shopkeeper, had lived honoured and respected for forty years.

On the evening of October 13, 1761, he, his family, and a young friend sat at supper in his house over his shop, at No. 16 Rue des Filatiers.

Jean Calas, the father, was sixty-three years old, and rather infirm; kind, benevolent, and serene; anything but a bigot, in that Louis, one of his sons, who was a Toulouse apprentice, had embraced the Roman faith with the full consent of his father, who supposed the matter to be one in which each must judge for himself.

Madame Calas, though of English extraction, was an excellent type of the best kind of French *bourgeoise*—practical, vigorous, alert—aged about forty-five.

Peter, the second son, was an amiable but rather weak youth of about five-and-twenty. There were two daughters, Rose and Nanette, who were away from home upon this particular evening, as was also Louis (who was still in receipt of a money allowance from his father); and Donat, the youngest boy, who was living at Nîmes.

Mark Anthony, the eldest son of the family, was the only unsatisfactory person in it. Only twenty-eight years old, he was one of those gloomy and discontented characters who, the world being "a looking-glass which gives back to every man the reflection of his own face," saw all life *en noir.*

His character had been further soured by the discovery that the profession he had set his heart on was not open to a Protestant; and that he could not be admitted to the Bar without producing a certificate from his curé declaring him a Catholic.

Mark Anthony endeavoured to gain this certificate by simply suppressing his Protestantism. But he failed. Change his religion he would not. If there was a bigot among the Calas, he was the one. He alone of the family had bitterly opposed the conversion of Louis.

Another situation he desired he had to give up through his father's lack of capital. He grew more and more morose. He hung about the cafés and the billiard saloons, bitter and idle. In a theatrical company he had joined he would declaim, it is said, Hamlet's monologue on death, and other pieces dealing with suicide, with an "inspired warmth."

The establishment at the Rue des Filatiers was completed by Jeannette Viguière, the *bonne à tout faire*, an ardent Roman Catholic and the faithful friend and servant of the family for thirty years.

On the evening of this October 13, 1761, a friend of the Calas, Gaubert Lavaysse, a youth about twenty, came in unexpectedly just as the Calas were going to sit down to supper.

Hospitable Madame bade Mark Anthony, who was sitting in the shop, "plunged in thought," go and buy some Roquefort cheese to add to their simple meal. He did as he was asked. He joined the party at supper in the parlour, next to the kitchen. They talked on indifferent topics. It was remembered afterwards that the conversation, among other things, fell upon some antiquities to be seen at the City Hall, and that Mark Anthony spoke of them too. At the dessert, about eight o'clock, he got up, *as was his custom*, from the table and went into the adjoining kitchen.

"Are you cold, *M. l'Aîné?*" said Jeannette, thinking he had come to warm himself.

"On the contrary—burning hot," he answered. And he went out.

The little supper-party meantime had gone into the salon, where, except Peter, who went to sleep, they talked until a quarter to ten, when Lavaysse left. Peter was roused to light him out.

When the two got downstairs into the shop a sharp cry of alarm reached the salon. Jean Calas hurried down. Madame stood at the top of the stairs for a moment, wondering and trembling. Then she went down.

Lavaysse came out of the shop and gently forced her upstairs, saying she should be told all.

In the shop Lavaysse and Peter had found the dead body of the unhappy Mark Anthony suspended from a wooden instrument used in binding bales of cloth, which the poor boy had placed between two doorposts, and on which he had hanged himself. On the counter lay his coat and vest, neatly folded.

Jean Calas cut the cord, lifted the body down, put it on the ground, and used all possible means to restore life. Impelled by that awful sense of unknown disaster, Madame and Jeannette came down too, and with tears, and calling the boy's name, tried all remedies—unavailingly.

Meanwhile, Calas had bidden Peter go for the doctor. He came, by name one Gorse, but he could do nothing. Then Peter, beside himself, would have rushed into the street to tell their misfortune abroad. His father caught hold of him: "Do not spread a report that he has killed himself; at least save our honour."

The feeling was in any case a perfectly natural one. But how much more natural in that dreadful day when, as Calas knew well, the body of a man proven a suicide was placed naked on a hurdle with the face turned to the ground, drawn thus through the streets, and then hanged on a gibbet.

Lavaysse had also run out of the house. Peter, finding him at a neighbour's, told him to deny that Mark Anthony had committed suicide. Lavaysse agreed. Voltaire spoke hereafter of that decision as "a natural and equitable" one. It was. But it was one of the most fatal ever uttered.

The neighbours were roused by now. Many rushed in to give assistance. Among others was an old friend of the family's, Cazeing by name. Clausade, a lawyer, said the police ought to be fetched. Lavaysse ran to fetch them.

Meanwhile a crowd had gathered outside the house. It had the characteristics of most crowds—perhaps of all French crowds—it was intensely excited; it was exceedingly inventive; and it would follow a leader like sheep. What *had* happened in that house? In 1835 there still stood over the door a signboard with the inscription, "Jean Calas, *Marchand d'Indiennes*". It stood there then. Calas? Calas? Why, Calas was a Huguenot. From among the people came a word—one of those idle words for which men shall give account in the Day of Judgment—"These Huguenots have killed their son to prevent him turning Catholic!" The idea was dramatic and pleased. The crowd caught it up. It was the match to the fagot, and the whole bonfire was ablaze at once.

But there was one man there at least, David de Beaudrigue, one of the chief magistrates of the city, whom, from his position, it should have been impossible to move a hair's breadth by an irresponsible word, and who is eternally infamous that, hearing such a cry, he believed it. But, for the doom of Calas, Beaudrigue was both bigot and fanatic. It has been well said by Parton, one of Voltaire's biographers, that "if the words had blazed ... across the midnight sky in letters of miraculous fire," Beaudrigue "could not have believed them with more complete and instantaneous faith."

He hastened into the house with his officers and arrested every person in it, including young Lavaysse, who had fought his way back there through the crowd, and Cazeing the friend. Through the ill-lit streets, thronged with an excited mob, the little party were taken to the Hôtel de Ville. Mark Anthony's body was borne on a bier before them. The Calas and their friends thought, as they might well think, that they were only going to give testimony of what had occurred. Grief, not fear, was in their hearts. So little did they anticipate not returning to their house that evening that Peter had put a lighted candle in one of the windows to light them when they came back. "Blow it out," said David. "You will not return so soon."

On every step of that dreadful journey to the Hôtel de Ville the ardent imagination of that southern crowd grew hotter. From saying that Calas had murdered his son to prevent him turning Catholic, it was only a step to the assertion that among the Huguenots such an act was common, encouraged, and esteemed a virtue. Before that town hall was reached Mark Anthony had become a martyr to the true faith; and Jean, his father, was already condemned to the most horrible of all deaths, on the most horrible of all accusations.

When the prisoners reached the place they still persisted in that most natural but most fatal falsehood, that Mark had not committed suicide. It still did not occur to their simplicity and their innocence that they could ever be accused of murdering one so dear to them. They were soon to be enlightened. They were separated, locked, with irons on their feet, into separate cells. Jean Calas and Peter were left in complete darkness. Cazeing was soon released. But Lavaysse, the unhappy young visitor, was imprisoned too. On the days following they were each separately examined on oath. All then confessed that the boy had committed suicide, and all told stories which tallied with each other. Their depositions were such that if clear evidence, reason, and justice ever appealed to bigots, they would have been liberated at once.

But David had been occupying his time in still further infuriating the people. The priests seconded him. One of his own colleagues warned him not to go so fast.

"I take all the responsibility," he answered. "It is in the cause of religion."

It is noticeable that, in his bloody haste, and though he assumed the case to be one of murder, he had never examined the shop at the Rue des Filatiers to see if it bore marks of a struggle, or the clothes of the supposed murderers. Yet how could it be thought that "the most vigorous man in the province," eight-and-twenty years old, would allow his feeble father of sixty-three to strangle and hang him without making any resistance? And if resistance was made, where were the rents and the bloodstains?

If, too, the boy had been killed because he was about to change his religion, should not his room have been searched for some object of Catholic piety, some signs of the dreadful struggle of the soul? His person *was* searched. On it were found a few papers of ribald songs.

For three weeks the body of this strange martyr was kept embalmed, lying in the torture chamber of the Hôtel de Ville. As it had been assumed without a shred of evidence that Mark Anthony had been about to join the Roman Church, it was equally easy to assume that he had also been about to enter one of the monastic orders. Popular fancy chose the White Penitents as the order of Mark's intentions. He was buried on a Sunday afternoon, "with more than royal pomp," in the great cathedral, and with the full and splendid rites of the Roman Church. Thousands of persons were present, and a few days after a solemn service for the repose of the soul of their Brother was held by the White Penitents.

For three successive Sundays from the pulpits in all the churches was read an admonition to give testimony, "by hearsay or otherwise," against Jean Calas.

To be sure, such testimony would never be difficult to obtain in any case or in any place, but in priest-ridden Toulouse, against Jean Calas, it might well have been on all lips.

After the five prisoners had spent five months in separate dungeons, chained by the feet, the trial began. It must be remembered that of the accused one was Jeannette, an ardent Roman Catholic, who had not only helped to convert Louis, but who had given no offence to his Protestant relatives by so doing.

On March 9, 1762, Jean Calas was tried first, and alone, for the murder of his son on the previous October 13th. He was tried by thirteen members of the Toulouse Parliament who held ten sessions. The witnesses against him were of this kind: a painter named Mattei said that his wife had told him that a person named Mandrille had told her that some person unnamed had told *her* that he had heard Mark Anthony's cries at the other end of the town. Some of the witnesses against Calas disappeared before the trial came on, feeling the strain on their inventive powers too great.

It was assumed by the prosecution that Mark Anthony *could* not have hanged himself in the place where the Calas swore they had found him; but, as has been noted, the prosecution never went to see the place.

For the prisoner, on the other hand, was the most overwhelming evidence.

First, it was the most unnatural of crimes. Secondly, it was impossible at the father's age and weakness that he should have murdered his strong son alone. If he had not murdered him alone, it must have been with the assistance of the family party, of whom one was Jeannette, the ardent Catholic, and another was Lavaysse, the casual visitor.

The testimony of all these people *for* Calas agreed absolutely—except on one or two minor and wholly immaterial points.

But, in the case of this prisoner, it was not merely that the law of his day declared him guilty until he was proved innocent. Calas was declared guilty without being allowed a chance of proving himself innocent. The accused was never then permitted a counsel. But with Calas, the people sat on the judgment seat with Pilate; assumed the prisoner's guilt, not without evidence, but in the teeth of it, and had condemned him before he was tried. Some of the magistrates themselves belonged to the confraternity of the White Penitents.

One of them only—M. de Lasalle—had the courage to object to the mockery of the proceedings. "You are all Calas," said a brother judge. "And you," answered Lasalle, "are all People."

By eight votes to five, then, "a weak old man was to be condemned to the most awful of all deaths" (first the torture, and then to be broken on the wheel) "for having strangled and hanged with his feeble hands, in hatred of the Catholic religon, his robust and vigorous son who had no more inclination towards that religion than the father himself." The words are the words of him who, said Madame du Deffand, became all men's *avocat*, Voltaire.

Out of those thirteen judges three voted for torture only, and two suggested that it might be better to examine the shop at the Rue des

Filatiers and see if a suicide *were* impossible. One hero alone voted for complete acquittal.

The terms of the sentence display a savage ferocity, of which only a religious hatred is capable. To the exquisite tortures to which Calas was condemned, even the brutes who, drunk with blood and believing in neither God nor devil committed the worst excesses of the French Revolution, never fell.

This mock trial had taken place on March 9th. On March 10th that sentence of ghoulish and delighted cruelty was read to the victim. He was taken straight to the torture-room, the oath was administered, and with the rack in front to remind him of the fate awaiting him, he was cross-examined. He answered as he had always answered—He was innocent. When asked who were his accomplices, he replied that as there had been no crime there could be no accomplices. One witness speaks of his "calmness and serenity." Yet he was a feeble man, not young, who for five months had been chained in a dark dungeon, accused of the most awful of crimes, and knowing that in his downfall he had dragged down with him everything he loved best in the world.

He was then put to the first torture—the *Question Ordinaire*. The very record of such horrors still makes the blood run cold. But what man could bear, man can bear to hear. First bound by the wrists to an iron ring in the wall, four feet above the ground, "and his feet to another ring in the floor of the room," with an ample length of rope between, "the body was stretched till every limb was drawn from its socket." The agony was then "increased tenfold by sliding a wooden horse under the lower rope." Thus, in mortal torment, Calas was questioned again. He maintained his innocence, and "neither wavered nor cried out."

After a rest—a rest!—of half an hour, during which the magistrates and a priest questioned him again, he was put to the *Question Extraordinaire*. Water was poured into his mouth by force until "he suffered the anguish of a hundred drownings."

He was then questioned again; and again maintained his innocence. Then more water was poured into him, until his body was swollen to twice its natural size. He was again questioned; with the same results.

Then the devils called Christians, who persecuted him in the name of Christ, saw that their aim would be defeated. Calas would not confess. But he could die.

He was taken on a tumbril in his shirt only—how many were to go thus to doom after him!—to the place of execution. From time to time he said "I am innocent." The crowd—in temper and intent the crowd who eighteen hundred years before had cried "Crucify Him!"—reviled him as he went, as they had reviled his Master. At the scaffold a priest, whom he knew personally, once more exhorted him to confess. "What, Father!" he said. "Do you too believe that a man could kill his own son?" Then, again like the Truth for Whom he suffered, he was bound on a cross. The executioner broke each of his limbs in two places with an iron bar. He lived thus for two hours, praying for his judges.

A few moments before his death a priest again exhorted him to confess. "I have said it," he answered. "I die innocent." At that supreme moment he mentioned Lavaysse—the boy upon whom he had brought so unwittingly ruin and disgrace. Then David de Beaudrigue, who felt that he was in some sort cheated of his prey without a confession, bade him turn and look at the fire which was to burn him, and confess all. He turned and looked. The executioner strangled him; and he died without a word.

His noble courage at least saved the lives of his family. Peter was condemned to perpetual banishment, "which if he was guilty was too little; and if he was innocent was too much." He was forced into a monastery; and, being a weak character and told that if he did not abjure his religion he should die as his father had died, he recanted in a terror not unnatural.

His mother was liberated. She crept away with Jeannette into the country near Toulouse, to hide her broken heart. Her two daughters were flung each into a separate convent. Young Lavaysse was sent back to his family, ruined alike in health and in prospects.

Donat Calas, the youngest of the family, the apprentice at Nîmes, had had to leave France when the trial came on, for fear of being indicted as an accomplice. He went to Geneva.

On March 22, 1762, only twelve days after the death of Jean Calas, Voltaire mentioned the case in writing to Le Bault. He was not at once moved to take any side. The affair was not his. But if he did take any, it was the side of Catholicism. "We are not worth much," he said airily, "but the Huguenots are worse than we are. *They* declaim against comedy."

But the affair made him think. Two days later he wrote that it "took him by the heart." Then he learnt that Donat was near him—at Geneva; that the boy had fled there on hearing of the trial. *That* seemed like guilt. "I am interested as a man, and a little as a philosopher. I want to know *on which side* is this horror of fanaticism." At the end of March, Audibert, a merchant of Marseilles, who had happened to be in Toulouse when the Calas tragedy was enacted, called on Voltaire and told him the facts of the case as they had appeared to him. Foul play somewhere, thinks Alain's pupil and Arouet's son, putting those facts together. But where? "I told him

(Audibert) that the crime of Calas was not probable; but it was still more improbable that disinterested judges should condemn an innocent man to be broken on the wheel."

Disinterested? There lay the crux. Voltaire's feelings were roused; but they had not run away with him. On March 27th, he wrote to d'Argental: "You will ask me, perhaps, why I interest myself so strongly in this Calas who was broken on the wheel? It is because I am a man.... Could you not induce M. de Choiseul to have this fearful case investigated?"

Every day, nay every hour, a mind far keener and shrewder than any Choiseul's was investigating it then: collecting evidence; writing innumerable letters; working, working; tempering with cool discretion a zeal that burnt hotter every moment as the innocence of Calas forced itself upon his soul; labouring with that "fiery patience," that critical judiciousness, which in such a case alone could win.

At the end of April he went from Ferney to Délices, that he might be nearer Donat Calas; study him; hear an account of his family from his own lips. The boy was only fifteen; cried when he told that piteous story; and spoke of both his father and mother as infinitely kind and indulgent to all their children.

Lest he should be moved by those emotions which grew stronger every day, or by a moral conviction in the innocence of Calas not fully borne out by physical facts, Voltaire sought the opinion of wise and capable friends. He employed Végobre, an able (and notably unimaginative) lawyer of Geneva, to investigate legal points; and for hours and hours would remain closeted with him. Ribotte-Charon, a merchant of Toulouse, himself warmly interested in the case, Voltaire induced to examine the site of the supposed murder and to study local details. Chazel, a solicitor of Montpellier, he engaged to interview the leading magistrates of the Languedoc district and to procure documents.

But to obtain a formal investigation of the affair it was necessary to get the ear of the Chancellor of France, the Count of Saint-Florentin. Voltaire incited every powerful friend he had in the world to assail this person. Villars and Richelieu were made to bombard him. What was the use of Dr. Tronchin's famous and influential patients if they could not be induced to attack M. Florentin too? Tronchin roused them, and they did as they were told. At Geneva was the Duchesse d'Enville, also a Tronchin patient, clever, powerful, and enlightened. Voltaire fired her with his own enthusiasm, and she wrote direct to Saint-Florentin. As for Madame de Pompadour and Choiseul, Voltaire undertook them himself. The Pompadour was always "one of us" in her heart; and while she hated the Jesuits, Choiseul did not love them.

By the end of June, Voltaire had brought Madame Calas up to Paris and begged his Angels, "in the name of humankind," to take her broken life under their wings. She had not been easy to persuade to come. She was crushed to the earth, as she might well be. Hope for the future, or hope for vengeance for the past, she had none. Only one passionate desire seems to have been left her—to get back her daughters from the convents into which they had been forced. The property of criminals was then confiscated to the King, and she had not a farthing in the world. But Voltaire paid all her expenses—content to wait until the generosity of Europe should refund him. For counsel he gave her d'Alembert and the famous *avocat*, Mariette. On June 11th, he appointed Élie de Beaumont as Mariette's colleague. It is always a part of cleverness to discover the cleverness of others. Beaumont was young and unknown; but he was a most able choice.

On July 4th, Peter Calas escaped from his monastery, and joined Donat at Geneva. Voltaire had thus the two brothers under observation. He put them through searching inquiries. Peter was naturally a most important witness.

On July 5th, Voltaire first spoke to d'Argental of the "Original Documents concerning the Calas" which in this month he gave to the world. They are for all time a model of editorial genius. They consist only of an extract from a letter from Madame Calas, and of a letter from Donat Calas to his mother. Voltaire's name did not appear at all. They contain that most damning of all evidence—a perfectly clear and simple statement of plain facts. If the editor contributed order and brevity, he left the quiet pathos of the woman and the passionate eagerness of the boy to speak for themselves.

The "Original Documents" he quickly followed up by a "Memoir and Declaration": the "Memoir" purporting to be by Donat Calas, the "Declaration" by Peter.

Once again he wholly obliterated himself. Only a Voltaire's genius could have curbed a Voltaire's passion and made him rein in, even for a while, his own fiery eloquence, speak as those poor Calas would have spoken, and wait.

He knew now, by every proof which can carry conviction to the mind, that they were innocent: and he had given those proofs to the world.

But that was not enough. In August he published "The History of Elizabeth Canning and of the Calas." Nothing he ever wrote shows more clearly how perfectly he understood that April nation, his countrymen. "Documents" and "Declarations"! Why, they at least *sounded* dull; and eighteenth-century Paris was not even going to run the risk of a yawn. "One might break half a dozen innocent people on the wheel, and in Paris people would only talk of the new comedy and think of a good supper." But Paris loved to be made to laugh one moment and to weep the next; to have its quick pity touched and its quick humour tickled—in a breath.

"The History of Elizabeth Canning" is sarcastically amusing—an account of that enterprising young Englishwoman who nearly had another woman hanged on the strength of a story invented by herself and her relatives.

"It is in vain that the law wishes that two witnesses should be able to hang an accused. If the Lord Chancellor and the Archbishop of Canterbury depose that they have seen me assassinate my father and my mother, and eat them whole for breakfast in a quarter of an hour, the Chancellor and the Archbishop must be sent to Bedlam, instead of burning me on their fine testimony. Put on one hand a thing absurd and impossible, and on the other a thousand witnesses and reasoners, and the impossibility ought to give the lie to all testimonies and reasonings."

"The History of the Calas" was that sombre and terrible story told by a master mind: passionate, and yet cool; moving, and yet cautious in argument; the work at once of the ablest, keenest, shrewdest lawyer in the case, and of the man who said of himself, almost without exaggeration, that for three years, until Calas was vindicated, a smile never escaped him for which he did not reproach himself as for a crime.

He did not appeal to "that great and supreme judge of all suits and causes, public opinion," in vain. The Calas case became the talk of Europe. Men felt, as Donat had been made to say in his Memoir, that "the cause was the cause of all families; of Nature; of religon; of the State; and of foreign countries."

Voltaire had his Calas pamphlets translated and published in Germany and England. Generous England came forward with a subscription list for the unhappy family, headed by the young Queen of George III., and to which the Empress of Russia and the King of Poland became contributors.

But still, to rouse men's interest was but a means to an end. The end was to obtain first from the Council of Paris a decree ordering that the case should be re-tried, and then that fresh trial itself. The obstacles were not few or trifling. Louis XV. and Saint-Florentin, in spite of the influence brought to bear upon them, were both opposed to such a course. A too strict and searching justice did not suit the monarchy of France. Louis XV. was always wise enough to let sleeping dogs lie if he could, instead of convening States-General and dismissing and recalling ministers to please the people they governed, like that weak fool, his successor. "Why can't you leave it alone?" was the motto of both King and Chancellor over the Calas case. And they would have lived up to it, but that the public opinion which had a Voltaire as its mouthpiece was too strong for them.

Another difficulty lay in the fact that Lavaysse *père* was so terrified by the Parliament of Toulouse that he took much persuading before he would appear openly on the side of Voltaire and as a witness for his own son. Then, too, the natural passionate eagerness of Madame Calas to get back her daughters, immediately and before the time was ripe, had to be curbed; and, far worse than all, that miserable Toulouse Parliament had so far entirely declined to furnish any of the papers concerning the trial, or even the decree of arrest.

MADEMOISELLE CLAIRON

From an Engraving after a Picture by Carle Van Loo

In September, Élie de Beaumont was ready with an able "Memoir" on the case, signed by fifteen of his brother barristers. He showed that there were "three impossibilities" in the way of Calas having murdered his son.

"The fourth," said Voltaire, "is that of resisting your arguments." The "Memoir" was naturally more technical than Voltaire's, but it was not more clever, nor half so moving.

Another friend of the case, the brave Lasalle, who had become "the public *avocat* for Calas in all the houses of Toulouse," and had been challenged to a duel on the subject by a brother magistrate, was also in Paris in November. In December, through the untiring exertions of the Duchesse d'Enville, herself a mother, Nanette and Rose, the daughters, were restored to Madame Calas.

On December 29th, Voltaire wrote that this restoration was an infallible test of the progress of the case. But, he added, "it is shameful that the affair drags so long."

Drags so long! Through the kindly veil that hides the future, even a Voltaire's keen eyes could not penetrate. For nine months he had now dreamt Calas, worked Calas, lived Calas. Every letter he wrote is full of him. For that one man whom he had never seen, and who died as, after all, thousands of others had died, the victim of religious hatred, Voltaire forgot the drama which his soul loved, and that aggravating Jean Jacques's latest novel, "Émile," which his soul scorned. Calas! Calas! For those nine months the thing beat upon his brain as regularly and unremittingly as the sea breaks on the shore. For Calas was more than a case: he was a type.

Voltaire had first thought that he saw in that dreadful story *l'infâme* in the garb of a cold and cruel Calvinism, changing the tenderest instincts of the human heart into a ferocity which made a father the murderer of his own son. And then he had discovered that it was that old *l'infâme* he knew better—*l'infâme* who in the person of priest and magistrate kept the people ignorant, and then inflamed that ignorance for their shameful ends.

What Calas had suffered, others might suffer. While he was unavenged, while that criminal law and procedure which condemned him went unreformed, while his judges were not rendered execrable to other men and hateful to themselves, who was safe?

To Voltaire the cause of Calas was the cause of Tolerance; that Tolerance which was the principle and the passion of his life.

CHAPTER XXXVII

THE "TREATISE ON TOLERANCE"

ONE of the disadvantages of biography as compared with fiction is, that in real life many events occur simultaneously, and the dramatic effect of a crisis is often spoilt by that crisis being extended over a long period of time and being interrupted by trivialities.

The Calas case, at whose "dragging" Voltaire had cried out at the end of nine months, lasted for three years—a period which is certainly a severe test of enthusiasm. Voltaire's triumphantly survived that test. At the end of those three years he was only more eager, passionate, and laborious than he had been at the beginning.

But in the meantime there were Ferney, Tourney, and Délices to manage; Madame Denis always needing amusement and Marie Corneille always needing instruction; that busy, hot-headed rival, Rousseau, to be taken into account, to say nothing of friends and enemies, visitors and plays.

On March 25, 1762—just about the time when the first rumours of the Calas story reached Voltaire—"Olympie" took what may be called its trial trip at Ferney. Two or three hundred people sobbed all through it in the most satisfactory manner, and all felt cheerful enough to enjoy a ball and a supper afterwards.

In April, these enthusiastic amateurs were once more delighted by a visit from the great actor Lekain. He had been at Délices in 1755; but there was a beautiful new little theatre at Ferney now, where "Olympie" was played again. Lekain looked on as a critic; and Voltaire did the same, being debarred from his dear acting by a cold in the head. "Tancred" was played too, and when there came that line:

Oh cursed judges! in whose feeble hands—

the whole house got upon its feet and howled itself hoarse. It would not have been like Voltaire to hide from his friends, even if he could have done so, a subject that so possessed him as the subject of Calas. "It is the only reparation," he said, writing of the scene, "that has yet been made to the memory of the most unhappy of fathers."

Charming the audience with her soft voice and round girlish freshness, Marie Corneille was now always one of the actresses. She had by this time a pretty *dot* as well as a pretty face; and Papa Voltaire, in addition to the proceeds of the Corneille Commentary, had settled a little estate upon her. A suitor naturally appeared soon upon the *tapis*. But though he was warmly recommended by the d'Argentals, M. Vaugrenant de Cormont seems to have been chiefly remarkable for large debts, a very mean father, and the delusion that he was conferring a very great honour on Mademoiselle by marrying her. He had taken up his abode at Ferney, and when he had received his *congé* was not to be dislodged without difficulty. Mademoiselle was serenely indifferent to him; so no harm was done.

Marrying and giving in marriage was to the fore in the Voltaire *ménage* just then. In May, Madame de Fontaine became the wife of that Marquis de Florian who had stayed with her at Ferney and long been her lover. Voltaire was delighted—not in the least on the score of morality—but because he thought the pair would suit each other, which they did.

On June 11, 1762, "Émile, or Education," Jean Jacques's new novel, was publicly burnt in Paris. Nine days after, it was condemned to the same fate in Geneva. "Émile" expresses in nervous and inspired language some of those theories which Voltaire's friend, Dr. Tronchin, had worked so hard to bring into practice. It was not so much the education of children that "Émile" dealt with as the education of parents. To abolish the fatal system of foster-motherhood, instituted that the real mothers might have more time for their lovers, their toilettes, and their pleasures, to portray a child brought up in natural and virtuous surroundings—even an eighteenth-century censor could not have found matter meet for burning in this. But "Émile" was only a scapegoat. "The Social Contract," published a little earlier, was what the authorities really attacked.

Neither the publication of "Émile," nor its burning, particularly attracted Voltaire's notice at first. Like Lasalle, he was all Calas. On July 21st, he wrote indifferently to Cideville that Rousseau had been banished from Berne and is now at Neufchâtel, "thinking he is always right, and regarding other people with pity." For the "Profession of Faith of a Savoyard Vicar" which was "imbedded in 'Émile,'" Voltaire indeed not only felt, but expressed, a very sincere admiration. But your "Eloïsa" and your "Émile," and your hysterics generally, why, they bore me, my dear Jean Jacques! And you are so dreadfully long-winded, you know! However, the "Savoyard Vicar" had shown that Rousseau had the courage of his unbelief. It was the kind of heroism in which Voltaire was not going to be behindhand. In July, 1762, appeared his "Sermon of Fifty," whose excellent brevity was a reproach and a corrective to the four immense volumes of "Émile," and whose virulent attack upon the Jewish faith was at least as outspoken and unmistakable as the Vicar's "Profession."

This fifty-page pamphlet is noticeable as the first of Voltaire's works which is openly anti-Christian. Goethe declared that for it, in his youthful fanaticism, he would have strangled the author if he could have got hold of him.

Rousseau, of course, took "The Sermon of Fifty" amiss, as he was fast coming to take amiss everything Voltaire did. Jean Jacques was quite persuaded, for instance, that it was Voltaire who had incited the Council of Geneva to burn "Émile"; and, presently, that it was Voltaire's hand which guided the pen of Robert Tronchin's "Letters from the Country," which favoured the burning of "Émile," and to which Rousseau was to make reply in the brilliant and splendid inspiration of his famous "Letters from the Mountain."

The truth seems to have been that Voltaire laughed at Jean-Jacques instead of losing his temper with him; or, rather, that he lost his temper with him for an occasional five minutes, and then laughed and forgave him. Végobre, the lawyer, who is described as having "no imagination" to invent such stories, was once breakfasting at Ferney when some letters came detailing the persecution inflicted on Rousseau for his "Vicar." "Let him come here!" cried Voltaire. "Let him come here! I would receive him like my own son."

The Prince de Ligne also records how, after Voltaire had vehemently declared that Jean Jacques was a monster and a scoundrel for whom no law ever invented was sufficiently severe, he added, "Where is he, poor wretch? Hunted out of Neufchâtel, I dare say. Let him come here! Bring him here: he is welcome to everything *I* have."

All the sentiments were genuine, no doubt. It would have been perfectly in Voltaire's character to abuse Rousseau by every epithet in a peculiarly rich vituperative vocabulary, and to have received him with all generous hospitality and thoughtful kindness as a guest in his house for months; to have quarrelled with him and abused him again, and once more to have received him as a brother.

After all, Voltaire was not a perfect hater.

That sodden, worthless Theriot came to Délices for a three months' visit in July, with all *his* treachery and ingratitude amply forgotten; and in October that very showy hero, Richelieu, who was always in money debt to Voltaire, descended upon his creditor with a suite of no fewer than forty persons. They had to be accommodated at Tourney, and *fêtes* and theatricals devised for their master's benefit. The Duchesse d'Enville and the Duke of Villars were also staying with Voltaire, who was quite delighted to discover that a Richelieu of sixty-six still kept up his character for gallantry, and to surprise him at the feet of a charming Madame Ménage, a Tronchin patient. The pretty face and wit of Madame Cramer also quite vanquished the susceptible elderly heart of the conqueror. Voltaire offered to get rid—temporarily—of her husband. But Richelieu had reckoned, not without his host indeed, but without his hostess. Sprightly Madame Cramer laughed in his face.

The first authorised publication of a work which had been suggested at Richelieu's supper-table thirty-two years earlier belongs, by some *bizarrerie* of destiny, to this 1762, which also saw the noblest work of Voltaire's life—the defence of Calas and the preaching of the Gospel of Tolerance.

Whoso has followed its author's history has also followed the "Pucelle's."

Alternately delight and torment, danger and refuge; now being read in the Cirey bathroom to the ecstatic bliss of Madame de Graffigny, now passed from hand to hand and from salon to salon in Paris, now being copied in Prussia, and then burnt in Geneva, hidden in Collini's breeches at Frankfort, and stolen from Émilie's effects by Mademoiselle du Thil—the adventures of the "Pucelle" would form a volume.

Considered intrinsically, it is at once Voltaire's shame and fame. It is to be feared that there are still many people who are only interested in him as the author of the "Pucelle"; while there are others to whom the fact that he wrote it blots out his noble work for humanity, and the bold part he played in the advancement of that civilisation which they, and all men, enjoy to-day.

That Voltaire took in vain the name of that purest of heroines, Joan of Arc, is at least partially forgivable. He did not know, and could not have known, the facts of her life as everybody knows them to-day. His offences against decency may be judged in that well-worn couplet:

Immodest words admit of no defence,
And want of decency is want of sense.

Only one excuse need even be offered. Voltaire wrote to the taste of his age. As the coarse horseplay and boisterous mirth of the novels of Fielding perfectly portrayed humour as understood by eighteenth-century England, so the gay indelicacies of the "Pucelle" represent humour as understood by eighteenth-century France.

The fact that women, and even women who were at least nominally respectable, were not ashamed to listen to and laugh at those airy, shameful *doubles ententes*, proves that the thing was to the taste of the time; as the fact that "Tom Jones" and "Joseph Andrews" were read aloud to select circles of admiring English ladies proves that Fielding likewise had not mistaken the taste of his public.

The "Pucelle" is infinitely bright, rollicking, and amusing. Voltaire's indecency was never that of a diseased mind like Swift. He flung not a little philosophy into his licence, and through sparkling banter whispered his message to his age. Those ten thousand lines of burlesque terminated, it has been said, the domination of legends over the human mind. Condorcet goes so far as to declare that readers need only see in the author of the "Pucelle" the enemy of hypocrisy and superstition.

But the fact seems to be that though Voltaire was constantly hitting out, as he always was hitting, at hypocrisy and superstition, the blows this time were only incidental; and that he wrote first to amuse himself, and then to amuse his world.

That he succeeded in both cases, condemns both it and him.

If Voltaire's connection with Madame du Châtelet was a blot on his moral character, the "Pucelle" was a darker blot. It spread wider to do harm. His passionate and tireless work for the liberation of men's souls and bodies, for light and for right, make such blots infinitely to be regretted. That the best work in the world is not done by morally the best men is a hard truth, but it is a truth.

Of the "Pucelle" it can only be said,

But yet the pity of it, Iago!—O Iago, the pity of it!

On February 12th of 1763 the man who had not only written the most scandalous of epics, but had tended Marie Corneille with as honest a respect and affection as if she had been his own innocent daughter, married her to M. Dupuits, cornet of dragoons, handsome, delightful, three-and-twenty, and head over ears in love with Mademoiselle. M. Dupuits united to his other charms the fact that his estates joined Ferney, and that he was quite sufficiently well off. One little trouble there had been. Père Corneille disapproved not only of this marriage, but of any marriage, for his daughter. Voltaire sent him a handsome present of money to assuage his wounded feelings, but did not invite him to the ceremony lest young Dupuits should have cause to be ashamed of his father-in-law, and that graceless Duke of Villars, who was also at Ferney, should laugh at him. The ceremony took place at midnight on February 12th, and the wedding dinner was at least magnificent enough to give Mama Denis as Marie called her, an indigestion. There were no partings. The young couple took up their abode at Ferney, where their love-making gave the keenest delight to a large element of romance still left in Voltaire's old heart, and where presently their children were born.

It was not wonderful that the good fortunes of Marie Corneille should have incited many other offshoots of that family to "come pecking about," as Voltaire said, to see if there was anything for them. Only a month after she was married, Claude Étienne Corneille, who was in the direct line of descent from the great Corneille, and not in the indirect, like lucky Marie, appeared at Ferney. But Voltaire, though he thought Claude an honest man and was sorry for him, could not adopt the whole clan. His mood was still adoptive, however.

In this very year he took to live with him Mademoiselle Dupuits, Marie's sister-in-law; and a certain Father Adam. Mademoiselle Dupuits was not less pretty than Marie, and very much more intelligent. Several of the noble Ferney visitors amused themselves by falling in love with her.

On March 2d, Voltaire had written, "We are free of the Jesuits, but I do not know that it is such a great good."

The suppression of the Order of Ignatius (it was not confirmed by royal edict until 1764) first occurred to him as a splendid tilt at *l'infâme*—as the happiest omen for the future that those who had been so intolerant should themselves be tolerated no more. But reflection cooled him. What is the good of being rid of Jesuit foxes if one falls to Jansenist wolves? "We expel the Jesuits," he wrote to that good old friend of his, the Duchess of Saxe-Gotha, in July, "and remain the prey of the convulsionists. It is only Protestant princes who behave sensibly. They keep priests in their right place."

None of these reflections taken singly, nor all of them taken together, prevented Voltaire from receiving into his house—"as chaplain," he said sardonically—the Jesuit priest called Father Adam, whom he had known at Colmar in 1754, and whose acquaintance he had since renewed at neighbouring Ornex. To be sure, Voltaire had no need to be afraid of any priestly influence, especially from one of whom he was fond of saying, that though Father Adam, he was not the first of men.

Like the Protestant princes, Voltaire knew very well how to keep *his* priest in his proper place. The Father was an indolent man, with a little fortune of his own and a rather quarrelsome disposition. But he made himself useful at Ferney for thirteen years by entertaining the visitors and playing chess with his lord and master. One of the visitors declared that Adam was Jesuit enough to let himself be beaten at the game—his opponent so dearly loved to win! But another, La Harpe, who was at

Ferney a whole year, denies this and declares that Voltaire frequently lost the game, and his temper, and when he saw things were going badly with him told anecdotes to distract his adversary's attention. A third authority states that when the game was practically lost to him, M. de Voltaire would begin gently humming a tune. If Adam did not take the hint and retire at once, Voltaire flung the chessmen one after another at the Father's head. Prudent Adam, however, usually left at once. When Voltaire had become calmer, he would call out profanely, "Adam, where art thou?" The Father came back; and the game was resumed as if nothing had happened.

Another member of a colony, which, as Voltaire said, was enough to make one die of laughter, was the fat Swiss servant, Barbara or Bonne-Baba, who showed her contempt for her illustrious master quite plainly and to his great enjoyment, and assured him she could not understand how anybody could be silly enough to think he had an ounce of common-sense.

If it was a laughable household, it was, as its master also said, a household that laughed from morning till night, and could be, that lively cripple d'Aumard included, as light-hearted as childhood.

But through all, never forgotten for a moment or put aside for a day, was the affair of Calas.

On March 7, 1763, that affair had its first triumph. On that day the Council of Paris met at Versailles, the Chancellor presiding, and all the councillors and ministers, religious and civil, attending, and decreed that there should be a new trial and that the Toulouse Parliament should produce the records of the old. Madame Calas and her two girls were present. All through the winter it had been considered an honour to call upon them, or to meet them at the d'Argentals' house. Councillors and officials vied with each other in thoughtful attentions to them all. During the sitting of the court one of the girls fainted, and was nearly killed with kindness. Some person, thought to be young Lavaysse, with a style charmingly candid and simple, has written an account of the day. Not only was the court "all Calas"—its eighty-four members unanimously voted for the case to be retried—but her Catholic Majesty, Marie Leczinska herself, who had by no means forgotten to hate their great *avocat*, Voltaire, received Madame Calas and her daughters with kindness. The King himself had "formally approved" that the papers of the procedure at Toulouse should be sent to the Council of Paris. The hostile influence of Saint-Florentin had been more than counteracted by the favourable, though secret, influence of Choiseul.

When Voltaire, waiting feverishly at Ferney, heard the long-hoped-for decree, his heart gave one great leap of joy. "Then there *is* justice on the earth; there *is* humanity," he wrote. "Men are not all rogues, as people say;

... it seems to me that the day of the Council of State is a great day for philosophy."

He eagerly concluded that this at last was the beginning of the end. But there was still infinite room for that slow courage called patience.

Now being passed from hand to hand in Paris, and having been so passed since the beginning of the year 1763, was what may be called the fruit of the Calas case: fruit of which men to-day may still eat and live: the pamphlet of two hundred pages which advanced by many years the reign of justice, of mercy, and of humanity—the "Treatise on Tolerance."

That sermon, of which the text is Calas, is one of the most powerful indictments ever written against the religious who have enough religion to hate and persecute, but not enough to love and succour. Voltaire was no Protestant, but that "Treatise" helped the "definite affranchisement" of the Protestant in Catholic countries as no party tract ever did. It gave the fatal blow to that "Gothic legislation" which, if it was dying, still showed now and then a superhuman strength in acts of fiendish barbarism. Sooner or later, said Choiseul, such seed as is sown in Voltaire's Gospel of Tolerance *must* bear fruit. What if the author of it had thrown decency to the winds in the "Pucelle"? What if, basing his attack on seemingly irreconcilable statements and incorrect dates, he had in keen mockery attacked the Scripture and Christianity? Not the less "the true Christian, like the true philosopher, will agree that in making tolerance and humanity prevail, Voltaire, whether he wished it or no, served the religion of the God of peace and mercy: and, instead of anger, will feel a reverent admiration for the ways of a Providence which, for such a work, chose such a workman."

Voltaire did not avow his little Treatise. What censor would or could have licensed such a thing? For a long time it was not even printed. By Voltaire? What could make you think so? The old owl of Ferney screwed up his brilliant eyes and chuckled. "Mind you do not impute to me the little book on Tolerance.... It will not be by me. It could not be. It is by some good soul who loves persecution as he loves the colic."

That he foresaw it would be one of his best passports to posterity, did not make him in the least degree more anxious to own it to his contemporaries. Abundant experience had proved to him that if it is "an ill lot to be a man of letters at all, there is something still more dangerous in loving the truth."

So through the year 1763 the "Treatise on Tolerance" was passed from hand to hand in Paris: by a good priest, you understand; by nobody in particular. And at Ferney, Voltaire, having preached tolerance, practised it.

At the convent into which Nanette Calas had been thrown was a good Superior who had loved and pitied the girl and poured out upon her the thwarted maternal instincts of her woman's heart. It is very pleasant to see how a hot partisan like Voltaire not only gave the Sister her due, but dwelt tenderly on her tenderness; sent on to his brethren, the philosophers, her kind little letters to Nanette; and warmed his old heart at the pure flame of the affection of this "good nun of the Visitation."

Then, too, when in June the liberal-minded citizens of Geneva appealed against the condemnation of rival Rousseau's "Émile," and when on August 8th that condemnation was revoked at their request, Voltaire was quite as delighted as if Jean Jacques had always been his dearest friend, and as if he had thought anything about that hysterical "Émile," except the "Profession of the Savoyard Vicar," worth the paper it was written on. Tolerance! Tolerance!

About the same time he produced the "Catechism of an Honest Man," which had a like burden; and before the year 1763 was out he was deeply engaged in helping other unfortunates whom the case of Calas and that "Treatise" threw at his feet.

In 1740, a daring Protestant gentleman of that fatal Languedoc, called Espinas, or Espinasse, gave supper and a bed to a minister of his faith. For this heinous crime he was condemned to the galleys for life, and had been there three-and-twenty years when his story reached Ferney. Through Voltaire's exertions he was released in 1763, and came to Switzerland, where his wife and children were living as paupers, on public charity. After interceding passionately for them for not less than three years, Voltaire succeeded in getting back a small part of the property which Espinas had forfeited on his imprisonment.

After Espinas came the case of Chaumont. In February, 1764, Voltaire was writing to Végobre to say that Choiseul had delivered from the galleys one Chaumont, whose crime had consisted in listening to an open-air Protestant preacher—"praying to God in bad French." He had companions in irons whom Voltaire's power and pity could not free. But Chaumont himself came to Ferney to thank his benefactor; and all Voltaire's little *entourage* made him compliments, including Father Adam.

Though that "Tolerance" was not yet tolerated in Paris; though at the beginning of 1764 it was forbidden to go through the post, as if it contained the germs of some infectious disease; though Calas was still unexculpated, and even powerful Choiseul could not push his authority far enough to liberate the innocent companions of Chaumont, still Voltaire thought that he saw light in the sky, and in the east the beginning of a beautiful day. "Everything I see," he wrote in prophetic utterance on April

2d, "sows the seeds of a Revolution which must infallibly come. I shall not have the pleasure of beholding it. The French reach everything late, but they do reach it at last. Young people are lucky: they will see great things." And again: "I shall not cease to preach Tolerance upon the housetops ... until persecution is no more. The progress of right is slow, the roots of prejudice deep. I shall never see the fruits of my efforts, but they are seeds which must one day germinate."

Tolerance! Tolerance! Between writing it, living it, dreaming it, the thing might have become a monomania, a possession. Only its great apostle was also a Frenchman—the most versatile son of the most versatile people on earth.

At the end of 1763 he had been privately circulating in Paris a gay novelette in verse called "Gertrude, or the Education of a Daughter"; and a little later he was reviewing English books for a Parisian literary paper.

Then, too, in the autumn of 1763 the young Prince de Ligne— eighteen years old, bright, shallow, amusing, "courtier of all Courts, favourite of all kings, friend of all philosophers"—had been staying at Ferney. It is said that before his arrival Voltaire, dreadfully fearing he should be bored, took some strong medicine, so that he could say (truthfully this time) he was too ill to appear. The very self-pleased and much-admired young Prince is now chiefly known to the world by the account he has given of Voltaire *intime.*

He writes vividly both of his host's greatness and littleness; tells how he loved the English, bad puns, and his best clothes; how his torrents of visitors wearied him, and what artful designs he invented to get rid of them; how good he was to the poor; how "he made all who were capable of it think and speak"; was charmed to find a musical talent in his shoemaker— "*Mon Dieu!* Sir, I put you at *my* feet—I ought to beat yours"—how he thought no one too obscure and insignificant to cheer with the liveliest wit and the most amazing vivacity ever possessed by a man of sixty-nine.

Ligne says he was quite delighted with the "sublime reply" of a regimental officer to the question "What is your religion?"

"My parents brought me up in the Roman faith." "Splendid answer!" chuckles Voltaire. "He does not say what *he* is!"

Early in 1764, young Boufflers, the son of that Madame de Boufflers who was the mistress of King Stanislas, and perhaps Madame du Châtelet's predecessor in the heart of Saint-Lambert, also came to Ferney. Boufflers was travelling *incognito* as a young French artist. He did not forget to write and tell his mother of his warm reception by her old acquaintance. Voltaire, with that rare adaptability of his, easily accommodated himself to his guest's youth and treated him *en camarade*; while Boufflers, on his part, drew with his artist's pencil a clever rough sketch of his host when he was losing at chess with Father Adam.

A further distraction from "Tolerance" and the Calas came in the shape of the first public performance of "Olympie" in Paris, on March 17, 1764. It had already been named by the public "O l'impie!"—a title the author was by no means going to apply to himself; while as for it applying to the piece—"Nothing is more pious. I am only afraid that it will not be good for anything but to be played in a convent of nuns on the abbess's birthday."

"Olympie" was well received. But it was feeble, in spite of those many alterations of which the indefatigable author vigorously said "You must correct if you are eighty. I cannot bear old men who say 'I have taken my bent.' Well, then, you old fools, take another!"

He also said that he had written it chiefly to put in notes at the end on suicide, the duties of priests, and other subjects in which he was interested; so it was not wonderful that even his friends had to own it a failure.

When another play of his, called "The Triumvirate," was performed in July—purporting to be the work of an ex-Jesuit, and having cost its dauntless master more trouble in rewriting and altering than any of his other pieces—it was confessed a disaster by everyone.

But, after all, both pieces had served as a distraction to their author; so they had their worth and use.

Another event in the spring of 1764 also changed the current of his thoughts, turned them back to his far-away youth, and to the strifes and weariness of a Court he had renounced for ever. On April 15th died Madame de Pompadour. Voltaire was not behindhand in acknowledging that he owed her much. To be sure, she had supported "that detestable Crébillon's detestable 'Catilina,'" and had not been always a faithful friend in other respects; but she had been as faithful as her position permitted. She had had, too "a just mind": she "thought aright."

Of the easy manner in which Voltaire and his century regarded her morals it need only be said that it affords an excellent insight into theirs.

"Cornélie-Chiffon" (as Voltaire called Marie Dupuits) "gave us a daughter" in June. Before that date, Mademoiselle Dupuits, her sister-in-law, portioned out of the "Corneille Commentary," had been married. Ferney was the resort of innumerable English, who came to see M. de Voltaire's plays, and told him what they thought of them with their native candour. The first volume of "The Philosophical Dictionary" slipped out in

July, 1764, anonymously, "smelling horribly of the fagot." Voltaire of course swore industriously that he had nothing to do with that "infernal Portatif," and of course deceived nobody.

In September, he smuggled it, by a very underhand trick and with the connivance of some booksellers of Geneva, into that town.

His friends, the Tronchins, were so angry at the *ruse* that through their agency the "Dictionary" was burnt there in the same month by the executioner.

And then that great work, the rehabilitation of the Calas, was completed at last. In June, 1764, the new trial had been begun. On March 9, 1765, exactly three years since he had paid for it the extreme penalty of that savage law, Calas was declared innocent of the murder of his son. With his innocence was re-established that of his whole family, of Jeannette Viguière, and of young Lavaysse. The accused had to constitute themselves prisoners at the Conciergerie as a matter of form. There all their friends visited them, including Damilaville, who wrote of the visit to Voltaire. Still well known is Carmontel's famous engraving of this prison scene, with Lavaysse reading to the family, including Jeannette, his "Memoir" on their case.

The Council who tried them had five sittings, each four hours in length, and a sixth which lasted eight hours. There were forty judges who were unanimous in their verdict—"Perfectly innocent."

As all the money subscribed for Madame Calas by Voltaire's efforts had been swallowed up in law expenses and long journeys, these forty judges petitioned the King for a grant to her and her children. And his Majesty presented them with handsome gifts of money. The family then asked him if he would object to them suing the Toulouse magistrates for damages.

But of this course Voltaire disapproved. "Let well alone," he said in substance: and they did.

It must be observed that not only had the sullen Parliament of Toulouse put every obstacle in the way of the new trial taking place, but that it never ratified the judgment of the Council of Paris. But that mattered little. The worst that Toulouse could do was done.

One of the magistrates, the infamous David de Beaudrigue, "paid dearly for the blood of the Calas." In February, 1764, he was degraded from his office. He afterwards committed suicide. That innocent blood was indeed on him and his children. His grandson fell a victim to the fury of the tigers of the Revolution, who had not forgotten the drama of the Rue des Filatiers.

When the courier came with the news of the verdict to Ferney, young Donat Calas was with Voltaire, and Voltaire said that his old eyes wept as many tears as the boy's. In a passion of delight he wrote to Cideville that this was the most splendid fifth act ever seen on a stage.

But he had not done with the Calas yet. The King's gifts of money were insufficient. So Voltaire got up subscriptions for engravings of Carmontel's picture, and made all his rich friends subscribe handsomely for copies. One hung over his own bed for the rest of his life.

Peter and Donat Calas settled in Geneva. When in 1770 their mother and Lavaysse visited them there, they all came on to Ferney. Voltaire said that he cried like a child. He never forgot to do everything in his power to benefit and help the two young men, and gave at least one of them employment in his weaving industry when he established it at Ferney.

The Calas case was not without wide results on current literature, art, and the drama.

Coquerel, who wrote a history of the case, states that there are no fewer than one hundred and thirteen publications relating to it. It forms the subject of ten plays and "seven long poems."

Besides Carmontel's engraving, there are pictures of "Jean Calas saying Good-bye to his Family," "Voltaire promising his support to the Calas Family," and many others.

But its most important, its one immortal result, was the "Treatise on Tolerance"—the work of the man without whom Calas would never have been avenged, and *l'infâme* been left unchecked till the Revolution.

It is hardly possible to overestimate the nobility of Voltaire's part in the redemption of the Calas.

A man who did not love him said justly that such a deed would cover a multitude of sins. "*Oh mon amie! le bel emploi du génie!*" wrote Diderot to Mademoiselle Voland.... "What are the Calas to him? Why should he stop the work he loves to defend them? If there were a Christ, surely Voltaire would be saved."

When one reflects on the enormous expenditure of time, labour, and money the case required of him, and the fact that he thoroughly knew the value of each, Diderot's words do not seem greatly exaggerated.

To suppose he had any thought of his own glory in the matter is not reasonable. He persistently gave the lion's share of the credit to Élie de

Beaumont. He himself had already as much fame as man could want. If he *had* wanted more, he knew to it a thousand avenues quicker and safer than the long Via Dolorosa of a legal reparation.

That kind of fame would only endanger his person and prestige, and make his chances of being well received by King and Court weaker than ever.

But that he *did* recognise Calas as one of the best works of his nobler self seems likely from a trifling incident.

Thirteen years later, on his last visit to Paris, someone, seeing the crowds that surrounded him whenever he went out into the street, asked a poor woman who this person was who was so much followed.

"It is the saviour of the Calas," she replied.

No flattery, no honour, no acclamation of that glorious time gave Voltaire, it is said, so keen a pleasure as that simple answer.

CHAPTER XXXVIII

THE SIRVENS AND LA BARRE

DESNOIRESTERRES has well observed that this mad eighteenth century produced the extraordinary anomaly of being at once that of scepticism and intolerance, of the most degraded superstition and the most barefaced irreligion. It might be thought—it is generally thought—that persecution would certainly not proceed from persons who were too indifferent to their faith to make the slightest attempt to live up to it. But if the history of religious hatred be closely followed, it will be seen that it is precisely these persons who are the cruellest persecutors. Perhaps they act on that old principle of compensation—"Give me the desire of my soul, and the gratification of my flesh, and by the scaffold, the torture, and the wheel, I will bring souls to the faith *I* only profess." There seems no other explanation of the fact that this "rotten age whose armies fled without a fight before a handful of men; this age which laughed at everything and cared for nothing but wit," was as fiercely intolerant and besottedly bigot as the age of Ignatius Loyola and Catherine de' Medici.

The case of Calas was but one of many. It was not finished when another, scarcely less sombre and terrible, was brought under Voltaire's notice.

In 1760 there lived near fanatic Toulouse, at a place called Castres, a Protestant family of the name of Sirven. Sirven *père*, aged about fifty-one, was a professional *feudiste*; that is to say, he was a person learned in feudal tenures, who kept registers and explained the obsolete terms of ancient leases, and thus was brought much in contact with the great families of the province. Thoroughly honest, honourable, and respectable, his wife shared these qualities with him. They had three daughters—Marie Anne, who was now married, Jeanne and Elizabeth, who both lived at home.

Elizabeth, the youngest, was feeble-minded: but on that very account—on that old, tender parental principle of making up by love for the cruelty of fortune—she was the dearest to her parents. On March 6, 1760, the poor girl suddenly disappeared. After vainly hunting for her all day, when Sirven reached his home at night he was told that the Bishop of Castres desired to see him. He went. The Bishop informed him that Elizabeth, whose deficient brain was certainly not equal to weighing the *pros* and *cons* of different religions, had ardently desired to become a Roman Catholic, and that to receive instruction in that faith she had been placed in the Convent of the Black Ladies. The poor father received the news more calmly than might have been expected. He said that he had no idea his daughter wished to change her religion; but that if the change was to be for her good and happiness, he would not oppose it.

The situation was a strange one. But it had a very common solution. The Bishop had a strong-minded sister who had caught that "epidemic of the time," which the infected called religious zeal.

Meanwhile poor Elizabeth in her convent, having been first "taught her catechism by blows," as Voltaire said, began, like many another weak intellect under strong suggestion, to see visions and to dream dreams. She became, in short, what a nun might call a saint, but what a doctor would call a lunatic. The Black Ladies declared that she implored them to corporally chastise her for the good of her soul; and it was certainly a fact that when she was returned to her parents in the October of 1760, quite insane, her body was "covered with the marks of the convent whip." If her father complained loudly of her treatment, such complaints, though natural, were infinitely imprudent. My Lord Bishop and the authorities kept a very keen official eye on M. Sirven, and harried him on the subject of his daughter whenever a chance offered. The sheep had gone back to the wolves, the brand to the burning. Rome never yet sat down with folded hands, as other Churches have done, and calmly watched her children desert her.

In the July of 1761 the Sirvens moved to a village called St. Alby, that Sirven might be near some business on which he was engaged.

On December 17, 1761, when he was staying at the château of a M. d'Esperandieu, for whom he was working, Elizabeth slipped out of her home at night, and never returned. Her mother and sister had at once given notice of her disappearance, and prayed that a search might be made. Sirven, called home, arrived on the morning of the 18th, and caused a still further search to be prosecuted. But in vain. A fortnight passed. On January 3, 1762, the unhappy father, who fancied, not unnaturally, that Elizabeth might have been decoyed away by her Roman friends, had to go in pursuit of his trade to a place called Burlats.

That same night the body of Elizabeth was discovered in a well at St. Alby.

The authorities were at once communicated with, and the judge of Mazamet, the David de Beaudrigue of the case. The body was taken to the Hôtel de Ville. There was abundant local testimony to the effect that the poor girl, had often been seen looking into the well, muttering to herself.

The case was clearly one of suicide or misadventure. Either was possible. But that it was one of the two was morally certain.

A lodger in the Sirvens' house at St. Alby could swear that only the footsteps of one person had been heard descending the stairs of the house on the night of December 17th, before Jeanne had hastened to those lodgers and told them of Elizabeth's flight. In addition to this, while the poor girl herself had been tall and strong, her mother was feeble and old; her married sister, who was staying with her parents, was also feeble and in ill-health; and Elizabeth could easily have resisted Jeanne, had she attempted, unaided, to be her murderess.

Singly, then, none of the three could have killed Elizabeth; and that they had done it together, apart from the inherent improbability and the inhuman nature of such a crime, there was not an iota of evidence to prove. As in the case of Calas, no cries had been heard, and there were no signs of a struggle.

As for Sirven himself, he could declare an *alibi*. On the night in question he had supped and slept at the château of M. d'Esperandieu.

But such evidence, or any evidence, weighed nothing with a people who had at the moment innocent Calas in irons in the dungeon of Toulouse. "It passes for fact among the Catholics of the province," wrote Voltaire in irony that came very near to being the literal truth, "that it is one of the chief points of the Protestant religion that fathers and mothers should hang, strangle, or drown all their children whom they suspect of having any *penchant* for the Roman faith." Sirven's public, like Calas's, had "a need of dramatic emotion enough to change truth into a legend."

What use to examine the body? No facts will alter *our* conviction. Beaudrigue, savage bigot though he was, had known his profession; the Beaudrigue of this case, Trinquier, the judge of Mazamet, was a little ignorant tradesman, who through the whole affair showed himself to be a tool in clever hands, a wire pulled—at Rome.

At first, Sirven was mad enough to rely on his own innocence, and the innocence of his family, to save them all. January 6 to 10, 1762, was spent in examining the witnesses. The honest Catholic villagers of St. Alby bore testimony to a man in favour of Sirven. But the attitude of the doctors who examined the body might well have alarmed him. It alarmed his friends; on their advice he employed an *avocat*, Jalabert.

Jalabert was devoted and expert. But the devotion of a saint and the brilliancy of a genius would not have helped the Sirvens.

They were charged with the murder of Elizabeth, and instantly took their decision. Proofs had not freed Calas—why should they save them? Remembering the fury of the people of Toulouse, "they fled while there was yet time."

They stayed at their old home, Castres, at the house of a friend, for one night. Under the cover of the next they walked through rain, mire, and darkness to five-miles distant Roquecombe. So far, they had at least been together.

But they saw very clearly now that they could not hope to escape notice if they travelled *en famille*.

On January 21st or 22d, the unhappy father tore himself from them, and for a month remained hidden among the mountains, only ten miles from Castres. Then he moved on. Through the snows of an icy winter he crossed the frontier, arrived at Geneva, and early in the April of 1762, at Lausanne.

His family, after having endured infinite perils and hardships, arrived there in June. On the way, among the glaciers and in the bitter cold of a mountain winter, Marie Anne had borne a dead child.

They had one consolation. Their flight was not unnecessary. Three Declarations had been published against them; though it was not until March 29, 1764, that the court formally sentenced the parents to be hanged, and the daughters to witness that execution, and then to perpetual banishment under pain of death.

On September 11th this sentence was carried out in effigy.

By that time the generous republicans of Berne had given Madame and her daughters, who were living at Lausanne, a little pension; their property having, of course, been confiscated to the King. Père Sirven was working at his trade at Geneva, and so was a near neighbour of Voltaire's.

Moultou, the friend and correspondent of Rousseau, brought the Sirvens one day to Ferney. Voltaire already knew their history. But the time was not ripe for another Quixotic knight-errantry. Calas was not yet vindicated. Apart from the inordinate amount of work it would entail, to take a second case in hand might militate against the interests of the first. Then the affair of the Sirvens would present far greater legal difficulties. They had fled the kingdom. They would have to be acquitted, if they were to be acquitted, not by the Parliament of Paris, but by the Parliament of Toulouse. And Voltaire was too much of an artist not to be perfectly aware that this cause would not have the *éclat* and the dramatic effects of the Calas'. "It lacked a scaffold."

But when the Sirvens clung with tears about his feet and implored him, as the saviour of Calas, to save them also—"What was I to do? What would you have done in my place?" "It is impossible to picture so much innocence and so much wretchedness." When the d'Argentals reproached him as unwise, "Here are too many parricide lawsuits indeed," he wrote. "But, my dear angels, whose fault is that?" And, again, as his excuse, "I have only done in the horrible disasters of Calas and the Sirvens what all men do: I have followed my bent. That of a philosopher is not to pity the unfortunate, but to serve them." He records himself how a priest said to him, "Why interfere? Let the dead bury their dead"; and how he replied, "I have found an Israelite by the roadside: let me give him a little oil and wine for his wounds. You are the Levite: let me be the Samaritan."

That priest's answer, if any, is not recorded.

In short the thing was done.

On March 8, 1765, the day before the Calas suit was triumphantly concluded, Voltaire wrote joyfully that the generous Élie de Beaumont would also defend the Sirvens. After that March 9th Voltaire could throw himself yet more thoroughly into the case. Calas is vindicated! So shall the Sirvens be!

But if there had been need for patience in the first affair, there was a hundred times greater need in the second.

The Parliament of Toulouse declined to give up its papers, as it had declined before. And then that flight—"the reason of their condemnation is in their flight. They are judged by contumacy."

In June, too, the death of Madame Sirven—"of her sorrows"—removed a most important and most valuable witness for the defence. Then the Sirvens had no money. Voltaire had to supply all—brains, wealth, influence, labour, literary talent. For seven years he worked the case with an energy that never tired, an enthusiasm that never cooled. When it had been going on for four years, he wrote that it "agitated all his soul." "This ardour, this fever, this perpetual exaltation"—what worker, however hot and persevering he fancy himself, is not ashamed by it, and astounded?

Voltaire wrote Memoirs for the Sirvens. He won over the disapproving d'Argentals to be as "obstinate" about it (the phrase is his own) as he was himself. He got up a subscription to which the great Frederick and the great Catherine of Russia gave generously; and Madame Geoffrin made her *protégé*, Stanislas Augustus Poniatowski—now King of Poland—contribute too.

Finally, Voltaire succeeded in persuading Sirven to return to Mazamet, where the case was re-tried; and on December 25, 1771, when Voltaire was seventy-seven years old, the Parliament of Toulouse met and completely exculpated the accused. As Voltaire said, it had taken them two hours to condemn innocence, and nine years to give it justice. Still, the thing was done.

In 1772, the Sirvens came to Ferney to thank their benefactor, and afforded him one of the highest of human pleasures: "the sight of a happiness which was his own work."

The year 1765, in which Voltaire showed so much public spirit, was not privately uneventful. In it he gave up Délices, which he had bought in 1755, and whose place Ferney had altogether usurped in his heart. In 1829, Délices was still in possession of the Tronchin family, from whom Voltaire had rented it. In 1881, it was a girls' school.

In 1766, he also gave up the lease of Chêne, his house in Lausanne.

In the January of 1765, Voltaire and Frederick the Great were again reconciled after a quarrel and a break in their correspondence which had lasted four years. Frederick, forsooth, had chosen to take as a personal insult the fact that Voltaire should waste his talents writing that stupid history about "the wolves and bears of Siberia"! And why in the world should he want to dedicate his "Tancred" to that old enemy of the Prussian monarch's, Madame de Pompadour? Voltaire, on his side, was minded to write any history he chose, and dedicate his plays to anybody he liked, and would thank Frederick not to interfere.

Then, at the end of 1764 he hears that Frederick is ill—and to the wind with both his heat and his coldness at once.

Frederick replied rather witheringly to the peace overtures on January 1, 1765: "I supposed you to be so busy crushing *l'infâme* ... that I did not dare to presume you would think of anything else."

But the ice was broken. Both succumbed to the old, old, fatal, potent charm. They wrote to each other about "once a fortnight"; discussed everything in heaven and earth; and until they should be mortal enemies again, were, once more, more than friends.

Frederick was once again, too, the friend not only of Voltaire, but of Voltaire's country. The Seven Years' War had been concluded in 1763 by the peace of Hubertsburg. Frederick kept Silesia; and France, with her feeble ministry and her doddering King, lost, to England, Canada, Saint Vincent, Grenada, Minorca.

Changes were rife elsewhere too. Voltaire's friend Elizabeth, Empress of Russia, had died in 1762, and was succeeded nominally by the miserable Peter, but really by his wife, Catherine the Great. In 1763, Peter disappeared under strong suspicions of poison, and Catherine reigned in his stead.

Many kings and potentates have been named the Great, but few so justly as Catherine.

If she was the perpetrator of great crimes, this woman of three-and-thirty was, even at her accession, of vast genius, of extraordinary capacity as a ruler, broad and liberal in her aims, and an enlightened lover of the arts. She declared that since 1746 she had been under the greatest obligations to Voltaire; that his letters had formed her mind. With the telepathy of intellect, these two master-minds had from their different corners of the world detected each other's greatness. They never met in the flesh. But from their correspondence it is easy to see their close spiritual affinity. Their earliest letters, which are preserved, date from the July of this 1765.

Voltaire shocked even Paris and Madame du Deffand by the airy way in which he took that little peccadillo of the Empress's, "that *bagatelle* about a husband." "Those are family affairs," he said, not without a wicked twinkle in his eyes, "with which I do not mix myself." It is certain that, whether or no he believed Catherine a murderess, he regarded her as a great woman and served her when he could.

There came an opportunity in August. Her Majesty is pleased to admire girls' education as conducted in Switzerland, and sends Count Bülow to arrange for a certain number of Swiss governesses to be brought to Moscow and Petersburg to instruct the noble *jeunes filles* of those cities.

Splendid idea! says Voltaire. But that "*bagatelle* about a husband" weighs on the Puritan conscience of Geneva. It is extraordinary now to think that any civilised Government could have dared so to interfere with personal liberty as to prevent women over age going to teach anyone they chose, anywhere they liked. But this is precisely what Geneva did. Voltaire was exceedingly angry. The refusal reflected on him. But he had done his best for Catherine, though in vain.

While this little affair was going on, a new friend, the young playwright La Harpe, of whom Voltaire was to see more hereafter, and an old friend, whom he had not seen for seventeen years, were both staying with him at Ferney.

On July 30th had arrived there "the sublime Clairon." She had been the first actress of her day when Voltaire had known her in Paris. Now she was the finest tragic actress of the eighteenth century, and in the rich maturity of her two-and-forty years a most clever and cultivated woman. She had helped Voltaire's plays enormously; some she had made for him. He said so, at least. Further, she was one of the philosophers. In 1761 she had protested against the excommunication of actors as a class; and Voltaire, remembering Adrienne Lecouvreur, had seconded her with all the force and irony of his style.

When she reached Ferney her host was so ill that she had to declaim her *rôle* in his "Orphan of China," which cured him on the spot. Part of her visit he hobbled about on crutches, crippled by an attack of sciatica and half blind from an affection of the eyes, but as mentally lively and alert as if he had had both of those requisites for happiness, "the body of an athlete and the soul of a sage."

Mademoiselle was not well herself, and under Tronchin. But she went on acting against the express orders of that good physician. It was in her blood, as it was in Voltaire's. He had entirely rebuilt his theatre for her. He went quite mad over her superb talent; and declared that for the first time in his life he had seen perfection in any kind. Blind though his avuncular affection might be, when he beheld Clairon in the flesh he did not suggest that Madame Denis (who, with her sister, was acting too) could in any way be her rival.

Clairon was still at Ferney in August. Soon after she left, that faithful Damilaville paid a visit there; and during the summer had come, under the chaperonage of Lord Abingdon, the famous John Wilkes. "Voltaire is obliging to me beyond all description" was Wilkes's record of his reception; while Voltaire, on his part, bore enthusiastic testimony to the great demagogue's inexhaustible life and wit.

On the 8th or 9th of that August, when Voltaire was acting or telling stories, nimbly gesticulating with those crutches, events of sinister importance to him, and of importance to all men who hated *l'infâme*, were taking place in Abbeville.

On one of those days, two large crucifixes in the town, one on a bridge, the other in a cemetery, were shamefully and blasphemously mutilated. The town was naturally very angry. It set itself busily to work to find the culprits. A few days later three suspected persons, all boys under one-and-twenty, were brought up before the authorities and questioned.

While their examination was proceeding, the Bishop of the diocese organised a solemn procession through the streets to the places where the sacrilege had been committed, and, kneeling there, invoked pardon for the blasphemers in ominous words, as "men who, though not beyond the reach of God's mercy, had rendered themselves worthy of the severest penalty of this world's law."

The mutilated crucifixes were placed in a church, to which the people flocked in crowds, and in a temper of mind very different from that of Him who hung there in effigy and in the supreme agony had prayed for His murderers.

On September 26th, a formal decree of arrest was issued against the three young men, d'Étallonde de Morival, Moisnel, and the Chevalier de la Barre.

D'Étallonde had already fled to Prussia; partly, no doubt, because his conscience was ill at ease, but partly, too, because he, or his friends, knew the times and the people. In Prussia he was afterwards made, through Voltaire's influence, an officer in Frederick's army.

Moisnel was a timid and foolish boy of eighteen.

Jean François Lefebre, Chevalier de la Barre, was a young Norman, not yet twenty years old. He had been educated by a country curé. His aunt, the Abbess of Willancourt, had given him masters, and he had rooms assigned to him in her convent. It is thought, but is not certain, that La Barre was in the army. What *is* certain is that this clerical education had been a very bad one. The Abbess, if not a wicked woman, was certainly one who loved pleasure; who enjoyed a joke, even if it were against the religion she professed; who gave rollicking little supper-parties; adored her good-looking lively young scapegrace of a nephew, and permitted him not only to sing roystering and indecent drinking songs with foolish companions within her sacred walls, but to keep there a library which included not only some very indecorous books—but that little volume which "smelt of the fagot," "The Philosophical Dictionary."

At her supper-parties young La Barre had often met one Duval, or Belleval, who, it is said, had been in love with the Abbess, and was not a little jealous of her handsome nephew. It was Duval who had heard young La Barre chant Rabelaisian ditties, and quote "what he could recollect" from the "Pucelle" and the "Epistle to Uranie." It was Duval who hated him, and Duval who denounced him.

On October 1, 1765, La Barre was arrested in the Abbey of Longvilliers, near Montreuil. Moisnel was also arrested.

On October 4th, the Abbess burnt her nephew's library, which would have been a prudent act if she had done it thoroughly, but she did not. On October 10th, the authorities searched the boy's rooms, and found in a press some indecent literature—*and* that "Philosophical Dictionary."

After five cross-examinations, unhappy young Moisnel said practically what his judges told him to say, not only respecting himself, but respecting La Barre. He swore that d'Étallonde had mutilated the crucifixes, an assertion to which La Barre also swore. D'Étallonde was safe in Prussia. Moisnel, who was delicate in health and in horrible fear of death, lost in the trial the very little sense he had ever had. Young La Barre, on the other hand, kept all his pluck, wit, and coolness.

To a charge that, on the Feast of the Holy Sacrament, he and his two companions had lingered near a religious procession in the street, and neither knelt nor uncovered as reverence and custom demanded, he pleaded "Guilty." He was in a hurry, he said, and had no evil intentions.

To the charge that to a person who bade him take another route if he could not behave himself, he had replied that he looked upon the Host as nothing but a piece of pastry and for his part could not swallow all the apostolic assertions, he answered that he might have used some such words.

It is not unworthy of remark that, though under torture he confessed to having mutilated the crucifix in the cemetery, the judges discovered no proof, and no proof ever was discovered, that he had mutilated the crucifix on the bridge. It is very much more remarkable that in his sentence the affair of the crucifixes was not even mentioned, and that he and absent d'Étallonde were condemned for "impiously and deliberately walking before the Host without kneeling or uncovering; uttering blasphemies against God, the Saints, and the Church; singing blasphemous songs, and rendering marks of adoration to profane books."

Now it will be allowed by any fair-minded person—whatever be his religion or irreligion—that to thus insult a faith, dear to millions of people for hundreds of generations, merited a sharp punishment.

As Voltaire said, "it deserved Saint Lazare."

On February 28, 1766, d'Étallonde and La Barre were condemned to have their tongues torn out with hot irons, their right hands to be cut off, and to be burnt to death by a slow fire. In the case of La Barre this sentence was so far graciously remitted that he was to be beheaded before he was burnt; but, on the other hand, he was further condemned to the torture Ordinary and Extraordinary, to extract from him the names of his accomplices. Even for that time the sentence was so brutal—"could they have done more if he had killed his father?"—that no one believed it would be carried out. Against absent d'Étallonde, of course, it could not be. A public appeal was made to the King. Ten of the best *avocats* of Paris declared the sentence illegal. La Barre was taken to the capital, and his case retried there, where "a majority of five voices condemned to the most horrible torments a young man only guilty of folly." He was taken back to Abbeville. All through the trial he had borne himself with a high courage. It did not leave him now. He recognised many old acquaintances on the way, and saluted them gaily. On the last evening of his life he supped with his confessor—a priest whom he had often met at his aunt's gay table. "Let us have some coffee," he is reported to have said; "it will not prevent my sleeping." Bravado, perhaps. But *bravado* and *brave* are of the same origin. The next day, July 1, 1766, began with the torture. On his way to the scaffold the poor boy recognised among the cruel crowd of spectators not only many men whom he had called friend, but, to their everlasting shame, women too. That "barbarism which would have made even drunken savages shudder," the pulling out of the tongue, was so barbarous that the five executioners only pretended to do it. On his way up to the scaffold La Barre's shoe dropped off. He turned and put it on again. He bound his own eyes, and talked calmly to the executioners, and then died with "the firmness of Socrates"—a harder death.

It is said that the executioner who cut off the head did it so cleverly that the spectators *applauded*. The body was thrown to the flames—with "The Philosophical Thoughts" of Diderot; the "Sopha" of the younger Crébillon; two little volumes of Bayle; and "The Philosophical Dictionary," which was supposed to have inspired the indecent impiety of which the unhappy boy had been guilty, but which certainly does inspire a religion not so unlike the religion of Christ as the savage hatred which killed La Barre.

The event caused a fearful sensation, even in the eighteenth century. The victim was so young, and had so nobly played the man. To the last moment, popular opinion had believed in a reprieve. One of the people who so believed was Voltaire. Vague reports of the case had reached him at first. Some young fools had been profaning a church, and then declaring in cross-examination that they had been led to do so by the books of the "Encyclopædia"! But then wild boys who commit drunken frolics do not read books of philosophy!

And when the tidings of that 1st of July had come—"My dear brother, my heart is withered." Grimm wrote boldly and significantly of the event that "humanity awaited an avenger." But this time how could the avenger be Voltaire? On the lips of all the churchmen were the words— Philosophy hath done this thing. This is where your fine freethinking, your mental emancipation, lead men! Certainly, it might have been answered that La Barre was not the product of philosophy, but of the Church; educated by a curé, finished by my Lady Abbess; sheltered, after his sin, in the Abbey of Longvilliers; given for his last confessor a priestly boon companion of those wild suppers at the convent. If the philosophers mocked at religion, what of the licentious priests of that wicked day? Châteauneuf, Chaulieu, Desfontaines—the names of a score of others must have come to Voltaire's lips. This boy had put the teaching of such men into action. The more fool he; but not the greater criminal. There were a thousand excuses for him; and "tears come easily for the youth which has committed sins which in ripe age it would have redeemed."

But Voltaire, with a guilty conscience one may hope, seems to have remembered that he had written not only "The Philosophical Dictionary," but the ribald "Pucelle." He might thereby have had some hand in La Barre's undoing; and when he saw that men flung the whole responsibility for that sin on him and his brothers, the Encyclopædists, he feared.

By July 14th he had gone to Rolle in Vaud. He had been there in the spring for his health; now he went for his safety.

But, safe or dangerous, he must write his view of the case. By the 22d of the same month his account of "The Death of the Chevalier de la Barre" was complete. Clear, masterly, succinct, it is perhaps one of the finest tracts in the cause of humanity ever written, even by Voltaire himself. On July 25th, he was asking clever young Élie de Beaumont if there was any law, date 1681, by which those guilty of indecent impieties could be sentenced to death. He had himself looked everywhere in vain; which was not wonderful. There was no such law. The ignorance and fanaticism of the judges had "supposed its existence." "This barbarity occupies me day and night." True, La Barre was past the reach of human help. But Voltaire could hope that his cries "might frighten the carnivorous beasts from others." They did that. The popular fury to which he gave mighty voice saved feeble Moisnel. After La Barre's death the judges did not dare to proceed with the suit.

In 1775, when d'Étallonde was staying with him at Ferney, Voltaire wrote a pamphlet called "The Cry of Innocent Blood," which had as its object the restitution of his civil rights to that young officer, to whom Frederick had accorded a long leave of absence. If he never obtained that restitution or full justification for the memory of La Barre, at least he never ceased to try. He worked the case for twelve years, and his labours were only stopped by death.

Partly for his own safety; partly in horror of a country which could sanction a vengeance so awful; partly in longing for an Elysium where he and his brothers might live and speak as free men, in this July of 1766, at Rolle, this boy Voltaire conceived the mad and hot-headed scheme of retiring, with all the enlightened, to Cleves, and forming there a literary society, with a printing press.

A dream! A dream! The other philosophers would not entertain the idea for a moment. Some of them, at least, felt "little suppers and the *opéra-comique*" to be among the necessities of existence. D'Alembert, chief of them all, who had refused the Presidency of the Berlin Academy and to be tutor to Catherine the Great's son for a quiet life, and Mademoiselle de Lespinasse, was not going to be tempted from either—for Cleves!

"I see," wrote Voltaire, "that M. Boursier" (which was one of his innumerable *noms de guerre*) "will have no workmen." So he went back to Ferney.

"The suit and the sacrifice of the Chevalier de la Barre remain one of the indelible stains with which the magistracy of the eighteenth century tarnished and defiled its robes."

That "Philosophical Dictionary"—of which the thin first volume had been burnt with La Barre; which in March, 1765, had been publicly destroyed in Paris by the hangman; which Rome anathematised, and of which liberal London had already demanded a fifth edition—is one of the greatest of Voltaire's works, and one which should still be popular. It stands alone, without rival or counterpart. Brief articles on an enormous variety of subjects gave infinite scope for Voltaire's versatility. Since he had written that first article, "Abraham," which had made even sullen Frederick laugh, the thing had been its author's commonplace book. If an article is too daring even for the "Encyclopædia"—put it in the "Dictionary." If one feels gay, write buffoonery; or seriously, write with passion. The "Dictionary" had room for everything. Mockery, sarcasm, lightness, wit, gaiety, profundity, the most earnest thought, the most burning zeal, banter, irony, audacity—they are all here. "The Philosophical Dictionary" has well been said to be "the whole of citizen Voltaire."

He had smuggled it into Geneva, and then gaily and without a pang of conscience denied that he had anything to do with its authorship. "If there is the least danger about it, please warn me, and then I can disown it in all the public papers with my usual candour and innocence."

He kept it by his side, and wrote, now in this mood, now in that, first one article and then another, until it numbered eight volumes.

Even in this age of many books there is always room for another, if it be sufficiently piquant and out of the common. The astonishing variety of the subjects, and the not less marvellous versatility of the style, the ease, the life and the humour of those eight volumes are qualities which may well appeal to the most jaded of modern readers. Its frequent profanity, indeed, is a blot dyed too deeply into the texture of the book to be eradicable by any editor. But, apart from this, to the bored person—always in search of a new literary sensation, of something which has not been done a thousand times before, of something that will not be done a thousand times again—may be well recommended a volume of "The Philosophical Dictionary."

CHAPTER XXXIX

VOLTAIRE AND GENEVA: VOLTAIRE AND LA HARPE

NOW Voltaire was not only genius and philanthropist, he was also a country gentleman.

He played the part to the life. He amicably exchanged seeds and bulbs with his neighbours, and admired their gardens in return for their admiration of his; he invited them to dinner-parties and theatricals; and, like many another of his class, could not for the life of him help interfering in local politics.

Geneva was a republic. But its constitution was not to modern ideas—or to Voltaire's ideas—at all republican.

In the governing class, which consisted of the Great Council of Two Hundred, the Little Council of Twenty-Five, and the Consistory of the Clergy, the people were not represented at all.

These people were divided into the shopkeepers, or Bourgeoisie, who demanded a share of political power; and the journeymen mechanics, who were not only without any political rights, but could not even set up in business for themselves, occupy any official post, or go into the liberal professions. These (so-called) Natives, a very large class, were the descendants of foreigners who had settled in Geneva. They asked for the rights enjoyed by the Bourgeoisie; while the Bourgeoisie, scornfully refusing the demands of the Natives, themselves asked for some of the privileges enjoyed by the Councils.

Voltaire, now as ever, was on the side not of the governing class, but of the people who had a right to share in the government, but did not; and, now as ever, he was irresistibly tempted to interfere in what was not his business.

In the autumn of 1765, "in spite of Espinas, Calas, and Sirven, who surround me; of wheels, gallows, galleys, and confiscations; and of Chevaliers de la Barre who do not precisely pour balm in the blood," he began to take upon himself the highly unnecessary and stormy *rôle* of peacemaker between the Genevan Bourgeoisie and Magistracy.

He first tried to get up some mediatory dinner-parties at Ferney, at which the heads of these two parties were to meet and amicably discuss their differences! The Council of Twenty-Five responded with a chilly dignity that it was very much obliged to M. de Voltaire, but it was not going to settle political disputes in *that* way; while four of the Bourgeoisie joyfully accepted so pleasant an invitation, and arrived at Ferney in M. de Voltaire's carriage, graciously sent for their convenience.

These four guests showed such a sweet reasonableness on all topics under discussion, that, says Voltaire, writing to that haughty Council, there is surely hope of a reconciliation?

The Council, in response, will be obliged if the Lord of Ferney will consider the matter closed.

Not he.

At the request of the Bourgeoisie he drew up a document stating their claims, sent it to France and begged her to step in and settle the dispute.

She selected as mediator her new envoy at Geneva, M. Hennin, who arrived on December 16, 1765, whose mediation did not prosper at all, but who was, and remained, much Voltaire's friend.

By this time the Bourgeoisie had become not a little aggressive and dictatorial, and the long mediatory dinner-parties had begun to bore Voltaire.

After all, the most oppressed class were the Natives. Two of them called at Ferney, and presently brought its lord a written statement of their grievances against the Bourgeoisie, which were not few or slight. He promised help, entered into the smallest details, and dismissed them with memorable words: "You are the largest part of a free and industrious people, and you are in slavery.... If you are forced to leave a country which your labours make prosperous, I shall still be able to help and protect you."

He wrote a little introductory letter to that statement which the Natives purposed to present to M. de Beauteville, the new mediator sent by France, to succeed, if that might be, where Hennin had failed.

"What is the Third Estate?" said the Abbé Sieyès. "Nothing." "What ought it to be? Everything."

In 1766 it was nothing. In the eye of the law, said de Beauteville, it positively did not exist.

He dismissed the petition with contumacy, and sent the Natives to the Councils, who received them in the same way.

Then M. de Voltaire himself wrote a petition for them; but before they sent it to the mediators (three had now been appointed, one by France, one by Berne, one by Geneva), he warned them of their probable failure, in a prophecy which Geneva long remembered. "You are like little flying-fish. Out of the water, you are eaten by birds of prey; in it, by larger fish. You are between two equally powerful parties: you will fall victims to the interests of one or the other, or perhaps of both together."

When the petition was presented on April 28, 1766, the unlucky Natives were threatened with imprisonment if they did not reveal its authorship. They did. Notwithstanding, a few days later, Auzière, their leader, was thrown into prison, a result Voltaire had long foreseen. Here the affair ended, for a time at least. Voltaire summed up his own position, with his usual neatness, in writing to d'Argental on May 6th. "The Natives say that I take the part of the Bourgeois, and the Bourgeois that I take the part of the Natives. The Natives and Bourgeois both pretend I pay too much deference to the Councils, and the Councils say I am too friendly to both the Bourgeois and Natives."

The Councils, in point of fact, were exceedingly angry with Voltaire, to whom happened precisely what happens to the foolish person who separates fighting dogs. The dogs growl at him and begin fighting again, and their master considers his interference uncommonly impertinent.

The air of Geneva was sultry with storms in this season of 1766; or Voltaire had upon him one of those pugnacious moods in which he had rent limb from limb Pompignan, Fréron, Desfontaines. To be sure, he seldom gave the first blow; but the moment he saw a chance of a fight he was as agog to join in it at seventy-two as he had been at twenty-two.

The Protestant minister called Jacob Vernet was the unlucky person who offended him now. Vernet was clever, and himself a writer. He had been friendly with Voltaire until 1757, when he sharply criticised the "Essay on the Manners and Mind of Nations." Then they further fell out on that vexed topic, a theatre in Geneva; and when d'Alembert's famous article appeared in the "Encyclopædia," Vernet broke off all intercourse with Voltaire, telling him the reason. Then Vernet drew a portrait of Voltaire in his "Critical Letters of an English Traveller." The likeness was not sufficiently flattering to please the original, who thereupon attacked Vernet in a "Dialogue between a Priest and a Protestant Minister." Vernet complained to the Councils that he had been libelled. And in May, 1766, Voltaire wrote against Vernet one of the most virulent of personal satires which ever fell from his pen—"The Praise of Hypocrisy." It lent his hand cunning for that kind of work. His next was the famous poem entitled "The Civil War of Geneva."

The excuse for this savage personal polemic was the case of one Covelle, who in 1763 had been condemned, for an offence against morals, to make confession of the same to the Consistory of Geneva, to kneel to the President of the Consistory, be reprimanded, and ask pardon. He confessed, but more than that he declined to do.

The mode of punishment has long been decided to be an unwise one. Voltaire, always in advance of his age, considered it an unwise one then. He took the part of Covelle, who personally was a wretched creature, as deficient in brains as in morals. But he stood for a cause.

After having been remanded for a fortnight for consideration, he presented to the Consistory a paper, the substance of which had been supplied by Voltaire, and which stated that the ecclesiastical laws did not compel kneeling to the Consistory, being reprimanded by it, or asking pardon from it.

Covelle published this statement, or rather Voltaire did, and between my Lord of Ferney and the authorities began a battle of pamphlets. They fill three large volumes, and may still be seen in Geneva. Voltaire also wrote twelve public letters in the name of Covelle, allowed him a small pension, and then made him the hero of "The Civil War of Geneva."

The hatred expressed in that poem redounded, as hatred is apt to do, on the hater. Bitterness and anger are not gay. They spoilt, artistically, "The Civil War of Geneva."

The poem is, unluckily for Voltaire, not only a satire on parties, though it is a satire on that retrograde and conservative faction which he held was ruining Geneva. It is also a savage satire against individuals. It attacks with a sudden blind fury (Voltaire having hitherto been temperate in his dislike of him) "that monster of vanity and contradictions, of pride and of meanness," Jean Jacques Rousseau. It tore Vernet's reputation to shreds. It descended to personal insult, and, that there might be no possible mistake, its victims were spoken of by name. The malice kills the wit. More indecent than the "Pucelle," "The War of Geneva" is much less clever and amusing. A picture of a travelling Englishman, that Lord Abingdon who had introduced Wilkes at Ferney and must needs put *his* spoke into the wheel of the Genevan party quarrels, is certainly happy. The young gentleman who, with his "phlegmatic enthusiasm," drags his dogs and his boredom all over Europe, and expects, no matter where he is, the mere fact of his being English to remove all obstacles and alter all conditions which he is pleased to dislike, will be certainly recognised as a type.

But as a whole "The Civil War of Geneva" contains Voltaire's vices without his virtues. The poem, like all his writings, certainly *did* something. In 1769 the decree to which Covelle had refused to submit was abolished.

"The War of Geneva," which was brought out canto by canto, appeared complete in 1768.

The strife of parties which that poem celebrated, and should have celebrated exclusively, had not been healed by the mediators sent by France. Very well, says France—if persuasion will not do, we will try force. By the January of 1767 French troops were quartered along the Lake of Geneva with the view of bringing the aggravating little Genevan republic to its senses by famine and blockade, and unlucky, and comparatively innocent, Ferney was almost unable to get the necessaries of life.

Voltaire was not the person to starve in silence. The soldiers were spoiling the trees in his park; poor d'Aumard could not get his plasters; Adam was very ill and could have neither doctor nor medicine ("so he is sure to recover"); and the household generally lacked everything except snow, "and we have enough of that to stock Europe." Choiseul must be written to! Voltaire wrote to him and pointed out that it was not the Genevans France was punishing, but Ferney; and on January 30th Choiseul sent an order exempting Ferney from the general rule and giving Voltaire an unlimited passport for himself and his household.

It was a very large one by now. Durey de Morsan, an amiable elderly ne'er-do-weel, had joined it, and lived there on Voltaire's charity, sometimes doing a little copying in return for his board and lodging.

There was also a *protégé* of Richelieu's, called Gallien, who repaid Voltaire's hospitality with the basest ingratitude; and an ex-Capuchin monk, known to Ferney as Richard, who, when he had been generously entertained for two years, decamped with money, manuscripts, and jewels belonging to his host.

And then, besides its regular inmates, there poured through the house a continual stream of visitors. In 1766 there had stayed there Madame Saint-Julien, a gay, good-natured, and highly connected little lady, whom Voltaire called his "butterfly philosopher"; and La Borde, playwright for himself, and first *valet de chambre* for the King.

Here, too, also in 1766, had come James Boswell, Esquire, of Auchinleck, for whose benefit M. de Voltaire is pleased to assume the manner and style of Mr. Boswell's great patron, and to speak of that patron as "a superstitious dog."

Voltaire would hardly have been his vain old French self if he had not modified his opinion of the great Doctor when Boswell told him that Johnson had said that Frederick the Great wrote as Voltaire's footboy, who had acted as his amanuensis, might do.

To be sure, when Boswell got home and asked the Doctor if he thought Rousseau as bad a man as Voltaire, that staunch old bigot had replied, "Why, Sir, it is difficult to settle the proportion of iniquity between them."

But Voltaire did not know of that answer.

Also in 1766, Grétry the musician, then only five-and-twenty, had often come over from Geneva, where he was staying, to visit Voltaire. Madame Cramer had first introduced him. The conversation often turned on comic opera, which Voltaire had once hated, but which, as expounded by Grétry, he was soon to love and at seventy-four to write gaily himself.

When Grétry spoke of his host's prodigious reputation, he records that Voltaire characteristically replied that he would give a hundred years of immortality for a good digestion.

Chabanon, friend of d'Alembert, musician, poet, dramatist, had also paid a first visit here in 1766. He came back again on May 1, 1767, and stayed seven months. He has left behind him a good account of that visit. He evidently guessed—what not all Voltaire's friends did guess—that one day the world would be interested in them only as having known Voltaire, and would be grateful to them for writing as little about themselves, and as much about their host, as possible.

While Chabanon was at Ferney, the leisure Voltaire's "devouring ardour" for study allowed him was spent, of course, in play-acting. He had just written a new play, "The Scythians," and loved it as he always loved his latest born. He was not a little disgusted when Ferney would have none of it, and demanded an old favourite, "Adélaïde du Guesclin," instead.

"I cannot think what they see in that 'Adélaïde,'" says its author discontentedly to Madame Denis.

Ferney and Chabanon only ratified the judgment of Paris in disliking "The Scythians." Played there on March 26th of this same 1767, the rude *parterre* had "no respect for the old age which had written it," and made such a noise that the first performances were "regular battles." There were only four in all.

The French officers of the blockading troops came *en masse* to Ferney in this spring to witness the theatricals. Colonel Chabrillant, the colonel of Conti's regiment, stayed for a long time as a guest at the château; and if he did, after the visit, forget to write a single word of thanks to his host or Mama Denis, why, that was a sort of ingratitude to which Voltaire should have been accustomed.

Three companies of the same regiment were quartered in the village of Ferney, and some of the grenadiers often came as audience to the performances, and at least once as actors. As a reward for their services Voltaire gave them supper and offered them money.

"We will not take anything," they said "We have seen M. de Voltaire. That is our payment."

The celebrity was as delighted as a boy. My "brave grenadiers!" he cried, and invited them all, whenever they wanted a meal or well-paid work, to come to Ferney.

When his guests were tired of acting themselves, they could, and did, now go to Geneva and see other people act. Through the influence of Voltaire upon M. de Beauteville, that French envoy had so far worked upon the prim Councils of Geneva that they had allowed a theatre to be opened in their Puritan town in April, 1766. "Olympie" was played there, and the loveliest comic operas. Voltaire had the whole troupe come to Ferney, where they acted four for his benefit. The Geneva theatre had only a short life. It was burnt in February, 1768. The townspeople hated it so, that when they saw it in flames they made no attempt to save it.

In the light of subsequent events, it seems almost certain that Voltaire received many of his visitors and gave many of his entertainments to keep Madame Denis in a good temper, and reconcile her to the country which she hated; while other festivities he arranged for the benefit of the light-hearted young people he always liked to have about him.

When there was a supper and a dance after theatricals he himself appeared for a moment only, and then retired to his room, which adjoined that where, not the guests, but the servants were dancing, and where he tranquilly worked or slept to the sound of the music. Sometimes he did not even appear to do the honours of the house at all; and declared of himself that he would have been dead in four days if he had not well known how to live quietly in the midst of uproar, and alone in a mob.

He had the usual quarrel on hand to keep him busy. That conceited La Beaumelle, who had been a thorn in his flesh in Prussia, assailed him in the summer of 1767 with no fewer than ninety-four abusive anonymous letters. Voltaire put the matter into the hands of the police. But in 1770 La Beaumelle, who had further complicated the situation by marrying the sister of young Lavaysse, the Calas' unfortunate friend, began an objectionable commentary on Voltaire's works, and would have finished it but that he (La Beaumelle) died in 1773.

That Voltaire spent energy and time in trying to inspire, and that he knew no greater delight than when he did inspire, his visitors with his own passion for hard work in place of idle pleasure, is on the testimony of Chabanon and of a fellow-visitor of Chabanon's, the famous La Harpe.

La Harpe from the first came to Ferney to be a brilliant pupil to this great past master of so many arts; to learn from the author of "Zaire" and of "Alzire," of "Mahomet" and of "Mérope," of "The Princess of Navarre," "The Prodigal Son," "Brutus," and "The Scotch Girl," how to write every kind of play that ever playwright has written. It has been mentioned that La Harpe had been at Ferney in 1765—part of the time with that noblest exponent of the drama, Clairon. He was here also in 1766 with Chabanon. And now, in the beginning of 1767, he came once again— this time with his young wife, and for a visit which lasted more than a year.

La Harpe was a clever, arrogant, and very self-satisfied young man of about eight-and-twenty. His tragedy, "Warwick," produced in 1763, made him famous in his own age. In this, he is only celebrated as the first writer in France who "made criticism eloquent." He had led a disreputable youth, and had just married his landlady's daughter as a reparation for wrong done to her. But in that age almost everybody was disreputable; and if virtue had been a *sine qua non* in society, there would have been no society at all.

Voltaire took this promising youth to his warm and sanguine old heart at once. He was poor! He was clever! He could act! What more did one want? With Voltaire's help he had gained a prize at the Academy. And with further help he should do greater things than that. Nothing is pleasanter in Voltaire's character as an old man than the enthusiastic interest and delight he took in his young literary *protégés*. He worked with them, corrected them, praised them, went into raptures over their talents to his friends, financed them, fathered them, housed them, and in the desire for their fame quite forgot his own.

The memorable La Harpe visit of 1767 opened under the rosiest aspects. The little bride had the youth in which Voltaire delighted, and she turned out to be "a comedian without knowing it." If "The Scythians" had been hissed in Paris, Madame de la Harpe reciting Act II. made Ferney sob. La Harpe, too, "declaimed verses as well as he wrote them," and was "the best actor in France."

So there were theatricals galore.

If thorns pricked on the rose stems and there were clouds in the bluest of skies, it was not Voltaire who spoke of them.

It is Chabanon, the fellow-guest, who sketches La Harpe as overbearing, impatient of correction, uncommonly quarrelsome, and quite forgetful of the fact that his host's position and seniority of nearly fifty years demanded some sort of respect.

Old Voltaire was good-natured enough to criticise the young man's plays for him, and La Harpe received the criticisms with the sulkiness of offended dignity. Voltaire was not patient by nature, heaven knows. But he kept his coolness and his temper with this irritating young man to a degree quite extraordinary. It was always "the little La Harpe," or "my dear child," or "Ah! the little one is angry!" with a good-natured laugh.

When one day the conceited visitor went so far as to rewrite some verses in his part in Voltaire's "Adélaïde"—"which seemed to me feeble"—"Let us hear them, my son," says Voltaire. And when he had heard them, as improved by La Harpe—

"Good," he said. "Yes, that is better. Go on making such changes. I shall only gain by them."

On another occasion, La Harpe, at a dinner-party of twenty persons, recited an ode by one old foe of Voltaire's, Pompignan, on the death of another, J. B. Rousseau, without stating the name of the author.

"Very good," says Voltaire. "Who wrote it?"

The audacious La Harpe makes him guess. And at last tells him.

"Pompignan."

That name, as La Harpe himself said, was a *coup de théâtre* indeed. There was a silence. "Repeat the lines again," says Voltaire. As La Harpe repeats them, the Patriarch listens with fixed attention. "There is no more to be said. It *is* a beautiful stanza."

Was this the same man whom the mere suggestion that d'Arnaud's sun was rising and his setting, had spurred to the folly of the Prussian visit? Was this the man so thin-skinned that every gnat-bite of a criticism made him raw and mad? The truth seems to be that Voltaire had a very weak spot in his heart for La Harpe, and loved him better than his own glory.

Not many years ago, in a grocer's shop in Paris, was discovered an autograph letter of Voltaire's in which he begged the Controller-General for a pension for his *protégé*.

"It seems to me that, M. de la Harpe having no pension, mine (from the King) is too large by half, and that it should be divided between us."

If this could be arranged—"La Harpe, and everyone else, can easily be made to think that this pension is a just recompense for the services he has rendered to literature."

The request was not granted. La Harpe never even knew that it had been made. But its singular generosity and delicacy are not altered by those facts. Well might Voltaire's bitterest enemy, Jean Jacques Rousseau, write of him: "I know no man on earth whose impulses have been more beautiful."

But his treatment of La Harpe was something better even than a noble impulse.

In the beginning of 1768, after the young couple had been guests in his house for more than a year, and after one of them at least had received full measure, pressed down and running over, of help, forbearance, and kindness, Voltaire discovered that valuable manuscripts had been stolen from him. Among others were those secret Memoirs written in 1759, which expressed the feelings of an angry, younger Voltaire, but not of a wiser and older one. To Paris had been sent not only copies of "The Civil War of Geneva," but anecdotes for his Histories which Voltaire was keeping until the death of the persons concerned left him at liberty to publish them.

There was a loud domestic explosion at Ferney. The strongest and gravest suspicion fell upon La Harpe. He vehemently denied everything, and accused a certain Antoine, a sculptor, of the crime. Antoine simply said La Harpe was a liar.

Madame Denis, who herself was suspected of a foolish elderly *tendresse* for La Harpe and of complicity in the affair with him, took his side, with, one may safely assume, a torrent of eloquence. But eloquence, not proof, was all either she or La Harpe had to offer. From his room La Harpe, "putting arrogance in the place of repentance," wrote his generous old host many impertinent little notes. He might have spared him.

Voltaire had often had manuscripts stolen from him before, and always alas! by his own familiar friends whom he trusted. But this time he felt the treachery with peculiar bitterness. He was not passionate and furious as he generally was. His attitude was that of knowing La Harpe to be guilty and longing to find him innocent. He made as little of it as he could. "This little roguery of La Harpe's is not serious," he wrote. "But it is certain and proven." In the November of 1767 La Harpe had been in Paris for a time, when "he gave the third canto of 'The Civil War of Geneva' to three persons of my acquaintance."

"I did not reproach him," Voltaire wrote sadly to Hennin, "but his own conscience did. He never alluded to the affair and looked me straight in the face, or spoke of it without turning pale with a pallor not that of innocence." Still, if I can help him in the future as I have done in the past, I shall do so; "only, if Madame Denis brings him back to Ferney I must lock up my papers." "His imprudence has had very disagreeable consequences for me, but I pardon him with all my heart; he has not sinned from malice."

Only to his intimate friends did he admit La Harpe had sinned at all. The sinner was dear to him. He must lie, if need be, to prove his innocence to the world.

Naturally, the La Harpes had to go away. And since they must go, would it not be better for their accomplice, Denis, to go too? It was not her first offence. She had helped Ximenès to steal manuscripts in 1754. Then, too, she was bored to death with Ferney; and her "natural aversion to a country life," wrote poor Voltaire "in confidence" to her sister, had had very ill effects upon her temper. Not all the *fêtes* and the visitors could make up to her for Paris. Voltaire said that he had been the innkeeper of Europe for fourteen years and was tired of the profession. "This tumult does not suit my seventy-four years or my feebleness." "Madame Denis has need of Paris." Here was one excuse for getting rid of her. And if more were wanted, there was her health which required the air of the capital and fashionable doctors; there were business affairs there which she might see to for her uncle; and a necessity of economising at Ferney brought about by her extravagance, and "muddle, which," said Grimm, "is carried by Mama Denis to a degree of perfection difficult to imagine."

To his friends Voltaire gave her health and the business to be looked after in Paris as reasons for her visit. They were that lesser part of the truth which is useful to conceal the greater. If he was loyal to La Harpe, so he was to Madame Denis. Of her share in the theft of the manuscripts he uttered not a word.

He gave her twenty thousand francs to spend in Paris, over and above the yearly income which he had settled on her.

Before March 1, 1768, the two La Harpes, Madame Denis, Marie Dupuits, and her husband, who had fallen under the ban of suspicion too, and declined to utter a word or give an iota of evidence on either side, had all started for the capital.

Voltaire dismissed the servants—except a couple of lacqueys and a valet. He sold his horses. "An old invalid recluse" had no need of them. Seven visitors who were staying in the house at the time, seeing their host's evident need of solitude, tactfully departed. There only remained Father Adam, faithful Wagnière, a colleague of Wagnière's called Bigex—a Savoyard, who had formerly been trusted servant and copyist in the service of Grimm—and two of the usual ne'er-do-weels, de Morsan and an ex-American officer called Rieu. Both these persons seem to have suppressed themselves with great success when they were not wanted, and to have been regarded by their benefactor as part of the household effects. He always spoke of himself as being entirely alone. Ferney was cleaned and put in order, and the stream of visitors ceased to flow.

It was certainly not because Voltaire was idle, but because his seventy-four years did not prevent him still being what the French call *malin*, that this Easter he decided to do what he had done at Colmar: play once more that 'deplorable comedy,' *faire ses Pâques*.

A priest was dining with him one night at Ferney. "Father D——," says Voltaire, "I wish, for example's sake, *faire mes Pâques* on Easter Day. I suppose you will give me absolution?"

"Willingly," says the priest. "I give it you." No more was said.

On Easter Day, 1768, Voltaire, accompanied by Wagnière and two gamekeepers, went solemnly to church, preceded by a servant carrying "a superb Blessed Loaf" which the Lord of Ferney was in the habit of presenting every Easter Sunday. After the distribution of this bread Voltaire mounted the pulpit and turned round and preached a little sermon. Protestant Wagnière had warned him against doing this. He felt sure it was illegal. But his master's mood was a wicked one; and, moreover, several thefts had been committed of late in his parish while all the people were at church, which gave him a text. His remonstrances were "vigorous, pathetic, and eloquent," and he warmly exhorted the people to the practice of virtue. The unhappy curé, not knowing what to do, hurried to the altar and proceeded with the mass. Voltaire spoke a few words in his praise, and then got down from the pulpit and resumed his own seat.

The story got noised abroad. Good Marie Leczinska mistook it for a conversion. The philosophers for once were at one with the orthodox, and condemned the deed. And so of course did Biort, Bishop of Annecy, who was also Prince and Bishop of Geneva, and of whose diocese Ferney was part.

In that wicked world of the eighteenth century there were few good bishops. But the Prelate of Annecy was one of them. He was also of strong character and of sound judgment and reason, with a fine capacity for irony.

On April 11, 1768, he wrote Voltaire a very excellent letter. He could not take, he said, as hypocrisy a deed which, if hypocritical, would tarnish a great man's glory and make him despicable in the eyes of all thoughtful persons. "I hope your future life will give proof of the integrity and sincerity of your act"; and then, in language of great dignity and even beauty, he attempted to recall the sinner to a sense of sin, and reminded him of that hour which could not now be far distant, when the faith would be his only hope, and his fame and glory the shadows of a dream.

Voltaire replied on April 15th, purposely misunderstanding the Bishop's letter and taking his remarks as compliments. He felt the act needed excuse. To d'Alembert, who was as freethinking as any man in

Paris, he wrote apologetically, that, finding himself between two fourteenth-century bishops, he was obliged to "howl with the wolves." He abused Biort as a fanatic and an imbecile. But he knew very well that he was neither. He was not so imbecile, at least, that he put any faith in a devout and serious letter M. de Voltaire was pleased to write to him on April 29th, and replied on May 2d in terms which showed very clearly that he knew his Voltaire—to the soul.

He had already issued a mandate to the clergy of his diocese forbidding them to give the Sacrament to this profane person. He now sent the whole correspondence to the King, and, as the only punishment adequate to the offence, he begged for a *lettre de cachet* for M. de Voltaire. Saint-Florentin was bidden to write the culprit a formal epistle, saying that the King strongly condemned "this enterprise" on the part of his ex-Gentleman-in-Ordinary. But there was no *lettre de cachet*. The incident had amused the Court. *That* covered a multitude of sins.

For the time the affair was over. But alas! only for the time.

Though there were few visitors in Madame Denis's absence, there were some. In the August of this 1768 two very lively young men, both about twenty years old, came over from Geneva to call upon the Patriarch of Ferney. One of them, named Price, told a friend more than forty years after, the little he recollected of the occasion. His companion was then known as the son of Lord Holland, but later and now as Charles James Fox. He had first visited Ferney in 1764 when he was sixteen.

Voltaire was delighted to see his visitors, but, as usual, declared that they had only come to bury him; and though he walked about the garden and drank chocolate with them, did not invite them to dinner.

The only part of their conversation Price recollected after that interval of forty years was that the host gave them the names of such of his works as might open their minds and "free them from religious prejudice," adding, "Here are the books with which to fortify yourselves."

Charles paid other visits to Ferney, and Voltaire soon learnt to love him, as all the world loved that generous and brilliant youth. "Y^r son is an English lad and j an old Frenchman," the Patriarch wrote to Lord Holland after Charles's next visit. "He is healthy and j sick. Yet j love him with all my heart, not only for his father but himself." Voltaire gave the young man dinner this time, in his "little caban"; and Charles became a *persona grata* at Ferney, as in all the world.

Another Englishman with whom Voltaire was brought into relation in the summer of 1768 was Horace Walpole. Voltaire had seen Horace's "Historic Doubts on Richard III.," and characteristically wrote that it was fifty years since *he* took a vow to doubt, and reminded Horace that he had known his father and uncle in England. Horace sent a copy of his book, and the correspondence drifted on to that favourite topic of contention between literary Englishmen and Voltaire—Shakespeare. Voltaire, who wrote in his own language—what need to write in English to "the best Frenchman ever born on English soil"?—pointed out with just pride in reply that he had been the first to make Shakespeare, Locke, and Newton known to the French, and that, in spite of the persecutions of a clique of fanatics. "I have been your apostle and your martyr: truly English people have no reason to complain of me."

If some new friends came into Voltaire's life in this solitary 1768, more old ones went out of it.

On June 24th of this year died Marie Leczinska. Friend? Well, once. There was that pension *sur sa cassette*, and "my poor Voltaire."

In the autumn died Olivet—a friend indeed—the best of Latinists, the kindly schoolmaster at Louis-le-Grand.

In December, that silent staunch laborious worker for the philosophic faith, Damilaville, met death with the resolute courage with which he had faced life, and left the world poorer for one of those rare people who say nothing and do much.

Voltaire mourned him as a public as well as a personal loss. He mourned him characteristically—that such a man should die while Fréron waxed fat! But since they did, the less time to sit idle and weeping.

Up then, and at them with those little deadly arrows of which the Voltairian quiver was always full—the arrows called Pamphlets.

CHAPTER XL

THE COLONY OF WATCHMAKERS AND WEAVERS

"WHAT harm can a book do that costs a hundred crowns?" Voltaire had written to Damilaville on April 5, 1765. "Twenty volumes folio will never make a revolution; it is the little pocket pamphlets of thirty sous that are to be feared."

He had acted on that principle all his life. But he had never acted upon it so much as in his hand-to-hand battle with *l'infâme*. He never acted upon it so often as in his eighteen months' solitude at Ferney in 1768-69.

For many years, from that "manufactory" of his, as Grimm called it, he poured forth a ceaseless stream of dialogues, epistles, discourses, reflections, novelettes, commentaries, burlesques, reviews. Hardly any of them were more than a few pages in length. But each dealt with some subject near to his wide heart; cried aloud for some reform which had not been made, and must be made; pointed out with mocking finger some scandal in Church or State; satirised with killing irony some gross abuse of power; turned on some miscarriage of civil justice the searchlight of truth; laughed lightly, in dialogue, at the education of women by nuns in convents to fit them to be wives and mothers in the world; drew up damning statistics of the 9,468,800 victims "hanged, drowned, broken on the wheel, or burnt, for the love of God" and their religion from the time of Constantine to Louis XIV.; pleaded vivaciously against the eighty-two annual holidays set apart by the Church on which it was criminal to work but not to be drunken and mischievous; enumerated the "Horrible Dangers of Reading," of knowing, of thinking; and lashed with the prettiest of stinging little whips a corrupt ministry, a wicked priesthood, and *l'infâme*, *l'infâme*.

"*Il fait le tout en badinant.*" Serious? Why, no. "Our French people want to learn without studying"; and they shall. Instruct! Instruct! but as one instructs a child with a lesson in the form of a story, or the simplest little sermon with a sugar-plum of a joke at the end. This was such a laughing philosopher that many persons have doubted if he really could have been a philosopher at all. He turned so many somersaults, as friend Frederick put it plaintively. But the somersaults gained him an audience, and once gained he knew very well how to keep and teach it. It was one of his own sayings that ridicule does for everything and is the strongest of arms. He proved the truth of that assertion himself—in the pamphlets by which he held the attention and commanded the intellect of the eighteenth century.

Read them now—they are the must amusing reading in the world—and beneath the sparkling mockery, see the burning meaning.

They are, considered as works of art alone, much more than brilliant burlesques. Each of them is endowed with Voltaire's "unquenchable life," and "stamped with the express image" of his whole personality. Gay, crisp, and clear, expressing his ideas in the fewest and easiest words and in the most vivacious and graceful of all literary styles, they conveyed to his generation "the consciousness at once of the power and the rights of the human intelligence."

Through these pamphlets "the revolution works in all minds. Light comes by a thousand holes it is impossible to stop up." "Reason penetrates into the merchants' shops as into the nobles' palaces."

What better proof could Voltaire himself have wanted of the growth of that liberty and tolerance which he loved, and strove to make all men love and have, than the fact that the government, autocratic and all-powerful as it was, could not prevent those pamphlets selling and working in their midst?

"Opinion rules the world," said Voltaire himself. At last he had made his opinion, Public Opinion. "From 1762 to the end of Voltaire's life it was on the side of the philosophers."

True, the authorities still burnt his works. In 1768 he had written "The Man with Forty Crowns," a burlesque story "on the financial chaos which fifteen years later brought France to bankruptcy." That must be burnt of course. France hated unfavourable prophecies. It *was* burnt. But by now Voltaire's pamphlets were like Shadrach, Meshach, and Abednego. Flames could not hurt them. And when they came out of the fiery furnace it was only with an added lustre and glory.

Well for Voltaire if those pamphlets could have engrossed all his solitude. In Beuchot's edition of his writings they fill ten large volumes. Here surely was occupation enough for a lifetime! But Voltaire had time for everything, and was for ever the spoilt boy who loved his own way.

The Easter of 1769 reminded him of last Easter and the fact that the Bishop of Annecy had forbidden his priesthood to allow him to confess or communicate. Very well then! I will do both.

His feeble body had been ill and ailing for a year—a condition of things which is apt to make the mind unreasonable. There was a recent case of a man called Boindin, who, dying unfortified by the Sacraments, had been refused Christian burial. There was always the case of Adrienne Lecouvreur—"thrown into the kennel like a dead dog."

Voltaire declared, to persons whom he could have no object in deceiving, that he had lately had "twelve accesses of fever." He was seventy-five years old. And death always was and had been a far more present reality to him than to most people.

These things taken together form, not at all a valid excuse, but some sort of honest excuse for an act that needs a great deal of excusing.

Voltaire was in bed one day in the March of 1769, dictating to Wagnière, when he saw from his window Gros, the Ferney curé, and a Capuchin monk who had come to help him with the Easter confessions, walking in the garden. Voltaire sent for the Capuchin and told him that he was too ill to leave his bed, but as a Frenchman, an official of the King, and seigneur of the parish, he wished there and then to make his confession. And he put the usual fee of six francs into the Capuchin's hand. The poor man, with the fear of his Bishop before his eyes, nervously temporised, said he was very busy and would return in a few days.

"Trust me to get even with him!" cries the patient when M. le Capuchin had retired. Burgos, "a kind of surgeon," is sent for, and having felt the invalid's pulse, is fool enough to say that it is excellent.

"What, you ignorant fellow! Excellent?" roars the sick man.

Burgos feels it again. It is a very different pulse this time, and M. de Voltaire is in a high fever.

"Then go and tell the priest."

Six days elapsed and no priest appeared. So the very active-minded invalid caused the whole household to be roused in a body in the middle of the night, and to hurry off to the curé saying their master was dying and presenting a certificate signed by himself, Wagnière, Bigex, and Burgos, which declared the invalid's pious desire to die fortified with the Sacraments and in the bosom of the faith in which he was born and had lived.

Neither curé nor Capuchin appeared.

Then Voltaire sent a lawyer to the curé, saying that if he did not come, the Lord of Ferney would denounce him to the Parliament as having refused the Sacraments to a dying man.

The poor curé was in such a fright that he was attacked on the spot, says Wagnière, by the colic.

On March 31st, Voltaire drew up before a notary a statement in legal form declaring himself, in spite of calumnies, to be a sincere Catholic. Among others the complaisant Father Adam witnessed this statement.

The next day, April 1st, the Capuchin appeared at Ferney. The Bishop of Annecy had been consulted, and now sent by the Capuchin a profession of faith for Voltaire to sign.

The invalid, who had already recited a hurried jumble of the Pater, the Credo, and the Confiteor, replied that the Creed was supposed to contain the whole faith; and though the unhappy Capuchin went on presenting to him at intervals the Bishop's paper to sign, he would do nothing but repeat his statement about the Creed. After having delivered to the Capuchin a long homily on morality and tolerance (which Wagnière found "very touching and pathetic") the sick man suddenly called out loudly, "Give me absolution at once," which the terrified confessor, who had entirely lost his head, did. Then Voltaire sent for the curé, who administered the Sacrament.

The notary was also present. "At the very instant the priest gave the wafer to M. de Voltaire" he declared aloud that he sincerely pardoned those who had calumniated him to the King "and who have not succeeded in their base design, and I demand a record of my declaration from the notary." He recorded it. No sooner was Voltaire left to himself than this amazing invalid jumped out of bed and went for a walk in the garden.

Meanwhile, curé and Capuchin laid their terrified heads together and bethought themselves of some means to avoid the consequences of having absolved and given the mass to the scoffer without his having signed the declaration drawn up by the Bishop.

On April 15th, they summoned seven witnesses whom they had persuaded to declare on oath that they had heard M. de Voltaire pronounce a complete and satisfactory confession of faith, which confession they invented and sent to the Bishop.

The hocus-pocus was on both sides, it will be seen. But Voltaire was responsible for it all. Paris—even Paris—received the news of his "unpardonable buffoonery" "pretty badly." The d'Argentals entirely disapproved of it, and Dr. Tronchin condemned it with severity.

"Useless *méchancétés* are very foolish," Voltaire had said. He regarded this one as indispensable. When he wrote to his Angels excusing himself, he declared that he had need of a buckler to withstand the mortal blows of sacerdotal calumny, and that such a duty, neglected, might at his death have had very unpleasant consequences for his family. These were not sufficient reasons for his act. But they at least free him from "the reproach of erecting hypocrisy into a deliberate doctrine." As Condorcet says, "such deceptions did not deceive, while they did protect." "Disagreeable as these temporisings are to us," they damn deeper the time which made them a pressing expedient, than the time-server.

As the Bishop of Annecy had accused Voltaire of holding impious conversations at his dinner-table, he now took advantage of Madame Denis's absence to have pious works read aloud to him at that meal. When a President of the Parliament of Dijon was dining with him, Massillon, of whom Voltaire was a warm admirer, was the author chosen. "What style! What harmony! What eloquence!" cries the Patriarch of Ferney as he listens to those magnificent periods, to the denunciations like a god's. The reader continued for three or four pages.

"Off with Massillon!" cries Voltaire, and "he gave himself up to all the folly and *verve* of his imagination." Irreverence? Malicious mockery? It has been generally thought so. May it not rather have been that both sentiments were perfectly genuine? that in one there expressed itself the passionate admiration and in the other the irresponsible liveliness, of which this extraordinary character was equally capable?

Though he had nearly harried the life out of one poor Capuchin of Gex, though he had wantonly insulted the faith of all the Capuchins, almost his next act was to obtain for them, through Choiseul, an annuity of six hundred francs for the Gex monastery, in return for which benefit the Brothers gave him the title of Temporal Father of the Capuchins of Gex. He derived a monkeyish delight from it; used to sign his letters with a cross, "✝, Brother Voltaire unworthy Capuchin"; but then he also derived an honest delight from the good he had been able to do the monastery.

Who can explain him?

Presently he was writing to Cardinal Bernis to obtain the Pope's permission for Father Adam to wear a wig on his bald head during mass. The climate was cold, the poor Father rheumatic, and his Holiness had been obliged to forbid wigs to the priesthood as they had so often been used as a disguise for unworthy purposes.

All through religious controversies and irreligious acts, Voltaire was engaged in a long, constant and very flattering

VOLTAIRE

From the Etching by Denon

correspondence with Catherine the Great. Even Frederick, in the beguiling days before the Prussian visits, had not so gratified Voltaire's self-love. Voltaire was the teacher, and Catherine, the greatest of queens and the cleverest of women, his humble pupil. In 1768 she had taken his advice—there is no subtler form of flattery—upon inoculation, and herself submitted to the operation. And in this 1769 she sent him the loveliest pelisse of Russian sable, a snuff box she had turned with her own royal hands, her portrait set in diamonds, and an epitome of the laws with which she governed her great empire. Here surely was balm for solitude, calumny, sickness, old age, every mortal misfortune! Voltaire warmed body and soul through the snowy Swiss spring in that gorgeous pelisse. In March, he had another present, which delighted his queer old heart hardly less. Saint-Lambert—Saint-Lambert, who had robbed him of his mistress and wounded him with a wound which another man could never have forgiven or forgotten—sent him his poem, "The Seasons." And the poet Voltaire writes to his brother of the lyre the most charming compliments and congratulations.

Before this, he was writing the kindest letters to La Harpe again. When Madame Denis, in the latter half of this October, 1769, and after an absence of a little less than eighteen months, burst into Ferney, her uncle seems to have folded her in his arms, received her with as much delight as if she had always been trustworthy, practical, sensible, and considerate, and to have let bygones be bygones as only he knew how.

The Dupuits were already home again; and Voltaire was busy with a new business which had been in his mind since he first came to Ferney, and in practical existence at least since 1767.

From the moment he had bought his estates he had felt the full weight of his responsibilities as a landowner, and realised as keenly as Arthur Young, the philosophic farmer who rode through France prophesying her downfall, that agriculture is the true wealth of a nation.

"The best thing we have to do on earth is to cultivate it."

At more than threescore years and ten, this old son of the pavement had set himself to learn, and did learn, the whole *technique* of agriculture. Directly he bought Ferney he began putting the barren land round it under cultivation, and so occupied all persons on his estates who were out of work. When he was seventy-eight he was still hard at work with his own hands on that field which had been called Voltaire's Field, because he cultivated it entirely himself.

It has been seen how he planted avenues of trees. Four times over he lined his drive with chestnut and walnut trees, and four times they nearly all died, or were wantonly destroyed by the peasants. "However, I am not daunted. The others laugh at me. Neither my old age nor my complaints nor the severity of the climate discourage me. To have cultivated a field and made twenty trees grow is a good which will never be lost."

He entered into a long correspondence with Moreau—that rare being, a practical Political Economist. He delighted in Galiani's famous "Dialogues on Corn"—never was man in the right so wittily before—and in this very 1769 he was thanking Abbé Mords-les-Morellet for his "Dictionary of Commerce."

For, after all, the Land meant the People; and commerce there must be, if the work of the People on the Land were to be remunerative.

Many terrible accounts have been given of the condition of the French poor before the Revolution. But theirs was a misery which no passion and eloquence can overstate.

Forbidden at certain seasons to guard their wretched pieces of land by fences lest they should interfere with my lord's hunt, or to manure their miserable crops lest they should spoil the flavour of my lord's game; forbidden, at hatching seasons, to weed those crops lest they should disturb the partridges; and forbidden, without special permission, to build a shed in which to store their grain—the fruit of their lands and their labour, if there was any such fruit, was always lost to them.

Taxes alone deprived them of three quarters of what they earned. On one side was the *corvée*, or the right of the lord to his peasants' labour without paying for it; and the *taille*, or the tax on property, which exacted a certain sum from each village: so that if the rich would not pay, the poor *must*.

Add to this the toll-gates, so numerous that fish brought from Harfleur to Paris paid eleven times its value *en route*; the fines exacted when land was bought or sold; above all, the enormous tax upon salt, which soon was as the match to fire the gunpowder of the Revolution; the tithes exacted by the Church: the fees for masses for the dead, for burying, christening, and marrying, coupled with the bitter injustice that the clergy of that Church were themselves exempt from all taxation.

Add to these regular taxes the irregular ones.

On the accession of Louis XV. one was levied, called the Tax of the Joyful Accession. Joyful! The people who paid it lived in a windowless, one-room hut of peat or clay; clothed in the filthiest rags; ignorant, bestial, degraded; creatures who never knew youth or hope: who died in unrecorded thousands, of pestilence and famine; or lived, to their own cruel misery, a few dark years "on a little black bread, and not enough of that."

Such were the fifty poor of Ferney as Voltaire found them, but not the twelve hundred he left.

Whatever his sins were—and they were many—he had one of the noblest and most difficult of virtues—a far higher conception of his duty to others than the men of his time. It was fashionable to talk philanthropy in the eighteenth century, but dangerous, as well as unmodish, to practise it.

"True philosophy ..." wrote the great Doer in the midst of the Dreamers, "makes the earth fertile and the people happier. The true philosopher cultivates the land, increases the number of the ploughs, and so of the inhabitants; occupies the poor man, and thus enriches him; encourages marriages, cares for the orphan; does not grumble at necessary taxes, and puts the labourer in a condition to pay them promptly."

He had begun by getting back for the Ferney poor that tithe of which Ancian had deprived them, and by making the peasants mend and make roads—at fair wages. Later, he petitioned the King for "some privileges for my children"; and Gex was at last declared free from all the taxes of the farmers-general, and salt, which used to be ten sous the pound, came down to four.

His building operations at both the church and château gave occupation to many masons. Then the masons must have decent dwellings in which to live themselves; and here was more work.

In 1767, he could write that he had formed a colony at Ferney; that he had established there three merchants, artists, and a doctor, and was building houses for them. By 1769 he recorded with an honest pride that he had quadrupled the number of the parishioners, and that there was not a poor man among them; that he had under his immediate supervision two hundred workers, and was the means of life to everyone round him.

Nor did he forget to provide them with pleasure as well as with work. Every Sunday the young people of the colony used to come up to the château to dance. Their host provided them with refreshments, and was the happiest spectator of their happiness.

Then he started a school, and himself paid the schoolmaster. There had been a time when he had thought that "it is not the labourer one must teach, it is the *bon bourgeois*, the inhabitant of towns: that enterprise is grand and great enough," which, for his day, it certainly was. It was a hundred years in advance of his time. Even that drastic reformer, Frederick the Great, had announced superbly, "The vulgar do not deserve enlightenment." So what wonder that in 1763 even a clear-sighted Voltaire prayed for "ignorant brothers to follow my plough?"

The wonder rather is that by 1767 his views had so enormously progressed that when Linguet, the barrister, wrote to him that in his opinion all was lost if the *canaille* were shown that they too could reason, he emphatically answered, instancing the intelligent Genevans who read as a relaxation from manual labour—"No, Sir; all is not lost when the people are put into a condition to see that they too have a mind. On the contrary, all is lost when they are treated like a herd of bulls, for sooner or later they will gore you with their horns."

Prophetic—but if many heard that voice crying in the wilderness, none acted on his words, save himself.

But in prospering Ferney there was room not only for a school and a doctor, masons and labourers, but for special industries. From the first, Voltaire had cultivated silkworms. He was never the man for an idle hobby. Why should no use be made of the silk? Before 1769, the Ferney theatre, which Madame Denis had lately used as a laundry, was turned into a silkworm nursery. From busy Geneva came stocking weavers, only too glad to colonise in a place where the lord, and master lent them money "on very easy terms," built decent dwellings for them, and gave them the full benefit of his knowledge of affairs.

By September 4, 1769, Voltaire, always alive to the advantages of a good advertisement, sent to the Duchesse de Choiseul the first pair of silk stockings ever made on his looms. If she would but wear them they *must* be the mode! What stocking would not look beautiful on a foot so charming? Voltaire found time to engage his Duchess to wear them, in a gay, coquettish, and essentially French correspondence. Madame had made a mistake, it appears, and sent him, as a pattern, a shoe much too large for her. Neither his thousand schemes and labours nor his seventy-five years had spoiled his talent for flattering badinage. His Duchess accepted his stockings and his compliments, showed both to her friends, and thus put some fifty to a hundred people, including young Calas who was helping his benefactor, out of the way of want.

On February 15, 1770, the party quarrels in Geneva came to a climax—and bloodshed.

The Natives had not forgotten the promise made to them four years earlier. "If you are forced to leave your country ... I shall still be able to help and protect you."

Neither had Voltaire.

On February 10, 1767, in writing to de Beauteville, the French mediator, he had suggested the scheme of a working colony—the nucleus of the idea of some enterprising person enticing the great watchmaking industry of quarrelsome Geneva to form a settlement, which should be managed by its founder and should bear his name. The scheme had appealed to Choiseul. In 1768, with Voltaire's co-operation and approval, that minister founded the colony of Versoix—or Versoy, as Voltaire spells it—which was designed to be what Ferney actually became.

The crisis of February 15, 1770, caused great numbers of the Native watchmakers of Geneva to flee from the city and take refuge at Versoix and at Ferney. Versoix was unequal to the emergency. There were no houses for the workers. But Ferney rose to the occasion. That was always part of its old master's genius.

Only a few months after the Natives had first consulted him, this far-seeing person had begun to build workmen's dwellings in his village. The overflow from those "pretty houses of freestone," he now took into the château itself. So far, so good.

The next thing to do was to obtain the permission for his settlement from the authorities. The authorities were personified by M. de Choiseul. Voltaire had helped him with his Versoix. So Choiseul could not, and did not, refuse to help Voltaire with Ferney.

To start the watchmakers in their new home at their old trade, Voltaire advanced sixty thousand livres. He at once found occupation for fifty Genevan workmen, not counting the inhabitants of Gex. He himself bought gold, silver, and jewels for the work, a better bargain than the work-people could do for themselves.

In six weeks he had watches ready for sale—of exquisite workmanship, artistic design, and to be sold at least one third cheaper than they could be in Geneva. The Duke of Choiseul bought the first six watches ever made by Voltaire's manufactory.

By April 9th the old courtier was promising the Duchess that she should soon have one worthy to wear even at *her* waist.

Then he began his system of personal advertisement. The handsomest commission in the world on every watch he sold could not have made the neediest agent work harder or more cunningly than did this Voltaire, who received at first no commission, never could expect a large one, and had need of neither large nor small.

On June 5, 1770, he sent round a circular to all the foreign ambassadors—"diplomacy *en masse*"—a most beautiful circular from "The Royal Manufactory of Ferney" (in capital letters), and recommending watches—"plain silver," from three louis, to repeaters at forty-two. That flaming document is still preserved.

The advertiser wrote a letter with it. "I never write for the sake of writing," he said; "but when I have a subject I do not spare my pen, old and dying as I am."

Catherine the Great was appealed to; and in answer to her "vaguely magnificent order for watches" to "the value of some thousands of roubles," Voltaire had to apologise for his workmen having taken advantage of her goodness, and sent her watches to the value of eight thousand!

The Empress replied imperially—as she was obliged to do—that such an expense would not ruin her. And in his next letter her artful old friend warmly recommended his pendulum clocks—"which we are now making"—and asked her to assist him in promoting a watch trade between Ferney and China. She did.

Ferney was soon sending watches not only to China, but to Spain, Italy, Russia, Holland, America, Turkey, Portugal, and North Africa, besides carrying on an enormous trade with Paris.

"Give me a chance and I am the man to build a city," said Voltaire to Richelieu. With a chance he could have done anything. Kings and commoners, cardinals, great ladies—he appealed to them all. Is not rosy-faced Bernis at Rome? Well, why should not he promote the sale of watches for me in the Imperial City?

Bernis totally ignored the commission. He was almost the only person to whom Voltaire applied who behaved so badly. And Ferney wrote him such a stinging reproach for his neglect that poor Bernis must have regretted he had not been more obliging.

As for Frederick the Great, he did better even than buy watches by the cartload like the other great potentate, Catherine.

He gave for twelve years free lodging in Berlin, with exemption from all taxation, to eighteen families of refugee Genevan watchmakers. This started the watchmaking industry in his capital.

To Madame Dubarry, who had succeeded to the honours and dishonour of the Pompadour, the Gentleman-in-Ordinary-to-the-King sent presently the loveliest little watch set in diamonds.

He left no stone unturned. He supervised every detail. In 1773, Ferney sold "four thousand watches worth half a million of francs." All losses Voltaire bore himself. Capable and alert as he was, they were sometimes heavy.

He had had a royal order, for instance, on the occasion of the marriage of the Dauphin with Marie Antoinette, which was encouraging but expensive. He was never paid.

Nothing daunted him however. By the June of 1770 he had begun building those much-needed houses in the rival, or rather the sister, colony of Versoix. And then, as if he found weaving and watchmaking insufficient for his energy, by 1772 he had started a lacemaking industry. That butterfly Madame Saint-Julien must make this airiest of gossamer fabrics—"the beautiful blonde lace which was made in our village"—the fashion. "The woman who made it can make more very reasonably. She can add a dozen workers to the staff, and we shall owe to you a new manufactory." The vigorous boy who wrote the words, originated the scheme, and carried it to successful issue, was only seventy-eight. He personally negotiated with the shop which was to buy and sell his new wares when made. Cannot one see him haggling and bargaining and enjoying himself, with a twinkle in his bright old eyes and a very humorous shrewdness in the curves of his thin lips?

But if he wanted a reward for all his trouble, he had it. The miserable hamlet had become a thriving village and the desert place blossomed like a rose. The master's corn fed his people and his bad wine ("which is not harmful") gave them drink. His bees produced excellent honey and wax, and his hemp and flax, linen.

Here dwelt together, as one family, Catholics and Huguenots. "Is not this better than St. Bartholomew?" "When a Catholic is sick, Protestants go and take care of him"; and *vice versa*. The good Protestant women prepared with their own hands the little portable altars for the Procession of the Holy Sacrament, and the curé thanked them publicly in a sermon. Gros had died—of drink, said Voltaire—and his place had been taken by Hugenot, an excellent priest, generous and liberal-minded, the friend of all his people whatever their faith, and of M. de Voltaire, who was supposed to have none at all.

Here surely was the tree of Tolerance he had planted, bearing beautiful fruit. It might well warm his old heart to see his little colony firm on "those two pivots of the wealth of a state, be it little or great, freedom of trade and freedom of conscience."

The man who worked the case of Calas for three years, the case of Sirven for seven, and the cases of Lally and d'Étallonde for twelve, was not likely to grow tired of the little colony always beneath his eyes. Nor was he unmindful of the claims not only Ferney, but all Gex, had upon his bounty. When it was devastated by famine in 1771 he had corn sent him from Sicily, and sold it much under cost price to his starving children and the poor people of the province. Their sufferings and sorrows were his own. He pleaded passionately for those who were, and had been for generations, miserable with the hopeless misery that is dumb; but who, before many years were past, were to cry aloud their wrongs with a great and terrible voice which would reach to the ends of the earth.

All Voltaire's letters in his later years are full of his watchmakers and weavers, their prosperity or their poverty, what he had done for them or what he would do. Did his own glorification play no part in his schemes? It doubtless played some. But the fact that he may have been vain does not alter the fact that he set an example which Christians have nobly followed, but which, in his day at least, they certainly did not set *him*.

Voltaire, sceptic and scoffer, too often of evil life and unclean lips, was not only the High Priest of Tolerance, but the first great practical philanthropist of his century.

LOUIS XVI.

From the Portrait by Callet in the Petit Trianon

CHAPTER XLI

THE PIGALLE STATUE, AND THE VINDICATION OF LALLY

ONE spring evening of the year 1770 the idea was suggested, at the table of the Neckers in Paris, of erecting a statue to the great Voltaire.

Necker was a prosperous banker, and, to be, Comptroller-General.

Madame, his wife, once the beloved of Gibbon, was the daughter of a Swiss minister and one of the first *salonières* in the capital.

The plan was immediately approved and acted upon by her seventeen guests. They formed themselves into a committee to receive subscriptions, and decided that the work should be entrusted to the famous Pigalle, who was to fix his own price, which he did very modestly.

Madame Necker herself communicated the plan to Voltaire.

He was boyishly delighted at the compliment. He answered gaily that he was seventy-six and had just had a long illness which had treated both his mind and body very badly, and that if Pigalle was to come and model his face he must first have a face to model. "You would hardly guess where it ought to be. My eyes have sunk three inches; my cheeks are like old parchment; ... the few teeth I had are gone.... This is not coquetry, it is truth."

It was. Dr. Burney, who visited Ferney in this year, spoke of his host as a living skeleton—"mere skin and bone"—but he spoke, too, like everybody else, of the gleaming eyes full of living fire; and d'Alembert wrote to the model himself: "Genius ... has always a countenance which genius, its brother, will easily find."

Subscriptions had flowed in from the first with unprecedented generosity. The magnificent Richelieu contributed magnificently. Frederick, one of the first to wish to give, wrote to ask d'Alembert of what amount his gift should be.

"An écu, Sire, and your name," says d'Alembert. But Frederick gave more than money. In noble words and a most generous eulogy, he blotted out Frankfort and the past for ever. "The finest monument to Voltaire is the one he has erected himself. His work will endure when the Basilisk of St. Peter, the Louvre, and all the buildings which human vanity supposes eternal, have perished."

Voltaire was delighted at Frederick's subscription (which of course was not limited to words), not only because that great name would look nobly, but for a more characteristic reason. "It would save money to too generous literary men, who have none."

Among the "too generous literary men" were four old enemies—Rousseau, Fréron, Palissot, and La Beaumelle. Their money was returned—except that of Rousseau. And peace-making d'Alembert had very hard work to get *vif* Voltaire to accept Jean Jacques's gift as a "reparation."

Another foe more unforgiving—or more honest—declined to give at all. "I will not give a sou to the *sub*scription," says Piron, "but I will undertake the *in*scription."

About June 16th, Pigalle, sculptor to the King and Chancellor of the Academy of Painting, arrived at Ferney, on work intent. But the model was so agreeable a host! True, in spite of the parties and distractions, he gave the sculptor a sitting every day. But as he never kept still a moment and was dictating letters, with much vivid French gesticulation, to Wagnière the whole time, it was not wonderful that on the seventh day of a visit which was to last eight, M. Pigalle discovered that he had done nothing at all. Fortunately, on that seventh day—June 23, 1770—the conversation turned upon the Golden Calf of the Children of Israel. Voltaire was so childishly delighted when Pigalle declared that such a thing would take at least six months to make—as disproving the Mosaic testimony that it was made in twenty-four hours—that during the rest of the sitting the model was as quiet and obedient as possible. The results were so satisfactory that Pigalle resolved not to attempt another interview, and the next morning left Ferney quietly and without seeing anyone.

The Golden Calf incident so pleased Voltaire that he at once wrote it down and dated it. He repeated it, with much chuckling, to all his correspondents; wrote an article on Casting for his dear "Philosophical Dictionary," where he introduced it again, most amusingly; and in 1776 wrote a pamphlet—"A Christian against Six Jews"—in which he put Pigalle's professional testimony in opposition to that of the sacred writers.

Another account of the episode declares that Pigalle kept his sitter quiet by talking of his dear "Pucelle."

There seems no reason why both stories should not be true.

Pigalle's statue disappointed his own generation, and is only a curiosity to ours.

The best statue of Voltaire is usually considered to be the one by Houdon, of a very old, sitting, draped figure, with a face far from unamiable or unkindly, excessively able and shrewd, with the most steady, penetrating old eyes, and mocking lips closed over the toothless mouth.

Pigalle represented his subject entirely unclad—for the best of all reasons, said Grimm, he could not do drapery. Good Madame Necker, mindful of her Calvinistic education, objected to the nakedness. But not old Voltaire. "It is all one to me," he said airily; and added sensibly, "M. Pigalle must be left absolute master of his statue.... It is a crime ... to put fetters on genius."

The want of clothing, however, gave rise to many doubtful jokes in eighteenth-century Paris, and his enemies made very spiteful epigrams on the meagreness of the figure. "Posterity will not want to count M. de Voltaire's ribs," says Fréron sarcastically. And though Voltaire pretended to laugh at such gibes—and laughed himself at all his bodily defects—he was still morally thin-skinned. "A statue is no consolation," he wrote dismally to d'Argental, "when so many enemies conspire to cover it with mud."

But there were more friends to cover it with adulation. In 1772, Mademoiselle Clairon surprised the *habitués* of her rooms one evening by drawing back a curtain and showing them the bust of Voltaire on an altar. She put a laurel crown on the head, and in her "noble and beautiful voice" recited an ode of Marmontel's which, particularly in its Apostrophe to Envy, produced a great effect.

When Voltaire heard of the incident, he got out his old lyre and thanked Mademoiselle in verse of extraordinary freshness—"very pretty for a young man of only seventy-nine," says Grimm.

While his statue was the topic of Paris, the original was entertaining at least three celebrated visitors at Ferney: Dr. Burney, d'Alembert, and Condorcet.

Dr. Burney, the father of Johnson's dear *protégée*, Fanny, came to Geneva in the course of his Musical Tour through France and Italy.

Hearing that Voltaire relentlessly snubbed the curious idle who only came "to look at the wild beast," the good pompous Doctor was a little nervous of the reception he might meet. But all went well.

A servant, presumably Wagnière, introduced Burney to his master's sanctum, and to the library, where Burney saw a portrait of young Dupuits, whom he supposed to be Voltaire's brother, though Wagnière told him Voltaire was seventy-eight (he was really seventy-six), and the difference in age between the "brothers" must have been forty years at the least.

Then Dr. Burney was introduced to the great man himself, who still worked, said Wagnière, ten hours a day and wrote constantly without spectacles. The conversation turned on English literature, and Voltaire observed how England had now no one "who lords it over the rest like Dryden, Pope, and Swift"; and remarked, when critics are silent it proves not so much that the age is correct, as that it is dull. Burney was shown the model village—"the most innocent and the most useful of all my works"—and tactfully departed before he should have taken more than his share of the great man's time.

D'Alembert arrived at Ferney in the September of 1770. He was supposed to be *en route* to see Rome and die. Frederick the Great had sent him six thousand francs for the tour. But either, as d'Alembert told the King, the prospect of the fatigue and the bad inns daunted him, or, as Duvernet says, Voltaire's society was too seductive. D'Alembert returned the King half of his money, and in two months was back in Paris.

The Marquis de Condorcet, who then was celebrated as a philosophic and freethinking noble who had wholly broken with the religion and the traditions of his caste, and now is celebrated as the philosopher and *littérateur* who wrote a brief and scholarly Life of Voltaire and who poisoned himself to escape the guillotine, was a fellow-guest with d'Alembert.

Is it difficult to fancy the conversation between these three men over the Ferney supper-table at the magic hour when Voltaire was always at his best, "at once light and learned," brilliant and subtle? The tranquil cheerfulness of that true philosopher, d'Alembert—"his just mind and inexhaustible imagination"—soothed the vexations with which he found his irritable host overwhelmed.

Condorcet, whom Voltaire spoke of as having "the same hatred of oppression and fanaticism, and the same zeal for humanity" as he had himself, was as exempt from what it was then modish to call "prejudices," as the gentle d'Alembert.

Of that brilliant little party there was but one man who still clung to some tenets of the old faith; and that man was Voltaire. Du Pan records how he heard him give an "energetic lesson" at his supper-table to his two guests, by sending all the servants out of the room in the middle of their conversation. "Now, gentlemen, continue your attack on God. But as I do not want to be strangled or robbed to-night by my servants they had better not hear you."

"*Si Dieu n'existait pas il faudrait l'inventer,*" Voltaire had said in one of the most famous lines in the world.

Baron Gleichen, who was at Délices in 1757, records how a young author sought to recommend himself to the great man's favour by saying "I am an atheist apprentice at your service." "But I," replied Voltaire, "am a master Deist."

But the pupils he had taught had gone far beyond his teaching. Diderot spoke of him as "*cagot*"; and the story runs that some fine lady of Paris dismissed him scornfully in the words, "He is a Deist, he is a bigot."

He had no further bigotries, it is certain. A thousand stories are told to illustrate his indignation against what he took to be a debasing fanaticism.

A Genevan lady brought to see him her little girl, who was as intelligent as she was pretty and could learn everything but her Catechism, and that she could not understand. "Ah!" says Voltaire. "How reasonable! A child always speaks the truth. You do not understand your Catechism? Do you see these fine peaches? Eat as many as you like."

It is recorded, too, that Voltaire had always a special grudge against Habakkuk: and when someone showed him that he had misrepresented facts in that prophet's history, "It is no matter," he replied; "Habakkuk was capable of anything."

There are many other such stories told of him. All profane jests are fathered on Voltaire. Some of them have lost their point with the circumstances and surroundings among which they were uttered. Some grow clumsy in translation. Some are without authenticity. That a searching wit like Voltaire, quite unhampered by reverence, must have found abundant subject for witticism in the degraded state of the established religion of his country in his time, is palpable enough.

D'Alembert left. It was his last visit to Ferney.

On December 24, 1770, the powerful Choiseul was disgraced and exiled by the far more powerful Dubarry. "The coachman of Europe," as Frederick called him, had been infinitely clever and infinitely unlucky. If he had made the army and remade the fleet, expelled the Jesuits, and promoted trade, art, and literature, he had involved his country in wars, for which she had wept tears of blood. He fell: and great was the fall of him.

The tidings were received at Ferney with the utmost consternation. For Voltaire personally Choiseul had done much. He had helped in the affairs of Calas and of Chaumont, in that of the Corneille Commentary, and of the blockade of Ferney. And, more than all, he had protected, with the absolutely necessary protection none but a powerful minister could afford, the colony of watchmakers and weavers.

His disgrace ruined Versoix: and Ferney rocked on her foundations.

The steady resolution, and perhaps the fighting renown, of her old master tided his children over the crisis. But there was famine as well as disturbance abroad in the land, and for a while things looked black indeed.

On January 23d of the new year 1771, Louis XV., d'Aiguillon, the successor of Choiseul, and Maupeou, the Chancellor, suppressed the Parliament of Paris, to the general disgust. Voltaire did not share it. That Parliament, if it had been forced at last to reinstate the Calas, had condemned La Barre, d'Étallonde, and General Lally: it "was defiled with the blood of the weak and the innocent"; had burnt the works of the Encyclopædists; and been so fiercely Jansenist that wise men regretted the Jesuits it had ruined. In its place were to be established six Superior Councils or Local Parliaments, which were to give justice gratuitously and to be the final courts of appeal, thereby saving the nation the enormous expense of conveying accused persons to the capital. To be sure, the jury system as practised in ideal England was better still. But in an imperfect world one must be satisfied with imperfect progress.

Voltaire believed the six sovereign Councils to be "the salvation of France"—"one of the best ideas since the foundation of monarchy." As far back as 1769 he had attacked the old Parliament, under a very transparent anonymity, in his "History of the Parliament of Paris."

All things considered, there was no wonder that a shrewd Maupeou, knowing how bitterly public opinion was against him, should call to his aid the man "who had led it and fashioned it to his taste." Voltaire put himself at the disposition of Maupeou, and for many a month deafened the enemy with blast upon blast from his famous old trumpet.

If he was quite disinterested—and he was—in working under Maupeou for what he felt convinced was "the liberty, salvation, and well-being of whole populations," it was not at all unnatural that Choiseul should find it hard to forgive this active devotion to the policy of his supplanters.

The Duchess, with whom Voltaire had coquetted so charmingly over that pair of silk stockings, was as much offended as her husband. Madame du Deffand, her dearest friend, was offended too. And Voltaire spared himself neither pains nor time to restore confidence, to assure the dear exiles of Chanteloup in immense letters of his sincere and unaltering devotion to them: of his gratitude for the powerful protection of the one, and the gracious kindness of the other. Of course such letters had no effect. The haughty little Duchess begged that the correspondence might end. And the most obstinate of men went on writing to her exactly the same.

There was division in his own house on the subject of the Parliament too. His nephew, Mignot, that short-sighted, good-natured, roundabout abbé, the son of Catherine, and the brother of Mesdames Denis and Florian, was, like his uncle, on the side of the reforms, and on May 20, 1771, was made senior clerk of the new Parliament.

D'Hornoy, on the other hand, Voltaire's great-nephew, had been a councillor of the old Parliament and was exiled with it.

However, politics apart, Voltaire liked both nephews, thought them honest souls, and made them, as has been noted, handsome allowances.

Brochures against the old Parliament and for the new occupied the Hermit of Ferney very actively during the whole of the year 1771, but they did not prevent him carrying on a correspondence with four sovereigns— Catherine, Frederick, Stanislas Augustus Poniatowski, and Gustavus III. of Sweden.

On December 18th he began a new tragedy, "The Laws of Minos." It was that dismal thing, a play with a purpose—"to make superstition execrable, and prove that when a law is unequal there is nothing for it but to abolish it." It was written in honour of Maupeou. The Chancellor's enemies did Voltaire a good turn by preventing it from being played.

Death was busy just now among both friends and foes of Voltaire. He was fast reaching the age when he was naturally the last leaf on the tree. In the December of 1771 died Helvétius, philosopher and farmer-general; in the spring of 1772, Duclos, who had replaced Voltaire as Historiographer of France, and preceded d'Alembert as Secretary to the Academy. Then fell a leaf from the Arouet branch itself. Madame de Florian, always delicate, went the way of all flesh; and by February 1, 1772, her widowed husband had arrived at Ferney in that loud desolation which is the herald of speedy consolation.

He met at Ferney a very pretty, vivacious little Protestant who had been divorced from her first husband for incompatibility of temper. The pair were gaily married before April 1, 1772—to the disgust of Madame Denis, who rightly thought her sister was forgotten too soon, but to the delight of that old matchmaker, Voltaire.

Besides the bride and bridegroom, there was also at hospitable Ferney, Florian's nephew, whom Voltaire called Florianet, an observant youth who lived to write "The Youth of Florian, or Memoirs of a Young Spaniard," and who had stayed here before when he was a boy of ten or eleven. He had acted then as a sort of page to Voltaire, and Father Adam had furthered his education by setting him Latin exercises. Voltaire used to help the child out of those intricacies concerning Hostages and the Gate of a City, play games with him, and try to wake in him liveliness and wit. "Seem witty, and the wit will come" was the advice of the wittiest man of his century.

Florianet was seventeen now, and amused himself, during a visit of two months, with balls, hunting, a quarrel with his new aunt, and games with Marie Dupuits's little girl. She was eight years old and very intelligent, and Voltaire was fond of her with that fondness for all young creatures which is surely an amiable trait in a busy man.

He was hardly less fond of Wagnière's children (the Genevan boy was a married man by this time, rearing a family at Ferney), who used to play about the room while the Patriarch dictated to their father.

In this spring of 1772, Voltaire was occupied in building a pretty little house in the neighbourhood for the Florian husband and wife. The poor bride was not destined to enjoy it long. She died two years later of a disease which was called by many extraordinary names and received the most extraordinary treatment, but which appears to have been consumption. The Marquis immediately fell violently in love with someone else.

The only significance of his third Marquise lies in the fact that she was the bearer of a conciliatory letter and a copy of his "Natural History" from the famous Buffon to Voltaire—the two having previously been on bad terms.

More visitors flocked to Ferney in the autumn of 1772. Lekain paid a third visit, and, the Genevan theatre having been burnt, "bewitched Geneva" at Châtelaine instead.

Châtelaine was a playhouse which Voltaire had built on French soil, but only a few yards from the territory of the republic, to the great umbrage of "Tronchins and syndics."

They did not hate it less in this September, when Lekain's seductive genius drew their young people within its walls by half-past eleven A.M. for a performance which was to take place at four, and the women wept and fainted at his pathos. Old Voltaire had a box reserved for him, cried like a schoolgirl at one moment, and the next applauded as if he were possessed, by thumping his stick violently on the floor and crying aloud, "It's splendid! It couldn't be better!"

A cool-headed English visitor, Dr. John Moore, who was here during one of Lekain's visits, described the performances as only "moderately good."

Traveller, physician, and writer, the author of a popular novel, "Zeluco," and the father of the hero of Coruña, Moore had frequent opportunities of conversing with the famous old skeleton who had so "much more spirit and vivacity than is generally produced by flesh and blood." He understood Voltaire far better than most of the English visitors. To be sure, he could not forgive him his adverse criticisms on Shakespeare—the king who can do no wrong. But Dr. Moore, himself a sincere Christian, was one of the very few who admitted that Voltaire was as sincere an unbeliever; that his Deism was not an offensive affectation to shock the devout, but a

VOLTAIRE'S DECLARATION OF FAITH

From the Original in the Bibliothèque Nationale, Paris

profound conviction; and that "as soon as he is convinced of the truths of Christianity he will openly avow his opinion, in health as in sickness, uniformly to his last moment."

Dr. Moore also perceived that here was the man who was not afraid of dying—only of dying before he had said all he had to say. He records Voltaire's famous comparison of the British nation to a hogshead of its own beer—"the top of which is froth, the bottom dregs, the middle excellent." Moore's "Society and Manners in France" contains one of the best, if not the best, accounts of Voltaire written from personal observation by an Englishman.

In the midst of theatrical gaieties news reached Voltaire of the death of Theriot, on November 23, 1772. Old age, that merciful narcotic, helped to deaden the blow for Theriot's old friend. Also, Theriot had long been proven worthless, and he had a great many of Voltaire's letters in his possession, which roused Voltaire from grief to anxiety lest they should appear incontinently in print.

On December 8th he was writing to d'Alembert to recommend "brother La Harpe" (who had so grievously failed him) for the post, left vacant by Theriot's death, of Parisian correspondent to Frederick the Great.

At the end of 1772, the jealousy of foolish Denis made another little *fracas* at Ferney. A girl of seventeen, Mademoiselle de Saussure, the daughter of a famous doctor, and "a very wide-awake little person," said Grimm, had the good fortune to amuse, and often visit, a Voltaire of seventy-eight. Madame Denis, who disliked Mademoiselle, not only for herself, but as being a relative of her sister's supplanter, the second Madame Florian, made a scandal of the affair.

If ever that homely proverb, "Give a dog a bad name and hang him," was true of anybody, it was certainly true of Voltaire.

It was wonderful that that sensitive niece did not find a cause of jealousy when, in the June of 1773, an old friend, La Borde, came back to Ferney, bearing with him as a present for Voltaire the portrait of Madame Dubarry, on which that charming and disreputable lady had imprinted two kisses. Her favour was worth having. Only twenty-seven years old, and but recently picked up from the gutter, she was the real ruler of France. She had dismissed Choiseul; she had made Terrai, that dissolute Comptroller-General of Finances, whose "edicts fell in showers"; and she used the public treasury as if it were her private purse.

Voltaire knew King and Court too well to neglect such a power. Somehow, in Geneva the winters had been getting longer and more snowy than ever; and always, in his mind, was that old, old idea of seeing Paris once again before he died. And there was no chance of a return if the Omnipotent Woman was unfavourable.

So Voltaire replied with that happy mixture of grace and effrontery for which his youth had been so famous, and in September, 1773, as has been noted, he sent Madame the sweetest little watch set in diamonds.

She repaid him for his compliments—on the spot. She helped him to vindicate General Lally.

It must not be thought that statues and visitors, old age in the present, and death in a near future, made Voltaire forget to fight *l'infâme*, or the iniquitous legal system which was often *l'infâme's* strongest support. He never forgot anything; and his mind had room for a thousand interests that never jostled or hurt each other.

In 1772, it had been greatly occupied by the case of the Bombelles.

Madame de Bombelles, a Protestant, had the misfortune to be the wife of a French officer who grew tired of her, and in order that he might marry someone else, discarded his wife on the excuse that they had been married by Protestant rites. The unhappy woman pleaded her case at law. It was decided against her; her marriage declared null and void; ordained that she should pay the costs of the suit; that her child should be educated as a Catholic, at its father's expense. Voltaire pleaded long and loud against a decision so shameful, and pleaded, as usual, as if the interest in hand were the only one he had in the world.

But though *l'infâme* was responsible for much, the cruelly unjust justice of the day had upon its guilty soul crimes with which *l'infâme* had nothing to do.

There had been the case of Martin—condemned to the wheel "on an equivocal meaning." The wretched man, arraigned on a wholly unfounded suspicion of murder, when one of the witnesses said that he did not recognise him as the person he had seen escaping from the scene of action, cried out, "Thank God! There is one who has not recognised me!" Which the judge took to mean, "Thank God! I committed the murder but have not been recognised by the witness."

The real murderer confessed before long, but not before Martin had been tortured and broken on the wheel, his little fortune confiscated, and his innocent family dispersed abroad, so that they never even knew perhaps that their father was proved innocent—too late.

Voltaire wrote an account of the case to d'Alembert. "Fine phrases! Fine phrases!" he said once to an admirer complimenting him on his style. "I never made one in my life!" He never did. He wrote to make men act, as he had always written; and the substance of his tale was ever so great and so moving that the simpler the form of it, the more effective.

In 1773, he wrote the "Fragment on the Criminal Lawsuit of the Montbaillis."

It is only four pages long. It tells, in language to be understood by any child, the story of a husband and wife, snuff-makers of St. Omer, who in July, 1770, had been accused of murdering their drunken old mother.

The inventive French temperament concluded that they *must* have murdered her, because a drunken mother is a trial, and her loss would be a gain. A quarrel they had had with her on the last evening of her life (the reconciliation which followed was conveniently forgotten) lent colour to the theory.

The positive facts that the doctor, who was at once called, attributed the old woman's death to apoplexy; that she not only left no money behind her, but that with her death expired the licence to make snuff, which was her son's only means of livelihood; that the accused were known to have been patient and affectionate in their filial relationship; were themselves of quiet and gentle character; and that there was not a single witness to the crime for which they were arraigned—had no weight with either the populace or the magistrates.

On November 19, 1771, Montbailli was tortured and broken on the wheel; and his wife, aged only twenty-four, was left in prison in irons, awaiting the birth of her child, and then death by the hand of the executioner.

But that dreadful reprieve gave her relatives time to appeal to the only man in France who could save her.

Voltaire laid the matter before the Chancellor Maupeou. The case was re-tried. Both the Montbaillis were declared innocent. And that fickle and dangerous people who had compassed the death of her husband, and who, but for Voltaire, would have compassed her own, received back the wife with tears of joy.

Voltaire had not spared himself. If he wrote briefly, he wrote often. That style, so simple to read, was not nearly so simple to write. Before things are made clear to the reader they have to be still clearer to the writer, who must know at least twice as much as he tells. Then, too, every fresh case brought Voltaire others. While he was writing pamphlets for the Montbaillis, he was also writing pamphlets on the case of a certain Comte de Morangiés; he was working hard for young d'Étallonde; he was appealing for his own poor people of Ferney and Gex; and he was in the midst of the suit for the vindication of Lally.

General Lally was a hot-headed Irish Jacobite, who had plotted in France for the restoration of the Stuarts, and who, when he was sent to India in the service of France, had declared his policy to be "No more English in India."

A clerk called Clive frustrated that little plan. Among a shipload of French prisoners sent to England was General Lally. England released him on parole. He returned to France—a country never noted for her tenderness to the unsuccessful. Besides popular indignation, he had to face that of the disappointed shareholders in the East India Company, and the ill-will of a government that supposed the best way to appease England would be to maltreat Lally.

He "was accused of all crimes" of which a man could be capable. He demanded an investigation. "I bring here my head and my innocence," he wrote to Choiseul, "and await your orders."

He awaited them for fifteen months in the Bastille—untried.

Then a special court was formed of fifteen members of the dying and rotten Parliament of Paris; and this man, who had "spent his last rupee in the public service," was accused of having sold Pondichery to his bitterest foes, the English, and upon no fewer than one hundred and fifty-nine other counts.

In the teeth of all testimony the unanimous voice of those fifteen judges condemned him to be beheaded. Surly, churlish, and embittered, imprudent speech was proven against him. But no worse offence. "He is the only man who has had his head cut off for being ungracious." That coward, the King, shut himself up in Choisy, so that no petition for mercy might reach him.

On May 6, 1766, Lally, General, sixty-four years old, and six times wounded in the service of his adopted country, was taken, gagged and handcuffed, to the Place de Grève and there beheaded. The gag was removed at the foot of the scaffold. But he was wise enough to disappoint the mob, and died without a word.

"It is expedient that one man should die for the people." That spirit is not extinct in France yet.

But if Lally's innocent blood cried in vain from the ground to King, magistracy, and mob, it reached old ears that to their last hour would never be deaf to the tale of wrong.

"I have the vanity to think that God has made me for an *avocat*," said Voltaire.

He had closely followed the General's trial. His prosecutor was Pasquier, who had received a royal pension for condemning poor mad Damiens to horrible tortures—Pasquier, "with the snout of an ox and the heart of a tiger," and Voltaire's especial detestation.

It may have been that hatred which first made him examine the documents concerning this trial. Also, he had met Lally at Richelieu's, and worked with him at d'Argenson's.

On June 16, 1766, he wrote to d'Alembert, "I will stake my neck on it he was not a traitor"; and a few days later, to d'Argental, "It is my fate to be dissatisfied with the sentences of the Parliament. I dare to be so with that which has condemned Lally."

Dissatisfied with wrong? There have been thousands of men good enough for that, who have lived and died dissatisfied with it, without lifting a finger to put right in its place.

Months passed, and years. Voltaire inserted in his "History of Louis XV." an able exculpation of Lally. It was something. But it was not enough.

In 1769, he wrote that Lally and his gag, Sirven, Calas, Martin, the Chevalier de la Barre, came before him sometimes in dreams. "People think our century only ridiculous, but it is horrible." In 1773, he wrote that he still had on his heart the blood of Lally and the Chevalier de la Barre.

Still? For ever till they were avenged. He had read English books on Lally's case. The English had had no reason to love Lally, but they regarded his sentence as a barbarous injustice.

And then, early in this year 1773, Lally's young son, whom the father had charged to avenge his memory, sent his first Memoir on the case to Voltaire and asked his assistance.

Voltaire had been very ill—really ill, not fancifully so—with the gout, and he was in his eightieth year. But this *"avocat* of lost causes" had his old burning zeal.

He first began by telling the young Chevalier de Lally-Tollendal, out of his abundant experience, and in a letter dated April 28, 1773, what to do and what not to do. "As for me, I will be your secretary." Lally-Tollendal, then two-and-twenty years old, had at fifteen written a Latin poem on Jean Calas. He thus already knew his Voltaire. The King had paid for his education—a confession of, or an *amende* for, the injustice which had killed his father. He was to be one of the aristocratic democrats of the French Revolution, a refugee in England, and, in 1815, peer of France. But now he was nothing and nobody, and alone could never have fulfilled his father's trust.

For many weeks the labour of "The Historical Fragments of the History of India and of General Lally" occupied Voltaire "day and night." It cost him, he told Madame du Deffand, more than any other work of his life. It had to be amusing in the history because the monkeys, who formed one half of the nation, would not read history unless it was amusing; and pathetic enough, as touching General Lally, to melt the hearts of the tigers who formed the other half.

Then there were pamphlets to be written, and Madame Dubarry to be won over. Through her, Lally-Tollendal got his commission in the army. Through Voltaire, on May 26, 1778, Louis XVI. in council publicly vindicated General Lally.

In a room in the Hôtel Villette, at the corner of the Rue de Beaune in Paris, a dying old Voltaire received that news. The splendid intellect which had served him for more than eighty years, as never mind served man before, was waning too. But for a moment its strength came back. To Lally-Tollendal Voltaire dictated his last letter.

"The dead returns to life on learning this great news; he tenderly embraces M. Lally; he sees that the King is the Defender of Justice; and will die, content."

With a last flash of his old spirit, he made someone write in a large hand, on a sheet of paper which he had pinned to the bed hangings where everyone could see it, the following words:

"On May 26th the judicial murder committed by Pasquier (Councillor to the Parliament) upon the person of Lally was avenged by the Council of the King."

If ever man carried into the other life the hatred of that oppression and injustice which have made the wretchedness of this to more than half the human race, surely that man was Voltaire.

CHAPTER XLII

LATTER DAYS

VOLTAIRE'S old age was naturally something less eventful than the "crowded hour" of his youth and manhood. But if ever his private life afforded him a chance of quiet, public events always stepped in to disturb it.

On May 10, 1774, Louis XV. died of the smallpox, to the good and blessing of the world. His old courtier at Ferney no sooner heard the news than he put pen to paper and wrote his Majesty's *Éloge*, "to be pronounced before an Academy on May 25th."

Of course a eulogy had to be eulogistic. The old hand had not lost its cunning. To flatter the dear departed, to speak of him as a good father, a good husband and master, and "as much a friend as a king can be"; to offer for his little failings that courtly excuse, "One cannot be always a king: one would be too much to be pitied," and to imply that the man was a fool so that the insult sounded like a compliment, why, Voltaire was the one writer in the world who could do it. And he did it.

He turned the occasion to practical use, by preaching against the neglect of inoculation; and then looked to the future.

What wonder that, for the moment, even this prophet should forget to prophesy Revolution; should think that he saw already the beginning of the Golden Age—Millennium—all things made new?

To be sure, he told the government plainly that there were still Frenchmen who were "in the same legal condition as the beasts of that land they watered with their tears." And the young King answered by repealing the Tax of the Joyful Accession; by disgracing Terrai, for whom old Ferney was keeping his last tooth; by appointing first as Minister of Finance, then as Comptroller-General, and then as Secretary of State, the great reforming Turgot, one of the most enlightened men in France and already the personal friend of Voltaire. "If any man can re-establish the finances," wrote Ferney on September 7th, "he is the man." And a few days later, when Turgot obtained free trade in grain, the enthusiastic old invalid thanked Nature for having made him live long enough to see that day. Free trade in grain had a very personal application to this master of a town, this founder of a colony. He had d'Étallonde staying with him now; and next to his arduous and passionate work for the restitution of that young officer's civil rights ("he is calm about his fate, and I—I die of it"), his four hundred children had the largest share of his mind. That they returned his affection and repaid him as they could, was proved when, on Madame Denis's recovery from a dangerous chest complaint in the spring of 1775, they fêted that "niece of her uncle" "with companies of infantry and cavalry, cockades and kettledrums"—all the mummery and millinery which they loved, and their master had loved all his life.

Madame Denis was, it must be remembered, already the legal owner of Ferney. She was to be its practical owner. And it was her old uncle's too sanguine hope that she would maintain the manufactory after him. She was certainly pleased at the colonists' rejoicings, and the colonists were pleased themselves, and Voltaire was highly delighted; and a quite cool observer, Hennin, the Resident, noted that it was a grand thing to see a cavalcade of nearly a hundred men, mounted and in uniform, from a village where, twelve years before, there were twenty families of wretched peasants.

So that, although the year 1775, which was to usher into Ferney such a succession of visitors as might make the most sociable heart quail, began with sickness, it began with rejoicing too.

D'Étallonde was still staying there. Nephew d'Hornoy was helping Voltaire to work his case. The Marquis and Marquise de Luchet came to join the party in the spring, and were here two months—the Marquis, who was to be one of Voltaire's biographers, always engaged in mad schemes for making money out of gold mines; and the Marquise turning her good-natured and laughter-loving self into a hospital nurse and nursing the Ferney invalids unremittingly.

Then came the Florians; and the Marquis's third wife brought with her another lively visitor, her young sister, whom Voltaire called "Quinze Ans," "who laughed at everything and laughed always."

They were followed by ecstatic little Madame Suard, who worshipped Voltaire with the tiresome adoration of a schoolgirl; kissed his hands and clasped her own; flattered, adored, and coquetted with him; and went so far as to declare in the long and rapturous accounts she wrote of him, that his every wrinkle was a charm.

With her came her brother, Panckoucke, who wanted to edit Voltaire's works, but did not yet obtain that favour. She also found with Voltaire, Audibert, that merchant of Marseilles, the earliest friend of the Calas; and Poissonnier, Catherine the Great's doctor.

In July, Chabanon, and Abbé Morellet were both staying at Ferney. Also in July, an audacious and wholly unsnubbable person called Denon had forced his way there too; asked for his host's bust; was refused; and revenged himself by sending the poor old Patriarch a most hideous sketch of his lean features which he, Denon, had made himself. It was very far from being the only offensive likeness of the great man. Still extant is a caricature called "Déjeuner at Ferney," which Voltaire used to think was by Huber, and which contains grotesque portraits of Voltaire and Father Adam, and represents poor Madame Denis, who *was* inclined to *embonpoint*, enormously fat. But, after all, it was in the January of this 1775 that Frederick had sent Voltaire, Voltaire's bust in porcelain with *Immortali* written beneath it. Here was compensation for many caricatures.

Little Madame Saint-Julien, who had made Ferney lace the mode, and was a fashionable philanthropist when philanthropy was not the fashion, paid another long visit to Ferney in the autumn, and went back to Paris to intercede with her influential relatives for Voltaire's children. She and their father were so successful that the day soon came when, "in spite of the obstinate resistance of the farmers-general," they obtained for the colonists that "moderate and fixed tariff which freed the country from the despotism of a pitiless tax," extorting from the poverty-stricken province of Gex alone the exorbitant sum of not less than forty thousand livres annually.

The grateful colonists had fireworks and illuminations on that good Butterfly's birthday; and in December they fêted old Voltaire himself, filled his carriage with flowers, and decorated the horses with laurels.

The visitors did not cease with the new year 1776. Nay, one came who came to stay. Mademoiselle Reine-Philiberte de Varicourt was the niece of those six poor gentlemen whose estates Voltaire had reclaimed in 1761 from the Jesuits of Ornex. Bright, honest, and good, well deserving that charming name of Belle-et-Bonne with which old Voltaire immediately christened her, the unfortunate girl had no *dot* and was destined to a convent.

But Madame Denis took one of her good-natured likings to her. She was girlishly kind to old Voltaire, while he on his part soon worshipped her pretty face, virgin heart, and bright intelligence. No "narrowing nunnery walls" for her! Marie Dupuits had husband and child to think of now, and Marie had never had Reine-Philiberte's dignified good sense.

Belle-et-Bonne fell into place at once. She became a regular, and not the least delightful, member of the heterogeneous Ferney household.

Another Englishman, Martin Sherlock, visited it in April, 1776, and wrote his experiences, in his "Letters of an English Traveller," in French, which has been retranslated into his native tongue.

Voltaire, who was accompanied by d'Hornoy, met his guest in the hall, showed him his gardens, spoke a few words to him in English, told an anecdote of Swift, talked of Pope, of Chesterfield, of Hervey, and with his old passionate admiration of Newton. Stopping before his bust, he exclaimed, "This is the greatest genius that ever existed!" There was no dimming of the old mind, no lack-lustre, no weariness. The England he had not seen for nearly fifty years was still a vivid and a present reality.

On one of his visits—Sherlock paid two—Voltaire showed his guest his shelves filled with English books—Robertson, "who is your Livy"; Hume, "who wrote history to be applauded"; Bolingbroke, "many leaves and little fruit"; Milton, Congreve, Rochester.

He criticised the English language—"energetic, precise, and barbarous." He explained to Madame Denis the scene in Shakespeare's "Henry V." where the King makes love to Katharine in bad French. He spoke "with the warmth of a man of thirty."

Quaintly dressed in white shoes and stockings, red breeches, embroidered waistcoat and bedgown, and a gold and silver nightcap over his grey peruke, old Voltaire apologised for this singular appearance to his guest by saying in English that at Ferney they were for Liberty and Property. "So that I wear my nightcap and Father Adam his hat." Later, he added gravely, "You are happy, you can do anything.... We cannot even die as we will."

During the conversation he had uttered what his visitor called "horrors" about Moses and Shakespeare.

Nothing proves better the young vigour of this marvellous old mind than the strength of its animosities. The "let-it-alone" spirit of old age was never this man's while there was breath left in his body. At the end of 1773 he had attacked another literary foe—an ungrateful *protégé*, "the inclement Clement"—in the "Cabals," a satire in which ring out clearly the notes a younger hand had struck in "Akakia" or in "Vanity."

Then on March 10, 1776, Fréron died of mortification at the suppression of his "Literary Year," and up gets Voltaire and says he has received an anonymous letter asking him, if you please, to endow Frélon-Fréron's daughter! This is too much. Voltaire suggests that Madame Fréron wrote that letter. And the Frélons say Voltaire invented it himself. And Voltaire is as spry and alert and angry as when he first hated Fréron, thirty years ago.

But these enemies he knew, or had known, in the flesh.

To admire or to despise Shakespeare was but a literary question. Old Eighty-two in this July of 1776 took it as a burning personal one. He had not precisely adored Shakespeare in the "English Letters." A barbarian, a monster—but of very great genius. For the sake of that genius he had permitted the polished French people to condone that "heavy grossness" and the shocking lack of taste; and in his famous criticism on "Hamlet," written in 1748, though he *had* called its author "a drunken savage," he had found in the play, not the less, "sublime touches worthy of the loftiest genius." To Sherlock, but three months ago, though he had uttered "horrors" in his criticism, he had admitted that "amazing genius" again.

And now one Letourneur publishes a new translation of the great William, and takes upon himself to call him the "god of the theatre," the only model for true tragedy; and ignores Corneille and Racine (to say nothing of the author of "Zaire") *in toto.*

Then Voltaire beat his breast and tore his hair to think that it was I—I—who showed to the French the pearls in this English dunghill; that I suffered persecution for telling them that though the god had feet of clay, the head and heart were gold.

So in a rage M. de Voltaire sat down and wrote a letter to the Academy—"his factotum against Shakespeare"; gave himself the lie; literally translated many passages, knowing, as he had said himself, that in a translation the letter killeth and the spirit giveth life; presented, as he meant to do, a gross and coarse Shakespeare, an indecent buffoon who had "ruined the taste of England for two hundred years." Various persons rushed into the fray on either side.

On August 25th, Voltaire's letter was read at a public meeting at the Academy, and a good-natured Marquis de Villevieille galloped off post-haste to Ferney to tell of its success. But there had been dissentient voices. Anglomania was already a power in the land. The young Queen had her Crawfords and Dillons, her English garden, her English jockeys, her English billiards. D'Alembert was too cool, too cool! The untrammelled nature of the great Diderot was formed to appreciate the broad and daring genius of the great Englishman. And Madame Necker, with the sure instincts of a clever woman, criticised Voltaire's letter in a letter to Garrick. Voltaire had but shown Shakespeare's dead body—"But I—I have seen the soul animating it, and know it is something more even than a majestic ghost which Garrick, the enchanter, summons from the grave."

The letter to the Academy was the last utterance on the great Englishman of the man who—whether he hotly regretted it, as he did now and in the famous Preface to "Semiramis," or was, or said he was, proud of it, as when he wrote to Walpole—first revealed Shakespeare to the people of France.

August saw the arrival of a visitor who was hereafter herself to be a celebrity, Madame de Genlis. Now only thirty years old, she was not yet famous for her literary works or that grave and religious turn of mind which did not prevent her occupying the very equivocal position of *gouvernante* to the children of the Duke of Orleans. As Madame Suard came to Ferney prepared to go into raptures, so Madame Genlis came prepared to disapprove.

The serious lady carried out her intention as thoroughly as the frivolous one. Her account of her visit contains much more about herself than about Voltaire, but states, no doubt very truly, that the impiety of his conversation was shocking, and, certainly untruly, that his manners lacked tact and urbanity. For this too particular lady the very trees in the Ferney garden grew too low and upset her temper and her hair; while the wild enthusiasm for their host of her companion, a painter, M. Ott, quite distressed a person who had so firmly resolved not to make a fool of herself in that direction.

As her point of view was unfavourable, her testimony as to her host's "ingenuous goodness" to his colonists, to the perfect modesty and simplicity with which he regarded his great work for them, is the more valuable. She confirmed the opinion of many others as to the piercing brilliancy of the old eyes—"which have in them an inexpressible sweetness." Madame Saint-Julien was there at the same time—little and gay and kind—and presently Marie Dupuits's little girl ran into the room and put her arms round Grandpapa Voltaire's neck.

During this August, Voltaire, rather proud of the transaction, "borrowed Lekain," who was acting at Court, from Marie Antoinette. The Hermit of Ferney was too toothless to act himself, but his earliest passion was also his latest. There was the most charming little theatre in the village of Ferney now. Lekain acted in that and at Châtelaine. The young Queen's graciousness in lending her player made artful old Voltaire long to have "Olympie" acted before her; to have her for his protectress; to see with his own eyes "her whose least charm," as he said, "was loveliness."

Picture the delight of the whilom author of "The Princess of Navarre" when he was commissioned to write a *divertissement* for her benefit. He wrote, or rather reproduced a sketch of a *fête* given at Vienna by the Austrian Court sixty years before, and called it "The Host and Hostess." The thing was meritless, but not objectless, though it failed in its object—the *rapprochement* of Ferney and Versailles.

Then M. de Voltaire must needs write an allegory, "Sésostris," to flatter the *beaux yeux* of the Queen, and to show what a King might do for the good of his people.

To the year 1776, besides the Battle of Shakespeare, belong two more fights—the last of Voltaire's life. Beauregard, Rohan, Jore—how far they were away! But the spirit of their old antagonist had not waxed faint.

The first fight was only a skirmish, it is true. Father Adam had been spoilt, of course. From being an inoffensive, lazy person—"the only idler in a houseful of busy people"—he had become assertive, worrying, and quarrelsome. He had fallen out with Bigex, the copyist, in 1769; and as a result Bigex had had to leave. And now the Father must go himself. It was characteristic of the man who had allowed Jore a pension for life, that he should send after this ungrateful priest who owed him thirteen years' hospitality, presents of money.

In the second fight, the very last of his life, occurring in the December of 1776, Voltaire matched steel with a worthier foe. It was in answer to an attack made upon him by an Abbé Guénée that he wrote the bold and brilliant, if neither deep nor sound, "Christian against Six Jews," which advanced Pigalle's evidence on the subject of the Golden Calf, and might have better confuted Guénée if that reasoner had not been on his own ground and most cool and subtle in argument.

But if his foes did not spare this old Voltaire, neither did his friends. In the early days of 1777 Moultou introduced at Ferney a wearisome playwright called Berthe, who would persist in reading aloud his tedious play to their host. "Here the Chevalier laughs," read Berthe, as a stage direction. "Happy man!" murmured Voltaire. When the listener could bear it no longer, he feigned the most violent colic that ever man had suffered. The next day Berthe came again, and so did the colic. "If God had not come to my aid," said Voltaire to Grimm, "I should have been lost."

It was in 1777 that Voltaire amused himself by competing under a pseudonym, for a prize offered by the French Academy for the best translation of the sixth book of the "Iliad." It did not gain a prize. It was not even good. But that such a man at such an age should have been "sleeplessly active" enough to enter into such a competition, makes the thing worth recording.

But worse than unsuccessful translations and dull plays, worse than being beaten in a verbal quibble with a priest, was a mortification this vain old heart received in the June of 1777.

Joseph II., the young Emperor of Austria, brother of Marie Antoinette, and himself something of a philosopher, had been the lion of the spring in Paris. It was confidently expected by d'Alembert, Frederick the Great—everyone, including Voltaire himself—that on his return home the celebrity would do what all celebrities did—visit the King of their kind at Ferney.

On June 27th, Voltaire wrote airily to say that he did not expect his Majesty. What in the world was there for him to see in this manufactory of watches and verses? But all the same, when the day came, Ferney rose up very early in the morning and from eight o'clock was ready in its best clothes, with its master in his great peruke, waiting. A splendid dinner had been prepared. The condition of the road from Ferney to Versoix had been improved by its owner. All was in readiness.

Presently the sound of the rumbling of the travelling carriage is heard in the distance. If his Majesty had not meant to call at the château, why choose this route? There were others. "This is Ferney!" says the coachman. "Whip up the horses!" cries the Emperor. And the imperial *cortège* dashes through Ferney, and past the windows of the expectant château itself, at a gallop. When it is added that his Majesty alighted at Versoix and examined that infant colony, and that when he reached Berne he paid a special visit to Voltaire's great rival, Haller, it will be seen that he meant to offend.

It is to the credit of a plucky old heart that Voltaire quite refused to acknowledge himself snubbed, pointed out that he had always said his Majesty would not come, and that "my age and maladies prevented me from finding myself on his route." But if he swallowed it with a smile, the pill was a bitter one not the less. "This disgrace" the poor old man called it, writing in confidence to his Angel. But the "disgrace," if any, was not Voltaire's, but the man's who, privately confessing himself a philosopher, was afraid to visit Voltaire lest he should be openly accounted one, and offend an austere mother.

The Emperor's neglected visit was the last mortification of the man who had had many, and had felt all with an extraordinary sensitiveness.

But, after all, "the end of all ambition is to be happy at home," and Voltaire had many consolations.

The good, fat, Swiss servant, Barbara, was one. Voltaire was at last learning a little how to grow old, and now went to bed at ten and slept till five, when Baba would bring him his coffee. One day he took it into his head to mix some rose-water with it, as an experiment. The result was an acute indigestion. He rang the bell violently. Enter Baba. "I am in the agonies of death. I put some rose-water in my coffee and am dying of it." "Sir," says the indignant Baba, "with all your cleverness you are sillier than your own turkeys."

But nearer and dearer than a Baba could be was Belle-et-Bonne. By this time she had become like the old man's daughter. With rare tact she had succeeded in endearing herself to him without offending Madame Denis. She would arrange his papers for him, and keep the desk which hung over his bed, and "which he could lower or raise at pleasure," in that order and neatness his soul loved.

"Good morning, *belle nature*," he would say when she greeted him in the morning; and when she kissed his old parchment face would declare it was Life kissing Death. It was Belle-et-Bonne who could soothe his irritability or impatience—"You put me on good terms with life."

And it was Voltaire of eighty-three who taught Mademoiselle Reine-Philiberte de Varicourt how to dance.

In the summer of this 1777 there arrived unexpectedly one day at Ferney a worn-out *roué* of a Marquis de Villette, who had passed two or three months here in 1765, and with whom Voltaire had since corresponded. Rich, gallant, well born, a society versemaker, this "ne'er-do-weel of good company" was the sort of person who sounds attractive on paper, and in real life is wholly objectionable. Voltaire—Voltaire!—had tendered him moral advice and urged him to reform. He had known the young man's mother—herself a woman of irregular morals—and from these two facts arose an entirely unfounded scandal, that Voltaire was Villette's father.

He was soon to be a sort of father-in-law. Villette, now some forty years old, and having run away from an intrigue and a duel in Paris, met Belle-et-Bonne at Ferney; saw her walking in the procession of the *fête* of St. Francis (always kept enthusiastically by the colony of François Marie Arouet), with flowers at her breast, a basket with doves in it in her hand, and her face bright, beautiful, and blushing.

What was there to do but to fall in love with her? Wagnière, who hated Villette, said that he played fast and loose with Mademoiselle for three months. However that may have been, Voltaire approved of his suit. To be sure, Belle-et-Bonne was too good for him. But she had no *dot*—if a pretty face, an innocent heart, youth, dignity, and intelligence count for nothing—so she would have no choice. And any husband is better than none—when none means a convent. *Enfin*, where to find a French marquis of stainless reputation in the eighteenth century? It was said that Voltaire *had* offered Villette a *dot* with his wife, and the disinterested Villette had refused it. And if that is not a sign of reformation—what is?

So in November, 1777, Mademoiselle de Varicourt was married in the Ferney chapel at midnight, with her six uncles preceding her up the aisle, and Papa Voltaire, in Catherine's sable pelisse, to give her away.

The young couple spent the honeymoon at Ferney, and through it Voltaire was working at his last two plays, "Irène" and "Agathocle."

It is marvellous, not so much that a man of eighty-three should write bad plays, as that he should write any.

No wonder that the new tragedy, "Irène," went ill at first. And not so very wonderful that the old playwright should follow his immemorial habit and rewrite till it satisfied him. He lost three months over it. And, as he remarked most truly, "Time is precious at my age."

So when "Irène" was impossible he turned to "Agathocle."

Madame Denis's easy tears and laughter over the two pieces were no sound criticism. Villette and Villevieille, then staying at Ferney, admired politely as visitors. The playwright, whose vanity has been excellently defined as "a gay and eager asking of assurance from others that his work gave them pleasure," was delighted with the compliments. But he accepted correction in that spirit which showed that his vanity "never stood in the way of self-knowledge."

"If I had committed a fault at a hundred," he said, "I should want to correct it at a hundred-and-one." So when Condorcet, more honest than the visitors, paid him the finer compliment of assuring him that such work as he had produced in "Irène" was not worthy of his genius, he took that assurance in excellent part; and though by January 2, 1778, "Irène" had been read and welcomed by the Comédie Française, he went on correcting and altering it to the end of the month.

He was spurred to do his best by the fact that Lekain declined to play the *rôle* written for him. No letters could have been kinder, wiser, or more conciliatory than those his old host and friend wrote to the great player.

The part should be rewritten for him!

He was also spurred to do his best by the fact that "Irène" was to be the means, the excuse, the reason to take him to Paris.

Paris! The idea had been simmering long. Paris! It was twenty-eight years since he had left it, for a few months at the most. To be sure, he had been far happier at Ferney than in the riot and fever of that over-rated capital. In answer to those who talked about the stagnation of the country, and talked of it as if it were some narcotic trance which numbed brain and use, Voltaire could point to the best work of his life. Near him, bound to his heart by many cords, was the smiling cosmos of the industrial Ferney which he had drawn from the chaos of a barren and starving province. Here were his gardens and farms; the house he had built, and loved as one can only love the work of one's own brain; the books and pictures he had collected; the thousand household gods from which the young part easily, but which the old regard with a personal affection.

Then, Ferney was safe. And in Paris—"Do you not know there are forty thousand fanatics who would bring forty thousand fagots to burn me? That would be my bed of honour." If Louis XV. was dead, so was a friendly Pompadour. Choiseul and Madame Dubarry were banished.

Good Louis XVI. hated this infidel of a Voltaire, and was just shrewd enough in his dulness to fear him. It was Louis, still a king, who, asked what play should be performed at the theatre, replied, "Anything, so long as it is not Voltaire." It was Louis Capet in the Temple who is reported to have said, pointing to the works of Rousseau and Voltaire in the library of the tower, "Those two men have lost France."

The brilliant Queen, who had permitted M. de Voltaire to write her a *divertissement* and to steal Lekain, was something more favourable. But the Queen—extravagant and childless—was the most unpopular woman in France. In 1776, she had compassed the fall of Turgot, Voltaire's friend, the hope of his country. In Paris, now, there was but one minister who was even tepidly favourable to the great recluse of Ferney, and that was Maurepas.

Altogether, the time seemed hardly ripe. But "if I want to commit a folly," Voltaire had written to Chabanon in 1775, "nothing will prevent me."

If a king had once been too strong for Voltaire, he may well have known now that he was stronger than any king. Besides, he had never been formally banished. "I do not wish Voltaire to return to France" was not an edict after all. Had he ever forgotten he was still Gentleman-in-Ordinary? And as for the danger to his person—seriously, what could be done to an old man of nearly eighty-four. Then, too, he needed a change. His health, though he was fond of repeating that he had as many mortal diseases as he had years, was quite good enough to permit him to take one.

Then there was "Irène," which he could see put into rehearsal himself: and then—then—then—there was the domestic influence of all Ferney urging him to take the step, to make up his mind, to go back to glory, to honour, to life.

Madame Denis, of course, longed for Paris. Her sixty-eight years and a chest complaint had not cooled her zest for pleasure and admirers. And if you do not go, Uncle Voltaire, whether you are banished or no, three parts of Europe will think you are! She had long ago inspired Marie Dupuits with her own love of amusement. The Marquis de Villette was constitutionally even less able to endure the country than Mama Denis. He had the finest house in the capital, which had once been the Bernières' house, where Voltaire had stayed as a young man, which stood at the corner of the Rue de Beaune on what is now the Quai Voltaire, opposite the Tuileries, and which is entirely at Papa Voltaire's service! Put all these persuadings and persuaders together before a man already more than half inclined to go, and the result is easily foreseen.

On the evening of February 3, 1778, Madame Denis and the *ménage* Villette left Ferney to prepare the Hôtel Villette in Paris against the arrival of M. de Voltaire.

On February 5th, Voltaire himself, accompanied only by Wagnière and a cook, set out in their travelling carriage. There was a painful farewell from the colonists. The poor people felt that their protector was leaving them for ever. It was in vain he promised them that he would be back in six weeks at the latest. That he really intended thus to return is partially proved by the fact that he did not even arrange his manuscripts and papers before leaving.

The first night was spent at Nantua.

At Bourg, where the horses were changed, Voltaire was recognised and had to escape from the crowd who surrounded him by locking himself up in a room in the post-house. Of course the innkeeper produced his best horses, and called out in his enthusiasm, "Drive fast! Kill the horses—I don't care about them! You are carrying M. de Voltaire!"

The *incognito* Voltaire had resolved to maintain was already a thing of the past. He had begun to taste what are called the delights or the drawbacks of fame, according to the temperament of the speaker.

The second night was passed at Sanecey. On the third, at Dijon some of his adorers insisted on dressing up as waiters and waiting upon him at supper in order to get a good view of him. Others serenaded the poor man outside his bedroom window. In Dijon he made an appointment with a lawyer, and transacted some business.

The next stop was at Joigny. A spring of the carriage broke when they were near Moret, but Villette arrived to rescue them from that very common dilemma, and met them with *his* carriage, in which they pursued the journey.

The nearer they approached to the capital, the higher rose Voltaire's spirits. He told stories with inimitable gaiety. "He seemed twenty."

At half-past three on the afternoon of February 10th they reached Paris. When the custom-house officer inquired if they had anything against regulations, Voltaire replied that there was nothing contraband except himself. He grew more and more lively every moment. They had no sooner arrived at the Hôtel Villette than this gay young traveller must step round to the Quai d'Orsay to see the Comte d'Argental. Friends for sixty years, their friendship had been strong enough to bridge a gulf of separation which had lasted more than half their long lives. Madame d'Argental had died in the December of 1774. There was but one Angel now. He had taken wing too, for the moment, Voltaire found when he reached the house. But the old man was no sooner back in the Hôtel Villette than d'Argental arrived, and the two fell on each other's necks. "I have left off dying to come and see you," says Voltaire. But there was a shadow on their happiness. D'Argental brought bad news. Two days earlier, on February 8th, Lekain, whose first part had been Titus in Voltaire's "Brutus," played his last part in "Adélaïde du Guesclin." He died, in spite of all the skill of Tronchin. Voltaire "uttered a great cry." Lekain had been his friend. Lekain was to have played in "Irène."

Belle-et-Bonne tells how the two old men sat up late into the night discussing the additions Voltaire had made in that play.

But for it, but for the thousand distractions of this new world, the loud acclamations, the surging stream of visitors the moment brought, Voltaire might have mourned Lekain longer.

But he was back in Paris. When he left it, he was a power, a danger, a fear. He had returned to it a king, and awaited his crowning.

CHAPTER XLIII

THE LAST VISIT

MORLEY speaks of Voltaire's last visit as "one of the historic events of the century," "the last great commotion in Paris under the old *régime*." "A ghost, a prophet, an apostle," says Grimm, "could not have excited a more fervent interest."

The Salons worshipped the man who for sixty years had been the first wit of the wittiest age in history—the author of that dear, daring, ribald, wicked "Pucelle."

The Philosophers kissed the hem of the garment of the author of "The Philosophical Dictionary."

The Academy fell at the feet of him who had attempted every kind of literature and failed in none.

The Drama welcomed not only the most famous playwright since Corneille and Racine, but the man who for sixty years had not ceased to try to improve the civil status of actors.

The thrifty *bourgeois* left their shops and stood in crowds outside the Hôtel Villette, waiting to see him who was himself of their order and had fought for its rights and rent earth and heaven with cries against its wrongs.

The Protestant came to worship him who had preached Tolerance, defended the Calas, and flung all the weight of his scorn and passion against a law which proclaimed the heretic's wife his mistress, and their children bastards.

The submerged, the *canaille*, fierce and hungry-eyed, were among the street crowds to see him who had pleaded against a criminal code which punished petty theft, blasphemy, and desertion in time of peace, by death; meted to the hapless imbeciles, called sorcerers, the vengeance of superstition and

"TRIOMPHE DE VOLTAIRE"

From a Contemporary Print

fear; and robbed the children of the condemned by confiscating their goods to the King.

Court and Church paid him the higher compliment of fearing him.

The preachers denounced the apostate from their pulpits. Here is he who has not only, having examined the evidences of Christianity, boldly declared that he finds them absurd and inadequate, but has also dared to attack the evil lives of the believers, tyranny, oppression, persecution, calling them the inevitable consequence of the Faith, and so the most powerful of all arguments against it.

Anti-Christ! Anti-Christ!

King and ministers turned and looked at each other in consternation. Surely there was somewhere an edict of banishment against this person? But where? If it had been found, no one would have dared to put it into execution.

The Paris which had once imprisoned him for teaching it how to become free, and persecuted him for opposing persecution, was at last the Paris of Voltaire, and not the antechamber of the Kings of France.

On the day after his arrival, Wednesday, February 11, 1778, he received three hundred visitors. In an outer room were Madame Denis and Villette. And within, his crown an old nightcap and his royal robes an ancient bedgown, sat the King of intellectual France. The courtier bred in

Courts knew well how to play his Majesty. Easy and gracious in manner, no visitor went away without a *mot*, an anecdote, a happy quotation he could repeat to his friends—"I heard it from the great Voltaire." One of the guests was the perfidious La Harpe, who had not seen his old friend since they parted in anger at Ferney ten years ago, and who found, he said, the wit undimmed, the memory unimpaired.

In intervals between the departure of one guest and the admission of the next—if there could have been any such intervals—the old playwright dictated a new line or a correction for "Irène" to Wagnière, and then went on receiving half Paris. "All Parnassus was there, from the mire to the summit," said Madame du Deffand. In that crowded day, her old friend found time to write her a little note and tell her how he had arrived, dead, but was risen again to throw himself at the feet of his Marquise.

Thursday, February 12th, brought a congratulatory deputation from the Academy, which was represented by three personal friends of Voltaire—Saint-Lambert, Marmontel, and the Prince de Beauvau. His Majesty received them with "a lively recognition," and sent a cheerful message to the Academy that he hoped to visit it in person.

Gluck, the great musician, and Piccini the lesser, came to do homage, one after the other, on February 13th. "Ah! that's as it should be!" says old Voltaire. "Piccini comes after Gluck."

The Comédie Française sent a congratulatory deputation on Saturday, the 14th, and much laboured flattery in an address delivered by Bellecour and Madame Vestris. Voltaire responded in the same manner— exaggerated. "We all played comedy beautifully!" he said, with a twinkle, afterwards.

For the rest of that day his talk to his guests was graver than usual. He discussed politics with them—and the French politics of 1778 were enough to sober Folly itself. A weak King, a ruined Treasury, a corrupt Church— and, as Voltaire himself wrote to Florian a week or two later, in the social state "a revolting luxury and a fearful misery."

He showed his guests a letter he had just received from another King who was neither fool nor feeble, and who ruled a kingdom which beside starving France was Utopia, El Dorado, Paradise.

By Sunday, February 15th, Voltaire was ill. But then Tronchin was in Paris! Voltaire had not written to that old friend for a matter of ten years— except "a *billet-doux* on arriving" in the capital. But though Tronchin disapproved of almost everything Voltaire did and thought, the good Doctor loved the man as a woman loves an engaging and ill-trained child.

He forgave the ten years' silence and the Châtelaine theatre, even old Voltaire's truculent unbelief—came to him, looked at him with those serene, wise eyes, forbade all going out, and commanded absolute rest.

Voltaire had been going to the theatre to-morrow. Well, he could give that up. But rest? Madame Necker called to see him this very day—Sunday. And how, pray, could he decline to receive the wife of her husband, the woman who had done so much for him in the matter of the Pigalle statue, and who, distantly related to Belle-et-Bonne, had sternly disapproved of her innocence being used to reform a wickedness like Villette's and had only brought herself with difficulty to enter that scoundrel's house? Voltaire received her with the most delightful *empressement*.

And then, waiting to see him was the "wise and illustrious" Franklin, philosopher and politician, who until Voltaire's arrival had himself been the lion of Paris. How to refuse *him*? He came into the presence chamber, bringing with him his grandson. Voltaire spoke in English until Madame Denis told him that Franklin perfectly understood French. There were twenty persons or so in the room. The two great men talked of the government and constitution of the United States. "If I were forty," says Voltaire, "I should go and settle in your happy country."

Then Dr. Franklin presented his grandson, a lad about seventeen. Voltaire raised his hands above the boy's head and blessed him, "uttering only these words," and in English—"God and Liberty."

He told the story himself to several of his correspondents. It moved his old heart. And the persons who saw the scene—to be sure, they were French and ready to be affected at anything—shed tears.

The Franklins had not been gone an hour before Voltaire was receiving Lord Stormont, the English ambassador, and Belbâtre, a famous performer on the harpsichord. Rest? Dr. Tronchin already knew the temper and disposition of his invalid, and something, though not yet all, of the selfish and pleasure-loving character of his Denis and his Villette. Voltaire was sent to bed. And prudent Tronchin inserted a notice in the "Journal de Paris" stating that M. de Voltaire had lived since he came to Paris on the capital of his strength instead of only on the income, as all his friends must wish; that that capital would very soon be exhausted, "and we shall be the witnesses, if we are not the accomplices, of his death."

The notice did not appear until February 20th, and by the 19th this marvellous old man was at least well enough to be assigning the parts in "Irène." Richelieu, himself eighty-two, came to help him in this delicate task. The magnificent marshal, in spite of the care and splendour of his dress, did not look nearly so young and vigorous as the attenuated figure in bedgown and nightcap, with his sunken eyes afire and all his old keenness and spirit. Besides settling parts, he was now rewriting the play itself so enthusiastically, that wretched Wagnière did not even have time to dress himself.

The next day, February 20th, that poor, shameful, tawdry favourite, Madame Dubarry, came out of her social banishment to see this new king, Arouet. Le Brun, poet, and once benefactor of Marie Corneille, who had written an inflammatory ode in praise of the monarch and wanted to see if it had been appreciated, closely followed the Dubarry. He tells how Voltaire contrasted the fresh, fair innocence of Belle-et-Bonne with the stale and painted charms of the last avowed mistress of a King of France.

Le Brun himself was characteristically received with "You see, Sir, a poor old man of eighty-four, who has committed eighty-four follies." The story runs that Voltaire had said the same to Sophie Arnould, and that that sprightly person had replied, "Why, that's nothing! I am only forty and I have committed a thousand."

It was on this same day, February 20th, that Voltaire received a letter from Abbé Gaultier, who had been a Jesuit for seventeen years and a curé for twenty, and now had a post at the Hospital of the Incurables. Gaultier was anxious for the salvation of Voltaire's soul, and that he should have the saving of it. Voltaire responded favourably; and the next day, the 21st, received the priest. Gaultier and Wagnière both give accounts of the interview. Both may have lied. One must have. The truth seems to be that Gaultier was ushered into a salon full of people, whom Voltaire soon dismissed. He took the priest into his private room, where—to make a long matter short—Gaultier offered himself as Voltaire's confessor. The Patriarch asked if anyone had suggested to him to make that offer—the Archbishop of Paris, for instance, or the Curé of Saint-Sulpice, in whose parish Villette's house was situated. Gaultier replied, No; and Voltaire said he was glad of the assurance. A long conversation ensued. Voltaire declared that he loved God; and Gaultier answered that he must give proofs of it. They were three times interrupted—by the Marquis de Villevieille, nephew Mignot, and Wagnière. Madame Denis came in to beg that her uncle might not be tired and worried. When Gaultier was dismissed, it was with the promise that he should be received again.

When Wagnière asked Voltaire what he thought of Gaultier, Voltaire replied that he was "a good fool." He appears to have thought that he would be more easily satisfied than shrewder men, and that if it came to the dreadful necessity of a confession as an insurance of decent and honourable burial, Gaultier would be the best confessor.

A few days later a certain Abbé Martin thrust himself in and imperatively insisted that the sceptic should make confession then and there to him. "I have come for that. I shall not move an inch."

"From whom do you come, M. l'Abbé?"

"From God Himself."

"Well, well, Sir—your credentials?"

The Abbé was dumb. The inconsistent old Patriarch, feeling that he had been severe, went out of his way to be more than usually kind and agreeable during the rest of the visit.

But such incidents made one ponder. To avoid the sickness which would make confession a necessity was the obvious thing to do. But to keep well meant to rest. And every hour that struck, every turn of the wheel, brought fresh excitements, fresh work, fresh visitors.

On the very day of Gaultier's visit, February 21st, came Madame du Deffand, whose long friendship and "herculean weakness" had enabled her to brave the crowds that surrounded Voltaire, and visit him first about a week earlier, on February 14th. Her account of that occasion has been lost. But the most ennuied and world-weary worldling of any time confessed that it had been delightful.

On this February 21st the event had lost the one great antidote to boredom—novelty. Denis was "*gaupe*," and Villette "*a plat* person of comedy," and Belle-et-Bonne damned with faint praise as "said to be amiable."

But in the presence of Voltaire, her correspondent since her youth, her warmest sympathiser when blindness fell upon her, even Madame du Deffand forgot again for a while what a bitter and empty world that is where Pleasure is the only god and amusement the be-all and end-all of existence. Old Voltaire entertained her with a lively account of Gaultier's visit.

But, all the same, he had not forgotten that that incident had a very serious side.

Four days later, on February 25th, about midday, he was dictating in bed, when suddenly, in a violent fit of coughing, he broke a blood-vessel. Wagnière, terrified, rang the bell loudly. Madame Denis ran into the room, and Tronchin was summoned immediately. It had been so easy to laugh at Gaultier with a blind old *mondaine* when one felt lively and well! But now—call him at once! Turning to the persons in his room, the old man bade them all remember that he had fulfilled "what they call here one's duties."

Tronchin came, bled the patient, and, what was likely to be far more useful, sent him a very excellent and strong-minded young nurse who was to refuse admission to all visitors, and a surgeon who was to stay in the house all night.

Meanwhile, Protestant Wagnière, who regarded his master's dealings with the priests as disgraceful to his honour in this world and very unlikely to save his soul for the next, had not summoned Gaultier.

The next day, February 26th, Voltaire wrote the priest a little note: "You promised, Sir, to come and hear me. Come as soon as you can." Madame Denis added her entreaties in a postscript. But, it being nine o'clock at night when Gaultier received the letter, he did not come to the Hôtel Villette till the next day, when his penitent could not, or would not, see him.

By Sunday, March 1st, he was well enough to listen to La Harpe reading a canto of "La Pharsale"—so loudly that he could be heard in the street.

On the Monday morning d'Alembert came to see the sick man. Voltaire told him that he had "taken the leap," and sent for Gaultier. There had been other priests, said d'Alembert, writing to Frederick the Great, who had thrust themselves into his room, preaching at him like fanatics, "whom the old Patriarch, from goodness of heart, had not ordered to be thrown out of the window." Gaultier was more moderate and reasonable than his brethren; and, thinks d'Alembert, if Voltaire has the natural weakness to feel that it is of consequence what becomes of the remains of poor humanity after death, he is right to do as he proposes to do—as all the world does, the good Protestant as well as the godless pagan. This is d'Alembert's attitude toward the matter throughout.

Later on that same day, Gaultier reappeared. He was ushered into the sick room. Voltaire sent the servants out of it. Wagnière listened at the door, which was luckily only a sort of paper screen. He was very much agitated by those fears for his master's honour. When Voltaire called him and bade him bring writing materials, the servant was too moved to answer the question as to what ailed him. Voltaire took the pen, wrote his statement or profession of faith, which declared that he had confessed to Gaultier, that he died in the Catholic religion in which he was born, and that if he had scandalised the Church he asked pardon of God and of it. D'Alembert—the truthful d'Alembert—says that Voltaire told him he added the last phrase at the request of the priest "and to have peace."

But to that "zeal in concessions," which had always made him as vigorously thorough in his lies as he was thorough in his good deeds, the addenda may in part be attributed.

The Marquis de Villevieille and Abbé Mignot readily signed what Gaultier lightly called "a little declaration which does not signify much." Wagnière hotly declined.

Before leaving, Gaultier proposed to give the sick man the Communion. Voltaire excused himself. He coughed too much, he said. He gave Gaultier, according to the custom, twenty-five louis for the poor of the parish, and the priest left.

There was one man about Voltaire, but only one, who wished him to declare, not what it was expedient to think, but what he really thought: what were the convictions of his soul, and the creed of his heart.

A few days earlier, on February 28th, at the earnest request of Wagnière and at a moment when he solemnly believed that his last hour had come, Voltaire had written down, clearly and firmly, his real faith:

"I die adoring God, loving my friends, not hating my enemies, and detesting superstition. February 28, 1778. Voltaire."

So far as a few weak words can express any man's attitude towards the Supreme Being and his own fellow-sinners, this confession expresses Voltaire's.

It is still preserved in the National Library at Paris.

On the Tuesday, March 3d, Gaultier returned. He wanted, or rather his superiors, the Archbishop of Paris and de Tersac, the Curé of Saint-Sulpice, to whom he had showed the confession, said that *they* wanted, one more detailed and less equivocal. The truth was Saint-Sulpice would have liked the credit of such a conversion himself. This "man of little understanding and a bigoted fanatic," as d'Alembert called him, was not a person to be offended. He had, as parish priest, the disposal of the bodies of those who died in his parish.

Voltaire would not see Gaultier. But from that stormy sick bed, on March 4th, he wrote the most graceful of conciliatory letters to offended de Tersac; and laconically announced to poor Gaultier, in a note, that Villette had given orders that until M. de Voltaire was better, no priest, except the Curé of Saint-Sulpice, should be admitted to the house.

Persistent Gaultier returned in a week and was again refused admission. Death-bed conversions were his speciality, and he was not going to be cheated of this one without a struggle. Meanwhile Voltaire upset all his plans by recovering rapidly. Paris, who had heard much more than the truth concerning this illness and confession, avenged herself for her anxiety by epigrams. It was right that the Curé of the Incurables should attempt such a conversion! The patient himself (whose every utterance was reported) declared that if he had lived on the banks of the Ganges he would have died with a cow's tail in his mouth. To die with a lie in it did not shock Paris in the least.

To find excuses for Voltaire's act, it is as necessary, as it is now impossible, to realise fully the conditions of life and death under a government which permitted no liberty of conscience, and in which men were either orthodox or anathema.

There were other troubles besides religious ones to harry this old patient of eighty-four out of a sick bed to the grave before his time.

Tronchin wanted Voltaire's real good, and Voltaire's real good meant Ferney and repose; while Villette was all for himself, pleasure, and Paris. One day the doctor turned the Marquis by force out of the sick-room. Villette called in a rival practitioner, Lorry—famous and freethinking—and no doubt was disappointed when Tronchin worked amicably side by side with his *confrère*.

A College of Physicians could not have kept Voltaire, when he began to recover a little, from doing as he liked. He was soon sitting up in bed, working on "Irène" and dictating to Wagnière as usual. Visitors thrust themselves in again. Poets came to read their complimentary odes. One writer announced to Voltaire in most wearisome prepared speech, that to-day he had come to visit Homer, to-morrow he would visit Euripides, the next Sophocles, the next Tacitus, the next ——"Sir, I am very old," says the voice from the bed; "if you *could* pay all these calls in one——"

Another flatterer said that, having surpassed his brethren in everything Voltaire would surpass Fontenelle himself in length of days.

"Ah! no, Sir. Fontenelle was a Norman: he cheated even Nature."

By March 10th the invalid was not unnaturally worse again, and Tronchin kept him in bed, although, or perhaps because, there was a rehearsal of "Irène" actually going on in the house at the moment.

The next day, Madame Vestris, who was to play in "Irène," was allowed to see him about her part. The maddening placidity with which she delivered lines intended to be passionately pathetic did not help to soothe the invalid's irritable and nervous condition. He told her how fifty years ago he had seen Mademoiselle Duclos reduce the whole house to tears by a single line; and talking to Mademoiselle Clairon afterwards, he hit the imperturbable Vestris hard in a mot well understood by all Paris.

He had himself recited with extraordinary feeling a few lines out of his last play. "Ah!" said Clairon, "where will you find an actress to render them like that? Such an effort might kill her."

"So much the better," answers the poor old playwright viciously. "I should be only too glad to render the public such a service."

The mediocrity of the other actors also grievously afflicted the overwrought mind and body of the sick man. There came, indeed, times when he sank into a sort of stupor: when nothing seemed to matter; when he was indifferent or unconscious that Madame Denis was conducting rehearsals and giving away the first-night tickets on her own responsibility, and that d'Argental and La Harpe were making such alterations in "Irène" as they deemed fit. He must have been really ill. In four days, it is said, he had aged four years. The trumpet blasts of adulation in prose or verse, always appearing in the newspapers, had no power to rouse him; and as for the abuse—"I received such abominations every week at Ferney," he said, "and had to pay the postage; here I get them every day, but they cost me nothing—so I am the gainer."

On March 14th, Madame Denis presided over the last rehearsal of "Irène," and on March 16th was the first performance.

The playwright, who had written and rewritten it, laboured at it, as he said himself, as if he had been twenty, was in bed in the Hôtel Villette, not too ill to be interested in its success, but past any great anxiety concerning it.

The house was crowded. Marie Antoinette was there—Marie Antoinette, who had been brilliantly imprudent enough to inquire why if Madame Geoffrin, "the nurse of the philosophers," had been received at Court, Voltaire should not be? She had a notebook in her hand, and put down therein all the pious and edifying passages to prove to her absent lord that M. de Voltaire's conversion was real! Her brother-in-law, d'Artois, was there; the Duke and Duchess of Bourbon: all Versailles, but the King.

The play, or more correctly the playwright, was received with tumultuous applause. "Irène" was feeble and tired, like the old hand that had written it. But here and there, where the bright flame of a dying genius flickered up for a moment, the house applauded madly, and to parts wholly meritless listened in respectful silence. After each act, messengers were despatched to tell Voltaire all was well. At the end of the last, Dupuits rushed to announce a general success, and the sick-room quickly filled with congratulating friends. "What you say consoles but does not cure me," said the poor old invalid. But he roused himself enough to inquire which verses were the most applauded, and to chuckle joyfully when he heard of the delighted reception of those which smote the clergy hip and thigh.

On March 19th, the "Journal de Paris" published a very sanguine account of Voltaire's health. "His recent indisposition has left no after-effects." It was certainly true that he was better again. He received a deputation from the Academy congratulating him on "Irène," and by March 21st was well enough to go out in a carriage. He was recognised and surrounded by the people in the streets, and when he regained the Hôtel Villette there was a deputation of Freemasons waiting to see him. There was no peace for him, in fact, at home or abroad. His whole visit to Paris was like the progress of a popular sovereign who has no officials to ensure his comfort and privacy.

Being better, the most natural thing to do was to go over "Irène." He sent for an acting copy. Directly he saw how it had been tampered with, he fell into the greatest rage in which Wagnière, after twenty-four years' service and a much richer experience of his master's *vifness* than Collini, had ever seen him. He forced Madame Denis to confess. He pushed her away so that she fell into an armchair, or rather, says Wagnière spitefully, into the arms of Duvivier, that dull young man she afterwards married. Then the indignant uncle sent the niece out (it was raining too) to d'Argental's house to fetch the manuscripts and plays with which he had intrusted that old friend. His rage lasted for twelve hours. He roundly abused both d'Argental and La Harpe. And then, for he was the same Voltaire, he apologised to both with a most generous humility.

On March 28th, he went to see Turgot—"Sully-Turgot"—the man who had "saved the century from decadence," and whose disgrace in 1776 Voltaire had felt as a keen personal grief and an irreparable public disaster. The meeting was very French and effusive. But it was not, for that, insincere. "Let me kiss the hands of him," cries old Voltaire, "who has signed the salvation of the people."

The day of this King's coronation had been fixed for March 30th. The nominal King sat aloof and sulky at Versailles. But what did that matter? The Queen, keener-eyed, saw in Voltaire a rival force not to be disregarded. And when d'Artois heard of Voltaire's death—"There has died a great rogue and a great man," said he. From a d'Artois it was no bad testimony.

At four o'clock in the afternoon of this March 30th a gorgeous blue, star-spangled coach waited at the door of the Hôtel Villette.

And presently there gets into it, amid the shouts and acclamations of his subjects, a very, very lean old figure, in that grey peruke whose fashion he had not altered for forty years, a square cap on the top of it, a red coat lined with ermine, Ferney white silk stockings on the shrunken legs, large silver buckles on the shoes, a little cane in the hand with a crow's beak for a head, and over all this extraordinary fancy dress (it was only rather less remarkable in Paris in 1778 than it would be in Paris to-day) Catherine's sable pelisse.

Thus dressed, he was driven through tumultuous crowds to the Louvre, where two thousand persons received him with shouts of "Long live Voltaire!"

The Academy met him in their outer hall—an honour never accorded to anyone, even to princes. Twenty Academicians were present. The absentees were all churchmen. The King was conducted to the Presidential Chamber, and there unanimously elected to the next three months' Presidency. Then the Perpetual Secretary, friend d'Alembert, rose and read a so-called Eulogy of Boileau, which was really a Eulogy of Voltaire. The serene dignity of the Secretary contrasted not a little with old Voltaire's painful efforts after self-command. It was twenty-eight years since he had been among them. It was thirty-five since, as a body, they had refused him admission. And now——!

He paid a brief visit to d'Alembert's office, and then got into his carriage again. The crowds had increased. All sorts and conditions of men were here to welcome him who had pointed the way to freedom—who, unlike all other kings, was of the people, and so, for them. Frenzied, as in another frenzy they had hooted the Calas to judgment through the streets of Toulouse, and as but a very few years later they might have hooted Voltaire himself to the Place de la Guillotine, they applauded and worshipped him now. The Villettes and Madame Denis met him at the Comédie Française. Their protection was necessary. The people clambered on the carriage itself to see him, to touch him. One man seized Belle-et-Bonne's little hand instead of the Patriarch's. "Ma foi!" he said. "This is a plump hand for eighty-four!"

She and Madame Denis preceded him to the box set aside for the Gentlemen-in-Ordinary. Then, with the women pressing on him and plucking the fur from his pelisse to keep as souvenirs, Voltaire made his way through the house to the passionate acclamations of the crowded audience. He would fain have concealed himself behind Belle-et-Bonne and his portly niece. "To the front!" cried the gods. And to the front he came. Opposite him was the royal box, in which was d'Artois who had been with the Queen at the opera, but had slipped away to do homage to a greater royalty.

Then another cry shook the house. "The crown!"

Brizard, the actor, came forward and put a laurel crown on the old poet's head. "Ah, God! You will kill me with glory!" he said. He took it off and put it on Belle-et-Bonne's. And the house bade her give it back to him. He resisted. And then Prince de Beauvau came forward and crowned him again. By this time the whole auditorium was on its feet. The passages were full to suffocation. The actors, dressed for their parts, came before the curtain to join in the enthusiasm. The delirium lasted for twenty minutes. The air of the theatre was black with the dust caused by the movement of so great a multitude, struggling to see.

At last the play began. It was "Irène," of course—"Irène," now at its sixth representation.

The audience had read their own meaning into its lines. They applauded wildly throughout. At the end the curtain was raised again. On the stage was a pedestal, and on the pedestal the bust of Voltaire which had been brought from the hall of the Comédie where it had recently been placed. Actors and actresses were grouped round it, holding garlands of flowers. Some of the audience, despite the new regulations, had crowded on to the stage for a better view.

Then Brizard, dressed for his part of monk in "Irène," placed his laurel garland on the head, and the whole company followed his example. From the house burst a roar which sounded as if it was from one throat as it was from one heart. For the first time in France, said Grimm, there was no dissentient voice. "Envy and hatred, fanaticism and intolerance, dared not murmur." Perhaps even at that delirious moment the old Patriarch recognised the triumph, not as his, but as philosophy's: and rejoiced the more. "It is then true, Sire," he wrote on April 1st, in his last letter to Frederick the Great, "that in the end men *will* be enlightened, and those who believe that it pays to blind them will not always be victorious."

March 30, 1778, is a great day in the history of France as celebrating, not the honour of Voltaire, but of that "happy revolution he had effected in the mind and the conduct of his century."

Villette drew him forward to the front of the box, and while he stood there for a moment the applause redoubled.

Then Madame Vestris, who had played "Irène," came forward and recited an ode by the Marquis de Saint-Marc. Voltaire, writing to Saint-Marc the next day, thanked him for having made him immortal in the prettiest verses in the world. The ode was not bad; but if it had been it would have been applauded and encored just the same. Copies were circulated through the house.

On the stage one woman came forward and impulsively kissed the bust, and other enthusiasts followed her example.

A stranger, entering at the moment, supposed himself to be in a madhouse.

The curtain fell again; and again rose, this time on "Nanine." Once more, it was not the play that counted, but the playwright. When the curtain fell for the last time, he made his royal way to his carriage between lines of women sobbing with emotion. Some persons seized his hands and kissed them with tears. Others fell upon the horses to stop them and cried for torches. Thus lighting him, crowds accompanied his carriage home, shouting, dancing, and weeping. When at last he reached the Hôtel Villette, worn out with the glory and the high-pitched emotions of the day, the poor old Patriarch himself wept like a child. "If I had known the people would commit such follies I would never have gone to the Comédie."

But it was the next morning which, like all next mornings, was the real time for reflection. Here was the man who, more than any other Frenchman who ever lived, understood the national temperament. "Capable of all excesses," "the Parisians pass their time in hissing and clapping—in putting up statues and pulling them down again." "You do not know the French," he said to Genevan Wagnière; "they would have done as much for Jean Jacques." "They want to stifle me under roses."

The reflections showed a just judgment. But, coming at such a time, they showed, too, a man old, tired, and at the end of his tether. Tronchin had long said that to survive such a life as he had been living the last few weeks, his body must be made of steel.

Long and bitterly discussed, but this "next morning" become a pressing and imminent question, was the return to Ferney. To go—or to stay? On the one side were Villette and Madame Denis. They were not the rose, but it was delightful to live near the rose. The one, despite the good and pretty wife, had already been drawn back again into the vile dissipations of the capital. The other was not only out at entertainments all day, but at sixty-eight was coyly coquetting with her Duvivier.

In the second camp was Wagnière, who besides having left home, wife, and children at Ferney, was sincerely devoted to his master's real good; the judicious, clear-seeing d'Alembert, young Dupuits, and above all, Dr. Tronchin. Fearless and upright, the great doctor made one last passionate appeal to his patient to go while there was time. "I would give a hundred louis to see you back at Ferney. Go in a week."

"Am I fit to travel?" says the poor old Patriarch.

"I will stake my head on it," says Tronchin.

The thin trembling hand grasped the strong one.

"You have given me back my life."

Voltaire was so much moved that the serene Tronchin, nay, the very cook who happened to be in the room at the same moment, was moved too.

Tronchin wrote off immediately to Ferney for Voltaire's coachman and carriage. Madame Denis's vociferous indignation was wasted on him. Little Madame Suard, the sprightly visitor of Ferney, must have been as delighted as all others who put Voltaire's life above their own pleasure. She came to see her old host. "We shall kill him," she said, "if he stays here."

But Madame Denis was not going back to the dismal solitude and the ice and snow of Ferney without a fight. Is it the Villette house you do not like? She hurried out, and nearly took one in the Faubourg Saint-Honoré, with a beautiful garden where Uncle Voltaire could fancy himself in the country. The negotiations for it fell through. But there is what might be made a very fine house in the Rue Richelieu, and which has the enormous advantage of being quite close to the home of your butterfly philosopher, Madame Saint-Julien! Voltaire at eighty-four, and with, as he pointed out to his every correspondent, at least two mortal complaints, actually consented to buy this unfinished house. He would live there eight months of the year, and the other four at Ferney. Still, those other four were to be taken at once. He would go now—soon! If he *could* go, that is. But had he not just been elected to three months' Presidency of the Academy? His vacillations were the despair of Tronchin—ay, and the despair of himself. He longed to go, but he could not go. Madame Denis, with the most limitless capacity for nagging ever vouchsafed to mortal woman, volubly assured him that influential friends had told her that if he did go, he would never be allowed to return.

True, on April 2d "Irène" had been performed at Court. That did not look like a new edict of banishment. But then the author had not been asked to see his play. Perhaps that *did?* Then it was said the Queen herself had had an idea of slipping into the theatre on that great 30th of March to see the crowning of the people's King—only—only—the other King had peremptorily forbidden her. A dog Voltaire had been fond of at Ferney came to Paris with one of the Ferney servants and bounded in to lick his master's hand with the touching, dumb joy of animal affection. "You see I am still beloved at Ferney," says the old man. Villette and Madame Denis took very good care that that dog should never enter the house again. They tried to get rid of Wagnière—his influence was so bad and so powerful. They failed in this. But, after all, they succeeded in their main object.

When a man's foes are those of his own household, resistance is peculiarly difficult.

"I have seen a great many fools," Tronchin wrote on April 6th, "but never such an old fool as he is."

The exhaustion consequent on his crowning had passed away. With it passed away, too, the idea of an immediate return to Ferney.

By that day, April 6th, the "old fool" was well enough to go on foot, in spite of adoring crowds, to the Academy.

A seller of books on the way naïvely begged him "to write me some and my fortune will be made." "You have made so many other people rich! Write me some books. I am a poor woman." Among the people he heard himself often called by that name which was a sweeter flattery to his soul than all odes and plaudits—"the man of Calas."

The next day he was made a Freemason, and in the evening went to see the unacknowledged actress-wife of the Duke of Orleans.

On April 11th he returned Madame du Deffand's visit. She forgave him for not coming before; but the Convent of St. Joseph, in which she lived, found it hard to forgive him for coming at all and profaning their holy place with his presence. He paid other visits. One old friend, the Comtesse de Ségur, was dying when he saw her. For a little, the charm of his reminiscences brought back to her their youth. When he visited her again, remembering only that he, like herself, stood on the brink of eternity, she passionately conjured him to cease his "war against religion." He turned upon her fiercely, forgetting her womanhood and her dying. That stern, terse creed he had hammered and forged for himself was as dear to him as was to her the fuller faith she had accepted without trouble or thought. The room was full of people. The guests paused to listen. Voltaire remembered himself: offered sympathy, suggested remedies, and left, greatly moved.

Another visit was yet more pathetic. He went to see Egérie de Livri, once the vivacious poor companion of the Duchesse de Sully and would-be actress, and now the Marquise de Gouvernet. In this withered old woman of eighty-three what traces were there of the brilliant girl to whom a Voltaire of five-and-twenty had taught declamation and love, who had gaily forgotten him for de Génonville, and graciously remembered him when he had immortalised her in "Les Vous et Les Tu"? Above him, on the wall, smiled the picture he had given her—his dead self, by Largillière. A ghost! A ghost! He left her, profoundly saddened. She sent the portrait to him at the Hôtel Villette, and he gave it to Belle-et-Bonne.

Another friend came to see him one morning—Longchamp—from whom he had parted eight-and-twenty years ago, and with whom were connected many memories, of the Court and of Paris, of Cirey and Madame du Châtelet.

If the man had cheated his master, he had loved him too. The things are not incompatible.

These meetings made the old heart yearn again for quiet and Ferney. But there was still so much to do!

Besides his plays to be corrected and personally supervised in rehearsal, a new grand scheme had been filling his mind, quickening his last energies, bringing back the resolute passion of his youth.

On April 27th, he attended a *séance* at the Academy. Abbé Délille read a translation of Pope's "Epistle to Arbuthnot." Well, one Academician had known the thing in the original and the author in the flesh. He sat and listened attentively. Then he got up. An admirable translation, gentlemen. But our language is, after all, poor—poorer than it need be in poetic expression. Why, for instance, should we not call an actor who plays tragedy, a tragedian? And why—why should this Academy not undertake the reconstruction of the French Dictionary? The one we have is unworthy of us—dull, inadequate, impossible. The Academy is called the lawgiver of language to the people of France. Let it worthily prove itself so! The work shall not only be useful, but patriotic. Each member shall take a letter. As for me, gentlemen, I am willing to consecrate to such a task the brief remainder of my days. The old man spoke with the fire and the vigour of youth. Some of his auditors were incompetent for the task he proposed to them; many were lazy and apathetic.

But the octogenarian who had suggested it went home with his soul on fire, drew paper and pen towards him, and began, through domestic disturbance and the ceaseless round of visits, to elaborate his scheme.

Two days later he received an ovation from the Academy of Sciences. D'Alembert read a Eulogy, written by Condorcet, of Trudain, Councillor of State, who had helped Voltaire with his colony at Ferney. To eulogise Voltaire himself followed in natural sequence. Franklin was there too. Old Voltaire spoke to him. "Embrace in the French fashion!" cried a voice: and they did.

At the end of April it was decided that Wagnière should leave for Ferney, to get there papers and books of which Voltaire had need. It was a bitter parting. The servant had done his best to make his master go with him. But Tronchin was not always at his side, and Denis and Villette were. Then there were his plays still needing correction. And now that Dictionary scheme, so hotly resolved upon—how to abandon *that*? Then, too, the Abbé Beauregard had preached in glowing vituperation at Versailles against all the philosophers, and one philosopher in particular. The kingly party, as well as the ecclesiastical, was mad to hound this Voltaire out of Paris.

There had been many times in his life when he had perforce to turn his back on the enemy and fly. But those had gone by for ever.

On April 27th, he signed the contract of purchase for the new house in the Rue Richelieu.

On the 29th, Wagnière left. Both knew the parting was their last. But neither could face the fact.

Life went on with a madder rush when the secretary had gone. Visits succeeded to visits. One ovation brought another. All the *mots* the Patriarch uttered (and numbers he did not) were recorded in the newspapers. His every action was noted—his very motives guessed. Through all he was working feverishly—without the invaluable help of Wagnière and with his strength kept up by drugs—on that scheme for the Dictionary.

It was ready by May 7th. He went to the Academy. Upon some of the brethren at least—they were almost all young enough to be his grandsons—had fallen that fatal mental inertia, that deadly sleep which paralysed the brains of half aristocratic France just before the Revolution. Nothing matters! Nothing is worth while! With eyes and heart aglow, this old Voltaire read aloud his brief and masterly plan. It remains that upon which all great dictionaries in Europe and America have been modelled to this day.

He recommended it with a zeal of which he alone was capable. Tronchin speaks of it as his "last dominant idea, his last passion." If he had been a boy of twenty, with name and fortune to make by this Dictionary alone, he could not have been more eager. In the end he obtained a unanimous consent to his scheme. But it was cool—cool! He insisted on the immediate division of the letters among the members. He himself took A. It meant the most work. That he also wrote a part of T is certain.

One old member reminded him of his age, and he turned upon him in reply with "something more than vivacity." The *séance* ended.

"Gentlemen," says old Voltaire, "I thank you in the name of the alphabet."

"And we," replied Chastellux, "thank you in the name of letters."

That evening Voltaire was present *incognito* at the performance of "Alzire." Of course he was recognised. For three quarters of an hour the howls of applause never ceased. Then he himself begged silence from the house. As he left it, the people, pressing on him, thrust odes of inflammatory flattery into his hand. This mob was enthusiastic enough. But those Academicians, his brothers, with all the world to conquer—their apathy lay heavily on his soul. If death came to him, the only young man of them all, would they go on with his scheme? He doubted them. "They are sluggards," he said passionately to Tronchin, "who wallow in idleness; but I will make them march." He must write them a Discourse to sting them and shame them. No man in the world had so much and so ably used the fine, pliant, delicate machinery of the French language, as he had. In the most perfect French in the world he had alike coquetted with women in drawing-rooms and spoken his great message to the race. He loved the tool with which he had carved immortal work. The day was not long enough to say what he had to say upon the language he had adorned. Far on into the night—brain and nerve stimulated by strong coffee—he wrote on the subject that possessed his soul. The sleep he had banished deserted him now when he called it. He wrote on. There was so little time! There was so much to do! Not afraid of death, but of dying before he had finished his work—that description was true to the finest shade of meaning. The coffee aggravated the internal disease from which he suffered. But he wrote on. On May 11th he could not go to a meeting of the Academy. But he could still write. The strong sun of that long life was fast sinking below the horizon, and the night coming when no man can work. The old brain nerved itself to one last effort. The old hand wrote on:

"Whoso fears God, fears to sit at ease."

Doubtful in morals, and a most trenchant unbeliever, the scoffer Voltaire yet sets a splendid example to all inert Christians who, comfortably cultivating the selfish virtues, care nothing for the race and recognise no mission but to save their own miserable souls.

Who has done more good for the world—the stainless anchorite, be his cloister a religious one or his own easy home; or this sinner, of whom it was said at his death, with literal truth, that the history of what had been accomplished in Europe in favour of reason and humanity was the history of his writings and of his deeds?

CHAPTER XLIV

THE END

THE accounts of the dying of Voltaire would fill a volume. Round this great deathbed were gathered persons who each had a different end to serve by differently describing it.

Villette wanted to prove himself the wise and unselfish friend; and Madame Denis must appear the tenderly devoted niece.

The Abbé Depery published an awful description of these last moments, which he declares he heard from Belle-et-Bonne. She was dead when he made the statement; and "it is easy to make the dead speak." But if that fearful story had been true, this girl, who passionately loved her more than father and dedicated the remainder of her days to his memory, would hardly have repeated it. Lady Morgan, who saw her in Paris forty years later, declared that she spoke of the dying man's peace, tranquillity, and resignation.

D'Alembert, Grimm, and Condorcet naturally wished to see a death, firm, consistent, and philosophic: and they saw it.

Dr. Tronchin, the sincere Christian, would fain have beheld a repentant sinner. Failing that, what could he see but the "frightful torment" of the wicked to whom Death is the King of Terrors, "the furies of Orestes," the *sæva indignatio* of Swift?

Gaultier naturally did not wish to own that he had missed so illustrious a conversion. He did not own it: he said the convert's mind was wandering.

But, after all, it matters not how one dies, but how one has lived. Death-bed utterances, even if truly reported, are to be attributed less to the illumined soul than to the diseased body. If at last the horrors of the Great Change and the awful prospect of the unknown Eternity overwhelmed this unbeliever, as at such an hour they have overwhelmed many sincere Christians, that fact is no confession that Voltaire gave the lie to the convictions of his life.

For more than sixty years they had been those not of a man in the careless vigour of health, or of a thoughtless profligate, or of an indifferent, but of one who had always known his tenure of life to be frail; who had realised the consolations of the religion he could not believe, and yearned for that faith he could never have.

If, at the last, his priestly counsellors did succeed in terrifying the old dying mind, enfeebled by the dying body, by their threats of Judgment and Eternity, what use to his soul, or the cause of their Christianity?

It is the eighty-four years of vigorous life and passionate utterance that count before God and man, and not the dying minutes.

Out of lies innumerable, then—some witnesses took their testimony of the death-bed of Voltaire from the cook of the Hôtel Villette—the following account has been sifted.

On some day, which was either May 12th or shortly after it, the old man met Madame Denis and Madame Saint-Julien when he was out walking.

He said he was ill and going to bed. Two hours later his good Butterfly came to see him. She found him very feverish, and begged that Tronchin might be sent for.

Madame Denis, remembering the Doctor's counsels, declined to summon him.

The patient grew worse. Villette sent for a local apothecary, who came with medicine which the sick man was at first too wise to take. But he was ill and old, and Madame Denis was naggingly persistent. He took, not enough said Madame Denis; too much said Madame Saint-Julien, who tasted it. Anyhow, he grew worse. That evening old Richelieu came to see him and recommended a remedy—laudanum—which he had himself been in the habit of taking for the gout.

With the night the patient's sufferings increased. He sent for the laudanum.

Madame Saint-Julien and a relative (most likely d'Hornoy), who were there when it came, implored caution. The audacious ignorance of Madame Denis had no fears.

Wagnière, who of course was not present, declares that his master characteristically seized the remedy and took too much, too often. D'Alembert—the notoriously truthful—says that he never took any: the bottle was broken. However that may be, he grew alarmingly worse.

At last Dr. Tronchin was called. But the patient was already past human aid. Suffering agonies from his internal disease, a fearful and most exhausting nausea, all the torments of ruined nerves and exhausted brain and unable to eat or sleep, the old man could still turn to the good physician and apologise to him for the liberty he had taken with his dying body. Tronchin had been right! He should have gone back to Ferney.

Often and often he called for Wagnière. By his side, always one may hope, was the good and gentle woman he had married to Villette. Constantly in and out of the sick room were a motley crowd—Madame Denis, Abbé Mignot, d'Hornoy, Lorry, Villette himself, besides Tronchin and a servant, Morand.

On May 16th the poor old man revived a little. To this day belong the last verses of the easiest and most limpid verse-writer of all time. They were written in reply to some lines of the Abbé Attaignant, and appeared in the "Journal de Paris." To them the dying writer added a few piteous words in prose. "I can do no more, Monsieur.... The mind is too much affected by the torments of the body."

On May 25th, d'Hornoy wrote to Wagnière urging his instant return. The patient was kept alive only by spoonfuls of jelly; and his exhaustion and feebleness were terrible.

By the next day the watchers had abandoned all hope. He revived, indeed, to hear the news of the vindication of Lally. That would have roused him from the dead. He dictated his last letter. For the moment, joy made mind triumph over matter, as it had done with this man all his life long. But his doctors could not be deceived. He was dying.

One of them was watching anxiously now for the signs of that repentance he longed for. "Religious toleration, the most difficult conquest to wring from the prejudices and passions of men," Voltaire had not been able to wring from one of the best friends he ever had. Tronchin wrote bitterly of this death-bed. In his zeal for some proof, some confession of the fallacy of that stern creed of negation, since called Voltairism, the great Doctor almost forgot his compassion and his friendship.

D'Alembert records that on May 28th Mignot went to fetch de Tersac.

De Tersac replied to the effect that it was no use visiting a man whose reason was already dimmed, but that unless he made a far fuller and more orthodox profession of faith than he had yet made, he would not accord him Christian burial.

Mignot, himself a personage, a member of the Grand Council and the head of an abbey, threatened to apply to the Parliament for justice. De Tersac replied that he could do as he pleased.

For two days more, Voltaire lingered—sometimes quite unconscious, but sometimes wholly sensible. On the morning of Saturday, May 30th, Gaultier again wrote to him offering his services.

At six o'clock in the evening of that day, Mignot fetched Gaultier and de Tersac.

D'Alembert told Frederick the Great that de Tersac approached Voltaire, saying loudly, "Jesus Christ!" and that Voltaire, rousing a little from his stupor, made a motion with his hand—"Let me die in peace."

Grimm and La Harpe tell the same story with unimportant variations. It may be true. "Spare me three things," said Madame du Deffand on her death-bed—perhaps remembering Voltaire's—"Let me have no question, no arguments, and no sermons."

Saint-Sulpice thought, or said that he thought, Voltaire too ill to make a confession. The persons about the bed took no pains to contradict him.

At nine o'clock in the evening the priests left. For three hours Voltaire was dying—calmly and peacefully, say some; in "all the terrors of the damned," say others. But the truth, none knows.

Ten minutes before he died he took Morand's hand. "Farewell, my dear Morand. I am dying." He never spoke again.

At a quarter-past eleven on the evening of Saturday, May 30, 1778, in the eighty-fourth year of his age, died François Marie Arouet de Voltaire.

His relatives had concealed the dangerous nature of his illness from the world. Madame Denis had written, even to Wagnière, and as late as May 26th, a letter of pretended hopefulness. King, priests, and prejudice were strong. Mignot and d'Hornoy knew well that it would be necessary to act cautiously, and to act at once. They had been professionally advised not to contest at law the question of burial.

From de Tersac they obtained a formal consent in writing that the body of Voltaire might be removed without ceremony. "I relinquish to that end all parochial rights."

Gaultier declared, also in writing, that he had been to Voltaire at his request, and found him "not in a state to be heard in confession."

On the night of May 30th the body was embalmed. The heart was taken out and given by Madame Denis to Villette.

Early in the morning of Sunday, May 31st, Mignot, taking with him the two priests' declarations and Voltaire's confession of faith made a few weeks before, left Paris in a post-chaise for his Abbey of Scellières, at Romilly-on-Seine, in Champagne, one hundred and ten miles from Paris.

On the same evening, when the capital was dark and the streets deserted, two other carriages left the Hôtel Villette. In one was the body of the dead man, dressed, and lying on the seat like a sleeping traveller. A servant was also in the carriage. In the next came d'Hornoy and two distant cousins of Voltaire, who, after Mignot, were his nearest male relatives. This dreadful *cortège* "stopped at no inn, alighted at no post-house."

At midday on June 1st it reached Scellières. The Abbé Mignot had obtained, on the strength of the clerical certificates and Voltaire's written profession of faith, the consent of his prior that the great man should be buried there.

At three o'clock in the afternoon the body was laid in the choir, and vespers for the dead were sung over it. It remained there all night, surrounded by torches.

Early the next morning, June 2d, before many of the assembled clergy of the district whom the prior had summoned, Voltaire was buried with full rites and the honourable and decent burial he had desired.

Only a small stone marked his resting-place, with the bald inscription "Here lies Voltaire."

After all, he needed no epitaphs. He had avenged the oppressed and enlightened the ignorant.

On June 3d, the bishop of the diocese sent a mandate forbidding the burial. It was too late. On that day Mignot and the other relatives returned to Paris.

The city had heard of Voltaire's death by now: the devout with exultation, the philosophers with profound grief. The authorities had, indeed, forbidden the newspapers to publish any obituary notice of Voltaire or even to mention his decease. At the theatre no piece written by him was to be played for twenty-one days. The Academy was forbidden to hold the service at the Cordeliers customary on the death of a member.

But these restrictions of a petty tyranny had the effect of all such restrictions—the exact opposite to what was intended.

The heart of Paris would have throbbed the quicker for a Voltaire's death in any case. But for those prohibitions it throbbed with indignation too.

"You are right, Saint-Sulpice," said one of many bitter epigrams the occasion produced. "Why bury him?... Refuse a tomb, but not an altar."

In this June following his death, his will, made at Ferney in September, 1776, was proved. Terse, lucid, and able, it is characteristic of the man who wrote it. Voltaire appointed Madame Denis his residuary legatee. To Mignot and d'Hornoy he left one hundred thousand francs each; to Wagnière, eight thousand livres; to Madame Wagnière and Bonne-Baba, his clothes, and to Bonne-Baba eight hundred livres as well. Each servant was to have a year's wages. To Rieu, that ex-American officer, were left such English books from the library as he might choose: to the poor of the parish of Ferney—"if there are any poor"—three hundred livres; and to the curé a diamond, five hundred livres in value. Voltaire also appointed fifteen hundred francs to be given to the lawyer who was to help Madame Denis in the execution of his will.

It will be observed that the legacies to the servants, and particularly to faithful Wagnière, were very small. Hoping against the knowledge he had of her character, Voltaire had supposed that Madame Denis would continue his generosity towards them. Wagnière, true to his master's person and honour in life, was true to his memory after death. He uttered not a word of complaint.

In the August of 1778, d'Alembert chose Voltaire as the subject for the prize poem of the Academy; and until his own death, five years later, never ceased to work for the posthumous glory of the man he had loved.

The once false La Harpe also eulogised Voltaire, and wrote a play in his honour; and the scholarly Condorcet wrote his Life.

But it was not Paris alone which did homage to this greatness. If ever man had been a citizen of the world, Voltaire had been.

On November 26, 1778, Frederick the Great, now President of his own Academy, read to it Voltaire's Eulogium. It is a most generous testimony to the character of that brilliant, irritable, and delightful child of genius whom the great King had so hotly loved and loathed. As an appreciation of his works, it is worthless. Frederick the Great was no literary critic. But it poured burning contempt on the "imbecile priests" of Paris who had refused such a man the last offices of the dead, and not all the authorities in the world could keep it out of their capital.

In the May of the following year, to shame those "imbecile priests" the deeper, although he had, as he put it, no idea of the immortality of the soul himself, Frederick had a mass for Voltaire's said in the Roman church at Berlin. A little later the faithful and persevering d'Alembert proposed that that King should erect a statue to his friend in that same church. Frederick did not see his way to this. He had in his own possession a finer monument to Voltaire's greatness—a part of that correspondence which is one of Arouet's "surest titles to immortality" and contains at once "the history of Voltaire *intime* and of the eighteenth century."

No one had mourned Voltaire more passionately than the other great sovereign, Catherine. "Since he is dead, wit has lost its honour; he was the divinity of gaiety." To her, he had been much more than that. He had "formed her mind and her head."

He had left his library, except its English books, with his other effects, to Madame Denis. In the December of 1778, Catherine completed the purchase of those 6,210 volumes with their copious marginal notes, with manuscripts, original letters, and papers concerning the trials in which Voltaire had been engaged. Some months later she sent for Wagnière to arrange them. When he had finished his work, she came to look at it. Bowing before Voltaire's statue she said, "There is the man to whom I owe all I know and all I am." Hearing that Wagnière was poorly provided for, she magnificently gave him a pension for life. He visited Frederick, and returned to live and die at Ferney. One of Voltaire's editors, passing through that village in 1825, found the secretary's son still living there—a Justice of the Peace.

To get rid of her uncle's library was for Madame Denis but to free herself of one useless encumbrance. There was another. What was the use of Ferney to such a woman? Ice and snow, weavers and watchmakers, country, retirement, solitude—she hated them all. Her uncle's poor people had never been anything to her—except when they fêted and made much of her on a birthday. Return to them? Never. She sold Ferney to Villette. To the indignation of her relations and of the whole Academy—particularly d'Alembert, who was as jealous for dead Voltaire's honour as a mother for her daughter's good name—she insisted on marrying her Duvivier. It is a little satisfactory to learn that that dull person (in society he was popularly known as the Extinguisher) avenged Voltaire by bullying the woman who had bullied him.

Madame Denis never had any interest but as the niece of her uncle. With his death she fades into the commonplace obscurity for which she was made.

The Villettes retired to Ferney. In her old home, when her husband had once more forgotten the fatal attractions of the capital, he and Belle-et-Bonne lived not unhappily. But the weaving and watchmaking industry declined. The pilot was no longer at the helm. The strong hand and all-directing brain which had turned starving idleness to affluent industry, and established trade on a sound business basis, were no longer there to hold and supervise. Ferney fell back into the nothingness from which a master-mind had drawn it.

Presently Villette became heavily inculpated in the famous Guéménée bankruptcy for thirty-three millions. He sold Ferney, where he had retained Voltaire's rooms as they had been at the time of his death, and where, a cherished possession, he had kept the dead man's heart enclosed in a silver vase. Husband and wife came up to Paris and lived in the Hôtel Villette, where Belle-et-Bonne continued the tender charities which were the solace of her life, and surrounded herself with relics and mementoes of her dead Voltaire.

In March, 1779, M. Ducis was installed in Voltaire's vacant chair in the French Academy. According to custom, he read the Eulogy of his predecessor. The time for official prohibitions was past. No government had been able to prevent the Hermit of Ferney being known to the whole world as "the great Voltaire" for many years before his death. He was the great Voltaire still. Grimm declares that no meeting of the Academy ever attracted such crowds. When some clerical member dared to suggest that all expressions contrary to religion and morals should be erased by some friendly hand from Voltaire's works, he was hissed and groaned into silence.

On the first anniversary of his death, "Agathocle," his last tragedy, still incomplete, was performed in Paris, with a prologue by d'Alembert.

A complete edition of Voltaire's works appeared in 1780.

In 1784 there were secretly circulating in Paris the "Memoirs for the Life of Voltaire," written by himself in 1759 and revenging himself on Frederick for Freytag and Frankfort with the most cool and deadly spite. The man who wrote them, in that perfectly easy and limpid French of which he was always master even when he was by no means master of himself, had never intended them to be published. He burnt the original manuscript; but he had two copies made. It will not be forgotten that La Harpe and Madame Denis were dismissed from Ferney for having stolen one of them. One became the property of Catherine the Great. The other, Madame Denis, remembering that "wearisome niece" and the "Golden Lion," sent in 1783 to Beaumarchais, then editing Voltaire's works. He did not dare to include the "Memoirs" therein, in Frederick's lifetime. But they were passed from hand to hand in Paris, and it was doubtless well for Voltaire's fame that Frederick had already eulogised him and said masses for the peace of his soul. The "Memoirs" are now always included in Voltaire's works. It is not, all things considered, wholly his fault that many people, ignorant of the circumstances under which it was drawn, have assumed the malicious caricature of Frederick therein contained to be a faithful portrait.

For thirteen years the body of him "who against monks had never rested, among monks rested peacefully" enough. The Revolution he foresaw had come, though not as he had foreseen it.

His ideal of government had been a purified and constitutional monarchy, but always a monarchy. "My muscles are not very flexible: I do not mind making one bow, but a hundred on end would fatigue me." By 1790 Louis XVI. was a king only in name. In that year the Abbey of Scellières, with all other religious houses, became the property of the nation. Villette had not merely fallen in with the views of the Revolution. They had been his when such convictions were dangerous and awkward, and he never forgot that Prophet of Revolution, Voltaire. It was through Villette that the Quai de Théatins, on which the Hôtel Villette stood, was renamed the Quai Voltaire.

In November, 1790, after a performance of "Brutus," Charles Villette, ex-Marquis, harangued the audience and passionately pleaded, "in the name of the country," that the remains of Voltaire might be brought to Paris and honourably buried. "This translation will be the dying sigh of fanaticism." The idea pleased a people agog for excitement and drunk with the first deep draughts of a liberty which for centuries they had not been allowed even to taste.

On June 1, 1791, the National Assembly made Louis XVI. sign the decree which ordained that the ashes of his great enemy should be transferred from the church of Romilly to that of Sainte-Geneviève in Paris—Sainte-Geneviève, which was henceforth to be called the Pantheon of France.

On July 6th, a funeral car, decked with laurels and oak leaves, drawn by four horses and escorted by a detachment of the National Guard, left Romilly-on-Seine and began its solemn triumphal progress to Paris. On the front of the car was written, "To the memory of Voltaire." On one side, "If man is born free, he ought to govern himself"; on the other, "If man has tyrants, he ought to dethrone them."

As it passed through the villages, the villagers came out to greet it with wreaths of flowers and laurels in their hands. Mothers held up their babies that they too might say that they had seen this great day; old men pressed forward to touch and be healed. At night the villages through which the procession passed were illuminated; by day could be seen triumphal arches, girls dressed in white, and garlands of flowers. Out of their ignorance and wretchedness, this *canaille* recognised him who had wept and clamoured for the rights of all men and made freedom a possibility even for them.

At nightfall on July 10th, the *cortège* reached Paris. The sarcophagus was placed on an altar on the ruins of that tower of the Bastille in which Voltaire had been twice a prisoner.

On the altar was the inscription, "On this spot, where despotism chained thee, receive the homage of a free people."

All Sunday night the sarcophagus remained there. At three o'clock on the sunny afternoon of Monday, July 11th, it was placed on a car designed by David, and drawn through Paris, escorted by an enormous company, organised, orderly, and representing every rank and condition. Here were the men who had demolished the Bastille, carrying its flag, and in their midst that terrible virago who had led them in the fray. Here were citizens with pikes, Swiss, Jacobins, actors, and bodies of soldiers. Some carried banners with devices from the dead man's writings. Some, dressed in Greek costume, carried a gilt model of the famous statue by Houdon. Among the self-constituted guard were many who, not a month before, had brought back that other King to his capital—from Varennes—with howls, insults, and imprecations.

Singers and music preceded the car itself. Supported on four great wheels of bronze, it looked like a magnificent altar. On the summit was the sarcophagus, and on that a full-length figure of Voltaire reclining in an attitude of sleep and with a winged Immortality placing a crown of stars on his head. On the sarcophagus was written, in words of noble simplicity, "He avenged Calas, La Barre, Sirven, and Montbailli. Poet, philosopher, historian, he gave a great impetus to the human mind: he prepared us to become free." The whole structure, forty feet high, was drawn by twelve white horses, two of which, it is said, had been furnished by Marie Antoinette. On the car were such inscriptions as—"He defended Calas." "He inspired toleration." "He claimed the rights of men."

Behind it walked Belle-et-Bonne and her husband, with their little girl in her nurse's arms. Then came deputations from the National Assembly and the Courts of Justice, and then another detachment of military.

The procession itself consisted of a hundred thousand persons. Six hundred thousand more witnessed it.

It first stopped at the Opera House. The operatic company came forward and sang that song in Voltaire's "Samson" which became, with the "Marseillaise," *the* song of the Revolution—

Wake, ye people! Break your chains!
After the Opera House, the Tuileries was passed. Every window was filled with spectators, save one. Behind that, closed and barred, sat the most unhappy of monarchs, Louis and Marie Antoinette, awaiting doom.

The next stop was in front of the Hôtel Villette. Upon a platform outside it were fifty young girls dressed in white, and before them the two daughters of Calas in deep mourning. They kissed the sarcophagus of "the man of Calas"; and Belle-et-Bonne lifted up her child as if "to consecrate her to reason, to philosophy, and to liberty."

The next stop was at the old Comédie Française—the scene of Voltaire's earliest dramatic triumphs, and where now was his bust with the inscription, "He wrote 'Œdipe' at seventeen."

At the Théâtre Français, become the Theatre of the Nation, were garlands and music and the inscription, "He wrote 'Irène' at eighty-four." And once more a chorus sang the spirited song out of "Samson."

At last, at ten o'clock at night and in a drizzling rain, the Pantheon was reached.

The sarcophagus was lifted into the place designed for it—near the tombs of Descartes and Mirabeau.

The history of Voltaire after death could be elaborated into a volume. But, after all, it throws no light on his life and character, only on those of the friends who loved him, the enemies who hated him, and the mob who went mad over him.

When it is considered that to the excesses of that mob he would have been passionately opposed, and that the only Revolution he desired was gradual, temperate, and unbloody, it may well be doubted if, had he lived till 1791, his last journey would not have been, like that of many other patriots, to a very different accompaniment and a very different destination.

For a while he was allowed to rest in that quiet and honoured grave.

But 1814 saw the restoration of those Bourbons whose hatred for him was hereditary.

With the connivance of the ministry, the tombs of both Voltaire and Rousseau were violated, their bones removed in a sack at night to a waste place outside the city, and emptied into a pit filled with quicklime. That long-dreaded fate—"thrown into the gutter like poor Lecouvreur"—was Voltaire's after all.

But those dishonoured ashes and that unhallowed burial keep his memory more vividly alive than the marble tomb of a Pantheon.

The violation was discovered in 1864, when, the Villette family becoming extinct, Voltaire's heart became the property of the nation.

It was decided to place it with his ashes in the Pantheon. But the tomb was empty.

The Marquis de Villette died in 1793, thereby escaping the guillotine, to which he had been condemned for refusing to vote for the death of the

King. Belle-et-Bonne, a widow at thirty-six, consecrated her life to Voltaire's memory.

In 1878, his centenary was celebrated with the warmest enthusiasm by the most fickle capital in the world.

Victor Hugo eulogised Voltaire with much emotion and applause, and fervent words which mean nothing in particular. But the fact that the Fighter had been dead a century did not prevent him from being still a cause of strife. Dupanloup, Bishop of Orleans, hotly attacked the infidel and demanded an injunction against a new edition of his works, which was refused.

This was the last famous assault on the Great Assaulter. France, perhaps even Catholic France, recognises in some sort the debt she owes to Voltaire. Is not the enemy who shows a nation her weak points, forces her to look to her ships and her armaments, to remedy abuses in her organisation, and feebleness, viciousness, and incompetency in her servants, something very like a friend in disguise?

It may be truly said that Voltaire did good to Roman Catholicism by attacking much that degraded it; by hooting out of it the superstition and tyranny which have made some of the noblest souls on earth decline it; and by forcing its children to give a reason for the faith that was in them.

Then, too, if the Church of Rome could withstand that deadly, breathless, and brilliant onslaught called Voltairism, she may well point triumphantly to the fulfilment of that ancient prophecy and consolation, "The gates of hell shall not prevail against it."

To the Church in France it may be acknowledged that Voltaire was not wholly an evil, while to her country he was a great glory.

In England there is still against him a prejudice, which, said Buckle, nothing but ignorance can excuse. To the ordinary Briton Voltaire is only a very profane scoffer who made some rather amusing and very doubtful jokes.

Yet this was he who, as Frederick the Great said, was extraordinary in everything. Here was the man who was poet, playwright, novelist, letter-writer, historian, critic, philosopher, theologian, socialist, philanthropist, agriculturist, humorist, reformer, wit, and man of the world.

England has no counterpart for him. But then neither has France, nor any other country. Think of the great names of earthly fame. Of which can it be said—with even approximate truth—"Here is another Voltaire?"

As a poet, he was the king of those society verses which he modestly said himself "are good for nothing but society and only for the moment for which they are written."

But such as they are—madrigal, epigram, epitaph, the gracefullest flattery in four lines, and the daintiest malice in a couplet—if Voltaire had written nothing else, his supremacy in these alone would have given him a perpetual place in the literature of his country.

His longer and graver poems are immortal for what he said, not for how he said it.

As a playwright, his tragedies were the most famous of his age. Ours applies to them those fatal adjectives—fluent, elegant, correct. Without any of the indomitable life and swing which characterise almost all his other works, they were perfectly suited to that exceedingly bad public taste which preferred smoothness before vigour, and a careful consideration of the unities to the genius of a Shakespeare.

Voltaire's comedies are only sprightly and fluent.

As a historian, whether in prose or verse, he is celebrated for his broad and comprehensive views, his enormous general knowledge (for his time), "the vehemence and sincerity of his abhorrence of the military spirit," his savage hatred of the religious *culte*, and his inimitably interesting and vivacious style. Until his day the learned rarely had wit and the witty rarely had learning. Voltaire set an example which has been singularly little followed: he made facts more amusing than fiction.

His fiction indeed is, with the multitude, one of his chief titles to fame. But all his fiction, rhyming or prose, was to teach fact; though his heart was so perfect that the facts never spoilt the fancy. He was the pioneer in France of the short story, the *conte*. There may be traced, in a slight degree, the influence of Swift. But Voltaire's satire is gayer, brighter, and cleaner than the great Dean's.

Voltaire is the first letter-writer in the world. He was himself interested in everything, and so interesting to everybody.

His letters contain not only his own best biography, and not only the literary history of the eighteenth century. They touch on all contemporary history—social, religious, scientific, political. They are at once the wittiest and the most natural extant. He wrote with that liquid ease with which a bird shakes out his song. His French is at one and the same time the most perfect French for the Frenchman and the stylist, and the simplest for the foreigner to understand.

Besides his letters, with their easy grace and wealth of world-wide knowledge, Horace Walpole's are but the gossip of a clique; Madame de Sévigné's the chit-chat of a boudoir; Lady Wortley Montagu's coarse and clumsy; and Pope's stilted and artificial. They are also comparatively free from the indecency which mars many other of Voltaire's writings and almost all the correspondence of his age. His letters remain (as early as 1872 there were seven thousand of them in print, and Beuchot thought at least as many more undiscovered) an almost inexhaustible gold mine of literary delight, and a most liberal education.

As a blasphemous mocker at some of the most sacred convictions of their souls, Voltaire has been naturally, when he touches on religion, anathema not only to Roman Catholics, but to all Christians. The liberal-minded will be ready to own that to attack a system he not only believed to be false but actively harmful, was well within his rights. It is his method which inspires just indignation. A profoundly serious subject has a right to profoundly serious treatment. But, after all, Voltaire's gibes and laugh turn against himself. Who believes a scoffer? If he had not jeered at the creed of Christendom, he would have made more converts to the creed of Voltaire.

What was his creed? It had only one article. "I believe in God." In that belief "one finds difficulties; in the belief that there is no God, absurdities." "The wise man attributes to God no human affections. He recognises a power necessary, eternal, which animates all Nature; and is resigned."

As for the immortality of the soul, it seems, contrary to the opinion of many of his biographers, that Voltaire rather longed to believe in it, than that he did so. "But your soul, Sir—your soul? What idea have you of it? From whence does it come? Where is it? What is it? What does it do? How does it act? Where does it go? I know nothing about it and I have never seen it." "For sixty years I have tried to discover what the soul is, and I still know nothing."

His practical scheme of religion he expressed himself. "To worship God; to leave each man the liberty to serve Him in his own fashion; to love one's neighbours; enlighten them if one can, pity them when they are in error; to attach no importance to trivial questions which would never have given trouble if no seriousness had been imputed to them. That is my religion, which is worth all your systems and all your symbols."

The stumbling-blocks he found in the road to Christianity—that is to Roman Catholicism, the only form of Christianity to which he addressed himself—were twofold. The mental stumbling-block was miracle; and the moral, the lives of the believers. He considered the second to be the natural fruit of the first: that the Christian belief must be destroyed to destroy the wickedness, darkness, cruelty, and tyranny he found in Christian lives; that men "will not cease to be persecutors till they have ceased to be absurd."

It should be remembered—it is not often remembered—that, in the words of Morley, "there is no case of Voltaire mocking at any set of men who lived good lives," and that "the Christianity he assailed was not that of the Sermon on the Mount."

Regarding the problems of the future life, of future awards, punishments, and compensations, and the manifold mysteries of this world, he was, broadly speaking, an Agnostic.

"Behold, I know not anything."

But Voltaire's real claim to eternal remembrance is far less how he thought or what he wrote, than what his writings *did*.

Some of them are obsolete to-day because they so perfectly accomplished their aim. Who wants to read now passionate arguments against torture, and scathing satires on a jurisdiction which openly accepted hearsay as evidence?

In his own day those writings produced many practical reforms, and paved the way to many more. Through them, he was himself enabled to be a philanthropist in an age when the prosperous elder brothers of the world looked up to God from stricken Abel with that scornful question, "Am I my brother's keeper?" Through them, he saved innocent lives and restored stolen honour.

But his Ferney, his Lally, Calas, Sirven, La Barre, were only types of his work for all the race.

He found the earth overspread with hideous under-growths of oppression and privilege, intolerance and cruelty; and he destroyed them.

He found the good land covered with abuses in Church and State and every social order; abuses political, personal; of the rights of the living, and the decent respect owed to the dead—and he uprooted them. With a laugh and blasphemy on his lips, but with eyes and soul afire and the nervous tireless hands trembling with eagerness, the most dauntless, passionate, dogged little worker in all human history hewed and hacked at the monstrous tyrannies of centuries, and flung them, dead, from the fair and beautiful soil they had usurped.

At last, after sixty years of superhuman effort, he had cleared the place and made it ready for the planting of the Tree of Liberty.

Whoso sits under that tree to-day in any country, free to worship his God as he will, to think, to learn, and to do all that does not intrench on the freedom of his fellow-men—free to progress to heights of light and knowledge as yet unseen and undreamt—should in gratitude remember Voltaire.

Booksophile
Your Local Online Bookstore

Buy Books Online from
www.Booksophile.com

Explore our collection of books written in various languages and uncommon topics from different parts of the world, including history, art and culture, poems, autobiography and bibliographies, cooking, action & adventure, world war, fiction, science, and law.

Add to your bookshelf or gift to another lover of books - first editions of some of the most celebrated books ever published. From classic literature to bestsellers, you will find many first editions that were presumed to be out-of-print.

Free shipping globally for orders worth US$ 100.00.

Use code "Shop_10" to avail additional 10% on first order.

Visit today
www.booksophile.com

CPSIA information can be obtained
at www.ICGtesting.com
Printed in the USA
LVHW031526020323
740520LV00008B/296

9 789356 898851